INTRODUCTION TO METAMATHEMATICS

BIBLIOTHECA MATHEMATICA

A Series of Monographs on Pure and Applied Mathematics

Volume I

*

Edited with the cooperation of

THE „MATHEMATISCH CENTRUM"

and

THE „WISKUNDIG GENOOTSCHAP"
at Amsterdam

*

Editors

INTRODUCTION TO METAMATHEMATICS

BY

STEPHEN COLE KLEENE
PROFESSOR OF MATHEMATICS AT THE UNIVERSITY
OF WISCONSIN (MADISON, WIS., U.S.A.)

1971

WOLTERS-NOORDHOFF PUBLISHING – GRONINGEN
NORTH-HOLLAND PUBLISHING COMPANY – AMSTERDAM · LONDON
AMERICAN ELSEVIER PUBLISHING COMPANY, INC. – NEW YORK

Library of Congress Catalog Card Number 70-97931

North-Holland ISBN 0 7204 2103 9
American Elsevier ISBN 0 444 10088 1

First published	1952
First reprint	1957
Second reprint	1959
Third reprint	1962
Fourth reprint	1964
Fifth reprint	1967
Sixth reprint	1971

Publishers:

WOLTERS-NOORDHOFF PUBLISHING – GRONINGEN
NORTH-HOLLAND PUBLISHING COMPANY – AMSTERDAM · LONDON

Sole distributors for the U.S.A. and Canada:

AMERICAN ELSEVIER PUBLISHING COMPANY, Inc.
52 Vanderbilt Avenue
New York, N.Y. 10017

Printed in The Netherlands

PREFACE

Two successive eras of investigations of the foundations of mathematics in the nineteenth century, culminating in the theory of sets and the arithmetization of analysis, led around 1900 to a new crisis, and a new era dominated by the programs of Russell and Whitehead, Hilbert and of Brouwer.

The appearance in 1931 of Gödel's two incompleteness theorems, in 1933 of Tarski's work on the concept of truth in formalized languages, in 1934 of the Herbrand-Gödel notion of 'general recursive function', and in 1936 of Church's thesis concerning it, inaugurate a still newer era in which mathematical tools are being applied both to evaluating the earlier programs and in unforeseen directions.

The aim of this book is to provide a connected introduction to the subjects of mathematical logic and recursive functions in particular, and to the newer foundational investigations in general.

Some selection was necessary. The main choice has been to concentrate after Part I on the metamathematical investigation of elementary number theory with the requisite mathematical logic, leaving aside the higher predicate calculi, analysis, type theory and set theory. This choice was made because in number theory one finds the first and simplest exemplification of the newer methods and concepts, although the extension to other branches of mathematics is well under way and promises to be increasingly important in the immediate future.

The book is written to be usable as a text book by first year graduate students in mathematics (and above) and others at that level of mathematical facility, irrespective of their knowledge of any particular mathematical subject matter.

In using the book as a text book, it is intended that Part I (Chapters I — III), which provides the necessary background, should be covered rapidly (in two or three weeks by a class meeting three times a week). The intensive study should begin with Part II (Chapter IV), where it is essential that the student concentrate upon acquiring a firm grasp of metamathematical method.

The starred sections can be omitted on a first reading or examined in a cursory manner. Sometimes it will then be necessary later to go back and study an earlier starred section (e.g. § 37 will have to be studied for § 72).

Gödel's two famous incompleteness theorems are reached in Chapter VIII, leaving a lemma to be proved in Chapter X. The author has found it feasible to complete these ten chapters (and sometimes a bit more) in the semester course which he has given along these lines at the University of Wisconsin.

The remaining five chapters can be used to extend such a course to a year course, or as collateral reading to accompany a seminar.

A semester course on recursive functions for students having some prior acquaintance with mathematical logic, or under an instructor with such acquaintance, could start with Part III (Chapter IX). There are other possibilities for selecting material; e.g. much of Part IV can follow directly Part II or even Chapter VII for students primarily interested in mathematical logic.

The author is indebted to Saunders MacLane for encouraging him to write this book and for valuable criticism of an early draft of several chapters. John Addison read the entire first printer's proof with great care, independently of the author. Among many others who have been of assistance are Evert Beth, Robert Breusch, Arend Heyting, Nancy Kleene, Leonard Linski, David Nelson, James Renno and Gene Rose. Scientific indebtedness is acknowledged by references to the Bibliography; especially extensive use has been made of Hilbert and Bernays' "Grundlagen der Mathematik" in two volumes 1934 and 1939.

July 1952 S. C. KLEENE

Note to the Sixth Reprint (1971). In successive reprints various errors have been corrected, the principal corrections being those listed in **Jour. symbolic logic** vol. 19 (1954) p. 216 and vol. 33 (1968) pp. 290-291, and: on p. 505 bottom paragraph $\overline{\mathrm{sg}}((r)_0) \cdot p((r)_1) + (r)_0 \cdot q((r)_1)$ replaced by a function $\chi(p, q, r)$ defined by Theorem XX (c); on p. 506 allowance made in the middle paragraph for x possibly occurring free in t, and line 5 from below „=" changed to „≃". Moreover, in this sixth reprint eleven bibliographical references have been updated (cf. end p. 517) and two short notes have been added (on pp. 65 and 316).

TABLE OF CONTENTS

PART I. THE PROBLEM OF FOUNDATIONS

PART II. MATHEMATICAL LOGIC

Part IV. MATHEMATICAL LOGIC (ADDITIONAL TOPICS)

PART I

THE PROBLEM OF FOUNDATIONS

Chapter I

THE THEORY OF SETS

§ 1. Enumerable sets. Before turning to our main subject, it will be appropriate to notice briefly Cantor's theory of sets.

A flock of four sheep and a grove of four trees are related to each other in a way in which neither is related to a pile of three stones or a grove of seven trees. Although the words for numbers have been used to state this truism on the printed page, the relationship to which we refer underlies the concept of cardinal number. Without counting the sheep or the trees, one can pair them with each other, for example by tethering the sheep to the trees, so that each sheep and each tree belongs to exactly one of the pairs. Such a pairing between the members of two collections or 'sets' of objects is called a *one-to-one* (1-1) *correspondence.*

In 1638 Galileo remarked that the ***squares of the positive integers*** can be placed in a 1-1 correspondence with the ***positive integers*** themselves, thus

$$1, \quad 4, \quad 9, \quad 16, \ldots, n^2, \ldots$$

$$1, \quad 2, \quad 3, \quad 4, \ldots, n, \ldots,$$

despite the ancient axiom that the whole is greater than any of its parts. Cantor, between 1874 and 1897, first undertook systematically to compare infinite sets in terms of the possibility of establishing 1-1 correspondences.

The two sets in Galileo's "paradox" and the set of the ***natural numbers***

$$0, \quad 1, \quad 2, \quad 3, \ldots, n-1, \ldots,$$

are examples of infinite sets which are 'enumerable'. Choosing the last named as the standard, we define an infinite set to be *enumerable* (or *denumerable* or *countable*), if it can be placed in a 1-1 correspondence with the natural numbers.

To show that an infinite set is enumerable, we need merely indicate how its members can be given (without repetitions) in an 'infinite list';

then the first in the list corresponds to 0, the second to 1, and so on. Although the list itself is infinite, each member occupies a finite position in the list.

A particular infinite list (without repetitions) of the members of the set, or 1-1 correspondence between the set and the natural numbers, is called an *enumeration* of the set; the number corresponding to a given member is the *index* of the member in the enumeration.

The members of a finite set can also be given in a list, i.e. a finite list. Hence the term *enumerable* is sometimes applied to sets which are either infinite and enumerable, i.e. *enumerably infinite*, or else finite.

The set of the ***integers*** can be enumerated, by listing them in the following order,

$$0, \quad 1, \quad -1, \quad 2, \quad -2, \quad 3, \quad -3, \ldots .$$

The set of the ***rational numbers*** is also enumerable, a fact which is surprising if one first compares them with the integers in the usual algebraic order. The points on the x-axis with integral abscissas are isolated, while those with rational abscissas are 'everywhere dense', i.e. between each two no matter how close there are others. The enumeration can be accomplished by a device which we shall present for the ***positive rational numbers***, leaving the case of all the rationals to the reader. Let the fractions of positive integers be arranged in an infinite matrix, thus,

$$\begin{array}{ccccccccc}
1/1 & & 1/2 & \rightarrow & 1/3 & & 1/4 & \rightarrow & \cdots \\
\downarrow & \nearrow & & \swarrow & & \nearrow & & & \\
2/1 & & 2/2 & & 2/3 & & 2/4 & & \cdots \\
& \swarrow & & \nearrow & & & & & \\
3/1 & & 3/2 & & 3/3 & & 3/4 & & \cdots \\
\downarrow & \nearrow & & & & & & & \\
4/1 & & 4/2 & & 4/3 & & 4/4 & & \cdots \\
& & & & \cdots & & & &
\end{array}$$

Then let these fractions be enumerated by following the arrows. A rational number is one which can be expressed as a fraction of integers. Go through the enumeration of fractions striking out each one which is equal in value to one that has preceded it. This leaves the following enumeration of the positive rational numbers,

$$1, \quad 2, \quad 1/2, \quad 1/3, \quad 3, \quad 4, \quad 3/2, \quad 2/3, \quad 1/4, \ldots .$$

The device of the matrix constitutes a general one for enumerating the ***ordered pairs of members of an enumerable set***, e.g. the ordered pairs of natural numbers, or the ordered pairs of integers. The rows of the matrix are the enumerations of the pairs with the first member of the pair fixed. The ***ordered triples of members of an enumerable set*** can then be enumerated by another application of the matrix, taking as the rows the enumerations already won of the triples with the first member of the triple fixed. Successively we can win enumerations of the ***ordered n-tuples of members of an enumerable set*** for each fixed positive integer n. All of these enumerations, including the enumeration of the original set, can be taken as the rows of a new matrix to obtain an enumeration of the ordered n-tuples for variable n, i.e. the ***finite sequences of members of an enumerable set.***

This result can be applied to obtain an enumeration of the ***algebraic equations***

$$a_0x^n + a_1x^{n-1} + \ldots + a_{n-1}x + a_n = 0 \qquad (a_0 \neq 0)$$

with integral coefficients, since each equation can be described by giving the sequence

$$(a_0, a_1, \ldots, a_{n-1}, a_n)$$

of its coefficients. A '(real) algebraic number' is a real root of an equation of this sort. Since a given equation has at most n different roots, the ***algebraic numbers*** are enumerable.

Another device will illustrate the possibilities for enumerating sets. In dealing with an enumerable set (finite or infinite), the numbers which correspond to the members in some specified enumeration can be used to designate or name the members individually. Now conversely, if a name or explicit expression can be assigned to every one of the members of a set individually, in a preassigned and unambiguous system of notation, the set is enumerable (finite or infinite). We stipulate that a name or expression shall be a finite sequence of symbols chosen from a given finite alphabet of available symbols. For example, the algebraic equations with integral coefficients can be written using decimal notation for the coefficients and exponents. The raised exponents are an inessential feature of the notation, which can be removed by a suitable convention. Indeed, so long as we are dealing only with these equations, we may simply write the exponents on the line. The symbols required are then precisely

$$0,\ 1,\ 2,\ 3,\ 4,\ 5,\ 6,\ 7,\ 8,\ 9,\ x,\ +,\ -,\ =.$$

The first symbol in an equation is not a 0. Reinterpret these symbols as the digits (!) in a quattuordecimal number system, i.e. a number system based on 14 in the same way that the decimal system is based on 10. Every equation becomes a natural number (distinct equations becoming distinct numbers). Enumerate the equations in the order of magnitude of these numbers.

§ 2. Cantor's diagonal method. That there are infinite sets considered in mathematics which cannot be enumerated was shown by Cantor's famous 'diagonal method'. The set of the ***real numbers*** is non-enumerable.

Let us first consider the ***real numbers x in the interval*** $0 < x \leq 1$. Each real number in this interval is represented uniquely by a proper non-terminating decimal fraction, i.e. a decimal fraction having its first significant digit to the right of the decimal point, and having infinitely many digits that are not 0. A number may have a terminating decimal fraction, i.e. one with repeating 0's, but that fraction is replaceable by a non-terminating fraction with repeating 9's. For example .483 or .483000... can be replaced by .482999.... Conversely every proper non-terminating decimal fraction represents a unique real number in the interval.

Now suppose that

$$x_0, \quad x_1, \quad x_2, \quad x_3, \ \ldots$$

is an infinite list or enumeration of some but not necessarily all of the real numbers belonging to the interval. Write down one below another their respective non-terminating decimal fractions,

$$\begin{array}{llllll}
.x_{00} & x_{01} & x_{02} & x_{03} & & \ldots \\
& \searrow & & & & \\
.x_{10} & x_{11} & x_{12} & x_{13} & & \ldots \\
& & \searrow & & & \\
.x_{20} & x_{21} & x_{22} & x_{23} & & \ldots \\
& & & \searrow & & \\
.x_{30} & x_{31} & x_{32} & x_{33} & & \ldots \\
& & \ldots\ldots & & \searrow &
\end{array}$$

Select the diagonal fraction shown by the arrows. In this change each of the successive digits x_{nn} to a different digit x'_{nn}, but avoid producing a terminating fraction. Say, let $x'_{nn} = 5$ if $x_{nn} \neq 5$, and $x'_{nn} = 6$ if $x_{nn} = 5$.

The resulting fraction

$$.x'_{00} \quad x'_{11} \quad x'_{22} \quad x'_{33} \quad \ldots$$

represents a real number x which belongs to the interval but not to the enumeration. For the fraction differs from the first of the given fractions in the tenths place, from the second in the hundredths place, from the third in the thousandths place, and so on.

Hence the given enumeration is not an enumeration of all the real numbers in the interval. An enumeration of all the real numbers in the interval is non-existent.

To apply the diagonal method to the real numbers without restriction to the interval $0 < x \leq 1$, it is only necessary to represent the real numbers in the characteristic-plus-mantissa form, e.g. $37.142\ldots = 37 + .142$, $-2.813\ldots = -3 + .186\ldots$, and to apply the method to the mantissas.

It is clear that an essential difference has been revealed between the set of the rational numbers or the set of the algebraic numbers on the one hand, and the set of the real numbers on the other.

It is interesting historically to note how Cantor's discoveries in 1874 (see the bibliography) illuminated an earlier discovery of Liouville in 1844. Liouville had been able to construct by a special method certain transcendental (i.e. non-algebraic) real numbers. Cantor's diagonal method makes the existence of transcendental numbers apparent from only the very general considerations presented above. In fact, to any given enumeration $x_0, x_1, x_2, x_3, \ldots$ of the algebraic numbers, particular transcendentals can be obtained by the diagonal method.

The (real) ***transcendental numbers*** are not enumerable. For if they were, like the algebraic numbers, enumerations of the two sets could be combined to produce an enumeration of all the real numbers. Thus, in a sense, most real numbers are transcendental.

Another example of a non-enumerable set is the set of the (single-valued) functions for which the independent and dependent variables each range on an enumerable set. For definiteness, consider the set of the ***functions of a natural number taking a natural number as value*** (or ***infinite sequences of natural numbers***). Suppose an enumeration is given of some but not necessarily all of them,

$$f_0(n), \quad f_1(n), \quad f_2(n), \quad f_3(n), \ldots.$$

Write the sequences of the values of the successive functions one below another, as the rows of an infinite matrix,

$$\begin{array}{ccccc} f_0(0) & f_0(1) & f_0(2) & f_0(3) & \dots \\ & \searrow & & & \\ f_1(0) & f_1(1) & f_1(2) & f_1(3) & \dots \\ & & \searrow & & \\ f_2(0) & f_2(1) & f_2(2) & f_2(3) & \dots \\ & & & \searrow & \\ f_3(0) & f_3(1) & f_3(2) & f_3(3) & \dots \\ & & \dots & & \searrow \end{array}$$

Take the sequence of values given by the diagonal. Change every one of these values to a different value, say by adding 1. The function $f(n)$ with the resulting sequence of values, which we may write

$$f(n) = f_n(n) + 1,$$

cannot belong to the enumeration, since it differs from the first of the enumerated functions in the value taken for 0, from the second in the value taken for 1, and so on.

To phrase the argument differently, suppose that the function $f(n)$ were in the enumeration; i.e. suppose that for some natural number q,

$$f(n) = f_q(n)$$

for every natural number n. Substituting the number q for the variable n in this and the preceding equation,

$$f(q) = f_q(q) = f_q(q) + 1.$$

This is impossible, since the natural number $f_q(q)$ cannot equal itself increased by 1.

Still another example of a non-enumerable set is the set of the ***sets of natural numbers***. (But the set of the finite sets of natural numbers is enumerable. Why?) We can represent a set of natural numbers by a *representing function*, which takes the value 0 for a natural number belonging to the set and the value 1 for a natural number not belonging to the set. The sequence of the values of the representing function of a set of natural numbers is an infinite sequence of 0's and 1's. For example, the sequence for a set containing 0, 2 and 3 but not 1 and 4 starts out 0 1 0 0 1 .... These sequences are taken as the rows of the infinite matrix. The alteration performed on the diagonal is the interchange of 0's and 1's.

Can these several non-enumerable sets be placed in 1-1 correspondence with one another, and are there still other types of infinite sets? The reader may profit by attempting to answer these questions himself (answers are given in § 5). We shall now look at Cantor's theory in its general formulation.

§ 3. Cardinal number. Cantor's theory of 'abstract sets' deals with sets in general. (He gave also a theory of 'point sets'.) Cantor describes his terms *set* and *element* as follows. "By a 'set' we understand any collection M of definite well-distinguished objects m of our perception or our thought (which are called the 'elements' of M) into a whole." (1895 p. 481.)

The sets include the *empty* or *null* or *vacuous* or *void* set which has no elements, and the *unit* sets which have a single element each. We write the empty set as 0; the unit set with sole element a as $\{a\}$; and the set having $a, b, c, \ldots$ as its elements as $\{a, b, c, \ldots\}$.

A set may also be called an *aggregate* or *collection* or *class* or *domain* or *totality*. That a is an element of M may also be expressed by saying that a is a *member* of M or *belongs* to M or is *in* M, or in symbols, $a \in M$. If a is not an element of M, in symbols, $a \notin M$.

We understand two sets M and N to be the same (in symbols, $M = N$), if they have the same elements; i.e. if for every object a, $a \in M$ if and only if $a \in N$.

Two sets M and N are said to be *equivalent* (in symbols, $M \sim N$), if there exists a 1-1 correspondence (§ 1) between them. (Sometimes we say "the correspondence $M \sim N$" to refer to a particular 1-1 correspondence between M and N, which must exist if $M \sim N$.)

The relation $M \sim N$ evidently possesses the 'reflexive', 'symmetric' and 'transitive' properties, i.e. for any sets M, N and P: $M \sim M$. If $M \sim N$, then $N \sim M$. If $M \sim N$ and $N \sim P$, then $M \sim P$.

The *cardinal number* of a set M is introduced as an object $\overline{\overline{M}}$ which is associated in common with all and only those sets (including M itself) which are equivalent to M. By this definition: $\overline{\overline{M}} = \overline{\overline{N}}$, if and only if $M \sim N$.

What cardinal numbers are, further than this, is perhaps immaterial; but we may notice several interpretations. Cantor describes them thus: "The general concept which with the aid of our active intelligence results from a set M, when we abstract from the nature of its various elements and from the order of their being given, we call the 'power' or 'cardinal number' of M." This double abstraction suggests his notation "$\overline{\overline{M}}$" for the cardinal of M. Frege 1884 and Russell 1902 identify the cardinal number $\overline{\overline{M}}$ with the set of the sets equivalent to M; while von Neumann 1928 chooses from each of these sets of sets ('equivalence classes') a particular set to serve as the cardinal of any set in the class.

The notion of a 'part' of a collection is introduced by the following definition. A set M_1 is a *subset* of a set M (in symbols, $M_1 \subset M$), if each element of M_1 is an element of M.

EXAMPLE 1. The set $\{a, b, c\}$ of three elements a, b, c has eight ($= 2^3$) subsets: O, $\{a\}$, $\{b\}$, $\{c\}$, $\{a, b\}$, $\{a, c\}$, $\{b, c\}$, $\{a, b, c\}$.

Note that the subsets of a set M include the vacuous set O, and the set M itself. The latter is the *improper* subset, and the other subsets are *proper*. Evidently, if $M_2 \subset M_1$ and $M_1 \subset M$ (abbreviated $M_2 \subset M_1 \subset M$), then $M_2 \subset M$.

The *union* or *sum* $M + N$ of two sets M and N is the set of the objects belonging to at least one of M and N (i.e. belonging to M or to N); and their *intersection* or *product* $M \cdot N$ is the set of the objects belonging to both of M and N (i.e. belonging to M and to N). Similarly for more than two sets. The *difference* $M - N$ of M and N (when $N \subset M$, also called the *complement* of N with respect to M) is the set of the objects belonging to M but not to N.

EXAMPLE 2. $\{a, b, c\} + \{b, d\} = \{a, b, c, d\}$, $\{a, b, c\} \cdot \{b, d\} = \{b\}$, $\{a, b, c\} - \{b, d\} = \{a, b, c\} - \{b\} = \{a, c\}$.

Evidently $M - M_1 \subset M$; and if $M_1 \subset M$, then (and only then) $M_1 + (M - M_1) = M$. Two sets M and N are *disjoint*, if they have no common elements, i.e. if $M \cdot N = \text{O}$. For example, M_1 and $M - M_1$ are disjoint sets. If M and N are disjoint, either $M \neq N$ or $M = N = \text{O}$.

We turn to the important question of comparing cardinal numbers. Given two sets M and N, it may or may not be possible to put M into 1-1 correspondence with some subset N_1 of N. Vice versa, there may or may not exist a subset M_1 of M which is equivalent to N. Combining these two pairs of alternatives gives four cases, exactly one of which must apply to any given pair of sets M and N:

(1a) For some N_1, $M \sim N_1 \subset N$; but for no M_1, $N \sim M_1 \subset M$.

(1b) For no N_1, $M \sim N_1 \subset N$; but for some M_1, $N \sim M_1 \subset M$.

(2) For some N_1, $M \sim N_1 \subset N$; and for some M_1, $N \sim M_1 \subset M$.

(3) For no N_1, $M \sim N_1 \subset N$; and for no M_1, $N \sim M_1 \subset M$.

In Case (1a), the cardinal of M is said to be *less* than the cardinal of N (in symbols, $\overline{\overline{M}} < \overline{\overline{N}}$). To justify considering $<$ as a relation between the cardinals $\overline{\overline{M}}$ and $\overline{\overline{N}}$, and not merely one between the sets M and N, we must observe that if $M' \sim M$ and $N' \sim N$, then Case (1a) applies to the pair of sets M', N' if and only if it applies to the pair M, N.

The order relation for cardinals is transitive, i.e. for any three cardinals $\overline{\overline{M}}$, $\overline{\overline{N}}$, $\overline{\overline{P}}$: If $\overline{\overline{M}} < \overline{\overline{N}}$ and $\overline{\overline{N}} < \overline{\overline{P}}$, then $\overline{\overline{M}} < \overline{\overline{P}}$.

We define $\overline{\overline{M}}$ to be $> \overline{\overline{N}}$, if $\overline{\overline{N}} < \overline{\overline{M}}$. Then $\overline{\overline{M}} > \overline{\overline{N}}$ exactly in Case (1b).

The relationship $\overline{\overline{M}} = \overline{\overline{N}}$, i.e. $M \sim N$, evidently falls under Case (2) by taking as N_1 and M_1 the improper subsets. Hence, for any two cardinals $\overline{\overline{M}}$ and $\overline{\overline{N}}$, the three relationships $\overline{\overline{M}} < \overline{\overline{N}}$, $\overline{\overline{M}} = \overline{\overline{N}}$ and $\overline{\overline{M}} > \overline{\overline{N}}$ are 'mutually exclusive', i.e. not more than one of them can hold.

It does not appear till an advanced stage of the theory (references in § 5) whether they are 'exhaustive', i.e. whether at least one of the three must hold. The situation is partially clarified by the next theorem, after which the question remains only whether Case (3) can arise.

***§ 4. The equivalence theorem, finite and infinite sets.** THEOREM A. *If* $M \sim N_1 \subset N$ *and* $N \sim M_1 \subset M$, *then* $M \sim N$. In other words: *In Case* (2) *of* § 3, $\overline{\overline{M}} = \overline{\overline{N}}$. (F. Bernstein 1898.)

PROOF. By the hypotheses, we may suppose given a particular 1-1 correspondence $M \overset{1}{\sim} N_1$ between M and the subset N_1 of N; and similarly $N \overset{2}{\sim} M_1$. Our problem is to find a third 1-1 correspondence $M \overset{3}{\sim} N$.

Let $A_0 = M - M_1$. In the given correspondence $M \overset{1}{\sim} N_1$, the elements of the subset A_0 of M will correspond to elements forming a subset B_1 of N_1 (and hence of N), or in symbols $A_0 \overset{1}{\sim} B_1$. Then in the other given correspondence $N \overset{2}{\sim} M_1$, the elements of the subset B_1 of N will correspond to elements forming a subset A_1 of M_1 (and hence of M), or in symbols $B_1 \overset{2}{\sim} A_1$; and so on. Thus

$$A_0 \overset{1}{\sim} B_1 \overset{2}{\sim} A_1 \overset{1}{\sim} B_2 \overset{2}{\sim} A_2 \overset{1}{\sim} B_3 \overset{2}{\sim} A_3 \overset{1}{\sim} \dots .$$

The situation may be grasped by picturing M and N as mirrors by which the part A_0 of M outside M_1 is reflected back and forth to produce an infinite succession of images $A_1, A_2, A_3, \dots$ in M and $B_1, B_2, B_3, \dots$ in N, as shown in the figure. (The sets M, M_1 and N are represented by

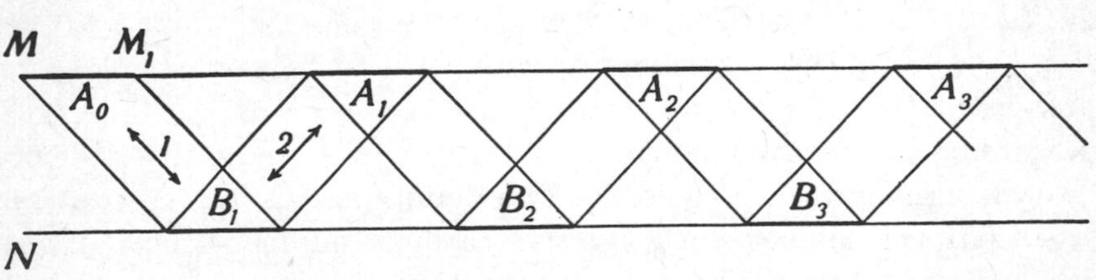

the parts of the horizontal lines to the right of the labels "M", "M_1" and "N"; the sets $A_0, B_1, A_1, \dots$ by the intercepted segments.)

Let $A = A_0 + A_1 + A_2 + A_3 + \dots$; i.e. A is the subset of M containing the elements which fall in A_0 or in any of its images A_1, A_2, $A_3, \dots$ in M. Also let $B = B_1 + B_2 + B_3 + \dots$; i.e. B is the subset of N containing the elements which fall in any of the images B_1, B_2, B_3, ... of A_0 in N.

To obtain the 1-1 correspondence $M \overset{3}{\sim} N$, we state a rule which determines to each element m of M a corresponding element n of N, and prove that the resulting correspondence is 1-1 between M and N.

RULE. Consider any element m of M. Either m belongs to the subset A, or m does not belong to A, i.e. m belongs to $M - A$. If m belongs to A, the corresponding element n of N shall be that which corresponds to m in the correspondence $M \overset{1}{\sim} N_1$. If m belongs to $M - A$ (in which case m belongs to M_1), the corresponding element n of N shall be that to which m corresponds in the correspondence $N \overset{2}{\sim} M_1$.

The resulting correspondence is 1-1 between M and N, for:

(a) To different elements m of M, say m_1 and m_2, there correspond different elements n_1 and n_2 of N. This is clear when m_1 and m_2 both belong to A or both to $M - A$. But it is also so when $m_1 \in A$ and $m_2 \in M - A$, since then $n_1 \in B$ and $n_2 \in N - B$.

(b) Each element of N corresponds to some element m of M. Namely, the elements of B all correspond to elements in A, and the elements of $N - B$ all correspond to elements in $M - A$.

The method of bringing M and N into 1-1 correspondence may be visualized as a shifting in the above picture of each of the parts A_0, A_1, A_2, A_3, ... of M one position to the right, so that A_0 takes the place of A_1, A_1 of A_2, A_2 of A_3, ... This changes $N \overset{2}{\sim} M_1$ into $N \overset{3}{\sim} M$.

COROLLARY A. *If* $M \subset N$, *then* $\overline{\overline{M}} \leq \overline{\overline{N}}$.

($\overline{\overline{M}} \leq \overline{\overline{N}}$ means: $\overline{\overline{M}} < \overline{\overline{N}}$ or $\overline{\overline{M}} = \overline{\overline{N}}$.) For if $M \subset N$, then either Case (1a) or Case (2) applies with M as the N_1.

The cardinal number of the empty set O we call 0. (NOTE: $M' \sim$ O only if $M' =$ O.) The cardinal number of any set $N + \{a\}$ where $a \notin N$ we call $\overline{\overline{N}} + 1$. (NOTE: For a given set $N + \{a\}$ with $a \notin N$, a set $M' \sim N + \{a\}$ if and only if $M' = N' + \{a'\}$ where $a' \notin N'$ and $N' \sim N$.)

Regarding the natural numbers 0, 1, 2, ..., n, $n + 1$, ... as a sequence of objects already known to us, the two definitions just stated correlate to each natural number n a respective cardinal number which we also write n. We call these cardinals *finite cardinals*, and sets which have these cardinals *finite sets*. The following two propositions will be proved in Example 1 § 7.

(I) *For each natural number n, the finite cardinal n is the cardinal of the set of the natural numbers which precede the natural number n in the usual order of the natural numbers; or in symbols,* $n = \overline{\overline{\{0, 1, 2, \ldots, n-1\}}}$.

(2) *If* $\overline{\overline{M}} = n$ *(for a natural number n) and* $M \sim M_1 \subset M$, *then* $M_1 = M$. Thus: *A finite set is not equivalent to any proper subset of itself.*

From these two propositions it is not hard to show that the equality relation $m = n$ and order relation $m < n$ as determined for finite cardinals by the definitions of § 3 agree with the familiar equality and order relation for the natural numbers (in particular, we do have $n < n + 1$ for finite cardinals). Thus no confusion will result from identifying the natural numbers with the finite cardinals when we choose to do so.

A set which is not finite we call *infinite*, and its cardinal an *infinite* or *transfinite cardinal*. The cardinal number of the set of the natural numbers, and therefore of every enumerably infinite set (§ 1), we call $\aleph_0$ (read "alef null").

COROLLARY B. *If n is a finite cardinal,* $n < \aleph_0$.

PROOF. Because n is the cardinal of the subset $\{0, 1, 2, \ldots, n-1\}$ of the natural numbers, by Corollary A, $n \leq \aleph_0$. Assume, contrary to the corollary, that $n = \aleph_0$. But $n + 1$ is also a finite cardinal, so similarly $n + 1 \leq \aleph_0$, which with $n = \aleph_0$ gives $n + 1 \leq n$, contradicting $n < n+1$. Hence the assumption $n = \aleph_0$ is untenable, and the remaining alternative $n < \aleph_0$ is established.

THEOREM B. *An infinite set M has an enumerably infinite subset.*

PROOF. M is not empty, since otherwise it would have the finite cardinal 0. Thus M has an element a_0. Then $M - \{a_0\}$ is not empty, since otherwise M would have the finite cardinal 1. Thus M has another element a_1. Continuing thus, we select distinct elements $a_0, a_1, a_2, a_3, \ldots$ corresponding to the natural numbers 0, 1, 2, 3, ..., which proves the theorem. If P is the set $M - \{a_0, a_1, a_2, a_3, \ldots\}$ of the elements of M not selected,

$$M = P + \{a_0, a_1, a_2, a_3, \ldots\}.$$

COROLLARY A. *If* $\overline{\overline{M}}$ *is an infinite cardinal, then* $\aleph_0 \leq \overline{\overline{M}}$.

By the theorem with Corollary A Theorem A.

COROLLARY B. *An infinite set M is equivalent to a proper subset of itself.*

For M (expressed as above) is equivalent to its proper subset

$$M - \{a_0\} = P + \{a_1, a_2, a_3, a_4, \ldots\}.$$

This with (2) above was proposed by Dedekind 1888 as an alternative definition of the distinction between finite and infinite sets. (We see that the property observed in Galileo's "paradox" is characteristic of infinite sets.)

COROLLARY C. *The cardinal number of an infinite set M is unchanged by the introduction of a finite or enumerably infinite set of elements.*

For new elements $b_0, b_1, b_2, b_3, \ldots$ can be introduced thus,

$$M + \{b_0, b_1, b_2, b_3, \ldots\} = P + \{a_0, b_0, a_1, b_1, \ldots\}.$$

Inversely, the corollary says that the removal of an enumerable set of elements from a set does not change the cardinal, provided the resulting set M is infinite. If the original set is non-enumerable, the resulting set must be infinite, as otherwise there would be an obvious enumeration of the original set. Thus:

COROLLARY D. *The cardinal number of a non-enumerable set is unchanged by the removal of a finite or enumerably infinite set of elements.*

***§ 5. Higher transfinite cardinals.** The first of the theorems of this section is a formulation in general terms of the situation which we met in the last example of § 2. The reader may also find it instructive to experiment with the theorem or its lemma for the case that M is a small finite set. The second of the theorems is a generalization of the situation encountered in Corollary B of Theorem A.

We take advantage of the equivalence theorem, via its Corollary A, to simplify the presentation of the proofs. The theorems however can be proved, with only slight modifications in the argument, without the use of the equivalence theorem.

LEMMA A. *If S is a set of subsets of M, and $M \sim \mathsf{S}$, then there is a subset T of M which does not belong to S.*

PROOF, by Cantor's diagonal method. A subset of M is defined when it is determined which of the elements of M belong to the subset. This can be arranged by stating a general criterion, which, for any element m of M, determines whether that element belongs to the subset or does not belong to the subset. We now give a criterion of this sort to define T.

CRITERION. In the 1-1 correspondence given by the hypothesis $M \sim \mathsf{S}$, any element m of M corresponds to an element S of S. But S is one of the subsets of M. Therefore either m belongs to S, or m does not belong to S. If m belongs to S, then m shall not belong to T. If m does not belong to S, then m shall belong to T.

Now suppose, contrary to what is to be shown, that T belongs to S. Select that element of M, call it m_1, which corresponds to T in the 1-1 correspondence $M \sim \mathsf{S}$.

Does m_1 belong to T? We apply the criterion, with m_1 as the m. Since m_1 corresponds to T, the S of the criterion is now T. The criterion gives a contradiction, either if m_1 belongs to T, or if m_1 does not belong to T.

The supposition that T belongs to S thus leads to absurdity. Hence, by the method of *reductio ad absurdum* (in which the negation of a proposition is proved by deducing a contradiction from the proposition), we conclude that T does not belong to S.

If M is a given set, then the set of the subsets of M, i.e. the set of which the elements are (all) the subsets of M, is designated as $\mathfrak{U}M$ ("$\mathfrak{U}$" from the German "Untermenge").

Theorem C. *For any set* M, $\overline{\overline{M}} < \overline{\overline{\mathfrak{U}M}}$. (Cantor's theorem.)

Proof. If N_1 is the set of the unit subsets of M, then $M \sim N_1 \subset \mathfrak{U}M$. Hence by Corollary A Theorem A, $\overline{\overline{M}} = \overline{\overline{N}}_1 \leq \overline{\overline{\mathfrak{U}M}}$. Suppose, contrary to the theorem, that $\overline{\overline{M}} = \overline{\overline{\mathfrak{U}M}}$, i.e. $M \sim \mathfrak{U}M$. Then $\mathfrak{U}M$ would satisfy the conditions for S in the lemma. By the lemma, there would be a subset T of M which does not belong to $\mathfrak{U}M$. This is absurd, since $\mathfrak{U}M$ is the set of all the subsets of M. Therefore the remaining alternative $\overline{\overline{M}} < \overline{\overline{\mathfrak{U}M}}$ must hold.

If we take as the M of the theorem a set with the transfinite cardinal $\aleph_0$, we discover sets $\mathfrak{U}M$, $\mathfrak{U}\mathfrak{U}M$, ... which have greater and greater transfinite cardinals. These new cardinals are denoted by $2^{\aleph_0}$, $2^{2^{\aleph_0}}$, ... (In fact, for any set M, the cardinal of $\mathfrak{U}M$ is denoted by $2^{\overline{\overline{M}}}$. Note that this accords with the usual arithmetic when M is finite.)

Lemma B. *If S is a set, and M is a set of subsets of S, and to each member M of M there is another member M' of M such that $\overline{\overline{M}} < \overline{\overline{M}}'$, then $\overline{\overline{M}} < \overline{\overline{S}}$ for every member M of M.*

Proof. Since $M \subset S$, by Corollary A Theorem A, $\overline{\overline{M}} \leq \overline{\overline{S}}$. Assume, contrary to the lemma, that $\overline{\overline{M}} = \overline{\overline{S}}$. But similarly, $\overline{\overline{M}}' \leq \overline{\overline{S}}$, which with $\overline{\overline{M}} = \overline{\overline{S}}$ gives $\overline{\overline{M}}' \leq \overline{\overline{M}}$, contradicting $\overline{\overline{M}} < \overline{\overline{M}}'$. Hence the assumption $\overline{\overline{M}} = \overline{\overline{S}}$ is false, and the alternative $\overline{\overline{M}} < \overline{\overline{S}}$ holds.

If M is a set of which the members are sets, then the set of (all) the objects each of which belongs to some member M of M is called the *sum* of the sets belonging to M and is designated by $\mathfrak{S}\mathsf{M}$. The set of the objects each of which belongs to every member M of M is called the *intersection* or *product* of the sets belonging to M and is designated by $\mathfrak{D}\mathsf{M}$ ("$\mathfrak{D}$" from the German "Durchschnitt"). These notions are the same as were introduced in § 3, except that now they are expressed as operations on the set M of the sets M which are added or multiplied. For example, $M + N = \mathfrak{S}\{M, N\}$, $M \cdot N = \mathfrak{D}\{M, N\}$.

THEOREM D. *If* M *is a set of sets, and if to each member* M *of* M *there is another member* M' *of* M *such that* $\overline{\overline{M}} < \overline{\overline{M'}}$, *then* $\overline{\overline{M}} < \overline{\overline{\mathfrak{S}\mathsf{M}}}$ *for every member* M of M.

PROOF. From the definition of $\mathfrak{S}\mathsf{M}$, every element M of M is a subset of $\mathfrak{S}\mathsf{M}$. The theorem now follows from the lemma with $\mathfrak{S}\mathsf{M}$ as the S of the lemma.

By this theorem, the sum of the sets $M, \mathfrak{U}M, \mathfrak{U}\mathfrak{U}M, \ldots$ which have the increasing transfinite cardinals $\aleph_0$, $2^{\aleph_0}$, $2^{2^{\aleph_0}}$, ... is a set having a transfinite cardinal greater still than any of those cardinals. This set can be used by Theorem C to start a new ascending series. This hierarchy extends indefinitely.

More will be found on Cantor's theory of abstract sets in Cantor 1895-7, Hausdorff 1914 or 1927, or Fraenkel 1928 or 1953, for example. There is a cognate branch of the theory dealing with "ordinal numbers". The "comparability theorem for cardinal numbers", which asserts that $\overline{\overline{M}} < \overline{\overline{N}}$, $\overline{\overline{M}} = \overline{\overline{N}}$ and $\overline{\overline{M}} > \overline{\overline{N}}$ are exhaustive (end § 3), appears as a corollary of the "well-ordering theorem" of Zermelo 1904 (cf. e.g. Hausdorff 1914 or 1927 p. 61, or Fraenkel 1928 p. 205). For a brief account of the celebrated "continuum problem", which deals with the question whether any cardinal lies between $\aleph_0$ and $2^{\aleph_0}$, see Gödel 1947.

We have begun with Cantor's theory for two quite opposite reasons. First, some of the ideas and methods which will prove basic later appear in it in their original and simplest form. Second, the theory, pursued too far, reveals logical difficulties, which are a point of departure for our main investigation. This will appear in Chapter III.

EXAMPLES. SETS OF CARDINAL $2^{\aleph_0}$. This is the cardinal assigned to the set of the subsets of the set of the natural numbers, which we described in § 2 as the set of the ***sets of natural numbers***. There we represented the elements of the set by the ***infinite sequences of*** 0's ***and*** 1's. The 0's and 1's can be interpreted as the digits in a dual (or dyadic) number system, i.e. a number system based on 2 as the decimal system is based on 10, so that we have the set of the ***proper dual fractions.*** Using Theorem B Corollary D to withdraw the terminating fractions, which are enumerable, we obtain the ***proper non-terminating dual fractions.*** These represent 1-1 the ***real numbers*** x ***in the interval*** $0 < x \leq 1$. From the proper non-terminating dual fractions we also obtain 1-1 the ***infinite sequences of natural numbers*** or ***functions of a natural number taking a natural number as value,*** by coordinating to a fraction that function $f(n)$ for which $f(0) =$ the number of 0's before the first 1 in the fraction, $f(1) =$ the number of 0's between the first 1 and the second 1, and so on (for example, the function n^2 corresponds to the fraction .1010000100000000 1 . . .).

Now omit from the interval $0 < x \leq 1$ the number $x = 1$, leaving the ***real numbers*** x ***in the interval*** $0 < x < 1$. A function $y = f(x)$ is easily found which, as x ranges over this interval, takes as value y exactly once each of the ***real numbers,*** e.g. the function $y = \cot \pi x$. Removing the rational numbers, the (real) ***irrational numbers*** are left; or removing the algebraic numbers, the ***transcendental numbers.*** In Cartesian coordinate geometry, the real numbers are coordinated to the ***points of the real Euclidean line.*** This set is the 'linear continuum', and accordingly the cardinal $2^{\aleph_0}$ is the 'power of the continuum'.

Next we can proceed as follows to obtain the set of the ***ordered pairs of real numbers,*** or regarding a pair (x, y) as Cartesian coordinates in the plane, the ***points of the real Euclidean plane.*** Under the equivalence already obtained between the real numbers and the infinite sequences of 0's and 1's, any two real numbers x, y correspond respectively to sequences of 0's and 1's

$$x_0 \quad x_1 \quad x_2 \quad x_3 \ldots,$$

$$y_0 \quad y_1 \quad y_2 \quad y_3 \ldots,$$

which can be combined into a single sequence

$$x_0 \quad y_0 \quad x_1 \quad y_1 \quad x_2 \quad y_2 \quad x_3 \quad y_3 \ldots,$$

corresponding to a single real number. Conversely, any single sequence breaks up into a determinate pair of sequences under this method of combination. Similar procedure gives the ***n-tuples of real numbers*** or the ***points of real Euclidean n-dimensional space*** for any fixed positive integer n, and even the ***infinite sequences of real numbers*** or the ***points of real Euclidean*** $\aleph_0$***-dimensional space.*** This last example is treated by using the method of § 1 to combine $\aleph_0$ sequences of 0's and 1's

$$\begin{array}{cccccccc}
x_{00} & & x_{01} & \rightarrow & x_{02} & & x_{03} & \rightarrow \cdots \\
\downarrow & \nearrow & & \swarrow & & \nearrow & & \\
x_{10} & & x_{11} & & x_{12} & & x_{13} & \cdots \\
& \swarrow & & \nearrow & & & & \\
x_{20} & & x_{21} & & x_{22} & & x_{23} & \cdots \\
\downarrow & \nearrow & & & & & & \\
x_{30} & & x_{31} & & x_{32} & & x_{33} & \cdots \\
& & & & \cdots & & &
\end{array}$$

into a single sequence

$$x_{00}\ x_{10}\ x_{01}\ x_{02}\ x_{11}\ x_{20}\ x_{30}\ x_{21}\ x_{12}\ x_{03} \cdots$$

in which each member of each of the given sequences has a determinate position.

For any one of the ***real continuous functions of a real variable***, all the values of the function are determined by the continuity property as soon as the values are given for the rational values of the independent variable. These values can be given as an infinite sequence of real numbers, by following the order of the rational numbers in some fixed enumeration of the latter. Therefore by Theorem A Corollary A, the set of these functions has at most the cardinal $2^{\aleph_0}$. But also it must have at least this cardinal, and hence exactly this cardinal, since the constant functions constitute a subset with the cardinal.

SETS OF CARDINAL $2^{2^{\aleph_0}}$. This is the cardinal of the ***sets of sets of natural numbers***. From the equivalence between the sets of natural numbers and the real numbers or the points in n-dimensional or $\aleph_0$-dimensional space, it follows that the ***sets of real numbers*** and the ***point sets in real Euclidean n-dimensional or $\aleph_0$-dimensional space*** have this cardinal. The ***real functions of a real variable*** can be represented by their graphs, which are point sets in the plane, and hence the set of them has at most the cardinal $2^{2^{\aleph_0}}$. It has exactly this cardinal, since those of the functions which take only 0 and 1 as values are the representing functions of the sets of real numbers, and so constitute a subset with the cardinal. If we extend geometric terminology to this example, we have the set of the ***points of real Euclidean $2^{\aleph_0}$-dimensional space.***

Chapter II

SOME FUNDAMENTAL CONCEPTS

§ 6. The natural numbers. The purpose of this chapter is to bring together, partly for reference and partly for closer inspection, some of the ideas and methods of mathematics.

When we write the natural number sequence

$$0, \quad 1, \quad 2, \quad 3, \quad \ldots,$$

we rely on the dots "..." to suggest the continuation of the sequence beyond the several members shown.

Kronecker remarked (1886), "God made the integers, all the rest is the work of man." We cannot expect that the cognizance of the natural number sequence can be reduced to that of anything essentially more primitive than itself.

But by elaborating upon what our conception of it comprises, we may succeed in making clearer the bases of our reasoning with the natural numbers.

We begin by describing the natural numbers as the objects which can be generated by starting with an initial object 0 (*zero*) and successively passing from an object n already generated to another object $n + 1$ or n' (the *successor* of n).

Here we conceive of it as possible, no matter how far we have already gone to reach n, to go the one step further to reach n'. The use of the accent notation "n'" instead of the more familiar "$n + 1$" emphasizes that $'$ is a primitive unary operation or function used in generating the natural numbers, while $+$ can be defined at a later stage as a binary operation or function of two natural numbers.

To obtain the natural numbers with the usual notations, it remains only to explain 0, 1, 2, 3, ... as standing for

$$0, \quad 0', \quad 0'', \quad 0''', \ldots,$$

respectively. This is a matter of detail concerning decimal notation.

In the foregoing description, we have evoked the conception of a succession of discrete steps. These consist in starting with 0, and proceeding repeatedly from a number n to the next n'. The description can be broken into several clauses, as follows.

1. 0 is a *natural number*. 2. If n is a *natural number*, then n' is a *natural number*. 3. The only *natural numbers* are those given by 1 and 2.

In this format, the succession of discrete steps becomes an application of Clause 1 and a succession of applications of Clause 2. The three clauses together constitute an example of what we call an *inductive definition*. The term ('natural number') which is being defined is italicized. The clauses except the last, which provide instances of the term being defined, are called *direct clauses*; the last clause, which says that the only instances are those provided by the preceding clauses, is the *extremal clause*.

Not stated in this inductive definition is the condition for distinctness, namely that numbers generated by applications of Clauses 1 and 2 in distinct ways should be distinct objects. This can be separated into two further propositions.

4. For any natural numbers m and n, $m' = n'$ only if $m = n$. 5. For any natural number n, $n' \neq 0$.

Also it is understood that $'$ is a univalent operator or single-valued function, so that conversely to 4: For any natural numbers m and n, $m' = n'$ if $m = n$.

To see that Propositions 4 and 5 do require the distinctness of every two differently generated numbers, we can reason as follows. Suppose that at a given stage in the generation of the numbers, all the numbers $0, 1, \ldots, n$ so far generated are distinct. Then the next one generated n' must be distinct from the successors $1, \ldots, n$ among those previously generated (by 4) and from 0 (by 5). So each successive step in the generation produces a new number.

For example, $0'''' \neq 0''$, as may also be seen thus. By 4 applied with $0'''$ as the m and $0'$ as the n, $0'''' = 0''$ only if $0''' = 0'$. By 4 again, $0''' = 0'$ only if $0'' = 0$. But by 5 with $0'$ as the n, $0'' \neq 0$.

These five propositions 1—5, with one difference, were taken by Peano (1889, 1891*) as axioms characterizing the natural number sequence. Peano stated Proposition 3 instead as the principle of mathematical induction (§ 7), and placed it fifth on his list, 4 and 5 being moved up to third and fourth, respectively.

Here we are not considering what the natural numbers are intrinsically, but only how they form the natural number sequence. A particular natural number is to be recognized as the object occupying a particular place in the sequence. In other words, a particular number is given when its generation under the inductive definition is given. For example, the natural number 4 is given as that object which is obtained by starting with the initial object 0 and applying the successor operation $'$ once, again, again and again; or briefly, 4 is given as $0''''$. A number such as 872656 in decimal notation could in principle be exhibited by applications of $'$ to 0, though in practice we do not do so.

Of course when we deal with propositions such as that a certain equation has two roots, we further employ the assignment of the natural numbers as cardinal numbers of finite sets (§ 4).

ORDER. Under the inductive definition of the natural numbers, they are generated in a certain order (the familiar one). Thus we define m to be $< n$, if m is generated before n in the course of generating n. Dissecting this, we have the following inductive definition of the relation $m < n$ (where m, n range over the natural numbers).

O1. $m < m'$. O2. If $m < n$, then $m < n'$. O3. $m < n$ only as required by O1 and O2.

When this definition is read, for a fixed m, as an inductive definition of the class of the numbers n greater than m, it has the form of the original inductive definition of the natural numbers, with m' replacing 0.

§ 7. Mathematical induction. Let P be a property of natural numbers. Suppose that:

(1) 0 has the property P.

(2) If any natural number n has the property P, then its successor n' has the property P.

Then: Every natural number n has the property P.

This is the principle of *mathematical induction*. We can state it a little more briefly using "n" as a natural number variable and "$P(n)$" as a notation for the proposition that n has the property P: If (1) $P(0)$, and (2) for all n, if $P(n)$ then $P(n')$, then, for all n, $P(n)$.

The justification of the induction principle is almost immediate, when the natural numbers are conceived as the objects generated under the inductive definition 1—3 of § 6. Suppose we have a property P for which (1) and (2) hold. Must then every natural number n have the property P? We interpret an affirmative answer to mean simply that, if any natural number n were given to us, we could be sure that that n has the property P. But a natural number n is given precisely when (actually or in principle) we are given its generation under the inductive definition, by starting with 0 and applying an exhibited number of times the successor operation $'$.

Under these circumstances, we can use (1) and (2) to conclude that n has the property P. For example, $P(4)$ holds because 4 is given as $0''''$; by (1), $P(0)$; thence by (2), $P(0')$; by (2) again, $P(0'')$; by (2) again, $P(0''')$; and by (2) again, $P(0'''')$.

Otherwise expressed, (1) and (2) are tools which enable us, while we are generating the natural numbers by Clauses 1 and 2 of the inductive definition, at the same time to verify for each number as we generate it that it has the property P.

This reasoning of course depends on the extremal clause 3 of the inductive definition. Conversely, the principle of induction can be used to prove Clause 3, by applying it with the following proposition as the $P(n)$: n is given as a natural number by Clauses 1 and 2, i.e. can be generated by starting with 0 and applying the successor operation $'$.

In connection with a proof by mathematical induction, we use the following terminology. The proposition $P(n)$ depending on a variable natural number n we call the *induction proposition*; and the variable n the *induction variable* or *induction number* or the variable *on* which the induction takes place. The part of the proof which consists in establishing (1), i.e. the proof that $P(0)$, we call the *basis* of the induction. The part which consists in establishing (2), i.e. the proof that if $P(n)$ then $P(n')$, we call the *induction step*. Within the induction step, the assumption $P(n)$, from which we deduce $P(n')$, we call the *hypothesis of the induction*.

Sometimes, in order to carry through the induction step, it is necessary to assume as hypothesis of the induction, not simply $P(n)$ but that $P(m)$ for all $m \leq n$. The reader may satisfy himself that the induction principle is valid in this modification, called a *course-of-values induction*. Induction may be applied to the proof of a proposition depending on a positive integer instead of a natural number, in which case the basis consists in proving $P(1)$.

The student encounters mathematical induction in elementary algebra courses. Formulas for summing progressions are often given as examples of propositions to be proved by induction which are not obvious before the proofs have been given. Many propositions which we commonly take for granted depend on induction when explicitly proved; and in other cases an induction step is so simple that it is passed off with the phrase "and so on" or the like (e.g. Theorems A and B § 4).

EXAMPLE 1. Prove the propositions (1) and (2) of § 4 by induction on n. We do so for (2), leaving (1) to the reader. The induction proposition is: *For any sets M and M_1, if $\overline{\overline{M}} = n$ and $M \sim M_1 \subset M$, then $M_1 = M$.*

Basis: $n = 0$. Let M and M_1 be sets such that $\overline{\overline{M}} = 0$, i.e. $M = O$, and $O \sim M_1 \subset O$. Then $M_1 = O$. Induction step. Assume the induction proposition as stated (as hypothesis of the induction). Now let M and M_1 be sets such that $\overline{\overline{M}} = n + 1$, i.e. $M = N + \{a\}$ where $\overline{\overline{N}} = n$ and $a \notin N$, and $N + \{a\} \sim M_1 \subset N + \{a\}$. We must prove that then $M_1 = N + \{a\}$. In the given 1-1 correspondence $N + \{a\} \sim M_1$, the element a of $N + \{a\}$ corresponds to some element b of M_1. Then $N \sim M_1 - \{b\} \subset (N + \{a\}) - \{b\}$. Moreover $(N + \{a\}) - \{b\} \sim N$. Hence $\overline{\overline{(N + \{a\}) - \{b\}}} = n$ and $(N + \{a\}) - \{b\} \sim M_1 - \{b\} \subset (N + \{a\}) - \{b\}$. By the hypothesis of the induction, applied using $(N + \{a\}) - \{b\}$ as the M and $M_1 - \{b\}$ as the M_1, $M_1 - \{b\} = (N + \{a\}) - \{b\}$. Hence (since $b \in M_1$ and $b \in N + \{a\}$), $M_1 = N + \{a\}$.

Example 2. In mathematical formulas parentheses are introduced in pairs to show which way the parts of the formula should be associated. In complicated cases different species of parentheses such as ( ), { }, [ ] may be employed; and very complicated cases may be avoided by various abbreviations. However, the question exists in principle whether, using one species of parentheses only, the association of a formula is unambiguously fixed by its parentheses. (The question is equivalent to a geometrical one concerning nesting of intervals.)

To make the question precise, suppose we have $2n$ parentheses, n of them being left parentheses (, and n of them right parentheses), and that they occur in linear order from left to right. This is the way they would occur in a mathematical formula, the other symbols of the formula which we need not notice now being interspersed among them.

We say that two pairs of parentheses *separate each other*, if they occur in the order $(_i\ (_j\ )_i\ )_j$, where the i's identify either pair and the j's the other, and other parentheses may occur interspersed among the four shown.

We define a 1-1 pairing of the n left parentheses with the n right parentheses (briefly, a pairing of the $2n$ parentheses) to be *proper*, if a left parenthesis is always paired with a right parenthesis to the right of it, and if no two of the pairs separate each other.

It is almost immediate that if $2n$ parentheses are properly paired, on removing any of the pairs, the remaining parentheses are properly paired. Also the parentheses included between a given pair in the proper pairing of the $2n$ parentheses are properly paired.

The following three lemmas contain the answer to the proposed question and some related information.

LEMMA 1. *A proper pairing of 2n parentheses ($n > 0$) contains an innermost pair, i.e. a pair which includes no other of the parentheses between them.*

Prove by a course-of-values induction on n. One may choose to consider n either a positive integer or a natural number. If the latter, the basis is *vacuously true*, i.e. true because its hypothesis is not satisfied. (HINT: Under the induction step, the leftmost parenthesis will be a left parenthesis $(_i$, and this with its mate $)_i$ either themselves constitute an innermost pair, or else include a set of parentheses lying between them to which the hypothesis of the induction can be applied.)

LEMMA 2. *A set of 2n parentheses admits at most one proper pairing.*

Prove by a (simple) induction on n. (HINT: Under the induction step, by Lemma 1 the given parentheses contain an innermost pair. Withdrawing this, the hypothesis of the induction applies to the set of the parentheses remaining.)

LEMMA 3. *If 2n parentheses and a consecutive subset of 2m of them both admit proper pairings, then the proper pairing in the subset forms a part of the proper pairing in the whole set, i.e. each parenthesis of the subset has the same mate in both pairings.*

Prove by induction on m.

For illustration, consider the 22 parentheses

$$(_7^1\ (_6^2\ (_4^3\ (_2^4\ (_1^5\ )_1^6\ )_2^7\ (_3^8\ )_3^9\ )_4^{10}\ (_5^{11}\ )_5^{12}\ )_6^{13}\ )_7^{14}\ (_{11}^{15}\ (_{10}^{16}\ (_8^{17}\ )_8^{18}\ (_9^{19}\ )_9^{20}\ )_{10}^{21}\ )_{11}^{22}.$$

A proper pairing, indicated by the subscripts, is discovered by the following 'algorithm' (suggested by the proof of Lemma 2): at each stage, proceeding from the left, search out the first innermost pair among those not already used, and let this pair belong to the pairing. By Lemma 2, it would be futile to search for any other proper pairing than this. The third to the twelfth parentheses are a consecutive subset, in which a proper pairing has already been established in the process of pairing the whole set. By Lemma 3, it would be futile to search for any consecutive subset admitting a proper pairing other than one of those already properly paired in pairing the whole.

§ 8. Systems of objects. By a system S of objects we mean a (nonempty) set or class or domain D (or possibly several such sets) of objects among which are established certain relationships.

For example, the natural number sequence (§ 6) constitutes a system of the type $(D, 0, ')$ where D is a set, 0 is a member of the set D, and $'$ a unary operation on a member of the set D. Another simple type of system is $(D, <)$ where D is a set and $<$ is a binary relation between members of the set.

When the objects of the system are known only through the relationships of the system, the system is *abstract*. What is established in this case is the structure of the system, and what the objects are, in any respects other than how they fit into the structure, is left unspecified.

Then any further specification of what the objects are gives a *representation* (or *model*) of the abstract system, i.e. a system of objects which satisfy the relationships of the abstract system and have some further status as well. These objects are not necessarily more concrete, as they may be chosen from some other abstract system (or even from the same one under a reinterpretation of the relationships).

Several representations of the abstract natural number sequence are (a) the natural numbers as cardinals of finite sets, (b) the positive integers (1 representing the abstract 0), (c) the even natural numbers (+2 representing the abstract $'$). (d) Commercial products are sometimes packaged in containers which carry advertizing matter including a picture of the container itself. Physically, the picture must be limited in accuracy. But if we suppose perfect accuracy, we can represent 0 by the container, 1 by the picture of the container on the container, 2 by the picture of the container in the picture of the container on the container, and so on.

Two representations of the same abstract system are (*simply*) *isomorphic*, i.e. can be put into a 1-1 correspondence preserving the relationships. More precisely, two systems $(D_1, 0_1, '_1)$ and $(D_2, 0_2, '_2)$ of the type $(D, 0, ')$ are simply isomorphic, if there exists a 1-1 correspondence between D_1 and D_2 such that 0_1 corresponds to 0_2 (in symbols, $0_1 \longleftrightarrow 0_2$), and whenever $m_1 \longleftrightarrow m_2$ then $m_1{'_1} \longleftrightarrow m_2{'_2}$. Two systems $(D_1, <_1)$ and $(D_2, <_2)$ of the type $(D, <)$ are simply isomorphic, if there exists a 1-1 correspondence between D_1 and D_2 such that, if $m_1 \longleftrightarrow m_2$ and $n_1 \longleftrightarrow n_2$ then: $m_1 <_1 n_1$ if and only if $m_2 <_2 n_2$.

Conversely, any two simply isomorphic systems constitute representations of the same abstract system, which is obtained by abstracting from either of them, i.e. by leaving out of account all relationships and properties except the ones to be considered for the abstract system.

As a second example of an abstract system of the type $(D, 0, ')$, let D have just two (distinct) objects 0 and 1, and let $0' = 1$ and $1' = 0$. We call this system the *residues modulo* 2. The natural number sequence becomes this when each number is replaced by its remainder after division by 2 (i.e. is *reduced* mod 2), thus,

$$0, \ 1, \ 0, \ 1, \ 0, \ 1, \ \ldots .$$

(Systems of residues were first considered by Gauss, 1801.)

As a third example, let S consist of two sequences

$$0, \ 1, \ 2, \ 3, \ldots; \ \omega, \ \omega+1, \ \omega+2, \ \omega+3, \ldots,$$

each by itself of the same structure as the natural numbers, and with no member of either sequence in the relation of successor to a member of the other.

We can modify each of these three examples obviously to consider it as a system of the type $(D, <)$. In the third example, we then take the elements in the order shown; and we call them the *ordinals* $< 2\omega$ (from Cantor's theory of ordinal numbers).

The residues mod 2 (or a representation of them) are not isomorphic with the natural numbers (or a representation of them), since it is impossible to establish a 1-1 correspondence. The ordinals $< 2\omega$ are not isomorphic with the natural numbers, for it is not possible in establishing a 1-1 correspondence to preserve the successor operation $'$ (or the order relation $<$).

In this section, we are writing "S" for a system and "D" for its set of objects, in the case of systems having one set. The notation can often be simplified without confusion to use one letter for both. It can e.g. in speaking of the natural numbers N as above. It cannot e.g. in speaking of the system $(N, <)$ consisting of the natural numbers, with the even numbers (odd numbers) ordered among themselves as usual, and all the even numbers preceding all the odd numbers. (This system is a representation of the ordinals $< 2\omega$.)

Systems of objects are introduced in mathematics under two contrasting methods or points of view (cf. Hilbert 1900).

The *genetic* or *constructive* method is illustrated by the inductive definition of the natural numbers (§ 6). There we conceived of the natural numbers as being generated or constructed in a certain orderly manner. (This did not prevent our treating them abstractly.)

In the *axiomatic* or *postulational* method, on the other hand, some propositions, called *axioms* or *postulates*, are put down at the outset as assumptions or conditions on a system S of objects. The consequences of the axioms are then developed as a theory about any existing system S of objects which satisfies the axioms.

To illustrate, we can take as the axioms Peano's five axioms. To

make the point clear, let us rewrite the Peano axioms substituting "member of D" for "natural number".
P1. $0 \varepsilon D$. P2. If $n \varepsilon D$, then $n' \varepsilon D$. P3. If $m \varepsilon D$ and $n \varepsilon D$, then $m' = n'$ only if $m = n$. P4. If $n \varepsilon D$, then $n' \neq 0$. P5. If $P \subset D$ and (1) $0 \varepsilon P$ and (2) whenever $n \varepsilon P$ then $n' \varepsilon P$, then $P = D$.

We already know that exactly one abstract system S satisfies these five axioms, namely the natural numbers which we previously introduced from the genetic standpoint.

But from the axiomatic standpoint, we can equally well consider other lists of axioms, for example P1—P4. Then S can be the natural numbers, or the ordinals $< 2\omega$, or any one of many other abstractly differing, i.e. non-isomorphic, systems.

If instead the axioms are P1 — P3, P5, then the different abstract systems which satisfy are precisely the natural numbers and the systems of residues mod m for each positive integer m.

Next suppose we not merely remove P4, but substitute for it:
P6. If $n \varepsilon D$, then $n' \neq n$ but $n'' = n$.
Now again exactly one abstract system satisfies, the residues mod 2.

The six axioms P1—P6 together are satisfied by no system S at all, since only the natural numbers satisfy P1—P5 and only the residues mod 2 satisfy P1—P3, P5, P6.

The axioms of an axiomatic theory are sometimes said to constitute an implicit definition of the system of the objects of the theory; but this can only mean that the axioms determine to which systems, defined from outside the theory, the theory applies. Then three cases arise. The axioms may be satisfied by no system of objects (e.g. P1—P6); or by exactly one abstract system, any two systems which satisfy being isomorphic (e.g. P1—P5, or P1—P3, P5, P6); or by more than one abstract system, i.e. non-isomorphic systems exist which satisfy (e.g. P1—P4, or P1—P3, P5). In the first case we may call the set of axioms *vacuous*; in the other two *non-vacuous*, and furthermore in the second *categorical* (Veblen 1904) and in the third *ambiguous*. (In the genetic method, on the other hand, the generation process is ordinarily intended to determine the abstract structure of the system completely, i.e. to constitute a categorical definition of the system.)

It may be by no means evident for a given axiomatic theory which of the three possibilities is the case. This is illustrated historically by the example of Euclidean geometry without Euclid's parallel postulate, on which depends the theorem that through a given point not on a given line there passes exactly one line parallel to the given line. From Euclid's

"Elements" (c. 330—320 B.C.) until the discovery of a non-Euclidean geometry by Lobatchevsky (1829) and Bolyai (1833), it was generally supposed that the axioms are categorical; or at least if the question had been asked in these terms, it would probably have been so answered.

The Greek's belief that they were dealing with a unique structure of space was not formulated in the present terminology. Euclid thought of his axioms as expressing certain fundamental properties of real space. The axiomatic method in this older sense, wherein the objects of the system S are supposed to be known prior to the axioms, may be distinguished as *informal* or *material axiomatics*. In this, the axioms merely express those properties of the objects which are being taken initially as evident from their construction, or in the case of theories applying to the empirical world as abstracted directly from experience or as postulated about that world.

The axiomatic method as described above, wherein the axioms are prior to any specification of the system S of objects which the axioms are about (and serve to introduce or "define implicitly" the S), was first developed systematically in Hilbert's "Grundlagen der Geometrie (Foundations of Geometry)" (1899), and may be distinguished as *formal* or *existential axiomatics*. We note that it is only from outside a formal axiomatic theory (i.e. in some other theory) that one can investigate whether one, or more than one, or no abstract system S satisfies the axioms. Within the formal axiomatic theory, the domain D for S plays the role of a fixed and completed set of objects, assumed as existing all at once apart from any order of generation, to which the operations, relations, etc. of S apply.

For a system S of the type $(D, 0, ')$, 0 and $'$, or D, 0 and $'$, are then called the *primitive* or *technical* or *undefined* notions, i.e. they are undefined prior to the introduction of the axioms. The other terms in the axioms are *ordinary* or *logical* or *defined*, i.e. their meanings must be previously understood. About D, 0 and $'$, it has only to be understood in advance that D is a set, 0 an object belonging to D, and $'$ an operation on a member of D; i.e. only the grammatical categories to which "D", "0" and "$'$" belong are defined in advance. Similarly for a system of the form $(D, <)$, the undefined notions are $<$, or D and $<$.

In mathematical practice there is often an interplay between the genetic and axiomatic methods of introducing systems of objects, as when an example of a system of objects satisfying the axioms is provided genetically. At other times an example may be drawn from another formal axiomatic theory. (In either case, as soon as the S for a given formal axiomatic theory is identified with a system of objects provided from outside the theory, we have an *application* of the formal axiomatic theory, in which application it becomes a material axiomatic theory.)

The formal axiomatic method is often used to advantage with ambiguous axiom systems, so as to develop simultaneously a common portion of theory for many different systems. The example of 'groups' in algebra is celebrated.

As another example, consider the following axioms for *linear order*, which apply to systems of the type $(D, <)$.

L1. If $m < n$ and $n < p$, then $m < p$. L2. At most one of $m < n$, $m = n$ and $m > n$ holds. L3. At least one of $m < n, m = n$ and $m > n$ holds.

Here $m > n$ means $n < m$. The variables m, n, p refer to any elements of D. These axioms are satisfied taking as D the natural numbers, the ordinals $< 2\omega$, the integers, the rational numbers, or the real numbers, and as $<$ the usual order relation for the same; and by many other systems. Omitting L3, we have a set of axioms for *partial order*.

***§ 9. Number theory vs. analysis.** *Arithmetic* or *number theory* may be described as the branch of mathematics which deals with the natural numbers and other (categorically defined) enumerable systems of objects, such as the integers or the rational numbers. A particular such system (or the theory of it) may be called *an arithmetic*. The treatment is usually abstract (§ 8). The objects are usually treated as *individuals* (i.e. they are not analyzed as composed out of other objects), except e.g. when the fundamental properties of non-negative rational numbers are being developed by representing them as ordered pairs of natural numbers.

In *arithmetic in the narrower sense* one is mainly concerned with particular operations called $+$ (addition) and $\cdot$ (multiplication), or also a few other related operations. In *arithmetic in the wider sense* or *number theory* a wider fund of concepts is employed.

These definitions are given to clarify our terminology. Sometimes "arithmetic" is encountered referring to the theory of $+$ and $\cdot$ for systems of numbers that are not enumerable (e.g. the 'arithmetic of transfinite cardinals').

While the cardinal numbers of the systems studied in arithmetic or number theory are $\aleph_0$ (or sometimes finite), *analysis* on the other hand deals with the real numbers and other systems of objects having the cardinal $2^{\aleph_0}$ (or sometimes a higher cardinal). As with number theory, the systems of objects employed in analysis are usually taken to be categorically determined.

Results of analysis are sometimes applied in number-theoretic investigations, which then constitute *analytic number theory*. Number theory without help from analysis is *pure* or *elementary number theory*.

We now examine briefly the fundamental system of objects for analysis, namely the continuum of the real numbers.

The theory of real numbers which is currently used as the basis for analysis (except by critics of its foundations) is the product of an earlier critical movement initiated by Gauss (1777—1855), Cauchy (1789—1857) and Abel (1802—1829).

This led late in the nineteenth century to the *arithmetization of analysis*, so called, by Weierstrass (1815—1897), Dedekind (1831—1916), Méray (1835—1911) and Cantor (1845—1918). Reliance on somewhat vague geometrical intuitions was replaced by a definition of the real numbers as certain objects constructed out of natural numbers, integers or rational numbers. The properties of the real numbers were thereby reduced ultimately to properties of natural numbers. As Poincaré said in 1900, "Today there remain in analysis only integers or finite or infinite systems of integers, interrelated by a net of relations of equality or inequality."

The definition of the real numbers from natural numbers, integers or rationals can be given in several ways. All lead to the same abstract structure of the real number continuum. In other words, what each of the definitions accomplishes is to provide a representation (§ 8) of the real numbers by objects constructed (directly or indirectly) out of natural numbers.

We have used the representations by the infinite decimal or dual fractions (§§ 2, 5). In principle any one of the sets proved equivalent to these (§ 5), e.g. the sets of natural numbers, could be used, but in practice one will choose a representation which makes it simple to define the properties of the real numbers.

A representation which makes the ordering of the real numbers especially perspicuous is that by Dedekind cuts (1872). Suppose the rational numbers R have been separated into two non-empty classes X_1, X_2 such that every rational in X_1 is $<$ every rational in X_2. Such a separation is called a *Dedekind cut* (*in* R). In case there is neither a greatest rational in the lower set X_1 nor a least in the upper X_2, the cut is called *open*. Dedekind's insight was that irrationals are called for exactly where the open cuts occur. A rational goes with either of two *closed* cuts, one for which it is the greatest in X_1, and the other for which it is the least in X_2. In order to have a unique representative of each real number (rational or irrational), we can use the lower sets X_1 of the cuts for which X_1 has no greatest. This gives us the following definition (writing **x** in place of X_1, and $R - \mathbf{x}$ in place of X_2).

A *real number* is a set **x** of rationals such that:
(a) Neither **x** nor $R - \mathbf{x}$ is empty. (b) **x** contains no greatest rational.
(c) Every rational in **x** is < every rational in $R - \mathbf{x}$.
The set C of reals is the set of all such sets **x** of rationals.

This definition makes use of the presupposed system R of rationals to construct the representatives of the reals, without taking R into the resulting system C as a subsystem. (If the members of R are individuals, the members of C are sets of those individuals.)

We now define a real number **x** to be *rational*, if $R - \mathbf{x}$ has a least member x, in which case **x** is said to *correspond* to the rational x (of the system R). Otherwise, **x** is *irrational*.

The rationals among the reals form a subsystem C_R of C which is isomorphic (§ 8) to the original system R of rationals, as we verify each time we use the representation to define a notion for the reals which has previously been defined for the rationals.

Examples. The real **2** is the set of the rationals < the rational 2, to which it corresponds. The real $\sqrt{\mathbf{2}}$ is the set of the rationals which are either negative or have squares < the rational 2 (among which there is no greatest). Since the square of no rational = 2 (as Pythagoras discovered in the sixth century B.C.), $R - \sqrt{\mathbf{2}}$ consists of the positive rationals having squares > 2 (among which there is no least), so $\sqrt{\mathbf{2}}$ is irrational.

The order relation for reals is defined thus: $\mathbf{x} < \mathbf{y}$, if there exists a rational r which is in **y** but not in **x**. (Now prove that C is linearly ordered by $<$, and that $(C_R, <)$ is isomorphic to $(R, <)$.)

A real number **v** is an *upper bound* of a set M of real numbers, if $\mathbf{v} \geq \mathbf{x}$ for every real number **x** belonging to M.

(A) *If a non-vacuous set* M *of real numbers has an upper bound, it has a least upper bound* **u** (= l.u.b. M).

Proof. We must construct **u** as a set of rationals having Properties (a) — (c). We are given M as a set of such sets of rationals. The definition of the set **u** is this: a rational $r \in \mathbf{u}$ when and only when, for some real number **x** which $\in$ M, $r \in \mathbf{x}$. In the symbolism of § 5, $\mathbf{u} = \mathfrak{S}$M. It is left to the reader to show now that **u** = l.u.b. M. (Prove that **u** is a real number, **u** is an upper bound of M, and M has no upper bound $\mathbf{v} < \mathbf{u}$.)

Lower bounds are defined similarly. If the real **x** is rational, let $\overline{\mathbf{x}} = \mathbf{x} + \{x\}$; otherwise, let $\overline{\mathbf{x}} = \mathbf{x}$. Let $-\mathbf{x}$ be the set of the rationals

$-r$ for $r \in R - \bar{\mathbf{x}}$. (If $\mathbf{x}$ is rational, then $-\mathbf{x}$ corresponds to $-x$.) Let $-\mathsf{M}$ be the set of the reals $-\mathbf{x}$ for $\mathbf{x} \in \mathsf{M}$. If $\mathbf{w}$ is a lower bound of M, then $-\mathbf{w}$ is an upper bound of $-\mathsf{M}$, so $-\mathsf{M}$ has a l.u.b., and $-$ (l.u.b. $-\mathsf{M}$) $=$ g.l.b. M.

Given reals $\mathbf{x}$ and $\mathbf{y}$, let $\mathbf{x}+\mathbf{y}$ be the set of the rationals $r+s$ for $r \in \mathbf{x}$ and $s \in \mathbf{y}$; let $\mathbf{x}-\mathbf{y} = \mathbf{x}+(-\mathbf{y})$; and let $|\mathbf{x}| = \mathbf{x}$ if $\mathbf{x} \geq \mathbf{0}$ and $|\mathbf{x}| = -\mathbf{x}$ if $\mathbf{x} < \mathbf{0}$. (Do not confuse $+$ and $-$ with addition and subtraction of sets, which are written $+$ and $-$.)

Given an infinite sequence $\mathbf{a}_0, \mathbf{a}_1, \ldots, \mathbf{a}_n, \ldots$ of reals and a real $\mathbf{a}$, we say that $\lim \mathbf{a}_n = \mathbf{a}$, if for every real $\mathbf{e} > \mathbf{0}$, there is a natural number $n_{\mathbf{e}}$ such that, for every $n > n_{\mathbf{e}}$, $|\mathbf{a}_n - \mathbf{a}| < \mathbf{e}$. For example, $\lim \mathbf{1/2}^n = \mathbf{0}$ (where $\mathbf{1/2}^n$ is the real corresponding to the rational $1/2^n$).

(B) *If* $\mathbf{u} =$ l.u.b. M *(as in* (A)), *there exists a sequence* $\mathbf{a}_0, \mathbf{a}_1, \ldots, \mathbf{a}_n, \ldots$ *of members of* M *such that* $\lim \mathbf{a}_n = \mathbf{u}$.

PROOF. Let $\mathsf{M}_n =$ the set of the reals which $\in \mathsf{M}$ and are $> \mathbf{u} - \mathbf{1/2}^n$. (Prove that M_n is not empty.) Let $\mathbf{a}_n$ be any real chosen from M_n. (Prove that $\lim \mathbf{a}_n = \mathbf{u}$.)

Notwithstanding that in this theory analysis is "arithmetized", the distinction between arithmetic and analysis remains sharp, in that analysis finds it necessary to employ infinite sets of the objects of arithmetic as its objects.

§ 10. Functions. In the most general sense, a (single-valued) *function* f or $f(x)$ or $y = f(x)$ *of one variable* x is a correspondence by which, to each element x of a set X there corresponds a single element y of a set Y.

The set X is the *range of the independent variable*, or the *domain of the function*. The function may be called a *function from* X *to* Y (or a *function of* a member of X *taking* a member of Y *as value*, or an *operation on* a member of X *producing* a member of Y, etc.).

The *range of the dependent variable* y or $f(x)$ is the subset Y_1 of Y comprising the elements of Y used in the correspondence, i.e. those which correspond by the function f to some element of X. Then X and Y_1 are in *many-one correspondence*, since to each element of X there corresponds just one element of Y_1, but an element of Y_1 will (in general) correspond to many elements of X. An element x of X is an *argument of the function* or a *value of the independent variable*. The corresponding element y of Y is the *corresponding value of the function* or *of the dependent variable*, or the *value of the function for that argument*. (Sometimes "argument" is encountered meaning "independent variable".)

A (single-valued) *function* f or $f(x_1, \ldots, x_n)$ or $y = f(x_1, \ldots, x_n)$ *of n variables* $x_1, \ldots, x_n$ is a correspondence by which, to each ordered n-tuple $(x_1, \ldots, x_n)$ of objects where $x_1 \varepsilon X_1$, $x_2 \varepsilon X_2, \ldots, x_n \varepsilon X_n$, there corresponds a single object y where $y \varepsilon Y$. A function of n variables can be considered as a function of one variable, with X as the class of all the ordered n-tuples $(x_1, \ldots, x_n)$. Similar terminology applies. Thus X_1 is the *range* of x_1, X_2 of $x_2, \ldots, X_n$ of x_n. Here $X_1, X_2, \ldots, X_n$ may all be the same set, or there may be several (up to n) different ranges. A particular sequence $x_1, \ldots, x_n$ of elements from $X_1, \ldots, X_n$, respectively, is a *set* (or *n-tuple*) *of arguments*.

In this plethora of terminology, one may recognize a mixture of terminologies based on two ideas: the idea of a function as a many-one correspondence, and the idea of a function as a variable y which ranges in relation to another variable x so that the value of y is always fixed by that of x.

The first idea is the more comprehensive one, which the student should keep uppermost in his mind. The second idea however gives rise in a natural way to the useful notational convention, whereby if "$f(x)$" for instance stands for a certain function of the independent variable x, and a, b, etc. are values of the independent variable (i.e. arguments), then "$f(a)$" stands for the value of the function for the argument a, "$f(b)$" for the value when $x = b$, etc.

One should be aware that then "$f(x)$" may have either of two meanings: 1. The function itself (i.e. the many-one correspondence between X and Y_1). 2. When x stands for an object from the domain, the corresponding value of the function (i.e. a member y of Y_1). When x is unspecified, the latter is called the *ambiguous value* of the function.

EXAMPLE 1. When we say "$x + y$ is symmetric" we mean by "$x + y$" the function. When we say "the sum $x + y$ of any two natural numbers x and y is $\geq x$", we mean by "$x + y$" not a function but a number (the ambiguous value of the function).

This situation can be avoided by using "f" instead of "$f(x)$" for the function, so long as we are talking only about functions for each of which a symbol such as "f", "g", "$+$" or "φ" has been introduced. But notations which show the independent variables are very convenient for naming other functions composed out of those functions (and constants), e.g. "$f(g(x))$", "$x^2 + 3x$" or "$\varphi(2, x)$".

EXAMPLE 2. To consider this in more detail, say that f and g are given *number-theoretic functions* of one variable each, i.e. functions from the set of the natural numbers to the same set. Let x be any natural number. Then $g(x)$ is a natural number, i.e. the value of g for x as argument, and $f(g(x))$ is a natural number, i.e. the value of f for the natural number $g(x)$ as argument. So to any natural number x, another number $f(g(x))$ is determined. Thus "$f(g(x))$" stands for the ambiguous value of a new function (Meaning 2); and it is also convenient to use it as a name for the new function itself (Meaning 1).

There is another notation (due to Church 1932) in which the independent variables appear, but which represents the function f as distinct from its ambiguous value, namely: "$\lambda x f(x)$", or for a function of n variables, "$\lambda x_1 \ldots x_n f(x_1, \ldots, x_n)$"; e.g. "$\lambda x f(g(x))$", "$\lambda x\, x^2 + 3x$", "$\lambda x\, \varphi(2, x)$". We shall use this λ-notation for emphasis in situations where especial care is required.

Example 3. Let φ be a function of two numbers. Using the λ-notation consistently, i.e. whenever we mean the function instead of the ambiguous value, we can distinguish (a) the number $\varphi(x, y)$, (b) the function $\lambda x\, \varphi(x, y)$ of one variable x, with y as parameter, (c) the function $\lambda xy\, \varphi(x, y)$ of two variables, with x as first and y as second variable, (d) the function $\lambda yx\, \varphi(x, y)$, with y as first and x as second variable, (e) the function $\lambda x \lambda y\, \varphi(x, y)$ of one variable x, whose values are functions of another variable y, etc. (Schönfinkel 1924 and Church identify (c) and (e), but that is not necessary for us.)

For any n-tuple $t_1, \ldots, t_n$ of arguments for f,

$$\{\lambda x_1 \ldots x_n f(x_1, \ldots, x_n)\}(t_1, \ldots, t_n) = f(t_1, \ldots, t_n).$$

For example, $\{\lambda x\, x^2 + 3x\}(2) = 10$, $\{\lambda x\, \varphi(x, y)\}(0) = \varphi(0, y)$, $\{\lambda yx\, \varphi(x, y)\}(0, 3) = \varphi(3, 0)$, $\{\lambda xy\, \varphi(x, y)\}(z, x) = \varphi(z, x)$.

We have described a function as a many-one correspondence. One may go further in saying what a many-one correspondence is to be, according to the kind of theory one is working in. In set-theoretic terms, the correspondence can be identified with the set of all the ordered pairs (x, y) of corresponding elements of X and Y_1. One may speak instead of the law or rule establishing the correspondence, at least in dealing with such functions that a law or rule in some understood sense can be given for each function. In the case that X is a finite set, a function can be given as a table.

Example 4. Let X and Y both be the residues modulo 2, i.e. $X = Y = \{0, 1\}$. The functions x' and $x \cdot y$ can be defined by the following tables:

x'

x	0	1
	1	0

$x \cdot y$

	y	0	1
x	0	0	0
	1	0	1

Thus by the second table, $0 \cdot 0 = 0 \cdot 1 = 1 \cdot 0 = 0$ and $1 \cdot 1 = 1$.

CHAPTER III

A CRITIQUE OF MATHEMATICAL REASONING

§ 11. The paradoxes. This chapter is intended to present the problem situation out of which the investigations to be reported in the rest of the book arose, i.e. the situation preceding those investigations (but not how it has since changed).

In the arithmetization of analysis (§ 9), an infinite collection (of rationals forming the lower half of a Dedekind cut, or of digits in sequence forming a non-terminating decimal, etc.) is constituted an object, and the set of all such objects is considered as a new collection. From this it is a natural step to Cantor's general set theory.

Hardly had these theories been consolidated, when the validity of the whole construction was cast into doubt by the discovery of paradoxes or antinomies in the fringes of the theory of sets.

(A) The *Burali-Forti paradox* 1897*, also known to Cantor in 1895, arises in Cantor's theory of transfinite ordinals.

(B) Somewhat similar antinomies occur in the theory of transfinite cardinals, particularly *Cantor's paradox* (found by him in 1899). Consider the set of all sets; call it M. By Cantor's theorem (Theorem C § 5), $\overline{\overline{\mathfrak{U}\mathsf{M}}} > \overline{\overline{\mathsf{M}}}$. Also, since M is the set of all sets, and $\mathfrak{U}\mathsf{M}$ is a set of sets (namely, the set of the subsets of M), $\mathfrak{U}\mathsf{M} \subset \mathsf{M}$. Hence by Corollary A Theorem A, $\overline{\overline{\mathfrak{U}\mathsf{M}}} \leq \overline{\overline{\mathsf{M}}}$; and so by § 3, not $\overline{\overline{\mathfrak{U}\mathsf{M}}} > \overline{\overline{\mathsf{M}}}$. Thus we have proved both that $\overline{\overline{\mathfrak{U}\mathsf{M}}} > \overline{\overline{\mathsf{M}}}$ and that not $\overline{\overline{\mathfrak{U}\mathsf{M}}} > \overline{\overline{\mathsf{M}}}$.

Starting with the same M, we can also reach a paradox thus. To each member M of M, i.e. to any set M, by Theorem C there is another member M' of M, namely $\mathfrak{U}M$, such that $\overline{\overline{M}} < \overline{\overline{M'}}$. Hence by Theorem D, $\overline{\overline{M}} < \overline{\overline{\mathfrak{S}\mathsf{M}}}$ for every member M of M. But M is the set of all sets, so $\mathfrak{S}\mathsf{M}$ is one of its members. Taking the M in the inequality just proved to be this member, we have $\overline{\overline{\mathfrak{S}\mathsf{M}}} < \overline{\overline{\mathfrak{S}\mathsf{M}}}$. But by § 3, for any set M, not $\overline{\overline{M}} < \overline{\overline{M}}$; hence in particular, not $\overline{\overline{\mathfrak{S}\mathsf{M}}} < \overline{\overline{\mathfrak{S}\mathsf{M}}}$.

The paradox with $\mathfrak{S}\mathsf{M}$ results likewise, if we start out with the set of all cardinal numbers, and choose as M a set containing, to each cardinal number, a set M having that cardinal.

If the notion of sets of arbitrary elements used here is thought to be too vague and hence unmathematical, we can prescribe as admissible elements of sets (a_1) the natural numbers 0, 1, 2, . . . (or (a_2) the empty set O) and (b) arbitrary sets whose members are admissible elements. With this prescription, the above paradoxes and the next arise as before (with (a_1), Gentzen 1936).

(C) The *Russell paradox* 1902-3*, discovered independently by Zermelo, deals with the set of all sets which are not members of themselves. Call this set T. Is T a member of itself?

Let us assume, for the sake of the argument, that T is a member of itself, i.e. in symbols $T \varepsilon T$. The assumption says that T is a member of T, i.e. T is a member of the set of all sets which are not members of themselves, i.e. T is a set which is not a member of itself, i.e. in symbols $T \bar{\varepsilon} T$. This contradicts the assumption $T \varepsilon T$. Thus far we have no paradox, as the contradiction between $T \varepsilon T$ and $T \bar{\varepsilon} T$ has arisen only under the assumption $T \varepsilon T$. By reductio ad absurdum, we conclude that the assumption is false. Thus we have now proved outright, without assumption, that $T \bar{\varepsilon} T$.

From the established result $T \bar{\varepsilon} T$, we can argue further. The result says that T is not a member of the set of all sets which are not members of themselves, i.e. T is not a set which is not a member of itself, i.e. T is a set which is a member of itself, i.e. in symbols $T \varepsilon T$. Now $T \bar{\varepsilon} T$ and $T \varepsilon T$ are both established, so we have a paradox.

This paradox can be extracted from Cantor's thus. If we prescribe (a_2) and (b) as admissible elements, so that sets have only sets as members, then when M is the set of all sets, $\mathfrak{U}\mathsf{M} = \mathsf{M}$, and the set T of the paradox is obtained by applying the proof of Lemma A § 5 to the identical 1-1 correspondence $\mathsf{M} \sim \mathfrak{U}\mathsf{M}$ in which each element of M corresponds to itself in $\mathfrak{U}\mathsf{M}$.

A popularization of the paradox (Russell 1919) concerns the barber in a certain village, who shaves all and only those persons in the village who do not shave themselves. Does he shave himself? (Of course here we can escape the paradox simply by concluding that there never was such a barber.)

Every municipality in Holland must have a mayor, and no two may have the same mayor. Sometimes it happens that the mayor is a non-resident of the municipality. Suppose a law is passed setting aside a special area S exclusively for such non-resident mayors, and compelling all non-resident mayors to reside there.

Suppose further that there are so many non-resident mayors that S

has to be constituted a municipality. Where shall the mayor of S reside? (Mannoury, cf. van Dantzig 1948.)

Suppose the Librarian of Congress compiles, for inclusion in the Library of Congress, a bibliography of all those bibliographies in the Library of Congress which do not list themselves. (Gonseth 1933.)

Russell also showed how to recast his paradox in logical instead of set-theoretic terminology. A property is called 'predicable' if it applies to itself, 'impredicable' if it does not apply to itself. For example, the property 'abstract' is abstract, and hence predicable; but 'concrete' is also abstract and not concrete, and hence is impredicable. What about the property 'impredicable'?

(D) The *Richard paradox* 1905, also substantially given by Dixon 1906, deals with the notion of finite definability. For definiteness, let this refer to a given language, say the English language with a preassigned alphabet, dictionary and grammar. The alphabet we may take as consisting of the blank space (to separate words), the 26 Latin letters, and the comma. By an 'expression' in the language we may understand simply any finite sequence of these 28 symbols not beginning with a blank space. The expressions in the English language can then be enumerated by the device which we applied at the end of § 1 to the enumeration of the algebraic equations.

An expression may define a number-theoretic function of one variable (i.e. a function of a natural number taking a natural number as value). From the specified enumeration of all the expressions in the English language, by striking out those which do not define a number-theoretic function, we obtain an enumeration (say $E_0, E_1, E_2, \ldots$) of those which do (say the functions defined are respectively $f_0(n), f_1(n), f_2(n), \ldots$).

Now consider the following expression, "the function whose value, for any given natural number as argument, is equal to one more than the value, for the given natural number as argument, of the function defined by the expression which corresponds to the given natural number in the last described enumeration".

In the quoted expression we refer to the above described enumeration of the expressions in the English language defining a number-theoretic function, without defining it. But we could easily have written in the definition of that enumeration in full, as part of the quoted expression. We should then have before us a definition of a function (briefly, the function $f_n(n) + 1$), by an expression in the English language. This function, by its definition, must differ from every function definable by an expression in the English language.

This paradox is especially interesting for its implications concerning languages such as English, and because it runs so close to Cantor's proof of the non-enumerability of the number-theoretic functions (§ 2). Richard gave the paradox in a form relating to the definition of a real number, paralleling Cantor's proof of the non-enumerability of the real numbers.

Consider the expression, "the least natural number not nameable in fewer than twenty-two syllables". This expression names in twenty-one syllables a natural number which by definition cannot be named in fewer than twenty-two syllables! (Berry 1906.)

(E) These modern paradoxes, which fall more or less within the context of set theory, are related to a very ancient one.

The statement "Cretans are always liars ..." is attributed to the philosopher Epimenides of Crete (sixth century B.C.). (The statement was quoted by Paul in "Epistle to Titus", I, 12, as by a Cretan "prophet", whom early Christian tradition, according to more recent sources, identified with Epimenides. Cf. Weyl 1949 p. 228.)

Suppose we distinguish two kinds of liars: liars of the first kind, who tell the truth some of the time, and liars of the second kind, who tell only lies. Let us interpret Epimenides' statement to mean that all Cretans are liars of the second kind. Suppose his statement were true. By what it says and the fact he is a Cretan, it must then be false. This is a contradiction; hence by reductio ad absurdum, the statement must be false. The falsity of the statement requires that there has been, or will eventually be, a Cretan who at some time tells the truth. Had the quoted statement been the only one any Cretan makes, we should have a paradox. It is logically unsatisfactory that we should escape paradox only through the historical accident that some Cretan existed who sometime told the truth.

The *Epimenides paradox*, known also as *the liar*, appears in stark form, if a person says simply, "This statement I am now making is a lie." The quoted statement can neither be true nor false without entailing a contradiction. This version of the paradox is attributed to Eubulides (fourth century B.C.), and was well known in ancient times. (Cf. Rüstow 1910. If the statement "Cretans are always liars ..." is not authentically Epimenides', or was not originally recognized as paradoxical, the Eubulides version of the Liar may then be older than the "lying Cretan" version.)

In the ancient "dilemma of the crocodile", a crocodile has stolen a child. The crocodile promises the child's father to return the child, provided that the father guesses whether the crocodile will return the child or not. What should the crocodile do, if the father guesses that the crocodile will not return the child? (Cf. Prantl 1855 p. 493.)

The following riddle also turns upon the paradox. A traveller has fallen among cannibals. They offer him the opportunity to make a statement, attaching the conditions that if his statement be true, he will be boiled, and if it be false, he will be roasted. What statement should he make? (A form of this riddle occurs in Cervantes' "Don Quixote" (1605), II, 51.)

§ 12. First inferences from the paradoxes. The reader may try his hand at solving the paradoxes. In the half century since the problem has been open, no solution has been found which is universally agreed upon.

The simplest kind of solution would be to locate a specific fallacy, like a mistake in a student's algebra exercise or geometry proof, with nothing else needing to be changed.

Ideas for solving the paradoxes in this sense come to mind on first considering them. One may propose that the error in the paradoxes (A) — (C) consists in using too large sets, such as the set of all sets or the set of all cardinal numbers; or in permitting sets to be considered as members of themselves, which again argues against the set of all sets. These suggestions are not necessarily wrong, but they are not after all simple. They leave us the problem of refounding set theory on a drastically altered basis, the details of which are not fully implicit in the suggestions. For example, if we ban the set of all cardinal numbers, we are unable to introduce the set of the natural numbers, unless we already know that they are not all the cardinal numbers; and the same difficulty will arise at higher stages. If we ban the set of all sets, we find ourselves in conflict with Cantor's definition of set. In order to have set theory at all, we must have theorems about all sets, and all sets then constitute a set under Cantor's definition. If not so, we must say what other definition of set we shall use instead, or we must supplement Cantor's definition with some further criterion to determine when a collection of objects as described in his definition shall constitute a set (Skolem 1929-30).

Axiomatic set theory. Reconstructions of set theory can be given, placing around the notion of set as few restrictions to exclude too large sets as appear to be required to forestall the known antinomies. Since the free use of our conceptions in constructing sets under Cantor's definition led to disaster, the notions of set theory are governed by axioms, like those governing 'point' and 'line' in Euclidean plane geometry. The first system of *axiomatic set theory* was Zermelo's (1908). Refinements in the axiomatic treatment of sets are due to Fraenkel (1922, 1925), Skolem (1922-3, 1929), von Neumann (1925, 1928), Bernays (1937-48), and others. Analysis can be founded on the basis of axiomatic set theory, which perhaps is the simplest basis set up since the paradoxes for the deduction of existing mathematics. Some very interesting discoveries have been made in connection with axiomatic set theory, notably by Skolem (1922-3; cf. § 75 below) and Gödel (1938, 1939, 1940).

THE BROADER PROBLEM OF FOUNDATIONS. Assuming that the paradoxes are avoided in the axiomatization of set theory — and of this the only assurance we have is the negative one that so far none have been encountered — does it constitute a full solution of the problem posed by the paradoxes?

In the case of geometry, mathematicians have recognized since the discovery of a non-Euclidean geometry that more than one kind of space is possible. Axiom systems serve to single out one or another kind of space, or certain common features of several spaces, for the geometer to study. A contradiction arising in a formal axiomatic theory can mean simply that an unrealizable combination of features has been postulated.

But in the case of arithmetic and analysis, theories culminating in set theory, mathematicians prior to the current epoch of criticism generally supposed that they were dealing with systems of objects, set up genetically, by definitions purporting to establish their structure completely. The theorems were thought of as expressing truths about these systems, rather than as propositions applying hypothetically to whatever systems of objects (if any) satisfy the axioms. But then how could contradictions have arisen in these subjects, unless there is some defect in the logic, some error in the methods of constructing and reasoning about mathematical objects, which we had hitherto trusted?

To say that now these subjects should instead be established on an axiomatic basis does not of itself dispose of the problem. After axiomatization, there must still be some level at which we have truth and falsity. If the axiomatics is informal, the axioms must be true. If the axiomatics is formal, at least we must believe that the theorems do follow from the axioms; and also there must be some relationship between these results and some actuality outside the axiomatic theory, if the mathematicians' activity is not to reduce to nonsense. The formally axiomatized propositions of mathematics cannot constitute the whole of mathematics; there must also be an intuitively understood mathematics. If we must give up our former belief that it comprises all of arithmetic, analysis and set theory, we shall not be wholly satisfied unless we learn wherein that belief was mistaken, and where now instead to draw a line of separation.

The immediate problem of eliminating the paradoxes thus merges with the broader problem of the foundations of mathematics and logic.

What is the nature of mathematical truth? What meaning do mathematical propositions have, and on what evidence do they rest? This broad problem, or complex of problems, exists for philosophy apart from the circumstance that paradoxes have arisen in the fringes of mathematics. Historically, this circumstance has led to a more intensive study of the problem on the part of mathematicians than would otherwise have been likely; and the paradoxes obviously impose conditions on the solution of the problem.

IMPREDICATIVE DEFINITION. When a set M and a particular object m are so defined that on the one hand m is a member of M, and on the other hand the definition of m depends on M, we say that the procedure (or the definition of m, or the definition of M) is *impredicative*. Similarly, when a property P is possessed by an object m whose definition depends on P (here M is the set of the objects which possess the property P). An impredicative definition is circular, at least on its face, as what is defined participates in its own definition.

Each of the antinomies of § 11 involves an impredicative definition. In (B), the set M of all sets includes as members the sets $\mathfrak{U}\mathsf{M}$ and $\mathfrak{S}\mathsf{M}$ defined from M. The impredicative procedure in the Russell paradox (C) stands out when the definition of T is elaborated thus. We divide the set M of all sets into two parts, the first comprising those members which contain themselves, and the second (which is T) those which do not. Then we put T (defined by this division of M into two parts) back into M, to ask into which part of M it falls. In the Richard paradox (D), the totality of expressions in the English language which constitute definitions of a function (real number, natural number) is taken as including the quoted expression, which refers to that totality. In the Epimenides paradox (E), the totality of statements is divided into two parts, the true and the false statements. A statement which refers to this division is reckoned as of the original totality, when we ask whether it is true or false.

Poincaré (1905-6, 1908) judged the cause of the paradoxes to lie in these impredicative definitions; and Russell (1906, 1910) enunciated the same explanation in his vicious circle principle: No totality can contain members definable only in terms of this totality, or members involving or presupposing this totality. Thus it might appear that we have a sufficient solution and adequate insight into the paradoxes, except for one circumstance: parts of mathematics we want to retain, particularly analysis, also contain impredicative definitions.

An example is the definition of $\mathbf{u} = \text{l.u.b. } \mathsf{M}$ (§ 9 (A)). Under the

Dedekind cut definition of the real numbers, the set C of real numbers is the set of all sets **x** of rationals having three properties (a), (b), (c). Now this totality has been divided into two parts, M and C – M. We define **u** as 𝔖M, and then reckon this set 𝔖M as a member of C. This definition **u** = 𝔖M depends on C in the general case, since in the general case M will have been defined from C as the set of those members of C which have a certain property P.

One can attempt to defend this impredicative definition by interpreting it, not as defining or creating the real number **u** for the first time (in which interpretation the definition of the totality C of real numbers is circular), but as only a description which singles out the particular number **u** from an already existing totality C of real numbers. But the same argument can be used to uphold the impredicative definitions in the paradoxes.

WEYL'S CONSTRUCTIVE CONTINUUM. The impredicative character of some of the definitions in analysis has been especially emphasized by Weyl, who in his book "Das Kontinuum (The continuum)" (1918) undertook to find out how much of analysis could be reconstructed without impredicative definitions. A fund of operations can be provided for constructing many particular categories of irrationals. Weyl was thus able to obtain a fair part of analysis, but not the theorem that an arbitrary non-empty set M of real numbers having an upper bound has a least upper bound. (Cf. also Weyl 1919.)

There have arisen three main schools of thought on the foundations of mathematics: (i) the logicistic school (Russell and Whitehead, English), (ii) the intuitionistic school (Brouwer, Dutch), and (iii) the formalistic or axiomatic school (Hilbert, German). (Sometimes "logistic" is used instead of "logicistic"; but "logistic" also has another meaning § 15.) This broad classification does not include various other points of view, which have not been as widely cultivated or do not comprise to a similar degree both a reconstruction of mathematics and a philosophy to support it.

LOGICISM. The logicistic thesis is that mathematics is a branch of logic. The mathematical notions are to be defined in terms of the logical notions. The theorems of mathematics are to be proved as theorems of logic.

Leibniz (1666) first conceived of logic as a science containing the ideas and principles underlying all other sciences. Dedekind (1888) and Frege (1884, 1893, 1903) were engaged in defining mathematical notions in terms of logical ones, and Peano (1889, 1894-1908) in expressing mathematical theorems in a logical symbolism.

To illustrate how mathematical notions can be defined from logical ones, let us presuppose the Frege-Russell definition of cardinal number (§ 3), and the definitions of the cardinal number 0 and of the cardinal number $n + 1$ for any cardinal number n (§ 4). Then a *finite cardinal* (or *natural number*) can be defined as a cardinal number which possesses every property P such that (1) 0 has the property P and (2) $n + 1$ has the property P whenever n has the property P. In brief, a natural number is defined as a cardinal number for which mathematical induction holds. The viewpoint here is very different from that of §§ 6 and 7, where we presupposed an intuitive conception of the natural number sequence, and elicited from it the principle that, whenever a particular property P of natural numbers is given such that (1) and (2), then any given natural number must have the property P. Here instead we presuppose the totality of all properties of cardinal numbers as existing in logic, prior to the definition of the natural number sequence. Note that this definition is impredicative, because the property of being a natural number, which it defines, belongs to the totality of properties of cardinal numbers, which is presupposed in the definition.

To adapt the logicistic construction of mathematics to the situation arising from the discovery of the paradoxes, Russell excluded impredicative definitions by his *ramified theory of types* (1908, 1910). Roughly, this is as follows. The primary objects or individuals (i.e. the given things not being subjected to logical analysis) are assigned to one type (say *type* 0), properties of individuals to *type* 1, properties of properties of individuals to *type* 2, etc.; and no properties are admitted which do not fall into one of these logical types (e.g. this puts the properties 'predicable' and 'impredicable' of § 11 outside the pale of logic). A more detailed account would describe the admitted types for other objects, such as relations and classes. Then, to exclude impredicative definitions within a type, the types above type 0 are further separated into orders. Thus for type 1, properties defined without mentioning any totality belong to *order* 0, and properties defined using the totality of properties of a given order belong to the next higher order. (The logicistic definition of natural number now becomes predicative, when the P in it is specified to range only over properties of a given order, in which case the property of being a natural number is of the next higher order.) But this separation into orders makes it impossible to construct the familiar analysis, which as we saw above contains impredicative definitions. To escape this outcome, Russell postulated his *axiom of reducibility*, which asserts that to any property belonging to an order above the lowest, there is a coextensive property (i.e. one possessed by exactly the same objects) of order 0. If only definable properties are considered to exist, then the axiom means that to every impredicative definition within a given type there is an equivalent predicative one.

The deduction of mathematics as a province of logic was carried out on this basis, using a logical symbolism, in the monumental "Principia mathematica" of Whitehead and Russell (three volumes, 1910-13). This work has had a great influence on subsequent developments in symbolic logic.

This deduction of mathematics from logic was offered as intuitive axiomatics. The axioms were intended to be believed, or at least to be accepted as plausible hypotheses concerning the world.

The difficulty is now: on what grounds shall we believe in the axiom of reducibility? If properties are to be constructed, the matter should be settled on the basis of constructions, not by an axiom. As the authors admitted in the introduction to their second edition (1925), "This axiom has a purely pragmatic justification: it leads to the desired results, and to no others [so far as is known]. But clearly it is not the sort of axiom with which we can rest content."

Ramsey 1926 found that the desired results and no others can apparently be obtained without the hierarchy of orders (i.e. with a *simple theory of types*). He classified the known antinomies into two sorts, now called 'logical' (e.g. the Burali-Forti, Cantor and Russell) and 'epistemological' or 'semantical' (e.g. the Richard and Epimenides); and he observed that the logical antinomies are (apparently) stopped by the simple hierarchy of types, and the semantical ones are (apparently) prevented from arising within the symbolic language by the absence therein of the requisite means for referring to expressions of the same language. But Ramsey's arguments to justify impredicative definitions within a type entail a conception of the totality of predicates of the type as existing independently of their constructibility or definability. This has been called "theological". Thus neither Whitehead and Russell nor Ramsey succeeded in attaining the logicistic goal constructively. (An interesting proposal for justifying impredicative definitions within a type, by Langford 1927 and Carnap 1931-2, is also not free of difficulties.)

Weyl 1946 says that, in the system of "Principia mathematica", "mathematics is no longer founded on logic, but on a sort of logician's paradise ..."; and he observes that one who is ready to believe in this "transcendental world" could also accept the system of axiomatic set theory (Zermelo, Fraenkel, etc.), which, for the deduction of mathematics, has the advantage of being simpler in structure.

Logicism treats the existence of the natural number series as an hypothesis about the actual world ('axiom of infinity'). A quite different handling of the problem of infinity is proposed by the intuitionists (§ 13) and the formalists (§ 14).

From both the intuitionistic and the formalistic standpoints, the (abstract) natural number sequence is more elementary than the notions of cardinal number and of all properties of cardinal numbers, which are used in the logicistic characterization of it.

The logicistic thesis can be questioned finally on the ground that logic already presupposes mathematical ideas in its formulation. In the intuitionistic view, an essential mathematical kernel is contained in the idea of iteration, which must be used e.g. in describing the hierarchy of types or the notion of a deduction from given premises.

Recent work in the logicistic school is that of Quine 1940*. A critical but sympathetic discussion of the logicistic order of ideas is given by Gödel 1944. Introductory treatments are provided by Russell 1919 and Black 1933.

§ 13. Intuitionism. In the 1880's, when the methods of Weierstrass, Dedekind and Cantor were flourishing, Kronecker argued vigorously that their fundamental definitions were only words, since they do not enable one in general to decide whether a given object satisfies the definition.

Poincaré, when he defends mathematical induction as an irreducible tool of intuitive mathematical reasoning (1902, 1905-6), is also a forerunner of the modern intuitionistic school.

In 1908 Brouwer, in a paper entitled "The untrustworthiness of the principles of logic", challenged the belief that the rules of the classical logic, which have come down to us essentially from Aristotle (384—322 B.C.), have an absolute validity, independent of the subject matter to which they are applied. Quoting from Weyl 1946, "According to his view and reading of history, classical logic was abstracted from the mathematics of finite sets and their subsets. ... Forgetful of this limited origin, one afterwards mistook that logic for something above and prior to all mathematics, and finally applied it, without justification, to the mathematics of infinite sets."

Two obvious examples will illustrate that principles valid in thinking about finite sets do not necessarily carry over to infinite sets. One is the principle that the whole is greater than any proper part, when applied to 1-1 correspondences between sets (§§ 1, 3, 4). Another is that a set of natural numbers contains a greatest.

A principle of classical logic, valid in reasoning about finite sets, which Brouwer does not accept for infinite sets, is the law of the excluded middle. The law, in its general form, says *for every proposition A, either A or not A*. Now let A be the proposition *there exists a member of the set* (*or domain*) *D having the property P*. Then *not A* is equivalent to *every member of D does not have the property P*, or in other words *every member of D has the property not-P*. The law, applied to this A, hence gives *either there exists a member of D having the property P, or every member of D has the property not-P*.

For definiteness, let us specify P to be a property such that, for any given member of D, we can determine whether that member has the property P or does not.

Now suppose D is a finite set. Then we could examine every member of D in turn, and thus either find a member having the property P, or verify that all members have the property *not-P*. There might be practical difficulties, e.g. when D is a very large set having say a million members, or even for a small D when the determination whether or not a given member has the property P may be tedious. But the possibility of completing the search exists in principle. It is this possibility which for Brouwer makes the law of the excluded middle a valid principle for reasoning with finite sets D and properties P of the kind specified.

For an infinite set D, the situation is fundamentally different. It is no longer possible in principle to search through the entire set D.

Moreover in this situation the law is not saved for Brouwer by substituting, for the impossible search through all the members of the infinite set D, a mathematical solution of the problem posed. We may in some cases, i.e. for some sets D and properties P, succeed in finding a member of D having the property P; and in other cases, succeed in showing by mathematical reasoning that every member of D has the property *not-P*, e.g. by deducing a contradiction from the assumption that an arbitrary (i.e. unspecified) member of D has the property P. (An example for the second kind of solution is when D is the set of all the ordered pairs (m, n) of positive integers, and P is the property of a pair (m, n) that $m^2 = 2n^2$. The result is then Pythagoras' discovery that $\sqrt{2}$ is irrational.) But we have no ground for affirming the possibility of obtaining either one or the other of these kinds of solutions in every case.

An example from modern mathematical history is afforded by Fermat's "last theorem", which asserts that the equation $x^n + y^n = z^n$ has no solution in positive integers x, y, z, n with $n > 2$. (For $n = 2$, there are triples of positive integers, called Pythagorean numbers, which satisfy, e.g. $x = 3, y = 4, z = 5$ or $x = 5, y = 12, z = 13$.) Here D is the set of all ordered quadruples (x, y, z, n) of positive integers with $n > 2$, and P is the property of a quadruple (x, y, z, n) that $x^n + y^n = z^n$. About 1637 Fermat wrote on the margin of his copy of Bachet's "Diophantus" that he had discovered a truly marvellous demonstration of this "theorem" which the margin was too narrow to contain. Despite an immense expenditure of effort, no one since then has succeeded in proving or disproving the alleged "theorem"; and moreover we lack the knowledge of any systematic method, the pursuit of which must in principle ultimately lead to a determination as to its truth or falsity. (Cf. Vandiver 1946 for details.)

Brouwer's non-acceptance of the law of the excluded middle for infinite sets D does not rest on the failure of mathematicians thus far to have solved this particular problem, or any other particular problem. To meet his objection, one would have to provide a method adequate in principle for solving not only all the outstanding unsolved mathematical problems, but any others that might ever be proposed in the future. How likely it is that such a method will be found, we leave for the time being to the reader to speculate. Later in the book we shall return to the question (§ 60).

The familiar mathematics, with its methods and logic, as developed prior to Brouwer's critique or disregarding it, we call *classical*; the mathematics, methods or logic which Brouwer and his school allow, we call *intuitionistic*. The classical includes parts which are intuitionistic and parts which are non-intuitionistic.

The non-intuitionistic mathematics which culminated in the theories of Weierstrass, Dedekind and Cantor, and the intuitionistic mathematics of Brouwer, differ essentially in their view of the infinite. In the former, the infinite is treated as *actual* or *completed* or *extended* or *existential*. An infinite set is regarded as existing as a completed totality, prior to or independently of any human process of generation or construction, and as though it could be spread out completely for our inspection. In the latter, the infinite is treated only as *potential* or *becoming* or *constructive*. The recognition of this distinction, in the case of infinite magnitudes, goes back to Gauss, who in 1831 wrote, "I protest ... against the use of an infinite magnitude as something completed, which is never permissible in mathematics." (Werke VIII p. 216.)

According to Weyl 1946, "Brouwer made it clear, as I think beyond any doubt, that there is no evidence supporting the belief in the existential character of the totality of all natural numbers .... The sequence of numbers which grows beyond any stage already reached by passing to the next number, is a manifold of possibilities open towards infinity; it remains forever in the status of creation, but is not a closed realm of things existing in themselves. That we blindly converted one into the other is the true source of our difficulties, including the antinomies — a source of more fundamental nature than Russell's vicious circle principle indicated. Brouwer opened our eyes and made us see how far classical mathematics, nourished by a belief in the 'absolute' that transcends all human possibilities of realization, goes beyond such statements as can claim real meaning and truth founded on evidence."

Brouwer's criticism of the classical logic as applied to an infinite set D (say the set of the natural numbers) arises from this standpoint respecting infinity. We see this clearly by considering the meanings which the intuitionist attaches to various forms of statements.

A generality statement *all natural numbers n have the property P*, or briefly *for all n, $P(n)$*, is understood by the intuitionist as an hypothetical assertion to the effect that, if any particular natural number n were given to us, we could be sure that that number n has the property P. This is a meaning which does not require us to take into view the classical completed infinity of the natural numbers.

Mathematical induction is an example of an intuitionistic method for proving generality propositions about the natural numbers. A proof by induction of the proposition *for all n, $P(n)$* shows that any given n would have to have the property P, by reasoning which uses only the numbers from 0 up to n (§ 7). Of course, for a particular proof by induction to be intuitionistic, also the reasonings used within its basis and induction step must be intuitionistic.

An existence statement *there exists a natural number n having the property P*, or briefly *there exists an n such that $P(n)$*, has its intuitionistic meaning as a partial communication (or abstract) of a statement giving a particular example of a natural number n which has the property P, or at least giving a method by which in principle one could find such an example.

Therefore an intuitionistic proof of the proposition *there exists an n such that $P(n)$* must be *constructive* in the following (strict) sense. The proof actually exhibits an example of an n such that $P(n)$, or at least indicates a method by which one could in principle find such an example.

In classical mathematics there occur *non-constructive* or *indirect* existence proofs, which the intuitionists do not accept. For example, to prove *there exists an n such that $P(n)$*, the classical mathematician may deduce a contradiction from the assumption *for all n, not $P(n)$*. Under both the classical and the intuitionistic logic, by reductio ad absurdum this gives *not for all n, not P(n)*. The classical logic allows this result to be transformed into *there exists an n such that P(n)*, but not (in general) the intuitionistic. Such a classical existence proof leaves us no nearer than before the proof was given to having an example of a number n such that $P(n)$ (though sometimes we may afterwards be able to discover one by another method). The intuitionist refrains from accepting such an existence proof, because its conclusion *there exists an n such that P(n)* can have no meaning for him other than as a reference to an example of a number n such that $P(n)$, and this example has not been produced. The classical meaning, that somewhere in the completed infinite totality of the natural numbers there occurs an n such that $P(n)$, is not available to him, since he does not conceive the natural numbers as a completed totality.

As another example of a non-constructive existence proof, suppose it has been shown for a certain P, by intuitionistic methods, that if Fermat's "last theorem" is true, then the number 5013 has the property P, and also that if Fermat's "last theorem" is false, then 10 has the property P. Classically this suffices to demonstrate the existence of a number n such that $P(n)$. But with the problem of the "last theorem" unsolved, Brouwer would disallow such an existence proof, because no example has been given. We do not know that 5013 is an example, nor do we know that 10 is an example, nor do we know any procedure which would in principle (i.e. apart from practical limitations on the length of procedures we can carry out) lead us to a particular number which we could be sure is an example. Brouwer would merely accept what has been given as proving the implication (or conditional statement) *if F or not F, then there exists an n such that P(n)*, where F is the statement *for all* $x, y, z > 0$ *and* $n > 2$, $x^n + y^n \neq z^n$. The classical mathematician, by his law of the excluded middle, has the premise *F or not F* of this implication, and so he can infer its conclusion *there exists an n such that P(n)*. But in the present state of knowledge, Brouwer does not accept the premise *F or not F* as known.

As appears in this example, intuitionistic methods are to be distinguished from non-intuitionistic ones in the case of definitions as well as in the case of proofs. In the present state of our knowledge, Brouwer does not accept *the number n which is equal to* 5013 *if F, and equal to* 10 *if not F* as a valid definition of a natural number n.

A disjunction *A or B* constitutes for the intuitionist an incomplete communication of a statement telling us that A holds or that B holds, or at least giving a method by which we can choose from A and B one which holds. A conjunction *A and B* means that both A and B hold. An implication *A implies B* (or *if A, then B*) expresses that B follows from A by intuitionistic reasoning, or more explicitly that one possesses a method which, from any proof of A, would procure a proof of B; and a negation *not A* (or *A is absurd*) that a contradiction *B and not B* follows from A by intuitionistic reasoning, or more explicitly that one possesses a method which, from any proof of A, would procure a proof of a contradiction *B and not B* (or of a statement already known to be absurd, such as $1 = 0$). Additional comments on these intuitionistic meanings will be given in § 82. See Note 1 on p. 65.

Quoting from Heyting 1934, "According to Brouwer, mathematics is identical with the exact part of our thinking. ... no science, in particular not philosophy or logic, can be a presupposition for mathematics. It would be circular to apply any philosophical or logical principles as means of proof, since mathematical conceptions are already presupposed in the formulation of such principles." There remains for mathematics "no other source than an intuition, which places its concepts and inferences before our eyes as immediately clear." This intuition "is nothing other than the faculty of considering separately particular concepts and inferences which occur regularly in ordinary thinking." The idea of the natural number series can be analyzed as resting on the possibility, first of considering an object or experience as given to us separately from the rest of the world, second of distinguishing one such from another, and third of imagining an unlimited repetition of the second process. "In the intuitionistic mathematics, one does not draw inferences according to fixed norms, which can be collected in a logic, but each single inference is immediately tested on its evidence." But also "There are general rules, by which from given mathematical theorems new theorems can be formed in an intuitively clear way; the theory of these connections can be treated in a 'mathematical logic', which is then a branch of mathematics and is not sensibly applied outside of mathematics."

We turn now to the question: How large a part do the non-intuitionistic methods play in the classical mathematics?

The fact that non-intuitionistic methods occur in classical elementary number theory is significant, since it enables elementary number theory to serve as the first and simplest testing ground in research on foundations growing out of the intuitionistic and formalistic thinking. We shall be almost wholly concerned with elementary number theory in this book.

Actually, in the existing body of elementary number theory, the non-intuitionistic methods do not play a large part. Most non-constructive existence proofs can be replaced by constructive ones.

On the other hand, in analysis (and still more transcendental branches of mathematics) the non-intuitionistic methods of definition and proof permeate the whole methodology. The real numbers in the Dedekind cut representation are infinite sets of rationals (§ 9). Thus to treat them as objects in the usual way, we are already using the completed infinite. In particular, we do apply the law of the excluded middle to these sets, in connection with the simplest definitions of the subject. For example, to show that for any two real numbers $\mathbf{x}$ and $\mathbf{y}$, either $\mathbf{x} < \mathbf{y}$ or $\mathbf{x} = \mathbf{y}$ or $\mathbf{x} > \mathbf{y}$, we use it twice, thus: Either there exists a rational r in $\mathbf{y}$ which does not belong to $\mathbf{x}$, or all rationals in $\mathbf{y}$ belong to $\mathbf{x}$; and similarly interchanging $\mathbf{x}$ and $\mathbf{y}$. In the impredicative definition of l.u.b. M (§ 9 (A), § 12), we use the totality of the real numbers in the same way. Another instance of non-constructive reasoning occurs in the proof of (B) § 9, where we assumed the right to choose an element $\mathbf{a}_n$ from a set M_n, simultaneously for infinitely many values of n, without giving any property to determine which element is chosen. (This is a case of the 'axiom of choice', first noticed as an assumption by Zermelo 1904. We used it also for Theorem B § 4.)

Although the completed infinite has been banned for magnitudes (as Gauss called upon us to do), it reappears in full force for collections. As Hilbert and Bernays describe the situation in their "Grundlagen der Mathematik (Foundations of mathematics)", vol. 1 (1934), p. 41, "The ... arithmetization of analysis is not without a residue left over, as certain systematic fundamental conceptions are introduced which do not belong to the domain of intuitive arithmetical thinking. The insight which has given us the rigorous foundation of analysis consists in this: that these few fundamental assumptions do suffice for building up the theory of magnitudes as a theory of sets of integers."

The next question is: What kind of a mathematics can be built within the intuitionistic restrictions? If the existing classical mathematics could be rebuilt within the intuitionistic restrictions, without too great increase in the labor required and too great sacrifices in the results achieved, the problem of its foundations would appear to be solved.

The intuitionists have created a whole new mathematics, including a theory of the continuum and a set theory (cf. Heyting 1934). This mathematics employs concepts and makes distinctions not found in the classical mathematics; and it is very attractive on its own account. As a substitute for classical mathematics it has turned out to be less powerful, and in many ways more complicated to develop. For example, in Brouwer's theory of the continuum, we cannot affirm that any two real numbers a and b are either equal or unequal. Our knowledge about the equality or inequality of a and b can be more or less specific. By $a \neq b$, it is meant that $a = b$ leads to a contradiction, while $a \# b$ is a stronger kind of inequality which means that one can give an example of a rational number which separates a and b. Of course $a \# b$ implies $a \neq b$. But there are pairs of real numbers a and b for which it is not known that either $a = b$ or $a \neq b$ (or $a \# b$). It is clear that such complications replace the classical theory of the continuum by something much less perspicuous in form.

Despite this, the possibility of an intuitionistic reconstruction of classical mathematics in a different way involving reinterpretation (recently undertaken) is not to be ruled out (cf. § 81).

§ 14. Formalism. Brouwer has revealed what the genetic or constructive tendency involves in its ultimate refinement; Hilbert does the same for the axiomatic or existential (§ 8). The axiomatic method had already been sharpened from the material axiomatics of Euclid to the formal axiomatics of Hilbert's "Grundlagen der Geometrie" (1899). Formalism is the result of a further step, to meet the crisis caused by the paradoxes and the challenge to classical mathematics by Brouwer and Weyl. This step was forecasted by Hilbert in 1904, and seriously undertaken by him and his collaborators Bernays, Ackermann, von Neumann and others since 1920 (cf. Bernays 1935a, Weyl 1944).

Hilbert conceded that the propositions of classical mathematics which involve the completed infinite go beyond intuitive evidence. But he refused to follow Brouwer in giving up classical mathematics on this account.

To salvage classical mathematics in the face of the intuitionistic criticism, he proposed a program which we can state preliminarily as follows: Classical mathematics shall be formulated as a formal axiomatic theory, and this theory shall be proved to be consistent, i.e. free from contradiction.

Prior to this proposal of Hilbert's, the method used in consistency proofs for axiomatic theories, especially in Hilbert's earlier axiomatic thinking, was to give a 'model'. A *model* for an axiomatic theory is simply a system of objects, chosen from some other theory and satisfying the axioms (§ 8). That is, to each object or primitive notion of the axiomatic theory, an object or notion of the other theory is correlated, in such a way that the axioms become (or correspond to) theorems of the other theory.

If this other theory is consistent, then the axiomatic theory must be. For suppose that, in the axiomatic theory, a contradiction were deducible from the axioms. Then, in the other theory, by corresponding inferences about the objects constituting the model, a contradiction would be deducible from the corresponding theorems.

In a famous early example, Beltrami (1868) showed that the lines in the plane non-Euclidean geometry of Lobatchevsky and Bolyai (the plane hyperbolic geometry) can be represented by the geodesics on a surface of constant negative curvature in Euclidean space. Thus the plane hyperbolic geometry is consistent, if the Euclidean geometry is consistent. (Another model for the same was given by Klein (1871) in terms of plane projective geometry with Cayley's metric (1859); this can be construed as a model in the Euclidean plane. Cf. Young 1911 Lectures II and III.)

The analytic geometry of Descartes (1619), i.e. the use of coordinates to represent geometrical objects, constitutes a general method for establishing the consistency of geometric theories on the basis of analysis, i.e. the theory of the real numbers.

Consistency proofs by the method of a model are relative. The theory for which a model is set up is consistent, if that from which the model is taken is consistent.

Only when the latter is unimpeachable does the model give us an absolute proof of consistency. Veblen and Bussey 1906 achieve absolute proofs of consistency for certain rudimentary projective geometries by setting up models using only a finite (sic!) class of objects to represent the points (cf. Young 1911 Lectures IV and V).

For proving absolutely the consistency of classical number theory, of analysis, and of set theory (suitably axiomatized), the method of a model offers no hope. No mathematical source is apparent for a model which would not merely take us back to one of the theories previously reduced by the method of a model to these.

The impossibility of drawing upon the perceptual or physical world for a model is argued in Hilbert and Bernays 1934 pp. 15—17. They illustrate it by considering Zeno's first paradox (fifth century B.C.), according to which a runner cannot run a course in a finite time. For before he can do so, he must run the first half, then the next quarter, then the next eight, and so on. But this would require him to complete an infinite number of acts. The usual solution of the paradox consists in observing that the infinite series of the time intervals required to run the successive segments converges. "Actually there is also a much more radical solution of the paradox. This consists in the consideration that we are by no means obliged to believe that the mathematical space-time representation of motion is physically significant for arbitrarily small space and time intervals; but rather have every basis to suppose that that mathematical model extrapolates the facts of a certain realm of experience, namely the motions within the orders of magnitude hitherto accessible to our observation, in the sense of a simple concept construction, similarly to the way the mechanics of continua completes an extrapolation in which a continuous filling of the space with matter is assumed .... The situation is similar in all cases where one believes it possible to exhibit directly an [actual] infinity as given through experience or perception .... Closer examination then shows that an infinity is actually not given to us at all, but is first interpolated or extrapolated through an intellectual process."

Therefore, if consistency is to be proved for number theory (including its non-intuitionistic portions), for analysis, etc., it must be by another method. It is Hilbert's contribution now to have conceived a new direct approach, and to have recognized what it involves for the axiomatization. This direct method is implicit in the meaning of consistency (at least as we now think of it), namely that no logical contradiction (a proposition A and its negation *not* A both being theorems) can arise in the theory deduced from the axioms. Thus to prove the consistency of a theory directly, one should prove a proposition about the theory itself, i.e. specifically about all possible proofs of theorems in the theory. The mathematical theory whose consistency it is hoped to prove then becomes itself the object of a mathematical study, which Hilbert calls "metamathematics" or "proof theory". How this is possible, and what the methods of the study may be, we shall examine in the next section.

Meanwhile let us consider further the import of Hilbert's proposal. Hilbert (1926, 1928) draws a distinction between 'real' and 'ideal' statements in classical mathematics, in essence as follows. The *real statements* are those which are being used as having an intuitive meaning; the *ideal statements* are those which are not being so used. The statements which correspond to the treatment of the infinite as actual are ideal. Classical mathematics adjoins the ideal statements to the real, in order to retain the simple rules of the Aristotelian logic in reasoning about infinite sets.

The addition of 'ideal elements' to a system to complete its structure and simplify the theory of the system is a common and fruitful device in modern mathematics. For example, in Euclidean plane geometry two distinct lines intersect in a unique point, except when the lines are parallel. To remove this exception, Poncelet in his projective geometry (1822) introduced a *point at infinity* on each of the original lines, such that parallel lines have the same point at infinity and non-parallel lines have different points at infinity. The totality of these points at infinity make up a *line at infinity*. As a line through a finite point of the projective plane rotates, its point at infinity traces out the line at infinity. By this device, the relationships of incidence between points and lines is simplified. Two distinct points determine a unique line (which is 'on' both points, i.e. through both of which the line passes); and two distinct lines determine a unique point (which is on both lines). These two propositions are *duals* of each other. There is a general principle, called the *principle of duality* for plane projective geometry, which says that to each theorem of the subject the statement obtained from it by interchanging the words "point" and "line" is also a theorem.

As other examples of the addition of elements to a previously constituted system of elements to serve some theoretical purpose, we may take the successive enlargements of the number system, starting say with the natural numbers, then adjoining the negative integers, then the fractions, then the irrationals, and finally the imaginary numbers. The adjunction of the negative integers simplifies the theory of addition by making the inverse operation (subtraction) always possible; etc.

Hilbert's problem is crudely analogous to the problem which existed when imaginary numbers first came into use. As they were then not clearly understood, one might have proposed to justify their use to doubters by proving that, if imaginaries are used according to prescribed rules to derive a result expressed in terms of reals only, then that result must be correct. Of course, this kind of justification for imaginaries relative to reals is not needed now, since their interpretation by points in the plane (Wessel 1799) and by pairs of reals (Gauss 1831) have become known.

This analogy suggests asking whether, if a proof of consistency in Hilbert's sense should succeed for a portion of classical mathematics comprising both real and ideal statements, we could then infer that the real statements proved therein by an excursion through the ideal are true intuitionistically? The extent to which we could will be discussed later (end § 42, end § 82); it will depend on what reasonings are covered by the consistency proof, and what class of statements is being taken as real. To this extent, success in Hilbert's program would give to classical mathematics a role as a method of proof for the intuitionists.

A sharp controversy arose between Brouwer and Hilbert in the early years after Hilbert's program took shape. Brouwer 1923 said, "An incorrect theory which is not stopped by a contradiction is none the less incorrect, just as a criminal policy unchecked by a reprimanding court is none the less criminal." Hilbert 1928 retorted, "To take the law of the excluded middle away from the mathematician would be like denying the astronomer the telescope or the boxer the use of his fists."

According to Brouwer (1928) and Heyting (1931-2, 1934), agreement between intuitionism and formalism is possible, provided (as in von Neumann 1931-2) the formalist refrains from attributing to the non-intuitionistic classical mathematics a material meaning or content, in terms of which the consistency proof justifies it. Such a justification, says Brouwer, "contains a vicious circle, because this justification depends on the (material (inhaltlichen)) correctness of the proposition that from the consistency of a statement the correctness of that statement follows, i.e. on the (material) correctness of the law of the excluded middle", which is part of the formalistic mathematics that is to be justified.

The delicate point in the formalistic position is to explain how the non-intuitionistic classical mathematics is significant, after having initially agreed with the intuitionists that its theorems lack a real meaning in terms of which they are true.

Classical mathematics constructs theories in quite a different sense from intuitionistic mathematics. Hilbert 1928 says, "It is by no means reasonable to set up in general the requirement that each separate formula should be interpretable taken by itself ...." In theoretical physics "only certain combinations and consequences of the physical laws can be checked experimentally — likewise in my proof theory only the real statements are immediately capable of a verification".

A theory in classical mathematics can be regarded as a simple and elegant systematizing scheme, by which a variety of (presumably) true real statements, previously appearing as heterogeneous and unrelated, and often previously unknown, are comprised as consequences of the ideal theorems in the theory. (Cf. von Neumann 1947, Einstein 1944 p. 288.)

The example of analytic number theory illustrates that theorems of analysis (lacking a meaning acceptable to the intuitionist) often entail theorems of number theory, which are meaningful intuitionistically, and for which either no non-analytic proofs have been discovered or only much more complicated ones.

For a theory to be valuable in this way, the real statements comprised must be true. Formerly mathematicians supposed this to be guaranteed by the truth of the theorems which we now recognize as ideal; now we hope to guarantee it instead by a consistency proof.

By easy stages of transition, the theorizing may climb to higher levels, from which it is only very indirectly concerned with systematizing the real propositions at the original level, but rather with systematizing ideal propositions at intermediate levels. In this connection it is of interest whether successively higher theoretical constructions actually add to the body of real propositions of the original sort which are comprised, as well as whether they do actually permit substantial simplifications of the proofs of those previously comprised. (Cf. end § 42.)

It is debatable how high a theoretical structure is justified for systematizing a given sort of real truths, e.g. whether classical analysis is justified as a systematization of number-theoretic truths. Historically analytic number theory was a by-product, and the actual impetus to the development of classical analysis came from the sciences, including geometry in its physical application.

Hilbert and Bernays 1934 emphasize that in the sciences "we have to do ... predominately with theories which do not reproduce the actual state of affairs completely, but represent a *simplifying idealization* of the state of affairs and have their meaning therein" (pp. 2—3). Analysis serves as a "formation of ideas (Ideenbildung)", in terms of which those theories can be expressed, or to which they can be reduced by the method of models. A proof of the consistency of analysis would assure us of the consistency of the idealizations effected in those theories (p. 19).

Weyl (1926, 1928, 1931) observes that in theoretical physics it is not the separate statements which are confronted with experience, but the theoretical system as a whole. What is afforded here is not a true description of what is given, but theoretical, purely symbolic construction of the world. (Also he argues that our theoretical interest is not exclusively or even primarily in the 'real statements', e.g. that this pointer coincides with that scale division, but rather in the ideal suppositions, e.g. the supposition of the electron as a universal electrical quantum.) It is a deep philosophical question what the 'truth' or objectivity is which pertains to this theoretical world construction going far beyond the given. This is closely connected with the question, what motivates us to take as basis the particular axiom system chosen. For this consistency is a necessary but not sufficient argument. When mathematics is taken for itself alone, he would restrict himself with Brouwer to the intuitive truths; he does not find a sufficient motive to go further. But when mathematics is merged completely with physics in the process of theoretical world construction, he sides with Hilbert.

A verdict on the formalists' thinking will depend partly on the fruits of the program they propose. This program calls for a subject called "metamathematics", in which they aim in particular to establish the consistency of classical mathematics.

We note in advance that metamathematics will be found to provide a rigorous mathematical technique for investigating a great variety of foundation problems for mathematics and logic, among which the consistency problem is only one. For example, metamathematical methods are applied now in studies of systematizations of mathematics arising from the logicistic and intuitionistic schools, as well as from Hilbert's. (Inversely, metamathematics owes much for its inception to the logicistic and intuitionistic investigations.) Our aim in the rest of this book is not to reach a verdict supporting or rejecting the formalistic viewpoint in any preassigned version; but to see what the metamathematical method consists in, and to learn some of the things that have been discovered in pursuing it.

§ 15. Formalization of a theory. We are now about to undertake a program which makes a mathematical theory itself the object of exact mathematical study. In a mathematical theory, we study a system of mathematical objects. How can a mathematical theory itself be an object for mathematical study?

The result of the mathematician's activity is embodied in propositions, the asserted propositions or theorems of the given mathematical theory. We cannot hope to study in exact terms what is in the mathematician's mind, but we can contemplate the system of these propositions.

The system of these propositions must be made entirely explicit. Not all of the propositions can be written down, but rather the disciple and student of the theory should be told all the conditions which determine what propositions hold in the theory.

As the first step, the propositions of the theory should be arranged deductively, some of them, from which the others are logically deducible, being specified as the axioms (or postulates).

This step will not be finished until all the properties of the undefined or technical terms of the theory which matter for the deduction of the theorems have been expressed by axioms. Then it should be possible to perform the deductions treating the technical terms as words in themselves without meaning. For to say that they have meanings necessary to the deduction of the theorems, other than what they derive from the axioms which govern them, amounts to saying that not all of their properties which matter for the deductions have been expressed by axioms. When the meanings of the technical terms are thus left out of account, we have arrived at the standpoint of formal axiomatics (§ 8).

The technical terms still have grammatical attributes, being nouns, adjectives, verbs, etc. Also there remain ordinary or logical terms, whose meanings are employed in the deductions. Indeed the point at which formal axiomatization stops is arbitrary, in so far as no absolute basis exists for the distinction between the technical and the ordinary terms.

At any rate, we are still short of our goal of making explicit all the conditions which determine what propositions hold in the theory. For we have not specified the logical principles to be used in the deductions. These principles are not the same for all theories, as we are now well aware (§ 13).

In order to make these explicit, a second step is required, which completes the step previously carried out for the so-called technical terms in respect to the non-grammatical part of their meanings. All the meanings of all the words are left out of account, and all the conditions which govern their use in the theory are stated explicitly. The logical principles which formerly entered implicitly through the meanings of the ordinary terms will now be given effect in part perhaps by new axioms, and in some part at least by rules permitting the inference of one sentence from another or others. Since we have abstracted entirely from the content or matter, leaving only the form, we say that the original theory has been *formalized*. In its structure, the theory is no longer a system of meaningful propositions, but one of sentences as sequences of words, which in turn are sequences of letters. We say by reference to the form alone which combinations of words are sentences, which sentences are axioms, and which sentences follow as immediate consequences from others.

Is such formalization possible? To what extent a given theory can be formalized we shall learn only after attempting it and studying the results (e.g. §§ 29, 42, 60, 72).

That at least a very considerable measure of formalization is possible for mathematical theories is a discovery which has been spread over a long stretch of man's intellectual history.

The discovery of the axiomatic-deductive method in mathematics is attributed by ancient Greek tradition to Pythagoras (sixth century B.C.), and comes to us from Euclid (365?—275? B.C.), whose "Elements" is said to have had the greatest circulation of any book except the Bible. Euclid failed to make explicit all of the postulates required in the deduction of his theorems. Others have been brought into the light in modern times, e.g. those governing the order of the points on a line by Pasch 1882.

The discovery of the formal treatment of logic, i.e. of the possibility of describing deductive reasoning with sentences in terms of their form, appears with Aristotle (384—322 B.C.). Again there have been modern refinements.

We use both discoveries when we formalize a mathematical theory. To do so fully rigorously, it is practically necessary to reconstruct the theory in a special symbolic language, i.e. to *symbolize* it. Instead of carrying out the steps described above on the theory as we find it in some natural word language, such as Greek or English, we build a new symbolic language specially for the purpose of expressing the theory. The natural word languages are too cumbersome, too irregular in construction and too ambiguous to be suitable. (The symbols in a symbolic language will usually correspond to whole words instead of to letters; and sequences of symbols which correspond to sentences will be called "formulas".)

This new language will be of the general character of the symbolism which we find in mathematics. In algebra we perform deductions as formal manipulations with equations, which would be exceedingly tedious to perform in ordinary language, as some of them were before the invention by Vieta (1591) and others of the modern algebraic notations. The discovery of simple symbolic notations which lend themselves to manipulation by formal rules has been one of the ways by which modern mathematics had advanced in power. However the ordinary practice in mathematics illustrates only a partial symbolization and formalization, since part of the statements remain expressed in words, and part of the deductions are performed in terms of the meanings of the words rather than by formal rules.

Since Leibniz (1666) conceived his idea of a universal characteristic, formal logic also has been receiving a symbolic treatment, with the aid of mathematical techniques, under De Morgan (1847, 1864), Boole (1847, 1854), Peirce (1867, 1880), Schröder (1877, 1890-1905) and others.

These concurrent developments have finally led to formalizations of portions of mathematics, in the strict sense, by Frege (1893, 1903), Peano (1894-1908) and Whitehead and Russell (1910-13). (The method of making a theory explicit which we have been describing is often called the *logistic* method.)

To Hilbert is due now, first, the emphasis that strict formalization of a theory involves the total abstraction from the meaning, the result being called a *formal system* or *formalism* (or sometimes a *formal theory* or *formal mathematics*); and second, his method of making the formal system as a whole the object of a mathematical study called *metamathematics* or *proof theory*.

Metamathematics includes the description or definition of formal systems as well as the investigation of properties of formal systems. In dealing with a particular formal system, we may call the system the *object theory*, and the metamathematics relating to it its *metatheory*.

From the standpoint of the metatheory, the object theory is not properly a theory at all as we formerly understood the term, but a system of meaningless objects like the positions in a game of chess, subject to mechanical manipulations like the moves in chess. The object theory is described and studied as a system of symbols and of objects built up out of symbols. The symbols are regarded simply as various kinds of recognizable objects. To fix our ideas we may think of them concretely as marks on paper; or more accurately as abstracted from our experience with symbols as marks on paper. (Proof theory must be to some extent abstract, since it supposes arbitrarily long sequences of symbols to be constructible, although the quantity of paper and ink in the world is finite.) The other objects of the system are analyzed only with regard to the manner of their composition out of the symbols. By definition, this is all that a formal system shall be as an object of study for metamathematics.

The metatheory belongs to intuitive and informal mathematics (unless the metatheory is itself formalized from a metametatheory, which here we leave out of account). The metatheory will be expressed in ordinary language, with mathematical symbols, such as metamathematical variables, introduced according to need. The assertions of the metatheory must be understood. The deductions must carry conviction. They must proceed by intuitive inferences, and not, as the deductions in the formal theory, by applications of stated rules. Rules have been stated to formalize the object theory, but now we must understand without rules how those rules work. An intuitive mathematics is necessary even to define the formal mathematics.

(We shall understand this to mean that the ultimate appeal to justify a metamathematical inference must be to the meaning and evidence rather than to any set of conventional rules. It will not prevent us in practice from systematizing our metamathematical results in theorems or rules, which can then be applied quasi-formally to abbreviate the intuitive reasoning. This is a familiar procedure in informal mathematics.

We shall sometimes even refer to principles of (intuitionistic) logic stated formally, when the formal derivation of those principles indicates the method by which the reasoning can be carried out informally.)

The methods used in the metatheory shall be restricted to methods, called *finitary* by the formalists, which employ only intuitively conceivable objects and performable processes. (We translate the German "finit" as "finitary", since the English "finite" is used for the German "endlich".) No infinite class may be regarded as a completed whole. Proofs of existence shall give, at least implicitly, a method for constructing the object which is being proved to exist. (Cf. § 13.)

This restriction is requisite for the purpose for which Hilbert introduces metamathematics. Propositions of a given mathematical theory may fail to have a clear meaning, and inferences in it may not carry indubitable evidence. By formalizing the theory, the development of the theory is reduced to form and rule. There is no longer ambiguity about what constitutes a statement of the theory, or what constitutes a proof in the theory. Then the question whether the methods which have been formalized in it lead to contradiction, and other questions about the effect of those methods, are to be investigated in the metatheory, by methods not subject to the same doubts as the methods of the original theory.

The finitary methods are of sorts used in intuitionistic elementary number theory. Some formalists attempt to circumscribe them still more narrowly (Hilbert and Bernays 1934 p. 43, and Bernays 1935, 1938).

We shall leave the discussion of this until later (§ 81). For the purpose of defending classical mathematics against the intuitionists, there is no need to use less than the intuitionists would allow. However it is natural to proceed on the basis of strictly elementary methods so long as they will suffice. All the examples of intuitionistic number-theoretic reasoning given in § 13 we shall take to be finitary. We shall find that up to a late stage in our metamathematical investigations, intuitionistic methods of an entirely elementary sort will suffice. The ultimate test whether a method is admissible in metamathematics must of course be whether it is intuitively convincing.

(Some authors use "meta-" to identify a language or theory in which another language or theory is made the object of a study not restricted to finitary methods. Also "syntax language" vs. "object language" is used in this connection. Cf. Carnap 1934; also cf. § 37. In this book, we only use "meta-" when the methods are finitary.)

The formal systems which are studied in metamathematics are (usually) so chosen that they serve as models for parts of informal mathematics and logic with which we are already more or less familiar, and from which they arose by formalization. The meanings which are intended to be attached to the symbols, formulas, etc. of a given formal system, in considering the system as a formalization of an informal theory, we call *the* (*intended*) *interpretation* of the system (or of its symbols, formulas, etc.). In other words, the interpretations of the symbols, formulas, etc. are the objects, propositions, etc. of the informal theory which are correlated under the method by which the system constitutes a model for the informal theory.

In the case of a formula which represents an ideal statement of classical mathematics (§ 14), the interpretation cannot constitute a wholly intuitive (or finitary) meaning, but must consist in whatever else it is the classical mathematician thinks in terms of in the informal (or not strictly formalized) development of classical mathematics, i.e. in the development which has taken place historically and takes place currently, when the procedure is not being consciously formalized in the strict sense of proof theory.

The interpretation motivates the metamathematician in his choice of the particular formal system which he introduces by his definitions. It guides him in choosing the problems relating to the system which he investigates. It may even provide him with essential clues toward achieving the solution of those problems. Only in the final statement and proof of his results is he prohibited (as a metamathematician) from using the interpretation.

How restrictive is this prohibition? Metamathematics must study the formal system as a system of symbols, etc. which are considered wholly objectively. This means simply that those symbols, etc. are themselves the ultimate objects, and are not being used to refer to something other than themselves. The metamathematician looks at them, not through and beyond them; thus they are objects without interpretation or meaning.

Now in studying those objects, metamathematics must bring to bear its own methods and tools. These may be any that are finitary. For example, metamathematics may employ the natural numbers in a finitary way. In the case of formulas admitting (outside of metamathematics) a finitary interpretation, it may be possible within metamathematics to define properties of those formal objects which (from outside the metamathematics) are equivalent to their interpretations. Thus the finitary interpretations may be brought in through the back door. But metamathematics cannot in any way deal with the non-finitary interpretations of the ideal propositions of classical mathematics.

In order to make it clear all along why we are interested in the formal systems which we are considering, and how they constitute formalizations of portions of logic and mathematics that we are already familar with informally, we shall in this book indicate the possibilities of interpretation, and use suggestive terminology, such as "proof" for formal derivations, and "and" for the name of the symbol &. This is necessary to our full purpose, even though the interpretation is extraneous to the metamathematics itself.

Let us briefly recapitulate. In the full picture, there will be three separate and distinct "theories": (a) the informal theory of which the formal system constitutes a formalization, (b) the formal system or object theory, and (c) the metatheory, in which the formal system is described and studied.

Here (b), which is formal, is not a theory in the common sense, but a system of symbols and of objects built from symbols (described from (c)), which however forms a kind of conventionalized image or model for (a). On the other hand, (a) and (c), which are informal, do not have an exactly determined structure, as does (b).

Then (c) is a theory with (b) as its subject matter, which must apply to (b) without looking at (a), or more precisely without looking at the interpretation of (b) in terms of (a).

Furthermore (c) is restricted to the use of finitary methods, while in general (a) will not be.

Note 1: At the top of p. 51, the seeming circularity that *not B* is used in explaining *not A* is to be avoided thus. Sameness and distinctness of two natural numbers (or of two finite sequences of symbols) are basic concepts (cf. p. 51 lines 20-24). For any B of the form $m = n$ where m and n are natural numbers, *not B* shall mean that m and n are distinct. The explanation of *not A* in lines 5-8 then serves for any A other than of that form, by taking the B in it to be of that form. Equivalently, since the distinctness of 1 from 0 is given by intuition (so *not* $1 = 0$ holds), *not A* means that one possesses a method which, from any proof of A, would procure a proof of $1 = 0$ (cf. lines 8-9).

PART II

MATHEMATICAL LOGIC

CHAPTER IV

A FORMAL SYSTEM

§ 16. Formal symbols. We shall now introduce a particular formal system. The system described in this chapter will be subject matter for the four following chapters and parts of later chapters. The system constitutes a formalization of a portion of classical elementary number theory including the logic required for it.

In setting up the system, we have made use of Hilbert and Ackermann 1928, Hilbert and Bernays 1934, 1939, Gentzen 1934-5, Bernays 1936, and less immediate sources.

Our undertaking has two distinct aspects. First, the formal system itself must be described and investigated, by finitary methods and without making use of an interpretation of the system. This is the metamathematics. Second, an interpretation of the system must be recognized, under which the system does constitute a formalization of number theory.

One approach would stress the second aspect. We could analyze existing informal mathematics, selecting and stereotyping fundamental concepts, presuppositions and deductive connections, and thus eventually arrive at a formal system.

Here instead, we shall place the initial emphasis on the first aspect. The formal system will be introduced at once in its full-fledged complexity, and the metamathematical investigations will be pursued with only incidental attention to the interpretation. The reader is asked to concentrate on learning precisely what the formal system is, and how it is investigated. The interpretation and the reasons for the choices made in setting up this particular system will then gradually unfold as we proceed.

The first step in setting up the formal system is to list the *formal symbols*. The list of formal symbols is analogous structurally to the alphabet of a language, although under the interpretation many of the formal symbols correspond to entire words and phrases rather than to single letters. The list of the formal symbols follows.

Logical symbols: $\supset$ (implies), & (and), $\vee$ (or), $\neg$ (not), $\forall$ (for all),

∃ (there exists). *Predicate symbols*: = (equals). *Function symbols*: + (plus), · (times), ′ (successor). *Individual symbols*: 0 (zero). *Variables*: *a*, *b*, *c*, ... *Parentheses*: (,).

The words shown parenthetically may be used in reading the symbols, and are intended to suggest the interpretations in a preliminary way, e.g. the interpretations of the logical symbols as 'logical constants'. The variables are interpreted as ranging over the natural numbers. An infinite list or enumeration of the variables is supposed to be at hand (potentially, cf. § 13).

We reiterate that the interpretations are extraneous to the description of the formal system as such. It must be possible to proceed regarding the formal symbols as mere marks, and not as symbols in the sense of symbols for something which they symbolize or signify. It is supposed only that we are able to recognize each formal symbol as the same in each of its recurrences, and as distinct from the other formal symbols. In the case of the variables this must include our being able to recognize a symbol which is a variable to be such.

The formal symbols constitute the first category of formal objects. We derive from this a second category by constructing finite sequences (of occurrences) of formal symbols, which we call *formal expressions*. The word "occurrence" is used here to refer to the members of the sequence in their status as members, and to emphasize that different members may be the same symbol (which agrees with our previous use of the term 'sequence', e.g. §§ 1, 2). The formal expressions include those consisting of a single (occurrence of a) formal symbol. Except when stated, the empty sequence (with no member) will not be included. For example, 0, (*a*)+(*b*), (*a*)=(0) and ((0∀00= are formal expressions. The last consists of seven (occurrences of) symbols, i.e. it has seven members; the third, fifth and sixth (occurrences of) symbols in it are each an (occurrence of) 0; and the (distinct) symbols which occur in it are (, 0, ∀, =. The formal expressions are analogous structurally to the words of a language; but under the interpretation some of them correspond to entire sentences, e.g. (*a*)=(0), and others are without significance, e.g. ((0∀00=. Again our terminology belies the fact that, for the formal system as such, the expressions express nothing, but are only certain recognizable and distinguishable objects.

We shall also use, as a third category of formal objects, the finite sequences of (occurrences of) formal expressions.

In discussing the formal objects we shall often, instead of exhibiting them, represent (i.e. denote) them by letters introduced for the purpose, or by expressions involving letters already so introduced. For example, the letter "s" might be used to represent the formal expression $(a)+(b)$, and "A" to represent $(a)=0$. Further illustrations will appear presently.

Letters and expressions so used are not formal symbols and expressions, but informal or metamathematical symbols and expressions, which stand as names for formal objects. In this, as compared with ordinary informal uses of symbolism, there is the new feature that the objects named are themselves symbols or objects constructed from symbols. We have thus a distinction to preserve between two kinds of symbolism, the formal symbolism about which we are speaking, and the intuitive or metamathematical symbolism in which we are speaking about the other. Differences in the kinds of type which will be used for the two purposes (a, b, t, x, $\mathcal{A}$, $\mathcal{B}$ vs. a, b, t, x, A, B) will assist in keeping the matter straight.

The use of symbols and expressions to name the objects we are talking about should not be considered as novel; our everyday method for constructing a sentence about an object requires this. What is novel, rather, is the other procedure, which we use somewhat in our metamathematics, of incorporating the object itself, i.e. a specimen of the object, directly into the sentence. Although this violates the usual canons of grammatical propriety, it is unambiguous when we are engaged in metamathematics. For in metamathematics we must treat the formal symbols as meaningless, and therefore the formal objects cannot serve as names for other objects, and a sentence containing a specimen of a formal object can only be about the formal object itself.

These remarks apply to our metamathematics. In an occasional passage, concerned with the interpretation and so labeled for the reader, we may give the formal symbols an informal status, treating them then as meaningful.

In our metamathematical study of the formal expressions, we shall make use of the operation of *juxtaposition* (or *concatenation*), in which two or more sequences of formal symbols are combined consecutively to produce a new sequence. For example, the juxtaposition of the two formal expressions $((0\forall 00=$ and $(a)+(b)$ in that order produces the new formal expression $((0\forall 00=(a)+(b)$; and the juxtaposition of the seven formal expressions $($, $(a)+(b)$, $)$, $\cdot$, $($, $(c)'$, $)$ in the given order produces the new formal expression $((a)+(b))\cdot((c)')$.

When some of the formal expressions to be juxtaposed are being represented by metamathematical letters or expressions, these latter may appear in place of the formal expressions which they represent in writing the result of the juxtaposition. For example, if the letter "s" represents some formal expression, the result of the juxtaposition of the seven formal expressions (, s,), ·, (, $(c)'$,) is written "(s)·($(c)'$)". Here "(s)·($(c)'$)" is a metamathematical expression representing a formal expression, the formal expression represented depending on what formal expression the letter "s" represents. In particular, if s is $(a)+(b)$, then (s)·($(c)'$) is $((a)+(b))\cdot((c)')$.

§ 17. Formation rules. We shall now define certain subcategories of the formal expressions, by definitions analogous to the rules of syntax in grammar.

First we define 'term', which is analogous to noun in grammar. The terms of this system all represent natural numbers, fixed or variable. The definition is formulated with the aid of metamathematical variables "s" and "t", and the operation of juxtaposition, as explained above. It has the form of an inductive definition, which enables us to proceed from known examples of terms to further ones.

1. 0 is a *term*. 2. A variable is a *term*. 3—5. If s and t are *terms*, then (s)+(t), (s)·(t) and (s)′ are *terms*. 6. The only *terms* are those given by 1—5.

Example 1. By 1 and 2, 0, a, b and c are terms. Then by 5, $(0)'$ and $(c)'$ are terms. Applying 5 again, $((0)')'$ is a term; and applying 3, $((c)')+(a)$ is a term.

We now give a definition of 'formula', analogous to (declarative) sentence in grammar.

1. If s and t are terms, then (s)=(t) is a *formula*. 2—5. If A and B are *formulas*, then (A) ⊃ (B), (A) & (B), (A) ∨ (B) and ¬(A) are *formulas*. 6—7. If x is a variable and A is a formula, then ∀x(A) and ∃x(A) are *formulas*. 8. The only *formulas* are those given by 1—7.

Example 2. Using 1 and the examples of terms already obtained, $(a)=(b)$ and $(((c)')+(a))=(b)$ are formulas. Then using 5 and 7, $\neg((a)=(b))$ and $\exists c((((c)')+(a))=(b))$ are formulas. Finally by an application of 2, the following is a formula:

$$\text{(A)} \qquad (\exists c((((c)')+(a))=(b))) \supset (\neg((a)=(b))).$$

The inductive definitions of term and formula have the consequence that each term or formula can be built up from 0 and variables by a series of steps, each of which steps corresponds to a direct clause of one of those definitions (§ 6), and may be called an *application* of that clause.

Each step, except an application of 1 or 2 of the definition of term, is of the following kind. At the start we have given an expression or pair of expressions previously obtained. We enclose the given expression or each of the given expressions in parentheses, and introduce an expression of one of the ten forms

(B) $\supset, \&, \vee, \neg, \forall x, \exists x, =, +, \cdot, '$,

where x is a variable. Let us call an expression of one of these ten forms an *operator*. In particular, $\supset$, &, $\vee$, $\neg$ are *propositional connectives*, and operators of the forms $\forall x$ and $\exists x$ are *quantifiers*, $\forall x$ being a *universal* and $\exists x$ an *existential quantifier*; these six are *logical operators.*

The given expression or pair of expressions we call the *scope* of the operator in the resulting expression. By following through the entire construction of a term or formula, establishing in the obvious way a correspondence between the parts of the given expression or pair of expressions and parts of the resulting expression at each step, we are led to an assignment of a *scope*, not merely to the operator last introduced in the completed term or formula, but to every operator in that term or formula.

EXAMPLE 3. In the formula (A) the scope of the first occurrence of $=$ consists of the part $((c)')+(a)$ and the first occurrence of b, and the scope of the $\exists c$ is the part $(((c)')+(a))=(b)$.

We now state the following fact, the rigorous proof of which we shall consider in a moment. In a given term or formula, the scopes of the operators can be recognized without ambiguity from the arrangement of the parentheses. In other words, the parentheses make it possible, given the term or formula as a finite sequence of formal symbols, to recover all essential details of its construction under the inductive definitions of term and formula.

The rigorous proof of this fact is afforded by Lemma 2 of § 7 Example 2, together with the following lemma which can be proved by induction from the inductive definitions of term and formula.

LEMMA 4. *In a given term or formula, there exists a proper pairing of the parentheses (which are 2n in number, n being left parentheses and n being right parentheses) such that the scope of each operator occurs as follows.*

(a) *For operators having one expression as scope, the scope is immediately enclosed within paired parentheses, and the operator stands immediately outside this pair of parentheses, i.e. immediately to the left of the left parenthesis (in the case of* $\neg$, $\forall x$, $\exists x$) *or immediately to the right of the right parenthesis (in the case of* ′).

(b) *For operators having two expressions as scope (namely* $\supset$, &, $\vee$, $=$, $+$, $\cdot$), *each of the two expressions is immediately enclosed within paired parentheses, and the operator stands immediately between the right parenthesis of the pair enclosing the left expression and the left parenthesis of the pair enclosing the right expression.*

EXAMPLE 3 (concluded). The displayed example (A) of a formula contains 22 parentheses. By Lemma 4, the 22 parentheses admit a proper pairing, which is discovered in the process of constructing the formula under the definitions of term and formula, and which indicates the scopes of the operators. Knowing that there exists a proper pairing, by Lemma 2 that pairing is unique, and can therefore be discovered by the algorithm of § 7, without prior knowledge of the construction of the formula under the definitions of term and formula. We actually did so at the end of § 7, where we examined the same 22 parentheses without looking at the intervening symbols. Using the resulting pairing of the 22 parentheses as they occur within the complete formula, we can see that the scope of the first occurrence of $=$ consists of the expression enclosed by the parentheses $(^{3}_{4}\ )^{10}_{4}$ and the expression enclosed by the parentheses $(^{11}_{5}\ )^{12}_{5}$. This agrees with our previous identification of that scope. Similarly, the scope of $\exists c$ is enclosed by the parentheses $(^{2}_{6}\ )^{13}_{6}$.

Lemma 3 of § 7, while not necessary to the proof that the scopes can be discovered from the arrangement of the parentheses, is useful in reasoning about the scopes in parts and the whole of a term or formula. For example, if M, N and A are formulas, and A occurs as a (consecutive) part, not the whole, of (M) $\supset$ (N), we can infer that this part (or each such part) is either a part of M or a part of N.

In choosing our definitions of term and formula, we of course provided the parentheses for the above described purpose of indicating the scopes unambiguously. Now evidently more parentheses will usually be introduced under the definitions than are strictly necessary for the purpose. Leaving the definitions as they stand, we can agree to omit superfluous parentheses as an abbreviation in the writing down of terms and formulas, or of metamathematical expressions representing them.

The possibilities in this direction are extended by employing conventions of a sort familiar from algebra, where "$a \cdot b+c$" is understood to mean $(a \cdot b)+c$. We say here that $+$ *ranks* ahead of $\cdot$, and rank our operators in the order in which we have listed them at (B) above. To restore any parentheses which are left out in abbreviating a term or formula, one may proceed step by step, each time selecting an operator which of those present comes earliest in the list, i.e. an operator of highest rank, and giving it the greatest scope compatible with the requirement that the whole be a term or formula.

We shall not always omit the maximum number of parentheses which our convention would allow, but aim at securing maximum readability. (With this aim, we also sometimes alter parentheses to square brackets or curly brackets.)

EXAMPLE 4. Restoring parentheses to "A ⊃ B ∨ C & D" gives successively "A ⊃ (B ∨ C & D)", "A ⊃ ((B ∨ C) & D)", "(A) ⊃ (((B) ∨ (C)) & (D))". We abbreviate the displayed example (A) of a formula as follows:

(A′) $$\exists c(c'+a=b) \supset \neg a=b.$$

Another kind of abbreviation is afforded by introducing a new symbol, with a method for translating an expression containing the new symbol back into one without it. For example, we abbreviate the terms (0)′, ((0)′)′, (((0)′)′)′, . . . as "1", "2", "3", . . . , respectively; and we abbreviate the formula $\neg a=b$ as "$a \neq b$", and the formula $\exists c(c'+a=b)$ as "$a<b$". The displayed formula (A) can then be written:

(A″) $$a<b \supset a \neq b.$$

The general rule for the abbreviation "≠" allows us to write "s≠t" as abbreviation for ¬s=t whenever s and t are terms. The general rule for the abbreviation "<" allows us to write "s<t" as abbreviation for ∃x(x′+s=t) whenever x is a variable and s and t are terms not containing x. In unabbreviating, when the introduction of the abbreviation has suppressed a variable, as in the case of "<", there is an ambiguity respecting the variable to be supplied. Thus in unabbreviating "s<t", we may choose as the x any variable which s and t do not contain. This ambiguity is of minor consequence, since the statements we shall wish to make about the formula abbreviated will hold regardless of what admissible variable is chosen.

We shall regard all this abbreviation as merely in the exposition of the metamathematics. This is adequate for our purposes, and thereby we keep the fundamental definitions, which establish the formal system, theoretically simpler. Metamathematical statements about terms and formulas of the system are hence to be understood to refer to the unabbreviated expressions in the literal sense of the definitions, whatever shorthand we may employ in writing the statements.

§ 18. Free and bound variables. An occurrence of a variable x in a formula A is said to be *bound* (or *as a bound variable*), if the occurrence is in a quantifier ∀x or ∃x or in the scope of a quantifier ∀x or ∃x (with the same x); otherwise, *free* (or *as a free variable*).

Example 1. In $\exists c(c'+a=b) \supset \neg a=b$, both occurrences of a and both occurrences of b are free, and both occurrences of c are bound. In $\exists c(c'+a=b) \supset \neg a=b+c$, the first two occurrences of c are bound and the third is free. In $\exists c(\exists c(c'+a=b) \supset \neg a=b+c)$ all occurrences of c are bound.

We also say that any occurrence of a variable x in a term t is *free*, as will follow from the above definition if applied reading "term t" instead of "formula A". The distinction between a free and a bound occurrence of a variable is always relative to the term or formula in which it is (at the moment) being considered as an occurrence.

Example 2. The third occurrence of c in $\exists c(\exists c(c'+a=b) \supset \neg a=b+c)$ is free when considered as an occurrence in the part c taken by itself or c' by itself or $c'+a$ by itself or $c'+a=b$ by itself, and bound as an occurrence in $\exists c(c'+a=b)$ by itself or $\exists c(c'+a=b) \supset \neg a=b+c$ by itself or in the whole formula.

A variable x which occurs as a free variable (briefly, occurs free) in A is called a *free variable of* A, and A is then said to *contain* x *as a free variable* (briefly, to *contain* x *free*); and likewise for bound variables.

Example 3. The free variables of $\exists c(c'+a=b) \supset \neg a=b+c$ are a, b and c, and the only bound variable is c.

A bound occurrence of a variable x in a formula A is bound *by* that particular one, of the quantifiers ∀x or ∃x (with the same x) in the scope of which it lies, which has the least scope (briefly, by the innermost quantifier in whose scope it lies), or in case it is an occurrence in a quantifier ∀x or ∃x, by that quantifier itself (or the latter *binds* the former).

Example 4. In $\exists c(\exists c(c'+a=b) \supset \neg a=b+c)$ the first and fourth occurrences of c are bound by the first quantifier $\exists c$, and the second and third occurrences of c by the second quantifier $\exists c$.

In building up a formula under the definitions of term and formula, a given bound occurrence of a variable in the resulting formula is bound by that one of the quantifiers whose introduction first converted it from a free to a bound occurrence (or if it is a variable in a quantifier, by the quantifier in which it is introduced).

EXAMPLE 5. Compare Example 4 with Example 2.

A few preliminary remarks are offered now on the interpretation of free and bound variables (sometimes called 'real' and 'apparent' variables). The remarks are of course not part of the metamathematics, but should help to explain the adoption of the metamathematical discriminations. An expression containing a free variable represents a quantity or proposition depending on the value of the variable. An expression containing a bound variable represents the result of an operation performed over the range of the variable. Our bound variables are associated with the logical operations of quantification, but examples occur with other sorts of operations familiar to mathematicians. In the following n and y are free, i and x are bound:

(A) $$\sum_{i=1}^{n} a_i, \quad \lim_{x\to 0} f(x, y), \quad \int_{-y}^{y} f(x, y)\, dx.$$

In the following the occurrence of t as upper limit of the integral is free and the occurrences in the integrand are bound:

(B) $$\int_{0}^{t} f(t)\, dt.$$

To go a little further with the interpretation, we may note some characteristic differences which it imposes on the way we may use the two kinds of variables in informal mathematics. A bound variable forms part of a circumlocution for expressing the result of an operation carried out over the range of the variable, and one can hence change the variable to any other having the same range without altering the meaning (subject to certain precautions). For example,

(C) $$\sum_{j=1}^{n} a_j, \quad \lim_{z\to 0} f(z, y), \quad \int_{-y}^{y} f(t, y)\, dt$$

would (ordinarily) mean the same as the respective expressions (A) above (but $\lim_{y\to 0} f(y, y)$ is not (usually) the same as $\lim_{x\to 0} f(x, y)$). If in an expression we substitute for a free variable an expression representing a constant or variable object from its range, we (ordinarily) obtain a meaningful result, while such a substitution would result in nonsense if applied to a bound variable. For example (substituting in (A)),

(D) $$\sum_{i=1}^{5} a_i, \quad \lim_{x\to 0} f(x, 2), \quad \int_{-z}^{z} f(x, z)\, dx$$

are (ordinarily) significant expressions, but not

$$\text{(E)} \qquad \sum_{5=1}^{n} a_5, \quad \lim_{2\to 0} f(2, y), \quad \int_{-z}^{z} f(0, z)\, d0.$$

When the same variable occurs both free and bound in an expression, the quantity represented by the expression depends only on the value of that variable in its free occurrences. Thus the integral (B) is a function of t, whose value for $t = 3$ is

$$\text{(F)} \qquad \int_0^3 f(t)\, dt, \quad \text{not} \quad \int_0^3 f(3)\, d3.$$

SUBSTITUTION. In stating the metamathematical definitions of the next section, we shall use an operation of substitution, which we define as follows. The *substitution of* a term t *for* a variable x *in* (or synonymously, *throughout*) a term or formula A shall consist in replacing simultaneously each free occurrence of x in A by an occurrence of t. To describe this in juxtaposition notation, let n be the number of free occurrences of x in A ($n \geq 0$); and write A as "$A_0xA_1x\ldots A_{n-1}xA_n$" showing these occurrences ($A_0, A_1, \ldots, A_{n-1}, A_n$ being parts possibly empty containing no occurrence of x free relative to A as a whole, and all the n occurrences of x shown being free). Then the result of the substitution of t for x in A is $A_0tA_1t\ldots A_{n-1}tA_n$.

A compact metamathematical notation will be useful in representing the result of a substitution. If substitution is to be performed for x, we first introduce a composite notation such as "A(x)" for the substituend, showing its dependence on x after the manner of notation for functions in mathematics (§ 10). The result of substituting t for x in A(x) is then written "A(t)".

EXAMPLE 6. Let x be c, and
A(x) or A(c) be $\exists c(c'+a=b) \supset \neg a=b+c$.
Then A(0) is $\exists c(c'+a=b) \supset \neg a=b+0$,
and A(a) is $\exists c(c'+a=b) \supset \neg a=b+a$.

EXAMPLE 7. Let x be a, and A(x) be $a+c=a$. Then A(0) is $0+c=0$, and A(b) is $b+c=b$.

The substitution which gives A(t) must always be performed for the original variable x in the original formula A(x), i.e. for the variable and in the formula for which the notation "A(x)" is first introduced.

EXAMPLE 7 (concluded). For the above x and A(x), A(c) is $c+c=c$. If we substitute b for c in A(c), we obtain $b+b=b$. This is not the same as A(b), which we obtained above correctly by substituting b for a in A(a), i.e. for the original x in the original A(x). (The same difficulty can occur by the misuse of the notation for a function in informal mathematics.)

We have not required that the variable x actually occur as a free variable in A(x). When x is not a free variable of A(x), the result A(t) of the substitution is the original expression A(x) itself.

Similarly, we define substitution performed simultaneously for a number of distinct variables; and we shall employ like notations, such as "$A(x_1, \ldots, x_n)$" for the substituend, and "$A(t_1, \ldots, t_n)$" for the result.

Henceforth we shall often introduce these composite notations, such as "A(x)" or "$A(x_1, \ldots, x_n)$" instead of "A", when we are interested in the dependence of A on a variable x or variables $x_1, \ldots, x_n$, whether or not we are about to make a substitution. For example, we usually designate a formula by "A(x)" instead of "A", when we want to use it in ∀xA(x) (read "for all x, A of x", or briefly "all x, A of x") or ∃xA(x) (read "there exists an x such that A of x", or briefly "exists x, A of x"). We repeat that by using "A(x)" (or "$A(x_1, \ldots, x_n)$") we do not imply that x (or each of $x_1, \ldots, x_n$) necessarily occurs free in the formula designated.

The preliminary remarks on the interpretation shed light on why we have elected to define our metamathematical substitution operation as applying only to the free occurrences of the variables.

We now say that a term t is *free at the free occurrences of* a variable x *in* a formula A(x) (or t is *free at the substitution positions for* x *in* A(x), or briefly t is *free for* x *in* A(x)), if no free occurrence of x in A(x) is in the scope of a quantifier ∀y or ∃y where y is a variable of t (i.e. occurs in t).

EXAMPLE 8. The terms d, $d+0'$ and $a \cdot d$ are free for a in the first but not in the second of the following formulas:

$$\text{(I)} \qquad \exists c(c'+a=b) \mathbin{\&} \neg d=0, \qquad \exists d(d'+a=b) \mathbin{\&} \neg d=0.$$

Under this definition, when t is free for x in A(x) and only then, the substitution of t for x in A(x) will not introduce t into A(x) at any place where a (free) variable y of t becomes a bound occurrence of y in the result A(t).

EXAMPLE 8 (concluded). Substituting $d+0'$ for a in (I) gives

$$\text{(II)} \qquad \exists c(c'+(d+0')=b) \mathbin{\&} \neg d=0, \quad \exists d(d'+(d+0')=b) \mathbin{\&} \neg d=0,$$

respectively. In the first of these, the d of the occurrence of $d+0'$ introduced by the substitution remains free in the whole formula, but not in the second.

We say that the substitution of t for x in A(x) is *free*, when t is free for x in A(x). With only the smattering of interpretation indicated above, it should be clear that a substitution is inappropriate when it is not free. The two formulas in (I) mean the same; but the two in (II) do not.

For an informal example, consider the second expression of (A) or (C). This stands for a function of y, call it

$$\text{(G)} \qquad f(y) = \lim_{x \to 0} f(x, y) = \lim_{z \to 0} f(z, y).$$

The value of $f(y)$ for $y = z$ is then given properly by

$$\text{(H)} \qquad f(z) = \lim_{x \to 0} f(x, z), \quad \text{not by} \quad f(z) = \lim_{z \to 0} f(z, z).$$

Example 9. To illustrate the handling of the terminology and notations explained in this section, say that x is (i.e. "x" denotes) a variable, A(x) is (i.e. "A(x)" denotes) a formula, and b is (i.e. "b" denotes) a variable such that (i) b is free for x in A(x) and (ii) b does not occur free in A(x) (unless b is x). Under our substitution notation, since "x" and "A(x)" are introduced first, (iii) A(b) is (by definition) the result of substituting b for (the free occurrences of) x in A(x). By (i), the occurrences of b in A(b) which are introduced by this substitution are free. By (ii), there are no other free occurrences of b in A(b). Thus the free occurrences of b in A(b) are exactly the occurrences introduced by the substitution. Hence (inversely to (i) — (iii)): (iv) x is free for b in A(b), (v) x does not occur free in A(b) (unless x is b), and (vi) A(x) is (in fact) the result of substituting x for (the free occurrences of) b in A(b). To make this example particular,

$$\text{x}, \quad \text{A(x)}, \quad \text{b}, \quad \text{A(b)}$$

may be respectively,

$$c, \quad \exists c(c'+a=b) \supset \neg a=b+c, \quad d, \quad \exists c(c'+a=b) \supset \neg a=b+d.$$

§ 19. Transformation rules. In this section we shall introduce further metamathematical definitions (called *deductive rules* or *transformation rules*) which give the formal system the structure of a deductive theory. To emphasize the analogy to an informal deductive theory, we shall start with a list of 'postulates'; however, for the metamathematics, these are not postulates in the sense of assumptions, as indeed they cannot be when officially they have no meaning, but only formulas and forms (or schemata) to which we shall refer when we give the definitions.

Before giving the postulate list, let us illustrate the types of postulates which will appear in the list. The simplest is an 'axiom', of which $\neg a'=0$ is an example. This is a formula of the formal system. Then we may have an 'axiom form' or 'axiom schema', of which "$B \supset A \vee B$" is an example. This is a metamathematical expression, which gives a particular axiom each time formulas are specified as represented by the metamathematical letters "A" and "B". For example, when A is $a'=0$ and B is $\neg a'=0$, we obtain the axiom $\neg a'=0 \supset a'=0 \vee \neg a'=0$. The axiom schema is thus a metamathematical device for specifying an infinite class of axioms having a common form.

We must also have another kind of postulates, which formalize the operations of deducing further theorems from the axioms. These are the 'rules of inference', of which the following is an example:

$$\frac{A, \ A \supset B}{B.}$$

This is a schema containing three metamathematical expressions "A", "$A \supset B$" and "B", which represent formulas whenever formulas are specified as represented by the metamathematical letters "A" and "B". The sense of the rule is that the formula represented by the expression written below the line may be 'inferred' from the pair of formulas represented by the two expressions written above the line. For example, by taking as A the formula $\neg a'=0$ and as B the formula $a'=0 \vee \neg a'=0$, the rule allows the inference from $\neg a'=0$ and $\neg a'=0 \supset a'=0 \vee \neg a'=0$ to $a'=0 \vee \neg a'=0$. Since $\neg a'=0$ and $\neg a'=0 \supset a'=0 \vee \neg a'=0$ are axioms (as we just saw), $a'=0 \vee \neg a'=0$ is a further 'formal theorem'. (Our terminology will include the axioms as theorems.)

We shall now display the full postulate list, and then give the definitions establishing the deductive structure of the formal system by referring to the list. The reader may verify that the cumulative effect of the series of definitions will be to define a subclass of the class of formulas called 'provable formulas' or 'formal theorems'.

Postulates for the formal system

Dramatis personae. For Postulates 1—8, A, B and C are formulas. For Postulates 9—13, x is a variable, A(x) is a formula, C is a formula which does not contain x free, and t is a term which is free for x in A(x).

GROUP A. Postulates for the predicate calculus.

GROUP A1. Postulates for the propositional calculus.

1a. $A \supset (B \supset A)$.

1b. $(A \supset B) \supset ((A \supset (B \supset C)) \supset (A \supset C))$.

2. $\dfrac{A, A \supset B}{B.}$

3. $A \supset (B \supset A \& B)$.

4a. $A \& B \supset A$.

4b. $A \& B \supset B$.

5a. $A \supset A \vee B$.

5b. $B \supset A \vee B$.

6. $(A \supset C) \supset ((B \supset C) \supset (A \vee B \supset C))$.

7. $(A \supset B) \supset ((A \supset \neg B) \supset \neg A)$.

8°. $\neg\neg A \supset A$.

GROUP A2. (Additional) Postulates for the predicate calculus.

9. $\dfrac{C \supset A(x)}{C \supset \forall x A(x).}$

10. $\forall x A(x) \supset A(t)$.

11. $A(t) \supset \exists x A(x)$.

12. $\dfrac{A(x) \supset C}{\exists x A(x) \supset C.}$

GROUP B. (Additional) Postulates for number theory.

13. $A(0) \& \forall x(A(x) \supset A(x')) \supset A(x)$.

14. $a'=b' \supset a=b$.

15. $\neg a'=0$.

16. $a=b \supset (a=c \supset b=c)$.

17. $a=b \supset a'=b'$.

18. $a+0=a$.

19. $a+b'=(a+b)'$.

20. $a \cdot 0=0$.

21. $a \cdot b'=a \cdot b+a$.

(The reason for writing "°" on Postulate 8 will be given in § 23.)

One may verify that 14—21 are formulas; and that 1—13 (or in the case of 2, 9 and 12, the expression(s) above, and the expression below, the line) are formulas, for each choice of the A, B, C, or x, A(x), C, t, subject to the stipulations given at the head of the postulate list.

The class of 'axioms' is defined thus. A formula is an *axiom*, if it has one of the forms 1a, 1b, 3—8, 10, 11, 13 or if it is one of the formulas 14—21.

The relation of 'immediate consequence' is defined thus. A formula is an *immediate consequence* of one or two other formulas, if it has the form shown below the line, while the other(s) have the form(s) shown above the line, in 2, 9 or 12.

This is the basic metamathematical definition corresponding to Postulates 2, 9 and 12, but we shall restate it with additional terminology which draws attention to the process of applying the definition. Postulates 2, 9 and 12 we call the *rules of inference*. For any (fixed) choice of the A and B, or the x, A(x) and C, subject to the stipulations, the formula(s) shown above the line is the *premise* (are the *first* and *second premise*, respectively), and the formula shown below the line is the *conclusion*, for the *application* of the rule (or the (*formal*) *inference* by the rule). The conclusion is an *immediate consequence* of the premise(s) (by the rule).

Carnap 1934 brings the two kinds of postulates under the common term 'transformation rules', by considering the axioms as the result of transformation from zero premises.

The definition of a '(formally) provable formula' or '(formal) theorem' can now be given inductively as follows.

1. If D is an axiom, then D is *provable*. 2. If E is *provable*, and D is an immediate consequence of E, then D is *provable*. 3. If E and F are *provable*, and D is an immediate consequence of E and F, then D is *provable*. 4. A formula is *provable* only as required by 1—3.

The notion can also be reached by using the intermediate concept of a '(formal) proof', thus. A (*formal*) *proof* is a finite sequence of one or more (occurrences of) formulas such that each formula of the sequence is either an axiom or an immediate consequence of preceding formulas of the sequence. A proof is said to be a proof *of* its last formula, and this formula is said to be (*formally*) *provable* or to be a (*formal*) *theorem*.

Example 1. The following sequence of 17 formulas is a proof of the formula $a=a$. Formula 1 is Axiom 16. Formula 2 is an axiom, by an application of Axiom Schema 1a in which the A and the B of the schema are both $0=0$; and Formula 3 by an application in which the A is $a=b \supset (a=c \supset b=c)$ and the B is $0=0 \supset (0=0 \supset 0=0)$. Formula 4 is an immediate consequence of Formulas 1 and 3, as first and second premise respectively, by an application of Rule 2 in which the A of the rule is $a=b \supset (a=b \supset b=c)$ and the B is $[0=0 \supset (0=0 \supset 0=0)] \supset [a=b \supset (a=c \supset b=c)]$. Formula 5 is an immediate consequence of Formula 4, by an application of Rule 9 in which the x is c, the A(x) is $a=b \supset (a=c \supset b=c)$, and the C is $0=0 \supset (0=0 \supset 0=0)$ (which, note, does not contain the x free). Formula 9 is an axiom by an application of Axiom Schema 10, in which the x is a, the A(x) is $\forall b \forall c[a=b \supset (a=c \supset b=c)]$, and the t is $a+0$ (which, note, is free for the x in the A(x)). The A(t), by our substitution notation (§ 18), is the result of substituting the t for (the free occurrences of) the x in the A(x), i.e. here the A(t) is $\forall b \forall c[a+0=b \supset (a+0=c \supset b=c)]$.

1. $a=b \supset (a=c \supset b=c)$ — Axiom 16.
2. $0=0 \supset (0=0 \supset 0=0)$ — Axiom Schema 1a.
3. $\{a=b \supset (a=c \supset b=c)\} \supset \{[0=0 \supset (0=0 \supset 0=0)] \supset [a=b \supset (a=c \supset b=c)]\}$ — Axiom Schema 1a.
4. $[0=0 \supset (0=0 \supset 0=0)] \supset [a=b \supset (a=c \supset b=c)]$ — Rule 2, 1, 3.
5. $[0=0 \supset (0=0 \supset 0=0)] \supset \forall c[a=b \supset (a=c \supset b=c)]$ — Rule 9, 4.
6. $[0=0 \supset (0=0 \supset 0=0)] \supset \forall b \forall c[a=b \supset (a=c \supset b=c)]$ — Rule 9, 5.
7. $[0=0 \supset (0=0 \supset 0=0)] \supset \forall a \forall b \forall c[a=b \supset (a=c \supset b=c)]$ — Rule 9, 6.
8. $\forall a \forall b \forall c[a=b \supset (a=c \supset b=c)]$ — Rule 2, 2, 7.
9. $\forall a \forall b \forall c[a=b \supset (a=c \supset b=c)] \supset \forall b \forall c [a+0=b \supset (a+0=c \supset b=c)]$ — Axiom Schema 10.
10. $\forall b \forall c[a+0=b \supset (a+0=c \supset b=c)]$ — Rule 2, 8, 9.
11. $\forall b \forall c[a+0=b \supset (a+0=c \supset b=c)] \supset \forall c[a+0=a \supset (a+0=c \supset a=c)]$ — Axiom Schema 10.
12. $\forall c[a+0=a \supset (a+0=c \supset a=c)]$ — Rule 2, 10, 11.
13. $\forall c[a+0=a \supset (a+0=c \supset a=c)] \supset [a+0=a \supset (a+0=a \supset a=a)]$ — Axiom Schema 10.
14. $a+0=a \supset (a+0=a \supset a=a)$ — Rule 2, 12, 13.
15. $a+0=a$ — Axiom 18.
16. $a+0=a \supset a=a$ — Rule 2, 15, 14.
17. $a=a$ — Rule 2, 15, 16.

EXAMPLE 2. Let A be any formula. Then the following sequence of five formulas is a proof of the formula A ⊃ A. (In other words, what we exhibit below is a 'proof schema', which becomes a particular proof on substituting any particular formula, such as 0=0, for the metamathematical letter "A"; and its last expression "A ⊃ A" is accordingly a 'theorem schema'.) Formula 1 is an axiom, by an application of Axiom Schema 1a in which the A and the B of the schema are the A of this example. Formula 2 is an axiom, by an application of Axiom Schema 1b in which the A and the C of the schema are the A of this example, and the B of the schema is the A ⊃ A of this example. Formula 3 is an immediate consequence of Formulas 1 and 2, as first and second premise, respectively, by an application of Rule 2 in which the A of the rule is the A ⊃ (A ⊃ A) of this example, and the B of the rule is the [A ⊃ ((A ⊃ A) ⊃ A)] ⊃ [A ⊃ A] of this example.

(1)
1. $A \supset (A \supset A)$ — Axiom Schema 1a.
2. $\{A \supset (A \supset A)\} \supset \{[A \supset ((A \supset A) \supset A)] \supset [A \supset A]\}$ — Axiom Schema 1b.
3. $[A \supset ((A \supset A) \supset A)] \supset [A \supset A]$ — Rule 2, 1, 2.
4. $A \supset ((A \supset A) \supset A)$ — Axiom Schema 1a.
5. $A \supset A$ — Rule 2, 4, 3.

The terms proof, theorem, etc. as defined for the formal system (i.e. formal proof, formal theorem, etc.) must be sharply distinguished from these terms in their ordinary informal senses, which we employ in presenting the metamathematics. A formal theorem is a formula (i.e. a certain kind of finite sequence of marks), and its formal proof is a certain kind of finite sequence of formulas. A metamathematical theorem is a meaningful statement about the formal objects, and its proof is an intuitive demonstration of the truth of that statement.

We mentioned three categories of formal objects (§ 16), but we shall be free to introduce others in the study of them, so long as the treatment is finitary. Besides this, a somewhat different extension of our subject matter occurs when we discuss the form of our metamathematical definitions and theorems in turn. If we chose to be meticulous in our way of doing this, it would constitute a metametamathematics. However, the same practice is common in (other branches of) informal mathematics; and we shall regard such discussions as incidental explanations, intended sometimes to make it easier to grasp quickly what is being done in the metamathematics, and sometimes to enable us to condense the statement of metamathematical theorems which could be stated without them.

CHAPTER V

FORMAL DEDUCTION

§ 20. Formal deduction. Formal proofs of even quite elementary theorems tend to be long. As a price for having analyzed logical deduction into simple steps, more of those steps have to be used.

The purpose of formalizing a theory is to get an explicit definition of what constitutes proof in the theory. Having achieved this, there is no need always to appeal directly to the definition. The labor required to establish the formal provability of formulas can be greatly lessened by using metamathematical theorems concerning the existence of formal proofs. If the demonstrations of those theorems do have the finitary character which metamathematics is supposed to have, the demonstrations will indicate, at least implicitly, methods for obtaining the formal proofs. The use of the metamathematical theorems then amounts to abbreviation, often of very great extent, in the presentation of the formal proofs.

The simpler of such metamathematical theorems we shall call *derived rules*, since they express principles which can be said to be derived from the postulated rules by showing that the use of them as additional methods of inference does not increase the class of provable formulas. We shall seek by means of derived rules to bring the methods for establishing the facts of formal provability as close as possible to the informal methods of the theory which is being formalized.

In setting up the formal system, proof was given the simplest possible structure, consisting of a single sequence of formulas. Some of our derived rules, called 'direct rules', will serve to abbreviate for us whole segments of such a sequence; we can then, so to speak, use these segments as prefabricated units in building proofs.

But also, in mathematical practice, proofs are common which have a more complicated structure, employing 'subsidiary deduction', i.e. deduction under assumptions for the sake of the argument, which assumptions are subsequently discharged. For example, subsidiary deduction is used in a proof by reductio ad absurdum, and less obtrusively when we place the hypothesis of a theorem on a par with proved propositions to deduce the conclusion. Other derived rules, called 'subsidiary deduction rules', will give us this kind of procedure.

We now introduce, by a metamathematical definition, the notion of 'formal deducibility under assumptions'. Given a list $D_1, \ldots, D_l$ ($l \geq 0$) of (occurrences of) formulas, a finite sequence of one or more (occurrences of) formulas is called a (*formal*) *deduction from* the *assumption formulas* $D_1, \ldots, D_l$, if each formula of the sequence is either one of the formulas $D_1, \ldots, D_l$, or an axiom, or an immediate consequence of preceding formulas of the sequence. A deduction is said to be a deduction *of* its last formula E; and this formula is said to be *deducible from* the assumption formulas (in symbols, $D_1, \ldots, D_l \vdash E$), and is called the *conclusion* (or *endformula*) of the deduction. (The symbol "$\vdash$" may be read "yields".)

The definitions of deduction and of deducibility are generalizations of those of proof and of provability (which they include as the case for $l = 0$) to permit the use of any formulas $D_1, \ldots, D_l$ we please, called assumption formulas for the deduction, as pro tempore on a par with the axioms.

Example 1. Let A, B and C be formulas. Then the following sequence of five formulas is a deduction of C from the three assumption formulas $A \supset (B \supset C)$, B and A. (We exhibit a 'deduction schema'.)

1. B — second assumption formula.
2. A — third assumption formula.

(2) 3. $A \supset (B \supset C)$ — first assumption formula.

4. $B \supset C$ — Rule 2, 2, 3.
5. C — Rule 2, 1, 4.

Example 2. Let the reader construct: (3) a deduction of A & B from A and B; (4) a deduction of C from $A \& B \supset C$, A, B.

By an *analysis* of a deduction or proof $A_1, \ldots, A_k$, we mean a specification, for each j ($j = 1, \ldots, k$), either that A_j is one of the assumption formulas and which one in the list $D_1, \ldots, D_l$, or that A_j is an axiom and by which axiom schema or particular axiom of the postulate list, or that A_j is an immediate consequence of preceding formulas and by which rule of inference and of which preceding formulas as the respective premises of that rule. In brief, an analysis of a deduction consists of the explanations employed to justify each occurrence of a formula in it (i.e. in our examples, the explanations given at the right of the formulas).

It may occasionally happen that an occurrence of a formula in a deduction (or proof) can be justified in more than one way, e.g. the formulas

A, B and C might be such that one of the five formulas in (2) is an axiom. Consequently, for some of the discussions below, the procedure to be applied to a given deduction is only determined uniquely, when along with the deduction itself there is given a particular analysis of it.

It is to be emphasized that the expression "$D_1, \ldots, D_l \vdash E$", which we use to state briefly that E is deducible from $D_1, \ldots, D_l$, is not a formula of the system, but a brief way of writing a metamathematical statement about the formulas $D_1, \ldots, D_l$, E, namely the statement that there exists a certain kind of a finite sequence of formulas. When $l = 0$, the notation becomes "$\vdash E$", meaning that E is provable. The symbol "$\vdash$" goes back to Frege 1879; the present use of it to Rosser 1935* and Kleene 1934*.

EXAMPLE 3. The following two statements (1′) and (2′) have been justified by exhibiting above the two deductions (1) and (2), respectively; and (3′) and (4′) by Example 2.

(1′) $\vdash A \supset A$. (2′) $A \supset (B \supset C), B, A \vdash C$.
(3′) $A, B \vdash A \& B$. (4′) $A \& B \supset C, A, B \vdash C$.

Notice that the symbol "$\vdash$" appears in context preceded by a finite sequence of zero or more formulas and followed by a single formula (or instead of formulas, metamathematical letters or expressions representing formulas). This makes unambiguous the scope of an occurrence of the symbol "$\vdash$" in a metamathematical sentence. In particular, the scopes of the formal operators are necessarily confined within formulas of the system, while "$\vdash$" is a metamathematical verb lying outside any formula of the system.

The definition of 'deducible from $D_1, \ldots, D_l$' can also be stated without using the intermediate concept of a deduction (cf. the first definition of 'provable' in § 19). We leave it to the reader to state the five clauses required. Briefly, "$D_1, \ldots, D_l \vdash E$" then means that it is possible to get from (zero or more of) the formulas $D_1, \ldots, D_l$ and (zero or more) axioms by the rules of inference to the formula E. The two versions of the definition are brought into agreement by observing that, when the formulas considered in the process of getting from $D_1, \ldots, D_l$ and axioms to E are put down in order of first consideration, we have a deduction of E from $D_1, \ldots, D_l$.

We shall use Greek capital letters, such as "Γ", "Δ", "Θ", etc., to stand for finite sequences of zero or more (occurrences of) formulas, when we wish to indicate sets of assumption formulas without naming the formulas individually (or sometimes "$\Gamma(x)$", "$\Delta(x_1, \ldots, x_n)$", etc., when we wish also to emphasize certain variables which may occur in them).

From the definition of the deducibility relation $\vdash$, there follow several *general properties of* $\vdash$ which can be seen to be true without reference to what particular postulates are in the postulate list for the formal system. (i) $\Gamma \vdash E$ when E is in the list Γ. (ii) If $\Gamma \vdash E$, then $\Delta, \Gamma \vdash E$ for any Δ. In particular, we can regard any provable formula as deducible from any assumption formulas we please. (iii) If $\Gamma \vdash E$, then $\Delta \vdash E$ where Δ comes from Γ by permuting the formulas Γ, or omitting any which are duplicates of others remaining. (iv) If $\Gamma \vdash E$, then $\Delta \vdash E$ where Δ comes from Γ by omitting any of the formulas Γ which are provable or deducible from those remaining. For, given a deduction of E from Γ, we can obtain one from Δ by inserting into the given deduction, in place of each occurrence of an assumption formula which we wish to suppress, a deduction of the same from the remaining assumption formulas. These four general properties can be analyzed into the simpler ones of the following lemma. However (while the inferences we make by general properties of $\vdash$ can actually all be made from (i)—(iv) or (I)—(V)), the reader is encouraged to reason flexibly with $\vdash$ on the basis of its meaning.

LEMMA 5. (I) $E \vdash E$. (II) *If* $\Gamma \vdash E$, *then* $C, \Gamma \vdash E$. (III) *If* $C, C, \Gamma \vdash E$, *then* $C, \Gamma \vdash E$. (IV) *If* $\Delta, D, C, \Gamma \vdash E$, *then* $\Delta, C, D, \Gamma \vdash E$. (V) *If* $\Delta \vdash C$ *and* $C, \Gamma \vdash E$, *then* $\Delta, \Gamma \vdash E$. (After Gentzen 1934-5.)

EXAMPLE 4. If $A \vdash B$ and $A, B, C \vdash D$ and $B, D \vdash E$, then $A, C \vdash E$. The reader may convince himself of this directly from the meaning of $\vdash$ (under both versions of its definition), and also verify that it follows from (i) — (iv) and from (I) — (V).

The definition which we have given for $\vdash$ is relative to a particular formal system as determined by a postulate list. Specifically, it is relative both to the part of the postulate list which determines the axioms, and to the rules of inference. Thus far we have been concerned only with the one formal system, but we shall make use of $\vdash$ in like sense in connection with other formal systems, e.g. subsystems of that one obtained by considering only part of the postulate list to be in force for determining the class of axioms and the relation of immediate consequence. We shall always understand $\vdash$ to be relative to the formal system we are studying at the given time.

Notice that $\Delta, \Gamma \vdash E$ for a given system is equivalent to $\Delta \vdash E$ for the system resulting from the given one by adding the formulas Γ to the set of axioms.

§ 21. The deduction theorem. We shall consider the following theorem first for the propositional calculus, i.e. with only the postulates of Group A1 in force.

THEOREM 1. *For the propositional calculus, if* Γ, A ⊢ B, *then* Γ ⊢ A ⊃ B. (The deduction theorem.)

PROOF. The hypothesis of the theorem says that there is a finite sequence of formulas such that: each formula of the sequence is either (a) one of the formulas Γ, (b) the formula A, (c) an axiom, or (d) an immediate consequence by Rule 2 of two preceding formulas (since Rule 2 is the only rule of inference here); and the last formula of the sequence is the formula B. This sequence we shall call the 'given deduction' of B from Γ, A.

The conclusion of the theorem says that there is a finite sequence of formulas such that: each formula of the sequence is either (a) one of the formulas Γ, (c) an axiom, or (d) an immediate consequence by Rule 2 of two preceding formulas; and the last formula of the sequence is the formula A ⊃ B. This sequence we shall call the 'resulting deduction' of A ⊃ B from Γ.

The theorem will be proved by a course-of-values induction on the length k of the given deduction (§ 7), taking the B of the theorem to be variable, but the Γ, A fixed for the induction.

The induction proposition $P(k)$ or $P(\Gamma, A, k)$ is: *For every formula* B, *if there is given a deduction of* B *from* Γ, A *of length k, then there can be found a deduction of* A ⊃ B *from* Γ.

BASIS (to prove the proposition for $k = 1$, i.e. to prove $P(\Gamma, A, 1)$). Suppose given a formula B and a deduction of B from Γ, A of length 1. We distinguish three cases, according to which of the possibilities (a)—(c) applies to the last (and since $k = 1$, only) formula B of the given deduction. The possibility (d) is excluded here, since B is the only formula.

For each case, we show how to construct the resulting deduction, leaving it to the reader to verify that the sequence of formulas which we submit as such does have the required features.

CASE (a): B is one of the formulas Γ. Then the following sequence of formulas is the resulting deduction.

1. B — one of the formulas Γ.
2. B ⊃ (A ⊃ B) — Axiom Schema 1a.
3. A ⊃ B — Rule 2, 1, 2.

CASE (b): B is A. The resulting deduction is the sequence of formulas (1) which was given in § 19 Example 2 as a proof of A ⊃ A. Since B is A, the formula A ⊃ A is A ⊃ B.

CASE (c): B is an axiom. The resulting deduction is the same as in Case (a), except that now the first step is justified on the ground that B is an axiom.

INDUCTION STEP. Assume (as hypothesis of the induction) that, for every $l \leq k$, $P(\Gamma, \mathrm{A}, l)$; i.e. that for every $l \leq k$ and every B, if there is given a deduction of B from Γ, A of length l, then there can be found a deduction of A ⊃ B from Γ. Now (to prove $P(\Gamma, \mathrm{A}, k+1)$) suppose given a formula B and a deduction of B from Γ, A of length $k+1$. We distinguish four cases, according to which of the possibilities (a) — (d) applies to the last formula B of the given deduction. The treatment of Cases (a) — (c) is the same as under the basis.

CASE (d): B is an immediate consequence by Rule 2 of two preceding formulas. By the statement of Rule 2, we may call these two formulas P and P ⊃ B. (We use the letter P now, instead of A as in the statement of the rule, since A is reserved here to designate the last assumption formula for the given deduction.) If we discard the part of the given deduction below the formula P, the part remaining will be a deduction of P from Γ, A of length $l \leq k$. By the hypothesis of the induction (with P as its B), we can hence find a deduction of A ⊃ P from Γ. Likewise, applying the hypothesis of the induction to the part of the given deduction down to P ⊃ B inclusive, we obtain a deduction of A ⊃ (P ⊃ B) from Γ. We use these two deductions (say they are of lengths p and q, respectively) in constructing the resulting deduction, as follows.

	. . .	deduction of A ⊃ P from Γ, given by the hypothesis of the induction.
p.	A ⊃ P	
	. . .	deduction of A ⊃ (P ⊃ B) from Γ, given by the hypothesis of the induction.
$p+q$.	A ⊃ (P ⊃ B)	

$p+q+1$. (A ⊃ P) ⊃ ((A ⊃ (P ⊃ B)) ⊃ (A ⊃ B)) — Axiom Schema 1b.
$p+q+2$. (A ⊃ (P ⊃ B)) ⊃ (A ⊃ B) — Rule 2, p, $p+q+1$.
$p+q+3$. A ⊃ B — Rule 2, $p+q$, $p+q+2$.

This completes the proof of the theorem by mathematical induction. The theorem includes the case that Γ is empty: *For the propositional calculus, if* A ⊢ B, *then* ⊢ A ⊃ B.

EXAMPLE. We were able to state, as (2′) above, that A ⊃ (B ⊃ C), B, A ⊢ C. By Theorem 1, we can thence infer that A ⊃ (B ⊃ C), B ⊢ A ⊃ C.

To examine this example more closely, let us take the deduction (2), which we exhibited in justification of (2′), as the given deduction of C from A ⊃ (B ⊃ C), B, A. By referring to the proof of Theorem 1, we should be able to find the resulting deduction of A ⊃ C from A ⊃ (B ⊃ C), B. Since the given deduction is of length > 1, and the last formula comes from preceding formulas by an application of Rule 2, the case which applies is Case (d) under the induction step. There we find some details, and instructions to find the rest by applying Theorem 1 to the deductions 1 and 1 — 4 occurring as parts of (2). Continuing in this manner, we eventually obtain the following as the resulting deduction.

1. B — second assumption formula.
2. B ⊃ (A ⊃ B) — Axiom Schema 1a.
3. A ⊃ B — Rule 2, 1, 2.
4. A ⊃ (A ⊃ A) — Axiom Schema 1a.
5. {A ⊃ (A ⊃ A)} ⊃ {[A ⊃ ((A ⊃ A) ⊃ A)] ⊃ [A ⊃ A]} — Axiom Schema 1b.
6. [A ⊃ ((A ⊃ A) ⊃ A)] ⊃ [A ⊃ A] — Rule 2, 4, 5.
7. A ⊃ ((A ⊃ A) ⊃ A) — Axiom Schema 1a.
8. A ⊃ A — Rule 2, 7, 6.

(5) 9. A ⊃ (B ⊃ C) — first assumption formula.

10. {A ⊃ (B ⊃ C)} ⊃ {A ⊃ (A ⊃ (B ⊃ C))} — Axiom Schema 1a.
11. A ⊃ (A ⊃ (B ⊃ C)) — Rule 2, 9, 10.
12. {A ⊃ A} ⊃ {[A ⊃ (A ⊃ (B ⊃ C))] ⊃ [A ⊃ (B ⊃ C)]} — Axiom Schema 1b.
13. [A ⊃ (A ⊃ (B ⊃ C))] ⊃ [A ⊃ (B ⊃ C)] — Rule 2, 8, 12.
14. A ⊃ (B ⊃ C) — Rule 2, 11, 13.
15. (A ⊃ B) ⊃ ((A ⊃ (B ⊃ C)) ⊃ (A ⊃ C)) — Axiom Schema 1b.
16. (A ⊃ (B ⊃ C)) ⊃ (A ⊃ C) — Rule 2, 3, 15.
17. A ⊃ C — Rule 2, 14, 16.

The deduction (5) is not the only deduction of A ⊃ C from A ⊃ (B ⊃ C), B. It happens that there is a shorter one, which we obtain from (5) by omitting Formulas 4—8 and 10—14, and citing 9 (instead of 14) as first premise for the inference by Rule 2 at Step 17.

But (5) is the particular one which results by the method used in proving Theorem 1 when (2) is taken as given deduction. We have carried through the exercise of finding (5) to emphasize the finitary character of the reasoning used in proof of Theorem 1, and in particular to show what is involved in the use of mathematical induction. Henceforth we shall be satisfied to know that the resulting deductions exist and could be found.

The proof of Theorem 1 will serve as a model for metamathematical proofs of certain types. In the future we shall often give such proofs in a more abbreviated way, when the reader could cast the argument into explicit applications of induction. A few proofs will be set up fully explicitly as models.

The above proof of Theorem 1 can be given in a more abbreviated way as follows. To each formula of the given deduction of B from Γ, A, let A ⊃ be prefixed. (In the example, from Formulas 1, 2, 3, 4, 5 of (2), we thus obtain Formulas 3, 8, 11, 14, 17 of (5).) The resulting sequence of formulas (with A ⊃ B as end-formula) is not (in general) a deduction from Γ, but can be made one by inserting additional formulas in the manner indicated in the treatment of the cases. (This simple plan of proof will be modified slightly, when we come to extend the theorem to the predicate calculus in § 22.)

From A ⊃ (B ⊃ C), B ⊢ A ⊃ C we infer by a second application of Theorem 1 that A ⊃ (B ⊃ C) ⊢ B ⊃ (A ⊃ C). A convenient arrangement of these inferences is the following.

1. A ⊃ (B ⊃ C), B, A ⊢ C — (2).
(5′) 2. A ⊃ (B ⊃ C), B ⊢ A ⊃ C — Theorem 1, 1.
3. A ⊃ (B ⊃ C) ⊢ B ⊃ (A ⊃ C) — Theorem 1, 2.

In this presentation, we have a sequence of expressions analogous to, but on a different level from, the sequence of formulas which constitutes a formal proof or deduction. The expressions in this sequence are metamathematical statements about the formal system, while in a formal proof or deduction they are formulas of the system.

Another example of a deduction and of a series of metamathematical statements follows.

1. A & B — second assumption formula.
2. A & B ⊃ A — Axiom Schema 4a.
3. A — Rule 2, 1, 2.
(6) 4. A ⊃ (B ⊃ C) — first assumption formula.
5. B ⊃ C — Rule 2, 3, 4.
6. A & B ⊃ B — Axiom Schema 4b.
7. B — Rule 2, 1, 6.
8. C — Rule 2, 7, 5.

(6′) 1. $A \supset (B \supset C), A \& B \vdash C$ — (6).
2. $A \supset (B \supset C) \vdash A \& B \supset C$ — Theorem 1, 1.

As further examples, the reader may establish:

(7′) $A \& B \supset C \vdash A \supset (B \supset C)$ — cf. (4′) § 20.

(8′) 1. $A \supset B, B \supset C \vdash A \supset C$.
2. $A \supset B \vdash (B \supset C) \supset (A \supset C)$ — Theorem 1, 1.

§ 22. The deduction theorem (concluded). Theorem 1 is a derived rule of the *subsidiary deduction* type (cf. § 20). For an application of the rule, the given deduction of B from Γ, A is the *subsidiary deduction*; and the deduction of $A \supset B$ from Γ obtained from the given deduction by the method indicated in the proof of the theorem we have called the *resulting deduction.* When we are stating the existence of deductions without actually exhibiting them, we may adopt an elliptical phraseology, speaking for example of "the deduction $\Gamma, A \vdash B$", when we mean the deduction which the statement "$\Gamma, A \vdash B$" asserts to exist.

In Theorem 1, the last assumption formula A of the subsidiary deduction $\Gamma, A \vdash B$ is not used in making up the list of assumption formulas for the resulting deduction $\Gamma \vdash A \supset B$; accordingly we say this (occurrence of A as) assumption formula of the subsidiary deduction is *discharged.* (There might also be occurrences of A in the list Γ, which would not be discharged.)

In general, a *subsidiary deduction rule* is a metamathematical theorem which has one or more hypotheses of the form $\Delta_i \vdash E_i$ called the *subsidiary deductions*, and a conclusion of the form $\Delta \vdash E$ called the *resulting deduction.* From each of the subsidiary deductions, one or more assumption formulas may be *discharged.*

Example 1. The rule "*If* $\Gamma, A \vdash C$ *and* $\Gamma, B \vdash C$, *then* $\Gamma, A \vee B \vdash C$", which will be established in the next section, has two subsidiary deductions, $\Gamma, A \vdash C$ and $\Gamma, B \vdash C$, from the first of which the last assumption formula A is discharged, and from the second the B.

A metamathematical theorem of the simple form $\Delta \vdash E$ is a derived rule of the *direct* type. It says that it is possible to proceed from the formulas Δ and the axioms directly to E by applications of the rules of inference.

There is the following important difference between these two kinds of derived rules. A direct rule necessarily remains true when the formal system is enlarged by adding new axioms and rules of inference, since the rule states simply that certain deductions can be constructed, and the new postulates only change the situation by providing additional means of constructing those same deductions. But a subsidiary deduction rule does not necessarily remain true when new postulates are added, since the enlargement of the system tends to create new instances of the subsidiary deductions, and it becomes a question whether resulting deductions exist to correspond to these new subsidiary deductions. Most of the subsidiary deduction rules which we shall state (in particular, all those of the present chapter) have an ambiguous set of assumption formulas Γ before the symbol "$\vdash$" throughout, so that the addition of new axioms can cause no trouble. But the addition of new rules of inference will create new cases to be considered in the proof of the rule.

We shall next treat Theorem 1 under the condition that all the postulates of Group A are in force, either exactly these, or also the ones of Group B (which are only an axiom schema and axioms). A certain restriction will be required in order to handle the new cases in the proof.

It seems easier to give this treatment now, while the proof of Theorem 1 for the propositional calculus is fresh; but some readers may prefer to postpone the remainder of this chapter, excepting the parts of § 23 referring to the propositional calculus, until after Chapter VI.

We begin by stating some definitions which are useful in formulating the restriction. Given a deduction $A_1, \ldots, A_k$ from assumption formulas $D_1, \ldots, D_l$ and a particular analysis of the deduction (§ 20), we define when (an occurrence of) a formula A_i in the deduction 'depends' on a given one D_j of the (occurrences of) assumption formulas $D_1, \ldots, D_l$, as follows.

1. If A_i in the given analysis is D_j, then A_i *depends* on D_j. 2. If A_{i_1} *depends* on D_j, and A_i in the given analysis is an immediate consequence of A_{i_1} (or of A_{i_1} and some A_{i_2}, in either order), then A_i *depends* on D_j. 3. A_i *depends* on D_j only as required by 1 and 2.

It is easily seen that A_i depends on D_j, if and only if there exists no subsequence of the deduction (not necessarily consecutive) which under the given analysis constitutes a deduction of A_i from the remaining assumption formulas $D_1, \ldots, D_{j-1}, D_{j+1}, \ldots, D_l$.

EXAMPLE 2. In the deduction (6), Formulas 4, 5 and 8 depend on the first assumption formula $A \supset (B \supset C)$, and the other formulas do not. Formulas 1, 6, 7 (with the given analysis) constitute a deduction of 7 from the other assumption formula $A \& B$.

We now say that a variable y is *varied in* a given deduction (with a given analysis) *for* a given assumption formula D_j, if (A) y occurs free in D_j, and (B) the deduction contains an application of Rule 9 or Rule 12 with respect to y (as the x for the application of the rule) to a formula depending on D_j (as the premise for the application of the rule). Otherwise, we say that y is *held constant in* the deduction *for* the assumption formula D_j.

EXAMPLE 3. Let x be a variable, A(x) a formula, and b a variable, such that (i) b is free for x in A(x) and (ii) b does not occur free in A(x) (unless b is x); and let C be a formula not containing b free. Then the following is a deduction of $C \supset \forall xA(x)$ from $C \supset A(b)$. In verifying that the stipulations for Postulates 9 and 10 are met, we use the facts (iv) — (vi) which were worked out in Example 9 § 18.

1. $\forall bA(b) \supset A(x)$ — Axiom Schema 10 (noting (iv) and (vi)).
2. $\forall bA(b) \supset \forall xA(x)$ — Rule 9, 1 (noting that, by (v), x does not occur free in $\forall bA(b)$).
3. $C \supset A(b)$ — assumption formula.
4. $C \supset \forall bA(b)$ — Rule 9, 3.
6. $C \supset (\forall bA(b) \supset \forall xA(x))$ — from 2 as in Case (a) for Theorem 1 § 21.
9. $C \supset \forall xA(x)$ — from 4, 6 as in Case (d) for Theorem 1.

If A(x) contains x free, then in this deduction b is varied, since (using (i) and (iii)) the assumption formula $C \supset A(b)$ contains b free, and Rule 9 is applied at Step 4 with respect to b to the premise 3, which depends on the assumption formula. But x is not varied, since the premise 1 for the application of Rule 9 with respect to x at Step 2 does not depend on the assumption formula.

In a given deduction (with a given analysis), a given variable y is always held constant for each assumption formula in which it does not occur free, while it may be varied for some of the assumption formulas in which it occurs free and held constant for others.

The above terminology suggests itself, since Rules 9 and 12 (the "$\forall$-rule" and the "$\exists$-rule") are the only two postulates of Group A in which a free variable participates as such. Axiom Schema 10, for example, can be applied using a free variable as the t, but in that case the variable is used in a way that a term not a variable (such as 0) can equally well be used. (The employment of free variables in stating the postulates of Group B is inessential.)

The restriction on Theorem 1 for the predicate calculus is that in the subsidiary deduction the free variables should be held constant for the assumption formula to be discharged. (This will be explained in terms of the interpretation in § 32.)

THEOREM 1 (concluded). *For the predicate calculus (or the full number-theoretic formal system), if* $\Gamma, A \vdash B$ *with the free variables held constant for the last assumption formula* A, *then* $\Gamma \vdash A \supset B$.

Proof is obtained from that given in § 21 by supplying the treatment of the two additional cases which can now arise under the induction step.

CASE (e): B is an immediate consequence of a preceding formula by an application of Rule 9. By the statement of Rule 9, that preceding formula is of the form $C \supset A(x)$, where x is a variable, A(x) a formula, and C a formula not containing x free. Then B is $C \supset \forall x A(x)$. We distinguish two subcases, according as in the given deduction (for a given analysis) that preceding formula $C \supset A(x)$ depends on the last assumption formula A or not.

SUBCASE (e1): $C \supset A(x)$ depends on A. Then A does not contain x free, since otherwise the hypothesis that the free variables are held constant for A in the given deduction would be contradicted. Since now neither A nor C contains x free, the formula A & C does not contain x free. This fact is used below in justifying the new application of Rule 9 at Step $p+q+1$. Applying the hypothesis of the induction to the segment of the given deduction ending with the formula $C \supset A(x)$, we obtain a deduction of $A \supset (C \supset A(x))$ from Γ. This deduction is incorporated in constructing the resulting deduction, as follows.

	. . .	deduction of $A \supset (C \supset A(x))$ from Γ, given by the hypothesis of the induction.
p.	$A \supset (C \supset A(x))$	deduction of $A \,\&\, C \supset A(x)$ from $A \supset (C \supset A(x))$, given by (6′): 2 (end of § 21).
	. . .	
$p+q$.	$A \,\&\, C \supset A(x)$	
$p+q+1$.	$A \,\&\, C \supset \forall x A(x)$	— Rule 9, $p+q$.
	. . .	deduction of $A \supset (C \supset \forall x A(x))$ from $A \,\&\, C \supset \forall x A(x)$, given by (7′).
$p+q+r+1$.	$A \supset (C \supset \forall x A(x))$	

SUBCASE (e2): $C \supset A(x)$ (and hence $C \supset \forall x A(x)$) does not depend on A. Then some subsequence of the given deduction constitutes a deduction of $C \supset \forall x A(x)$ from the remaining assumption formulas Γ. We use this in constructing the resulting deduction, as follows.

	...	deduction of $C \supset \forall x A(x)$ from Γ, given by the hypothesis of independence.
p.	$C \supset \forall x A(x)$	
$p+1$.	$(C \supset \forall x A(x)) \supset (A \supset (C \supset \forall x A(x)))$ — Axiom Schema 1a.	
$p+2$.	$A \supset (C \supset \forall x A(x))$ — Rule 2, p, $p+1$.	

CASE (f): B is an immediate consequence of a preceding formula by an application of Rule 12. The treatment of this case is similar, using (5′):3 twice in the first subcase.

The deduction theorem was first proved as a derived rule by Herbrand 1930. (Cf. also Herbrand 1928, Tarski 1930, Church 1932, Hilbert-Bernays 1934 p. 155, Jaśkowski 1934.)

§ 23. Introduction and elimination of logical symbols. The following theorem contains a collection of derived rules, with row and column designations attached to provide convenient descriptive names for the rules. For example, "$\forall x A(x) \vdash A(t)$" is the rule of "generality elimination" or briefly "$\forall$-elimination".

The variable "x" written as superscript on the symbol "$\vdash$" in two of the rules is to mark the application of Rule 9 or 12 with respect to x in constructing the resulting deduction.

THEOREM 2. *For the following rules*, A, B *and* C, *or* x, A(x), C *and* t, *are subject to the same stipulations as for the corresponding postulates* (§ 19), *and* Γ *or* $\Gamma(x)$ *is any list of formulas.*

For the propositional calculus, the rules hold from "Implication" *to* "Negation", *inclusive.*

For the predicate calculus (or the full number-theoretic system), all the rules hold, provided that in each subsidiary deduction the free variables are held constant for the assumption formula to be discharged.

	(Introduction)	(Elimination)
(Implication)	*If* $\Gamma, A \vdash B$, *then* $\Gamma \vdash A \supset B$.	$A, A \supset B \vdash B$. (Modus ponens.)
(Conjunction)	$A, B \vdash A \& B$.	$A \& B \vdash A$. $A \& B \vdash B$.
(Disjunction)	$A \vdash A \vee B$. $B \vdash A \vee B$.	*If* $\Gamma, A \vdash C$ *and* $\Gamma, B \vdash C$, *then* $\Gamma, A \vee B \vdash C$. (Proof by cases.)

(Negation)	*If* Γ, A $\vdash$ B *and* Γ, A $\vdash \neg$B, *then* $\Gamma \vdash \neg$A. (Reductio ad absurdum.)	$\neg\neg$A $\vdash$ A. (Discharge of double negation.)°
(Generality)	A(x) $\vdash^x$ $\forall$xA(x).	$\forall$xA(x) $\vdash$ A(t).
(Existence)	A(t) $\vdash$ $\exists$xA(x).	*If* Γ(x), A(x) $\vdash$ C, *then* Γ(x), $\exists$xA(x) $\vdash^x$ C.

Proofs. The rule of $\supset$-introduction is Theorem 1. There remain ten direct and three other subsidiary deduction rules. The direct rules may be established by exhibiting the required deductions. The proofs of the subsidiary deduction rules are conveniently presented as sequences of metamathematical statements (certain of which statements are to be substantiated by exhibiting a deduction as in the proof of a direct rule, and others of which follow from preceding of the statements by Theorem 1 or by general properties of $\vdash$). In both cases appeal is made at some point to a corresponding one of the postulates. These proofs are given below for several of the rules of each type, the others being left to the reader. However here and in similar situations, the reader is urged first to attempt himself even those which we give.

Direct rules. $\supset$-elimination.

1. A — first assumption formula.
2. A $\supset$ B — second assumption formula.
3. B — Rule 2, 1, 2.

This rule is simply Rule 2 of the postulate list (the "$\supset$-rule", or "modus ponens" of traditional logic) restated as a derived rule.

&-introduction. We already have this as (3') § 20.

$\neg$-elimination, or discharge of double negation.

1. $\neg\neg$A — assumption formula.
2. $\neg\neg$A $\supset$ A — Axiom Schema 8.
3. A — Rule 2, 1, 2.

$\forall$-introduction. Let C be some axiom not containing x free.

1. A(x) — assumption formula.
2. A(x) $\supset$ (C $\supset$ A(x)) — Axiom Schema 1a.
3. C $\supset$ A(x) — Rule 2, 1, 2.
4. C $\supset$ $\forall$xA(x) — Rule 9, 3.
5. C — an axiom.
6. $\forall$xA(x) — Rule 2, 5, 4.

SUBSIDIARY DEDUCTION RULES. $\vee$-elimination.

1. $\Gamma, A \vdash C$ — hypothesis.
2. $\Gamma \vdash A \supset C$ — Theorem 1, 1.
3. $\Gamma, B \vdash C$ — hypothesis.
4. $\Gamma \vdash B \supset C$ — Theorem 1, 3.
5. $A \supset C, B \supset C \vdash A \vee B \supset C$ — using Axiom Schema 6 and Rule 2.
6. $A \vee B, A \vee B \supset C \vdash C$ — $\supset$-elimination (or using Rule 2).
7. $\Gamma, A \vee B \vdash C$ — 2, 4, 5, 6.

$\exists$-elimination.

1. $\Gamma(x), A(x) \vdash C$ — hypothesis.
2. $\Gamma(x) \vdash A(x) \supset C$ — Theorem 1, 1.
3. $A(x) \supset C \vdash^{x} \exists x A(x) \supset C$ — using Rule 12.
4. $\exists x A(x), \exists x A(x) \supset C \vdash C$ — $\supset$-elimination.
5. $\Gamma(x), \exists x A(x) \vdash^{x} C$ — 2, 3, 4.

DISCUSSION. These rules give a classification ot logical operations as introductions and eliminations of the logical symbols, adapted from Gentzen 1934-5.

The rule called "$\vee$-elimination" does serve to eliminate a disjunction symbol, when it is used as follows.

1. $\vdash A \vee B$ — suppose given.
2. $A \vdash C$ — suppose given, with the free variables held constant for A.
3. $B \vdash C$ — suppose given, with the free variables held constant for B.
4. $A \vee B \vdash C$ — $\vee$-elimination (with Γ empty), 2, 3.
5. $\vdash C$ — 1, 4.

This process corresponds to the familiar informal method of proof by cases: Either A or B. Case 1: A. Then C. Case 2: B. Then C. Hence C.

Similarly, $\exists$-elimination, used as follows, eliminates an existence symbol.

1. $\vdash \exists x A(x)$ — suppose given.
2. $A(x) \vdash C$ — suppose given, where C does not contain x as a free variable, and with the free variables held constant for A(x).
3. $\exists x A(x) \vdash C$ — $\exists$-elimination, 2.
4. $\vdash C$ — 1, 3.

This corresponds to the familiar argument: There exists an x such that A(x); consider such an x. Then C, which does not depend on x. Hence C.

Similarly, $\neg$-introduction corresponds to the method of reductio ad absurdum.

Using the Γ provided for in the theorem, any of these procedures can be carried out in the presence of any list of additional assumption formulas.

The following shows that $A, \neg A \vdash B$ (in words: from a contradiction A and $\neg$A, any formula B is deducible). This we shall cite as the rule of *weak $\neg$-elimination.*

1. $A, \neg A, \neg B \vdash A$.
2. $A, \neg A, \neg B \vdash \neg A$.
3. $A, \neg A \vdash \neg\neg B$ — $\neg$-introduction, 1, 2.
4. $\neg\neg B \vdash B$ — $\neg$-elimination.

(9′) 5. $A, \neg A \vdash B$ — 3, 4, as was to be proved.

Step 3 amounts to blaming the formula $\neg$B for the contradiction A and $\neg$A of 1 and 2. Continuing, we have:

6. $\neg A \vdash A \supset B$ — $\supset$-introduction, 5.
7. $\vdash \neg A \supset (A \supset B)$ — $\supset$-introduction, 6.

Our formal system was intended as a formalization of number theory, including methods only accepted under the classical viewpoint (cf. § 13). However, if Axiom Schema 8 ($\neg\neg A \supset A$) is replaced by the following (cf. (9′): 7), all the postulates express principles also accepted by the intuitionists (cf. end § 30):

$$8^{\mathrm{I}}. \quad \neg A \supset (A \supset B).$$

In terms of the derived rules of Theorem 2, this means replacing $\neg$-elimination by weak $\neg$-elimination. When we wish to consider this system also, we call the original system with Postulate 8 the *classical system,* and the system with Postulate 8^{I} instead the (*corresponding*) *intuitionistic system.* Our results are marked with the symbol "°" in every case when the demonstration we give is not valid for both systems, but only for the classical (and no demonstration which the reader is expected to discover for himself is available for the intuitionistic system).

Use of $\forall$-introduction followed by $\forall$-elimination gives us the following rule.

SUBSTITUTION FOR AN INDIVIDUAL VARIABLE. *If* x *is a variable,* A(x) *is a formula, and* t *is a term which is free for* x *in* A(x): $A(x) \vdash^{x} A(t)$.

We shall abbreviate the presentation of applications of our derived rules, using tacitly general properties of $\vdash$.

EXAMPLE 1. Consider the following argument.

1. A, B $\vdash$ C — suppose this given.
2. A & B $\vdash$ A — &-elimination.
3. A & B $\vdash$ B — &-elimination.
4. A & B $\vdash$ C — 1, 2, 3.

We condense this as follows.

1. A, B $\vdash$ C — suppose this given.
2. A & B $\vdash$ C — &-elim., 1.

Given "$\Gamma \vdash P$, $P \vdash Q$" (which means: $\Gamma \vdash P$ and $P \vdash Q$), we condense to "$\Gamma \vdash P \vdash Q$"; and similarly with longer chains of deductions, each of which after the first has as its only assumption formula the conclusion of the preceding. (But "$\Gamma \vdash P, \vdash Q$" means: $\Gamma \vdash P$ and $\vdash Q$.)

EXAMPLE 2.

1. $A \supset B$, A $\vdash$ B — $\supset$-elimination.
2. B $\vdash$ $B \vee C$ — $\vee$-introduction.
3. $A \supset B$, A $\vdash$ $B \vee C$ — 1, 2.

We condense this to:

1. $A \supset B$, A $\vdash$ B $\vdash$ $B \vee C$ — $\supset$-elim., $\vee$-introd.

***§ 24. Dependence and variation.** For the predicate calculus, in order to use a deduction obtained (i.e. proved to exist) by one of the derived rules of Theorem 2 as a subsidiary deduction for a new application of one of the rules, we shall need (so far as our information goes) to know not only that the deduction exists, but also that the free variables are held constant for the assumption formula to be discharged.

In order to have such information on hand when it is needed, we shall make it a practice in applying the rules to keep track of all cases when a variable may be varied in the resulting deduction. It is convenient to do this by writing any variables which may be varied as superscripts on the symbol "$\vdash$". This notation is not fully explicit, as it does not show for which of the assumption formulas a given superscript variable may be varied. We may then simply associate the superscript with the assumption formulas in which the variable occurs free. (When there is occasion to be more explicit, the facts may be stated verbally, e.g. as in Lemma 8a below.)

We recall that, under the definition of variation (§ 22), a variable y can be varied only for an assumption formula D_j in which it occurs free.

It is easily seen that, given any deduction $D_1, \ldots, D_l \vdash E$, assumption formula D_j, and variable y that occurs free in D_j, one can find another deduction of E from $D_1, \ldots, D_l$ in which y is varied for D_j. (HINT: introduce into the deduction some superfluous steps.) Therefore our interest will always be in whether there is some deduction $D_1, \ldots, D_l \vdash E$ in which y is not varied for D_j; and our statements to the effect that a variable y is varied only for such and such assumption formulas will mean that there is some deduction (with the given assumption formulas and conclusion) in which this is the case.

Similarly, given any deduction $D_1, \ldots, D_l \vdash E$, it is always possible to find another deduction of E from $D_1, \ldots D_l$ in which the conclusion E depends on D_j.

The procedure for keeping track of variation is entirely straightforward (likewise for dependence). Thus far our only derived rules which call for introducing a superscript are ∀-introduction, ∃-elimination and substitution. (Even then the superscript is not always necessary, e.g. when the A(x) for an ∀-introduction or substitution does not contain x free. Also cf. Lemma 7b below.) Moreover, once superscripts have been introduced, we must carry them forward in the obvious way from given deductions to resulting deduction (unless some reason to the contrary can be given), both in applying the subsidiary deduction rules of this section, and in combining deductions by general properties of $\vdash$ (§ 20).

The situations which arise in practice are simple enough so that we have little trouble in seeing what is happening. Variables which are being varied have usually just previously been introduced in that role for some immediate purpose, so that they are not likely to be overlooked. However, to make the theory of our derived rules complete, the facts are stated in more detail in the following lemmas.

LEMMA 6. *In Theorem* 1, $A \supset B$ *depends on a given one of the formulas* Γ *in the resulting deduction* $\Gamma \vdash A \supset B$, *only if* B *depends on the same one in the given deduction* $\Gamma, A \vdash B$. *Similarly, in the other subsidiary deduction rules of Theorem* 2, *the conclusion depends on a given one of the* Γ*'s in the resulting deduction, only if the conclusion depends on the same one in the given deduction* (*or in one at least of the two given deductions*).

For otherwise that assumption formula could be omitted from the Γ's in applying the rule, and afterwards introduced by (II) (and (IV)) of Lemma 5.

In ∨-elimination, if the C does not depend both on the A in $\Gamma, A \vdash C$ and on the B in $\Gamma, B \vdash C$, the ∨-elimination can be avoided altogether. Similarly in ∃-elimination, if the C does not depend on the A(x).

LEMMA 7a. *In Theorem* 1, *a variable is varied for a given one of the* Γ*'s in the resulting deduction* $\Gamma \vdash A \supset B$, *only if it is varied for the same one in the given deduction* $\Gamma, A \vdash B$. *Similarly in the other subsidiary deduction rules of Theorem* 2, *except that for the variable* x *of* $\exists$*-elimination the situation is as stated in Lemma* 7b.

LEMMA 7b. *In* $\exists$*-elimination, the* x *is varied in the resulting deduction* $\Gamma(x), \exists x A(x) \vdash^{x} C$ *only for those of the* $\Gamma(x)$*'s which contain the* x *free and on which the* C *depends in the given deduction* $\Gamma(x), A(x) \vdash C$. (*In* $\exists$*-elimination, no variable is varied for the* $\exists x A(x)$; *and likewise in* $\vee$*-elimination for the* $A \vee B$.)

These two lemmas may be verified by examining the proofs of Theorems 1 and 2. For $\exists$-elimination, if the x is varied in the given deduction for any one of the $\Gamma(x)$'s on which the C does not depend, that one of the $\Gamma(x)$'s may be omitted for the $\exists$-elimination.

The discussions of dependence and variation under steps performed by general properties of $\vdash$ (using the list of such properties provided in Lemma 5) are left to the reader, excepting that of variation for the Δ's of (V). Before treating this (in Lemma 9), we prove the following basic lemmas.

LEMMA 8a. *If*

$$\text{(I)} \qquad D_1, D_2, \ldots, D_l \vdash E,$$

where, for $j = 1, \ldots, l$, *only the distinct variables* $y_{j1}, \ldots, y_{jp_j}$ *are varied for* D_j (*but* $y_{j1}, \ldots, y_{jp_j}$ *need not be distinct from the variables* $y_{k1}, \ldots, y_{kp_k}$ *for* $j \neq k$), *then*

$$\text{(II)} \quad \vdash \forall y_{11} \ldots \forall y_{1p_1} D_1 \supset (\forall y_{21} \ldots \forall y_{2p_2} D_2 \supset \ldots (\forall y_{l1} \ldots \forall y_{lp_l} D_l \supset E) \ldots);$$

and conversely.

For (II) follows from (I) by $\forall$-eliminations and $\supset$-introductions. Conversely, (I) follows from (II) by $\forall$-introductions and $\supset$-eliminations.

LEMMA 8b. *Given a deduction of* E *from* $D_1, \ldots, D_l$, *another deduction* of E *from* $D_1, \ldots, D_l$ *can be found in which, for* $j = 1, \ldots, l$, *Rule* 9 *is applied, to premises dependent on* D_j, *only with respect to variables which are varied for* D_j *in the given deduction, and Rule* 12 *is applied to no premise dependent on an assumption formula.*

We take the given deduction as (I) for Lemma 8a, pass to (II), and thence conversely back to another deduction (I). In this the applications of Rules 9 and 12 which come from the proof (II) are to premises dependent on no assumption formulas. Those which come from the $\forall$-introductions used to obtain (I) from (II) are exactly as described in the present lemma.

LEMMA 9. *In* (V) *of Lemma* 5, *a variable* y *is varied for a given one of the* Δ*'s in the resulting deduction* Δ, Γ ⊢ E, *only* (a) *if* y *is varied for the same one of the* Δ's *in the first given deduction* Δ ⊢ C, *or* (b) *if* y *is varied for* C *in the second given deduction* C, Γ ⊢ E, *and* C *depends on that one of the* Δ*'s in the first given deduction* Δ ⊢ C, *and that one of the* Δ*'s contains* y *free.*

Lemma 9 would be immediate, except for the following contingency. In the second given deduction C, Γ ⊢ E there might be an application of Rule 9 or 12 with respect to y to a premise dependent on C, and yet y be held constant for C because C does not contain y free. If this deduction were combined with a deduction Δ ⊢ C in which C depends on one of the Δ's containing y free, then y would be varied for that one of the Δ's in the resulting deduction Δ, Γ ⊢ E. But we can use Lemma 8b to replace the given deduction C, Γ ⊢ E by another, after which the contingency described cannot arise for any variable y.

Hereafter, for new derived rules the facts respecting dependence and variation will be as one would expect, with any exceptions noted, and all cases when variation may be introduced indicated by superscripts on "⊢". In general, in a subsidiary deduction rule having assumption formulas for given and resulting deductions in obvious correspondence: The conclusion depends on (A given variable is varied for) a given one of the assumption formulas of the resulting deduction, only if it does on (is for) the corresponding assumption formula of the given deduction or of either given deduction. Examples are Theorems 3 and 4 § 25 (for dependence), 15 and 16 § 34, the formal induction rule § 38, 41 (b) and (c) § 73, 42 (III)—(V) and 43 (VIIa)—(VIIIb) § 74, 59 and 60 (b2)—(d) § 81.

STRONG $\forall$-INTRODUCTION AND $\exists$-ELIMINATION. Occasionally it is useful to employ $\forall$-introduction and $\exists$-elimination in a slightly strengthened version, which permits a change in the variable.

LEMMA 10. *Let* x *be a variable,* A(x) *a formula, and* b *a variable, such that* (i) b *is free for* x *in* A(x) *and* (ii) b *does not occur free in* A(x) (*unless* b *is* x). *Furthermore, for the* $\exists$*-elimination rule, let* C *be a formula not containing* b *free, and let the free variables be held constant for* A(b) *in the subsidiary deduction. Then*:

$A(b) \vdash^{b} \forall x A(x).$ (Strong $\forall$-introduction.)

If $\Gamma(b), A(b) \vdash C$, *then* $\Gamma(b), \exists x A(x) \vdash^{b} C.$ (Strong $\exists$-elimination.)

PROOFS. In Example 3 § 22 we derived the rule $C \supset A(b) \vdash^{b} C \supset \forall x A(x)$.

Using this instead of the postulated rule 9 in our former proof for $\forall$-introduction (§ 23), we obtain the strong version.

DERIVED RULES AND RESPECTIVE POSTULATES. We call Postulates 1a, 1b and 2 the *postulates for* $\supset$, Postulates 3, 4a and 4b the *&-postulates*, Postulates 7 and 8 (or for the intuitionistic system 7 and 8^{I}) the $\neg$-*postulates*, etc. Postulates for $\supset$ are used in establishing all the derived rules of Theorem 2.

LEMMA 11. *For each selection of one or more of the logical symbols* $\supset$, &, $\vee$, $\neg$, $\forall$ *and* $\exists$: *The rules of Theorem 2 for* $\supset$ *and those symbols (including for* $\forall$ *and* $\exists$ *the strong versions, and for* $\neg$ *in the intuitionistic system the weak* $\neg$*-elimination rule in place of the other) hold good in the formal system which has as postulates only the* $\supset$*-postulates and the postulates for the symbols in question, provided that in case the symbols include* $\forall$ *but not & the* $\forall$*-postulates include an additional axiom schema as follows, where* x, A(x) *and* C *are subject to the same stipulations as for Rule* 9:

$$9a. \quad \forall x(C \supset A(x)) \supset (C \supset \forall x A(x)).$$

PROOF. This may be verified by a perusal of the above proofs of the rules, with an exception in the case the symbols include $\forall$ but not &, since the treatment of Case (e) Subcase (e1) of Theorem 1 (§ 22) entails use of the &-postulates. With the additional $\forall$-schema, however, that can be replaced by the following.

p.	$A \supset (C \supset A(x))$	— as before.
$p+1$.	$A \supset \forall x(C \supset A(x))$	— Rule 9, p.
$p+2$.	$\forall x(C \supset A(x)) \supset (C \supset \forall x A(x))$	— Axiom Schema 9a.
	...	deduction from $p+1$ and $p+2$ given by (8′):1 (end § 21).
$p+q+2$.	$A \supset (C \supset \forall x A(x))$.	

DEDUCTIONS IN TREE FORM. We have been taking a deduction to be a linear sequence of (occurrences of) formulas. Sometimes it is useful instead to consider the (occurrences of) formulas in a partial ordering which represents the logical structure directly. In this ordering, the premises for each inference are written immediately over the conclusion, as in the statement of the rules of inference; and no (occurrence of a) formula serves as premise for more than one inference. A deduction (or proof) in the former arrangement we say is in *sequence form*; in this, in *tree form*.

The method of converting a deduction of E from Γ given in sequence form, with a given analysis, into one in tree form (called "resolution into proof threads" by Hilbert and Bernays 1934 p. 221), and inversely, will be clear from an example.

EXAMPLE 1. Consider the deduction (6) of § 21. By the analysis, the bottom formula 8 is an immediate consequence of 7 and 5. Let us write 7 and 5 immediately above 8. Then 7 is an immediate consequence of 1 and 6; so we write 1 and 6 just over 7; etc. Looking just at the numbers 1—8, we obtain the following figure.

(a)

$$\dfrac{\dfrac{1 \qquad 6}{7} \qquad \dfrac{\dfrac{1 \quad 2}{3} \qquad 4}{5}}{8}$$

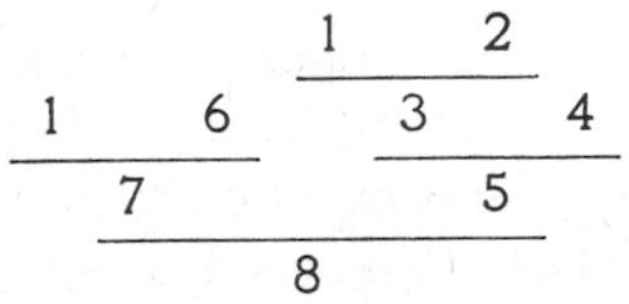

Writing in the formulas themselves (with new numbers 1′ — 9′ and the analysis), we have the deduction in tree form.

(b)

$$\dfrac{\dfrac{\begin{matrix}\text{second}\\ \text{assumption}\\ \text{formula}\\ 1'.\ A \& B\end{matrix} \qquad \begin{matrix}\text{Axiom}\\ \text{Schema 4b}\\ 2'.\ A \& B \supset B\end{matrix}}{3'.\ B}\,2 \qquad \dfrac{\dfrac{\begin{matrix}\text{second}\\ \text{assumption}\\ \text{formula}\\ 4'.\ A \& B\end{matrix} \qquad \begin{matrix}\text{Axiom}\\ \text{Schema 4a}\\ 5'.\ A \& B \supset A\end{matrix}}{6'.\ A}\,2 \qquad \begin{matrix}\text{first}\\ \text{assumption}\\ \text{formula}\\ 7'.\ A \supset (B \supset C)\end{matrix}}{8'.\ B \supset C}\,2}{9'.\ C}\,2$$

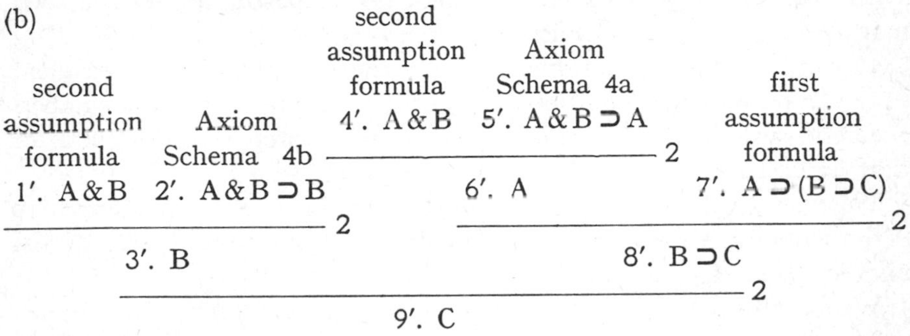

Inversely, from this deduction in tree form of C from A ⊃ (B ⊃ C) and A & B, by arranging the (occurrences of) formulas as a linear sequence say in the order of the numbers 1′—9′, we obtain one in sequence form (not the original one).

Briefly described, a *branch* of a deduction in tree form consists of the (occurrences of) formulas in linear sequence, passing downward within the tree structure, beginning with a formula occurring as an axiom or assumption formula, and terminating in the conclusion (or endformula) of the deduction. The *height* of a deduction in tree form is the length of a longest branch (or in other words, the number of levels). An (occurrence of) a formula is said to be *above* another (or the latter to be *below* the former), if the former is above the latter in the same branch.

EXAMPLE 1 (concluded). The deduction (b) has 5 branches, namely: 1′, 3′, 9′; 2′, 3′, 9′; 4′, 6′, 8′, 9′; 5′, 6′, 8′, 9′; 7′, 8′, 9′. The height is 4. The (occurrence of a) formula 4′ is above 8′ but not above 3′.

CHAPTER VI

THE PROPOSITIONAL CALCULUS

§ 25. Proposition letter formulas. In this chapter we single out for intensive study that part of the formal system which is obtained by using only the postulates of Group A1. The meanings of 'provable', 'deducible' and '$\vdash$' are to be understood accordingly.

Under the definition of 'formula' which was given for the full system in § 17 our formulas are all built up in terms of the number-theoretic symbolism. But so long as we are using only the postulates of Group A1, many details of this symbolism are irrelevant.

It is undesirable that we should restrict the generality of our treatment of the propositional calculus because we intend applying it in the number-theoretic system. On the other hand, we must prepare the ground for that application.

We now give, for use in the propositional calculus, an alternative definition of 'formula', which eliminates the irrelevant details of the number-theoretic definition.

We start by introducing formal symbols of a new kind,

$$\mathcal{A},\ \mathcal{B},\ \mathcal{C},\ \ldots,$$

called *proposition letters*, of which we suppose a (potentially) infinite list to be available. The new definition of 'formula' follows.

1. A proposition letter is a *formula*. 2—5. If A and B are *formulas*, then (A) $\supset$ (B), (A) & (B), (A) $\vee$ (B) and $\neg$(A) are *formulas*. 6. The only *formulas* are those given by 1 — 5.

Comparing this with the definition in § 17, Clause 1 of that definition is replaced by the new Clause 1, and Clauses 6 — 7 are suppressed. When we wish to distinguish between the two notions of formula, we shall call that of § 17 *number-theoretic formula*, and the present one *proposition letter formula*.

EXAMPLE 1. $\mathcal{A} \vee (\neg\mathcal{A} \,\&\, \mathcal{B})$ is a proposition letter formula (parentheses being omitted in continuation of practices established in § 17).

We henceforth agree, for this chapter, that when we say "formula" without specifying a particular sense, the word may be read either in the sense of proposition letter formula, or in the sense of predicate letter formula to be defined in the next chapter, or in the number-theoretic sense. (It might be read in still other suitable senses. But for definiteness we restrict it here to these three, leaving the question whether another sense is suitable to be considered when one has another sense in mind.)

Results stated in this chapter using simply "formula" will thus apply, at no extra expense, to any one of three formal systems, having in common Group A1 as postulate list, but differing in the sense of formula. These three systems we may distinguish respectively as the *pure propositional calculus*, the *predicate letter propositional calculus* and the *number-theoretic propositional calculus*.

Some of our results, however, will be stated using "proposition letter formula". These will also apply generally. The only difference in the case of these is that it is easier to explain them in terms of proposition letters, leaving it to the reader to translate them to other senses of formula, when he needs to, by means of two general rules for translation which we shall next provide (Theorems 3 and 4).

Let $P_1, \ldots, P_m$ be a list of distinct proposition letters. (Here "P_1", ..., "P_m" are metamathematical letters, used as names for proposition letters when we do not wish to limit our discussion by using particular proposition letters.)

A proposition letter formula A is said to be a proposition letter formula *in* $P_1, \ldots, P_m$, if no proposition letters other than $P_1, \ldots, P_m$ occur in A.

Example 2. $\mathcal{A} \vee (\neg \mathcal{A} \,\&\, \mathcal{B})$ is a proposition letter formula in $\mathcal{A}, \mathcal{B}, \mathcal{C}$.

Substitution for a proposition letter (or simultaneously for several distinct proposition letters) is defined as for a variable in § 18, except that it applies to all occurrences without exception (there being here no 'bound occurrences'). Also, later in the section, we use an operation called *replacement in all occurrences* of a formula (or simultaneously of several distinct formulas), defined similarly (the x in the definition of § 18 becoming a formula); this operation is unambiguous because the occurrences will be non-overlapping.

Theorem 3. Substitution for proposition letters. *Let* Γ *be proposition letter formulas, and* E *a proposition letter formula, in the distinct proposition letters* $P_1, \ldots, P_m$. *Let* $A_1, \ldots, A_m$ *be formulas. Let* Γ^* *and* E^* *result from* Γ *and* E, *respectively, by substituting simultaneously* $A_1, \ldots, A_m$ *for* $P_1, \ldots, P_m$, *respectively. If* $\Gamma \vdash E$, *then* $\Gamma^* \vdash E^*$. (For the case that Γ is empty: *If* $\vdash E$, *then* $\vdash E^*$.)

PROOF. For the postulates of Group A1, nothing is required of the A, B, C which appear in those postulates except that they be formulas fixed throughout a given application of a postulate. Now consider the given deduction of E from Γ in the pure propositional calculus. The formulas Γ and the formula E are proposition letter formulas in the distinct proposition letters $P_1, \dots, P_m$, and besides these some more P_{m+1}, $\dots, P_{m+r}$ may occur in other formulas of the deduction. Let $A_{m+1}, \dots,$ A_{m+r} be any formulas. For each of the proposition letters $P_1, \dots, P_{m+r}$, let the respective formulas $A_1, \dots, A_{m+r}$ be substituted throughout every formula of the given deduction. For each application of a postulate in the given deduction, the A, B, C of the application will be transformed by the substitution into expressions A*, B*, C* (every occurrence of A becoming an occurrence of A*, etc.). These expressions A*, B*, C* will be formulas, since to each application of one of Clauses 2 — 5 of the definition of proposition letter formula used in building up A, B, C from the proposition letters $P_1, \dots, P_{m+r}$ there will correspond an application of the same-numbered clause of the definition of formula used in building up A*, B*, C* from the formulas $A_1, \dots, A_{m+r}$. Hence we shall have again an application of the same postulate. Thus the sequence of formulas into which the given deduction is transformed is again a deduction with the same analysis. It is a deduction of E* from Γ*.

EXAMPLE 3. To illustrate the proof of the rule, consider the following deduction of $\mathcal{A} \supset \mathcal{B}$ from $\mathcal{B}$.

1. $\mathcal{B}$ — assumption formula.
(a) 2. $\mathcal{B} \supset (\mathcal{A} \supset \mathcal{B})$ — Axiom Schema 1a.
3. $\mathcal{A} \supset \mathcal{B}$ — Rule 2, 1, 2.

On substituting $\mathcal{B}, \neg\mathcal{A} \,\&\, \mathcal{C}$ (or $\exists c(a=c'), \neg a=0$) for $\mathcal{A}, \mathcal{B}$, we obtain the following deduction (b) (or (c)) with the same analysis as (a).

1. $\neg\mathcal{A} \,\&\, \mathcal{C}$ — assumption formula.
(b) 2. $\neg\mathcal{A} \,\&\, \mathcal{C} \supset (\mathcal{B} \supset \neg\mathcal{A} \,\&\, \mathcal{C})$ — Axiom Schema 1a.
3. $\mathcal{B} \supset \neg\mathcal{A} \,\&\, \mathcal{C}$ — Rule 2, 1, 2.

1. $\neg a=0$ — assumption formula.
(c) 2. $\neg a=0 \supset (\exists c(a=c') \supset \neg a=0)$ — Axiom Schema 1a.
3. $\exists c(a=c') \supset \neg a=0$ — Rule 2, 1, 2.

To illustrate the application of the rule with the same two examples, we know (by reference to (a)) that

(a′) $$\mathcal{B} \vdash \mathcal{A} \supset \mathcal{B}.$$

The rule allows us to infer, by the substitutions described,

(b′) $\neg\mathcal{A} \,\&\, \mathcal{C} \vdash \mathcal{B} \supset \neg\mathcal{A} \,\&\, \mathcal{C}$,

(c′) $\neg a{=}0 \vdash \exists c(a{=}c') \supset \neg a{=}0$.

In one case ((a′) to (b′)), we are using the rule within the pure propositional calculus, for which it is a derived rule of the subsidiary deduction type. In the other case, by substituting formulas in another sense, we have used the rule to infer (c′) in the number-theoretic propositional calculus from (a′) in the pure calculus.

Evidently (a′), (b′), (c′), etc. can all be included in the statement: If A and B are formulas, then

(10′) $\mathrm{B} \vdash \mathrm{A} \supset \mathrm{B}$.

The sense of the rule appears as simply that, having established a deducibility relationship in terms of particular proposition letters $\mathcal{A}$, $\mathcal{B}$, $\mathcal{C}$, . . . , we can assert the same relationship in the form of a schema with metamathematical letters "A", "B", "C",. . . representing any formulas.

Combining this remark with our earlier observation that a rule of the direct form $\Gamma \vdash \mathrm{E}$ always remains valid in the presence of additional postulates (§ 22), we see that all results of the form $\Gamma \vdash \mathrm{E}$ obtained in this chapter (whether or not stated in terms of proposition letters) will hold good for later chapters where we take into account more of the structure of the formulas and a larger part of the postulate list of the original formal system.

Remark 1. Within the pure propositional calculus, substitution can be performed for a single variable P_j at a time, by using the rule with $\mathrm{P}_1,\ldots, \mathrm{P}_{j-1}, \mathrm{P}_{j+1}, \ldots, \mathrm{P}_m$ as the $\mathrm{A}_1,\ldots, \mathrm{A}_{j-1}, \mathrm{A}_{j+1},\ldots, \mathrm{A}_m$.

A formula will be said to be *prime* (*for the propositional calculus*), if it does not have any one of the forms $\mathrm{A} \supset \mathrm{B}$, $\mathrm{A} \,\&\, \mathrm{B}$, $\mathrm{A} \vee \mathrm{B}$, $\neg\mathrm{A}$ where A and B are formulas.

Example 4. $a{=}0$, $\exists c(a{=}c')$ and $\forall c(a{=}c' \vee a{=}b)$ are prime, but $\neg a{=}0$ and $\neg a{=}0 \,\&\, \exists c(a{=}c')$ are not. A proposition letter formula is prime, only when it consists simply of a proposition letter.

From the fact that the scopes of the operators $\supset$, &, $\vee$, $\neg$ in a formula can be recognized without ambiguity (§ 17), it follows that any given formula is constructed in a uniquely determined manner out of prime formulas by applications of Clauses 2 — 5 of the definition of formula. We call the distinct prime formulas out of which a formula or several formulas are thus constructed the *distinct prime components* (*for the propositional calculus*) of that formula or set of formulas.

EXAMPLE 5. The distinct prime components of $a=0 \vee (\neg a=0 \,\&\, \exists c(a=c')) \supset \forall c(a=c' \vee a=b)$ are $a=0$, $\exists c(a=c')$, $\forall c(a=c' \vee a=b)$.

THEOREM 4. CONVERSE OF SUBSTITUTION FOR PROPOSITION LETTERS. *Under the same stipulations as in Theorem* 3, *and provided in addition that* $A_1, \ldots, A_m$ *are distinct prime formulas*: *If* $\Gamma^* \vdash E^*$, *then* $\Gamma \vdash E$.

PROOF. Consider a given deduction of E^* from Γ^*. The distinct prime components of the formulas Γ^* and E^* are the formulas $A_1, \ldots, A_m$. Other formulas of the deduction may contribute additional distinct prime components $A_{m+1}, \ldots, A_{m+r}$. Let $P_{m+1}, \ldots, P_{m+r}$ be proposition letters. Throughout the formulas of the given deduction, let $A_1, \ldots, A_{m+r}$ be replaced simultaneously in every occurrence by $P_1, \ldots, P_{m+r}$, respectively. Consider any postulate application of the given deduction of E^* from Γ^*. It is readily shown (using Lemma 3 as illustrated in § 17) that the replacements will take place within the A, B, C of the application, producing proposition letter formulas A′, B′, C′, every occurrence of A becoming an occurrence of A′, etc. Thus the sequence of proposition letter formulas into which the given deduction of E^* from Γ^* is transformed by the replacements is a deduction of E from Γ with the same analysis. As the method of this proof shows, the converse rule can also be formulated thus:

THEOREM 4 (second version). *Let* Γ^* *be formulas and* E^* *a formula having as their distinct prime components* $A_1, \ldots, A_m$. *Let* $P_1, \ldots, P_m$ *be proposition letters, not necessarily distinct. Let* Γ, E *result from* Γ^*, E^*, *respectively, by replacing, simultaneously in all occurrences,* $A_1, \ldots, A_m$ *by* $P_1, \ldots, P_m$, *respectively. Then* $\Gamma^* \vdash E^*$ *only if* $\Gamma \vdash E$.

Except when "formula" is read in another sense than proposition letter formula, Theorem 4 is included in Theorem 3.

EXAMPLE 6. To illustrate the proof, let $\neg a=0 \supset (\exists c(a=c') \supset \neg a=0)$ occur in the given deduction of E^* from Γ^* as an axiom by Schema 1a (as at Example 3 (c) Step 2). Replacing the distinct prime components $a=0$, $\exists c(a=c')$ by the proposition letters $\mathcal{A}$, $\mathcal{B}$, respectively (or both by $\mathcal{A}$), gives $\neg\mathcal{A} \supset (\mathcal{B} \supset \neg\mathcal{A})$ (or $\neg\mathcal{A} \supset (\mathcal{A} \supset \neg\mathcal{A})$), which is an axiom by Schema 1a in the pure propositional calculus. But replacing $a=0$, $\exists c(a=c') \supset \neg a=0$ (the latter not being prime) by $\mathcal{A}$, $\mathcal{B}$, or replacing the three prime parts $a=0$, $\exists c(a=c')$, $a=0$ (the first and third not being distinct) by $\mathcal{A}$, $\mathcal{B}$, $\mathcal{C}$, would not give an axiom by Schema 1a.

EXAMPLE 7. To illustrate the application of the converse rule, take the fact (which we will establish in § 28 Example 3) that $\mathcal{A} \vee (\neg \mathcal{A} \,\&\, \mathcal{B})$ is unprovable in the pure propositional calculus. It follows, by the converse rule, substituting $a=0$, $\exists c(a=c')$ for $\mathcal{A}$, $\mathcal{B}$, respectively, that $a=0 \vee (\neg a=0 \,\&\, \exists c(a=c'))$ is unprovable in the number-theoretic propositional calculus, i.e. this formula of our original system cannot be proved on the basis of the postulates of Group A1 only (although in fact it is provable using the complete list, § 39). But from the unprovability of $\mathcal{A} \vee (\neg \mathcal{A} \,\&\, \mathcal{B})$ in the pure calculus, it does not follow that $a=0 \vee (\neg a=0 \,\&\, \neg a=0)$ is unprovable in the number-theoretic propositional calculus. Why?

§ 26. Equivalence, replacement. Let A and B be formulas. We use "$A \sim B$" as abbreviation for $(A \supset B) \,\&\, (B \supset A)$. The symbol "$\sim$" may be read "equivalent". It functions as a formal operator, which placed between two formulas of the system gives another formula of the system. In omitting parentheses, it is then ranked ahead of the other formal operators (§ 17).

We say that A is *equivalent* to B in the propositional calculus or other formal system, if in that formal system $\vdash A \sim B$. Here the word "equivalent" functions as a metamathematical verb, which placed between two formulas of the system gives a statement about those formulas.

THEOREM 5. *If* A, B *and* C *are formulas*:

*1. $\vdash A \supset A$. *2. $A \supset B,\ B \supset C \vdash A \supset C$.

*3. $A \supset (B \supset C) \vdash B \supset (A \supset C)$.

*4. $A \supset (B \supset C) \vdash A \,\&\, B \supset C$. *5. $A \,\&\, B \supset C \vdash A \supset (B \supset C)$.

(Principle of identity, chain inference, interchange of premises, importation, exportation.)

*6. $A \supset B \vdash (B \supset C) \supset (A \supset C)$. *7. $A \supset B \vdash (C \supset A) \supset (C \supset B)$.

*8a. $A \supset B \vdash A \,\&\, C \supset B \,\&\, C$. *8b. $A \supset B \vdash C \,\&\, A \supset C \,\&\, B$.

*9a. $A \supset B \vdash A \vee C \supset B \vee C$. *9b. $A \supset B \vdash C \vee A \supset C \vee B$.

(Introduction of a conclusion, premise, conjunctive member, or disjunctive member, into an implication.)

*10a. $\neg A \vdash A \supset B$. *10b. $A \vdash \neg A \supset B$. *11. $B \vdash A \supset B$.

(Demonstration of an implication by refuting the premise, or by proving the conclusion.)

*12. $A \supset B \vdash \neg B \supset \neg A$. *13. $A \supset \neg B \vdash B \supset \neg A$.

*14°. $\neg A \supset B \vdash \neg B \supset A$. *15°. $\neg A \supset \neg B \vdash B \supset A$.

(Contraposition, and contraposition with double negations suppressed.)

*16. $A \supset B, B \supset A \vdash A \sim B$.

*17a. $A \sim B \vdash A \supset B$. *17b. $A \sim B \vdash B \supset A$.

*18a. $A \sim B, A \vdash B$. *18b. $A \sim B, B \vdash A$.

(From the definition of $\sim$ in terms of $\supset$ and &.)

*19. $\vdash A \sim A$. *20. $A \sim B \vdash B \sim A$. *21. $A \sim B, B \sim C \vdash A \sim C$.

(Reflexive, symmetric and transitive properties of equivalence.)

*22. $A \supset (B \supset C), \neg\neg A, \neg\neg B \vdash \neg\neg C$.

*23. $\neg\neg(A \supset B) \vdash \neg\neg A \supset \neg\neg B$.

*24. $\neg\neg(A \supset B), \neg\neg(B \supset C) \vdash \neg\neg(A \supset C)$.

*25. $\vdash \neg\neg(A \,\&\, B) \sim \neg\neg A \,\&\, \neg\neg B$; in particular, $\vdash \neg\neg(A \sim B) \sim \neg\neg(A \supset B) \,\&\, \neg\neg(B \supset A)$.

(Additional results of interest for the intuitionistic system.)

Proofs. Eight of these have already been established, as follows: *1 at § 20 (1′); *2 at § 21 (8′):1; *3 at (5′):3; *4 at (6′):2; 5* at (7′); *6 at (8′):2; *10a at § 23 (9′):6; and *11 at § 25 (10′). The reader may establish the others, using the derived rules of Theorem 2 for the propositional calculus (§ 23). For example:

*9a. 1. $A \supset B, A \vdash B \vdash B \vee C$ — $\supset$-elim., $\vee$-introd.
2. $A \supset B, C \vdash B \vee C$ — $\vee$-introd.
3. $A \supset B, A \vee C \vdash B \vee C$ — $\vee$-elim., 1, 2.
4. $A \supset B \vdash A \vee C \supset B \vee C$ — $\supset$-introd., 3.

*12. 1. $A \supset B, \neg B, A \vdash B$ — $\supset$-elim.
2. $A \supset B, \neg B, A \vdash \neg B$.
3. $A \supset B, \neg B \vdash \neg A$ — $\neg$-introd., 1, 2.
4. $A \supset B \vdash \neg B \supset \neg A$ — $\supset$-introd., 3.

*14. Similarly to *12, but now an application of $\neg$-elim. is added at Step 3.

*22. 1. $A \supset (B \supset C), B \vdash A \supset C$ — $\supset$-elim., *3 (or § 21 (5′):2).
2. $A \supset (B \supset C), B \vdash \neg\neg A \supset \neg\neg C$ — *12 twice, 1.
3. $A \supset (B \supset C), \neg\neg A \vdash B \supset \neg\neg C$ — $\supset$-elim., $\supset$-introd., 2.
4. $A \supset (B \supset C), \neg\neg A \vdash \neg\neg B \supset \neg\neg C$ — *13, *12, 3.

*23. Taking $A \supset B$, A, B as the A, B, C, respectively, in *22:
1. $(A \supset B) \supset (A \supset B), \neg\neg(A \supset B), \neg\neg A \vdash \neg\neg B$. But:
2. $\vdash (A \supset B) \supset (A \supset B)$ — *1. Hence:
3. $\neg\neg(A \supset B), \neg\neg A \vdash \neg\neg B$ — 1, 2.

*24. Taking $A \supset B$, $B \supset C$, $A \supset C$ for A, B, C, respectively, in *22:
1. $(A \supset B) \supset ((B \supset C) \supset (A \supset C))$, $\neg\neg(A \supset B)$, $\neg\neg(B \supset C) \vdash \neg\neg(A \supset C)$. But:
2. $\vdash (A \supset B) \supset ((B \supset C) \supset (A \supset C))$ — $\supset$-introd., *6.

*25. Taking A, B, A & B for A, B, C, respectively, in *22, and using Axiom Schema 3 (§ 19), $\neg\neg A, \neg\neg B \vdash \neg\neg(A \,\&\, B)$. Applying *12 twice to Axiom Schema 4a, $\vdash \neg\neg(A \,\&\, B) \supset \neg\neg A$; etc.

Replacement. Let A be a formal expression. Consider another formal expression C. It may happen that A occurs as a (consecutive) part of C; indeed, this may happen in more than one way. Suppose that it does happen, and that, if it happens in more than one way, a particular occurrence of A in C has been specified. We now denote C, with a particular occurrence of A in C specified, by "C_A". In juxtaposition notation, C_A is EAF, where E and F are the parts (possibly empty) which precede and follow the specified part A. Now let B be a formal expression. The result of *replacing* the specified part A of C by B is the expression EBF. This we denote by "C_B".

Contrast this definition of replacement with the definition of substitution given in § 18. Replacement takes place for a specified occurrence of an expression consisting of one or more symbols. Substitution takes place for all occurrences of a single symbol, unless there is a distinction between 'free' and 'bound' occurrences, in which case it takes place for all free occurrences. (In § 25 we used replacement in all occurrences. That is equivalent to replacement, as now defined, applied successively to each of the original non-overlapping occurrences of an expression in an expression.)

Example 1. If A is $\mathcal{A} \supset \mathcal{B}$, C_A is $(\mathcal{A} \supset \mathcal{B}) \,\&\, \neg((\underline{\mathcal{A} \supset \mathcal{B}}) \vee \neg\mathcal{A})$ and B is $\neg\mathcal{A} \vee \mathcal{B}$, then C_B is $(\mathcal{A} \supset \mathcal{B}) \,\&\, \neg((\neg\mathcal{A} \vee \mathcal{B}) \vee \neg\mathcal{A})$.

The foregoing definition of replacement is stated for formal expressions in general. For the case that A, C_A and B are proposition letter formulas (as in Example 1), we have the following situation (as can be demonstrated rigorously by applying the analysis of the scopes of operators (§ 17) to the definition of proposition letter formula (§ 25)): The formula C_A can be built up from the specified part A by applications of Clauses 2—5 of the definition of proposition letter formula, and C_B can be constructed from B by parallel steps. The number of steps in this construction of C_A from A, after A is given and exclusive of the steps required to build up the parts not containing the specified occurrence of A, we call the *depth* of that occurrence of A in C_A. In other words, the depth of the part A in C_A is the number of operators within the scopes of which it lies.

EXAMPLE 1 (continued). The parallel constructions of C_A from A and of C_B from B are as follows, and the depth is 3.

$\mathcal{A} \supset \mathcal{B}$	$\neg\mathcal{A} \vee \mathcal{B}$
$(\mathcal{A} \supset \mathcal{B}) \vee \neg\mathcal{A}$	$(\neg\mathcal{A} \vee \mathcal{B}) \vee \neg\mathcal{A}$
$\neg((\mathcal{A} \supset \mathcal{B}) \vee \neg\mathcal{A})$	$\neg((\neg\mathcal{A} \vee \mathcal{B}) \vee \neg\mathcal{A})$
$(\mathcal{A} \supset \mathcal{B}) \;\&\; \neg((\mathcal{A} \supset \mathcal{B}) \vee \neg\mathcal{A})$	$(\mathcal{A} \supset \mathcal{B}) \;\&\; \neg((\neg\mathcal{A} \vee \mathcal{B}) \vee \neg\mathcal{A})$

THEOREM 6. *If* A, B, C_A *and* C_B *are proposition letter formulas related as in the foregoing definition of replacement, then* $A \sim B \vdash C_A \sim C_B$. (Replacement theorem.)

PROOF, by induction on the depth of A in C_A, taking the A and B fixed for the induction. The induction proposition is that what is stated in the theorem is true, with the fixed A and B, for every C_A in which the specified occurrence of A is at depth *d*. BASIS: A is at depth 0 in C_A. Then C_A is A, C_B is B, and the conclusion of the theorem is simply $A \sim B \vdash A \sim B$, which holds as a general property of $\vdash$. INDUCTION STEP: A is at depth $d+1$ in C_A. As hypothesis of the induction, $A \sim B \vdash M_A \sim M_B$ for any proposition letter formula M_A in which the specified occurrence of A lies at depth *d*. Now C_A must have one of the seven forms $M_A \supset N$, $N \supset M_A$, $M_A \;\&\; N$, $N \;\&\; M_A$, $M_A \vee N$, $N \vee M_A$, $\neg M_A$, where M_A and N are proposition letter formulas, and A is at depth *d* in M_A. By the hypothesis of the induction, $A \sim B \vdash M_A \sim M_B$. Furthermore, by the appropriate one of the following lemmas (taking M_A as the A, M_B as the B, and N as the C of the lemma), $M_A \sim M_B \vdash C_A \sim C_B$. Therefore $A \sim B \vdash C_A \sim C_B$.

LEMMAS FOR REPLACEMENT. *If* A, B *and* C *are formulas*:

*26. $A \sim B \vdash A \supset C \sim B \supset C$. *27. $A \sim B \vdash C \supset A \sim C \supset B$.
*28a. $A \sim B \vdash A \;\&\; C \sim B \;\&\; C$. *28b. $A \sim B \vdash C \;\&\; A \sim C \;\&\; B$.
*29a. $A \sim B \vdash A \vee C \sim B \vee C$. *29b. $A \sim B \vdash C \vee A \sim C \vee B$.
*30. $A \sim B \vdash \neg A \sim \neg B$.

PROOFS.

*26. 1. $A \sim B \vdash B \supset A$ — &-elim. (*17b).
2. $A \sim B \vdash (A \supset C) \supset (B \supset C)$ — *6, 1.
3. $A \sim B \vdash (B \supset C) \supset (A \supset C)$ — similarly, using *17a and *6.
4. $A \sim B \vdash A \supset C \sim B \supset C$ — &-introd. (*16), 2, 3.

*27. Similarly, using *17a and *7, then *17b and *7.

EXAMPLE 1 (concluded). Let $\sim$ be written between each of the four pairs of formulas in the parallel constructions of C_A and C_B. The second of the resulting four formulas is deducible from the first by *29a, the third from the second by *30, and the fourth from the third by *28b. Combining these deductions consecutively, we have the deduction of $C_A \sim C_B$ from $A \sim B$ which is given by the method of proof of Theorem 6.

Theorem 6 has been stated in terms of proposition letter formulas. But by the substitution rule (Theorem 3 § 25), we can apply it for other senses of formula, provided that the A, B, C_A of the application can be obtained from proposition letter formulas by substituting formulas simultaneously for the proposition letters. Hence, or directly by the method of the above proof of Theorem 6:

THEOREM 6 (second version). *If* A *and* B *are formulas,* C_A *is a formula constructed from a specified occurrence of* A *using only the operators* $\supset$, &, $\vee$, $\neg$, *and* C_B *results from* C_A *by replacing this occurrence of* A *by* B, *then* $A \sim B \vdash C_A \sim C_B$.

EXAMPLE 2. Let x be a variable, and A, B and C(x) be formulas. By the theorem, $A \sim B \vdash A \vee \forall x(A \supset C(x)) \sim B \vee \forall x(A \supset C(x))$. (This can be considered as coming from $\mathcal{A} \sim \mathcal{B} \vdash \mathcal{A} \vee \mathcal{C} \sim \mathcal{B} \vee \mathcal{C}$ by substituting A, B, $\forall x(A \supset C(x))$ for $\mathcal{A}, \mathcal{B}, \mathcal{C}$, respectively.) But our present means are inadequate for deducing $A \vee \forall x(A \supset C(x)) \sim A \vee \forall x(B \supset C(x))$ from $A \sim B$. In this the occurrence of A to be replaced is within the part $\forall x(A \supset C(x))$, and so the C_A cannot be built up from the occurrence of A by using only the operators $\supset$, &, $\vee$, $\neg$.

COROLLARY. *Under the conditions of the theorem (in either version),* $A \sim B,\ C_A \vdash C_B$. (Replacement property of equivalence.)

From the theorem by *18a. (Conversely, the theorem is obtained from the corollary and *19 by taking $C_A \sim C_{\underline{A}}$ as the C_A of the corollary. The theorem includes the lemmas, as the cases when the depth is 1.)

Our results have been developed to give replacement of a single occurrence of A at a time. By iterated applications, we can then replace any set of occurrences.

CHAINS OF EQUIVALENCES. We can now present demonstrations of equivalence between proposition letter formulas in the following abbreviated way. Let us write

$$\vdash C_0 \sim C_1 \sim \ldots \sim C_{n-1} \sim C_n,$$

where for each i ($i = 1, \ldots, n$) either:

(a) C_i is the same formula as C_{i-1}; or

(b_1) $\vdash C_{i-1} \sim C_i$ or (b_2) $\vdash C_i \sim C_{i-1}$; or

(c) C_i comes from C_{i-1} by replacing one or more occurrences of A_i by B_i where (1) $\vdash A_i \sim B_i$ or (2) $\vdash B_i \sim A_i$.

Then we can regard "$C_0 \sim C_1 \sim \ldots \sim C_{n-1} \sim C_n$" as an abbreviation for $(\ldots((C_0 \sim C_1) \& (C_1 \sim C_2)) \& \ldots \& (C_{n-2} \sim C_{n-1})) \& (C_{n-1} \sim C_n)$; and we can understand that $\vdash C_j \sim C_k$ for all pairs j, k ($j, k = 0, \ldots, n$). For we have for each i either $\vdash C_{i-1} \sim C_i$ or $\vdash C_i \sim C_{i-1}$, by *19 in Case (a), immediately in Case (b), and by applications of Theorem 6 in Case (c). Then we have $\vdash C_j \sim C_k$ for all other pairs j, k by *19, *20 and *21. The method applies likewise when we have any list Γ of assumption formulas written before the symbol "$\vdash$" throughout. We may insert explanatory remarks in brackets between links of the chain. (For an example see the proof of *57 in § 27.)

The chain method will apply also when we have instead of $\sim$ some other relational symbol for which we have established the corresponding reflexive, symmetric, transitive and replacement properties. Furthermore in the absence of some of these properties (except transitivity) it can be modified to apply, as follows. When symmetry is absent, omit (b_2) and (c) (2), and require that $j \leq k$. When reflexiveness is also absent, omit also (a), and require that $j < k$. When replaceability is absent, omit (c). (Examples from Chapter VIII: with all properties present, $=$; lacking symmetry and replaceability, $\leq$; lacking also reflexiveness, $<$.)

§ 27. Equivalences, duality.

THEOREM 7. *If* A, B *and* C *are formulas:*

*31.	$\vdash (A \& B) \& C \sim A \& (B \& C)$.	*32.	$\vdash (A \vee B) \vee C \sim A \vee (B \vee C)$.
*33.	$\vdash A \& B \sim B \& A$.	*34.	$\vdash A \vee B \sim B \vee A$.
*35.	$\vdash A \& (B \vee C) \sim (A \& B) \vee (A \& C)$.	*36.	$\vdash A \vee (B \& C) \sim (A \vee B) \& (A \vee C)$.
*37.	$\vdash A \& A \sim A$.	*38.	$\vdash A \vee A \sim A$.
*39.	$\vdash A \& (A \vee B) \sim A$.	*40.	$\vdash A \vee (A \& B) \sim A$.

(Associative, commutative, distributive, idempotent and elimination laws.)

*41.	$A \vdash A \supset B \sim B$.	*42.	$B \vdash A \supset B \sim B$.
*43.	$\neg A \vdash A \supset B \sim \neg A$.	*44.	$\neg B \vdash A \supset B \sim \neg A$.
*45.	$B \vdash A \& B \sim A$.	*46.	$B \vdash A \vee B \sim B$.
*47.	$\neg B \vdash A \& B \sim B$.	*48.	$\neg B \vdash A \vee B \sim A$.

(Special cases of implication, conjunction and disjunction.)

*49°. $\vdash \neg\neg A \sim A$.

*50. $\vdash \neg(A \,\&\, \neg A)$. *51°. $\vdash A \vee \neg A$.

(Law of double negation, denial of contradiction, law of the excluded middle.)

*52°. $\vdash A \,\&\, (B \vee \neg B) \sim A$. *53. $\vdash A \vee (B \,\&\, \neg B) \sim A$.

*54. $\vdash A \,\&\, B \,\&\, \neg B \sim B \,\&\, \neg B$. *55°. $\vdash A \vee B \vee \neg B \sim B \vee \neg B$.

(For simplifying a disjunction of conjunctions, or a conjunction of disjunctions.)

*56°. $\vdash A \vee B \sim \neg(\neg A \,\&\, \neg B)$. *57°. $\vdash A \,\&\, B \sim \neg(\neg A \vee \neg B)$.

*58°. $\vdash A \supset B \sim \neg(A \,\&\, \neg B)$. *59°. $\vdash A \supset B \sim \neg A \vee B$.

*60°. $\vdash A \,\&\, B \sim \neg(A \supset \neg B)$. *61°. $\vdash A \vee B \sim \neg A \supset B$.

(Each two of $\supset$, &, $\vee$ in terms of the other and $\neg$.)

*62°. $\vdash \neg(A \,\&\, B) \sim \neg A \vee \neg B$. *63. $\vdash \neg(A \vee B) \sim \neg A \,\&\, \neg B$.

(Transfer of $\neg$ across & and $\vee$ (De Morgan's laws, 1847).)

*49a. $\vdash A \supset \neg\neg A$. *49b. $\vdash \neg\neg\neg A \sim \neg A$.

*49c. $\vdash A \vee \neg A \supset (\neg\neg A \supset A)$; hence $\vdash A \vee \neg A \supset (\neg\neg A \sim A)$.

*50a. $\vdash \neg(A \sim \neg A)$. *51a. $\vdash \neg\neg(A \vee \neg A)$.

*56a. $\vdash A \vee B \supset \neg(\neg A \,\&\, \neg B)$. *51b. $\vdash \neg\neg(\neg\neg A \supset A)$.

*56b. $\vdash \neg A \vee B \supset \neg(A \,\&\, \neg B)$. *57a. $\vdash A \,\&\, B \supset \neg(\neg A \vee \neg B)$.

*58a. $\vdash (A \supset B) \supset \neg(A \,\&\, \neg B)$. *57b. $\vdash A \,\&\, \neg B \supset \neg(\neg A \vee B)$.

*58b-d. $\vdash A \supset \neg B \sim \neg(A \,\&\, B) \sim \neg\neg A \supset \neg B \sim \neg\neg(\neg A \vee \neg B)$.

*58e, f. $\neg\neg B \supset B \vdash \neg\neg A \supset B \sim A \supset B \sim \neg(A \,\&\, \neg B)$.

*58g. $\vdash (\neg\neg A \supset B) \supset \neg(A \,\&\, \neg B)$. *59a. $\vdash \neg A \vee B \supset (A \supset B)$.

*60a. $\vdash A \,\&\, B \supset \neg(A \supset \neg B)$. *59b. $\vdash (A \supset B) \supset \neg\neg(\neg A \vee B)$.

*60b. $\vdash A \,\&\, \neg B \supset \neg(A \supset B)$. *59c. $\vdash (\neg A \supset B) \supset \neg\neg(A \vee B)$.

*60c. $\vdash \neg\neg A \,\&\, B \supset \neg(A \supset \neg B)$. *61a. $\vdash A \vee B \supset (\neg A \supset B)$.

*60d-f. $\vdash \neg\neg A \,\&\, \neg B \sim \neg(A \supset B) \sim \neg(\neg A \vee B) \sim \neg\neg(A \,\&\, \neg B)$.

*60g-i. $\vdash \neg\neg(A \supset B) \sim \neg(A \,\&\, \neg B) \sim A \supset \neg\neg B \sim \neg\neg A \supset \neg\neg B$.

*62a. $\vdash \neg A \vee \neg B \supset \neg(A \,\&\, B)$. *61b. $\vdash \neg(A \vee B) \sim \neg(\neg A \supset B)$.

(Additional results of interest for the intuitionistic system.)

Proofs for the classical system, excepting *32, *34, *36, *38, *40, *53, *55. A little work may be saved if one chooses by postponing proof of these seven until duality (Corollary Theorem 8) is available.

*35. 1. A, B ⊢ A & B ⊢ (A & B) ∨ (A & C) — &-introd., ∨-introd.
2. A, C ⊢ A & C ⊢ (A & B) ∨ (A & C) — &-introd., ∨-introd.
3. A, B ∨ C ⊢ (A & B) ∨ (A & C) — ∨-elim., 1, 2.
4. A & (B ∨ C) ⊢ (A & B) ∨ (A & C) — &-elim., 3.
5. ⊢ A & (B ∨ C) ⊃ (A & B) ∨ (A & C) — ⊃-introd., 4.
6. A & B ⊢ A — &-elim.
7. A & B ⊢ B ⊢ B ∨ C — &-elim., ∨-introd.
8. A & B ⊢ A & (B ∨ C) — &-introd., 6, 7.
9. A & C ⊢ A & (B ∨ C) — similarly.
10. (A & B) ∨ (A & C) ⊢ A & (B ∨ C) — ∨-elim., 8, 9.
11. ⊢ (A & B) ∨ (A & C) ⊃ A & (B ∨ C) — ⊃-introd., 10.
12. ⊢ A & (B ∨ C) ∼ (A & B) ∨ (A & C) — &-introd. (*16), 5, 11.

*49. 1. ⊢ ¬¬A ⊃ A — ¬-elim., ⊃-introd. (or Axiom Schema 8).
2. A, ¬A ⊢ A.
3. A, ¬A ⊢ ¬A.
4. A ⊢ ¬¬A — ¬-introd., 2, 3; etc.

*51. 1. ¬(A ∨ ¬A), A ⊢ A ∨ ¬A — ∨-introd.
2. ¬(A ∨ ¬A), A ⊢ ¬(A ∨ ¬A).
3. ¬(A ∨ ¬A) ⊢ ¬A — ¬-introd., 1, 2.
4. ¬(A ∨ ¬A) ⊢ ¬¬A — similarly.
5. ⊢ ¬¬(A ∨ ¬A) — ¬-introd., 3, 4.
6. ⊢ A ∨ ¬A — ¬-elim., 5.

REMARK 1. Thus in the formal system without Axiom Schema 8, ¬¬B ⊃ B ⊢ A ∨ ¬A where B is A ∨ ¬A. Conversely, in the intuitionistic system, A ∨ ¬A ⊢ ¬¬A ⊃ A, thus:

1. A ⊢ ¬¬A ⊃ A — *11.
2. ¬A ⊢ ¬¬A ⊃ A — *10b.
3. A ∨ ¬A ⊢ ¬¬A ⊃ A — ∨-elim., 1, 2.

Thus either of ¬¬A ⊃ A or A ∨ ¬A can be chosen as the one non-intuitionistic postulate of the classical system.

*52. By *45 and *51.

*54. Similarly, by *47 and *50. Parentheses have been omitted in the result, since by *31 it is immaterial which way the association is taken.

*56. 1. A, ¬A & ¬B ⊢ A.
2. A, ¬A & ¬B ⊢ ¬A — &-elim.
3. A ⊢ ¬(¬A & ¬B) — ¬-introd., 1, 2.
4. B ⊢ ¬(¬A & ¬B) — similarly.

5. $\vdash A \vee B \supset \neg(\neg A \& \neg B)$ — $\vee$-elim., 3, 4, $\supset$-introd.
6. $\neg(A \vee B), A \vdash A \vee B$ — $\vee$-introd.
7. $\neg(A \vee B), A \vdash \neg(A \vee B)$.
8. $\neg(A \vee B) \vdash \neg A$ — $\neg$-introd., 6, 7.
9. $\neg(A \vee B) \vdash \neg B$ — similarly.
10. $\vdash \neg(A \vee B) \supset \neg A \& \neg B$ — &-introd. 8, 9, $\supset$-introd.
11. $\vdash \neg(\neg A \& \neg B) \supset A \vee B$ — contraposition (*14), 10.

*57. Presented as a chain of equivalences: $\vdash \neg(\neg A \vee \neg B) \sim \neg\neg(\neg\neg A \& \neg\neg B)$ [*56] $\sim \neg\neg A \& \neg\neg B$ [*49] $\sim A \& B$ [*49].

*59-63. Set these up by the chain method.

Proofs for the intuitionistic system. *49c. By Remark 1; by *49a, *16 and *17a, $\vdash \neg\neg A \supset A \sim (\neg\neg A \sim A)$. *51a. By the proof of *51 omitting Step 6. *51b. Apply *12 twice to *49c, and use *51a. *58d. Use *63. *60f. Use *25.

To *interchange* two expressions A and B throughout a third expression C is to replace in C, simultaneously, all occurrences of A by B and all occurrences of B by A (examples will follow).

Theorem 8°. *Let* D *be a proposition letter formula constructed from the distinct proposition letters* $P_1, \ldots, P_m$ *and their negations* $\neg P_1, \ldots, \neg P_m$ *using only the operators* &, $\vee$. *Then a formula* $D^\dagger$ *equivalent to the negation* $\neg D$ *of* D *is obtained by the interchange throughout* D *of* & *with* $\vee$ *and of each letter with its negation.*

In other words, if D *be such a proposition letter formula, and* $D^\dagger$ *be the result of the described interchange performed on* D: $\vdash \neg D \sim D^\dagger$.

Example 1°. Taking $\neg\mathcal{A} \& (\neg\mathcal{B} \vee \mathcal{B})$ as the D, $\neg D$ is equivalent to $\mathcal{A} \vee (\mathcal{B} \& \neg\mathcal{B})$.

Proof amounts essentially to this: the $\neg$ of $\neg D$ can be transferred progressively to the interior by applications of *62 and *63, and any resulting double negations then discharged by applications of *49, in doing which D is transformed into $D^\dagger$ (details to follow).

Example 1 (concluded).

$$\begin{aligned}\vdash \neg(\neg\mathcal{A} \& (\neg\mathcal{B} \vee \mathcal{B})) &\sim \\ \neg\neg\mathcal{A} \vee \neg(\neg\mathcal{B} \vee \mathcal{B}) &\sim \\ \neg\neg\mathcal{A} \vee (\neg\neg\mathcal{B} \& \neg\mathcal{B}) &\sim \\ \mathcal{A} \vee (\mathcal{B} \& \neg\mathcal{B}).&\end{aligned}$$

To give the proof more explicitly, we take as the induction number (for a course-of-values induction) the number of occurrences of & and ∨ in D; call it the *grade* of D.

BASIS: D is of grade 0. Then for some proposition letter P, D is P or D is ¬P. CASE 1: D is P. Then ⊢ ¬D ∼ ¬P [case hypothesis] ∼ P† [definition of †] ∼ D† [case hypothesis]. CASE 2: D is ¬P. Similarly, using *49. INDUCTION STEP: D is of grade $g+1$. Then for some proposition letter formulas A and B of the type under consideration with grades $\leq g$, either D is A & B or D is A ∨ B. CASE 1: D is A & B. Then ⊢ ¬D ∼ ¬(A & B) [case hypothesis] ∼ ¬A ∨ ¬B [*62] ∼ A† ∨ B† [hypothesis of the induction] ∼ (A & B)† [definition of †] ∼ D† [case hypothesis]. CASE 2: D is A ∨ B. Similarly.

EXAMPLE 2°. By the substitution rule (Theorem 3 § 25), substituting $\mathcal{B}$, $\neg\mathcal{A} \vee \mathcal{C}$ for $\mathcal{A}$, $\mathcal{B}$ in the result of Example 1,

$$\vdash \neg(\neg\mathcal{B} \,\&\, (\neg[\neg\mathcal{A} \vee \mathcal{C}] \vee [\neg\mathcal{A} \vee \mathcal{C}])) \sim \mathcal{B} \vee ([\neg\mathcal{A} \vee \mathcal{C}] \,\&\, \neg[\neg\mathcal{A} \vee \mathcal{C}]).$$

In fact, for any formulas A and B,

$$\vdash \neg(\neg A \,\&\, (\neg B \vee B)) \sim A \vee (B \,\&\, \neg B).$$

As this example illustrates, the theorem can also be stated using any formulas $A_1, \ldots, A_m$ in place of the proposition letters $P_1, \ldots, P_m$, provided the $A_1, \ldots, A_m$ retain their identity throughout the construction of D, and are held intact in the interchange operation. (Second version of Theorem 8.)

COROLLARY°. *An equivalence between two letter formulas* E *and* F *of the type described in the theorem is preserved under the interchange throughout* E *and* F *of* & *with* ∨.

In other words, if E *and* F *be two such proposition letter formulas, and* E′ *and* F′ *be the results of the described interchange performed on* E *and* F, *respectively*: *If* ⊢ E ∼ F, *then* ⊢ E′ ∼ F′. (Principle of duality.)

EXAMPLE 3°. By *52, $\vdash \mathcal{A} \,\&\, (\mathcal{B} \vee \neg\mathcal{B}) \sim \mathcal{A}$. Hence (taking $\mathcal{A} \,\&\, (\mathcal{B} \vee \neg\mathcal{B})$ as the E and $\mathcal{A}$ as the F) $\vdash \mathcal{A} \vee (\mathcal{B} \,\&\, \neg\mathcal{B}) \sim \mathcal{A}$.

PROOF. By hypothesis, ⊢ E ∼ F. Let us substitute for each proposition letter P within E and F the negation ¬P of that letter, indicating this substitution operation by "*". By the substitution rule (Theorem 3 § 25), then ⊢ E* ∼ F*. Next let us replace within E* and F* each doubly negated letter ¬¬P by the simple letter P, indicating this operation by "‡". By the law of double negation (*49) and the replacement property of equivalence (Corollary Theorem 6), ⊢ E*‡ ∼ F*‡. The effect of these two operations is to interchange the proposition letters with their negations in the given equivalence. Now by Theorem 6 (or *30), $\vdash \neg E^{*\ddagger} \sim \neg F^{*\ddagger}$. Evaluating the negations by Theorem 8, $\vdash E^{*\ddagger\dagger} \sim F^{*\ddagger\dagger}$. These last two steps effect the interchange of & with V, and interchange the proposition letters with their negations a second time to restore them to their original condition. What we now have is therefore $\vdash E' \sim F'$.

EXAMPLE 3 (concluded).

$\vdash E \sim F.$	$\vdash \quad \mathcal{A} \,\&\, (\ \mathcal{B} \vee \neg\ \mathcal{B}) \sim \quad \mathcal{A}.$
$\vdash E^{*} \sim F^{*}.$	$\vdash \quad \neg\mathcal{A} \,\&\, (\neg\mathcal{B} \vee \neg\neg\mathcal{B}) \sim \quad \neg\mathcal{A}.$
$\vdash E^{*\ddagger} \sim F^{*\ddagger}.$	$\vdash \quad \neg\mathcal{A} \,\&\, (\neg\mathcal{B} \vee \quad \mathcal{B}) \sim \quad \neg\mathcal{A}.$
$\vdash \neg E^{*\ddagger} \sim \neg F^{*\ddagger}.$	$\vdash \neg\, (\neg\mathcal{A} \,\&\, (\neg\mathcal{B} \vee \quad \mathcal{B})) \sim \neg\neg\mathcal{A}.$
$\vdash E^{*\ddagger\dagger} \sim F^{*\ddagger\dagger}$, i.e. $\vdash E' \sim F'$.	$\vdash \quad \mathcal{A} \vee (\ \mathcal{B} \,\&\, \ \neg\mathcal{B}) \sim \quad \mathcal{A}.$

EXAMPLE 4°. Substituting any formulas A, B for $\mathcal{A}$, $\mathcal{B}$ in the result of Example 3 (by Theorem 3 § 25), $\vdash A \vee (B \,\&\, \neg B) \sim A$. This is *53.

Similarly *32, *34, *36, *38, *40, *55 follow from *31, *33, *35, *37, *39, *54, respectively, by duality (Corollary Theorem 8), when A, B, C are simple proposition letters; and thence by the substitution rule (Theorem 3), when A, B, C are any formulas.

EXAMPLE 5°. By duality (Corollary Theorem 8):

(a) If $\vdash \mathcal{A} \vee \mathcal{B} \sim \mathcal{A}$, then $\vdash \mathcal{A} \,\&\, \mathcal{B} \sim \mathcal{A}$.

But we cannot infer the following:

(b) "For any formulas A and B, if $\vdash A \vee B \sim A$, then $\vdash A \,\&\, B \sim A$." (Indeed, taking $\mathcal{A}$, $\mathcal{B} \,\&\, \neg\mathcal{B}$ for the A, B in (b), "$\vdash A \vee B \sim A$" becomes "$\vdash \mathcal{A} \vee (\mathcal{B} \,\&\, \neg\mathcal{B}) \sim \mathcal{A}$", which is true by *53; while "$\vdash A \,\&\, B \sim A$" becomes "$\vdash \mathcal{A} \,\&\, \mathcal{B} \,\&\, \neg\mathcal{B} \sim \mathcal{A}$", which is false as will be shown in Example 4 § 28.) Explain. (How does the present situation differ from Examples 2 and 4?) — To state a second version of the corollary, we must require that the $A_1, \ldots, A_m$ be distinct prime formulas (cf. Theorems 3 and 4). — Since (b) is false, by Theorem 3 so is:

(c) "$\mathcal{A} \vee \mathcal{B} \sim \mathcal{A} \vdash \mathcal{A} \,\&\, \mathcal{B} \sim \mathcal{A}$."

Thus duality holds only as a subsidiary deduction rule, not as a direct rule.

The recognition of duality in logic goes back to Schröder 1877.

In applying duality to a formula that has been abbreviated by omitting parentheses under the convention of § 17, which ranks & ahead of V, care must be taken to show the scopes of the operators without change in the result. (Hence we usually prefer in this connection not to apply the convention between & and V.)

As an exercise, the reader may verify the following addendum to the corollary, by reexamining the proof.

COROLLARY (second part)°. *Also: If* $\vdash$ E $\supset$ F, *then* $\vdash$ F′ $\supset$ E′. (Dual-converse relationship.)

EXAMPLE 6°. The axiom $\mathcal{A} \& \mathcal{B} \supset \mathcal{A}$ has as dual-converse the axiom $\mathcal{A} \supset \mathcal{A} \vee \mathcal{B}$. The provable formula $\mathcal{A} \& \mathcal{B} \supset \mathcal{A} \vee \mathcal{B}$ is its own dual-converse.

§ 28. Valuation, consistency. Since setting up the formal system, or in this chapter a subsystem, our metamathematical investigations have been devoted chiefly to establishing the provability of certain formulas, and the deducibility of certain formulas from other formulas, i.e. to developing logic and mathematics within the formal system. This is a necessary part of our program, and contributes to showing that the formal system does constitute a formalization of a certain part of mathematics.

But also in metamathematics questions are asked which relate to a formal system as a whole. One of these is the question of the 'consistency' of the system, which is fundamental in Hilbert's program (§ 14).

The propositional calculus (and generally, any formal system having the symbol $\neg$ for negation) is said to be (*simply*) *consistent*, if for no formula A are both A and $\neg$A provable in the system; and to be (*simply*) *inconsistent* in the contrary case that for some formula A, both $\vdash$ A and $\vdash \neg$A.

This is a strictly metamathematical definition. It refers only to the formal symbol $\neg$, and to the definitions of formula and provable formula. It thus becomes an exact mathematical problem, which we can consider in metamathematics, to prove the consistency of a given formal system.

The definition and problem of consistency take on significance from outside the metamathematics, under the interpretation of the formal system as a formalization of an informal theory, with the symbol $\neg$ expressing negation. The propositions expressed by two number-theoretic formulas A and $\neg$A, if A does not contain free variables (or the propositions expressed for each particular set of values of the variables, if A does contain free variables), taken together constitute a contradiction. Likewise, in the case of proposition letter formulas, on interpreting the proposition letters by any particular propositions. A metamathematical proof of the consistency of the formal system would hence afford security against a contradiction's arising in the informal theory.

For the propositional calculus (and generally, for any formal system which has &-elimination and weak $\neg$-elimination as postulated or derived rules), the above definition is equivalent to the following. The system is (*simply*) *consistent*, if there is some unprovable formula; (*simply*) *inconsistent*, if every formula is provable. For if both ⊢ A and ⊢ ¬A, then by use of weak ¬-elimination (§ 23), ⊢ B for every formula B. In the case of consistency, A & ¬A is an example of an unprovable formula, since otherwise by &-elimination both ⊢ A and ⊢ ¬A.

The definition of consistency (in the first form) and the definition of provable formula (say in the first form, § 19) suggest a plan of attack on the problem of proving consistency (not the only possible plan). Suppose we can find a metamathematical property of formulas such that (a) the axioms have the property, (b) if the premises for an application of a rule of inference have the property, so does the conclusion, and (c) two formulas of the forms A and ¬A cannot both have the property. Then using (a) and (b) every provable formula would have the property, and by (c) the system would be consistent. In this section we shall give a metamathematical proof of consistency for the propositional calculus following this plan.

The property of formulas which will be used is suggested by the logical interpretation of the propositional calculus. We conceive of each proposition letter as a variable whose values are propositions, and we conceive of these propositions as being each either true or false. The operators of the calculus ⊃, &, V, ¬ form from these propositions other propositions whose truth or falsity will depend only on the truth or falsity of the component propositions, according to tables to be given presently. (Hence the operators of the calculus are sometimes called 'truth-value functions of propositions'.) Then it will appear that the provable proposition letter formulas all have the property that they are identically true, in the sense that they represent true propositions for all possible permutations of true and false propositions as values of the proposition letters contained in them.

To use this idea for the purpose of a metamathematical consistency proof for the calculus, it is necessary to avoid the reference to 'propositions', 'truth' and 'falsity', which have connotations that are extraneous to the metamathematics. This we can do, since nothing essential in the argument outlined above depends on the values of the proposition letters being propositions, or on the nature of truth and falsity, except that true and false propositions are distinct from each other.

The purely mathematical character of what we shall do may be emphasized by an analogy to the elementary school arithmetic of positive integers. While the numbers 1, 2, 3, . . . in that arithmetic were intended to have a meaning for counting and measurement, so far as the addition and multiplication tables were concerned they could be any enumeration of distinct objects. From this standpoint, the arithmetic deals with operations, i.e. functions, $+$ and $\cdot$, over a domain of objects $\{1, 2, 3, \ldots\}$, and depends only on the possibility of recognizing and distinguishing between those objects, and not on their intrinsic nature.

We shall now set up an arithmetic in like sense for a domain of only two objects, with four functions $\supset$, &, $\vee$, $\neg$. This describes succinctly what we shall do. Since for metamathematics, $\supset$, &, $\vee$, $\neg$ are meaningless given objects, a more precise statement of what we shall do is the following. We introduce a metamathematical computation process (called a *valuation procedure*), by which a function in the arithmetic (or a table for such a function, called a *truth table*) is correlated to each of the symbols $\supset$, &, $\vee$, $\neg$, and thence to each proposition letter formula. Then we study metamathematical properties of proposition letter formulas defined in terms of the correlated functions (or tables).

Since only the distinctness of the two objects (*truth values*) is required for the abstract arithmetic, it is immaterial what they are called. We might designate them as "0" and "1", or "+" and "−", or "↑" and "↓", or "t" and "f", etc. We choose the last pair of symbols, which suggest respectively the notions 'true' and 'false' of the logical interpretation.

We begin by considering the proposition letters as variables ranging over the domain {t, f}.

We then consider the operators of the calculus as functions over this domain, defined by the following tables, analogous to the addition and multiplication tables in the arithmetic of positive integers. From the table, to any given value(s) of the independent variable(s), the corresponding value of the function can be read.

$\mathcal{A} \supset \mathcal{B}$

	$\mathcal{B}$: t	f
$\mathcal{A}$: t	t	f
f	t	t

$\mathcal{A}$ & $\mathcal{B}$

	$\mathcal{B}$: t	f
$\mathcal{A}$: t	t	f
f	f	f

$\mathcal{A} \vee \mathcal{B}$

	$\mathcal{B}$: t	f
$\mathcal{A}$: t	t	t
f	t	f

$\neg \mathcal{A}$

$\mathcal{A}$: t	f
f	t

(The tables for $\neg$ and $\vee$ are the same as were given in § 10 Example 4 for ′ and $\cdot$, when the two objects are written "0" and "1".)

Then each proposition letter formula A in a given list $P_1, \ldots, P_m$ of distinct proposition letters represents a function of those letters regarded as independent variables over the domain {t, f}. To each m-tuple of values of the letters, the corresponding value of the function can be computed by a series of applications of the fundamental tables.

EXAMPLE 1. The letter formula $\mathcal{A} \sim \mathcal{B}$, i.e. $(\mathcal{A} \supset \mathcal{B}) \& (\mathcal{B} \supset \mathcal{A})$ (§ 26), represents the function which has the following table.

$\mathcal{A} \sim \mathcal{B}$

	$\mathcal{B}$: t	f
$\mathcal{A}$: t	t	f
f	f	t

The computation of the value entered in the upper right square is as follows.

$$(\mathcal{A} \supset \mathcal{B}) \& (\mathcal{B} \supset \mathcal{A})$$
$$(\mathfrak{t} \supset \mathfrak{f}) \& (\mathfrak{f} \supset \mathfrak{t})$$
$$\mathfrak{f} \quad \& \quad \mathfrak{t}$$
$$\mathfrak{f}$$

The square arrangement of the tables is special to two variables (where it helps to suggest properties of the functions). For m variables $P_1, \ldots, P_m$ generally, we can arrange the 2^m possible m-tuples of arguments vertically one below another in some fixed order, and write the corresponding function values in a *value column* opposite these.

EXAMPLE 2.

$\mathcal{A}$	$\mathcal{B}$	$\mathcal{C}$	$\neg[\mathcal{A} \vee \mathcal{B} \supset (\mathcal{B} \& \mathcal{C}) \vee \neg\mathcal{A}]$
t	t	t	f
t	t	f	t
t	f	t	t
t	f	f	t
f	t	t	f
f	t	f	f
f	f	t	f
f	f	f	f

A proposition letter formula E in the distinct proposition letters $P_1, \ldots, P_m$ is said to be *identically true*, if the value column of its table contains only t's; *identically false*, if only f's. Two proposition letter formulas E and F in $P_1, \ldots, P_m$ are said to be *identically equal*, if their tables have the same value column. (In other words, an identically true E represents the constant function t, an identically false E the constant function f, and identically equal E and F the same function.)

These definitions so stated apply to E (to E and F) considered as proposition letter formula(s) in a specified list $P_1, \ldots, P_m$ of distinct proposition letters, not all of which (according to § 25) need occur in the formula(s). We may suppose first that $P_1, \ldots, P_m$ is the minimal eligible list, i.e. the list comprising exactly those distinct proposition letters which occur in E (in E or in F). Then if we add to the list other letters, each row in the table(s) for the formula(s) will simply be split into a number of rows (2^k of them if k letters are added) showing the possible assignments of values to these additional letters, without altering the computation process or value entry. Hence if we have identical truth or identical falsity (identical equality) with respect to the minimal list, we shall have it also with respect to any other list, and conversely. Therefore the reference to the list may be omitted.

THEOREM 9. *A necessary condition that a proposition letter formula* E *be provable* (*or deducible from identically true formulas* Γ) *in the propositional calculus is that it be identically true; i.e. if* ⊢ E, *then* E *is identically true.*

Proof is by course-of-values induction on the length of the given proof of E, using the two following lemmas.

LEMMA 12a. *A proposition letter formula which is an axiom is identically true.*

PROOF. For each of the ten axiom schemata of the propositional calculus (Postulates 1a, 1b, 3 — 8 § 19, or intuitionistically 8^{I} § 23 instead of 8), we can easily verify the following fact by computation: The table which is obtained by assigning the values t and f in all possible ways directly to the parts A, B, C which appear in the schema contains only t's in the value column. This amounts to verifying the lemma treating the A, B, C of the schemata as simple proposition letters $\mathcal{A}$, $\mathcal{B}$, $\mathcal{C}$.

The truth of the lemma follows from this. For consider any axiom which is a proposition letter formula. This comes from one of the schemata by taking as the A, B, C certain proposition letter formulas in say $P_1, \ldots P_m$ as joint list of distinct proposition letters. Now no matter what m-tuple of t's and f's is assigned as values to $P_1, \ldots P_m$, the triple of values for A, B, C to which it leads must in turn (as already verified) lead to the value t for the whole axiom.

LEMMA 12b. *If the premises for an application of the rule of inference are identically true proposition letter formulas, so is the conclusion.*

PROOF. By inspection of the following table, we see that the only pair of values of A, B which gives the value t to both premises A and A ⊃ B for the rule of inference of the calculus (Postulate 2) is the pair t, t; and this pair does give the value t to the conclusion B.

A	B	A	A ⊃ B	B
t	t	t	t	t
t	f	t	f	f
f	t	f	t	t
f	f	f	t	f

Hence, if A and B are proposition letter formulas in $P_1, \ldots, P_m$, any m-tuple of values of $P_1, \ldots, P_m$ which gives both premises the value t must give this value also to the conclusion. By hypothesis, the premises have the value t for all m-tuples of values of $P_1, \ldots, P_m$. Therefore the conclusion has also.

EXAMPLE 3. The formula $\neg[\mathcal{A} \vee \mathcal{B} \supset (\mathcal{B} \& \mathcal{C}) \vee \neg\mathcal{A}]$ is not provable in the propositional calculus, because there are f's in the value column of its table (Example 2). Likewise, $\mathcal{A} \vee (\neg\mathcal{A} \& \mathcal{B})$ is not provable, because it takes the value f when $\mathcal{A}$, $\mathcal{B}$ take the values f, f.

COROLLARY 1. *A necessary condition that two proposition letter formulas* E *and* F *be equivalent is that* E *and* F *be identically equal; i.e. if* $\vdash$ E $\sim$ F, *then* E *and* F *are identically equal.*

PROOF. If E and F are equivalent, then by definition of equivalence, E $\sim$ F is provable. Hence by the theorem, E $\sim$ F is identically true. Referring to the table for $\sim$ (Example 1), we see that E $\sim$ F can only receive the value t when E and F receive either both the value t or both the value f, i.e. when they receive the same value. Since E $\sim$ F is identically true, i.e. does always receive the value t, E and F do always receive the same value, i.e. they are identically equal.

EXAMPLE 4. $\mathcal{A} \& \mathcal{B} \& \neg\mathcal{B}$ and $\mathcal{A}$ are not equivalent, because they take different values (namely, f and t, respectively) when e.g. $\mathcal{A}$, $\mathcal{B}$ are given the values t, t

COROLLARY 2. *The propositional calculus is (simply) consistent; i.e. for no formula* A, *both* $\vdash$ A *and* $\vdash \neg$A.

PROOF. Using the second version of the definition of simple consistency (above), this is already proved by Example 3.

To give the proof directly from the original definition, suppose one of A and $\neg$A is provable. Then by the theorem it is identically true; then using the table for $\neg$, the other is identically false, hence not identically true, and hence by the theorem unprovable.

This establishes the consistency for the propositional calculus in terms of proposition letter formulas. If A* and ¬A* be provable formulas in the calculus for another notion of formula, then by the converse of the substitution rule (Theorem 4 § 25), there would be provable proposition letter formulas A and ¬A. Thus the consistency extends to the other senses of formula.

This consistency proof, of course, does not hold good for the addition of another group of postulates, even should that group by itself be consistent.

The consistency proof for the propositional calculus was first given by Post 1921. (Cf. also Łukasiewicz 1925, Hilbert-Ackermann 1928.)

The arithmetic of a domain of two objects, used in this section to give the consistency proof, may be thought of as *an* interpretation of the calculus in the following sense. The valuation tables provide arithmetical significances for the operators of the calculus. The proposition letters are considered as independent variables ranging over the domain {t, f} of the arithmetic. Each proposition letter formula is interpreted as expressing the proposition that its value is t for all choices of the values of its independent variables. By Theorem 9, only formulas which are true under this interpretation are provable. For the proposition expressed by a formula under this interpretation is equivalent to the formula's having the metamathematical property of identical truth, as defined above in terms of a computation procedure using t and f.

On the other hand, in *the* (*usual*) *logical interpretation*, the proposition letters are considered as independent variables ranging over some domain of propositions. A proposition letter formula then expresses the general proposition that all the particular propositions, expressed by it for different choices of propositions from that domain as values of its independent variables, are true. The logical interpretation is related to the arithmetical interpretation by putting the particular propositions (from the domain considered) into many-one correspondence with the two objects t, f, those propositions which correspond to t being true and those which correspond to f being false. The proposition expressed by a formula under this interpretation is not equivalent to a metamathematically definable property of the formula, except for specially restricted domains of the propositions allowed as values of the proposition letters.

§ 29. Completeness, normal form. Another problem which we may be able to treat in metamathematics is that of the 'completeness' of a given formal system. For example, we have listed eleven postulates for the propositional calculus (§ 19). Can we give a reason why we stop with just these? Might we with advantage attempt to discover others which could be added to the list to give more provable formulas? To be able to answer these questions, we must first provide some criterion as to what we want to be able to prove in the system. Different notions of completeness will result according to the criterion chosen.

We may give the criterion a positive form, and say that the system is complete, if its postulate list already provides all we need for some purpose. For example, suppose that some property has been defined for formulas of the system; or alternatively, that an interpretation has been given to the formulas of the system, in which case the property is that the formulas express true propositions under the interpretation. Relative to such a property or interpretation, definitions of both consistency and completeness can be given as follows.

The system is *consistent* with respect to the property (or interpretation), if only formulas which have the property (or express true propositions under the interpretation) are provable. The system is *complete* with respect to the property (or interpretation), if all formulas which have the property (or express true propositions under the interpretation) are provable.

Unlike the notion of simple consistency given in the preceding section, these notions of consistency and completeness relative to a property or interpretation may not always belong to metamathematics. Whether or not they do we shall have to consider from case to case, according to whether the property (or interpretation) is one which can be formulated within metamathematics.

For the propositional calculus we have the property of identical truth (or if we prefer, the interpretation of the calculus as an arithmetic of a domain of two objects), which can be formulated in metamathematics. Theorem 9 is thus a metamathematical consistency theorem for a certain property of letter formulas (or interpretation of the calculus).

To recapitulate the idea of completeness relative to an interpretation: A system is complete under a given interpretation, if the deductive postulates (or transformation rules) enable us to prove in the system all the true propositions which its formation rules enable us to express in the system.

We are led to other formulations of completeness, if we give the criterion for what formulas should be provable a negative form, and say that the system is complete, if the postulates provide all that we can afford to have lest some undesirable effect ensue. An effect which comes to mind is simple inconsistency. The completeness notions obtained in this way will always be metamathematical, if the effect to be avoided is metamathematically describable (as in particular simple inconsistency is). Exact formulations will be given for particular formal systems as we come to them.

Notice that a consistency theorem will always be a theorem to the effect that at most such and such formulas are provable; and a completeness theorem one to the effect that at least such and such formulas are provable.

From this general introduction to the problem of completeness, we turn now to consider it for the propositional calculus. We shall show first (Theorem 10) that the calculus is complete with respect to the property of identical truth.

THEOREM 10° AND COROLLARY 1°. *The conditions of Theorem* 9 *and Corollary* 1 *are sufficient* (as well as necessary); *i.e. if* E *is identically true, then* $\vdash$ E, *and if* E *and* F *are identically equal, then* $\vdash \mathrm{E} \sim \mathrm{F}$.

The proof will be based on two lemmas. Let $\mathrm{P}_1, \ldots, \mathrm{P}_m$ be distinct proposition letters. Given an m-tuple of t's and f's as values of $\mathrm{P}_1, \ldots, \mathrm{P}_m$, by the *corresponding letter m-tuple* we shall mean the sequence $\mathrm{Q}_1, \ldots, \mathrm{Q}_m$ of letters and negated letters where, for each j ($j = 1, \ldots, m$), Q_j is P_j or $\neg \mathrm{P}_j$ according as the given value of P_j is t or f.

EXAMPLE 1. Let $\mathcal{A}$, $\mathcal{B}$, $\mathcal{C}$ take the values t, f, t, respectively. The corresponding letter m-tuple is $\mathcal{A}$, $\neg\mathcal{B}$, $\mathcal{C}$.

LEMMA 13. *Let* E *be a proposition letter formula in the distinct proposition letters* $\mathrm{P}_1, \ldots, \mathrm{P}_m$; *let an m-tuple of* t's *and* f's *be given as values of* $\mathrm{P}_1, \ldots, \mathrm{P}_m$; *and let* $\mathrm{Q}_1, \ldots, \mathrm{Q}_m$ *be the corresponding letter m-tuple. Then* $\mathrm{Q}_1, \ldots, \mathrm{Q}_m \vdash \mathrm{E}$ *or* $\mathrm{Q}_1, \ldots, \mathrm{Q}_m \vdash \neg\mathrm{E}$, *according as for the given m-tuple of values* E *takes the value* t *or the value* f.

EXAMPLE 2. Corresponding to the table in Example 2 § 28 for $\neg[\mathcal{A} \vee \mathcal{B} \supset (\mathcal{B} \,\&\, \mathcal{C}) \vee \neg\mathcal{A}]$, we now have eight deductions:

$$\begin{array}{rrrl}
\mathcal{A}, & \mathcal{B}, & \mathcal{C} & \vdash \neg\neg[\mathcal{A} \vee \mathcal{B} \supset (\mathcal{B} \,\&\, \mathcal{C}) \vee \neg\mathcal{A}]. \\
\mathcal{A}, & \mathcal{B}, & \neg\mathcal{C} & \vdash \neg[\mathcal{A} \vee \mathcal{B} \supset (\mathcal{B} \,\&\, \mathcal{C}) \vee \neg\mathcal{A}]. \\
\mathcal{A}, & \neg\mathcal{B}, & \mathcal{C} & \vdash \neg[\mathcal{A} \vee \mathcal{B} \supset (\mathcal{B} \,\&\, \mathcal{C}) \vee \neg\mathcal{A}]. \\
\mathcal{A}, & \neg\mathcal{B}, & \neg\mathcal{C} & \vdash \neg[\mathcal{A} \vee \mathcal{B} \supset (\mathcal{B} \,\&\, \mathcal{C}) \vee \neg\mathcal{A}]. \\
\neg\mathcal{A}, & \mathcal{B}, & \mathcal{C} & \vdash \neg\neg[\mathcal{A} \vee \mathcal{B} \supset (\mathcal{B} \,\&\, \mathcal{C}) \vee \neg\mathcal{A}]. \\
\neg\mathcal{A}, & \mathcal{B}, & \neg\mathcal{C} & \vdash \neg\neg[\mathcal{A} \vee \mathcal{B} \supset (\mathcal{B} \,\&\, \mathcal{C}) \vee \neg\mathcal{A}]. \\
\neg\mathcal{A}, & \neg\mathcal{B}, & \mathcal{C} & \vdash \neg\neg[\mathcal{A} \vee \mathcal{B} \supset (\mathcal{B} \,\&\, \mathcal{C}) \vee \neg\mathcal{A}]. \\
\neg\mathcal{A}, & \neg\mathcal{B}, & \neg\mathcal{C} & \vdash \neg\neg[\mathcal{A} \vee \mathcal{B} \supset (\mathcal{B} \,\&\, \mathcal{C}) \vee \neg\mathcal{A}].
\end{array}$$

PROOF OF LEMMA 13, by course-of-values induction on the number of (occurrences of) logical symbols in E; call this number the *degree.*

BASIS: E is of degree 0. Then E is P_j for some j. In the given m-tuple of values, the value of P_j is $\mathfrak{t}$ or is $\mathfrak{f}$. CASE 1: the value of P_j is $\mathfrak{t}$. Then Q_j is P_j, i.e. Q_j is E; and so by general properties of $\vdash$, $Q_1, \ldots, Q_m \vdash E$, as was to be shown since in this case E takes the value $\mathfrak{t}$. CASE 2: the value of P_j is $\mathfrak{f}$. Then similarly Q_j is $\neg E$, and so $Q_1, \ldots, Q_m \vdash \neg E$, as was to be shown.

INDUCTION STEP: E is of degree $d+1$. Then for some proposition letter formulas A and B in $P_1, \ldots, P_m$ of degrees $\leq d$, E is $A \supset B$ or $A \,\&\, B$ or $A \vee B$ or $\neg A$. CASE 1: E is $A \supset B$. Four subcases arise, according as for the given m-tuple of values of $P_1, \ldots, P_m$, the formulas A, B take the respective values $\mathfrak{t}, \mathfrak{t}$ or $\mathfrak{t}, \mathfrak{f}$ or $\mathfrak{f}, \mathfrak{t}$ or $\mathfrak{f}, \mathfrak{f}$. SUBCASE 2: A, B take the values $\mathfrak{t}, \mathfrak{f}$. Then (by the upper right entry in the table for $\supset$) E takes the value $\mathfrak{f}$, so we are to show that $Q_1, \ldots, Q_m \vdash \neg E$. But by the hypothesis of the induction, $Q_1, \ldots, Q_m \vdash A$ and $Q_1, \ldots, Q_m \vdash \neg B$. Also, using *41 or *44, $A, \neg B \vdash \neg(A \supset B)$; i.e. $A, \neg B \vdash \neg E$. Hence $Q_1, \ldots, Q_m \vdash \neg E$, as was to be shown. The treatment of the other cases and subcases is similar, using *41—*48, *49a.

LEMMA 14. *Let* E *be a proposition letter formula in the distinct proposition letters* $P_1, \ldots, P_m$. *If for each of the* 2^m *m-tuples of* $\mathfrak{t}$'s *and* $\mathfrak{f}$'s, $Q_1, \ldots, Q_m \vdash E$ *where* $Q_1, \ldots, Q_m$ *is the corresponding letter m-tuple, then* $P_1 \vee \neg P_1, \ldots, P_m \vee \neg P_m \vdash E$.

PROOF OF LEMMA 14. By $2^{m-1} + 2^{m-2} + \ldots + 1$ applications of $\vee$-elimination. For example when $m = 2$, by hypothesis:

$$\text{(a)} \qquad \begin{cases} P_1, \quad P_2 \vdash E. \\ P_1, \neg P_2 \vdash E. \\ \neg P_1, \quad P_2 \vdash E. \\ \neg P_1, \neg P_2 \vdash E. \end{cases}$$

By two applications of $\vee$-elimination:

$$\text{(b)} \qquad \begin{cases} P_1, P_2 \vee \neg P_2 \vdash E. \\ \neg P_1, P_2 \vee \neg P_2 \vdash E. \end{cases}$$

By one additional application,

$$\text{(c)} \qquad P_1 \vee \neg P_1, P_2 \vee \neg P_2 \vdash E,$$

as was to be shown.

PROOF OF THEOREM 10. Say E is a proposition letter formula in $P_1, \ldots, P_m$. By hypothesis E is identically true, i.e. takes the value $\mathfrak{t}$

for each m-tuple of t's and f's as values of $P_1, \ldots, P_m$. Then by Lemma 13, the hypothesis of Lemma 14 is satisfied; so by Lemma 14, $P_1 \vee \neg P_1, \ldots, P_m \vee \neg P_m \vdash E$. Thence using *51, $\vdash E$.

REMARK 1. All but the final step of this proof is good for the intuitionistic system also. Hence in that, for any letter formula E in $P_1, \ldots, P_m$:

(a) $P_1 \vee \neg P_1, \ldots, P_m \vee \neg P_m \vdash E$, if E is identically true.

(b) $P_1 \vee \neg P_1, \ldots, P_m \vee \neg P_m \vdash E \vee \neg E$.

The theorem expresses the completeness of the deductive rules of the propositional calculus for the purpose of establishing letter formulas which are identically true under the arithmetic interpretation; and Corollary 1 says that the deductive theory gives a complete account of the equality of functions definable in the arithmetic.

COROLLARY 2°. *The addition to the postulate list for the propositional calculus of an unprovable letter formula for use as an axiom schema would destroy the simple consistency.*

PROOF. By Theorem 10, this letter formula must receive the value f for some set of values of the proposition letters which it contains. Select such a set of values, and use the new axiom schema by substituting $\mathcal{A} \vee \neg \mathcal{A}$ for the letters which have the value t, and $\mathcal{A} \& \neg \mathcal{A}$ for those which have the value f. The resulting new axiom would be identically false. Hence by Corollary 1 it would be equivalent to $\mathcal{A} \& \neg \mathcal{A}$ which is also identically false. So (using *18a) $\mathcal{A} \& \neg \mathcal{A}$ would also be provable, and the system would thus be inconsistent (§ 28).

Corollary 2 says that the propositional calculus is incapable of being enlarged by postulates of the same character as those already listed without destroying the simple consistency. This is a completeness property of the second type described in the introductory remarks.

Given an m-tuple of t's and f's as values of $P_1, \ldots, P_m$, and letting $Q_1, \ldots, Q_m$ be the corresponding letter m-tuple, we call $Q_1 \& \ldots \& Q_m$ ($Q_1^{\dagger} \vee \ldots \vee Q_m^{\dagger}$, § 27) the *corresponding elementary conjunction* (*disjunction*).

EXAMPLE 1 (concluded). The corresponding elementary conjunction (disjunction) is $\mathcal{A} \& \neg \mathcal{B} \& \mathcal{C}$ ($\neg \mathcal{A} \vee \mathcal{B} \vee \neg \mathcal{C}$).

THEOREM 11°. *A proposition letter formula* E *in the distinct proposition letters* $P_1, \ldots, P_m$ *is equivalent to a formula* F (called a *principal disjunctive normal form of* E) *having one of two forms, as follows. If* E *takes the value* t *for some m-tuples of* t's *and* f's *as values of* $P_1, \ldots, P_m$, *then* F *is the disjunction (in some order) of the corresponding elementary conjunctions. If* E *is identically false, then* F *is* $P_1 \& \neg P_1$. (*Dually,* E *has a principal conjunctive normal form* G, *in which the roles of* V *and* & *and of* t *and* f *are interchanged;* $\vdash E \sim G$).

Example 2 (continued)°. $\neg[\mathcal{A} \vee \mathcal{B} \supset (\mathcal{B} \& \mathcal{C}) \vee \neg \mathcal{A}]$ has as a p.d.n.f. $(\mathcal{A} \& \mathcal{B} \& \neg \mathcal{C}) \vee (\mathcal{A} \& \neg \mathcal{B} \& \mathcal{C}) \vee (\mathcal{A} \& \neg \mathcal{B} \& \neg \mathcal{C})$, and as a p.c.n.f. $\neg\mathcal{A} \vee \neg\mathcal{B} \vee \neg\mathcal{C} \& \mathcal{A} \vee \neg\mathcal{B} \vee \neg\mathcal{C} \& \mathcal{A} \vee \neg\mathcal{B} \vee \mathcal{C} \& \mathcal{A} \vee \mathcal{B} \vee \neg\mathcal{C} \& \mathcal{A} \vee \mathcal{B} \vee \mathcal{C}$.

Proof. By Theorem 10 Corollary 1, since (as is easily seen from the specified form of a p.d.n.f., and the valuation tables for ¬, &, V) E and F are identically equal.

The propositional calculus, besides being deductively complete in two senses (Theorem 10 and Corollary 2), is also notationally complete in the sense that each of the 2^{2^m} possible truth-value functions of m variables $P_1, \ldots, P_m$ can be represented by a letter formula in those letters. For, given the table for the function, we can build a p.d.n.f. (uniquely determined to within the order of its disjunctive members) to represent it.

These three completeness results appeared first in Post 1921; the present method of proof of Theorem 10 is due to Kalmár 1934-5. (The writer also used it, as an application of V-elimination in another context, in a first draft of 1934.)

Hilbert and Ackermann 1928 gave a version of Post's proof, which consists in establishing the normal form theorem first, by reduction techniques going back in part to the nineteenth century workers on symbolic logic. Briefly, a letter formula E can be reduced to a p.d.n.f. (or p.c.n.f.), using the chain method § 26, as follows. First, *58 or *59 is used to remove the occurrences of ⊃. Second, the occurrences of ¬ are transferred to the interior by repeated applications of Theorem 8. Third, the resulting expression is "multiplied out" using the distributive law *35 (with *33) as in ordinary algebra with V, & in the role of +, · (or vice versa, using *36 with *34, for p.c.n.f.). Fourth, simplifications are performed, based (besides on *31—*34) on the idempotent laws *37, *38 and on *52—*55, so that the resulting disjunctive members (for p.c.n.f., conjunctive members) or "terms" contain each at most one occurrence of each letter, except if the p.d.n.f. $P_1 \& \neg P_1$ (the p.c.n.f. $P_1 \vee \neg P_1$) is reached. Fifth, in the non-exceptional case, missing letters are introduced into the terms using *52 and *35 (*53 and *36). Sixth, using *31—*34, *37, *38, the letters and negated letters are brought to the normal order within terms, so that the terms become elementary conjunctions (elementary disjunctions), and duplications of terms are suppressed.

EXAMPLE 2 (concluded)°. Although our proof of Theorem 11 establishes that $\neg[\mathcal{A} \vee \mathcal{B} \supset (\mathcal{B} \,\&\, C) \vee \neg \mathcal{A}]$ is equivalent to

$$(\mathcal{A} \,\&\, \mathcal{B} \,\&\, \neg C) \vee (\mathcal{A} \,\&\, \neg \mathcal{B} \,\&\, C) \vee (\mathcal{A} \,\&\, \neg \mathcal{B} \,\&\, \neg C),$$

the reader may find it of interest to reduce the one to the other by the procedure just described. The fourth operation leads to $(\mathcal{A} \,\&\, \neg \mathcal{B}) \vee (\mathcal{A} \,\&\, \neg C) \vee (\mathcal{B} \,\&\, \neg C \,\&\, \mathcal{A})$. — From this by *40 we get as a "disjunctive normal form" (not "principal") $(\mathcal{A} \,\&\, \neg \mathcal{B}) \vee (\mathcal{A} \,\&\, \neg C)$, and thence using *35 the still shorter equivalent (not a d.n.f.) $\mathcal{A} \,\&\, (\neg \mathcal{B} \vee \neg C)$.

§ 30. Decision procedure, interpretation. We know examples in mathematics of general questions, such that any particular instance of the question can be answered by a preassigned uniform method. More precisely, in such an example, there is an infinite class of particular questions, and a procedure in relation to that class, both being described in advance, such that if we thereafter select any particular question of the class, the procedure will surely apply and lead us to a definite answer, either "yes" or "no", to the particular question selected.

EXAMPLE 1. Let $f(x)$ and $g(x)$ be polynomials with given integral coefficients. Is $f(x)$ a factor of $g(x)$? We can divide $g(x)$ by $f(x)$. This division is performable step by step by a preassigned method. It will terminate in a finite number of steps (how many will depend on how we count the steps, but this could be made precise so that the number will depend on the degrees of the polynomials and the size of the coefficients). We shall then have the remainder before us. This remainder we can recognize to be either 0 or different from 0. If it is 0, the answer to the question is "yes". If it is different from 0, the answer is "no".

EXAMPLE 2. Does the equation $ax + by = c$, where a, b, c are given integers, have a solution in integers for x and y? There is a well-known method for answering the question, using Euclid's algorithm.

A method of this sort, which suffices to answer, either by "yes" or by "no", any particular instance of a general question, we call a *decision procedure* or *decision method* or *algorithm* for the question. The problem of finding such a method we shall call the *decision problem* for the question. The problem appears in modern logic with Schröder 1895, Löwenheim 1915 and Hilbert 1918. The present account is only introductory, and we shall attempt a more precise definition of what constitutes a decision method later (§§ 60, 61). For the present, it will be enough that we should be able to recognize particular examples of decision procedures.

Similarly, we may have a *calculation procedure* or *algorithm* (and hence a *calculation problem*) in relation to a general question which requires for an answer, not "yes" or "no", but the exhibiting of some object.

Now, in connection with a given formal system, such as the one we have been studying, there are some general questions, such as 'Is a given formal expression a formula?' and 'Is a given finite sequence of formal expressions a proof?', for which a decision method is provided directly by the definitions establishing the system. In fact, this must be the case if the formalization by means of the system is to accomplish what was intended. Of a different nature is the question 'Is a given formula provable?' To see this difference, let us compare the definitions of the three notions: 'formula', 'proof', 'provable formula'. For each of the three definitions, in applying it to a particular given object, we have to recognize that the given object belongs to the class defined (if it does belong) through the consideration of a sequence of objects, namely respectively: the formulas obtained on the way in the construction of the given formula, the segments of the given proof, the formulas in a proof of the given provable formula. In the cases of formula and proof, this sequence of objects is contained within the given object, from which it can be regained for our consideration. But in the case of provable formula, this sequence of objects is not contained within the given object. Hence, for the last question, if a decision method exists, it must consist in something else than a direct or nearly direct application of the definition, and the decision problem for this question is not trivial. It is often called *the decision problem* for the formal system. This problem is solved for the pure propositional calculus by Theorems 9 and 10 (§§ 28, 29):

THEOREM 12°. *A decision procedure (or algorithm) for determining whether or not a proposition letter formula* E *is provable in the propositional calculus is afforded by the process of calculating the table for the function of* t *and* f *represented by* E. *According as only* t's *occur in the value column or not,* E *is provable or not.*

Furthermore, the decision procedure extends to the other senses of formula, as we may first pass to a corresponding letter formula by simultaneously replacing the distinct prime components by respective distinct proposition letters (Theorems 3 and 4 § 25). A decision procedure for equivalence is included in that for provability, by the definition of equivalence (§ 26), or can be based similarly on the Corollaries 1. The decision problem for deducibility is reduced to that for provability by noting, from the derived rules for $\supset$ and & (Theorem 2 § 23) that, in the propositional calculus, $D_1, \ldots, D_l \vdash E$ if and only if $\vdash D_1 \& \ldots \& D_l \supset E$. (A second set of decision procedures is afforded by the process of reduction to p.d.n.f., end § 29.)

INTERPRETATION. Our metamathematical result that the propositional calculus admits an arithmetical interpretation, with two objects $\mathfrak{t}$, $\mathfrak{f}$ in the arithmetic, illuminates the usual logical interpretation (cf. end of § 28). We see that our propositional calculus is a suitable logical instrument (1) when the particular propositions are such that each is definitely either true or false, or (2) when we wish to make it an assumption of a theory which we are developing that each is either true or false. For an intuitionist, Situation (1) is represented in the mathematics of a finite domain of objects, and also in reasoning with propositions about the objects of an infinite domain when those propositions are of a type for which there are decision procedures (cf. Remark 1 § 29). The use of the propositional calculus in classical mathematics can be taken as an example of Situation (2).

The truth tables now make it definite exactly how the operators of the calculus are to be interpreted as truth-value functions of propositions. For example, we see that $\vee$ is the *inclusive* 'or': $A \vee B$ is true, if either A is true or B is true or both. (The *exclusive* 'or' is expressible thus: $(A \vee B) \& \neg(A \& B)$.)

The implication $A \supset B$ means the same as $\neg A \vee B$ (*59 § 27), and is called *material implication*. The holding of $A \supset B$ does not require a necessary connection of ideas between A and B. For example, the moon is made of green cheese materially implies $2+2=5$ (because the premise is false). Fermat's "last theorem" materially implies $2+2=4$ (because the conclusion is true). This is considered paradoxical by some writers (Lewis 1912, 1917). Without attempting to enter fully into a controversial question, we offer the following brief remarks. The role of material implication is best understood, when it is considered in a wider context, such as that provided by the full number-theoretic system. $\forall x(A(x) \supset B(x))$ expresses a relationship between A(x) and B(x) as variable propositions (or 'propositional functions of x'), called *formal implication*. The property of material implication of holding whenever the first member is false, when the material implication is used in combination with generality to build a formal implication, allows a theorem $\forall x(A(x) \supset B(x))$ to hold *vacuously* for certain values of x. This is a device, of a piece with the admission of 0 into the number system and of the vacuous set into the theory of sets, which conduces to simpler and more comprehensive formulations of theorems. The same is true of the property of material implication of holding whenever the second member is true. From the standpoint of lay English, $\supset$ is probably better rendered as "if ..., then ..." or "only if". Notwithstanding, "implication" is a handy name for $\supset$. In using it, we follow the practice common in mathematics of employing the same designation for analogous notions arising in related technical theories. (An example is the many different kinds of "addition" and "multiplication" in mathematics.) The operator $\supset$ does have the character of an implication in our formal system, in consequence of the two properties of it expressed by the deduction theorem and Rule 2 (i.e. the two $\supset$-rules of Theorem 2). So it does represent logical consequence, not in some a priori sense, but in the sense defined for the formal system by the deductive postulates of the system.

Other forms of the calculus. In view of *56—*61, the notational completeness of the propositional calculus (end of § 29) could have been obtained by taking $\neg$ and only one of the three other operators $\supset$, &, $\vee$ as primitive operators for the calculus (formal symbols), and defining the other two of $\supset$, &, $\vee$ from those as symbols of abbreviation (as $\sim$ was defined in § 26). The still further reduction can be made to a single primitive operator | (called 'alternative denial', or the 'Sheffer stroke', 1913*), with the table:

$\mathcal{A} \mid \mathcal{B}$

	$\mathcal{B}$	t	f
$\mathcal{A}$	t	f	t
	f	t	t

Thence one defines $\neg\mathcal{A}$ as $\mathcal{A} \mid \mathcal{A}$, and $\mathcal{A} \vee \mathcal{B}$ as $(\neg\mathcal{A}) \mid (\neg\mathcal{B})$.

The propositional calculus may be set up taking the substitution rule, which we derived as a subsidiary deduction rule in Theorem 3 § 25, instead as a direct postulated rule:

$$\frac{\text{E}}{\text{E}^*.}$$

In this case, the proposition letters are called *proposition variables*, and particular axioms using the formal variables $\mathcal{A}$, $\mathcal{B}$, C can be used in place of the axiom schemata using the metamathematical variables "A", "B", "C". The direct substitution rule is usually construed to apply to a single variable at a time (cf. Remark 1 § 25).

EXAMPLE 3. We then have $\mathcal{A} \supset (\mathcal{B} \supset \mathcal{A})$ as Axiom 1a. To construct thence a proof of A ⊃ (B ⊃ A), for any given formulas A and B, we proceed thus. If A does not contain $\mathcal{B}$, first substitute A for $\mathcal{A}$, then B for $\mathcal{B}$. If A contains $\mathcal{B}$, let P be a proposition letter distinct from $\mathcal{A}$ and not occurring in A, and substitute successively P for $\mathcal{B}$, A for $\mathcal{A}$, B for P.

This is the more usual method of setting up the propositional calculus; the method we have chosen using axiom schemata is due to von Neumann 1927. In either case, the rules of inference must have the character of schemata, i.e. they must employ metamathematical variables, since infinitely many applications have to be provided for. For the calculus with the direct substitution rule, while the provability notion is the same (as the reader may demonstrate), the deducibility relation is more extensive. The deduction theorem, and other subsidiary deduction rules depending on it, must then carry a restriction on the use of proposition variables in the subsidiary deductions, stated with reference to applications of the new substitution rule exactly like the one we have stated with reference to Rules 9 and 12 for individual variables in the predicate calculus.

With either of these variations in the way of setting up the propositional calculus as a formal system (and there exist others), we still have essentially the same calculus. Allowing for differences in the selection of the operators, the class of provable formulas and the interpretation as an arithmetic of two objects remain the same. All these systems, and the common theory if we abstract from the particular formulation, may be called *classical* or *two-valued propositional calculus*.

OTHER PROPOSITIONAL CALCULI. There are other systems of propositional calculus, which are propositional calculi in that they analyze propositions only with respect to how they are formed from other propositions taken as wholes, and which have therefore a definition of formula of the same character (to within the particular choice of operators), but which differ essentially from the system studied here.

One class of examples is obtained by generalizing from the two-valued propositional calculus to the *n-valued propositional calculi* for any positive integer $n \geq 2$. These for $n > 2$ were discussed by Lukasiewicz 1920 ($n = 3$) and Post 1921 (any n). They are calculi which can be treated on the basis of truth tables in an arithmetic of n objects, as the classical system is treated on the basis of two. (Cf. e.g. Łukasiewicz and Tarski 1930, Rosser and Turquette 1945, 1949, 1952.)

Another example is the *intuitionistic propositional calculus* (Heyting

1930), which is intended as a formalization of intuitionistic mathematical reasoning with propositions. As noted in § 23, we obtain a postulate list for it (for the intuitionistic predicate calculus) from our postulate group A1 (group A) simply by replacing Axiom Schema 8 by Axiom Schema 8^{I}. This is not Heyting's original postulate list, but one suggested by Gentzen's 1934-5. (Heyting's postulates for the predicate calculus are in 1930a.) Whether our numbered results and italicized theorems marked with the symbol "°" as not being established intuitionistically, so far as our discussion has gone, actually do not hold for the intuitionistic system is a question which in each case requires further consideration. We shall return to this later in the book (§§ 80, 82). The result of this section, that a decision procedure exists for the propositional calculus, is one such result which does hold for the intuitionistic system (Theorem 56 (d) § 80). It is known that in the intuitionistic propositional calculus none of the four operators can be expressed in terms of the remaining ones (Wajsberg 1938, McKinsey 1939); and that the calculus cannot be treated on the basis of truth tables for any finite n (Gödel 1932), but can be for $n = \aleph_0$ (Jaśkowski 1936*).

Still further apart from the standpoint of the classical calculus studied here are the *propositional calculi of strict implication* (Lewis 1912), and the *modal propositional calculi* which deal with 'possibility', 'necessity', etc. (Cf. Lewis and Langford 1932, Feys 1937-8, McKinsey and Tarski 1948, Feys 1965*.)

Chapter VII

THE PREDICATE CALCULUS

§31. Predicate letter formulas. In this chapter, we study the part of the formal system obtained by using exactly the postulates of Group A.

The propositional calculus, studied in the preceding chapter, is a formalization of logical relationships which depend only on the analysis of the way certain propositions are composed out of simpler propositions, using operations of composition in which the simpler propositions enter as unanalyzed wholes.

In the predicate calculus, the analysis goes a step further, and we are allowed to consider also what may be called the 'subject-predicate' structure of the simpler propositions, and to use operations of composition which depend on that structure.

This analysis still does not take into account all features of the structure of number-theoretic propositions. This we can emphasize, just as in the preceding chapter, by introducing an alternative notion of formula, which eliminates the irrelevant details of the number-theoretic definition of formula, and leaves the way open to other applications as well.

We start by introducing formal expressions of a new species, constituting a generalization of the proposition letters introduced in § 25, as follows,

$$\mathcal{A},\ \mathcal{A}(a),\ \mathcal{A}(a, b), \ldots,\ \mathcal{B},\ \mathcal{B}(a),\ \mathcal{B}(a, b), \ldots,\ \mathcal{C},\ \mathcal{C}(a),\ \mathcal{C}(a, b), \ldots.$$

These expressions we call *predicate letters* (*with attached* or *name form variables*). Each of the symbols formerly used as a proposition letter forms a different predicate letter with each different number $n \geq 0$ of attached variables, and for $n = 0$ a predicate letter is a proposition letter. The n attached variables may be any n distinct variables. Different choices of the n attached variables with a given predicate letter are said to give different *name forms* of the same predicate letter, e.g. $\mathcal{A}(a, b)$, $\mathcal{A}(b, a)$ and $\mathcal{A}(c, d)$ are three name forms of the predicate letter formed by using $\mathcal{A}$ with two attached variables, but $\mathcal{A}(a)$ and $\mathcal{A}(a, b, c)$ are other predicate letters, and $\mathcal{A}(a, a)$ is not a predicate letter. It ordinarily suffices throughout a discussion to consider each of the distinct predicate letters employed in the discussion as represented by just one name form, i.e. as taken with a fixed sequence of n attached variables throughout the discussion; and usually we take these n attached variables to be the first n variables in order from a given infinite list $a_1, a_2, a_3, \ldots$ of variables (usually here the list $a, b, c, \ldots$).

For the definition of *predicate letter formula*, given inductively as follows, the only terms shall be the variables. However we elect to say "term" at some places and "variable" at others, so that it will be clear how the discussion generalizes, if we later wish to allow a wider class of terms than simply the variables.

1. If $P(a_1, \ldots, a_n)$ is a predicate letter with attached variables, and $t_1, \ldots, t_n$ are terms, then $P(t_1, \ldots, t_n)$ is a *formula*. 2 — 5. If A and B are *formulas*, then $(A) \supset (B)$, $(A) \& (B)$, $(A) \vee (B)$ and $\neg(A)$ are *formulas*. 6 — 7. If x is a variable, and A(x) is a *formula*, then $\forall x(A(x))$ and $\exists x(A(x))$ are *formulas*. 8. The only *formulas* are those given by 1 — 7.

Example 1. By 1, $\mathcal{A}(b, a)$, $\mathcal{B}$, $\mathcal{A}(a, b)$ and $\mathcal{A}(a, a)$ are predicate letter formulas. Here it suffices to start from the two name forms $\mathcal{A}(a, b)$ and $\mathcal{B}$. By successive applications of 3 and 2 (omitting parentheses under the usual conventions § 17), $\mathcal{A}(b, a) \& \mathcal{B}$ and $\mathcal{A}(b, a) \& \mathcal{B} \supset \mathcal{A}(a, b)$ are predicate letter formulas. Finally by 6, $\forall b(\mathcal{A}(b, a) \& \mathcal{B} \supset \mathcal{A}(a, b))$ is a predicate letter formula.

For this chapter, when we say "term" and "formula" without specifying the senses, the words may be understood either in the respective senses of free variable and predicate letter formula, or else in their respective number-theoretic senses (§ 17). The two formal systems, having in common Group A (§ 19) as postulate list, but differing thus in their formation rules, we distinguish as the *pure predicate calculus* and the *number-theoretic predicate calculus*.

Before going ahead with the metamathematics, let us see how the formalism is interpreted as a calculus of predicates.

In word languages, a proposition is expressed by a sentence. Then a 'predicate' is expressed by an incomplete sentence or sentence skeleton containing an open place. For example, "___ is a man" expresses a predicate. When we fill the open place with the name of a subject such as "Socrates", a sentence such as "Socrates is a man" is obtained. The situation is conveniently described by using the modern mathematical notion of a 'function' (§ 10). The predicate is then a function of one variable. This variable ranges over some domain, including as members Socrates, Chiron, etc. To each member of this domain, the function correlates a proposition; i.e. when the independent variable takes a member of the domain as value, the predicate takes a proposition as corresponding value. Thus the predicate is a *propositional function of one variable.* Predicates are often called 'properties', e.g. in Chapters II, III. In this terminology "___ is a man" expresses the property P of being a man, and "Socrates is a man" expresses the proposition that Socrates has the property P. Another term used in this connection is 'class'; "Socrates is a man" expresses that Socrates belongs to the class C of men. ('Predicate' in its strict grammatical meaning of that which a sentence says about its subject is narrower than 'propositional function of one variable' or 'property', since for a predicate the omitted noun in the sentence skeleton must be the subject of the sentence.)

As a second illustration, consider the sentence skeleton "___ loves ___". In grammatical terminology, this consists of a transitive verb and two open places, one to be filled by the name of a subject such as "Jane", and the other of an object such as "John". Whether the resulting sentence expresses a true or a false proposition we are not saying. The sentence skeleton in this illustration expresses a *binary relation*, i.e. a relation among two members, or in other words a *propositional function of two variables.*

In other examples, there may be several correlated open spaces to be filled with the same name. For example, "___$_1$ is the father of ___$_2$, or ___$_1$ is the mother of ___$_2$" expresses a binary relation, also expressed by "___$_1$ is a parent of ___$_2$".

The reader may easily make up examples of sentence skeletons containing any greater number n of open places or of sets of correlated open places. Such a sentence skeleton expresses an *n-ary relation*, or *propositional function of n variables.*

From the standpoint of functions, the distinction between a 'predicate' in the traditional sense of the first illustration and a 'relation' is of minor significance; and likewise the distinction between 'subject' and 'object' in the first two examples. It will be more convenient henceforth to say simply "predicate" and "object" in all cases. By a *predicate* (*of n variables*) we shall accordingly mean a propositional function of n variables, where n may be 0 giving a proposition, or 1 giving a predicate in the traditional sense or a property, or > 1 giving an n-ary relation. We call the values of the independent variables (when $n > 0$) *objects*, and the independent variables *object variables.*

The predicate calculus will treat of the logic of predicates in this general sense of 'predicate', i.e. as propositional function. Some writers hence say "functional calculus" instead of "predicate calculus".

We shall consider here only the case of predicate calculus which has one domain of objects for all its object variables, in which case the objects may be called also *individuals*, and the object variables *individual variables*. This case suffices for the intended application to our number-theoretic system, for which the domain is the set of the natural numbers.

The treatment of the predicate calculus will not depend on any supposition about the object domain, except that it be non-empty, i.e. contain at least one element. For the pure form of the calculus, no provision is made for referring to particular objects of the domain, i.e. there are individual variables but no individual constants.

Now let us see how we come to choose the symbolism which we use to represent predicates. The blanks employed above to show the open places in a sentence skeleton we replace by the device customary in mathematics of letters called "variables". Thus instead of "$\_\__1$ is father of $\_\__2$, or $\_\__1$ is mother of $\_\__2$", we more conveniently write (1) "a is father of b, or a is mother of b". Some mathematical examples are (2) "a is even", (3) "a equals b", and (4) "a is less than b".

Furthermore, since a predicate is a kind of a function, namely one whose values are propositions, we employ functional notation (§ 10) in naming predicates, except in cases when some other notation is in common usage. Thus we might designate the predicate of (1) as "$P(a, b)$" (for "a is a parent of b") and of (2) as "$E(a)$", using the functional notation with the predicate symbol ("P" or "E") written ahead of the independent variables. (We have already done so in § 7 in using "$P(n)$" to express that n has the property P.) For (3) and (4), we use the customary relational notations "$a=b$" and "$a<b$", with the predicate symbol ("$=$" or "$<$") written between the independent variables.

For the pure predicate calculus, the predicate letters such as $\mathcal{A}(a, b)$, $\mathcal{B}$, etc. are to be interpreted as standing for unspecified predicates, i.e. $\mathcal{A}(a, b)$ for a predicate of two variables, $\mathcal{B}$ for a predicate of zero variables (i.e. a proposition), etc. Then any predicate letter formula can be interpreted as standing for a predicate which is determined by the predicates represented by the distinct predicate letters from which it is constructed, e.g. $\forall b(\mathcal{A}(b, a) \,\&\, \mathcal{B} \supset \mathcal{A}(a, b))$ represents a predicate of one variable (corresponding to the free a) determined by the predicate of two variables represented by $\mathcal{A}(a, b)$ and the proposition represented by $\mathcal{B}$.

Note that when we are using $\mathcal{A}(a, b)$ as the name form for the predicate letter $\mathcal{A}$ with two attached variables, then for the interpretation, after choosing independently what predicate $\mathcal{A}(a, b)$ shall stand for, the meanings of $\mathcal{A}(c, b)$, $\mathcal{A}(a, a)$, $\mathcal{A}(b, a)$, etc. depend upon that, by the standard convention for functional notation (§ 10).

Similarly, any formula in the number-theoretic system can be interpreted as expressing a predicate, under the usual number-theoretic meanings of the symbols. For example, $\exists c(a=0''\cdot c)$ expresses $E(a)$ or *a is even*, $a=b$ expresses $a=b$, and $\exists c(c'+a=b)$ (abbreviated $a<b$ in § 17) expresses $a<b$.

Let $x_1, \ldots, x_n$ be distinct variables, and $A(x_1, \ldots, x_n)$ a formula (under either notion of formula). When we are interpreting $A(x_1, \ldots, x_n)$ by a predicate, or performing formal operations with it which are in keeping with an interpretation by a predicate (even though the interpretation is not involved in the formal operations), we call $A(x_1, \ldots, x_n)$ a *name form* in $x_1, \ldots, x_n$ as the *name form variables*, and say that $x_1, \ldots, x_n$ have the *name form interpretation* or the *predicate interpretation*. The name form $A(x_1, \ldots, x_n)$ is the formula of the system; "$A(x_1, \ldots, x_n)$" is our metamathematical name for that formula (under our substitution notation § 18); and we may on occasion introduce "$A(x_1, \ldots, x_n)$" as a name for the predicate $A(x_1, \ldots, x_n)$ which the formula $A(x_1, \ldots, x_n)$ expresses under the interpretation.

It is natural to interpret a formula with free variables by a predicate, e.g., when we are concerned with the formation rules of the system, and the formula in question is being considered as a constituent of other formulas. A discussion of the interpretations of a formula by a proposition will be given at the end of § 32.

§ 32. Derived rules, free variables. In using the derived rules of Theorem 2 (§ 23) for the predicate calculus, we must observe carefully the restrictions on the handling of variables: (1) The t for an $\forall$-elimination or $\exists$-introduction must be free for the x in the A(x) (cf. § 18). (2) The x for an $\exists$-elimination must not occur free in the C. (3) In a subsidiary deduction the free variables must be held constant for the assumption formula to be discharged (cf. § 22). At first parenthetical remarks will call attention to the precautions taken. Later it will be left increasingly to the reader to observe them.

THEOREM 13. *For *64—*68, let* $x_1, \ldots, x_n$ *be distinct variables,* $A(x_1, \ldots, x_n)$ *be a formula, and* $t_1, \ldots, t_n$ *be terms (not necessarily distinct) which are free for* $x_1, \ldots, x_n$*, respectively, in* $A(x_1, \ldots, x_n)$. *For *67,* *also let* C *be a formula not containing any of* $x_1, \ldots, x_n$ *free, and* $\Gamma(x_1, \ldots, x_n)$ *be a finite sequence of zero or more formulas, and suppose that the free variables are held constant for the last assumption formula* $A(x_1, \ldots, x_n)$ *in the subsidiary deduction. Then:*

*64. $A(x_1, \ldots, x_n) \vdash^{x_1 \ldots x_n} \forall x_1 \ldots \forall x_n A(x_1, \ldots, x_n)$.

*65. $\forall x_1 \ldots \forall x_n A(x_1, \ldots, x_n) \vdash A(t_1, \ldots, t_n)$.

*66. $A(x_1, \ldots, x_n) \vdash^{x_1 \ldots x_n} A(t_1, \ldots, t_n)$.

*68. $A(t_1, \ldots, t_n) \vdash \exists x_1 \ldots \exists x_n A(x_1, \ldots, x_n)$.

*67. *If* $\Gamma(x_1, \ldots, x_n), \; A(x_1, \ldots, x_n) \vdash C$, *then* $\Gamma(x_1, \ldots, x_n), \exists x_1 \ldots \exists x_n A(x_1, \ldots, x_n) \vdash^{x_1 \ldots x_n} C$.

(n-fold ∀-introduction, ∀-elimination, substitution, ∃-introduction and ∃-elimination.)

If x *is a variable, and* A(x) *and* B(x) *are formulas:*

*69. $A(x) \supset B(x) \vdash^{x} \forall x A(x) \supset \forall x B(x)$.

*70. $A(x) \supset B(x) \vdash^{x} \exists x A(x) \supset \exists x B(x)$.

PROOFS. *64. By n successive applications of the simple ∀-introduction rule (§ 23).

For *65 and *66 (and later *68), we make two cases. CASE 1: $t_1, \ldots, t_n$ do not contain $x_1, \ldots, x_n$. CASE 2: otherwise.

*65 CASE 1. By n-successive simple ∀-eliminations,

$\forall x_1 \ldots \forall x_n A(x_1, \ldots, x_n) \vdash \forall x_2 \ldots \forall x_n A(t_1, x_2, \ldots, x_n) \vdash \forall x_3 \ldots \forall x_n A(t_1, t_2, x_3, \ldots, x_n) \vdash \ldots \vdash \forall x_n A(t_1, \ldots, t_{n-1}, x_n) \vdash A(t_1, \ldots, t_n)$.

The case hypothesis and the hypothesis of the theorem that $t_1, \ldots, t_n$ are free for $x_1, \ldots, x_n$, respectively, in $A(x_1, \ldots, x_n)$, together insure that t_1 is free for x_1 in $\forall x_2 \ldots \forall x_n A(x_1, x_2, \ldots, x_n)$, t_2 for x_2 in $\forall x_3 \ldots \forall x_n A(t_1, x_2, x_3, \ldots, x_n)$, etc. (Case 2 will follow *66 Case 1.)

*66 CASE 1. By combining *64 and *65 Case 1 (or by n successive applications of the simple substitution rule § 23).

*65 CASE 2. Let $w_1, \ldots, w_n$ be variables distinct from each other and from $x_1, \ldots, x_n$, and not occurring in $A(x_1, \ldots, x_n)$ or $t_1, \ldots, t_n$. Then, by Cases 1 of *65 and *66,

$$\forall x_1 \ldots \forall x_n A(x_1, \ldots, x_n) \vdash A(w_1, \ldots, w_n) \vdash^{w_1 \ldots w_n} A(t_1, \ldots, t_n).$$

*68 CASE 2. $A(t_1, \ldots, t_n) \vdash \exists w_1 \ldots \exists w_n A(w_1, \ldots, w_n)$. Also $A(w_1, \ldots, w_n) \vdash \exists x_1 \ldots \exists x_n A(x_1, \ldots, x_n)$, whence by *67,

$$\exists w_1 \ldots \exists w_n A(w_1, \ldots, w_n) \vdash \exists x_1 \ldots \exists x_n A(x_1, \ldots, x_n).$$

*69. 1. $A(x) \supset B(x), A(x) \vdash B(x) \vdash^x \forall x B(x)$ — $\supset$-elim., $\forall$-introd.

2. $A(x) \supset B(x), \forall x A(x) \vdash^x \forall x B(x)$ — $\forall$-elim., 1 [the term x is free for x in A(x) by use of the definition § 18].

3. $A(x) \supset B(x) \vdash^x \forall x A(x) \supset \forall x B(x)$ — $\supset$-introd., 2 [the variable x is held constant in the subsidiary deduction 2 for the assumption formula $\forall x A(x)$ which is being discharged, since x does not occur free in $\forall x A(x)$].

*70. 1. $A(x) \supset B(x), A(x) \vdash B(x) \vdash \exists x B(x)$ — $\supset$-elim., $\exists$-introd. [cf. *69 Step 2].

2. $A(x) \supset B(x), \exists x A(x) \vdash^x \exists x B(x)$ — $\exists$-elim., 1 [$\exists x B(x)$ does not contain x free, and x is held constant in the subsidiary deduction 1].

3. $A(x) \supset B(x) \vdash^x \exists x A(x) \supset \exists x B(x)$ — $\supset$-introd., 2 [x does not occur free in $\exists x A(x)$].

The $\exists$-elimination rule required at Step 2 for *70 is a subsidiary deduction rule, while the $\forall$-elimination rule used at Step 2 for *69 was established in the stronger direct form (although under an abbreviation introduced in § 23 Example 1 the step is presented in the same format). Hence the greater care required in justifying Step 2 for *70.

Example 1. $\forall$-introduction can be applied to the formula $\mathcal{A}(a, a)$ in only one way, while $\exists$-introduction (simple or 2-fold) can be applied in several ways, as follows.

$\mathcal{A}(a,a) \vdash^a \forall a \mathcal{A}(a,a)$ — $\forall$-introd., letting x be a; A(x) be $\mathcal{A}(a,a)$.

$\mathcal{A}(a,a) \vdash \exists a \mathcal{A}(a,a)$ — $\exists$-introd., letting x be a; A(x) be $\mathcal{A}(a,a)$; t be a.

$\mathcal{A}(a,a) \vdash \exists b \mathcal{A}(a,b)$ — $\exists$-introd., letting x be b; A(x) be $\mathcal{A}(a,b)$; t be a.

$\mathcal{A}(a,a) \vdash \exists b \mathcal{A}(b,a)$ — $\exists$-introd., letting x be b; A(x) be $\mathcal{A}(b,a)$; t be a.

$\mathcal{A}(a,a) \vdash \exists a \exists b \mathcal{A}(a,b)$ — 2-fold $\exists$-introd., letting x_1, x_2 be a, b; $A(x_1, x_2)$ be $\mathcal{A}(a,b)$; t_1, t_2 be a, a.

$\mathcal{A}(a,a) \vdash \exists a \exists b \mathcal{A}(b,a)$ — 2-fold $\exists$-introd., letting x_1, x_2 be a, b; $A(x_1, x_2)$ be $\mathcal{A}(b,a)$; t_1, t_2 be a, a.

Interpretation of formulas with free variables. The restriction for our subsidiary deduction rules of Theorem 2, that the free variables should be held constant for each assumption formula to be discharged, can be illuminated by some remarks on the interpretation, which of course are not part of the metamathematics.

In Example 2 following, we have in Step 1 a deduction from the assumption formula $b \neq 0$ with b held constant, so that $\supset$-introduction is applicable at once. In Example 3, $\supset$-introduction is not applicable at once because b is varied, although it can be applied after an $\forall$-elimination.

In Example 4, we see how a false result (for the number-theoretic interpretation) is obtainable, if we violate the restriction on subsidiary deduction.

EXAMPLE 2. 1. $b \neq 0 \vdash a+b \neq a$ — can be established, holding b constant, in the number-theoretic system (§ 39; "s≠t" abbreviates ¬s=t, § 17).
2. $\vdash b \neq 0 \supset a+b \neq a$ — ⊃-introd., 1.
3. $\vdash \forall b(b \neq 0 \supset a+b \neq a)$ — ∀-introd., 2.

EXAMPLE 3. 1. $b \neq 0 \vdash^{b} 0 \neq 0$ — substitution (§ 23), b being varied.
2. $\forall b(b \neq 0) \vdash 0 \neq 0$ — ∀-elim., 1.
3. $\vdash \forall b(b \neq 0) \supset 0 \neq 0$ — ⊃-introd., 2.

EXAMPLE 4. 1. $b \neq 0 \vdash^{b} 0 \neq 0$ — same as Example 3 Step 1.
2? $\vdash b \neq 0 \supset 0 \neq 0$ — ⊃-introd., misapplied to 1.
3? $\vdash \forall b(b \neq 0 \supset 0 \neq 0)$ — ∀-introd., 2.
4? $\vdash 0' \neq 0 \supset 0 \neq 0$ — ∀-elim., 3.
5. $\vdash 0' \neq 0$ — by substitution in Axiom 15.
6? $\vdash 0 \neq 0$ — Rule 2, 5, 4.

The only violation of the formal rules in Example 4 is at Step 2. It is suggested that the reader undertake himself to explain the fallacy in terms of the interpretation, before reading the further discussion below. Especially he should note the difference between the formulas at Step 3 of Examples 3 and 4. The reader may also supply the formal details for the following two examples, and compare the results.

EXAMPLE 5. Given A(x) ⊢ B and A(x) ⊢ ¬B with x held constant, then ⊢ ¬A(x) and ⊢ ∀x¬A(x).

EXAMPLE 6. Given A(x) $\vdash^{x}$ B and A(x) $\vdash^{x}$ ¬B with x not necessarily held constant, then ⊢ ¬∀xA(x).

The rules of ∨-elimination and ∃-elimination may be discussed in like manner.

In informal mathematics, we know two different ways of using free variables in stating propositions, as illustrated in algebra by an *identical equation* $(x+y)^2 = x^2 + 2xy + y^2$ and a *conditional equation* $x^2 + 2 = 3x$.

The first of these interpretations is the one which applies to the free variables in the axioms and formal theorems of our system, and we call it the *generality interpretation*. For example, Axiom 14, which is $a'=b' \supset a=b$, means that, for every pair a and b of natural numbers, if $a' = b'$, then $a = b$; and the formal theorem $a=a$, proved in Example 1 § 19, expresses that every natural number equals itself.

But when a formula A(x) with a free variable x is taken as an assumption formula for a formal deduction, we have a choice. We may intend the assumption in the sense "Suppose that, for all x, $A(x)$", so that x has the generality interpretation. Or we may intend the assumption in the sense "Let x be a number such that $A(x)$", in which case we say x has the *conditional interpretation*.

In the second case, the use in the deduction of operations which depend, considered in terms of the meaning, on the possibility of allowing x to range over the object domain will be out of keeping with the interpretation. For the generality interpretation, there is no such limitation. Step 1 Example 2 is a deduction constructed in keeping with the conditional interpretation; and Step 1 Examples 3 and 4 only with the generality interpretation. That the assumption formula $b \neq 0$ is false under the latter interpretation is beside the point here, and the concluding formula of Example 3 is quite correct (although not very interesting).

The student of elementary mathematics is acquainted with the distinction between symbols classified as constants and symbols classified as variables. Close inspection shows that the distinction in the use of the symbols is always relative to a context. A given symbol is introduced as name for an object, and throughout a certain context every occurrence of the symbol is as name for the same object. From outside the context, it is indicated that the object may be any one (some one, etc.) of the members of some set. Fundamentally then, the symbol is constant, i.e. its meaning cannot be changed, within the context, while from outside the context it is variable.

(The terminology actually employed in a given theory is generally that suitable to the context constituted by the theory as a whole. Sometimes symbols which are constant throughout an important subcontext, but variable for the theory as a whole, are called "parameters" or "arbitrary constants".)

For the generality interpretation of a variable x in a formula A(x), the context within which all (free) occurrences of x must represent the same object is exactly the whole formula A(x). The formula A(x) then means the same as ∀xA(x), and in analogy to the scope of the quantifier ∀x, we also call A(x) the *scope* of the generality expressed by the free variable x.

For the conditional interpretation, the context within which all (free) occurrences of x have the same meaning is not just A(x) but the whole deduction from A(x) (or the part of it dependent on A(x)).

In Example 4 Step 1, under the generality interpretation the scope of the generality expressed by b is exactly the assumption formula $b \neq 0$. Were the formula of Step 2 provable, the generality interpretation would then apply to it as a whole, and the scope would become $b \neq 0 \supset 0 \neq 0$, not just the part $b \neq 0$.

The universal quantifier $\forall x$ functions in our logical symbolism as a device to restrict the scope of generality to a part of a formula. The formulas of Steps 2 and 3 Example 4 (or of the two conclusions of Example 5) are synonymous under the generality interpretation of the free variable in the first. No formula without a quantifier can be written which is synonymous with the formula of Step 3 Example 3 (or of the conclusion of Example 6).

Let A be a formula containing free exactly the distinct variables $x_1, \ldots, x_n$ in order of first occurrence. According as $n > 0$ or $n = 0$, we call A *open* or *closed*. The closed formula $\forall x_1 \ldots \forall x_n A$ (sometimes abbreviated "$\forall$A") we call the *closure of* A. By *64 and *65, A and $\forall$A are *interdeducible* (i.e. each can be deduced from the other), with $x_1, \ldots, x_n$ varied in the deduction of $\forall$A from A. Under the generality interpretation A and $\forall$A are synonymous.

§ 33. Replacement. Let C_A be a formula in which there is a specified occurrence of a formula A, and let C_B be the result of replacing this occurrence by B (§ 26). There will then exist parallel constructions of C_A from A and of C_B from B by Clauses 2—7 of the definition of formula (§ 17 or § 31). The number of steps in this construction of C_A (or of operators in the scopes of which the part A lies) we call the *depth* of the part A in C_A.

EXAMPLE 1. Let A be $\mathcal{A}(b, a)$, C_A be $\forall b(\mathcal{A}(b, a) \,\&\, \mathcal{B} \supset \mathcal{A}(a, b))$ (the specified occurrence here being the only occurrence), and B be $\exists d\mathcal{A}(d, a, c)$. Then C_B is $\forall b(\exists d\mathcal{A}(d, a, c) \,\&\, \mathcal{B} \supset \mathcal{A}(a, b))$. The parallel constructions of C_A from A and of C_B from B are as follows, and the depth is 3.

$\mathcal{A}(b, a)$	$\exists d\mathcal{A}(d, a, c)$
$\mathcal{A}(b, a) \,\&\, \mathcal{B}$	$\exists d\mathcal{A}(d, a, c) \,\&\, \mathcal{B}$
$\mathcal{A}(b, a) \,\&\, \mathcal{B} \supset \mathcal{A}(a, b)$	$\exists d\mathcal{A}(d, a, c) \,\&\, \mathcal{B} \supset \mathcal{A}(a, b)$
$\forall b(\mathcal{A}(b, a) \,\&\, \mathcal{B} \supset \mathcal{A}(a, b))$	$\forall b(\exists d\mathcal{A}(d, a, c) \,\&\, \mathcal{B} \supset \mathcal{A}(a, b))$

THEOREM 14. *If* A, B, C_A *and* C_B *are formulas related as in the foregoing discussion of replacement, then*

$$A \sim B \vdash^{x_1 \ldots x_n} C_A \sim C_B$$

where $x_1, \ldots, x_n$ *are the free variables of* A *or* B *which belong to a quantifier of* C_A *having the specified occurrence of* A *within its scope.* (Replacement theorem.)

In other words, $x_1, \ldots, x_n$ are the free variables of $A \sim B$ which are quantified in the construction of C_A from the specified part A. Proof of the theorem is by induction on the depth as before (Theorem 6 § 26), using now two additional lemmas.

ADDITIONAL LEMMAS FOR REPLACEMENT. *If* x *is a variable, and* A(x) *and* B(x) *are formulas*:

*71. $A(x) \sim B(x) \vdash^{x} \forall x A(x) \sim \forall x B(x)$.

*72. $A(x) \sim B(x) \vdash^{x} \exists x A(x) \sim \exists x B(x)$.

PROOFS. From *69 and *70, respectively.

EXAMPLE 1 (concluded). Let $\sim$ be written between the formulas of each pair in the parallel columns. The resulting formulas are deducible, each from the preceding, using successively *28a, *26 and *71 (varying b).

COROLLARY 1. *Under the conditions of the theorem*:
If $\vdash A \sim B$, *then* $\vdash C_A \sim C_B$.

EXAMPLE 2°. By *49 (and *20), $\vdash A(x) \sim \neg\neg A(x)$. Hence

$$\vdash \neg\neg\forall x A(x) \sim \neg\neg\forall x \neg\neg A(x).$$

EXAMPLE 3. Now (cf. Example 2 § 26), if A and B do not contain x free: $A \sim B \vdash A \vee \forall x(A \supset C(x)) \sim A \vee \forall x(B \supset C(x))$. If A and B may contain x free: $A \sim B \vdash^{x} A \vee \forall x(A \supset C(x)) \sim A \vee \forall x(B \supset C(x))$. If $\vdash A \sim B$, then $\vdash A \vee \forall x(A \supset C(x)) \sim A \vee \forall x(B \supset C(x))$.

COROLLARY 2. *Under the conditions of the theorem*:
$A \sim B, C_A \vdash^{x_1 \ldots x_n} C_B$, *with* $x_1, \ldots, x_n$ *varied only for the first assumption formula. If* $\vdash A \sim B$, *then* $C_A \vdash C_B$. (Replacement property of equivalence.)

A replacement may be preceded by a substitution for individual variables (*66).

EXAMPLE 4. $b+0=a \sim a=b \vdash^{b} b'+0=a \sim a=b' \vdash^{b} \exists b(b'+0=a) \sim \exists b(a=b')$. But in § 38 we will have $\vdash b+0=a \sim a=b$. Hence then $\vdash \exists b(b'+0=a) \sim \exists b(a=b')$.

The interpretation illuminates the treatment of the variables in replacement. In informal mathematics, knowing that sin x is the same function as cos $(\pi/2 - x)$, i.e. having sin x $=$ cos $(\pi/2 - x)$ as an identical equation (with x taking the generality interpretation § 32), we are justified in replacing "sin x" by "cos $(\pi/2-x)$" in "$\int_0^t \sin x\,dx$", and in replacing "sin $2x$" by "cos $(\pi/2-2x)$". But assuming the conditional equation $\sin x = 1 - x$ gives us no right to replace "sin x" by "$1-x$" in "$\int_0^t \sin x\,dx$", or to replace "sin $2x$" by "$1-2x$".

CHANGE OF BOUND VARIABLES. Two formulas A and B will be said to be *congruent*, if A and B have the same number k of symbols, and for each i ($i = 1, \ldots, k$): (I) If the i-th symbol of A is not a variable, then the i-th symbol of B is the same symbol. (II) If the i-th symbol of A is a free occurrence of a variable, then the i-th symbol of B is a free occurrence of the same variable. (III) If the i-th symbol of A is an occurrence of a variable bound by the j-th quantifier of A, then the i-th symbol of B is an occurrence of a variable (not necessarily of the same variable) bound by the j-th quantifier of B.

In brief, two formulas are congruent, if they differ only in their bound variables, and corresponding bound variables are bound by corresponding quantifiers.

EXAMPLE 5. The two following formulas are congruent:
$\forall a(\mathcal{A}(a,c) \vee \exists a\mathcal{B}(a) \supset \exists b\mathcal{C}(a,b)), \quad \forall b(\mathcal{A}(b,c) \vee \exists c\mathcal{B}(c) \supset \exists a\mathcal{C}(b,a))$.
This can be made apparent by introducing indices to show which occurrences of variables are bound by the same quantifier:
$\forall a_1(\mathcal{A}(a_1,c) \vee \exists a_2\mathcal{B}(a_2) \supset \exists b_3\mathcal{C}(a_1,b_3)), \forall b_1(\mathcal{A}(b_1,c) \vee \exists c_2\mathcal{B}(c_2) \supset \exists a_3\mathcal{C}(b_1,a_3))$.
If we erase out the bound variables themselves, leaving blanks numbered with the indices, identical expressions will be obtained.

LEMMA 15a. *If* x *is a variable,* A(x) *is a formula, and* b *is a variable such that* (i) b *is free for* x *in* A(x), *and* (ii) b *does not occur free in* A(x) (*unless* b *is* x), *then*:
*73. $\vdash \forall$xA(x) $\sim \forall$bA(b). *74. $\vdash \exists$xA(x) $\sim \exists$bA(b).

PROOFS. *73. By Example 3 § 22 (Steps 1—2), $\vdash \forall$bA(b) $\supset \forall$xA(x), and similarly $\vdash \forall$xA(x) $\supset \forall$bA(b). — Note by Example 9 § 18 that (i) and (ii) are necessary and sufficient in order that $\forall$bA(b) be congruent to $\forall$xA(x) (or $\exists$bA(b) to $\exists$xA(x)).

LEMMA 15b. *Congruent formulas are equivalent; i.e. if* A *is congruent to* B, *then* $\vdash$ A $\sim$ B.

PROOF. Let A contain in order exactly r quantifiers with respective variables $u_1, \ldots, u_r$ (not necessarily distinct). Let $w_1, \ldots, w_r$ be distinct variables occurring neither in A nor in B. Let C come from A by changing each u_j $(j = 1, \ldots, r)$ to w_j in exactly the occurrences which the j-th quantifier binds. By r successive replacements, using *73 or *74 and Corollary 1 Theorem 14, $\vdash A \sim C$. Similarly, $\vdash B \sim C$. Hence (*20, *21), $\vdash A \sim B$.

EXAMPLE 5 (concluded). $\vdash \forall a(\mathcal{A}(a, c) \vee \exists a\mathcal{B}(a) \supset \exists b\mathcal{C}(a, b)) \sim \forall d(\mathcal{A}(d, c) \vee \exists a\mathcal{B}(a) \supset \exists b\mathcal{C}(d, b))$ [*73] $\sim \forall d(\mathcal{A}(d, c) \vee \exists e\mathcal{B}(e) \supset \exists b\mathcal{C}(d, b))$ [*74] $\sim \forall d(\mathcal{A}(d, c) \vee \exists e\mathcal{B}(e) \supset \exists f\mathcal{C}(d, f))$ [*74]. Similarly $\vdash \forall b(\mathcal{A}(b, c) \vee \exists c\mathcal{B}(c) \supset \exists a\mathcal{C}(b, a)) \sim \forall d(\mathcal{A}(d, c) \vee \exists e\mathcal{B}(e) \supset \exists f\mathcal{C}(d, f))$.

REMARK 1. (a) Similarly to Theorem 14, by using *6—*9b, *12, *69, *70 (instead of *26—*30, *71, *72) as the lemmas: *Let the part* A *stand in* C_A *within the scopes of only certain of the symbols* $\supset$, &, $\vee$, $\neg$, $\forall$, $\exists$. *Then* $A \supset B \vdash^{x_1 \ldots x_n} C_A \supset C_B$ *or* $B \supset A \vdash^{x_1 \ldots x_n} C_A \supset C_B$ *in the system having as postulates only the* $\supset$*-postulates and the postulates for the symbols in question, provided that in case the symbols include* $\forall$ *but not* & *the* $\forall$*-postulates include Axiom Schema* 9a *of Lemma* 11 § 24. (Cf. Herbrand 1930 § 3.2, MacLane 1934 pp. 28 ff., Curry 1939 pp. 290—291.)

(b) $\vdash \forall x A(x) \supset \forall b A(b)$ *and* $\vdash \forall b A(b) \supset \forall x A(x)$ (*similarly with* $\exists$) *using only Postulates* 9 *and* 10 (11 *and* 12). (c) Therefore: *If* A *is congruent to* B, *then* $\vdash A \supset B$ *and* $\vdash B \supset A$ (*and hence* A *and* B *are interdeducible*) *using only the* $\supset$*-postulates and the postulates for* (*at most*) *the logical symbols which* A *contains, provided as in* (a).

PERMANENT ABBREVIATIONS. Our use of permanent abbreviations, such as "$a<b$" (discussed at the end of § 17) will differ from that of temporary abbreviations, such as "A(x)", "$A(x_1, \ldots, x_n)$", etc. (§ 18), in two respects. First, they shall not contain free variables not shown in the abbreviation ('anonymous free variables'). Second, instead of avoiding the substitution of terms not free at the substitution positions, we permit the bound variables suppressed by the abbreviation ('anonymous bound variables') to be chosen at will to make whatever terms we wish to substitute free at the substitution positions. All legitimate unabbreviations of a given abbreviation are congruent, and hence by Lemma 15b equivalent. Thus it is immaterial in considering questions of deducibility and provability which legitimate unabbreviation is used.

For the question whether a postulate applies, the manner of unabbreviating may make a difference, e.g. $s<t \supset (B \supset s<t)$ is an axiom by Schema 1a only if both occurrences of "$s<t$" are unabbreviated alike. Hereafter in our statements that a postulate applies we shall be tacitly supposing that like appearing abbreviations are unabbreviated alike.

***§ 34. Substitution.** The use of a formal substitution rule for predicate letters can be largely avoided by stating results in the schematic form, with metamathematical letters instead of particular predicate letters. We then substitute informally in applying the results with a change in the signification of the metamathematical letters, but this substitution does not constitute application of a formal substitution rule. We have been doing this continually, from the very beginning of our study of the formal system. One new example is given to show what is meant.

EXAMPLE 1°. As *83 (§ 35) we will establish that, if x is any variable and A(x) any formula, $\vdash \exists x A(x) \sim \neg \forall x \neg A(x)$. Now let x be any variable and A(x) any formula. By taking the negation $\neg A(x)$ of this A(x) as the A(x) of *83, we have $\vdash \exists x \neg A(x) \sim \neg \forall x \neg\neg A(x)$. This and Example 2 § 33 explain the second and third steps of the following chain: $\vdash \forall x A(x) \sim \neg\neg \forall x A(x)$ [*49] $\sim \neg\neg \forall x \neg\neg A(x)$ [*49] $\sim \neg \exists x \neg A(x)$ [*83].

The only essential use we shall make of the formal substitution rule for the predicate calculus (Theorem 15) is in establishing duality (Corollary Theorem 18 § 35), where we substitute negations of the predicate letters for the letters. That substitution can be justified by reasoning already used in proving the substitution rule for the propositional calculus (Theorem 3 § 25), with no new complications. A further application of formal substitution occurs in passing from a number of results, first proved by duality in terms of particular predicate letters, to the general results of the same form with metamathematical letters. That application could be avoided by using the substitution rule only heuristically, to discover proofs that we can afterwards validate without use of it. The reader may therefore, if he wishes, omit the detailed treatment of substitution given in the remainder of this section.

A generalized notion of 'occurrence' is appropriate to the name form interpretation. In informal mathematics, "sin x" as an expression for a function occurs in "3 sin x + cos x", in "$\int_0^t \sin x\, dx$" and in "cos x sin $2x$", although as an expression for a number it occurs only in the first.

To simplify the notation in this section, we shall analyze each substitution taking the attached variables for each of the distinct predicate letters to be the first n variables from an infinite list $a_1, a_2, a_3, \ldots$ of variables (cf. § 31). However this list may have to be chosen differently for different substitutions (see below).

By an *occurrence* of a predicate letter $P(a_1, \ldots, a_n)$ with attached variables in a predicate letter formula E we shall mean a (consecutive) part of E of the form $P(t_1, \ldots, t_n)$ where $t_1, \ldots, t_n$ are terms. A predicate letter formula E is said to be a predicate letter formula *in* the distinct predicate letters

(1) $\quad P_1(a_1, \ldots, a_{n_1}), \ldots, P_m(a_1, \ldots, a_{n_m}) \qquad (n_1, \ldots, n_m \geq 0;\ m \geq 1),$

if no predicate letters other than (1) occur in E.

EXAMPLE 2. The predicate letter $\mathcal{A}(a, b)$ occurs twice in $\forall b(\mathcal{A}(b, a) \,\&\, \mathcal{B} \supset \mathcal{A}(a, b))$, first as the part $\mathcal{A}(b, a)$ and second as the part $\mathcal{A}(a, b)$. The formula $\forall b(\mathcal{A}(b, a) \,\&\, \mathcal{B} \supset \mathcal{A}(a, b))$ is a predicate letter formula in $\mathcal{A}(a, b)$, $\mathcal{B}$, $C(a, b, c)$.

The *substitution* of formulas (in either sense § 31)

(2) $\qquad A_1(a_1, \ldots, a_{n_1}), \ldots, A_m(a_1, \ldots, a_{n_m}),$

considered as name forms in the respective variables shown, for the predicate letters (1) in E (with result E*) shall consist in replacing, simultaneously for each j ($j = 1, \ldots, m$), each occurrence $P_j(t_1, \ldots, t_{n_j})$ of $P_j(a_1, \ldots, a_{n_j})$ in E by $A_j(t_1, \ldots, t_{n_j})$.

The name form variables (i.e. the a's) do not appear as such in E and E*. In asking whether a given formula E* does come from another given formula E by substitution for certain predicate letters, it suffices to ask the question taking as the name form variables ones not occurring in E and E*, though we are not restricting ourselves to such a choice of the name form variables when others will do also.

The substitution is said to be *free*, if for each j ($j = 1, \ldots, m$), $A_j(a_1, \ldots, a_{n_j})$ is 'free' for $P_j(a_1, \ldots, a_{n_j})$ in E, in the following sense: $A(a_1, \ldots, a_n)$ is *free* for $P(a_1, \ldots, a_n)$ in E, if, for each occurrence $P(t_1, \ldots, t_n)$ of $P(a_1, \ldots, a_n)$ in E, (A1) $t_1, \ldots, t_n$ are free for $a_1, \ldots, a_n$, respectively, in $A(a_1, \ldots, a_n)$, and (A2) $P(t_1, \ldots, t_n)$ does not stand in E within the scope of a quantifier $\forall y$ or $\exists y$ where y is a free variable of $A(a_1, \ldots, a_n)$ other than one of the name form variables $a_1, \ldots, a_n$.

EXAMPLE 3. Let $m = 1$; $n = n_1 = 2$; a_1, a_2 be c, d; $P(a_1, a_2)$ be $\mathcal{A}(c, d)$; $A(a_1, a_2)$ be $\forall b\mathcal{B}(a, b, c, d) \vee \mathcal{A}(d, c)$; and E be $\exists c\mathcal{A}(c, a)$. Then E* is $\exists c(\forall b\mathcal{B}(a, b, c, a) \vee \mathcal{A}(a, c))$. The substitution is free.

It is convenient to refer to the free occurrences of $a_1, \ldots, a_n$ in $A(a_1, \ldots, a_n)$ as *explicit occurrences*; and to other occurrences of variables in $A(a_1, \ldots, a_n)$ as *anonymous occurrences*. Variables occurring explicitly [anonymously] free (bound) in $A(a_1, \ldots, a_n)$ are *explicit* [*anonymous*] *free* (*bound*) *variables* of $A(a_1, \ldots, a_n)$. The terminology extends generally to situations in which formulas or parts of formulas are being represented by metamathematical letters.

EXAMPLE 4. In considering $\mathcal{A}(a, b)$ & $\exists a\mathcal{B}(a, b, c)$ as a name form in a, b, and in using "$\mathrm{A}(a, b)$" (or "$\mathrm{A}(\mathrm{a}_1, \mathrm{a}_2)$" where "$\mathrm{a}_1$", "$\mathrm{a}_2$" stand for a, b) to stand for it, the first occurrence of a and both occurrences of b are explicit, the second and third occurrences of a and the occurrence of c are anonymous. So a and b are explicit free variables, c is an anonymous free variable, and a is an anonymous bound variable. In using "$\forall a\mathrm{A}(a, b)$" to stand for $\forall a(\mathcal{A}(a, b)$ & $\exists a\mathcal{B}(a, b, c))$, the first two occurrences of a are explicit, the other two anonymous; so a is both an explicit bound variable and an anonymous bound variable. The $\forall a$ is an explicit quantifier, and the $\exists a$ an anonymous quantifier.

In our further examples of substitution, the variables $\mathrm{a}_1, \mathrm{a}_2, \mathrm{a}_3, \ldots$ will be $a, b, c, \ldots$. (This choice can always be made, except when as in Example 3 it would interfere with the anonymous variables for the substitution.)

Failure of (A1) or (A2) is always due to the presence of anonymous variables.

EXAMPLE 5. The formula $\exists c\mathcal{A}(c, a, b)$ is not free for $\mathcal{A}(a)$ in $\mathcal{A}(c) \supset \mathcal{B}$, because (A1) is violated (after substitution, with result $\exists c\mathcal{A}(c, c, b) \supset \mathcal{B}$, the c of $\mathcal{A}(c)$ would become bound by the anonymous quantifier $\exists c$ of $\exists c\mathcal{A}(c, a, b)$), nor in $\forall b(\mathcal{A}(a) \supset \mathcal{B}(b))$, because (A2) is violated (after substitution, with result $\forall b(\exists c\mathcal{A}(c, a, b) \supset \mathcal{B}(b))$, the anonymous free b of $\exists c\mathcal{A}(c, a, b)$ would become bound by the $\forall b$ of $\forall b(\mathcal{A}(a) \supset \mathcal{B}(b))$).

The conditions (A1) and (A2) can be regarded as conditions that each part $\mathrm{A}(\mathrm{t}_1, \ldots, \mathrm{t}_n)$ of E*resulting by the substitution of $\mathrm{A}(\mathrm{a}_1, \ldots, \mathrm{a}_n)$ for $\mathrm{P}(\mathrm{a}_1, \ldots, \mathrm{a}_n)$ should constitute an *occurrence of* $\mathrm{A}(\mathrm{a}_1, \ldots, \mathrm{a}_n)$ *as a name form in* $\mathrm{a}_1, \ldots, \mathrm{a}_n$.

EXAMPLE 6. The a's in this example shall be a, b, c. But we supply indices to assist in referring to different occurrences of the variables. Let E be

(i) $\forall b_1(\mathcal{A}(b_2, a_3)$ & $\mathcal{B} \supset \mathcal{A}(a_4, b_5))$.

Let $\mathrm{A}(a, b)$, B, $\mathrm{C}(a, b, c)$ (to be substituted for $\mathcal{A}(a, b)$, $\mathcal{B}$, $C(a, b, c)$, respectively) be

(ii) $\exists c_6 C(c_7, a, b, b)$, $\neg\mathcal{B}(a_8)$, $\mathcal{A}(a, b)$

(the indexed occurrences of variables being anonymous). Then E* (the result of the substitution performed on E) is

(iii) $\forall b_1(\exists c_6 C(c_7, b_2, a_3, a_3)$ & $\neg\mathcal{B}(a_8) \supset \exists c_6 C(c_7, a_4, b_5, b_5))$.

The substitution is free.

The meaning of the next lemma will be made clear by the example following it.

LEMMA 16a. *If the substitution of* (2) *for* (1) *in* E *is free, then in the result* E* *each free occurrence of a variable originates as a free occurrence of the variable either in* E *or anonymously in some* $A_j(a_1, \ldots, a_{n_j})$, *and each bound occurrence of a variable and the quantifier binding it originate together in the same relationship either in* E *or anonymously in some* $A_j(a_1, \ldots, a_{n_j})$.

EXAMPLE 6 (concluded). The two free a_3's in (iii) originate as the free a_3 in (i). The free a_8 originates as the anonymous free a_8 in (ii). The two b_5's bound by $\forall b_1$ originate together as the b_5 bound by $\forall b_1$ in (i). The c_7 bound by $\exists c_6$ (either such pair) originate as the anonymous c_7 bound by $\exists c_6$ in (ii).

OUTLINE OF PROOF. Consider a given occurrence of a variable in E*. This is either (Case 1) not in any of the parts $A_j(t_1, \ldots, t_{n_j})$ (e.g. b_1), or (Case 2) in one of the parts $A_j(t_1, \ldots, t_{n_j})$ but not in any t_i (e.g. c_6, c_7, a_8), or (Case 3) in one of the occurrences of t_i which is introduced into $A_j(t_1, \ldots, t_{n_j})$ by substitution for a free occurrence of a_i in $A_j(a_1, \ldots, a_{n_j})$ (e.g. b_2, a_3, a_4, b_5). The lemma follows, using in Case 2 the condition (A2) for freedom, and in Case 3 the condition (A1).

LEMMA 16b. *Let*

$$(\tilde{2}) \qquad \tilde{A}_1(a_1, \ldots, a_{n_1}), \ldots, \tilde{A}_m(a_1, \ldots, a_{n_m})$$

be formulas respectively congruent to the formulas (2), *and let* $\tilde{F}$ *be a formula congruent to* F. *If the substitution of* (2) *for* (1) *in* F *with result* F*, *and the substitution of* $(\tilde{2})$ *for* (1) *in* $\tilde{F}$ *with result* $\tilde{F}^\dagger$, *are both free, then* $\tilde{F}^\dagger$ *is congruent to* F*.

By Lemma 16a, noting that, if the p-th symbol of F* originates as the q-th of F (of $A_j(a_1, \ldots, a_{n_j})$), the p-th symbol of $\tilde{F}^\dagger$ originates as the q-th of $\tilde{F}$ (of $\tilde{A}_j(a_1, \ldots, a_{n_j})$).

LEMMA 17. *Given a proof of* F, *and a list of variables* $z_1, \ldots, z_q$, *we can find a formula* $\tilde{F}$ *congruent to* F *and containing none of the variables* $z_1, \ldots, z_q$ *bound, and a proof of* $\tilde{F}$ *containing no applications of Rule* 9 *or* 12 *with respect to any of* $z_1, \ldots, z_q$.

PROOF. Let the distinct free variables of F be $b_1, \ldots, b_s$, and call F also "$F(b_1, \ldots, b_s)$". Let $u_1, \ldots, u_r$ be all the distinct variables occurring free or bound in any formula of the given proof of F (including $b_1, \ldots, b_s$). Let $\bar{u}_1, \ldots, \bar{u}_r$ be new variables, distinct from each other and from $u_1, \ldots, u_r, z_1, \ldots, z_q$. For the definition of what constitutes a proof in the predicate calculus (Postulate Group A § 19), all variables are on a par initially. Hence if, throughout the given proof of F, we change $u_1, \ldots, u_r$ simultaneously in all occurrences free and bound to $\bar{u}_1, \ldots, \bar{u}_r$, respectively, the resulting figure must also be a proof. Say it is a proof of $\tilde{F}(\text{ƀ}_1, \ldots, \text{ƀ}_s)$; so (a) $\vdash \tilde{F}(\text{ƀ}_1, \ldots, \text{ƀ}_s)$. Now by *n*-fold substitution (*66), (b) $\tilde{F}(\text{ƀ}_1, \ldots, \text{ƀ}_s) \vdash^{\text{ƀ}_1 \cdots \text{ƀ}_s} \tilde{F}(b_1, \ldots, b_s)$. Referring to the proof of *66, since $b_1, \ldots, b_s$ are distinct from $\text{ƀ}_1, \ldots, \text{ƀ}_s$, the deduction (b) requires the use of Rule 9 only with respect to $\text{ƀ}_1, \ldots, \text{ƀ}_s$ (and Rule 12 not at all). Let $\tilde{F}$ be $\tilde{F}(b_1, \ldots, b_s)$. Combining (a) and (b), we obtain a proof of $\tilde{F}$ in which Rules 9 and 12 are used only with respect to the new variables $\bar{u}_1, \ldots, \bar{u}_r$ (including $\text{ƀ}_1, \ldots, \text{ƀ}_s$), therefore not with respect to any of $z_1, \ldots, z_q$.

THEOREM 15. SUBSTITUTION FOR PREDICATE LETTERS. *Let* $D_1, \ldots, D_l$, E *be predicate letter formulas in the distinct predicate letters* (1). *Let* $D_1^*, \ldots, D_l^*$, E* *result by the substitution of* (2) (*as name forms in the variables shown*) *for* (1) *throughout* $D_1, \ldots, D_l$, E, *respectively. Then, provided that*
(A) *the substitution is free, and*
(B) *for* $j = 1, \ldots, m$, *the anonymous free variables of* $A_j(a_1, \ldots, a_{n_j})$ *are held constant in the given deduction for each assumption formula which contains the corresponding predicate letter* $P_j(a_1, \ldots, a_{n_j})$:
If $D_1, \ldots, D_l \vdash E$, *then* $D_1^*, \ldots, D_l^* \vdash E^*$.

(Proviso (B) is of course satisfied, if all the anonymous free variables of (2) are held constant in the given deduction. In the case $l = 0$, Proviso (B) disappears, and we have simply: *If* $\vdash$ E, *then* $\vdash$ E*, *provided* (A) *the substitution is free.*)

PROOF. We take the given deduction $D_1, \ldots, D_l \vdash E$ as (I) for Lemma 8a (§ 24), and pass to a proof (II). The long formula in (II) we now write as "F". The substitution of (2) for (1) in F is free, as we see by using Proviso (A), and also Proviso (B) to insure that the condition (A2) is met respecting the y's of (II). If we can show now that $\vdash$ F*, then by using Lemma 8a in the converse direction, it will follow that $D_1^*, \ldots, D_l^* \vdash E^*$, as is to be proved.

Accordingly, consider a given proof of F. In formulas of this proof there may occur some other predicate letters than (1). Let (1′) be the list (1) increased to include these; and let (2′) be (2) increased correspondingly, using as the additional name forms formulas which contain no anonymous variables.

Suppose we were to substitute (2′) for (1′) throughout the given proof of F. Then we could reason, exactly as in the proof of the substitution rule for proposition letters (Theorem 3 § 25), that the resulting figure is a proof of F*, except for two contingencies.

First, the C for an application of Rule 9 or 12 may be transformed by the substitution into a formula C* which contains the x of the application free, so that the rule no longer applies. This can happen only if the x of the application is one of the anonymous free variables $z_1, \ldots, z_q$ of (2). Using Lemma 17, we can replace the given proof of F by a proof of a formula $\tilde{F}$ congruent to F and containing none of $z_1, \ldots, z_q$ bound, so that in the new proof there are no applications of Rules 9 and 12 with respect to $z_1, \ldots, z_q$.

Second, the t for an application of Axiom Schema 10 or 11 may after the substitution no longer be free for the x in the A(x), due to the introduction of anonymous quantifiers in the formulas (2) with variables occurring in the t. Let us choose formulas ($\tilde{2}'$) congruent to (2′) and containing bound no variables occurring either free or bound in any formula of the proof of $\tilde{F}$.

Now if we substitute ($\tilde{2}'$) for (1′) in the proof of $\tilde{F}$, neither contingency can arise; and so, denoting the substitution of ($\tilde{2}'$) by "†", the resulting sequence of formulas will be a proof of $\tilde{F}^\dagger$. Thus $\vdash \tilde{F}^\dagger$.

By the choice of the bound variables in ($\tilde{2}'$), condition (A1) for freedom is satisfied in the substitution of ($\tilde{2}$) for (1) in $\tilde{F}$. Because $\tilde{F}$ does not contain bound any of the anonymous free variables $z_1, \ldots, z_q$ of (2), hence of ($\tilde{2}$), condition (A2) is satisfied also. Thus the substitution of ($\tilde{2}$) for (1) in $\tilde{F}$ is free. So is that of (2) for (1) in F (as remarked above). Hence by Lemma 16b, $\tilde{F}^\dagger$ is congruent to F*; and by Lemma 15b, $\vdash \tilde{F}^\dagger \sim F^*$. This with $\vdash \tilde{F}^\dagger$ (and *18a) gives $\vdash F^*$, as remained to be shown.

Example 7°. We shall prove (Example 2 § 35) that
(a) $\vdash \mathcal{A} \vee \forall a\mathcal{B}(a) \sim \forall a(\mathcal{A} \vee \mathcal{B}(a))$. Thence by Lemma 15b,
(b) $\vdash \mathcal{A} \vee \forall x\mathcal{B}(x) \sim \forall x(\mathcal{A} \vee \mathcal{B}(x))$, where x is any variable. Thence by Theorem 15, (c) $\vdash A \vee \forall xB(x) \sim \forall x(A \vee B(x))$, where B(x) is any formula, and A any formula not containing x free (as otherwise (A2) for Proviso (A) would be violated). This is *92 with the same stipulations as appear in Theorem 17. From (b) we easily infer (d) $\mathcal{A} \vee \forall x\mathcal{B}(x) \vdash \mathcal{A} \vee \mathcal{B}(x)$ and (e) $\mathcal{A} \vee \mathcal{B}(x) \vdash^x \mathcal{A} \vee \forall x\mathcal{B}(x)$. Substitution for $\mathcal{A}$ of a formula A containing x free is permissible in (d), but Proviso (B) prevents it in (e).

The situations which the provisos of the substitution rule, or the stipulations on our metamathematical letters, prevent always involve a variable occurring both anonymously and explicitly. A blanket rule that could be used, in place of the more detailed conditions stated from case to case, is simply that the anonymous variables be distinct from the explicit variables. This is of course a little more restrictive than is necessary, e.g. anonymous bound x's in the A of *92 are clearly innocuous.

Remark 1. *If* Γ, E *are predicate letter formulas in the predicate letters* (1), *and* Γ ⊢ E, *then there is a deduction of* E *from* Γ *in (each formula of) which no predicate letters other than* (1) *occur*. For in the given deduction we can substitute (2′) for (1′), where (2) is the same as (1), and the additional name forms in (2′) contain only (1), e.g. each of them can be $\forall x_1 \dots \forall x_{n_1} P_1(x_1, \dots, x_{n_1})$.

Converse of substitution. A formula $A(a_1, \dots, a_n)$ will be called a *prime name form* (in the distinct variables $a_1, \dots, a_n$), provided (i) it has none of the forms $A \supset B$, $A \& B$, $A \vee B$, $\neg A$, $\forall x A(x)$ or $\exists x A(x)$, where A and B are formulas, x is a variable, and A(x) is a formula, and (ii) it contains exactly the variables $a_1, \dots, a_n$. Two prime name forms $A_i(a_1, \dots, a_{n_i})$ and $A_j(a_1, \dots, a_{n_j})$ will be said to be *distinct* (as prime name forms), if $A_i(t_1, \dots, t_{n_i})$ and $A_j(u_1, \dots, u_{n_j})$ are not the same formula for any terms $t_1, \dots, t_{n_i}, u_1, \dots, u_{n_j}$. For example, $a+a=b$ and $0=a\cdot b$ are distinct, but $a+a=b$ and $a=b\cdot c$ are not distinct.

Theorem 16. Converse of substitution for predicate letters. *Under the same stipulations as in Theorem* 15, *without Provisos* (A) *and* (B), *but provided instead that* (2) *be distinct prime name forms: If* $D_1^*, \dots, D_l^* \vdash E^*$, *then* $D_1, \dots, D_l \vdash E$.

This can be proved using the same ideas as Theorem 4 (§ 25), and likewise admits a second version.

Name form replacement. Using the notion of name form occurrence indicated above (following Example 5), the replacement theory (Theorem 14 with *66, cf. § 33 following Corollary 2) can be formulated thus: $A(x_1, \dots, x_n) \sim B(x_1, \dots, x_n) \vdash^{x_1 \dots x_n} C_{A(t_1, \dots, t_n)} \sim C_{B(t_1, \dots, t_n)}$, provided the parts $A(t_1, \dots, t_n)$ and $B(t_1, \dots, t_n)$ constitute occurrences of $A(x_1, \dots, x_n)$ and $B(x_1, \dots, x_n)$, respectively, as name forms in $x_1, \dots, x_n$.

Remark 2. Results similar to Theorems 15 and 16 and Remark 1 hold for individual variables. We shall state only the following. (a) *If* $z_1, \dots, z_q$ *are distinct variables not occurring bound in* $D(z_1, \dots, z_q)$ *and* $E(z_1, \dots, z_q)$, *and* $D(z_1, \dots, z_q) \vdash E(z_1, \dots, z_q)$ *with* $z_1, \dots, z_q$ *held constant, then there is a deduction of* $E(z_1, \dots, z_q)$ *from* $D(z_1, \dots, z_q)$ *in which* $z_1, \dots, z_q$ *do not occur bound*. Proof, stated for $q = 1$ and with just one variable y varied. By Lemma 8a, ∀-introd. (on z), and change to a new variable $\bar{z}$, $\forall\bar{z}[\forall y D(\bar{z}) \supset E(\bar{z})]$ is provable. This formula does not contain z at all. For the definition of what constitutes a proof in the predicate calculus of a given formula, all variables not in the formula are on a par. Therefore there is a proof of $\forall\bar{z}[\forall y D(\bar{z}) \supset E(\bar{z})]$ not containing z. From this formula and D(z) we can deduce E(z) by $\forall$-elim. (on $\bar{z}$), $\forall$-introd. (on y) and $\supset$-elim. (b) *Let* $z_1, \ldots, z_q$ *be distinct variables not occurring bound in* $D(z_1, \ldots, z_q)$ *and* $E(z_1, \ldots, z_q)$; *and let* $t_1, \ldots, t_q$ *be distinct prime terms (i.e. individual symbols or variables) none of which occurs in* $D(z_1, \ldots, z_q)$ *or* $E(z_1, \ldots, z_q)$ *unless it is one of* $z_1, \ldots, z_q$. *Then* $D(z_1, \ldots, z_q) \vdash E(z_1, \ldots, z_q)$ *with* $z_1, \ldots, z_q$ *held constant, if and only if* $D(t_1, \ldots, t_q) \vdash E(t_1, \ldots, t_q)$ *with (the variables among)* $t_1, \ldots, t_q$ *held constant.* For by (a), $z_1, \ldots, z_q, t_1, \ldots, t_q$ can be eliminated as bound variables from the given deduction, after which every inference will remain valid on substituting throughout $t_1, \ldots, t_q$ for $z_1, \ldots, z_q$, or vice versa.

§ 35. Equivalences, duality, prenex form.

THEOREM 17. *If* x *and* y *are distinct variables,* A, B, A(x), B(x) *and* A(x, y) *are formulas,* A *and* B *do not contain* x *free, and for* *79 *and* *80 *if* x *is free for* y *in* A(x, y), *then*:

*75. $\vdash \forall x A \sim A$.

*76. $\vdash \exists x A \sim A$.

*77. $\vdash \forall x \forall y A(x,y) \sim \forall y \forall x A(x,y)$.

*78. $\vdash \exists x \exists y A(x,y) \sim \exists y \exists x A(x,y)$.

*79. $\vdash \forall x \forall y A(x,y) \supset \forall x A(x,x)$.

*80. $\vdash \exists x A(x,x) \supset \exists x \exists y A(x,y)$.

*81. $\vdash \forall x A(x) \supset \exists x A(x)$.

*82. $\vdash \exists x \forall y A(x,y) \supset \forall y \exists x A(x,y)$.

(Alterations of quantifiers.)

*83°. $\vdash \exists x A(x) \sim \neg\forall x \neg A(x)$.

*84°. $\vdash \forall x A(x) \sim \neg\exists x \neg A(x)$.

(Each of $\exists$ and $\forall$ in terms of the other and $\neg$.)

*85°. $\vdash \neg\forall x A(x) \sim \exists x \neg A(x)$.

*86. $\vdash \neg\exists x A(x) \sim \forall x \neg A(x)$.

*87. $\vdash \forall x A(x) \,\&\, \forall x B(x) \sim \forall x(A(x) \,\&\, B(x))$.

*88. $\vdash \exists x A(x) \vee \exists x B(x) \sim \exists x(A(x) \vee B(x))$.

*89. $\vdash A \,\&\, \forall x B(x) \sim \forall x(A \,\&\, B(x))$.

*90. $\vdash A \vee \exists x B(x) \sim \exists x(A \vee B(x))$.

*91. $\vdash A \,\&\, \exists x B(x) \sim \exists x(A \,\&\, B(x))$.

*92°. $\vdash A \vee \forall x B(x) \sim \forall x(A \vee B(x))$.

*93. $\vdash \exists x(A(x) \,\&\, B(x)) \supset \exists x A(x) \,\&\, \exists x B(x)$.

*94. $\vdash \forall x A(x) \vee \forall x B(x) \supset \forall x(A(x) \vee B(x))$.

(Transfer of $\neg$, & and $\vee$ across quantifiers).

*83a. $\vdash \exists x A(x) \supset \neg\forall x\neg A(x)$. *84a. $\vdash \forall x A(x) \supset \neg\exists x\neg A(x)$.

*85a. $\vdash \exists x \neg A(x) \supset \neg\forall x A(x)$. *92a. $\vdash A \vee \forall x B(x) \supset \forall x(A \vee B(x))$.

(Additional results of interest for the intuitionistic system.)

*95. $\vdash \forall x(A \supset B(x)) \sim A \supset \forall x B(x)$.

*96. $\vdash \forall x(A(x) \supset B) \sim \exists x A(x) \supset B$.

*97°. $\vdash \exists x(A \supset B(x)) \sim A \supset \exists x B(x)$.

*98°. $\vdash \exists x(A(x) \supset B) \sim \forall x A(x) \supset B$.

*99°. $\vdash \exists x(A(x) \supset B(x)) \sim \forall x A(x) \supset \exists x B(x)$.

*97a. $\vdash \exists x(A \supset B(x)) \supset (A \supset \exists x B(x))$.

*98a. $\vdash \exists x(A(x) \supset B) \supset (\forall x A(x) \supset B)$.

*99a. $\vdash \exists x(A(x) \supset B(x)) \supset (\forall x A(x) \supset \exists x B(x))$.

(Transfer of quantifiers across $\supset$, with comparison of classical and intuitionistic results.)

PROOFS, for the classical system, of *75—*94, excepting *76, *78, *80, *88, *90, *92, *94. Work is saved by postponing these seven until we have duality (or for *80 and *94, the dual-converse relationship). Then, classically, *95—*99 will follow by using *59 (§ 27) with *88, *90, *92 and *85, *86.

*75 If we redesignate A as "A(x)", then since A does not contain x free, A(t) is also A(x) (§ 18). The result follows, using $\forall$-elim. and $\supset$-introd. (or Axiom Schema 10), and $\forall$-introd. and $\supset$-introd. [x is not varied in the $\forall$-introd., since A(x) does not contain it free], and *16.

*79. 1. $\forall x\forall y A(x, y) \vdash A(x, x) \vdash^{x} \forall x A(x, x)$ — double $\forall$-elim. (*65) [x, x is a pair of terms free for x, y in A(x, y)], $\forall$-introd.

2. $\vdash \forall x\forall y A(x, y) \supset \forall x A(x, x)$ — $\supset$-introd., 1 [x is not varied in 1, since $\forall x\forall y A(x, y)$ does not contain x free].

*82. 1. $A(x, y) \vdash \exists x A(x, y) \vdash^{y} \forall y\exists x A(x, y)$ — $\exists$-introd., $\forall$-introd.

2. $\forall y A(x, y) \vdash \forall y\exists x A(x, y)$ — $\forall$-elim., 1.

3. $\exists x\forall y A(x, y) \vdash \forall y\exists x A(x, y)$ — $\exists$-elim., 2 [$\forall y\exists x A(x, y)$ does not contain x free, and no variable is varied in 2, since y (cf. 1) does not occur free in $\forall y A(x, y)$].

4. $\vdash \exists x\forall y A(x, y) \supset \forall y\exists x A(x, y)$ — $\supset$-introd., 3 [no variable is varied in 3 (cf. Lemma 7b § 24)].

Note how the attempt to give a corresponding demonstration of the converse of *82 (i.e. of *82 with the direction of $\supset$ reversed) is defeated by the restriction on the use of subsidiary deduction in the predicate calculus:

1. $A(x, y) \vdash^{y} \forall y A(x, y) \vdash \exists x\forall y A(x, y)$ — $\forall$-introd., $\exists$-introd.

2? $\exists x A(x, y) \vdash \exists x \forall y A(x, y)$ — $\exists$-elim., 1. But this is illegitimate, since the rule of $\exists$-elimination (in contrast to the $\forall$-elimination rule used at Step 2 for *82) is a subsidiary deduction rule, and is inapplicable here because in the subsidiary deduction 1 the variable y is varied for the assumption formula A(x, y) to be discharged (except if A(x, y) does not contain y free).

There is no way around this difficulty, and the converse of *82 should not be provable for arbitrary A(x, y). In terms of the interpretation, the formula $\exists x \forall y A(x, y)$ says that there is one x such that for every y, A(x, y); and $\forall y \exists x A(x, y)$ says merely that for every y there is some x, not necessarily the same x for different y's, such that A(x, y). The distinction is familiar to mathematicians from the example of uniform convergence vs. ordinary convergence of a sequence of functions $a_n(x)$ to a limit function $a(x)$ on an interval or other range X of x. Using the present logical symbolism, and variables p, n and N ranging over natural numbers, and x over X, the properties of uniform convergence and ordinary convergence are expressed respectively by

(i) $\forall p \exists N \forall x \forall n (n > N \supset | a_n(x) - a(x) | < 1/2^p)$,

(ii) $\forall p \forall x \exists N \forall n (n > N \supset | a_n(x) - a(x) | < 1/2^p)$.

Then *82 says that uniform convergence implies ordinary convergence; but the converse is not generally true. (Similarly for uniform and ordinary continuity.)

A metamathematical demonstration that $\forall b \exists a \mathcal{A}(a, b) \supset \exists a \forall b \mathcal{A}(a, b)$ is unprovable in the predicate calculus will be given in Example 2 § 36.

*83. 1. $A(x), \forall x \neg A(x) \vdash \neg A(x)$ — $\forall$-elim.

2. $A(x), \forall x \neg A(x) \vdash A(x)$.

3. $A(x) \vdash \neg \forall x \neg A(x)$ — $\neg$-introd., 1,2 [no variable of $\forall x \neg A(x)$ is varied in 1 or 2].

4. $\exists x A(x) \vdash \neg \forall x \neg A(x)$ — $\exists$-elim., 3 [$\neg \forall x \neg A(x)$ does not contain x free, and no variable is varied in 3].

5. $\vdash \exists x A(x) \supset \neg \forall x \neg A(x)$ — $\supset$-introd., 4 [no variable is varied in 4].

6. $\neg \exists x A(x), A(x) \vdash \exists x A(x)$ — $\exists$-introd.

7. $\neg \exists x A(x), A(x) \vdash \neg \exists x A(x)$.

8. $\neg \exists x A(x) \vdash \neg A(x) \vdash^{x} \forall x \neg A(x)$ — $\neg$-introd., 6, 7 [no variables are varied in 6, 7], $\forall$-introd.

9. $\vdash \neg \exists x A(x) \supset \forall x \neg A(x)$ — $\supset$-introd., 8 [x does not occur free in the assumption formula $\neg \exists x A(x)$ of 8 which is being discharged].

10. $\vdash \neg \forall x \neg A(x) \supset \exists x A(x)$ — contraposition (*14), 9.
11. $\vdash \exists x A(x) \sim \neg \forall x \neg A(x)$ — &-introd. (*16), 5, 10.

*84. See Example 1 § 34.

*87. 1. $A(x), B(x) \vdash A(x) \& B(x) \vdash^x \forall x(A(x) \& B(x))$ — &-introd., $\forall$-introd.
2. $\forall x A(x), \quad \forall x B(x) \vdash \forall x(A(x) \& B(x))$ -- $\forall$-elim. twice, 1.
3. $\forall x A(x) \& \forall x B(x) \vdash \forall x(A(x) \& B(x))$ — &-elim., 2.
4. $\vdash \forall x A(x) \& \forall x B(x) \supset \forall x(A(x) \& B(x))$ — $\supset$-introd., 3 [no variable is varied in 3, since x (cf. 1) does not occur free in $\forall x A(x) \& \forall x B(x)$].
5. $A(x) \& B(x) \vdash A(x) \vdash^x \forall x A(x)$ — &-elim., $\forall$-introd.
6. $A(x) \& B(x) \vdash B(x) \vdash^x \forall x B(x)$ — &-elim., $\forall$-introd.
7. $A(x) \& B(x) \vdash^x \forall x A(x) \& \forall x B(x)$ — &-introd., 5, 6.
8. $\forall x(A(x) \& B(x)) \vdash \forall x A(x) \& \forall x B(x)$ — $\forall$-elim., 7.
9. $\vdash \forall x(A(x) \& B(x)) \supset \forall x A(x) \& \forall x B(x)$ — $\supset$-introd., 8 [no variable is varied in 8, since x (cf. 7) does not occur free in $\forall x(A(x) \& B(x))$].
10. $\vdash \forall x A(x) \& \forall x B(x) \sim \forall x(A(x) \& B(x))$ — &-introd., 4, 9.

*89, *91, *93. If we read "A" for "A(x)" and "$\forall x A(x)$" in the preceding, omitting one $\forall$-elimination at Step 2 and the $\forall$-introduction at Step 5, it reads as a demonstration of *89. Then substituting $\exists$ for $\forall$ throughout, we get a demonstration of *91. The reader may write this out, and verify that the conditions for the $\exists$-eliminations are satisfied. But substitution of $\exists$ for $\forall$ in the proof of *87 does not work. Why? We thus obtain only *93 but not the converse.

As a further exercise, the reader may attempt to give a corresponding proof of *92, and see how this is defeated by the restriction on subsidiary deductions. The result *92, which we shall infer from *91 after we have duality, is interesting as an example of a formula which does not contain $\neg$ but which we do not succeed in proving without Postulate 8.

In view of *49b § 27, there can be at most 18 (= 3·2·3) intuitionistically non-equivalent formulas formed from A(x) by quantifying x and possibly applying negation. (We use either 0, 1 or 2 $\neg$'s first, then either $\forall x$ or $\exists x$, then again either 0, 1 or 2 $\neg$'s.)

Corollary. *Each of the four tables* I — IV *comprises formulas equivalent to one another in the classical predicate calculus. For each table, in the intuitionistic system: Each two formulas not separated by a line are equivalent. Each formula implies any formula below it, i.e. the implication from the one to the other is provable. The double negation of the implication from each formula to any formula not separated from it by a double line is provable* (*and hence,* using *49a and *25, *of the equivalence*). (Heyting 1946.)

$$
\begin{array}{lr}
\multicolumn{2}{c}{\text{I}} \\
\text{a.} & \forall x A(x) \\ \hline
\text{b.} & \neg\neg\forall x A(x) \\ \hline\hline
\text{c}_1. & \forall x \neg\neg A(x) \\
\text{c}_2. & \neg\neg\forall x \neg\neg A(x) \\
\text{c}_3. & \neg\exists x \neg A(x)
\end{array}
\qquad
\begin{array}{lr}
\multicolumn{2}{c}{\text{II}} \\
\text{a.} & \exists x A(x) \\ \hline
\text{b.} & \exists x \neg\neg A(x) \\ \hline
\text{c}_1. & \neg\neg\exists x A(x) \\
\text{c}_2. & \neg\neg\exists x \neg\neg A(x) \\
\text{c}_3. & \neg\forall x \neg A(x)
\end{array}
$$

$$
\begin{array}{lr}
\multicolumn{2}{c}{\text{III}} \\
\text{a.} & \exists x \neg A(x) \\ \hline
\text{b}_1. & \neg\neg\exists x \neg A(x) \\
\text{b}_2. & \neg\forall x \neg\neg A(x) \\ \hline\hline
\text{c.} & \neg\forall x A(x)
\end{array}
\qquad
\begin{array}{lr}
\multicolumn{2}{c}{\text{IV}} \\
\text{a}_1. & \forall x \neg A(x) \\
\text{a}_2. & \neg\neg\forall x \neg A(x) \\
\text{a}_3. & \neg\exists x \neg\neg A(x) \\
\text{a}_4. & \neg\exists x A(x)
\end{array}
$$

PROOFS for Table II, in the intuitionistic system. $\vdash$ IIa $\supset$ IIb [*49a, *70]. $\vdash$ IIb $\supset$ IIc$_3$ [*85a]. $\vdash$ IIc$_3 \sim$ IIc$_1$ [*86]. $\vdash$ IIc$_3 \sim \neg\forall x\neg\neg\neg A(x)$ [*49b] $\sim$ IIc$_2$ [*86]. $\vdash \neg\neg$(IIc$_2 \supset$ IIb) [*51b]. Likewise, $\vdash \neg\neg$(IIc$_1 \supset$ IIa). Hence $\vdash \neg\neg$(IIb $\supset$ IIa), by *24 with $\vdash$ IIb $\supset$ IIc$_1$ and *49a.

THEOREM 18°. *Let* D *be a predicate letter formula constructed from the distinct predicate letters* $P_1(a_1, \ldots, a_{n_1}), \ldots, P_m(a_1, \ldots, a_{n_m})$ *and their negations* $\neg P_1(a_1, \ldots, a_{n_1}), \ldots, \neg P_m(a_1, \ldots, a_{n_m})$ *using only the operators* &, $\vee$, $\forall x$ *and* $\exists x$ (*for any variable* x). *Then a formula* $D^\dagger$ *equivalent to the negation* $\neg D$ *of* D *is obtained by the interchange throughout* D *of* & *with* $\vee$, *of* $\forall$ *with* $\exists$, *and of each letter with its negation.*

In other words, if D *be such a predicate letter formula, and* $D^\dagger$ *be the result of the described interchange performed on* D: $\vdash \neg D \sim D^\dagger$.

EXAMPLE 1°. $\vdash \neg\exists a(\forall b\neg\mathcal{A}(b) \;\&\; (\neg B \vee \exists c\;\; C(a, c, b))) \sim$
$\forall a(\exists b\;\; \mathcal{A}(b) \vee (\;\; B \;\&\; \forall c\neg C(a, c, b)))$.

Proof is by the same method as Theorem 8 (§ 27), using *85 and *86 to handle the two new cases which now arise under the induction step. The theorem as before admits a second version.

COROLLARY°. *An equivalence between two letter formulas* E *and* F *of the type described in the theorem is preserved under the interchange throughout* E *and* F *of* & *with* $\vee$ *and of* $\forall$ *with* $\exists$.

In other words, if E *and* F *be two such predicate letter formulas, and* E′ *and* F′ *be the results of the described interchange performed on* E *and* F, *respectively*: *If* $\vdash$ E $\sim$ F, *then* $\vdash$ E′ $\sim$ F′. (Principle of duality.) *Also, if* $\vdash$ E $\supset$ F, *then* $\vdash$ F′ $\supset$ E′. (Dual-converse relationship.)

The corollary follows from the theorem as before.

Example 2°. By *91, $\vdash \mathcal{A} \,\&\, \exists a \mathcal{B}(a) \sim \exists a(\mathcal{A} \,\&\, \mathcal{B}(a))$. Thence by duality, $\vdash \mathcal{A} \vee \forall a \mathcal{B}(a) \sim \forall a(\mathcal{A} \vee \mathcal{B}(a))$. Thence *92, as in Example 7 § 34.

Similarly, we obtain *76, *78, *88, *90 as duals of *75, *77, *87, *89 and *80, *94 as dual-converses of *79, *93, respectively. (Note that each of *81 and *82 is self-dual-converse.)

Theorem 19°. *Given any formula* C, *there can be found a formula* D (called a *prenex form of* C) *with the following two properties. The formula* C *is equivalent to* D, *i.e.* $\vdash$ C $\sim$ D. *In* D, *all the quantifiers* (*if any*) *stand at the front, i.e. all the other logical symbols* $\supset$, &, $\vee$, $\neg$ (*if any*) *stand within the scope of every quantifier* (such a formula we say is *prenex*).

Proof. To reduce a formula C to prenex form, we can, step by step, move all the quantifiers outside the scopes of the logical symbols $\supset$, &, $\vee$, $\neg$ by applications of *85, *86, *89—*92, *95—*98, noting the following. In case the formula for application of *89—*92, *95—*98 fails to meet the condition that the A or the B not contain the x free, a change of bound variables can be made by *73 or *74. In case the A for *89—*92 stands on the wrong side of the & or $\vee$, *33 or *34 can be used. (This procedure for reduction to prenex form does not require *87, *88 or *99; but at any point where one of them can be applied, the use of it will save steps and lead to a shorter prenex form.)

To prove that the procedure terminates, we can use as induction number the number of instances of a quantifier standing inside the scope of an $\supset$, &, $\vee$ or $\neg$, i.e. the total number of pairs, one member of which is an $\supset$, &, $\vee$ or $\neg$, and the other member is a quantifier standing inside the scope of that member. If this number is not 0, there must be some instance where there is no logical symbol of intermediate scope. A step is then carried out which removes this instance, leaving the others unchanged, so that the induction number is reduced by one. (If *87, *88 or *99 is used, the induction number is reduced by two or more.)

Example 3°. The numbered formulas which follow are successively equivalent, each to the next, by replacements based on the equivalences cited at the right. The last formula is a prenex form of the first, or indeed of any formula in the list.

1. $[\neg \exists a \mathcal{A}(a) \vee \forall a \mathcal{B}(a)] \,\&\, [C \supset \forall a \mathcal{D}(a)]$.
2. $[\forall a \neg \mathcal{A}(a) \vee \forall a \mathcal{B}(a)] \,\&\, \forall a[C \supset \mathcal{D}(a)]$ — *86, *95.
3. $\forall a[\forall a \neg \mathcal{A}(a) \vee \mathcal{B}(a)] \,\&\, \forall a[C \supset \mathcal{D}(a)]$ — *92.
4. $\forall a[\forall b \neg \mathcal{A}(b) \vee \mathcal{B}(a)] \,\&\, \forall a[C \supset \mathcal{D}(a)]$ — *73.
5. $\forall a \forall b[\neg \mathcal{A}(b) \vee \mathcal{B}(a)] \,\&\, \forall a[C \supset \mathcal{D}(a)]$ — *34, *92.
6. $\forall a\{\forall b[\neg \mathcal{A}(b) \vee \mathcal{B}(a)] \,\&\, [C \supset \mathcal{D}(a)]\}$ — *87.
7. $\forall a \forall b\{[\neg \mathcal{A}(b) \vee \mathcal{B}(a)] \,\&\, [C \supset \mathcal{D}(a)]\}$ — *33, *89.

§ 36. Valuation, consistency. The predicate calculus is intended to be a formalization of principles of predicate logic which hold good independently of the number of elements in the object domain, provided there is at least one element (§ 31). Hence the provable formulas should all be true, if we specify the number to be k, where k is any integer ≥ 1. We may combine this idea with the one used in § 28, where we abstracted from true and false propositions to obtain two arithmetic objects $\mathfrak{t}$ and $\mathfrak{f}$. This suggests a finitary valuation procedure, which will enable us to establish metamathematically the consistency of the predicate calculus.

In the valuation procedure, a predicate letter formula is considered as representing a function of the free individual variables and of the predicate letters (including proposition letters) which it contains, or possibly of these and other free variables and predicate letters as well. Then when we define the notion which will correspond to that of identical truth for the propositional calculus, we shall require that the formulas provable in the calculus should be true whatever predicate each predicate letter represents, and also, in view of the generality interpretation of the free individual variables (§ 32), whatever object from the object domain each free individual variable represents.

After choosing a fixed positive integer k for the number of distinct objects in the object domain, it does not matter for the valuation procedure what the objects themselves are. It is convenient to take them to be (or to call them) the numbers $1, \ldots, k$. These numbers are to be the values which the individual variables take.

As before (§ 28), the proposition letters (i.e. letters for predicates of 0 variables) take the values $\mathfrak{t}$, $\mathfrak{f}$.

Now consider the predicate letters. For any given integer $n > 0$, a predicate letter with n attached variables differs under the logical interpretation of the system from a proposition letter in that it represents not a proposition but rather a propositional function of n variables, i.e. a function which takes a proposition as value for each set of values of the attached variables (§ 31). The values which we give a predicate letter with n

attached variables in our valuation procedure, when the propositions are replaced by t and f, will accordingly be not t, f, but rather functions of n variables each over the domain $\{1, \ldots, k\}$ taking values in the domain {t, f}. There are exactly 2^{k^n} different such functions. We call them the *logical functions* of n variables over the domain of k objects. The truth values t, f, which we use for the case $n = 0$, can be considered as being the 2 ($= 2^{k^0}$) logical functions of 0 variables.

As before, we interpret ⊃, &, V, ¬ as fixed functions over the domain of two objects {t, f} taking values in the same domain, defined by the tables given previously (§ 28). We now interpret ∀ and ∃ as fixed functions over the logical functions of one variable taking values from the domain {t, f}, where the variable x in ∀x or ∃x indicates of what individual variable the operand shall be considered as logical function. These two fixed logical functions are defined as follows. For a given logical function A(x), the value of ∀xA(x) is t, if A(x) has the value t for every value of x in the domain $\{1, \ldots, k\}$; otherwise the value is f. The value of ∃xA(x) is t, if A(x) has the value t for some value of x in the domain $\{1, \ldots, k\}$; and otherwise the value is f.

Given a predicate letter formula, we are now in a position to compute a table expressing the values of the function, of the distinct free individual variables and predicate letters occurring in it (or of these and other variables and letters), which the formula represents. For the tabulation, it will be convenient first to list in some fixed order the logical functions which will be required as values of the predicate letters, and to introduce symbols to stand for them.

Example 1. For $k = 2$, let us construct the table for the predicate letter formula $\forall a(\mathcal{B} \supset \mathcal{A}(a)) \vee (\neg \mathcal{A}(b) \,\&\, \mathcal{B})$, for exactly the free variables and predicate letters contained in it. This formula then represents a function of three variables, namely b, $\mathcal{B}$ and $\mathcal{A}(a)$, where a is the attached variable of the name form used for $\mathcal{A}$ as a predicate letter with one variable (cf. § 31). Before constructing the table for the formula, we shall introduce notations for the logical functions of one variable, which we shall be employing as values of the variable $\mathcal{A}(a)$. Since $k = 2$, there are 4 ($= 2^{2^1}$) of them, $\mathfrak{l}_1(a)$, $\mathfrak{l}_2(a)$, $\mathfrak{l}_3(a)$, $\mathfrak{l}_4(a)$, defined by the following table of their values.

LOGICAL FUNCTIONS OF ONE VARIABLE IN A DOMAIN OF TWO OBJECTS

Value of the independent variable	Corresponding value of the respective function			
a	$\mathfrak{l}_1(a)$	$\mathfrak{l}_2(a)$	$\mathfrak{l}_3(a)$	$\mathfrak{l}_4(a)$
1	$\mathfrak{t}$	$\mathfrak{t}$	$\mathfrak{f}$	$\mathfrak{f}$
2	$\mathfrak{t}$	$\mathfrak{f}$	$\mathfrak{t}$	$\mathfrak{f}$

The table for the given formula is now as shown (the computation of a sample entry will follow).

Value of the respective independent variable			Corresponding value of the function
b	$\mathcal{B}$	$\mathcal{A}(a)$	$\forall a(\mathcal{B} \supset \mathcal{A}(a)) \vee (\neg \mathcal{A}(b) \,\&\, \mathcal{B})$
1	$\mathfrak{t}$	$\mathfrak{l}_1(a)$	$\mathfrak{t}$
1	$\mathfrak{t}$	$\mathfrak{l}_2(a)$	$\mathfrak{f}$
1	$\mathfrak{t}$	$\mathfrak{l}_3(a)$	$\mathfrak{t}$
1	$\mathfrak{t}$	$\mathfrak{l}_4(a)$	$\mathfrak{t}$
1	$\mathfrak{f}$	$\mathfrak{l}_1(a)$	$\mathfrak{t}$
1	$\mathfrak{f}$	$\mathfrak{l}_2(a)$	$\mathfrak{t}$
1	$\mathfrak{f}$	$\mathfrak{l}_3(a)$	$\mathfrak{t}$
1	$\mathfrak{f}$	$\mathfrak{l}_4(a)$	$\mathfrak{t}$
2	$\mathfrak{t}$	$\mathfrak{l}_1(a)$	$\mathfrak{t}$
2	$\mathfrak{t}$	$\mathfrak{l}_2(a)$	$\mathfrak{t}$
2	$\mathfrak{t}$	$\mathfrak{l}_3(a)$	$\mathfrak{f}$
2	$\mathfrak{t}$	$\mathfrak{l}_4(a)$	$\mathfrak{t}$
2	$\mathfrak{f}$	$\mathfrak{l}_1(a)$	$\mathfrak{t}$
2	$\mathfrak{f}$	$\mathfrak{l}_2(a)$	$\mathfrak{t}$
2	$\mathfrak{f}$	$\mathfrak{l}_3(a)$	$\mathfrak{t}$
2	$\mathfrak{f}$	$\mathfrak{l}_4(a)$	$\mathfrak{t}$

We now give the computation for the second value (line 2 of the table). For this purpose, when we come to the $\forall$-operation, we shall need the table for $\mathcal{B} \supset \mathcal{A}(a)$ with $\mathcal{B}$ having the value $\mathfrak{t}$ and $\mathcal{A}(a)$ the value $\mathfrak{l}_2(a)$. We give this table first (its computation to follow).

Value of the independent variable a	Corresponding value of the function $\mathfrak{t} \supset \mathfrak{l}_2(a)$
1	$\mathfrak{t}$
2	$\mathfrak{f}$

The computations of the two values in this subsidiary table, using the table for $\mathfrak{l}_2(a)$ given at the outset and the table for $\supset$ from § 28, are these:

$$\begin{array}{ll} \mathfrak{t} \supset \mathfrak{l}_2(a) & \qquad\qquad \mathfrak{t} \supset \mathfrak{l}_2(a) \\ \mathfrak{t} \supset \mathfrak{l}_2(1) & \qquad\qquad \mathfrak{t} \supset \mathfrak{l}_2(2) \\ \mathfrak{t} \supset \ \mathfrak{t} & \qquad\qquad \mathfrak{t} \supset \ \mathfrak{f} \\ \quad \mathfrak{t} & \qquad\qquad \quad \mathfrak{f} \end{array}$$

We now return to the original question of computing the entry for the second line of the table for $\forall a(\mathcal{B} \supset \mathcal{A}(a)) \vee (\neg \mathcal{A}(b) \,\&\, \mathcal{B})$, i.e. the value of this formula when b has the value 1, $\mathcal{B}$ the value $\mathfrak{t}$ and $\mathcal{A}(a)$ the value $\mathfrak{l}_2(a)$. We start out thus.

$$\begin{array}{l} \forall a(\mathcal{B} \supset \mathcal{A}(a)) \vee (\neg \mathcal{A}(b) \,\&\, \mathcal{B}) \\ \forall a(\mathfrak{t} \supset \mathfrak{l}_2(a)) \vee (\neg \mathfrak{l}_2(1) \,\&\, \mathfrak{t}) \end{array}$$

Since the value column of the table for $\mathfrak{t} \supset \mathfrak{l}_2(a)$ does not have all $\mathfrak{t}$'s, we can replace $\forall a(\mathfrak{t} \supset \mathfrak{l}_2(a))$ by $\mathfrak{f}$ under the interpretation given for $\forall$, and also we can replace $\mathfrak{l}_2(1)$ by its value $\mathfrak{t}$ from the table for $\mathfrak{l}_2(a)$, thus.

$$\begin{array}{l} \mathfrak{f} \vee (\neg \mathfrak{t} \,\&\, \mathfrak{t}) \\ \mathfrak{f} \vee (\mathfrak{f} \,\&\, \mathfrak{t}) \\ \mathfrak{f} \vee \quad \mathfrak{f} \\ \quad \mathfrak{f} \end{array}$$

The reader may verify that he understands the procedure by calculating other entries in our table for $\forall a(\mathcal{B} \supset \mathcal{A}(a)) \vee (\neg \mathcal{A}(b) \,\&\, \mathcal{B})$. Of course there are usually short cuts that can be used in ascertaining the table for a formula, so that it is not necessary to go through the whole calculation procedure separately for every entry of the table (e.g. here we can recognize at once that all eight entries for which $\mathcal{B}$ is $\mathfrak{f}$ are $\mathfrak{t}$). But this calculation illustrates the underlying definition of the function represented by a predicate letter formula for a given positive integer k.

If, for a given k, the value column of the table for a predicate letter formula, as a function of certain free variables and predicate letters including all contained in it, contains only $\mathfrak{t}$'s, we say that the formula is *k-identical*, or *valid in a domain of k objects*. If it contains some t's, the formula is said to be *satisfiable in a domain of k objects*.

As before (§ 28), if it is *k*-identical (or satisfiable in a domain of *k* objects) for the minimal list of free variables and predicate letters, then it is for any other list; and conversely. Hence again the reference to the list can be omitted.

If the value columns of the tables for two predicate letter formulas considered as functions of just those free variables and predicate letters contained in either (or of any others as well) are the same, the two formulas are said to be *k-equal*.

THEOREM 20. *For each fixed integer k* ($k \geq 1$): *A necessary condition that a predicate letter formula* E *be provable* (*or deducible from k-identical formulas* Γ) *in the predicate calculus is that* E *be k-identical.*

PROOF. The theorem follows from two lemmas, corresponding to those for Theorem 9, but now referring to the postulate list of the predicate calculus, predicate letter formulas and *k*-identity. The reasoning already given for the postulates of Group A1 carries over in its essentials to the present situation, and for the four postulates of Group A2 we show the treatment of two.

AXIOM SCHEMA 10. An axiom by this schema is ∀xA(x) ⊃ A(t), where the term t for the pure predicate calculus is simply a variable, and this variable t is free for x in A(x).

The variable t may be the same or distinct from x, and x may or may not occur free in A(x).

We must show that ∀xA(x) ⊃ A(t) takes the value t, for every assignment of logical functions as values of the predicate letters, and of the objects 1, . . . , *k* as values of the free variables, contained in ∀xA(x) ⊃ A(t).

Consider a particular such assignment. If the assigned values are given to the predicate letters and free variables of A(x), except (if x occurs free in A(x)) to the variable x, then A(x) represents a logical function of the variable x (whether or not x occurs free in A(x)).

Since t is free for x in A(x), in the sequence of symbols A(t) the free occurrences of t occupy the positions which are occupied in A(x) by free occurrences of either t or x. Therefore the value of the logical function represented by A(x), when x takes as value the assigned value of t, is the value of A(t) for the particular assignment under consideration.

Now there are two cases.

CASE 1: the logical function represented by A(x) has only t's as values. Then the value of A(t), which is one of these values, is t. Hence, by the valuation table for ⊃ (§ 28), ∀xA(x) ⊃ A(t) has the value t.

CASE 2: the logical function represented by A(x) has some f's in its value column. Then, by the definition of the valuation process for ∀, the formula ∀xA(x) has the value f; and again ∀xA(x) ⊃ A(t) has the value t.

RULE 12. The premise is A(x) ⊃ C, and the conclusion is ∃xA(x) ⊃ C, where C does not contain x free.

We have as hypothesis that A(x) ⊃ C takes the value t for every assignment of logical functions as values of the predicate letters, and of the objects 1, . . ., *k* as values of the free variables, contained in A(x) ⊃ C. We must show the like for ∃xA(x) ⊃ C.

Consider a particular assignment for ∃xA(x) ⊃ C, for just the predicate letters and free variables which it contains. Since ∃xA(x) ⊃ C does not contain x free, this does not include an assignment for x.

Now if the assigned values are given to the predicate letters and free variables of A(x), except (if x occurs free in A(x)) to x, then A(x) represents a logical function of the variable x.

CASE 1: the logical function represented by A(x) has some t's in its value column. Choose a value of x corresponding to one of these t's; and consider the given assignment for ∃xA(x) ⊃ C, together with this value of x, as an assignment for A(x) ⊃ C. Then A(x) has the value t; by hypothesis, A(x) ⊃ C has the value t; and hence by the valuation table for ⊃, C has the value t. Since C does not contain x free, this value of C is on the basis of the given assignment for ∃xA(x) ⊃ C, without regard to the value of x. Hence, by the valuation table for ⊃, ∃xA(x) ⊃ C takes the value t for the given assignment.

CASE 2: the logical function represented by A(x) has only f's as values. Then ∃xA(x) has the value f; and hence ∃xA(x) ⊃ C has the value t.

EXAMPLE 1 (concluded). $\forall a(\mathcal{B} \supset \mathcal{A}(a)) \vee (\neg\mathcal{A}(b)\ \&\ \mathcal{B})$ is not *k*-identical, since its value column contains f's, and hence it is unprovable in the predicate calculus.

EXAMPLE 2. For $k = 2$, when $\mathcal{A}(a, b)$ takes as value the logical function $\mathfrak{l}(a, b)$ such that $\mathfrak{l}(1, 1) = \mathfrak{l}(2, 2) = \mathfrak{t}$, $\mathfrak{l}(1, 2) = \mathfrak{l}(2, 1) = \mathfrak{f}$, the formula $\forall b\exists a\mathcal{A}(a, b) \supset \exists a\forall b\mathcal{A}(a, b)$ takes the value f, so it is unprovable.

Corollary 1. *For each integer $k \geq 1$, a necessary condition that two predicate letter formulas* E *and* F *be equivalent is that they be k-equal, i.e. if* $\vdash$ E $\sim$ F, *then* E *and* F *are k-equal.*

Example 3. For $k = 2$, with $\mathfrak{l}_1(a)$, $\mathfrak{l}_2(a)$, $\mathfrak{l}_3(a)$, $\mathfrak{l}_4(a)$ as in Example 1, we have the following tables for the top formulas of I — IV Corollary Theorem 17 written with a particular variable and predicate letter. Hence no two of the four are equivalent.

$\mathcal{A}(a)$	$\forall a\mathcal{A}(a)$	$\exists a\mathcal{A}(a)$	$\exists a \neg \mathcal{A}(a)$	$\forall a \neg \mathcal{A}(a)$
$\mathfrak{l}_1(a)$	t	t	f	f
$\mathfrak{l}_2(a)$	f	t	t	f
$\mathfrak{l}_3(a)$	f	t	t	f
$\mathfrak{l}_4(a)$	f	f	t	t

Corollary 2. *The predicate calculus is (simply) consistent, i.e. for no formula* A, *both* $\vdash$ A *and* $\vdash \neg$A.

Proof. If A is a predicate letter formula, then, for each k, A and $\neg$A cannot both be k-identical. (Here it would suffice to have proved the theorem for any one fixed k. In the original proof by Hilbert and Ackermann 1928, $k = 1$.) For the other sense of formula, the consistency follows by the converse of the substitution rule (Theorem 16 § 34).

***§ 37. Set-theoretic predicate logic, *k*-transforms.** The logical functions used in the valuation procedure for a given finite k are finite objects, in the sense that each is represented by a table having a finite number of entries.

The notion of a logical function of n variables can be stated similarly for the case that the object domain has an infinite number of elements, but with the difference that the functions cannot be described by finite tables. We can then define the notions of *validity*, and of *satisfiability*, in a given non-empty object domain. Clearly only the cardinal number of the object domain matters for this purpose, and not what the elements are themselves.

Then by reasoning as in the proof of Theorem 20, we can show that every provable predicate letter formula is valid in every non-empty object domain. In demonstrating this for the case of an infinite domain, the reasoning employed is no longer finitary. A non-finitary step appears, for example, in the treatment of Axiom Schema 10, where we distinguish two cases according as all of the values of a certain function are t's or some are f's, there being now infinitely many values under consideration.

This constitutes an application of the law of the excluded middle for an infinite set (§ 13). In fact the notion itself of validity, for the case of an infinite domain and a formula containing a predicate letter with $n > 0$ attached variables, is not finitary. For it requires that the value of a function be **t** for all logical functions of n variables as values of that predicate letter; and the class of those logical functions is non-enumerable, and so only conceivable (as we usually think) in terms of the completed infinite.

The result that every provable letter formula of the predicate calculus is valid in every non-empty object domain therefore does not belong to metamathematics (cf. § 15). It belongs rather to what may be called *set-theoretic predicate logic* (Hilbert-Bernays 1934 p. 125), which has in common with metamathematics that it makes the logical formalism an object of study, but differs from it in not being restricted in the study to finitary methods. While our main business is metamathematics, the extra-metamathematical conceptions and results of set-theoretic predicate logic may have heuristic value, i.e. they may suggest to us what we may hope to discover in the metamathematics.

Our success in proving the consistency of the predicate calculus (Theorem 20 Corollary 2) stems from the fact that we were able to fit to the formulas of the calculus a finitary interpretation, namely the interpretation by validity in a fixed finite domain (i.e. k-identity). But that does not correspond to the usual interpretation of the calculus, to which corresponds rather validity in an arbitrary non-empty domain.

On the basis of the set-theoretic result that every provable formula is valid in every non-empty domain, we shall now see heuristically that the totality of the necessary conditions given by Theorem 20, i.e. the property of being k-identical for every finite k, is insufficient for provability.

This will be a consequence of the fact that a formal axiom system (cf. § 8) about a set D of elements which requires D to be infinite can be expressed by a predicate letter formula. To convey the idea, we shall first give the axioms as three formulas in our logical symbolism, but using the predicate symbol $<$ to suggest that they are axioms for an order relation:

$$\neg a<a, \qquad a<b \;\&\; b<c \supset a<c, \qquad \exists b(a<b).$$

These are order properties which are satisfied (in the old intuitive sense, § 8) when the domain of elements is the set of the natural numbers, and $<$ is the usual order relation for them. It is easily seen that they cannot be satisfied in any finite non-empty domain of elements. (The details are left to the reader.)

Now let us express the axiom system as one predicate letter formula, using $\mathcal{A}(a, b)$ in place of $a<b$, and also using only bound variables:

$$\forall a \neg \mathcal{A}(a, a) \mathbin{\&} \forall a \forall b \forall c[\mathcal{A}(a, b) \mathbin{\&} \mathcal{A}(b, c) \supset \mathcal{A}(a, c)] \mathbin{\&} \forall a \exists b \mathcal{A}(a, b).$$

This formula, call it "F", is not satisfiable (in the new set-theoretic sense) in a domain of k objects, for any finite $k > 0$, but is satisfiable in the enumerable domain of the natural numbers. Its negation $\neg$F is then valid in a domain of k objects for every finite k, i.e. is k-identical for every finite k, but is not valid in the enumerable domain. Thus $\neg$F meets the totality of necessary conditions of Theorem 20, but by the set-theoretic result that every provable formula is valid in every non-empty domain, it cannot be provable in the predicate calculus. This example $\neg$F and others are given in Hilbert-Bernays 1934 pp. 123—124.

In terms of the set-theoretic interpretation, the completeness of the predicate calculus should mean that every predicate letter formula which is valid in every non-empty domain should be provable. This interpretation is not finitary, unlike the corresponding interpretation for the propositional calculus (§§ 28, 29), and so the corresponding completeness problem does not belong to metamathematics. These remarks suggest that the situation is not as simple as for the propositional calculus, when we come to the question of completeness and to the decision problem. We shall return to these problems in a later chapter on the predicate calculus, where several results will be presented, partly metamathematical and partly of the set-theoretic variety (Chapter XIV).

For later reference, we summarize our present conclusions in a theorem and corollary, which we mark with the letter "C" to show that they do not belong to our sequence of metamathematical theorems, but are only established here by use of non-finitary classical methods. Although we are using "set-theoretic" for the present kind of predicate logic, some of the results are only on the level of classical number-theory; e.g. while Theorem 21 in its full generality involves sets of arbitrarily high cardinal number, the corollary can be inferred also from a specialization of Theorem 21 relating to the enumerable domain of the natural numbers and the enumerable class of the logical functions which are expressible by the use of the logical symbolism applied to $<$ (where $a<b$ is $\mathfrak{t}$ or $\mathfrak{f}$, according as a is a lesser natural number than b or not).

THEOREM 21^{C}. *In each non-empty object domain: Every predicate letter formula which is provable (or deducible from valid formulas) in the predicate calculus is valid.*

COROLLARY[C]. *In order that a predicate letter formula be provable in the predicate calculus, it is not (in general) sufficient that the formula be k-identical for every positive integer k.*

ANALOGY BETWEEN ∀, ∃ AND &, V. When interpreted in a finite domain of k objects $1, \ldots, k$, the formula ∀xA(x) is synonymous with A(1) & ... & A(**k**), and ∃xA(x) with A(1) V ... V A(**k**), where 1, ..., **k** are names in the formal system for the objects. This suggests a slightly different approach to the results of the preceding section, from which we will obtain an intermediate metamathematical result of some interest in itself. (For the case $k=2$, cf. Hilbert-Ackermann 1928 pp. 66—68.)

We shall take 1, 2, ..., **k** to be the formal expressions 0′, 0″, ..., 0′⋯′ (the last having k accents) which we call *numerals from* 1 *to* **k**. (However it would serve our purpose equally well to use k individual symbols.)

We define *predicate letter formula with k individuals*, or briefly *k-predicate letter formula*, by allowing the terms for Clause 1 of the definition of predicate letter formula in § 31 to include now the numerals from 1 to **k** as well as the variables; and the predicate calculus with this notion of formula we call the *predicate calculus with k individuals*, or briefly the *k-predicate calculus*.

Then we define *k-proposition letter formula* either as a k-predicate letter formula containing no variables free or bound (and therefore no quantifiers); or equivalently by allowing the formulas for Clause 1 of the definition of proposition letter formula (§ 25) to include not only the proposition letters but now also the expressions resulting from the predicate letters by substituting numerals from 1 to **k** for each of their attached variables, e.g. for $k = 2$, $\mathcal{A}(1)$, $\mathcal{A}(2)$, $\mathcal{B}(1)$, $\mathcal{A}(1, 1)$, $\mathcal{A}(1, 2)$, $\mathcal{A}(2, 1)$.

A convenient abbreviation is to write the latter as "$\mathcal{A}_1$", "$\mathcal{A}_2$", "$\mathcal{B}_1$", "$\mathcal{A}_{11}$", "$\mathcal{A}_{12}$", "$\mathcal{A}_{21}$", respectively, so that in effect we merely augment the former list of proposition letters by the same alphabetical letters with finite numbers of positive integral subscripts $\leq k$. Our former theory for the pure propositional calculus obviously will apply unchanged, if now each two letters differing either alphabetically or in their subscripts are treated as distinct proposition letters.

Given any closed k-predicate letter formula, we define its *k-transform* to be the k-proposition letter formula which results from it by replacing, successively, each part of the form ∀xA(x) where A(x) is a k-predicate letter formula by A(1) & ... & A(**k**), and likewise each part ∃xA(x) by A(1) V ... V A(**k**), until all of the quantifiers are eliminated. It is easily seen that the order of the replacements does not affect the result.

EXAMPLE 1. The 2-transform of $\forall b \exists a \mathcal{A}(a, b) \supset \exists a \forall b \mathcal{A}(a, b)$ is $(\mathcal{A}(1, 1) \vee \mathcal{A}(2, 1)) \,\&\, (\mathcal{A}(1, 2) \vee \mathcal{A}(2, 2)) \supset (\mathcal{A}(1, 1) \,\&\, \mathcal{A}(1, 2)) \vee (\mathcal{A}(2, 1) \,\&\, \mathcal{A}(2, 2))$, or briefly

$$(\mathcal{A}_{11} \vee \mathcal{A}_{21}) \,\&\, (\mathcal{A}_{12} \vee \mathcal{A}_{22}) \supset (\mathcal{A}_{11} \,\&\, \mathcal{A}_{12}) \vee (\mathcal{A}_{21} \,\&\, \mathcal{A}_{22}).$$

Given a k-predicate letter formula $A(x_1, \ldots, x_n)$ with exactly the distinct free variables $x_1, \ldots, x_n$, the set of its *k-transforms* shall be the k-transforms of the k^n closed k-predicate letter formulas obtained from $A(x_1, \ldots, x_n)$ by substituting for $x_1, \ldots, x_n$ each of the k^n different n-tuples of numerals from 1 to $\boldsymbol{k}$.

EXAMPLE 2. The 2-transforms of $\forall a \mathcal{A}(a, c) \supset \mathcal{A}(b, c)$ are $\mathcal{A}_{11} \,\&\, \mathcal{A}_{21} \supset \mathcal{A}_{11}$, $\mathcal{A}_{12} \,\&\, \mathcal{A}_{22} \supset \mathcal{A}_{12}$, $\mathcal{A}_{11} \,\&\, \mathcal{A}_{21} \supset \mathcal{A}_{21}$, $\mathcal{A}_{12} \,\&\, \mathcal{A}_{22} \supset \mathcal{A}_{22}$.

THEOREM 22. *For each $k \geq 1$: If a formula* E *is provable (deducible from formulas* Γ*) in the pure or k-predicate calculus, then all of the k-transforms of* E *are provable (deducible from the k-transforms of the formulas* Γ*) in the propositional calculus.* (Hilbert-Bernays 1934, pp. 119 ff.)

Proof is left to the reader.

We easily see that a predicate letter formula is k-identical, if and only if all of its k-transforms are identically true (§ 28). Thus, using Theorem 9, Theorem 20 becomes a corollary of Theorem 22.

EXAMPLE 1 (concluded). The formula $(\mathcal{A}_{11} \vee \mathcal{A}_{21}) \,\&\, (\mathcal{A}_{12} \vee \mathcal{A}_{22}) \supset (\mathcal{A}_{11} \,\&\, \mathcal{A}_{12}) \vee (\mathcal{A}_{21} \,\&\, \mathcal{A}_{22})$ is not provable in the propositional calculus, since it takes the value $\mathfrak{f}$ when $\mathcal{A}_{11}$, $\mathcal{A}_{12}$, $\mathcal{A}_{21}$, $\mathcal{A}_{22}$ take the respective values $\mathfrak{t}$, $\mathfrak{f}$, $\mathfrak{f}$, $\mathfrak{t}$. Hence $\forall b \exists a \mathcal{A}(a, b) \supset \exists a \forall b \mathcal{A}(a, b)$ is unprovable in the predicate calculus. Comparing these values for $\mathcal{A}_{11}$, $\mathcal{A}_{12}$, $\mathcal{A}_{21}$, $\mathcal{A}_{22}$ with the table for $\mathfrak{l}(a, b)$ in Example 2 § 36, we see that this is basically the same refutation as there.

EXAMPLE 3. Is $\neg\neg\exists a \mathcal{A}(a) \supset \exists a \neg\neg\mathcal{A}(a)$ (which is of the form $\text{IIc}_1 \supset \text{IIb}$ of Corollary Theorem 17) provable in the intuitionistic predicate calculus? By Theorem 22 (with $k = 2$), it is only if $\neg\neg(\mathcal{A}_1 \vee \mathcal{A}_2) \supset \neg\neg\mathcal{A}_1 \vee \neg\neg\mathcal{A}_2$ is provable in the intuitionistic propositional calculus (a result to be used in § 80).

It is often useful heuristically in studying the predicate calculus to think of $\forall x A(x)$ as a conjunction extended over all the members of the object domain, and of $\exists x A(x)$ similarly as a disjunction, even though only in the case of a finite domain with a given number k of members are we able to construct synonymous formal expressions on this basis.

From this analogy between ∀ and & and between ∃ and V, and the notion of & as analogous to · and V to + (end § 29), some authors write ∀xA(x) as "Π_xA(x)" and ∃xA(x) as "Σ_xA(x)". (Compare also the definitions of the product and sum of a set of sets, § 5.)

In retrospect, we can see how the postulates 3 — 6 for & and V suggest those for ∀ and ∃. The actual postulates of Group A2 are what the analogy calls for, allowing for certain differences in detail. The analogy is clear in the corresponding derived rules of Theorem 2. Of the numbered results, e.g., *75, *76, *83, *84, *91, *92 are analogous to *37, *38, *56, *57, *35, *36, respectively.

PREDICATE CALCULUS WITH A POSTULATED SUBSTITUTION RULE. As in the case of the propositional calculus (§ 30), the predicate calculus is usually formulated with a postulated instead of a derived substitution rule, namely, in the notation of Theorem 15 § 34 and under Proviso (A):

$$\frac{E}{E^*}.$$

The predicate letters are then called *predicate variables*; the rule is usually construed to apply to a single variable at a time; and as before these variables must be held constant in subsidiary deductions for assumption formulas to be discharged. (The first accurate statement of the substitution rule seems to be that of Hilbert-Bernays 1939 pp. 377—378, or 1934 p. 98 understanding the restriction on "Einsetzung" to apply also to "Umbenennung".)

n-VALUED PREDICATE CALCULI. Cf. Rosser and Turquette 1948-51, 1952.

SEVERAL-SORTED PREDICATE CALCULI. As was implied in § 31, the predicate calculus may be studied with several object domains, some of the variables being specified as ranging over one of these domains, others over another, etc. If these several object domains are regarded as simply several different primary categories of objects, the only new feature involved is that no operation should be performed which substitutes a term or variable of one sort, i.e. referring to one of the domains, for one of another. For example, *79 would hold only when x and y are variables of the same sort. Each of the attached variables for a name form should be of a specified sort. (Cf. Herbrand 1930, Schmidt 1938, Wang 1952 and Example 13 § 74.)

HIGHER PREDICATE CALCULI. However, one may also obtain predicate calculi with several types of variables by starting with predicate calculus first with a single primary domain of objects called *individuals*; then with an additional domain of objects consisting of the predicates over the first domain of objects, thus admitting quantifiers $\forall P$ and $\exists P$ where $P(a_1, \ldots, a_n)$ is a predicate variable of the first system; and so on. When a hierarchy of predicate calculi built on this plan is being considered, the first is called the *restricted predicate calculus* or *predicate calculus of first order*, and the others *predicate calculi of second order*, *third order*, etc., or generally *higher predicate calculi*. Many difficult questions arise in considering hierarchies of systems of this sort, which are investigated by the logicistic school (§ 12). A brief introduction is provided by Chapter IV of the 2nd (1938) or 3rd (1949) edition of Hilbert-Ackermann 1928. The subject is treated in Church 1956 Chapters V (vol I) and VI (vol II).

CHAPTER VIII

FORMAL NUMBER THEORY

§ 38. Induction, equality, replacement. In this chapter we return to the study of the full formal system of Chapter IV.

We shall now state our results mainly with particular formal variables, as the postulates of Group B (after 13) were stated, so that the provable formulas will read as particular theorems of number theory formalized in the symbolism of the system. Results of the form $\vdash$ A stated with particular free variables can be applied with terms substituted for those variables, in view of the substitution rule for individual variables (§ 23 and *66 § 32).

From Postulate 13 (using $\supset$-introd., $\forall$-introd., &-introd. and $\supset$-elim.), we have the following formal rule of mathematical induction. Formal inductions by this rule are of course altogether separate from informal mathematical inductions used in proving metamathematical theorems.

INDUCTION RULE. *Let* x *be a variable,* A(x) *be a formula, and* Γ *be a list of formulas not containing* x *free. If* $\Gamma \vdash$ A(0), *and* Γ, A(x) $\vdash$ A(x′) *with the free variables held constant for* A(x), *then* $\Gamma \vdash$ A(x).

Beginning with the proofs of the next theorem, we shall frequently adopt a more informal presentation of demonstrations of formal provability or deducibility. The use above of the chain method in handling equivalences (§ 26) was a step in this direction. We now go further, omitting the symbol "$\vdash$" in many situations. Thus we shall say "assume A", meaning that we wish to take A as an assumption formula in constructing a deduction. Of course, properly we are not assuming anything, but indicating that the formulas to follow are to be formally deducible from A (and any other assumption formulas which we have introduced), until the discharge of the assumption formula A is indicated or implied by the context. At each stage in such informal presentation, the formulas given are to be understood as deducible from all the assumption formulas not yet discharged.

EXAMPLE 1. The following is a demonstration in this presentation that $\vdash \exists x A(x) \supset \neg \forall x \neg A(x)$ (cf. the first half of the proof of *83 § 35).

In preparation for $\supset$-introd., assume $\exists x A(x)$. Preparatory to $\exists$-elim. from this, assume $A(x)$. We shall deduce $\neg \forall x \neg A(x)$ by reductio ad absurdum (i.e. $\neg$-introd.). Assume for this purpose $\forall x \neg A(x)$. Then by $\forall$-elim. $\neg A(x)$, contradicting $A(x)$. [Then $\neg \forall x \neg A(x)$ by the $\neg$-introd., which discharges the assumption $\forall x \neg A(x)$. Since $\neg \forall x \neg A(x)$ does not contain x free, the $\exists$-elim. can be completed now, discharging $A(x)$. Finally we have $\exists x A(x) \supset \neg \forall x \neg A(x)$ by the $\supset$-introd., discharging $\exists x A(x)$.] The bracketed steps will often be tacit.

To analyze this, we list the formulas, showing by an arrow how long each assumption remains in force.

1. $\exists x A(x)$ — assumed.
2. $A(x)$ — assumed.
3. $\forall x \neg A(x)$ — assumed.
4. $\neg A(x)$ — $\forall$-elim., 3.
5. $\neg \forall x \neg A(x)$ — $\neg$-introd., 2, 4.
6. $\neg \forall x \neg A(x)$ — $\exists$-elim., 5.
7. $\exists x A(x) \supset \neg \forall x \neg A(x)$ — $\supset$-introd., 6.

Each formula is deducible from the assumption formulas whose arrows appear opposite it, e.g. Line 5 means that $\neg \forall x \neg A(x)$ is deducible from $\exists x A(x)$ (Line 1) and $A(x)$ (Line 2). Stating these facts in the $\vdash$-notation, our demonstration appears in the former style.

1.			$\exists x A(x)$	$\vdash \exists x A(x)$.
2.		$A(x)$,	$\exists x A(x)$	$\vdash A(x)$.
3.	$\forall x \neg A(x)$,	$A(x)$,	$\exists x A(x)$	$\vdash \forall x \neg A(x)$.
4.	$\forall x \neg A(x)$,	$A(x)$,	$\exists x A(x)$	$\vdash \neg A(x)$ — $\forall$-elim., 3.
5.		$A(x)$,	$\exists x A(x)$	$\vdash \neg \forall x \neg A(x)$ — $\neg$-introd., 2, 4.
6.			$\exists x A(x)$	$\vdash \neg \forall x \neg A(x)$ — $\exists$-elim., 5.
7.				$\vdash \exists x A(x) \supset \neg \forall x \neg A(x)$ — $\supset$-introd., 6.

Note that the columns of assumption formulas take the place of the arrows. For Step 5, we can supply $\forall x \neg A(x)$ as an additional assumption formula in 2 by general properties of $\vdash$. At Step 6, $\exists$-elim. gives $\exists x A(x)$, $\exists x A(x) \vdash \neg \forall x \neg A(x)$, and the extra $\exists x A(x)$ is omitted by general properties of $\vdash$. Actually it is immaterial whether $\exists x A(x)$ is considered as an assumption formula for 2—5 or not.

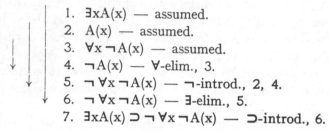

Applications of the rule of $\vee$-elimination will now often be described in the language of "cases" (cf. § 23). Applications of the formal induction rule will often be presented in the following manner, using the same terminology as in informal inductions (§ 7): Basis. ... A(0). Induction step. Assume A(x) (the hypothesis of the induction). Then ... A(x′). [At this point the induction step is completed, and A(x) ceases to be an assumption formula.] Hence A(x). [Other formulas Γ may have been in use as assumption formulas throughout. This proof that ⊢ A(x), or that Γ ⊢ A(x), we say is "by (formal) induction on x"; A(x) is the "induction formula".]

This informal presentation is convenient in situations where the formal development closely parallels intuitive reasonings. It saves space, and brings our procedures for demonstrating the facts about formal provability and deducibility still closer in appearance to the methods of informal mathematics (cf. § 20).

The reader should then understand at all times how the procedures can be made rigorous as applications of our derived rules stated in terms of the symbol "⊢". The ⊢-notation has been used to give concise and accurate statements of our derived rules, showing clearly their structure. We continue to use it when we have new rules to state, and in other passages where it helps to emphasize the form of the deducibility relationships or the fact that we are talking about the formulas of the system (and not in them).

We shall hereafter commonly abbreviate $a \cdot b$ to "ab".

THEOREM 23. (Properties of equality.)

*100. $\vdash a=a$. *101. $\vdash a=b \supset b=a$.

*102. $\vdash a=b \ \& \ b=c \supset a=c$.

(Reflexive, symmetric and transitive properties.)

*103 (Axiom 17). $\vdash a=b \supset a'=b'$.

*104. $\vdash a=b \supset a+c=b+c$. *105. $\vdash a=b \supset c+a=c+b$.

*106. $\vdash a=b \supset ac=bc$. *107. $\vdash a=b \supset ca=cb$.

(Special replacement properties of the function symbols ′, +, ·.)

*108 (Axiom 16). $\vdash a=b \supset (a=c \supset b=c)$.

*109. $\vdash a=b \supset (c=a \supset c=b)$.

(Special replacement properties of the predicate symbol =.)

PROOFS. *100. We exhibited a proof of this formula directly from the postulates as Example 1 § 19. Taking advantage of the derived rules established meanwhile, we can now summarize it thus. From Axiom 16 by substitution (*66 § 32), $a+0=a \supset (a+0=a \supset a=a)$. Thence by Axiom 18 (using ⊃-elim. twice), $a=a$.

*101. Using the informal presentation, assume $a=b$. By Axiom 16,

$a=c \supset b=c$. Substituting a for c, $a=a \supset b=a$. Thence by *100, $b=a$.

*104. Proof will be by the formal induction rule. In both the basis and the induction step, the method of a chain of equalities will be used (cf. end of § 26). Our use of this method depends on having already established *100—*102. Since we do not yet have the the general replacement property (Theorem 24 (a)), any step which entails replacing a term by another term given as equal to it will have to be justified by a special replacement result fitting the situation. Here we shall use Axiom 17 (*103) for the purpose. Substitution in an axiom or previously established formula will not be explicitly mentioned. Assume $a=b$. We deduce $a+c=b+c$ by induction on c, thus. BASIS. $a+0 = a$ [Axiom 18] $= b$ [assumption] $= b+0$ [Axiom 18]. INDUCTION STEP. Assume, as hypothesis of the induction, $a+c=b+c$. Then $a+c' = (a+c)'$ [Axiom 19] $= (b+c)'$ [hypothesis of the induction, Axiom 17] $= b+c'$ [Axiom 19].

*105. Let $a=b \supset c+a=c+b$ be abbreviated "A(a, b)". We shall prove $\forall b$A(a, b) by induction on a. We do the induction step, leaving the basis to be done similarly by the reader. IND. STEP. Assume $\forall b$A(a, b). By $\forall$-elim., A(a, b). We now deduce A(a', b) by induction on b. BASIS. Assume $a'=0$. But by Axiom 15, $\neg a'=0$. Hence by weak $\neg$-elim. (§ 23), $c+a'=c+0$. IND. STEP. (We do not need to use the hypothesis of the induction on b.) Assume $a'=b'$. Then by Ax. 14, $a=b$; and using A(a, b), $c+a=c+b$. Now $c+a' = (c+a)'$ [Ax. 19] $= (c+b)'$ [using $c+a=c+b$ with Ax. 17] $= c+b'$ [Ax. 19]. (Why did we take $\forall b$A(a, b) instead of A(a, b) as the induction formula for the induction on a? Cf. the statement of the induction rule. For the induction on b within the induction step of the induction on a, $\forall b$A(a, b) is the Γ.)

Another way to handle *105 is to prove *118 and *119 first, after which *105 can be inferred from *104.

*106 and *107. Similarly to *104 and *105. To justify replacing ac by bc in $ac+a$ after assuming $ac=bc$, we must use *104; etc.

REPLACEMENT. THEOREM 24. (a) *If* $\mathrm{u_r}$ *is a term containing a specified occurrence of a term* r, *and* $\mathrm{u_s}$ *is the result of replacing this occurrence by a term* s, *then*

$$\mathrm{r}=\mathrm{s} \vdash \mathrm{u_r}=\mathrm{u_s}.$$

(b) *If* $\mathrm{C_r}$ *is a formula containing a specified occurrence of a term* r (*not as the variable of a quantifier*), *and* $\mathrm{C_s}$ *is the result of replacing this occurrence by a term* s, *then*

$$\mathrm{r}=\mathrm{s} \vdash^{\mathrm{x}_1 \ldots \mathrm{x}_n} \mathrm{C_r} \sim \mathrm{C_s}$$

where $x_1, \ldots, x_n$ *are the variables of* r *or* s *which belong to a quantifier of* C_r *having the specified occurrence of* r *within its scope.* (Replacement theorem.)

Example to follow. Proof is by the same method as before (§§ 26, 33), using seven additional lemmas.

ADDITIONAL LEMMAS FOR REPLACEMENT. *If* r *and* s *are terms*:

$$*110.\quad r=s \vdash r'=s'.$$

*111. $r=s \vdash r+t=s+t$. *112. $r=s \vdash t+r=t+s$.

*113. $r=s \vdash rt=st$. *114. $r=s \vdash tr=ts$.

*115. $r=s \vdash r=t \sim s=t$. *116. $r=s \vdash t=r \sim t=s$.

PROOFS. The first five of these lemmas follow from *103—*107, respectively, by substitution (*66) and $\supset$-elim. The last two follow from *108 and *109 with *66, *101, $\supset$-elim. and *16.

EXAMPLE 2. Let r be b, s be a, C_r be $\exists d(d'+b=c)$. The parallel constructions of C_r from r and of C_s from s are as follows, and the depth is 3.

b	a
$d'+b$	$d'+a$
$d'+b=c$	$d'+a=c$
$\exists d(d'+b=c)$	$\exists d(d'+a=c)$

Let $=$ be written between the expressions in each of the top two lines, and $\sim$ in each of the bottom two. The resulting formulas are deducible, each from the preceding, using successively *112, *115, *72 (varying d). Using the abbreviation "<" (§ 17), the result can be written $b=a \vdash b<c \sim a<c$. (Why is d not varied in the result?)

COROLLARY 1. *Under the conditions of the theorem: If* $\vdash r=s$, *then* $\vdash u_r=u_s$ *and* $\vdash C_r \sim C_s$.

COROLLARY 2. *Under the conditions of the theorem*: $r=s, C_r \vdash^{x_1 \ldots x_n} C_s$ *with* $x_1, \ldots, x_n$ *varied only for the first assumption formula. If* $\vdash r=s$, *then* $C_r \vdash C_s$. (Replacement property of equality.)

EXAMPLE 2 (concluded). Using also *101: $a=b, b<c \vdash a<c$.

As before, a replacement may be preceded by a substitution for individual variables (cf. § 33 Example 4, and § 34 just above Remark 2).

§ 39. Addition, multiplication, order. Postulate Group B (§ 19) may be described as follows. Postulates 14, 15 and 13 express formally the last three of Peano's axioms (§ 6). (The first two enter in the present system, which has only natural number variables, through Clauses 1 and 5 in the definition of term, § 17.) Axioms 16 and 17 give properties of equality (including as 17 the univalence of the successor function $'$, which was implicit in Peano's formulation). Axioms 18 and 19 are what may be called 'recursion equations' defining the function $+$, and Axioms 20 and 21 are the like for the function $\cdot$.

For our abbreviations "$a \neq b$" and "1", "2", "3", ..., see § 17.

THEOREM 25. (Arithmetic laws.)

*117. $\vdash (a+b)+c=a+(b+c)$.

*118. $\vdash a'+b=(a+b)'$.

*119. $\vdash a+b=b+a$.

*120. $\vdash a(b+c)=ab+ac$.

*121. $\vdash (ab)c=a(bc)$.

*122. $\vdash a'b=ab+b$.

*123. $\vdash ab=ba$.

(Associative, commutative and distributive laws for $+$ and $\cdot$, with lemmas used in proving the commutative laws.)

*124 (Axiom 18). $\vdash a+0=a$.

*125 (Axiom 20). $\vdash a\cdot 0=0$.

*126. $\vdash a+1=a'$.

*127. $\vdash a\cdot 1=a$.

(Direct laws for 0 and 1.)

*128. $\vdash a+b=0 \supset a=0 \;\&\; b=0$.

*129. $\vdash ab=0 \supset a=0 \vee b=0$.

*130. $\vdash a+b=1 \supset a=1 \vee b=1$.

*131. $\vdash ab=1 \supset a=1 \;\&\; b=1$.

(Inverse laws for 0 and 1.)

*132. $\vdash a+c=b+c \supset a=b$.

*133. $\vdash c\neq 0 \supset (ac=bc \supset a=b)$.

(Inverse laws for $+$ and $\cdot$.)

PROOFS. In these proofs, since we now have Theorem 24 (a), we do not need to invoke the special cases of it *103—*107, as we did in the proofs for Theorem 23.

*117 and *118. By induction on c and b, respectively.

*119. By induction on a, using induction on b in the basis.

*122. By induction on b. IND. STEP. Assume $a'b=ab+b$. Then $a'b' = a'b+a'$ [Ax. 21] $= (ab+b)+a'$ [hyp. ind.] $= ((ab+b)+a)'$ [Ax. 19] $= (ab+(b+a))'$ [*117] $= (ab+(a+b))'$ [*119] $= ((ab+a)+b)'$ [*117] $= (ab'+b)'$ [Ax. 21] $= ab'+b'$ [Ax. 19].

*128. *If* $\vdash$ A(0) *and* $\vdash$ A(x'), *then* $\vdash$ A(x). For from $\vdash$ A(x') by general properties of $\vdash$, A(x) $\vdash$ A(x'), and so induction on x applies. This rule we call *induction cases* (*on* x). For *128, call the formula to be proved "A(a, b)". To prove A(a, b) by induction cases on a, it will suffice to prove

A(0, b) and A(a', b). To prove these two, by induction cases on b, it will suffice to prove the four formulas A(0, 0), A(0, b'), A(a', 0), A(a', b'), i.e. the formulas

$$0+0=0 \supset 0=0 \,\&\, 0=0, \qquad 0+b'=0 \supset 0=0 \,\&\, b'=0,$$
$$a'+0=0 \supset a'=0 \,\&\, 0=0, \qquad a'+b'=0 \supset a'=0 \,\&\, b'=0.$$

The proofs of these four are easy, as in each case we can either refute the premise of the implication (using Axiom 15) or prove the conclusion (cf. *10a and *11 § 26).

*130. This is established similarly, but with an iteration of the argument by cases, so that to prove A(x′), we prove A(0′) and A(x″). Altogether, to prove A(a, b), it thus suffices to prove the nine formulas

$$\text{A}(0, 0),\ \ \text{A}(0, 1),\ \ \text{A}(0, b''),\ \ \text{A}(1, 0),\ \ \text{A}(1, 1),$$
$$\text{A}(1, b''),\ \ \text{A}(a'', 0),\ \ \text{A}(a'', 1),\ \ \text{A}(a'', b'').$$

The treatment of each of the nine is routine (using Axioms 14 and 15).

*132. Induction on c, using Axiom 14.

*133. Let "A(a, b)" abbreviate $ac=bc \supset a=b$. Assume $c\neq 0$. We deduce $\forall a$A(a, b) by induction on b, as follows. (Cf. *95.) Basis. Assume $ac=0c$. By *125 (and *123), $ac=0$. But $c\neq 0$. Hence by *129 and propositional calculus, $a=0$. Ind. step. Assume $\forall a$A(a, b). By $\forall$-elim., A(a, b). We shall deduce A(a, b') by induction on a. Basis. Assume $0c=b'c$. By *125 (and *123, *101), $b'c=0$; and by *129, $b'=0 \vee c=0$. But $b'\neq 0$ by Ax. 15, and $c\neq 0$ by hypothesis; hence $\neg(b'=0 \vee c=0)$. From this contradiction, by weak $\neg$-elim. (§ 23), $0=b'$. Ind. step. Assume $a'c=b'c$. By *122, $ac+c=bc+c$. By 132*, $ac=bc$. Thence by A(a, b), $a=b$; and by *103, $a'=b'$.

Another way to handle *133 is to wait until *139 is established, after which it can be proved similarly to *146b.

We now use the abbreviation "$a<b$" for $\exists c(c'+a=b)$ under the conventions discussed in §§ 17, 33; and we read "$a>b$" as abbreviation for $b<a$; "$a\leq b$" for $a<b \vee a=b$; "$a\geq b$" for $b\leq a$; "$a<b<c$" for $a<b \,\&\, b<c$ (cf. end of § 26); etc.

Theorem 26. (Order properties.)

*134a. $\vdash a<b<c \supset a<c$. *134b. $\vdash a\leq b<c \supset a<c$.

*134c. $\vdash a<b\leq c \supset a<c$. *134d. $\vdash a\leq b\leq c \supset a\leq c$.

(Transitive laws.)

*135a. $\vdash a<a'$. *135b. $\vdash 0<a'$. *136. $\vdash 0\leq a$.

*137 (= *137_0). $\vdash a=0 \vee \exists b(a=b')$. *$137_1$. $\vdash a=0 \vee a=1 \vee \exists b(a=b'')$.

*137_2. $\vdash a=0 \vee a=1 \vee a=2 \vee \exists b(a=b''')$. ...

*138a. $\vdash a \leq b \sim a<b'$. *138b. $\vdash a>b \sim a \geq b'$.

(Order properties for 0 and $'$.)

*139. $\vdash a<b \vee a=b \vee a>b$.

*140. $\vdash \neg a<a$. *141. $\vdash a<b \supset \neg a>b$.

(Connexity, irreflexiveness, asymmetry.)

*142a. $\vdash a+b \geq a$. *143a. $\vdash b \neq 0 \supset ab \geq a$.

*142b. $\vdash b \neq 0 \supset a+b>a$. *143b. $\vdash a \neq 0 \,\&\, b>1 \supset ab>a$.

*143c. $\vdash b \neq 0 \supset a'b>a$; hence $\vdash b \neq 0 \supset \exists c(cb>a)$.

*144a. $\vdash a<b \sim a+c<b+c$. *145a. $\vdash c \neq 0 \supset (a<b \sim ac<bc)$.

*144b. $\vdash a \leq b \sim a+c \leq b+c$. *145b. $\vdash c \neq 0 \supset (a \leq b \sim ac \leq bc)$.

(Inequalities under addition and multiplication.)

*146a. $\vdash b \neq 0 \supset \exists q \exists r(a=bq+r \,\&\, r<b)$.

*146b. $\vdash a=bq_1+r_1 \,\&\, r_1<b \,\&\, a=bq_2+r_2 \,\&\, r_2<b \supset q_1=q_2 \,\&\, r_1=r_2$.

(Existence and uniqueness of quotient and remainder.)

Proofs. *134a. Assume $a<b<c$, i.e. $a<b \,\&\, b<c$, i.e. $\exists d(d'+a=b) \,\&\, \exists e(e'+b=c)$. Preparatory to $\exists$- and &-elim., assume $d'+a=b$ and $e'+b=c$. Then $e'+(d'+a)=c$, which can be reassociated as $(e'+d)'+a=c$. By $\exists$-introd., $\exists f(f'+a=c)$, i.e. $a<c$.

*134b. From *134a, with the help of proof by cases (§ 23). (Cf. Example 2 § 38.)

*136. By induction cases on a, using *135b.

*137, *137_k. By repeated use of induction cases; or thus: The formula of *136 is equivalent to that of *137, using Ax. 18 and properties of = (cf. Example 4 § 33); and *137_1, *137_2, ... follow successively.

*138a. Using $\exists$- and $\vee$-elim. and introd. with *137, $\vdash a<b' \sim 0'+a=b' \vee \exists c(c''+a=b')$. Using *119 and Axs. 19, 17, 14 and 18, $\vdash 0'+a=b' \sim a=b$. Using *119 and Axs. 19, 17 and 14 with *72 (or $\exists$-elim. and introd.), $\vdash \exists c(c''+a=b') \sim a<b$.

*139. By induction on b, using *136 in the basis, and *138a, b in the induction step.

*140. Assume $a<a$, i.e. $\exists b(b'+a=a)$. For $\exists$-elim., assume $b'+a=a$. Then by *132 with *124 and *119, $b'=0$, contradicting Ax. 15. Remark. Because the contradictory formulas $b'=0$ and $b' \neq 0$ contain b free, we cannot carry out the $\exists$-elim. immediately. But by

weak $\neg$-elim. (§ 23), we can first deduce a pair of contradictory formulas not containing b free, e.g. $0=0$ and $0\neq 0$.

By *140, $\vdash a=b \supset \neg a<b$.

*143b. Assume $a\neq 0$ & $b>1$. By $a\neq 0$ with *137, $\exists c(a=c')$; and by $b>1$ with *140, *141 and *135a, $b\neq 0$ & $b\neq 1$, and thence with *137$_1$, $\exists d(b=d'')$. Assume (preparatory to $\exists$-eliminations) $a=c'$ and $b=d''$.

*144a. From *104, *132, *117 and *72.

*145a. Assume $c\neq 0$. PART 1: to deduce $a<b \supset ac<bc$. (Left to the reader.) PART 2: to deduce $ac<bc \supset a<b$. Assume $ac<bc$. To deduce $a<b$, it will suffice by cases (V-elim.) from *139 to deduce $a<b$ under each of three case hypotheses. CASE 1: $a<b$. CASE 2: $a=b$. Then $ac=bc$. This with *140 gives $\neg ac<bc$, contradicting our assumption $ac<bc$. By weak $\neg$-elim., $a<b$. CASE 3: $a>b$, i.e. $b<a$. Then by the result of Part 1, $bc<ac$, i.e. $ac>bc$. Thence by *141, $\neg ac<bc$.

*146a. Use induction on a (after assuming $b\neq 0$). (Proof can also be based on *143c and *149.)

*146b. Assume $a=bq_1+r_1$ & $r_1<b$ & $a=bq_2+r_2$ & $r_2<b$. To deduce $q_1=q_2$, it will suffice by *139, using cases and weak $\neg$-elim., to deduce a contradiction from $q_1<q_2$ and again from $q_1>q_2$. Assume $q_1<q_2$. For $\exists$-elim. from this, assume $e'+q_1=q_2$. Now $bq_1+r_1 = a = bq_2+r_2 = b(e'+q_1)+r_2 = bq_1+(be'+r_2)$. So $r_1 = be'+r_2$ [*132] $\geq be'$ [*142a] $\geq b$ [*143a]. This contradicts $r_1<b$, by *140 and *141. The other case is similar. Having deduced $q_1=q_2$, we have $a = bq_1+r_1 = bq_1+r_2$, whence $r_1=r_2$ by *132.

***§ 40. The further development of number theory.** Our formal system of number theory differs from the informal theory in that the logic is made explicit. We have brought our acquaintance with the logic to a stage where the further development of number theory in the formal system will proceed much along lines already familiar to us from the informal theory. We shall not continue systematically with this development, but will only note several aspects of it, before turning to general metamathematical questions about the system.

For this section, *let* x *be a variable,* A(x) *be a formula, and* y *and* z *be variables distinct from* x *and each other which are free for* x *in* A(x) *and do not occur free in* A(x).

The *least number principle* (or *well-orderedness* of the natural numbers) says that, if there exists a natural number x such that $A(x)$, then there exists a least such x, call it y. The property of y can be expressed in the formal symbolism by $A(y) \& \forall z(z<y \supset \neg A(z))$, or in an equivalent form using:

*147. $\vdash z<y \supset \neg A(z) \sim A(z) \supset y \leq z$.

(By *13, *139.) We establish first:

*148°. $\vdash \exists y[y<x \& A(y) \& \forall z(z<y \supset \neg A(z))] \vee \forall y[y<x \supset \neg A(y)]$.

(Law of the excluded middle, and least number principle, for an initial segment of the natural numbers.)

*148a. $A(x) \vee \neg A(x) \vdash^{x} \exists y[y<x \& A(y) \& \forall z(z<y \supset \neg A(z))] \vee \forall y[y<x \supset \neg A(y)]$.

*148b. $\vdash \neg\neg\{\exists y[y<x \& A(y) \& \forall z(z<y \supset \neg A(z))] \vee \forall y[y<x \supset \neg A(y)]\}$.

(Intuitionistic versions of the same.)

Proofs. *148. By induction on x, thus. Let the formula of *148 be abbreviated "$P(x) \vee Q(x)$". Basis. From *136, *140, *141 and *10a, $\vdash Q(0)$, whence $\vdash P(0) \vee Q(0)$. Ind. step. Assume $P(x) \vee Q(x)$. We deduce $P(x') \vee Q(x')$ thence by cases (V-elim.). For Case 1, $P(x) \vdash P(x') \vdash P(x') \vee Q(x')$, using *135a, *134a. For Case 2, we use subcases from $A(x) \vee \neg A(x)$ (*51). For Subcase 2a, $Q(x), A(x) \vdash P(x') \vdash P(x') \vee Q(x')$, using *135a. For Subcase 2b, $Q(x), \neg A(x) \vdash Q(x') \vdash P(x') \vee Q(x')$, using *138a.

*148a. Since *51 is not available in the intuitionistic system, we now use $\forall x(A(x) \vee \neg A(x))$ as an assumption formula Γ for the induction.

*148b. From Axiom Schema 6, by ⊃-elim. and contraposition twice (*13, *12), $A \supset \neg\neg C, B \supset \neg\neg C \vdash A \vee B \supset \neg\neg C \vdash \neg\neg(A \vee B) \supset \neg\neg C$. Thence by the ⊃-rules: *If* $\Gamma, A \vdash \neg\neg C$ *and* $\Gamma, B \vdash \neg\neg C$ (*with the free variables held constant for* A *and* B, *respectively*), *then* $\Gamma, \neg\neg(A \vee B) \vdash \neg\neg C$. Thus we justify a modification of proof by cases, in which the case formula $A \vee B$ and the conclusion C are doubly negated. Hence, if we replace the induction formula in the proof of *148 by $\neg\neg(P(x) \vee Q(x))$, and the other case formula by $\neg\neg(A(x) \vee \neg A(x))$ (which is provable intuitionistically by *51a), the induction again works (using *49a), and gives us *148b.

Now we can infer the least number principle.

*149°. $\vdash \exists x A(x) \supset \exists y[A(y) \& \forall z(z<y \supset \neg A(z))]$.

(Least number principle.)

*149a. $A(x) \vee \neg A(x) \vdash^{x} \exists x A(x) \supset \exists y[A(y) \& \forall z(z<y \supset \neg A(z))]$.

*149b. $\vdash \neg\neg\{\exists x A(x) \supset \exists y[A(y) \& \forall z(z<y \supset \neg A(z))]\}$.

(Intuitionistic versions of the least number principle.)

PROOFS. *149 (or *149a). Assume $\exists x A(x)$; and for $\exists$-elim., A(x). Substitute x' for x in *148 (or in the conclusion of *148a) to obtain $P(x') \vee Q(x')$. CASE 1: $P(x')$. Thence $\exists y[A(y) \,\&\, \forall z(z<y \supset \neg A(z))]$. CASE 2: $Q(x')$. Thence with *135a, $\neg A(x)$, contradicting A(x). By weak $\neg$-elim., $\exists y[A(y) \,\&\, \forall z(z<y \supset \neg A(z))]$.

*149b. Using instead *148b and the modification of proof by cases, $\exists x A(x) \supset \neg\neg\exists y[A(y) \,\&\, \forall z(z<y \supset \neg A(z))]$. Now use *60h, g.

Other consequences of *148a are:

*150. $A(x) \vee \neg A(x) \vdash^{x} \exists y[y<x \,\&\, A(y)] \vee \neg\exists y[y<x \,\&\, A(y)]$.

*151. $A(x) \vee \neg A(x) \vdash^{x} \forall y[y<x \supset A(y)] \vee \neg\forall y[y<x \supset A(y)]$.

(Of interest for the intuitionistic system.)

PROOFS. *150. From *148a, $A(x) \vee \neg A(x) \vdash^{x} \exists y[y<x \,\&\, A(y)] \vee \forall y[y<x \supset \neg A(y)]$. But $\vdash \forall y[y<x \supset \neg A(y)] \sim \forall y \neg [y<x \,\&\, A(y)]$ [*58b] $\sim \neg\exists y[y<x \,\&\, A(y)]$ [*86].

*151. Similarly, applying *148a to $\neg A(x)$, and replacing $\neg\neg A(x)$ by A(x) (since by *49c, $A(x) \vee \neg A(x) \vdash \neg\neg A(x) \sim A(x)$).

As an example of a number-theoretic theorem requiring some further concepts, we shall treat Euclid's theorem that there exist infinitely many prime numbers. This may be expressed by saying that to any number a, there is a prime greater than a. In fact, there must be a prime between $a+1$ and $a!+1$, inclusive, by the following reasoning. Every positive integer $n \leq a$ divides $a!$. Hence none of them except 1 divides $a!+1$. But $a!+1 > 1$; so it is, or has as factor, a prime. This prime is between $a+1$ and $a!+1$, inclusive.

The two cases may be combined by noting that the least divisor of $a!+1$ greater than 1 is a prime greater than a. Also the reasoning holds good using in place of $a!$ any common multiple of $1, \ldots, a$.

Preparatory to the formal treatment of Euclid's theorem, we now introduce "$a|b$" (read "a divides b" or "a is a factor (divisor) of b") as abbreviation for $\exists c(ac=b)$. We can show:

*152. $\vdash a|ab$. *153. $\vdash a|a$. *154. $\vdash a|b \,\&\, b|c \supset a|c$.

*155. $\vdash a>1 \supset \neg(a|b \,\&\, a|b')$. *156. $\vdash b\neq 0 \supset (a|b \supset 0<a\leq b)$.

(Properties of |.)

(HINTS: For *155, use *137_1, *145a (with *135a), *132, Ax. 15. For *156, use *143a.) Next we introduce "Pr(a)" ("a is prime") as abbreviation for $a>1 \,\&\, \neg\exists c(1<c<a \,\&\, c|a)$. Then Euclid's theorem is expressed in the formal system by the formula $\exists b(\Pr(b) \,\&\, b>a)$.

A difficulty for formalizing the foregoing proof is that the system has no term to express the function $a!$. We avoid this by establishing:

*157. $\vdash \exists d[d>0 \mathbin{\&} \forall b(0<b\leq a \supset b|d)]$.

(Existence of common multiples of $1, \ldots, a$.)

(PROOF by induction on a. Call the formula "$\exists d\mathrm{A}(a, d)$". For the basis, $\vdash \mathrm{A}(0, 1)$. For the ind. step (preparatory to $\exists$-elim.), $\mathrm{A}(a, d) \vdash \mathrm{A}(a', da')$.) Now assume in preparation for $\exists$-elim.,

(1) $$d>0 \mathbin{\&} \forall b(0<b\leq a \supset b|d).$$

The variable d governed by this formula then has the role of $a!$; more precisely, it may represent under the interpretation any common multiple of $1, \ldots, a$.

By (1), *144a and *153, $d'>1 \mathbin{\&} d'|d'$. Hence $\exists e(e>1 \mathbin{\&} e|d')$. By the least number principle (*149), $\exists b[b>1 \mathbin{\&} b|d' \mathbin{\&} \forall c(c<b \supset \neg(c>1 \mathbin{\&} c|d'))]$. Assume, for $\exists$-elim.,

(2) $$b>1 \mathbin{\&} b|d' \mathbin{\&} \forall c(c<b \supset \neg(c>1 \mathbin{\&} c|d')).$$

Assume $1<c<b \mathbin{\&} c|b$. From $c<b$ by (2), $\neg(c>1 \mathbin{\&} c|d')$; but from $1<c$, $c|b$, $b|d'$ (from (2)) and *154, $c>1 \mathbin{\&} c|d'$. By $\neg$- and $\forall$-introd., $\forall c \neg(1<c<b \mathbin{\&} c|b)$; whence by *86, $\neg\exists c(1<c<b \mathbin{\&} c|b)$. Using also $b>1$ from (2), $\mathrm{Pr}(b)$.

By (2), $b>1 \mathbin{\&} b|d'$. Hence by *155, $\neg b|d$. Hence by (1), $b>a$.

By &- and $\exists$-introd., $\exists b(\mathrm{Pr}(b) \mathbin{\&} b>a)$. Since this formula does not contain b or d free, by $\exists$-elim. the assumptions (2) and (1) are discharged. This completes the proof of Euclid's theorem in the classical system.

To prove it in the intuitionistic system, using *149a instead of *149, it remains to establish $(e>1 \mathbin{\&} e|d') \vee \neg(e>1 \mathbin{\&} e|d')$. For this purpose, we first establish:

*158. $\vdash a=b \vee \neg a=b$. *159. $\vdash a<b \vee \neg a<b$.

*160. $\vdash a|b \sim \exists c(c\leq b \mathbin{\&} ac=b)$.

(For use in the intuitionistic treatment of Euclid's theorem.)

(Prove *158 and *159 by *139—*141; *160 similarly to *156.) Then we prove successively $e>1 \vee \neg e>1$ (by *159), $e|d' \vee \neg e|d'$ (by *160, *138a, *150, *158), and $(e>1 \mathbin{\&} e|d') \vee \neg(e>1 \mathbin{\&} e|d')$ (thence by Remark 1 (b) § 29 and Theorem 3 § 25). Thus, intuitionistically as well as classically:

*161. $\vdash \exists b(\mathrm{Pr}(b) \mathbin{\&} b>a)$. (Euclid's theorem.)

The process of recognizing that the proofs in an informal theory can be formalized in a given formal system is one of continual analysis and stereotyping of arguments which recur in the informal theory, to keep pace as the theory develops with the increasing condensation of the informal reasoning. We attempt to recognize successively these types of informal arguments as being formalizable, and we may record the results we thus obtain as derived rules for the formal system. This is very similar to the semi-formal process of developing an informal theory itself from explicitly stated postulates; but here we have gone further back to postulate the logical as well as the (in the ordinary sense) mathematical principles.

Informally, we have used mathematical induction not only in the simple (or ordinary) form, but also in a modification called 'course-of-values induction' (cf. § 7 including Example 2, the proof of Theorem 1 § 21, etc.). It is of interest now to recognize that in the formal system this modification can be derived from the simple form of induction which is postulated for the system. We shall state it as a theorem schema; the method of formulating a rule on the basis of the schema has been sufficiently illustrated on simple induction (cf. Axiom Schema 13 in § 19 with the induction rule in § 38).

In the first schema *162a, the expressions A(0) and $\forall x[\forall y(y \leq x \supset A(y)) \supset A(x')]$ formalize the basis and induction step, respectively; in the more compact form *162b, the two are brought together in the single expression $\forall x[\forall y(y < x \supset A(y)) \supset A(x)]$.

*162a. $\vdash A(0) \mathbin{\&} \forall x[\forall y(y \leq x \supset A(y)) \supset A(x')] \supset A(x)$.

*162b. $\vdash \forall x[\forall y(y < x \supset A(y)) \supset A(x)] \supset A(x)$.

(Course-of-values induction.)

PROOFS. *162a. Assume $A(0) \mathbin{\&} \forall x[\forall y(y \leq x \supset A(y)) \supset A(x')]$, deduce $\forall y(y \leq x \supset A(y))$ by simple induction on x, and infer A(x) by $\forall$-elim.

Sometimes inductions require a *double basis*; i.e. we establish as the basis $A(0)$ and $A(1)$, and then for the induction step infer $A(x'')$ from the two preceding cases $A(x)$ and $A(x')$. This can be treated formally as a course-of-values induction, using cases according as $x'=1$ or $x'>1$ under the induction step; or we can make it into a simple induction by using $A(x) \mathbin{\&} A(x')$ as the induction formula. This device of using a conjunction as the induction proposition applies similarly to *induction from a k-fold basis* for any fixed $k \geq 2$, and also to the *inductive proof of several propositions simultaneously*.

Inductive arguments are sometimes presented in the guise of a *descending induction* or proof by the *method of infinite descent*. This consists in establishing that $A(x)$ is false for every x, by showing that if $A(x)$ is true for any x, there is a lesser number for which it is also true.

*163. $\vdash \forall x[A(x) \supset \exists y(y<x \,\&\, A(y))] \supset \neg A(x)$.
(Method of infinite descent.)

*163a. $\vdash \forall x[A(x) \supset \neg\neg\exists y(y<x \,\&\, A(y))] \supset \neg A(x)$.
(Additional version of interest for the intuitionistic system.)

PROOFS. Assuming the premise of either *163 or *163a, $\neg A(x)$ follows by a course-of-values induction.

ANOTHER METHOD. Taking $\neg A(x)$ as the A(x) of *162b, the result is equivalent to *163a by the following steps.
$\vdash \forall y(y<x \supset \neg A(y)) \supset \neg A(x) \sim \neg[\forall y \neg(y<x \,\&\, A(y)) \,\&\, A(x)]$ [*58b twice] $\sim A(x) \supset \neg \forall y \neg(y<x \,\&\, A(y))$ [*33, *58b] $\sim$
$A(x) \supset \neg\neg\exists y(y<x \,\&\, A(y))$ [*86]. Then *163 follows from *163a.

Proofs of *163a and *163 can also be given by reductio ad absurdum from *149 or from *149b; and conversely *149b can be proved by reductio ad absurdum from *163a (using *60h, g). (In each case, the formula of the one is deducible in the intuitionistic predicate calculus from that of the other.)

These examples suggest that the forms of argumentation ordinarily encountered in informal elementary number theory will turn out to be formalizable in our formal system. The lack of such functions as $a!$ remains a cause for doubt (although we did get around it in proving Euclid's theorem). Attention will be given to this question concerning functions in §§ 41, 49, 59, 74, 82.

In § 42 we shall take up the question of the completeness of the formal system. From the standpoint of the interpretation, this includes whether all the possible reasonings of elementary number theory (not merely the commonly encountered ones) are formalizable in the system, at least in so far as they contribute to the proof of propositions expressible in the system. We shall also consider a more specific, strictly metamathematical notion of completeness.

§ 41. Formal calculation. A formula A is said to be (*formally*) *refutable*, if $\neg$A is provable.

A closed formula A (end § 32) is (*formally*) *decidable*, if A is either provable or refutable, i.e. if either $\vdash$ A or $\vdash \neg$A.

The formal number-theoretic system (or a system with formation rules of a like sort) is said to be (*simply*) *complete*, if every closed formula A is formally decidable; (*simply*) *incomplete* in the contrary case that there is a formally undecidable closed formula.

The restriction that A be closed is essential here, in order that the metamathematical notion of simple completeness should have the intended significance. Otherwise, under the generality interpretation of the free variables in both A and $\neg$A, the second formula would not express the negation of the proposition expressed by the first (§ 32).

EXAMPLE 1. The formula $2|a$ (i.e. $\exists c(0''\cdot c=a)$)expresses: every number a is even; and $\neg 2|a$ expresses: every number a is not even, i.e. every number a is odd. Neither proposition is true; and, we hope, neither formula is provable. But $\forall a 2|a$ expresses: every number a is even; and $\neg\forall a 2|a$ expresses: not every number a is even. By the classical law of the excluded middle, one of the two propositions should be true. In fact the second is; and the formula $\neg\forall a 2|a$ is provable.

We did not apply the notion of simple completeness to the propositional and predicate calculi, because the proposition and predicate letters had the role of free variables for the interpretation (§§ 28, 29, 36, 37). Simple completeness is another example of a notion of completeness with a positive criterion (§ 29).

The terms 0, 0′, 0″, ..., which represent the particular natural numbers under the interpretation of the system, we call *numerals*, and we abbreviate them by the same symbols "0", "1", "2", ..., respectively, as we use for the natural numbers intuitively (as in §§ 17, 37). Moreover, whenever we have introduced an italic letter, such as "x", to designate an intuitive natural number, then the corresponding bold italic letter "$\boldsymbol{x}$" shall designate the corresponding numeral $0^{(x)}$, i.e. $0'^{\cdots}{}'$ with x accents ($x \geq 0$) (as in § 37). In this connection, we can also use "$\boldsymbol{x}-1$" to designate the numeral with $x-1$ accents (for $x > 0$); there is no ambiguity, since we have no formal "$-$". But "$\boldsymbol{x}+1$" designates $0^{(x)}+0'$.

Let $P(x_1, \ldots, x_n)$ be an intuitive number-theoretic predicate. We say that $P(x_1, \ldots, x_n)$ is *numeralwise expressible* in the formal system, if there is a formula $\mathrm{P}(\mathrm{x}_1, \ldots, \mathrm{x}_n)$ with no free variables other than the distinct variables $\mathrm{x}_1, \ldots, \mathrm{x}_n$ such that, for each particular n-tuple of natural numbers $x_1, \ldots, x_n$,

(i) if $P(x_1, \ldots, x_n)$ is true, then $\vdash \mathrm{P}(\boldsymbol{x}_1, \ldots, \boldsymbol{x}_n)$, and

(ii) if $P(x_1, \ldots, x_n)$ is false, then $\vdash \neg\mathrm{P}(\boldsymbol{x}_1, \ldots, \boldsymbol{x}_n)$.

In this case, the formula $\mathrm{P}(\mathrm{x}_1, \ldots, \mathrm{x}_n)$ *numeralwise expresses* the predicate $P(x_1, \ldots, x_n)$ (with the formal variables $\mathrm{x}_1, \ldots, \mathrm{x}_n$ corresponding to the respective intuitive variables $x_1, \ldots, x_n$).

Our metamathematical use of this notion will be confined to cases when there is a decision procedure for the predicate $P(x_1,\ldots,x_n)$ (§ 30), so that for each n-tuple $x_1,\ldots,x_n$,

(iii) $P(x_1,\ldots,x_n)$ is true, or $P(x_1,\ldots,x_n)$ is false.

Using (iii) with (i) and (ii),

(iv) $\vdash \mathrm{P}(\boldsymbol{x}_1,\ldots,\boldsymbol{x}_n)$ or $\vdash \neg\mathrm{P}(\boldsymbol{x}_1,\ldots,\boldsymbol{x}_n)$;

thus $\mathrm{P}(\boldsymbol{x}_1,\ldots,\boldsymbol{x}_n)$ is decidable for each $x_1,\ldots,x_n$, or as we shall say $\mathrm{P}(\mathrm{x}_1,\ldots,\mathrm{x}_n)$ is *numeralwise decidable*. The formula $\neg\mathrm{P}(\mathrm{x}_1,\ldots,\mathrm{x}_n)$ then numeralwise expresses the predicate not-$P(x_1,\ldots,x_n)$.

The notion of numeralwise expressibility gives only one of the senses in which a formula $\mathrm{P}(\mathrm{x}_1,\ldots,\mathrm{x}_n)$ may express a predicate $P(x_1,\ldots,x_n)$. It requires more of the deductive apparatus of the system than merely that $\mathrm{P}(\mathrm{x}_1,\ldots,\mathrm{x}_n)$ should express $P(x_1,\ldots,x_n)$ under the interpretation of the symbolism (with the name form interpretation for $\mathrm{x}_1,\ldots,\mathrm{x}_n$, § 31), which after all requires nothing deductively. It does not require that formulas expressing various general properties of the predicate should be formally provable.

EXAMPLE 2. The formulas $\exists c(c'+a=b)$ and $\exists c(a+c'=b)$ each express $a<b$ (with a, b corresponding to a, b) under the meanings of the formal symbols, as we could see back in § 17 before we knew anything about the deductive rules.

The first formula $\exists c(c'+a=b)$ (which is the one we picked for our permanent abbreviation "$a<b$", §§ 17, 39) numeralwise expresses $a<b$ in the formal number-theoretic system, and even in the system without the induction schema (or Axioms 20 and 21), as we now establish.

For (i), we must show that, if a and b are any two natural numbers such that $a<b$, then $\vdash \exists c(c'+\boldsymbol{a}=\boldsymbol{b})$. For illustration, let $a=3$, $b=5$. Now $\vdash 0''+0''' = (0''+0'')'$ [Ax. 19] $= (0''+0')''$ [Ax. 19, Ax. 17] $= (0''+0)'''$ [Ax. 19, Ax. 17 twice] $= 0'''''$ [Ax. 18, Ax. 17 thrice]. Thus (tacitly using *102), $\vdash 0''+0'''=0'''''$. By $\exists$-introd., $\vdash \exists c(c'+0'''=0''''')$, i.e. $\vdash \exists c(c'+3=5)$. A similar series of steps will give us $\vdash \exists c(c'+\boldsymbol{a}=\boldsymbol{b})$ for any a and b such that $a<b$. To prove this in general, we may first establish as a lemma by informal induction on k that for any term t, using Axs. 17—19 (and *102), $\vdash \mathrm{t}+0^{(k)}=\mathrm{t}^{(k)}$.

For (ii) we must show that, if a and b are any two natural numbers such that a is not $<b$, then $\vdash \neg\exists c(c'+\boldsymbol{a}=\boldsymbol{b})$. If not $a<b$, then $a \geq b$. For illustration, let $a=3$, $b=2$. By applications of Axs. 17—19, exactly as above except that c' replaces $0''$ (or taking c' instead of $0''$ as the t of the lemma), $\vdash c'+0'''=c''''$. Thence $c'+0'''=0'' \vdash c''''=0''$ $\vdash c''=0$ [using Ax. 14 twice]. But by Ax. 15, $\vdash \neg c''=0$. By

reductio ad absurdum ($\neg$-introd.), $\vdash \neg c'+0'''=0''$; whence by $\forall$-introd. and *86 § 35, $\vdash \neg \exists c(c'+0'''=0'')$, i.e. $\vdash \neg \exists c(c'+3=2)$. Similarly for any other a and b such that $a \geq b$, $\vdash \neg \exists c(c'+\boldsymbol{a}=\boldsymbol{b})$.

Thus $\exists c(c'+a=b)$ numeralwise expresses $a<b$ in the formal system without Axiom Schema 13. But we cannot expect that in this system formulas expressing general properties of $<$, such as those of *134a—146b (with "$a<b$" as abbreviation for $\exists c(c'+a=b)$), will be provable, except in a few cases (e.g. *135b).

The other formula $\exists c(a+c'=b)$ (which by *119 is equivalent to $\exists c(c'+a=b)$ in the full system with Axiom Schema 13) seemingly does not numeralwise express $a<b$ in the system without Axiom Schema 13. Of course it does in the full system (or even without Axiom Schema 13, provided *118 or *119 is supplied as an axiom).

The numbered results of this section (beginning with *(164)) refer primarily to the full number-theoretic system (as throughout this chapter). But in fact for them we need no new applications of the formal induction rule (or Axiom Schema 13), provided certain particular formulas previously proved by means of it are available. More precisely, we can get along here with the predicate calculus, the particular number-theoretic axioms 14—21, the replacement property of equality which depends on having in addition only *104—*107 § 38, and *137 (or *136) § 39, except in a few cases which we will keep track of and list at the end of the section. (This subsystem of the full system was singled out by Raphael Robinson, 1950 abstract*, in a connection to be discussed in § 76.)

The predicates

*(164) $a=b$, *(165) $a<b$

are numeralwise expressed by the respective formulas $a=b$ *and* $a<b$, *i.e.* $\exists c(c'+a=b)$.

PROOFS. *(165). By Example 2; or (in the full number-theoretic system) using *135a, *134a, *140, *141.

If x *is a variable,* A(x) *and* B(x) *are formulas, k is a natural number,* y *is a variable distinct from* x *and free for* x *in* A(x) *and not occurring free in* A(x), *and* t *is a term not containing* x *and free for* x *in* A(x):

*166. $A(0), A(1), \ldots, A(\boldsymbol{k}-1) \vdash \forall x(x<\boldsymbol{k} \supset A(x))$.

*166a. $A(0), A(1), \ldots, A(\boldsymbol{k}) \vdash \forall x(x\leq\boldsymbol{k} \supset A(x))$.

*167. $\forall x(x<\boldsymbol{k} \supset A(x)) \vdash A(\boldsymbol{i})$ *for* $i = 0, 1, \ldots, k-1$.

*167a. $\forall x(x\leq\boldsymbol{k} \supset A(x)) \vdash A(\boldsymbol{i})$ *for* $i = 0, 1, \ldots, k$.

*168. $A(t) \vdash \forall x[x \geq t \supset \exists y(y \leq x \mathbin{\&} A(y))]$.

*169. $\forall x[x < t \supset A(x)], \forall x[x \geq t \supset B(x)] \vdash \forall x[A(x) \vee B(x)]$.

When $k = 0$, the list $A(0), A(1), \ldots, A(\boldsymbol{k}-1)$ of assumption formulas for *166 is empty, and there are no $A(\boldsymbol{i})$'s for *167.

PROOFS. *166. If we can show that $A(0), A(1), \ldots, A(\boldsymbol{k}-1), x<\boldsymbol{k} \vdash A(x)$, then *166 will follow by $\supset$- and $\forall$-introd. By *137_k (or via its proof, from *137 or *136), $\vdash x=0 \vee x=1 \vee \ldots \vee x=\boldsymbol{k}-1 \vee x=\boldsymbol{k} \vee \exists y(x=y^{(k+1)})$. Accordingly by $\vee$-elim. with weak $\neg$-elim. and $\exists$-elim., it will suffice to deduce either $A(x)$ or a contradiction from $A(0), A(1), \ldots, A(\boldsymbol{k}-1)$, $x<\boldsymbol{k}$ with each of $x=0$, $x=1$, $\ldots$, $x=\boldsymbol{k}-1$, $x=\boldsymbol{k}$, $x=y^{(k+1)}$ in turn. But (using now the informal presentation, beginning § 38) from each of $x=0, x=1, \ldots, x=\boldsymbol{k}-1$ with the corresponding one of $A(0), A(1), \ldots, A(\boldsymbol{k}-1)$, we obtain $A(x)$ by replacement (Corollary 2 Theorem 24 § 38). From $x=\boldsymbol{k}$ with $x<\boldsymbol{k}$ by replacement, $\boldsymbol{k}<\boldsymbol{k}$, contradicting $\neg\boldsymbol{k}<\boldsymbol{k}$ which is provable by *(165). From $x=y^{(k+1)}$ and $x<\boldsymbol{k}$ by replacement, $y^{(k+1)}<\boldsymbol{k}$, i.e. $\exists z(z'+y^{(k+1)}=\boldsymbol{k})$. Assume (for $\exists$-elim.) $z'+y^{(k+1)}=\boldsymbol{k}$. Thence by $k+1$ applications of Ax. 19 (with some applications of Ax. 17), $(z'+y)^{(k+1)}=\boldsymbol{k}$; whence by k applications of Ax. 14, $(z'+y)'=0$, contradicting Ax. 15. (Cf. the remark in the proof of *140 § 39.)

*167. Since $i < k$, by *(165) $\vdash \boldsymbol{i}<\boldsymbol{k}$.

*169. Using cases from *139. REMARK. We require *139 only with t substituted for b. When t is a numeral $\boldsymbol{k}$, this formula $a<\boldsymbol{k} \vee a=\boldsymbol{k} \vee a>\boldsymbol{k}$ can be proved from *137 or *136 similarly to *166. (Use *(165) in the first k cases. For the $k+2$-nd case, $a = b^{(k+1)} = (b')^{(k)} = (b'+0)^{(k)}$ [Axs. 18, 17] $= b'+\boldsymbol{k}$ [Axs. 19, 17].)

Although thus each of the formulas $a<0 \vee a=0 \vee a>0$, $a<1 \vee a=1 \vee a>1$, $a<2 \vee a=2 \vee a>2$, $\ldots$ is provable in the system lacking Axiom Schema 13 (and even Axs. 14, 15, 20, 21) but having the formula of *137 or *136 as additional axiom, we have no ground for believing that the formula $a<b \vee a=b \vee a>b$ of *139 itself is provable in that system.

The remainder of this section may be postponed, if the reader prefers, until just before § 49.

Under the interpretation of the formal symbolism, a number-theoretic function $\varphi(x_1, \ldots, x_n)$ is expressed by a term $t(x_1, \ldots, x_n)$.

EXAMPLE 3. The function $(a+1)^2$ is expressed under the interpretation by the terms $(a')\cdot(a')$, $aa+(2a+1)$, etc.

The only number-theoretic functions which can be thus directly expressed are the polynomials. However, we shall find that it is possible to paraphrase many propositions in which other number-theoretic functions occur, so that those propositions become expressible in the formal symbolism despite the lack of terms expressing the functions themselves.

For let $\varphi(x_1,\ldots, x_n)$ be a given number-theoretic function, and let $P(x_1,\ldots, x_n, w)$ be the predicate $\varphi(x_1,\ldots, x_n)=w$, which we call the *representing predicate* of the function $\varphi(x_1,\ldots, x_n)$. If the predicate $P(x_1,\ldots, x_n, w)$ is expressed in the system by a formula $\mathrm{P}(\mathrm{x}_1,\ldots, \mathrm{x}_n, \mathrm{w})$, and $C(x)$ is a predicate expressed by $\mathrm{C}(\mathrm{x})$, then $C(\varphi(x_1,\ldots, x_n))$ is expressed by $\exists\mathrm{w}(\mathrm{P}(\mathrm{x}_1,\ldots, \mathrm{x}_n, \mathrm{w}) \& \mathrm{C}(\mathrm{w}))$ (and also by $\forall\mathrm{w}(\mathrm{P}(\mathrm{x}_1,\ldots, \mathrm{x}_n, \mathrm{w}) \supset \mathrm{C}(\mathrm{w}))$).

This suggests that, if the representing predicate of a function is expressible in the system, we can hope to be able to express and develop the theory of the function in the system much as though a term for the function itself were available. A metamathematical investigation to confirm this conjecture will be undertaken later (§ 74).

We seek some information now (and in § 49) on the question for what functions the representing predicates are expressible, or briefly, what functions are 'representable'. Thus far we have been talking only about the interpretation of the symbolism, but presently we will introduce a notion for the representation of functions analogous to 'numeralwise expressibility' for the expression of predicates.

The necessary and sufficient condition that a predicate $P(x_1,\ldots, x_n, w)$ be the representing predicate of some (single-valued) function $\varphi(x_1,\ldots,x_n)$ is that for each n-tuple $x_1,\ldots, x_n$ there exists a unique w such that $P(x_1,\ldots, x_n, w)$. When this condition holds, the function $\varphi(x_1,\ldots, x_n)$ represented can be defined 'descriptively' from the predicate $P(x_1,\ldots, x_n, w)$ as *the w such that* $P(x_1,\ldots, x_n, w)$.

We now introduce "$\exists!\mathrm{x}\mathrm{A}(\mathrm{x})$" under the usual stipulations on the letters (beginning § 40, and end § 33) as abbreviation for $\exists\mathrm{x}[\mathrm{A}(\mathrm{x}) \& \forall\mathrm{y}(\mathrm{A}(\mathrm{y}) \supset \mathrm{x}=\mathrm{y})]$ (read "there exists a unique x such that A(x)"). Then if $P(x_1,\ldots, x_n, w)$ is expressed by the formula $\mathrm{P}(\mathrm{x}_1,\ldots, \mathrm{x}_n, \mathrm{w})$, the condition that $P(x_1,\ldots, x_n, w)$ be a representing predicate is expressed by the formula $\forall\mathrm{x}_1\ldots\forall\mathrm{x}_n\exists!\mathrm{w}\mathrm{P}(\mathrm{x}_1,\ldots, \mathrm{x}_n, \mathrm{w})$, or simply by $\exists!\mathrm{w}\mathrm{P}(\mathrm{x}_1,\ldots, \mathrm{x}_n, \mathrm{w})$ when $\mathrm{x}_1,\ldots, \mathrm{x}_n$ have the generality interpretation (§ 32).

If x, y *and* z *are distinct variables,* A(x) *is a formula,* t, r *and* s *are terms,* Γ *are formulas not containing* x *free,* y, z, r, s *and* t *are free for* x *in* A(x), z *and* x *do not occur in* t, *and* y *and* z *do not occur free in* A(x):

*170. *If* Γ, A(t), A(x) ⊢ t=x *with the free variables held constant for* A(x), *then* Γ, A(t) ⊢ ∃!xA(x).

*171. ⊢ ∃!x(t=x).

*172. $A(r), A(s), \exists!xA(x) \vdash r=s$.
*173. $r \neq s, A(r), \exists!xA(x) \vdash \neg A(s)$.

(Properties of $\exists!$.)

*174a. $A(t) \& \forall z(z<t \supset \neg A(z)) \vdash \exists!y[A(y) \& \forall z(z<y \supset \neg A(z))]$.
*174b. $\vdash \exists y[A(y) \& \forall z(z<y \supset \neg A(z))] \sim \exists!y[A(y) \& \forall z(z<y \supset \neg A(z))]$.

(Uniqueness of the least x such that A(x).)

PROOFS. *174a. Using *170, *139. Cf. the remark in the proof of *169.

An intuitive number-theoretic function $\varphi(x_1,\ldots,x_n)$ is said to be *numeralwise representable* in the formal system, if there is a formula $P(x_1,\ldots,x_n, w)$ with no free variables other than the distinct variables $x_1,\ldots,x_n$, w such that, for each particular n-tuple of natural numbers $x_1,\ldots,x_n$,

(v) if $\varphi(x_1, \ldots, x_n) = w$, then $\vdash P(\boldsymbol{x}_1,\ldots, \boldsymbol{x}_n, \boldsymbol{w})$, and

(vi) $\vdash \exists!wP(\boldsymbol{x}_1,\ldots, \boldsymbol{x}_n, w)$.

In this case, the formula $P(x_1,\ldots,x_n, w)$ *numeralwise represents* the function $\varphi(x_1,\ldots,x_n)$ (with the obvious correspondence of variables).

Our finitary (i.e. intuitionistic) use of this notion will be confined to cases when there is a calculation procedure for the function $\varphi(x_1,\ldots,x_n)$ (§ 30), so that the w of (v) can be found for any given $x_1,\ldots,x_n$ (or will make this tacitly an hypothesis).

If $\varphi(x_1,\ldots,x_n)$ is numeralwise represented by $P(x_1,\ldots,x_n, w)$, the latter numeralwise expresses the representing predicate $P(x_1,\ldots,x_n, w)$ of φ. For from (v) and (vi), we can infer that for every w,

(vii) if $\varphi(x_1,\ldots,x_n) \neq w$, then $\vdash \neg P(\boldsymbol{x}_1,\ldots, \boldsymbol{x}_n, \boldsymbol{w})$,

as follows. Take the $\boldsymbol{w}$ of (v) as the r and the $\boldsymbol{w}$ of (vii) as the s for *173. Use *(164) to get the provability of the $r \neq s$.

We have no ground to believe that, conversely, (vii) for every w together with (v) necessarily implies (vi).

We have used the $\exists!$-notation to state (vi) compactly. $\exists!xA(x)$ is equivalent to $\exists xA(x) \& \forall x\forall y(A(x) \& A(y) \supset x=y)$, in which the first part expresses existence and the second uniqueness. The existence part for (vi) follows already from (v); so what (vi) adds is the uniqueness.

In numeralwise representability of functions (just as in numeralwise expressibility of predicates), we are limiting ourselves to the consideration of the values for particular arguments, in contrast to general properties. The questions considered are in this way analogous to computational questions in informal arithmetic.

For example, we have not required in defining 'numeralwise representability' that the formula $\exists !wP(x_1,\ldots,x_n, w)$ should be provable with $x_1,\ldots,x_n$ as formal variables. That would be stronger than our demand that (vi) hold for every $\boldsymbol{x}_1,\ldots,\boldsymbol{x}_n$ with $x_1,\ldots,x_n$ as intuitive variables, which would follow from it by substitution (*66 § 32 with $\boldsymbol{x}_1,\ldots,\boldsymbol{x}_n$ as the $t_1,\ldots,t_n$). That stronger condition (without (v)) will be the prerequisite for the theory to be developed in § 74. For the six functions we consider now, we readily obtain that also.

The functions

*(175) a', *(176) $a+b$, *(177) ab

are numeralwise represented by the respective formulas $a'=b$, $a+b=c$, $ab=c$.

PROOFS. *(176) By *171 and the form of the representing formula $a+b=c$, (vi) is immediate (and even $\vdash \exists !c(a+b=c)$). For (v), we must show that for each pair a, b of natural numbers, if $c = a+b$, then $\vdash \boldsymbol{a}+\boldsymbol{b}=\boldsymbol{c}$. For example, if $a = 2$ and $b = 3$ (then $c = 5$), we have $\vdash \boldsymbol{a}+\boldsymbol{b}=\boldsymbol{c}$ (i.e. $\vdash 0''+0'''=0'''''$) as for (i) in Example 2.

*(177) Similarly. The proof of (v) can be conveniently arranged as an intuitive induction on b. IND. STEP. Say $c = ab$, $d = ab'$ $(= ab+a = c+a)$. Then $\vdash \boldsymbol{ab}' = \boldsymbol{ab}+\boldsymbol{a}$ [Ax. 21] $= \boldsymbol{c}+\boldsymbol{a}$ [hyp. ind., *104] $= \boldsymbol{d}$ [by (v) for *(176)].

Some general principles will illuminate our treatment of the next examples. A *prime* formula is one containing no logical symbols, i.e. here it is s=t for some terms s and t.

(A) *Each closed prime formula* s=t *is formally decidable* (*and* s=t *is provable or refutable according as the terms* s *and* t *express the same or different numbers under the usual interpretation of* 0, ′, +, ·). *Each prime formula is numeralwise decidable.*

PROOF. Use *(176), *(177), Theorem 24 § 38, and *(164).

EXAMPLE 4. Let s=t be $0'''\cdot 0''''+0'=(0'''\cdot 0'')''$, i.e. abbreviated $3\cdot 4+1=(3\cdot 2)''$. Now $\vdash 3\cdot 4+1=(3\cdot 2)'' \sim 12+1=(3\cdot 2)''$ [since by *(177), $\vdash 3\cdot 4=12$] $\sim 13=(3\cdot 2)''$ [since by *(176), $\vdash 12+1=13$] $\sim 13=8$ [since by *(177), $\vdash 3\cdot 2=6$; and noting that $6''$, i.e. $(0'''''')''$, is 8]. But by *(164), $\vdash \neg 13=8$. Hence $\vdash \neg 3\cdot 4+1=(3\cdot 2)''$. We have used tacitly Theorem 24 (b) or its Corollary 1, and *21 § 26, in concluding by the chain that $\vdash 3\cdot 4+1=(3\cdot 2)'' \sim 13=8$; and *30 *18b, or *20 and Corollary Theorem 6, in combining this with $\vdash \neg 13=8$ to infer that $\vdash \neg 3\cdot 4+1=(3\cdot 2)''$.

(B) *Let* $P(x_1,\ldots,x_n)$ *be a formula containing free only the distinct variables* $x_1,\ldots,x_n$, *and suppose* $P(x_1,\ldots,x_n)$ *is numeralwise decidable* *(and numeralwise expresses $P(x_1,\ldots,x_n)$). Then: If* $\mathrm{t}_1,\ldots,\mathrm{t}_n$ *are terms containing no variables (and therefore expressing numbers* $t_1,\ldots,t_n$*),* $\mathrm{P}(\mathrm{t}_1,\ldots,\mathrm{t}_n)$ *is decidable (and* $\mathrm{P}(\mathrm{t}_1,\ldots,\mathrm{t}_n)$ *is provable or refutable according as* $P(t_1,\ldots,t_n)$ *is true or false). If* $\mathrm{t}_1,\ldots,\mathrm{t}_n$ *are terms free for* $\mathrm{x}_1,\ldots,\mathrm{x}_n$ *in* $\mathrm{P}(\mathrm{x}_1,\ldots,\mathrm{x}_n)$, $\mathrm{P}(\mathrm{t}_1,\ldots,\mathrm{t}_n)$ *is numeralwise decidable.*

Proved like (A), which is the special case of (B) for which $\mathrm{P}(\mathrm{x}_1,\ldots,\mathrm{x}_n)$ is $\mathrm{x}_1=\mathrm{x}_2$.

(C) *A formula composed out of closed decidable formulas using only the operators* $\supset$, &, $\vee$, $\neg$ *of the propositional calculus is decidable (and whether it is provable or refutable can be determined by use of the classical 2-valued truth tables* § 28 *taking* $\mathfrak{t}$ *and* $\mathfrak{f}$ *as 'provable' and 'refutable', respectively).*

By Lemma 13 § 29 with Theorem 3 § 25.

(D) Hence: *Each formula without variables is decidable. Each formula without quantifiers is numeralwise decidable.*

(E) *Let* $\mathrm{A}(\mathrm{x}_1,\ldots,\mathrm{x}_n,\mathrm{y})$ *be a numeralwise decidable formula containing free only the distinct variables* $\mathrm{x}_1,\ldots,\mathrm{x}_n,\mathrm{y}$*; and let* z *be a variable distinct from* $\mathrm{x}_1,\ldots,\mathrm{x}_n,\mathrm{y}$. *Then* $\forall\mathrm{y}(\mathrm{y}<\mathrm{z}\supset\mathrm{A}(\mathrm{x}_1,\ldots,\mathrm{x}_n,\mathrm{y}))$ *and* $\exists\mathrm{y}(\mathrm{y}<\mathrm{z}\ \&\ \mathrm{A}(\mathrm{x}_1,\ldots,\mathrm{x}_n,\mathrm{y}))$ *are numeralwise decidable (and* $\forall\mathrm{y}(\mathrm{y}<\boldsymbol{z}\supset\mathrm{A}(\boldsymbol{x}_1,\ldots,\boldsymbol{x}_n,\mathrm{y}))$ *is provable or refutable, according as all of* $\mathrm{A}(\boldsymbol{x}_1,\ldots,\boldsymbol{x}_n,0)$, $\mathrm{A}(\boldsymbol{x}_1,\ldots,\boldsymbol{x}_n,1),\ldots,\mathrm{A}(\boldsymbol{x}_1,\ldots,\boldsymbol{x}_n,\boldsymbol{z}-1)$ *are provable or some are refutable;* $\exists\mathrm{y}(\mathrm{y}<\boldsymbol{z}\ \&\ \mathrm{A}(\boldsymbol{x}_1,\ldots,\boldsymbol{x}_n,\mathrm{y}))$*, according as some are provable or all are refutable). Similarly with* $\leq$ *in place of* $<$.

PROOF (for $<$). Use *166, *167, *(165) (also *58b § 27, *86 § 35).

Consider the division of two integers, a by b. For example, $13 = 5\cdot 2+3$ where $3 < 5$. In words, when 13 is divided by 5, the quotient is 2 and the remainder is 3. Customarily, the division process, and therewith the quotient function $[a/b]$ and the remainder function $\mathrm{rm}(a, b)$ are defined only for $b \neq 0$. To avoid the trouble of discussing partially defined functions now, we extend the definitions to the case $b = 0$ by setting $[a/0] = 0$, $\mathrm{rm}(a, 0) = a$. This preserves the law $a = b[a/b] + \mathrm{rm}(a, b)$. Then $b\,|\,a$ ("b divides a") if and only if $\mathrm{rm}(a, b) = 0$.

The functions

*(178) $[a/b]$, *(179) $\mathrm{rm}(a, b)$

are numeralwise represented by respective formulas $\mathrm{Q}(a, b, q)$ *and* $\mathrm{R}(a, b, r)$ *such that, for any numerals* $\boldsymbol{q}$ *and* $\boldsymbol{r}$:

*178a. $\mathrm{Q}(a, b, \boldsymbol{q}) \vdash \exists! q\mathrm{Q}(a, b, q)$. *179a. $\mathrm{R}(a, b, \boldsymbol{r}) \vdash \exists! r\mathrm{R}(a, b, r)$.

PROOFS. *(179) and *179a. Let $\mathrm{S}(a, b, r)$ be the formula

$$\exists q(q \leq a \;\&\; a = bq + r \;\&\; r < b) \vee (b = 0 \;\&\; r = a).$$

Then let $\mathrm{R}(a, b, r)$ be

$$\mathrm{S}(a, b, r) \;\&\; \forall e(e < r \supset \neg \mathrm{S}(a, b, e)).$$

Now *179a is immediate from *174a (with $\boldsymbol{r}$ as the t).

To establish (v) for *(179), consider any pair of numbers a and b, and let $r = \mathrm{rm}(a, b)$ and $q = [a/b]$. CASE 1: $b \neq 0$. Now $a = bq+r$; hence by (A), $\vdash \boldsymbol{a}=\boldsymbol{bq}+\boldsymbol{r}$. Also $r < b$; hence by *(165), $\vdash \boldsymbol{r}<\boldsymbol{b}$. By &-introd. (or (C)), $\vdash \boldsymbol{a}=\boldsymbol{bq}+\boldsymbol{r} \;\&\; \boldsymbol{r}<\boldsymbol{b}$. But $q \leq a$; so by (E), $\vdash \exists q(q \leq \boldsymbol{a} \;\&\; \boldsymbol{a}=\boldsymbol{b}q+\boldsymbol{r} \;\&\; \boldsymbol{r}<\boldsymbol{b})$. By $\vee$-introd., $\vdash \exists q(q \leq \boldsymbol{a} \;\&\; \boldsymbol{a}=\boldsymbol{b}q+\boldsymbol{r} \;\&\; \boldsymbol{r}<\boldsymbol{b}) \vee (\boldsymbol{b}=0 \;\&\; \boldsymbol{r}=\boldsymbol{a})$, i.e. $\vdash \mathrm{S}(\boldsymbol{a}, \boldsymbol{b}, \boldsymbol{r})$. Now let e be any number $< r$. Then $e < b$ (so by *(165), $\vdash \boldsymbol{e}<\boldsymbol{b}$). For any number p, $a \neq bp+e$ (since q, r is the only pair of numbers with $r < b$ such that $a = bq+r$); so by (A), $\vdash \neg \boldsymbol{a} = \boldsymbol{bp}+\boldsymbol{e}$. Thence by (C), $\vdash \neg(\boldsymbol{a}=\boldsymbol{bp}+\boldsymbol{e} \;\&\; \boldsymbol{e}<\boldsymbol{b})$. In particular this holds for $p = 0, 1, \ldots, a$; so by (E), $\vdash \neg\exists q(q \leq \boldsymbol{a} \;\&\; \boldsymbol{a}=\boldsymbol{b}q+\boldsymbol{e} \;\&\; \boldsymbol{e}<\boldsymbol{b})$. But $b \neq 0$; hence by *(164), $\vdash \neg \boldsymbol{b}=0$. By *(164), either $\vdash \boldsymbol{e}=\boldsymbol{a}$ or $\vdash \neg \boldsymbol{e}=\boldsymbol{a}$. Combining these results by (C), $\vdash \neg(\exists q(q \leq \boldsymbol{a} \;\&\; \boldsymbol{a}=\boldsymbol{b}q+\boldsymbol{e} \;\&\; \boldsymbol{e}<\boldsymbol{b}) \vee (\boldsymbol{b}=0 \;\&\; \boldsymbol{e}=\boldsymbol{a}))$, i.e. $\vdash \neg \mathrm{S}(\boldsymbol{a}, \boldsymbol{b}, \boldsymbol{e})$. This was for any $e < r$, i.e. it holds for $e = 0, 1, \ldots, r-1$; so by (E), $\vdash \forall e(e<\boldsymbol{r} \supset \neg \mathrm{S}(\boldsymbol{a}, \boldsymbol{b}, e))$. From this and $\vdash \mathrm{S}(\boldsymbol{a}, \boldsymbol{b}, \boldsymbol{r})$ by &-introd., $\vdash \mathrm{S}(\boldsymbol{a}, \boldsymbol{b}, \boldsymbol{r}) \;\&\; \forall e(e<\boldsymbol{r} \supset \neg \mathrm{S}(\boldsymbol{a}, \boldsymbol{b}, e))$, i.e. $\vdash \mathrm{R}(\boldsymbol{a}, \boldsymbol{b}, \boldsymbol{r})$, as was to be shown. CASE 2: $b = 0$. Similarly. (Summarizing: From the form of $\mathrm{R}(a, b, r)$, by (A), *(165), (C) and (E), $\mathrm{R}(a, b, r)$ is numeralwise decidable. By formal steps paralleling the interpretation, we verify that $\mathrm{R}(\boldsymbol{a}, \boldsymbol{b}, \boldsymbol{r})$ is provable rather than refutable when $r = \mathrm{rm}(a, b)$.)

Now (vi) for *(179) follows by substituting any numerals $\boldsymbol{a}, \boldsymbol{b}$ for a, b in *179a, and using (v).

The function

*(180) $\mathrm{rm}(c, (i' \cdot d)')$

is numeralwise represented by a formula B(c, d, i, w) *such that, for any numeral* $\boldsymbol{w}$:

*180a. B(c, d, i, $\boldsymbol{w}$) $\vdash \exists!$wB(c, d, i, w).

PROOF. Let "c", "d", "i", "v", "w" denote c, d, i, q, r, respectively; and let B(c, d, i, w) be R(c, (i′·d)′, w). Use *179a, substitution (*66), *(179) and (B).

The foregoing treatment does not give the stronger property that

$\vdash \exists! \mathrm{w} \mathrm{P}(\mathrm{x}_1, \ldots, \mathrm{x}_n, \mathrm{w})$ for the formulas numeralwise representing $[a/b]$, $\mathrm{rm}(a, b)$ and $\mathrm{rm}(c, (i' \cdot d)')$. However using *146a and *146b (with *123, *140, *141, *142a and *143a), this can be established also, and simpler representing formulas can be given equivalent to the former.

*178b. $\vdash \mathrm{Q}(a, b, q) \sim \exists r(a=bq+r \,\&\, r<b) \vee b=q=0$.

*179b. $\vdash \mathrm{R}(a, b, r) \sim \exists q(a=bq+r \,\&\, r<b) \vee (b=0 \,\&\, r=a)$.

*180b. $\vdash \mathrm{B}(\mathrm{c}, \mathrm{d}, \mathrm{i}, \mathrm{w}) \sim \exists \mathrm{v}(\mathrm{c}=(\mathrm{i}' \cdot \mathrm{d})' \cdot \mathrm{v}+\mathrm{w} \,\&\, \mathrm{w}<(\mathrm{i}' \cdot \mathrm{d})')$.

*178c. $\vdash \exists! q \mathrm{Q}(a, b, q)$. *179c. $\vdash \exists! r \mathrm{R}(a, b, r)$.

*180c. $\vdash \exists! \mathrm{w} \mathrm{B}(\mathrm{c}, \mathrm{d}, \mathrm{i}, \mathrm{w})$.

LEMMA 18a. *The results* *(164)—*180c *and* (A)—(E) *of this section, excepting* *169 *and* *174a *when* t *is not a numeral,* *174b, *178b, c, *179b, c *and* *180b, c, *hold good for the formal system lacking Axiom Schema* 13 *but having as additional particular number-theoretic axioms the formulas of* *104—*107 *and of* *137 *or* *136 ("Robinson's system").

§ 42. Gödel's theorem.

From a result of Presburger 1930, metamathematical proofs of consistency and completeness, and a decision procedure, can be given for the formal system with the formation rule and axioms for · omitted. (Cf. Example 2 § 79. Presburger deals with a classical system of the arithmetic of the integers, but Hilbert and Bernays 1934 pp. 359 ff. adapt his method to essentially the present classical system, and Joan Ross has verified that the adaptation works for the intuitionistic system as well.)

For the full system (or systems essentially equivalent to it), these questions proved to be very refractory. Consistency proofs by Ackermann 1924-5 and von Neumann 1927 lead to the result that the system is consistent under the restriction on the use of the induction postulate (Axiom Schema 13) to the case that the induction variable x does not occur free within the scope of a quantifier of the induction formula A(x). (Cf. Theorem 55 § 79. The restriction excludes e.g. our proofs of *105, *136 and *148.)

This situation was illuminated in 1931 by the appearance of two remarkable theorems of Gödel "on formally undecidable propositions of Principia Mathematica and related systems". We designate the first of these theorems, which entails the other as corollary, as "Gödel's theorem", although it is only one of a series of important contributions by its author. These two theorems, which became the most widely noted in the subject, bear on the whole program and philosophy of metamathematics.

The metamathematical results presented thus far in this book were reached along paths more or less suggested by the interpretation of the system. These results of Gödel are obtained by a kind of metamathematical reasoning which goes more deeply into the structure of the formal system as a system of objects.

As is set forth in § 16, the objects of the formal system which we study are various formal symbols, formal expressions (i.e. finite sequences of formal symbols), and finite sequences of formal expressions. There are an enumerable infinity of formal symbols given at the outset. Hence, by the methods of § 1, the formal objects form an enumerable class. By specifying a particular enumeration of them, and letting our metamathematical statements refer to the indices in the enumeration instead of to the objects enumerated, metamathematics becomes a branch of number theory. Therewith, the possibility appears that the formal system should contain formulas which, when considered in the light of the enumeration, express propositions of its own metamathematics.

It will appear, on further study, that this possibility can be exploited, and with the use of Cantor's diagonal method (§ 2), a closed formula A can be found which, interpreted by a person who knows this enumeration, asserts its own unprovability.

This formula A bears an analogy to the proposition of the Epimenides paradox (§ 11). But now there is a way of escape from the paradox. By the construction of A,

(1) A means that A is unprovable.

Let us assume, as we hope is the case, that formulas which express false propositions are unprovable in the system, i.e.

(2) false formulas are unprovable.

Now the formula A cannot be false, because by (1) that would mean that it is not unprovable, contradicting (2). But A can be true, provided it is unprovable. Indeed this must be the case. For assuming that A is provable, by (1) A is false, and hence by (2) unprovable. By (intuitive) reductio ad absurdum, this gives that A is unprovable, whereupon by (1) also A is true. Thus the system is incomplete in the sense that it fails to afford a proof of every formula which is true under the interpretation (if (2) is so, or if at least the particular formula A is unprovable if false).

The negation ¬A of the formula is also unprovable. For A is true; hence ¬A is false; and by (2), ¬A is unprovable. So the system is incomplete also in the simple sense defined metamathematically in the last section (if (2) is so, or if at least the particular formulas A and ¬A are each unprovable if false).

The above is of course only a preliminary heuristic account of Gödel's reasoning. Because of the nature of this intuitive argument, which skirts so close to and yet misses a paradox, it is important that the strictly finitary metamathematical proof of Gödel's theorem should be appreciated. When this metamathematical proof is examined in full detail, it is seen to be of the nature of ordinary mathematics. In fact, if we chose to make our metamathematics a part of number theory (now informal rather than formal number theory) by talking about the indices in the enumeration, and if we ignore the interpretations of the object system (now a system of numbers), the theorem becomes a proposition of ordinary elementary number theory. Its proof, while exceedingly long and tedious in these terms, is not open to any objection which would not equally involve parts of traditional mathematics which have been held most secure.

We can give the rigorous metamathematical proof now, by borrowing one lemma from results of the next two chapters. Our numbering of the lemmas and theorems corresponds to the logical order.

In making use of the idea of enumerating the formal objects, practical considerations dictate that the indices of formal objects should be correlated to the objects by as simple a rule as possible. We can modify the above heuristic argument (inessentially) by using, rather than an enumeration in the usual sense, an enumeration with gaps in the natural numbers, i.e. a correlation of distinct natural numbers to the distinct formal objects, not all of the natural numbers being used in the correlation. We call this a Gödel numbering, and the correlated number of a formal object its Gödel number. (Sometimes separate Gödel numberings are given of the formal symbols, of the formal expressions, and of the finite sequences of formal expressions. If that is done, then when one speaks of a number as the Gödel number of a symbol, or of an expression, or of a sequence of expressions, in each case a different correlation is being referred to.)

Relative to any specified Gödel numbering, for any n which is the Gödel number of a formula, let "A_n" designate the formula. (For other n's, we need not define A_n.) We may write this formula A_n also as "$\mathrm{A}_n(a)$", showing the free variable a for use with our substitution notation (§ 18).

LEMMA 21. *There is a Gödel numbering of the formal objects such that the predicates $A(a, b)$ and $B(a, c)$ defined as follows are numeralwise expressible* (§ 41) *in the formal system.*

$A(a, b)$: a is the Gödel number of a formula (namely $\mathrm{A}_a(a)$), and b is the Gödel number of a proof of the formula $\mathrm{A}_a(\boldsymbol{a})$.

$B(a, c)$: a is the Gödel number of a formula (namely $\mathrm{A}_a(a)$), and c is the Gödel number of a proof of the formula $\neg \mathrm{A}_a(\boldsymbol{a})$.

Now let A(a, b) and B(a, c) be particular formulas which numeralwise express the predicates $A(a, b)$ and $B(a, c)$, respectively, for the Gödel numbering given by the lemma. The two formulas A(a, b) and B(a, c) could actually be exhibited, after we have the proof of the lemma (to be completed in § 52).

Consider the formula $\forall b \neg \mathrm{A}(a, b)$ which contains a and no other variable free. This formula has a Gödel number, call it p, and is then the same as the formula which we have designated "$\mathrm{A}_p(a)$". Now consider the formula $\mathrm{A}_p(\boldsymbol{p})$, i.e.

$$\mathrm{A}_p(\boldsymbol{p}): \qquad \forall b \neg \mathrm{A}(\boldsymbol{p}, b),$$

which contains no variable free. Note that we have used Cantor's diagonal method in substituting the numeral $\boldsymbol{p}$ for a in $\mathrm{A}_p(a)$ to obtain this formula.

To relate this to the preliminary heuristic outline, we can interpret the formula $\mathrm{A}_p(\boldsymbol{p})$ from our perspective of the Gödel numbering as expressing the proposition that $\mathrm{A}_p(\boldsymbol{p})$ is unprovable, i.e. it is a formula A which asserts its own unprovability.

In the metamathematical argument, the assumptions of the heuristic argument that the system should not allow the proof of either of the formulas A or $\neg$ A if false will be replaced by metamathematical equivalents. For the unprovability of A if false, this equivalent will be the (simple) consistency of the system (§ 28). For the unprovability of $\neg$A if false, we shall need a stronger condition called 'ω-consistency' which we shall now define.

The formal system (or a system with similar formation rules) is said to be *ω-consistent*, if for no variable x and formula A(x) are all of the following true:

$$\vdash \mathrm{A}(0), \quad \vdash \mathrm{A}(1), \quad \vdash \mathrm{A}(2), \ldots; \quad \vdash \neg \forall \mathrm{x} \mathrm{A}(\mathrm{x})$$

(or in other words if not both $\vdash \mathrm{A}(\boldsymbol{n})$ for every natural number n and $\vdash \neg \forall \mathrm{x} \mathrm{A}(\mathrm{x})$). In the contrary case that for some x and A(x) all of A(0), A(1), A(2), ... and also $\neg \forall \mathrm{x} \mathrm{A}(\mathrm{x})$ are provable, the system is *ω-inconsistent.*

Note that ω-consistency implies simple consistency. For if A be any provable formula containing no free variables, writing it as "A(x)" where x is a variable, all of A(0), A(1), A(2), ... are provable (under our substitution notation § 18, each of these is simply A itself); and hence if the system is ω-consistent, $\neg \forall \mathrm{x} \mathrm{A}(\mathrm{x})$ is an example of an unprovable formula (cf. § 28).

THEOREM 28. *If the number-theoretic formal system is (simply) consistent, then not* $\vdash \mathrm{A}_p(\boldsymbol{p})$; *and if the system is ω-consistent, then not* $\vdash \neg \mathrm{A}_p(\boldsymbol{p})$.

Thus, if the system is ω-consistent, then it is (simply) incomplete, with $\mathrm{A}_p(\boldsymbol{p})$ *as an example of an undecidable formula.* (Gödel's theorem, in the original form.)

PROOF that, if the system is consistent, then not $\vdash \mathrm{A}_p(\boldsymbol{p})$. Suppose (for intuitive reductio ad absurdum) that $\vdash \mathrm{A}_p(\boldsymbol{p})$, i.e. suppose that $\mathrm{A}_p(\boldsymbol{p})$ is provable. Then there is a proof of it; let the Gödel number of this proof be k. Then $A(p, k)$ is true. Hence, since $\mathrm{A}(a, b)$ was introduced under the lemma as a formula which numeralwise expresses $A(a, b)$, $\vdash \mathrm{A}(\boldsymbol{p}, \boldsymbol{k})$. By $\exists$-introd., $\vdash \exists b \mathrm{A}(\boldsymbol{p}, b)$. Thence by *83a, $\vdash \neg \forall b \neg \mathrm{A}(\boldsymbol{p}, b)$. But this is $\vdash \neg \mathrm{A}_p(\boldsymbol{p})$. This, with our assumption that $\vdash \mathrm{A}_p(\boldsymbol{p})$, contradicts the hypothesis that the system is consistent. Therefore by reductio ad absurdum, not $\vdash \mathrm{A}_p(\boldsymbol{p})$, as was to be shown. (We could also have contradicted the consistency by using $\forall$-elim. to infer $\vdash \neg \mathrm{A}(\boldsymbol{p}, \boldsymbol{k})$ from $\vdash \mathrm{A}_p(\boldsymbol{p})$.)

PROOF that, if the system is ω-consistent (and hence also consistent), then not $\vdash \neg \mathrm{A}_p(\boldsymbol{p})$. By the consistency and the first part of the theorem, $\mathrm{A}_p(\boldsymbol{p})$ is not provable. Hence each of the natural numbers 0, 1, 2, ... is not the Gödel number of a proof of $\mathrm{A}_p(\boldsymbol{p})$; i.e. $A(p, 0)$, $A(p, 1)$, $A(p, 2)$, ... are all false. Hence, since $\mathrm{A}(a, b)$ numeralwise expresses $A(a, b)$, $\vdash \neg \mathrm{A}(\boldsymbol{p}, 0)$, $\vdash \neg \mathrm{A}(\boldsymbol{p}, 1)$, $\vdash \neg \mathrm{A}(\boldsymbol{p}, 2)$, ... By the ω-consistency, then not $\vdash \neg \forall b \neg \mathrm{A}(\boldsymbol{p}, b)$. But this is not $\vdash \neg \mathrm{A}_p(\boldsymbol{p})$, which was to be shown.

We have given the original Gödel form of the theorem first, as the proof is intuitively simpler and follows the heuristic outline. Rosser 1936 has shown, however, that by using a slightly more complicated example of an undecidable formula, the hypothesis of ω-consistency can be dispensed with, and the incompleteness proved from the (simple) consistency alone. Consider the formula $\forall b[\neg \mathrm{A}(a, b) \vee \exists c(c \leq b \;\&\; \mathrm{B}(a, c))]$. This has a Gödel number, call it q. Now consider the formula $\mathrm{A}_q(\boldsymbol{q})$, i.e.

$$\mathrm{A}_q(\boldsymbol{q}): \qquad \forall b[\neg \mathrm{A}(\boldsymbol{q}, b) \vee \exists c(c \leq b \;\&\; \mathrm{B}(\boldsymbol{q}, c))].$$

We can interpret the formula $\mathrm{A}_q(\boldsymbol{q})$ from our perspective of the Gödel numbering as asserting that to any proof of $\mathrm{A}_q(\boldsymbol{q})$ there exists a proof of $\neg \mathrm{A}_q(\boldsymbol{q})$ with an equal or smaller Gödel number, which under the hypothesis of simple consistency implies that $\mathrm{A}_q(\boldsymbol{q})$ is unprovable.

THEOREM 29. *If the number-theoretic formal system is (simply) consistent, then neither* $\vdash \mathrm{A}_q(\boldsymbol{q})$ *nor* $\vdash \neg \mathrm{A}_q(\boldsymbol{q})$; *i.e. if the system is consistent, then it is (simply) incomplete, with* $\mathrm{A}_q(\boldsymbol{q})$ *as an undecidable formula.* (Rosser's form of Gödel's theorem.)

PROOF that, if the system is consistent, then not $\vdash A_q(\boldsymbol{q})$. Suppose that $\vdash A_q(\boldsymbol{q})$. As before (using q instead of p), $\vdash A(\boldsymbol{q}, \boldsymbol{k})$. Also, under our hypothesis of consistency, the assumption that $\vdash A_q(\boldsymbol{q})$ implies that not $\vdash \neg A_q(\boldsymbol{q})$, i.e. $\neg A_q(\boldsymbol{q})$ is unprovable. Hence, in particular, each of $B(q, 0), B(q, 1), \ldots, B(q, k)$ is false. Since $\mathrm{B}(a, b)$ numeralwise expresses $B(a, b)$, therefore $\vdash \neg \mathrm{B}(\boldsymbol{q}, 0)$, $\vdash \neg \mathrm{B}(\boldsymbol{q}, 1), \ldots, \vdash \neg \mathrm{B}(\boldsymbol{q}, \boldsymbol{k})$. Hence by *166a, $\vdash \forall c(c \leq \boldsymbol{k} \supset \neg \mathrm{B}(\boldsymbol{q}, c))$. This with $\vdash A(\boldsymbol{q}, \boldsymbol{k})$ gives by &- and $\exists$-introd., $\vdash \exists b[A(\boldsymbol{q}, b) \,\&\, \forall c(c \leq b \supset \neg \mathrm{B}(\boldsymbol{q}, c))]$. Thence by *58b and *86, $\vdash \exists b[A(\boldsymbol{q}, b) \,\&\, \neg \exists c(c \leq b \,\&\, \mathrm{B}(\boldsymbol{q}, c))]$. Thence by *57b (and *70), $\vdash \exists b \neg[\neg A(\boldsymbol{q}, b) \vee \exists c(c \leq b \,\&\, \mathrm{B}(\boldsymbol{q}, c))]$. Thence by *85a, $\vdash \neg \forall b[\neg A(\boldsymbol{q}, b) \vee \exists c(c \leq b \,\&\, \mathrm{B}(\boldsymbol{q}, c))]$. But this is $\vdash \neg A_q(\boldsymbol{q})$. Hence as before, not $\vdash A_q(\boldsymbol{q})$, as was to be shown.

PROOF that, if the system is consistent, then not $\vdash \neg A_q(\boldsymbol{q})$. Suppose that $\vdash \neg A_q(\boldsymbol{q})$, i.e. that $\neg A_q(\boldsymbol{q})$ is provable. Then there is a proof of it; let the Gödel number of this proof be k. Then $B(q, k)$ is true. Hence $\vdash \mathrm{B}(\boldsymbol{q}, \boldsymbol{k})$. By *168, $\vdash \forall b[b \geq \boldsymbol{k} \supset \exists c(c \leq b \,\&\, \mathrm{B}(\boldsymbol{q}, c))]$. Also as before (with q instead of p), $\vdash \neg A(\boldsymbol{q}, 0)$, $\vdash \neg A(\boldsymbol{q}, 1), \ldots, \vdash \neg A(\boldsymbol{q}, \boldsymbol{k}-1)$. By *166, $\vdash \forall b[b < \boldsymbol{k} \supset \neg A(\boldsymbol{q}, b)]$. Now by *169, $\vdash \forall b[\neg A(\boldsymbol{q}, b) \vee \exists c(c \leq b \,\&\, \mathrm{B}(\boldsymbol{q}, c))]$. But this is $\vdash A_q(\boldsymbol{q})$. Hence not $\vdash \neg A_q(\boldsymbol{q})$, as was to be shown.

Observe that we have not shown outright that $A_p(\boldsymbol{p})$, $\neg A_p(\boldsymbol{p})$, $A_q(\boldsymbol{q})$, $\neg A_q(\boldsymbol{q})$ are unprovable, but only that if the system is (simply) consistent, $A_p(\boldsymbol{p})$, $A_q(\boldsymbol{q})$, $\neg A_q(\boldsymbol{q})$ are unprovable, and if the system is ω-consistent, $\neg A_p(\boldsymbol{p})$ is unprovable.

Consider our demonstration that $A_p(\boldsymbol{p})$ is unprovable, if the system is consistent. If a demonstration of the consistency of the system were now supplied, prefixing it to the former would complete a demonstration that $A_p(\boldsymbol{p})$ is unprovable.

Supposing such a demonstration that $A_p(\boldsymbol{p})$ is unprovable to exist, we could, using the representation of the formal objects by Gödel numbers, express it as a demonstration in informal number theory. We now ask whether the latter demonstration could be formalized in the system.

In formalizing it, the formula $A_p(\boldsymbol{p})$ would itself be the formalized statement of what is demonstrated, i.e. that $A_p(\boldsymbol{p})$ is unprovable. Thus a formalized demonstration that $A_p(\boldsymbol{p})$ is unprovable would be a formal proof of $A_p(\boldsymbol{p})$. By Theorem 28, such a proof cannot exist if the system is consistent.

Thus, if we had an informal demonstration that $A_p(\boldsymbol{p})$ is unprovable, the demonstration would be incapable of being formalized within the system, if the system is consistent. The supposed informal demonstration was to consist of two parts, first a supposed proof of the consistency of the system, and second the proof we have already given (for the first half of Theorem 28) that $A_p(\boldsymbol{p})$ is unprovable if the system is consistent.

By showing that the second part actually can be formalized in the system, we have a method of showing that the first cannot be if the system is consistent. This gives the next theorem. We shall recapitulate this argument before stating the theorem.

The assertion that the system is (simply) consistent can be expressed in the formal system via the Gödel numbering variously. Let $C(a, b)$ be ($D(a, c)$ be) the predicate: a is the Gödel number of a formula, namely A_a, and b is (c is) the Gödel number of a proof of A_a (of $\neg A_a$). There are formulas $\mathrm{C}(a, b)$ and $\mathrm{D}(a, c)$ expressing $C(a, b)$ and $D(a, c)$, respectively (§ 52). The original definition of consistency in § 28 is then rendered directly into the formalism by the formula $\neg \exists a[\exists b \mathrm{C}(a, b) \& \exists c \mathrm{D}(a, c)]$. By the second version of the definition, and the fact that $\neg 1=0$ is provable (Ax. 15), the system is consistent, if and only if the particular formula $1=0$ is unprovable. Let r be the Gödel number of this formula. Then $A_r(\boldsymbol{r})$ is the same formula, and consistency is expressed by $\neg \exists b \mathrm{A}(\boldsymbol{r}, b)$ or $\forall b \neg \mathrm{A}(\boldsymbol{r}, b)$. Let us call one of these formulas, at our preference, "Consis".

The assertion that $A_p(\boldsymbol{p})$ is unprovable is expressed, via the Gödel numbering, by $\forall b \neg \mathrm{A}(\boldsymbol{p}, b)$, which is $A_p(\boldsymbol{p})$.

The intuitive demonstration of the first half of Theorem 28 is a demonstration that

(I) {the system is consistent} implies {$A_p(\boldsymbol{p})$ is unprovable}.

It is now proposed that the entire metamathematical demonstration of (I) should be formalized in the system, using the Gödel numbering, so that we should then have

(II) $$\vdash \text{Consis} \supset A_p(\boldsymbol{p}).$$

Now assume metamathematically that $\vdash$ Consis. Then from (II) we should have by $\supset$-elimination, $\vdash A_p(\boldsymbol{p})$. By Theorem 28, this is impossible, if the system is consistent. By metamathematical reductio ad absurdum, this would give the following theorem. (The proof could also be based on Theorem 29, since $\vdash \forall b \neg \mathrm{A}(\boldsymbol{q}, b) \supset A_q(\boldsymbol{q})$.)

THEOREM 30. *If the number-theoretic formal system is (simply) consistent, then not* $\vdash$ Consis; *i.e. if the system is consistent, then there is no consistency proof for it by methods formalizable in the system.* (Gödel's second theorem.)

The proofs of Theorems 28 and 29 will be complete when we have established Lemma 21 in Chapter X. For the proof of Theorem 30, there will remain the gap to be filled in passing from (I) to (II). This is an exercise in formalizing an informally given proof of considerable length, which we shall not take the space to carry through in this book.

Hilbert and Bernays 1939 carry it out for a certain formal system Z_μ (cf. pp. 283 ff., especially pp. 306—324), and thence infer (pp. 324—328) that the theorem holds also for a system *Z* which differs from our classical number-theoretic system in inessential respects (mainly, in the use of predicate variables, cf. end § 37, and in the equality postulates, cf. § 73). Thence Theorem 30 holds for our classical system; and it can be inferred to hold for our intuitionistic system (at least when Consis is $\forall b \neg A(\mathbf{r}, b)$ or $\neg \exists b A(\mathbf{r}, b)$, and $A(a, b)$ is suitably chosen) by use of Gödel 1932-3 (cf. Theorem 60 (b2) § 81 and Nelson 1947 pp. 326—327).

It may be remarked that this exercise is required only for the sake of using as the formula Consis a direct formalization of the original definition of (simple) consistency or a close equivalent. Intuitively $A_p(\mathbf{p})$ itself expresses an equivalent, via the long intuitive proof of Gödel's theorem. For by Theorem 28, if the system is consistent, $A_p(\mathbf{p})$ is unprovable, and by § 28, if $A_p(\mathbf{p})$ is unprovable, the system is consistent; and the unprovability of $A_p(\mathbf{p})$ is expressed by $A_p(\mathbf{p})$.

What is the significance of these results for the proposed program of metamathematics? We certainly hope that the formal system is consistent. If so, then by Theorem 29 it is necessarily incomplete. We have not succeeded in formalizing informal number theory completely explicitly, so that each proposition or its negation is a consequence by explicitly stated rules of explicitly stated axioms (§ 15).

Taking the supposition of (simple) consistency in its finitary meaning, i.e. if the consistency is capable of being proved metamathematically, then the system is incomplete also in the sense that there are expressible in it propositions true on finitary grounds, but unprovable formally, three such propositions being expressed by $A_p(\mathbf{p})$, $A_q(\mathbf{q})$ and Consis.

For the problem of proving consistency metamathematically, Theorem 30 has the consequence that the methods which we must trust in the proof must include some which lie outside the collection of the methods formalized in the system. This is not a priori incompatible with the other requirement that the methods not include all which lie inside, our mistrust of some of which was the occasion for the formalist project of attempting the proof. It does pose the challenge to the metamathematician to bring to bear methods of finitary proof more powerful than those commonly used in elementary number theory.

There is a further implication for the completeness and consistency problems. Suppose our system is (simply) consistent. Then, as in the proof of the second half of Theorem 28, $A_p(\boldsymbol{p})$ is unprovable, but $\vdash \neg A(\boldsymbol{p}, 0)$, $\vdash \neg A(\boldsymbol{p}, 1)$, $\vdash \neg A(\boldsymbol{p}, 2)$, ... Thus we have a formula A(x) (namely $\neg A(\boldsymbol{p}, b)$) such that $\vdash$ A(0), $\vdash$ A(1), $\vdash$ A(2), ..., but not $\vdash \forall x A(x)$ (which is $A_p(\boldsymbol{p})$). Tarski 1933a gives the name *ω-incompleteness* to this situation. If in this situation $\vdash \neg \forall x A(x)$ (which is $\neg A_p(\boldsymbol{p})$), the system would be ω-inconsistent. The discovery that a system may be ω-incomplete reveals the possibility that it may be ω-inconsistent without being simply inconsistent. The system obtained from our system by taking $\neg A_p(\boldsymbol{p})$ as a new axiom definitely is, under the assumption that ours is simply consistent. To see that this system is simply consistent, we observe that if B and ¬B were provable in it, then in the original system B and ¬B would be deducible from $\neg A_p(\boldsymbol{p})$ (end § 20); hence by ¬-introd., $\neg\neg A_p(\boldsymbol{p})$ would be provable; and by ¬-elim. (or intuitionistically by $\text{IVa}_2 \supset \text{IVa}_1$ from Corollary Theorem 17 § 35), $A_p(\boldsymbol{p})$ would be provable, contradicting Theorem 28. There are evidently definable still higher orders of completeness and consistency.

We don't want our system to be ω-inconsistent, even if it is consistent. In particular, if the simple consistency were provable metamathematically, then the formula $\neg A_p(\boldsymbol{p})$ would under the interpretation express a proposition contradicting one that is true on finitary grounds; and in case $\neg A_p(\boldsymbol{p})$ were provable, following Hilbert and Bernays (1939 p. 282) we should call the system *externally inconsistent*, i.e. inconsistent with respect to the finitary interpretation. Thus a proof of simple consistency alone would not secure the formalized mathematics against the possibility of establishing something intuitively false. (This was first noted by Finsler 1926 in connection with a system that is not formal in our sense. Also cf. Gödel 1931-2a.)

Suppose our system is simply consistent. For brevity, call a formula "true" ("false"), if it expresses a true (false) proposition under the interpretation. Let B(x) be a formula which numeralwise expresses a predicate $B(x)$, which it shall express under the interpretation. Then for each natural number x, the formula $B(\boldsymbol{x})$ is provable if and only if it is true. The formula $\forall x B(x)$ is true if it is provable (in view of ∀-elim.); but not in general conversely (e.g. $A_p(\boldsymbol{p})$). The formula $\exists x B(x)$ is provable if it is true (in view of ∃-introd.); but we have not shown the converse metamathematically (e.g. $\exists b A(\boldsymbol{p}, b)$, from which $\neg A_p(\boldsymbol{p})$ follows by *83a, and which we thus know to be false, but do not know without assuming also ω-consistency to be unprovable).

Thus (cf. § 14) a proof of (simple) consistency would be sufficient to justify the use of our classical system for proving "real" statements intuitionistically by an excursion through the "ideal", for "real" statements of the forms B(**x**) and ∀xB(x), but not so far as we have yet shown for those of the form ∃xB(x).

Suppose that we add to the system $A_p(\boldsymbol{p})$, $A_q(\boldsymbol{q})$ or Consis as a new axiom, and iterate the whole process, to obtain a succession of systems. It can be shown that if these systems are consistent, then the class of provable formulas of the form ∀xB(x) is successively enlarged. Gödel 1931-2 states that the same is true of the systems obtained by admitting successively higher types of variables (at least, supposing ω-consistency). Except that we lack proofs of the appropriate consistency properties, this shows (cf. § 14) that successively higher theoretical constructions do add to the class of "real" statements of the original sort which are comprised. Gödel 1936 states also that in the higher systems infinitely many of the previously provable formulas have very much shorter proofs.

Thus far we have Gödel's theorem only for our particular formal system (except for the last remarks, which refer to a succession of systems). The question arises now whether it may not depend on some peculiarities of the present formalization of logic, and might be avoided in some other. In the next chapters, besides completing the proof of the required lemma for Gödel's theorem, we shall reach a standpoint from which we can discuss these questions for formal systems in general, with the formal system studied here as an example (§§ 60, 61).

PART III

RECURSIVE FUNCTIONS

CHAPTER IX

PRIMITIVE RECURSIVE FUNCTIONS

§ 43. Primitive recursive functions. To establish the lemma for Gödel's theorem, we shall develop an intuitive theory about a certain class of number-theoretic functions and predicates, eventually showing that every predicate of the class is numeralwise expressible in the formal system (§ 49), and that the two predicates $A(a, b)$ and $B(a, c)$ of the lemma belong to the class (§ 52). This will save us much of the labor of a step by step development within the formal system.

Except for the application just described, the theory of these functions and predicates will be developed independently of the formal system of the preceding chapters. In this theory, as in metamathematics, we shall use only finitary methods.

The series of the natural numbers

$$0, \quad 0', \quad 0'', 0''', \ldots,$$

or 0, 1, 2, 3, ..., we described as the class of the objects generated from one primitive object 0 by means of one primitive operation $'$ or $+1$. This constitutes an inductive definition of the class of the natural numbers (§ 6).

Proof by induction, as a method of proving a theorem $T(y)$ for all natural numbers y, corresponds immediately to this mode of generating the numbers (§ 7). *Definition by induction* (not to be confused with 'inductive definition', §§ 6, 53), also called *recursive definition*, is the analogous method of defining a number-theoretic function $\varphi(y)$ or predicate $P(y)$. First $\varphi(0)$ or $P(0)$ (the value of the function or predicate for 0 as argument) is given. Then, for any natural number y, $\varphi(y')$ or $P(y')$ (the next value after that for y) is expressed in terms of y and $\varphi(y)$ or $P(y)$ (the value for y). Analogously, we can conclude that under these circumstances the value $\varphi(y)$ or $P(y)$ of the function or predicate is defined for every natural number y. For the two parts of the definition enable us, as we generate any natural number y, at the same time to determine the value $\varphi(y)$ or $P(y)$.

To examine this in more detail, let us write the pair of equations

$$(1) \qquad \begin{cases} \varphi(0) = q, \\ \varphi(y') = \chi(y, \varphi(y)), \end{cases}$$

to express the definition of a function $\varphi(y)$ by induction on y, where q is a given natural number, and $\chi(y, z)$ is a given number-theoretic function of two variables.

Then for example, the value $\varphi(4)$ is determined thus. To generate 4, we generate successively 0, 1, 2, 3, 4. By the first equation, the value $\varphi(0)$ shall be the given number q; then by the second equation, the value $\varphi(1)$ shall be $\chi(0, \varphi(0))$, i.e. (using the value $\varphi(0)$ already found) $\chi(0, q)$, which (since $\chi(y, z)$ is a given function) is a given number; again the value $\varphi(2)$ shall be $\chi(1, \varphi(1))$, i.e. $\chi(1, \chi(0, q))$; the value $\varphi(3)$ shall be $\chi(2, \varphi(2))$, i.e. $\chi(2, \chi(1, \chi(0, q)))$; and finally the value $\varphi(4)$ shall be $\chi(3, \varphi(3))$, i.e. $\chi(3, \chi(2, \chi(1, \chi(0, q))))$.

Thus we have a process by which, to each natural number y, on the basis of the generation of y in the natural number sequence, a corresponding number $\varphi(y)$ is determined. Since a number $\varphi(y)$ is thus associated with y, for each y, a particular number-theoretic function φ is defined with these numbers $\varphi(y)$ as its respective values.

This function φ satisfies the equations (1), when (1) are considered as functional equations in an unknown function φ, since every particular equation comprised in (1) (namely, $\varphi(0)=q$, $\varphi(0')=\chi(0, \varphi(0))$, $\varphi(1')= \chi(1, \varphi(1))$, ...) is satisfied in the course of selecting the successive numbers $\varphi(0)$, $\varphi(1)$, $\varphi(2)$, ... Also this φ is the only function satisfying (1) as functional equations, since the process by which we determined the successive numbers $\varphi(0)$, $\varphi(1)$, $\varphi(2)$, ... from the equations (1) can be interpreted as showing that any function φ satisfying the equations must have the values selected.

In other definitions by induction, the function φ defined depends on additional variables $x_2, \ldots, x_n$, called *parameters*, which have fixed values throughout the induction on y.

EXAMPLE 1. Consider intuitively the equations

$$\begin{cases} a+0 = a, \\ a+b' = (a+b)', \end{cases}$$

which we encountered in the formal symbolism as Axioms 18 and 19. These define the function $a+b$ by induction on b, with a as parameter, and $'$ as a previously known function. Then the equations

$$\begin{cases} a \cdot 0 = 0, \\ a \cdot b' = (a \cdot b)+a \end{cases}$$

define $a \cdot b$ by induction on b, with $a+b$ as a known function; and

$$\begin{cases} a^0 = 1, \\ a^{b'} = a^b \cdot a \end{cases}$$

define a^b by induction on b, with $a \cdot b$ as a known function.

An example of a definition of a predicate by induction will be given later (Example 2 § 45).

What number-theoretic functions are definable by induction? To make this question precise, we must specify what functions are to be taken as known initially, and what operations, including what forms of definition by induction, are to be allowed in defining further functions.

We shall now select the specifications with a view to obtaining functions definable by induction in an elementary manner. These functions will be called 'primitive recursive'.

Each of the following equations and systems of equations (I)—(V) defines a number-theoretic function φ, when n and m are positive integers, i is an integer such that $1 \leq i \leq n$, q is a natural number, and $\psi, \chi_1, \ldots, \chi_m, \chi$ are given number-theoretic functions of the indicated numbers of variables.

(I) $$\varphi(x) = x'.$$

(II) $$\varphi(x_1, \ldots, x_n) = q.$$

(III) $$\varphi(x_1, \ldots, x_n) = x_i.$$

(IV) $$\varphi(x_1, \ldots, x_n) = \psi(\chi_1(x_1, \ldots, x_n), \ldots, \chi_m(x_1, \ldots, x_n)).$$

(Va) $$\begin{cases} \varphi(0) = q, \\ \varphi(y') = \chi(y, \varphi(y)). \end{cases}$$

(Vb) $$\begin{cases} \varphi(0, x_2, \ldots, x_n) = \psi(x_2, \ldots, x_n), \\ \varphi(y', x_2, \ldots, x_n) = \chi(y, \varphi(y, x_2, \ldots, x_n), x_2, \ldots, x_n). \end{cases}$$

((Va) constitutes the case of (V) for $n = 1$, and (Vb) for $n > 1$.)

A function is *primitive recursive*, if it is definable by a series of applications of these five operations of definition.

This definition can be given in more detail, analogously to the definition of provable formula for the formal system (§ 19), say using the second version, as follows.

We refer to the above equations and equation pairs (I)—(V) as schemata. They are analogous to the postulates, with (I)—(III) in the role of axiom schemata (or more strictly, (I) to a particular axiom), and (IV) and (V) in the role of rules of inference.

A function φ is called an *initial function*, if φ satisfies Equation (I), or Equation (II) for a particular n and q, or Equation (III) for a particular n and i.

A function φ is called an *immediate dependent* of other functions, if φ satisfies Equation (IV) for a particular n and m with $\psi, \chi_1, \dots, \chi_m$ as the other functions, or Equations (Va) for a particular q with χ as the other function, or Equations (Vb) for a particular n with ψ, χ as the other functions.

A function φ is called *primitive recursive*, if there is a finite sequence $\varphi_1, \dots, \varphi_k$ $(k \geq 1)$ of (occurrences of) functions (called a *primitive recursive description of* φ), such that each function of the sequence is either an initial function, or an immediate dependent of preceding functions of the sequence, and the last function φ_k is the function φ.

§ 44. Explicit definition. The first problem of this chapter is to recognize as primitive recursive various functions which may already be known to us in other ways. (Analogously, in studying the formal system, we deduced from the axioms further formal theorems, and derived rules as general methods for finding still others.)

The schemata have been given stereotyped forms to simplify the definition of the class of primitive recursive functions. In the remainder of this section, we shall learn to telescope several applications of them.

Schema (I) gives the *successor function* as one of the initial functions. In this connection, we designate it as S. The initial functions given by Schema (II) we call the *constant functions*, and we designate them as C^n_q. The initial functions given by Schema (III) we call the *identity functions*, and we designate them as U^n_i.

Schema (IV) we call the schema of *definition by substitution*. The expression for the ambiguous value of φ is obtained by substituting expressions for the ambiguous values of $\chi_1, \dots, \chi_m$ for the variables of ψ (cf. § 10). The function φ defined by an application of this schema we sometimes write as $\mathrm{S}^n_m(\psi, \chi_1, \dots, \chi_m)$.

An *explicit definition* of a function consists in giving an expression for its ambiguous value constructed syntactically from its independent variables (with no other variables occurring free) and symbols for given functions, constants, operators, etc. In particular, we say that a function φ is *definable explicitly* from (or is *explicit* in) functions $\psi_1, \dots, \psi_l$ and constants $q_1, \dots, q_s$, if an expression for its ambiguous value $\varphi(x_1, \dots, x_n)$ can be given in terms of the variables $x_1, \dots, x_n$, the constants $q_1, \dots, q_s$ and the functions $\psi_1, \dots, \psi_l$ (cf. Example 2 § 10). In this case φ can be obtained from $\psi_1, \dots, \psi_l$ by a series of applications of Schemata (II) — (IV). For Schemata (II) and (III) introduce each constant and each of the variables $x_1, \ldots, x_n$ as a function of all the variables $x_1, \ldots, x_n$; and then the substitutions used in building up the expression for the ambiguous value $\varphi(x_1, \ldots, x_n)$ all fit the standard form (IV).

EXAMPLE 1. Consider the explicit definition

(a) $$\varphi(x, z, y) = \zeta(x, \eta(y, \theta(x)), 2).$$

Considering x, y and 2 on the right as each a function of x, z, y,

$$\varphi(x, z, y) = \zeta(U_1^3(x, z, y), \eta(U_3^3(x, z, y), \theta(U_1^3(x, z, y))), C_2^3(x, z, y)).$$

Thence we see that the following series of applications of Schemata (II) — (IV) can be used to define φ from ζ, η, θ. The successive functions used are named or defined at the left; and the applications of the schemata are analyzed at the right. For example, at Step 5, Schema (IV) is applied with $n = 3$ and $m = 1$ and with the preceding functions of Steps 3 and 4 as the ψ and χ of (IV).

1. ζ — first given function.
2. η — second given function.
3. θ — third given function.
4. $U_1^3(x, z, y) = x$ — (III), $n = 3$, $i = 1$.
5. $\theta_1(x, z, y) = \theta(U_1^3(x, z, y))$ — (IV), $n = 3$, $m = 1$; 3, 4.
6. $U_3^3(x, z, y) = y$ — (III), $n = 3$, $i = 3$.
7. $\psi(x, z, y) = \eta(U_3^3(x, z, y), \theta_1(x, z, y))$ — (IV), $n = 3$, $m = 2$; 2, 6, 5.
8. $C_2^3(x, z, y) = 2$ — (II), $n = 3$, $q = 2$.
9. $\varphi(x, z, y) = \zeta(U_1^3(x, z, y), \psi(x, z, y), C_2^3(x, z, y))$ — (IV), $n = 3$, $m = 3$; 1, 4, 7, 8.

Note that this definition of φ from ζ, η, θ can be expressed symbolically thus,

(b) $$\varphi = \mathsf{S}_3^3(\zeta, U_1^3, \mathsf{S}_2^3(\eta, U_3^3, \mathsf{S}_1^3(\theta, U_1^3)), C_2^3).$$

If ζ, η, θ are primitive recursive, then so is φ; and a primitive recursive description $\varphi_1, \ldots, \varphi_k$ of φ is then $\ldots, \zeta, \ldots, \eta, \ldots, \theta, U_1^3, \theta_1, U_3^3, \psi, C_2^3, \varphi$ where $\ldots, \zeta; \ldots, \eta; \ldots, \theta$ are descriptions of ζ, η, θ, respectively.

This use of the identity functions U_i^n in the analysis of explicit definition is due to Gödel 1934.

Schema (V) is the schema of *primitive recursion*, without parameters (Va) or with parameters (Vb). We sometimes write the function φ so defined as $\mathsf{R}_q^1(\chi)$ (for (Va)) or $\mathsf{R}^n(\psi, \chi)$ (for (Vb)). However in speaking of a "primitive recursion", we shall now understand that the application of (V) may have lumped with it some steps of explicit definition.

EXAMPLE 2. To analyze the primitive recursion for $a+b$ (Example 1 § 43), first let us restate it writing $\varphi(b, a)$ for $a+b$,

$$\begin{cases} \varphi(0, a) = a & [= U_1^1(a)], \\ \varphi(b', a) = (\varphi(b, a))' & [= \chi(b, \varphi(b, a), a), \\ & \quad \text{if } \chi(b, c, a) = c' = S(U_2^3(b,c,a))]. \end{cases}$$

This fits Schema (Vb) when the right members are expressed as shown in brackets. So we accomplish the definition thus:

1. $S(a) = a'$ — (I).
2. $U_1^1(a) = a$ — (III), $n = 1$, $i = 1$.
3. $U_2^3(b, c, a) = c$ — (III), $n = 3$, $i = 2$.
4. $\chi(b, c, a) = S(U_2^3(b, c, a))$ — (IV), $n = 3$, $m = 1$; 1, 3.
5. $\begin{cases} \varphi(0, a) = U_1^1(a) \\ \varphi(b', a) = \chi(b, \varphi(b, a), a) \end{cases}$ — (Vb), $n = 2$; 2, 4.

This shows that $a+b$ considered as $\varphi(b, a)$ (i.e. $\varphi = \lambda ba\ a+b$, cf. Example 3 § 10) is primitive recursive, with S, U_1^1, U_2^3, χ, φ as a primitive recursive description. We can obtain $a+b$ as $\varphi_1(a, b)$ (i.e. $\varphi_1 = \lambda ab\ a+b$) by three more steps. Symbolically,

$$\lambda ba\ a+b = \mathsf{R}^2(U_1^1,\ \mathsf{S}_1^3(S,\ U_2^3)),$$
$$\lambda ab\ a+b = \mathsf{S}_2^2(\mathsf{R}^2(U_1^1,\ \mathsf{S}_1^3(S,\ U_2^3)),\ U_2^2,\ U_1^2).$$

This illustrates the general method. By the commutative property of $a+b$, $\varphi_1(a, b) = \varphi(a, b)$, so the last three steps could be omitted here; but not e.g. in treating the recursion for a^b.

We now use these techniques to establish the primitive recursiveness of a series of functions. Each of the functions listed below at the left is primitive recursive. To verify this, the reader may recognize, first, that the explicit definitions and primitive recursions exhibited at the right do generate primitive recursive functions, and second that the functions generated are the same as those defined or named at the left.

#1. $a+b$. $\qquad \begin{cases} a+0 = a, \\ a+b' = (a+b)'. \end{cases}$

#2. $a \cdot b$. $\qquad \begin{cases} a \cdot 0 = 0, \\ a \cdot b' = a \cdot b + a. \end{cases}$

#3. a^b (also written: $a \exp b$). $\qquad \begin{cases} a^0 = 1, \\ a^{b'} = a^b \cdot a. \end{cases}$

#4. $a!$. $\qquad \begin{cases} 0! = 1, \\ a'! = a! \cdot a'. \end{cases}$

#5. $\text{pd}(a) = \begin{cases} \text{predecessor} \\ \text{of } a \text{ if } a > 0, \\ 0 \text{ if } a = 0. \end{cases}$ $\begin{cases} \text{pd}(0) = 0, \\ \text{pd}(a') = a. \end{cases}$

#6. $a \dot{-} b = \begin{cases} a - b \text{ if } a \geq b, \\ 0 \text{ if } a < b. \end{cases}$ $\begin{cases} a \dot{-} 0 = a, \\ a \dot{-} b' = \text{pd}(a \dot{-} b). \end{cases}$

#7. $\min(a,b)$. $\min(a,b) = b \dot{-} (b \dot{-} a)$.

#7a. $\min(a_1, \ldots, a_n)$. $\min(a_1, \ldots, a_n) = \min(\ldots \min(\min(a_1, a_2), a_3) \ldots, a_n)$.

#8. $\max(a,b)$. $\max(a,b) = (a+b) \dot{-} \min(a,b)$.

#8a. $\max(a_1, \ldots, a_n)$. Similarly to #7a.

#9. $\overline{\text{sg}}(a) = \begin{cases} 1 \text{ if } a = 0, \\ 0 \text{ if } a > 0. \end{cases}$ $\overline{\text{sg}}(a) = 1 \dot{-} a$, or $\overline{\text{sg}}(a) = 0^a$, or $\begin{cases} \overline{\text{sg}}(0) = 1, \\ \overline{\text{sg}}(a') = 0. \end{cases}$

#10. $\text{sg}(a) = \begin{cases} 0 \text{ if } a = 0, \\ 1 \text{ if } a > 0. \end{cases}$ $\text{sg}(a) = \overline{\text{sg}}(\overline{\text{sg}}(a))$, or $\text{sg}(a) = \min(a, 1)$, or $\begin{cases} \text{sg}(0) = 0, \\ \text{sg}(a') = 1. \end{cases}$

#11. $|a - b|$. $|a - b| = (a \dot{-} b) + (b \dot{-} a)$.

#12. $\text{rm}(a,b)$ (cf. § 41). $\begin{cases} \text{rm}(0,b) = 0, \\ \text{rm}(a',b) = (\text{rm}(a,b))' \cdot \text{sg}\, |b - (\text{rm}(a,b))'|. \end{cases}$

#13. $[a/b]$. $\begin{cases} [0/b] = 0, \\ [a'/b] = [a/b] + \overline{\text{sg}}\, |b - (\text{rm}(a,b))'|. \end{cases}$

REMARK 1. The particular list (I) — (V) of schemata for generating the primitive recursive functions (BASIS A) is a handy one. If constants be allowed as primitive recursive functions of 0 variables, a basis is obtained by changing (II) to

(II_B) $$\varphi = 0,$$

allowing $n = 0$ or $m = 0$ in (IV), omitting (Va), and allowing $n = 1$ in (Vb) (BASIS B). This basis emphasizes the fundamental role of 0 and ′. The constant functions C_q^0 for $q > 0$ are introduced by successive applications of (IV) with $n = 0$, $m = 1$, S as the ψ, and C_{q-1}^0 as the χ; and C_q^n for $n > 0$ by (IV) with $m = 0$, and C_q^0 as the ψ. Substantial reductions in the basis for generating primitive recursive functions have been given by Péter 1934 (see also David Nelson 1947 Part II) and Raphael Robinson 1947. (It shall be understood throughout the chapter, outside of the present remark and Remark 1 end § 47, that we are using Basis A.)

§ 45. Predicates, prime factor representation. The following notion of relative primitive recursiveness enters naturally into our theory for showing functions to be primitive recursive, just as the notion of deducibility entered into our theory for showing formulas to be provable.

A function φ is *primitive recursive in* $\psi_1, \ldots, \psi_l$ (briefly Ψ), if there is a finite sequence $\varphi_1, \ldots, \varphi_k$ of (occurrences of) functions (called a *primitive recursive derivation of* φ *from* Ψ) such that each function of the sequence is either one of the functions Ψ (the *assumed functions*), or an initial function, or an immediate dependent of preceding functions, and the last function φ_k is φ.

Since this definition has the same form as that of deducibility, to each of the general properties of $\vdash$ (§ 20) a corresponding principle can be stated now. For example, if φ is primitive recursive in Ψ, and some of the functions Ψ are primitive recursive, then φ is primitive recursive in the rest of the functions Ψ. An example (with $l = 1$) will be given later in which "if $\psi_1, \ldots, \psi_l$ are primitive recursive, then φ is primitive recursive" is true, but "φ is primitive recursive in $\psi_1, \ldots, \psi_l$" is false (Example 2 § 55).

EXAMPLE 1. In Example 1 § 44, φ is primitive recursive in ζ, η, θ, with $\zeta, \eta, \theta, U_1^3, \theta_1, U_3^3, \psi, C_2^3, \varphi$ as a primitive recursive derivation.

Our general result on explicit definition (§ 44) can be stated now thus.

#A. *A function* φ *definable explicitly from functions* Ψ *and constants* $q_1, \ldots, q_s$ *is primitive recursive in* Ψ.

By $\sum_{y<z} \psi(x_1, \ldots, x_n, y)$ we mean the sum of the numbers $\psi(x_1, \ldots, x_n, y)$ for all natural numbers y such that $y < z$, if $z > 0$; and 0, if $z = 0$. It is a function of $x_1, \ldots, x_n, z$ for any given function $\psi(x_1, \ldots, x_n, y)$. By $\prod_{y<z} \psi(x_1, \ldots, x_n, y)$ we mean similarly the product of the numbers $\psi(x_1, \ldots, x_n, y)$ for $y < z$, if $z > 0$; and 1, if $z = 0$.

#B. *The finite sum* $\sum_{y<z} \psi(x_1, \ldots, x_n, y)$ *and product* $\prod_{y<z} \psi(x_1, \ldots, x_n, y)$ *are primitive recursive in* ψ.

PROOF. The sum $\sum_{y<z} \psi(x_1, \ldots, x_n, y)$ is given from $\psi(x_1, \ldots, x_n, y)$ by the following recursion on z:

$$\begin{cases} \sum_{y<0} \psi(x_1, \ldots, x_n, y) = 0, \\ \sum_{y<z'} \psi(x_1, \ldots, x_n, y) = \psi(x_1, \ldots, x_n, z) + \sum_{y<z} \psi(x_1, \ldots, x_n, y). \end{cases}$$

Other finite sums and products reduce to these by explicit definition; e.g. $\sum_{y \leq z} \psi(y) = \sum_{y=0}^{z} \psi(y) = \sum_{y<z'} \psi(y)$, $\sum_{w<y<z} \psi(y) = \sum_{y<z \dot{-} w'} \psi(y+w')$, $\sum_{w \leq y \leq z} \psi(y) = \sum_{y=w}^{z} \psi(y) = \sum_{y<z' \dot{-} w} \psi(y+w)$.

Although in this chapter we are developing an intuitive and not a formal theory, we shall sometimes wish the conciseness of expression which a logical symbolism affords, and in particular we shall have a need for such a symbolism in forming notations for predicates and functions. For these two purposes, we now introduce a new logical symbolism. This symbolism is to be taken as informal and meaningful, in contrast to that of the formal system as subject matter for metamathematics. An expression in the new intuitive symbolism is to be distinguished from a formula in the old formal symbolism by the differences in the symbols excepting "&", and by context. This distinction between two symbolisms is introduced in this book (and in Gödel 1931) for the named purposes, and is not an established usage in the literature. (Our intuitive logical symbolism, excepting "$\equiv$", "$(E!y)$", and the operators with "$x<y$" etc., is the formal symbolism of Hilbert and Bernays 1934, 1939; and our formal logical symbolism, excepting "$\sim$" and "$\exists!\mathrm{y}$", is that of Gentzen 1934-5.)

Symbols in the intuitive symbolism.	Words in the English language.	Symbols in the formal symbolism.
$Q \equiv R$.	Q is equivalent to R.	$\mathrm{Q} \sim \mathrm{R}$.
$Q \rightarrow R$.	Q implies R (if Q, then R).	$\mathrm{Q} \supset \mathrm{R}$.
Q & R.	Q and R.	Q & R.
$Q \vee R$.	Q or R.	$\mathrm{Q} \vee \mathrm{R}$.
$\overline{Q}$.	not Q.	$\neg\mathrm{Q}$.
$(y)R(y)$.	for all y, $R(y)$.	$\forall\mathrm{y}\mathrm{R}(\mathrm{y})$.
$(Ey)R(y)$.	there exists a y such that $R(y)$.	$\exists\mathrm{y}\mathrm{R}(\mathrm{y})$.
$(E!y)R(y)$.	there exists a unique y such that $R(y)$.	$\exists!\mathrm{y}\mathrm{R}(\mathrm{y})$.
$(y)_{y<z}R(y)$.	for all $y < z$, $R(y)$.	$\forall\mathrm{y}(\mathrm{y}<\mathrm{z} \supset \mathrm{R}(\mathrm{y}))$.
$(Ey)_{y<z}R(y)$.	there exists a $y < z$ such that $R(y)$.	$\exists\mathrm{y}\,(\mathrm{y}<\mathrm{z}\ \&\ \mathrm{R}(\mathrm{y}))$.
$\mu y_{y<z}R(y)$.	the least $y < z$ such that $R(y)$, if $(Ey)_{y<z}R(y)$; otherwise, z.	

Similar notations are formed by using "(y)", "(Ey)" and "μy" with the inequalities "$y \leq z$", "$w<y<z$", "$w<y\leq z$", "$w\leq y<z$", "$w\leq y\leq z$". When

the indicated range of y is empty, the "(y)" expression is true, and the "(Ey)" expression is false. When the indicated range contains no y such that $R(y)$, the value of the "μy" expression is the cardinal number of the range.

In the present theory we often talk about the truth values 'true' (briefly $\mathfrak{t}$) and 'false' (briefly $\mathfrak{f}$) of propositions, instead of the propositions themselves. (Context will distinguish this use of "$\mathfrak{t}$" and "$\mathfrak{f}$" to stand for the truth values of propositions from the analogous use of them in §§ 28, 36 in a valuation procedure applying to formulas.) When we do this, we have immediately four types of functions. (a) Functions from $\{0, 1, 2, \ldots\}$ to $\{0, 1, 2, \ldots\}$, called *number-theoretic functions* or briefly here *functions*. (b) Functions from $\{0, 1, 2, \ldots\}$ to $\{\mathfrak{t}, \mathfrak{f}\}$, called *number-theoretic predicates* or briefly here *predicates*. (c) Functions from $\{\mathfrak{t}, \mathfrak{f}\}$ to $\{\mathfrak{t}, \mathfrak{f}\}$, called *truth-value functions* or *propositional connectives*. We use five of them $\equiv$, $\rightarrow$, &, $\vee$, $\overline{}$, defined by the same tables as were given in § 28 for the respective formal operators $\sim$, $\supset$, &, $\vee$, $\neg$. (d) Functions from $\{\mathfrak{t}, \mathfrak{f}\}$ to $\{0, 1, 2, \ldots\}$. The function of this type which correlates 0 to $\mathfrak{t}$ and 1 to $\mathfrak{f}$ enters into the definition of 'representing function' given below.

Of course, when the propositions are not being identified with their truth values, 'predicate' means *propositional function of natural numbers* (§ 31). Our practice of at times talking about the truth values $\mathfrak{t}$, $\mathfrak{f}$ instead of the propositions calls for comment. In fact it is immaterial in many contexts whether we think of the values of the predicates as propositions or truth values $\mathfrak{t}$, $\mathfrak{f}$. This is because the essential mathematical meaning of the propositions comes from the definition of the predicates which take them as values. For example, consider the two propositions $3<5$ and $3\leq 5$. They are distinct propositions, differing in meaning. At first sight something appears to be lost if we identify them both with the one object $\mathfrak{t}$. However, if we identify the proposition $3<5$ with $\mathfrak{t}$, at the same time stating that this is the value of the predicate $<$ for 3 and 5 as arguments, we express all the meaning of the original proposition. In other words, the proposition $3<5$ is synonymous with the proposition that the predicate $<$, interpreted as having its values in the domain $\{\mathfrak{t}, \mathfrak{f}\}$, takes the value $\mathfrak{t}$ for 3 and 5 as respective arguments. (Moreover, here it is immaterial whether "$\mathfrak{t}$" and "$\mathfrak{f}$" mean 'true' and 'false' as we provide above, or are simply any two distinct objects as in §§ 28, 36. The predicates under the two interpretations are isomorphic, so the abstract mathematical content of the proposition that the value of $3<5$ is $\mathfrak{t}$ is the same.)

In working closely with functions, we need to be aware of two meanings of the common functional notation, as noted in § 10. For predicates, there are three possible meanings (or six if we distinguish between propositions and truth values).

Meanings of "$P(x_1,\ldots,x_n)$".	Alternative notations.
1. The predicate $P(x_1,\ldots,x_n)$.	P, or $\lambda x_1\ldots x_n P(x_1,\ldots,x_n)$.
2. The value of the predicate P for $x_1,\ldots,x_n$ as arguments (the ambiguous value).	No alternative notation.
3. The proposition that $P(x_1,\ldots,x_n)$ is true for all $x_1,\ldots,x_n$.	$(x_1)\ldots(x_n)P(x_1,\ldots,x_n)$.

These three senses correspond, respectively, to the name form (§ 31), conditional (§ 32), and generality (§ 32), interpretation of the free variables $\mathrm{x}_1,\ldots,\mathrm{x}_n$ in a formula $\mathrm{P}(\mathrm{x}_1,\ldots,\mathrm{x}_n)$ of the formal system.

Example 2. The two statements

$$\begin{cases} E(0) \text{ (or } E(0) \equiv \mathfrak{t}), \\ E(a') \equiv \overline{E}(a), \end{cases}$$

define the predicate $E(a)$ ($\equiv$ {a is even}) by recursion. — We can define a function $\varepsilon(a)$ by the primitive recursion

$$\begin{cases} \varepsilon(0) = 0, \\ \varepsilon(a') = \overline{\mathrm{sg}}(\varepsilon(a)) \end{cases}$$

(cf. #9 § 44). Then $E(a) \equiv \varepsilon(a)=0$.

We say that a function $\varphi(x_1,\ldots,x_n)$ is the *representing function* of a predicate $P(x_1,\ldots,x_n)$, if φ takes only 0 and 1 as values and satisfies the equivalence

$$P(x_1, \ldots, x_n) \equiv \varphi(x_1, \ldots, x_n)=0;$$

or in other words, when the values of P are given as $\mathfrak{t}$ and $\mathfrak{f}$, if $\varphi(x_1,\ldots,x_n)$ is 0 when $P(x_1,\ldots,x_n)$ is $\mathfrak{t}$, and $\varphi(x_1,\ldots,x_n)$ is 1 when $P(x_1,\ldots,x_n)$ is $\mathfrak{f}$.

We say that a predicate $P(x_1,\ldots,x_n)$ is *primitive recursive*, if its representing function $\varphi(x_1,\ldots,x_n)$ is primitive recursive (e.g. $E(a)$ in Example 2). This definition follows Gödel 1931.

As another example, we list the equality predicate, the representing function being shown at the right (cf. ##10, 11).

#14. $a=b$. $\qquad\qquad$ $\mathrm{sg}\,|\,a-b\,|$.

We furthermore say that a function φ or predicate P is *primitive recursive in* predicates and functions Ψ, if the corresponding statement holds replacing the predicates among P, Ψ by their representing functions.

Gödel 1931 gave some theorems concerning primitive recursive functions and predicates, which we state as follows (##C—E). The facts had also been obtained by Skolem 1923.

#C. *A predicate P obtained by substituting functions* $\chi_1, \ldots, \chi_m$ *for the respective variables of a predicate Q is primitive recursive in* $\chi_1, \ldots, \chi_m, Q$.

PROOF. If the given predicate is $Q(y_1, \ldots, y_m)$ with the representing function $\psi(y_1, \ldots, y_m)$, and the functions substituted are $\chi_1(x_1, \ldots, x_n)$, $\ldots, \chi_m(x_1, \ldots, x_n)$, the representing function of the new predicate $Q(\chi_1(x_1, \ldots, x_n), \ldots, \chi_m(x_1, \ldots, x_n))$ is $\psi(\chi_1(x_1, \ldots, x_n), \ldots, \chi_m(x_1, \ldots, x_n))$. This function is primitive recursive in $\psi, \chi_1, \ldots, \chi_m$ by Schema (IV). We know from § 44 that no generality is lost by considering the substitution as of this particular form; and similarly in #D:

#D. *The predicate* $\overline{Q}(x_1, \ldots, x_n)$ *is primitive recursive in the predicate Q. The predicates* $Q(x_1, \ldots, x_n) \vee R(x_1, \ldots, x_n)$, $Q(x_1, \ldots, x_n) \,\&\, R(x_1, \ldots, x_n)$, $Q(x_1, \ldots, x_n) \rightarrow R(x_1, \ldots, x_n)$ *and* $Q(x_1, \ldots, x_n) \equiv R(x_1, \ldots, x_n)$ *are primitive recursive in Q and R.*

PROOF. Let the representing functions of $Q(x_1, \ldots, x_n)$ and $R(x_1, \ldots, x_n)$ be $\psi(x_1, \ldots, x_n)$ and $\chi(x_1, \ldots, x_n)$, respectively. Then the representing function of $\overline{Q}(x_1, \ldots, x_n)$ is $\overline{\mathrm{sg}}(\psi(x_1, \ldots, x_n))$ (#9), which is primitive recursive in ψ. The representing function of $Q(x_1, \ldots, x_n) \vee R(x_1, \ldots, x_n)$ is $\psi(x_1, \ldots, x_n) \cdot \chi(x_1, \ldots, x_n)$, which is primitive recursive in ψ and χ. The rest of the theorem follows by known equivalences for &, $\rightarrow$, $\equiv$ in terms of $^{-}$ and $\vee$ (cf. Chapter VI, allowing for the differences in the symbolism).

#E. *The predicates* $(Ey)_{y<z}R(x_1, \ldots, x_n, y)$ *and* $(y)_{y<z}R(x_1, \ldots, x_n, y)$ *and the function* $\mu y_{y<z}R(x_1, \ldots, x_n, y)$ *are primitive recursive in the predicate R.*

PROOF. Let $\chi(x_1, \ldots, x_n, y)$ be the representing function of $R(x_1, \ldots, x_n, y)$. Then $\prod_{y<z} \chi(x_1, \ldots, x_n, y)$ is the representing function of $(Ey)_{y<z}R(x_1, \ldots, x_n, y)$. This is primitive recursive in χ by #B. Similarly, $\mathrm{sg}(\sum_{y<z} \chi(x_1, \ldots, x_n, y))$ is the representing function of $(y)_{y<z} R(x_1, \ldots, x_n, y)$ (#10). We illustrate the proof for $\mu y_{y<z}R(x_1, \ldots, x_n, y)$ with an example. Let the values of $x_1, \ldots, x_n$ be fixed, and write simply "$\chi(y)$" for $\chi(x_1, \ldots, x_n, y)$ with the fixed values of $x_1, \ldots, x_n$. Suppose that $z = 7$, and that for $y = 0, 1, \ldots, 6$ (first row below) $\chi(y)$ takes the values shown (second row).

y	0	1	2	3	4	5	6	$7 = z$
$\chi(y)$	1	1	1	0	1	0	0	
$\pi(y) = \prod_{s \leq y} \chi(s)$	1	1	1	0	0	0	0	
$\sigma(y) = \sum_{t<y} \pi(t)$	0	1	2	3	3	3	3	3

The desired number $\mu y_{y<z} R(y)$ is the least y (first row) $< z$ for which $R(y)$ is true, i.e. for which a 0 appears in the second row, if there is such a y. In our example, there is, and the least is 3. This number also appears as the last number $\sigma(z)$ in the fourth row. The device illustrated will evidently work in any case. To change the example, if $\overline{(Ey)_{y<z}R(y)}$, so that no 0 occurs in the second row, then $\sigma(z)$ will be z, which is what $\mu y_{y<z} R(y)$ was defined to be in this case. The function $\sigma(z)$ written out in full is $\sum_{t<z} \prod_{s \leq t} \chi(x_1, \ldots, x_n, s)$. By #B, this is primitive recursive in χ.

In using these theorems, we may combine several applications into one step. By #14 with #C, $\psi(x_1, \ldots, x_n) = \chi(x_1, \ldots, x_n)$ is primitive recursive in ψ, χ; e.g. using § 44, $c' + a = b$ is primitive recursive. By ##E, C and § 44, $(Ey)_{y<\psi(x_1, \ldots, x_n)} R(x_1, \ldots, x_n, y)$ is primitive recursive in ψ, R; e.g. using § 44 further, the following is primitive recursive.

#15. $a<b$. $\qquad a<b \equiv (Ec)_{c<b}[c' + a = b]$, or $\mathrm{sg}(a' \dot{-} b)$.

The inequality "$y<z$" in #E can be changed to "$y \leq z$", "$w<y<z$", "$w<y \leq z$", "$w \leq y<z$" or "$w \leq y \leq z$"; for example, $(y)_{w \leq y \leq z} R(x_1, \ldots, x_n, y) \equiv (y)_{y<z' \dot{-} w} R(x_1, \ldots, x_n, y+w)$.

A set of predicates $Q_1, \ldots, Q_m$ is *mutually exclusive*, if for each set of arguments not more than one of them is true (cf. § 3).

#F. *The function* φ *defined thus*

$$\varphi(x_1, \ldots, x_n) = \begin{cases} \varphi_1(x_1, \ldots, x_n) & \textit{if } Q_1(x_1, \ldots, x_n), \\ \quad \cdots & \\ \varphi_m(x_1, \ldots, x_n) & \textit{if } Q_m(x_1, \ldots, x_n), \\ \varphi_{m+1}(x_1, \ldots, x_n) & \textit{otherwise,} \end{cases}$$

where $Q_1, \ldots, Q_m$ *are mutually exclusive predicates* (*or* $\varphi(x_1, \ldots, x_n)$ *shall have the value given by the first clause which applies*) *is primitive recursive in* $\varphi_1, \ldots, \varphi_{m+1}, Q_1, \ldots, Q_m$. (Definition by cases.)

PROOF, for $Q_1, \ldots, Q_m$ mutually exclusive. FIRST METHOD. Let $\psi_1, \ldots, \psi_m$ be the representing functions of $Q_1, \ldots, Q_m$. Then (omitting "$(x_1, \ldots, x_n)$" to save space)

$$\varphi = \overline{\mathrm{sg}}(\psi_1) \cdot \varphi_1 + \ldots + \overline{\mathrm{sg}}(\psi_m) \cdot \varphi_m + \psi_1 \cdot \ldots \cdot \psi_m \cdot \varphi_{m+1}.$$

SECOND METHOD.

$$\varphi = \mu y_{y \leq \varphi_1 + \ldots + \varphi_{m+1}} (Q_1 \,\&\, y = \varphi_1) \vee \ldots \vee (Q_m \,\&\, y = \varphi_m) \vee (\bar{Q}_1 \,\&\, \ldots \,\&\, \bar{Q}_m \,\&\, y = \varphi_{m+1}).$$

PRIME FACTOR REPRESENTATION. Let the prime numbers in order of magnitude be $p_0, p_1, p_2, \ldots, p_i, \ldots$ (i.e. $p_0=2$, $p_1=3$, $p_2=5$, ...). The fundamental theorem of arithmetic (Gauss 1801) states that a given positive integer a can be factored into a product of prime factors which is unique to within the order of the factors. Thus we have a unique representation of a of the form

(1) $$a = p_0^{a_0} \cdot p_1^{a_1} \cdot p_2^{a_2} \cdot \ldots \cdot p_i^{a_i} \ldots \qquad (a \neq 0),$$

where a_i is the number of times p_i occurs in a as factor (0 if p_i is not a factor of a). We can regard the product (1) as extending indefinitely, all but a finite number of the exponents being 0.

We now add to our list of particular primitive recursive functions and predicates.

#16. $a|b \equiv a$ divides b. $\qquad a|b \equiv (Ec)_{c \leq b}[ac = b]$, or $\mathrm{sg}\,\mathrm{rm}(b, a)$.

#17. $\Pr(a) \equiv a$ is a prime number. $\qquad \Pr(a) \equiv a > 1 \,\&\, \overline{(Ec)}_{1<c<a}[c|a]$.

#18. $p_i =$ the $i+1$-st prime number. $\qquad \begin{cases} p_0 = 2, \\ p_{i'} = \mu x_{p_i < x \leq p_i!+1} \Pr(x), \end{cases}$

where the upper bound $p_i!+1$ for x is given by Euclid's demonstration that to any p there exists a prime $> p$ and $\leq p!+1$ (§ 40). The combining of an application of #E with a primitive recursion is legitimate, as it merely condenses what could be accomplished by first introducing $\chi(c) = \mu x_{c<x\leq c!+1} \Pr(x)$, and then writing the second recursion equation as $p_{i'} = \chi(p_i)$.

#19. $(a)_i = \begin{cases} \text{the exponent } a_i \text{ of } p_i \\ \text{in (1), if } a \neq 0; \\ 0, \text{ if } a = 0. \end{cases} \qquad (a)_i = \mu x_{x<a}[p_i^x|a \,\&\, \overline{p_i^{x'}|a}].$

We may write $((a)_i)_j$ as $(a)_{i,j}$, $(((a)_i)_j)_k$ as $(a)_{i,j,k}$, etc.

#20. $\mathrm{lh}(a) = \begin{cases} \text{the number of non-} \\ \text{vanishing exponents} \\ \text{in (1), if } a \neq 0; \\ 0, \text{ if } a = 0. \end{cases} \qquad \begin{cases} \mathrm{lh}(0, a) = 0, \\ \mathrm{lh}(i', a) = \begin{cases} \mathrm{lh}(i,a)+1 \text{ if } p_i|a, \\ \mathrm{lh}(i,a) \text{ otherwise.} \end{cases} \\ \mathrm{lh}(a) = \mathrm{lh}(a, a). \end{cases}$

We can represent the finite sequences $a_0, \ldots, a_s$ of positive integers by the numbers $a = p_0^{a_0} \cdot \ldots \cdot p_s^{a_s}$; then $\mathrm{lh}(a)$ is the length $s+1$ of the sequence represented by a.

#21. $a * b = a \cdot \prod_{i<\mathrm{lh}(b)} p_{\mathrm{lh}(a)+i}^{(b)_i}.$

Then if $a = p_0^{a_0} \cdot \ldots \cdot p_s^{a_s}$ $(a_0, \ldots, a_s > 0)$ and $b = p_0^{b_0} \cdot \ldots \cdot p_t^{b_t}$ $(b_0, \ldots, b_t > 0)$, $a*b = p_0^{a_0} \cdot \ldots \cdot p_s^{a_s} \cdot p_{s+1}^{b_0} \cdot \ldots \cdot p_{s+t+1}^{b_t}$. For any a and any such b, $a*1 = a$, $1*b = b$, $1*1 = 1$.

§ 46. Course-of-values recursion. In proving a theorem $T(y)$ by induction, it may happen that the case $T(y')$ of the theorem depends not simply on the immediately preceding case $T(y)$, but on one or more preceding cases. This kind of a proof by induction we have called a 'course-of-values induction'. It can be reduced to a simple induction, by first proving the lemma $(s)_{s \leq y} T(s)$ by simple induction, after which the theorem follows by setting $s = y$ (cf. *162a § 40).

The analogous situation arises in definition by induction. The function value $\varphi(0)$ is given outright; and the function value $\varphi(y')$ is expressed in terms of y and one or more of the preceding values $\varphi(s)$ for $s \leq y$. The recursion is then called a *course-of-values recursion.* We shall see that it can be reduced to a primitive recursion by an analogous device (cf. Péter 1934).

The two cases of the definition of φ may be combined (cf. *162b), by saying that $\varphi(y)$ is expressed in terms of y and $\varphi(s)$ for $s < y$. When $y = 0$, this means that $\varphi(0)$ is given outright, since the set of values $\varphi(s)$ for $s < y$ is then empty.

More generally, let the function to be defined be $\varphi(y, x_2, \ldots, x_n)$ where $x_2, \ldots, x_n$ are parameters (remaining fixed throughout the recursion). As an auxiliary function, we introduce

(1) $$\tilde{\varphi}(y; x_2, \ldots, x_n) = \prod_{i<y} p_i^{\varphi(i, x_2, \ldots, x_n)},$$

called the *course-of-values function* (*in* y) for the given function $\varphi(y, x_2, \ldots, x_n)$.

Given the sequence of the values $\varphi(s, x_2, \ldots, x_n)$ of our original function for $s < y$, by (1) we obtain the value $\tilde{\varphi}(y; x_2, \ldots, x_n)$ of the course-of-values function. Conversely, given $\tilde{\varphi}(y; x_2, \ldots, x_n)$, we can extract all the values $\varphi(s, x_2, \ldots, x_n)$ for $s < y$ with the help of #19 thus,

(2) $$\varphi(s, x_2, \ldots, x_n) = (\tilde{\varphi}(y; x_2, \ldots, x_n))_s \text{ if } s < y.$$

So in a sense the knowledge of the value $\tilde{\varphi}(y; x_2, \ldots, x_n)$ of the course-of-values function is equivalent to the knowledge of the sequence of values $\varphi(0, x_2, \ldots, x_n), \ldots, \varphi(y-1, x_2, \ldots, x_n)$ of the original function.

#G. *If* φ *satisfies the equation*

(3) $$\varphi(y, x_2, \ldots, x_n) = \chi(y, \tilde{\varphi}(y; x_2, \ldots, x_n), x_2, \ldots, x_n),$$

then φ *is primitive recursive in* χ.

PROOF. First we set up a primitive recursion for $\tilde{\varphi}$,

$$(4) \quad \begin{cases} \tilde{\varphi}(0; x_2, \ldots, x_n) = 1, \\ \tilde{\varphi}(y'; x_2, \ldots, x_n) = \tilde{\varphi}(y; x_2, \ldots, x_n) \cdot p_y^{\chi(y, \tilde{\varphi}(y; x_2, \ldots, x_n), x_2, \ldots, x_n)}. \end{cases}$$

Then we obtain φ from $\tilde{\varphi}$ by the explicit definition,

$$(5) \quad \varphi(y, x_2, \ldots, x_n) = (\tilde{\varphi}(y'; x_2, \ldots, x_n))_y.$$

EXAMPLE 1. Let

$$(a) \quad \varphi(y) = \prod_{s<y} (y + \varphi(s)).$$

The sequence of the values of this function, and of its course-of-values function, are as shown.

y	0	1	2	3	4	...
$\varphi(y)$	1	2	12	300	145920	...
$\tilde{\varphi}(y)$	1	2^1	$2^1 \cdot 3^2$	$2^1 \cdot 3^2 \cdot 5^{12}$	$2^1 \cdot 3^2 \cdot 5^{12} \cdot 7^{300}$	...

Note that the last exponent in $\tilde{\varphi}(y')$ is always the value of $\varphi(y)$; e.g. $(\tilde{\varphi}(3))_2 = 12 = \varphi(2)$. To apply #G, note that by (2)

$$(b) \quad \varphi(y) = \prod_{s<y} (y + (\tilde{\varphi}(y))_s).$$

This is of the form (3), and by ##1, 19, B and G, φ is primitive recursive.

This version of #G accomplishes the reduction of course-of-values recursion to primitive recursion, for cases when the course-of-values recursion is already given in the form (3) of a dependence of $\varphi(y, x_2, \ldots, x_n)$ on the number $\tilde{\varphi}(y; x_2, \ldots, x_n)$ besides on $y, x_2, \ldots, x_n$.

We illustrate further how to reduce course-of-values recursions not already so given to the form (3).

EXAMPLE 2. RECURSION FROM A DOUBLE BASIS.

$$(a) \quad \begin{cases} \varphi(0) = q_0, \\ \varphi(1) = q_1, \\ \varphi(y'') = \chi(y, \varphi(y), \varphi(y')). \end{cases}$$

First we restate this in the more compact form for course-of-values recursion (using ##6, F), thus

$$(b) \quad \varphi(y) = \begin{cases} q_0 \text{ if } y = 0, \\ q_1 \text{ if } y = 1, \\ \chi(y \dot{-} 2, \varphi(y \dot{-} 2), \varphi(y \dot{-} 1)) \text{ otherwise.} \end{cases}$$

Then we express $\varphi(y \dot{-} 2)$, $\varphi(y \dot{-} 1)$ as $(\tilde{\varphi}(y))_{y \dot{-} 2}$, $(\tilde{\varphi}(y))_{y \dot{-} 1}$, respectively.

The method applies also to definitions of predicates by course-of-values recursion.

EXAMPLE 3. Consider the equivalence

(a) $T(y) \equiv y=23 \vee V(y) \vee [y=2^{17}\cdot 3^{(y)_1}\cdot 5^{(y)_2} \;\&\; T((y)_1) \;\&\; T((y)_2)] \vee$
$[y = 2^{19}\cdot 3^{(y)_1}\cdot 5^{(y)_2} \;\&\; T((y)_1) \;\&\; T((y)_2)] \vee [y=2^{21}\cdot 3^{(y)_1} \;\&\; T((y)_1)]$,

where V is a given predicate. This defines $T(y)$ by course-of-values induction on y. For when $y=0$, all disjunctive members on the right are false except perhaps the second; so $T(0) \equiv V(0)$. When $y > 0$, $(y)_1 < y$ and $(y)_2 < y$.

Thus $T(y)$ is expressed in terms of y, V and $T(s)$ for $s < y$ only. Let $\tau(y)$ be the representing function of $T(y)$; and let $T((y)_1)$, $T((y)_2)$ in the right member of (a) be expressed as $(\tilde{\tau}(y))_{(y)_1}=0$, $(\tilde{\tau}(y))_{(y)_2}=0$, respectively. Now the definition of T has the form

(b) $$T(y) \equiv R(y, \tilde{\tau}(y))$$

where, by ##2, 3, 14, 19, A, C and D, $R(y, z)$ is primitive recursive in V. This means simply that the representing function ρ of R is primitive recursive in the representing function υ of V; so we have an equation of the form

(c) $$\tau(y) = \rho(y, \tilde{\tau}(y))$$

where ρ is primitive recursive in υ. By #G, τ is primitive recursive in ρ, and hence in υ, i.e. T is primitive recursive in V (and is primitive recursive if V is).

In these examples we do always succeed in reducing the given course-of-values recursion to the form (3) by use of (2). Closer examination in § 47 will show why, and enable us to formulate a version of #G which includes that reduction.

EXAMPLE 4. SIMULTANEOUS RECURSION. The function values $\varphi_1(y)$ and $\varphi_2(y)$ are expressed in terms of y and values $\varphi_1(s)$ and $\varphi_2(s)$ for $s < y$. Reduce to #G by using as auxiliary function

$$\varphi(y) = 2^{\varphi_1(y)}3^{\varphi_2(y)}.$$

***§ 47. Uniformity.** In ##A — G (considering for the moment only functions and not predicates), our concern was not primarily with any particular functions φ and Ψ, but with methods by which a function φ is defined from Ψ as unspecified functions. In showing for a particular such method that a function φ of n variables is primitive recursive in Ψ, our applications of the schemata (I) — (V) did not depend on what functions Ψ are, so long as their number l and the respective numbers $m_1, \ldots, m_l$ of arguments which they take is fixed. In other words, we gave a *primitive recursive derivation schema of* φ *from* Ψ, with a fixed *analysis*. The definition of 'analysis' is analogous to that given in § 20. For an application of Schema (II) it includes the specification of the n and q; for (III) of the n and i; etc. (Analogously we often obtained derived rules for the formal system by exhibiting a 'deduction schema' with metamathematical letters standing for unspecified formulas, variables, etc.) Under these circumstances, we say that φ is *primitive recursive uniformly in* Ψ.

We can also explain this uniformity notion as follows. For a particular method of defining a number-theoretic function φ from number-theoretic functions Ψ, we can write $\varphi = \mathsf{F}(\Psi)$ to express the fact that what function φ shall be is determined by what functions Ψ are. Then F is a fixed mathematical function of higher type, namely one from l number-theoretic functions Ψ of $m_1, \ldots, m_l$ variables respectively to a number-theoretic function φ of n variables. We call such a function F a *scheme function* or *schema* or *scheme* or *functional*. We can also write $\varphi(x_1, \ldots, x_n) = \mathsf{F}(\Psi; x_1, \ldots, x_n)$ (with the same F) to express the fact that (by the schema F) what natural number $\varphi(x_1, \ldots, x_n)$ shall be is determined by what functions Ψ are and what numbers $x_1, \ldots, x_n$ are.

For any fixed n and m, Schema (IV) constitutes a functional, which we have already denoted by S^n_m. For fixed n (and when $n = 1$, fixed q) Schema (V) constitutes a functional R^1_q or R^n. The other three schemata (I) — (III) define particular number-theoretic functions S, C^n_q, U^n_i (or constitute functionals with $l = 0$).

Now we say that a functional (or schema) $\varphi = \mathsf{F}(\Psi)$ is *primitive recursive*, or that φ is *primitive recursive uniformly in* Ψ, if F is definable explicitly from the functionals S^n_m, R^1_q, R^n and constants S, C^n_q, U^n_i.

EXAMPLE 1. In Example 1 § 44, φ is primitive recursive uniformly in ζ, η, θ. Under the first version of the definition of uniformity, we see this from the fact that the analysis of the primitive recursive derivation schema ζ, η, θ, U^3_1, θ_1, U^3_3, ψ, C^3_2, φ (consisting of the explanations opposite 1 — 9 at the right) is fixed. Under the second version, we see it from the fact that (b) expresses $\varphi = \mathsf{F}(\zeta, \eta, \theta)$ explicitly in terms of S^3_3, S^3_2, S^3_1 and U^3_1, U^3_3, C^3_2.

Sometimes a method for determining a function φ from functions Ψ is specified only under some restriction on the Ψ's. To establish uniform primitive recursiveness, we show then that there is a fixed succession of applications of Schemata (I) — (V) which leads from Ψ to the same function φ as the given method, for any Ψ to which the given method applies (or is intended to apply). The succession of applications of Schemata (I) — (V) then leads in fact to some function φ from any Ψ, since each of (I) — (V) has this property. Thus: The given method constitutes a functional $\varphi = \mathsf{F}(\Psi)$ defined only for a restricted range of Ψ. The succession of applications of (I) — (V) constitutes a completely defined functional $\varphi = \mathsf{F}_1(\Psi)$, which is primitive recursive and such that $\mathsf{F}_1(\Psi) = \mathsf{F}(\Psi)$ on the range of definition of F.

Example 2. Let a function φ be defined thus,

(a) $$\varphi(x) = \begin{cases} \varphi_1(x) \text{ if } \psi_1(x)=0, \\ \varphi_2(x) \text{ if } \psi_2(x)=0, \\ \varphi_3(x) \text{ otherwise,} \end{cases}$$

where $\varphi_1, \varphi_2, \varphi_3, \psi_1, \psi_2$ are given functions such that, for each x, $\psi_1(x)$ and $\psi_2(x)$ are each either 0 or 1 and not both 0. Then we can write

(b) $$\varphi(x) = \overline{\text{sg}}(\psi_1(x))\cdot\varphi_1(x) + \overline{\text{sg}}(\psi_2(x))\cdot\varphi_2(x) + \psi_1(x)\cdot\psi_2(x)\cdot\varphi_3(x),$$

and conclude that φ is primitive recursive uniformly in $\varphi_1, \varphi_2, \varphi_3, \psi_1, \psi_2$ (cf. the first proof of #F § 45). The φ of (a) was only defined for ψ_1, ψ_2 satisfying the restriction stated; but (b) defines a φ without any restriction, which is the same φ as the former when the restriction is satisfied.

For schemes involving predicates, we say that a function φ or predicate P is *primitive recursive uniformly in* predicates and functions Ψ, if the corresponding statement holds replacing the predicates among P, Ψ by their representing functions. The interpretation just explained applies when the functions introduced as representing functions of the predicates among Ψ are then treated as unrestricted function variables in applying the schemata (I) — (V).

Using the explained interpretation, we can say that a function φ (or predicate P) is primitive recursive uniformly in Ψ, even when some of the Ψ's are particular functions (or predicates). Then if any of those Ψ's which are particular are primitive recursive, φ (or P) is primitive recursive uniformly in the rest of the Ψ's.

If φ is primitive recursive uniformly in θ, Ψ as function variables, and we then take θ to be θ^*, the resulting function φ^* is primitive recursive uniformly in θ^*, Ψ (and hence if θ^* is primitive recursive, in Ψ). This principle works whether θ^* is a particular function, or a function variable, including the case that it depends on additional number variables $c_1, \ldots, c_p$ as parameters. The principle is stated accurately as Lemma I. To make it clear how many (and which) independent variables the functions have, we write $\theta = \lambda s_1 \ldots s_q \theta(s_1, \ldots, s_q)$ (a function of q variables), $\theta^* = \lambda s_1 \ldots s_q c_1 \ldots c_p\ \theta^*(s_1, \ldots, s_q, c_1, \ldots, c_p)$ (a function of $q+p$ variables), and $\lambda s_1 \ldots s_q\ \theta^*(s_1, \ldots, s_q, c_1, \ldots, c_p)$ for the function of q variables $s_1, \ldots, s_q$ which we get from θ^* whenever $c_1, \ldots, c_p$ are fixed numbers.

LEMMA I. *Given a functional* $\varphi = \mathsf{F}(\theta, \Psi)$ *as follows*

$$\varphi(x_1, \ldots, x_n) = \mathsf{F}(\lambda s_1 \ldots s_q\ \theta(s_1 \ldots s_q), \Psi; x_1, \ldots, x_n),$$

let a functional $\varphi^* = \mathsf{G}(\theta^*, \Psi)$ *be defined as follows*

$$\varphi^*(x_1, \ldots, x_n, c_1, \ldots, c_p) =$$

$$\mathsf{G}(\lambda s_1 \ldots s_q c_1 \ldots c_p\ \theta^*(s_1, \ldots, s_q, c_1, \ldots, c_p), \Psi; x_1, \ldots, x_n, c_1, \ldots, c_p) =$$

$$\mathsf{F}(\lambda s_1 \ldots s_q\ \theta^*(s_1, \ldots, s_q, c_1, \ldots, c_p), \Psi; x_1, \ldots, x_n).$$

If F *is primitive recursive, so is* G.

PROOF. The essence of the proof is that both explicit definitions and primitive recursions remain such when parameters are introduced.

To give the proof in more detail, we use course-of-values induction on the length k of a primitive recursive derivation schema $\varphi_1, \ldots, \varphi_k$ of φ from θ, Ψ. Seven cases arise according as φ $(= \varphi_k)$ is θ, or one of the Ψ's (say ψ_i), or an initial function by Schema (I), (II) or (III), or an immediate dependent of preceding functions by Schema (IV) or (V).

CASE 6: $\varphi(x_1, \ldots, x_n) = \psi(\chi_1(x_1, \ldots, x_n), \ldots, \chi_m(x_1, \ldots, x_n))$, where ψ, $\chi_1, \ldots, \chi_m$ precede φ $(= \varphi_k)$ in $\varphi_1, \ldots, \varphi_k$. Then

$\varphi^*(x_1, \ldots, x_n, c_1, \ldots, c_p) =$

$$\psi^*(\chi_1^*(x_1, \ldots, x_n, c_1, \ldots, c_p), \ldots, \chi_m^*(x_1, \ldots, x_n, c_1, \ldots, c_p), c_1, \ldots, c_p).$$

By the hypothesis of the induction, ψ^*, $\chi_1^*, \ldots, \chi_m^*$ are primitive recursive uniformly in θ^*, Ψ. By #A, φ^* is primitive recursive uniformly in ψ^*, $\chi_1^*, \ldots, \chi_m^*$; and hence, in θ^*, Ψ.

EXAMPLE 3. Not every number-theoretic function is primitive recursive. (Why? Cf. §§ 1, 2: Is every real number algebraic?) Let $\xi(c)$ be a particular function which is not primitive recursive. Let φ be defined from an unspecified function θ thus,

$$\varphi(x) = \xi(\theta(0)).$$

Then, for each particular θ, the resulting φ is a constant function, and so is primitive recursive, by an application of Schema (II) with $n=1$, $q = \xi(\theta(0))$. A fortiori, for each θ, φ is primitive recursive in θ, with C_q^1 for $q = \xi(\theta(0))$ as a primitive recursive derivation of φ from θ. But, because the analysis of this derivation depends on θ, we cannot conclude that φ is primitive recursive uniformly in θ. Indeed if it were, by Lemma I taking $U_2^2(s, c)$ (which is primitive recursive) as the $\theta^*(s, c)$, the resulting function $\varphi^*(x, c)$ would be primitive recursive, and hence so would be $\varphi^*(0, c)$. But $\varphi^*(0, c) = \xi(U_2^2(0, c)) = \xi(c)$. — Thus also Lemma I does not hold, if the hypothesis that F is primitive recursive, i.e. that φ is primitive recursive uniformly in θ, Ψ, is weakened to: φ is primitive recursive in θ, Ψ, for each θ, Ψ. — In this example, of course φ is primitive recursive uniformly in ξ, θ.

Since the former proofs actually establish uniformity:

##A—G (second versions). *Reread the original versions with "primitive recursive uniformly" in place of "primitive recursive".*

Usually a course-of-values recursion arises in the following form. The ambiguous value $\varphi(y, x_2, \ldots, x_n)$ is given in terms of $y, x_2, \ldots, x_n$, other functions and predicates Ψ, and $\varphi(s, x_2, \ldots, x_n)$ as a function of s for the given $x_2, \ldots, x_n$. The expression by which it is given is the result of substituting $\varphi(s, x_2, \ldots, x_n)$ for a function variable $\theta(s)$ of a primitive recursive functional. This functional has the property that its value is not changed, if values of $\theta(s)$ are changed for $s \geq y$ only. In other words, there is a primitive recursive functional $\mathsf{F}(\lambda s\, \theta(s), \Psi; y, x_2, \ldots, x_n)$ such that

(6) $$\varphi(y, x_2, \ldots, x_n) = \mathsf{F}(\lambda s\, \varphi(s, x_2, \ldots, x_n), \Psi; y, x_2, \ldots, x_n),$$

(7) $$\mathsf{F}(\lambda s\, \theta_1(s), \Psi; y, x_2, \ldots, x_n) = \mathsf{F}(\lambda s\, \theta_2(s), \Psi; y, x_2, \ldots, x_n) \quad \text{whenever } \theta_1(s) = \theta_2(s) \text{ for all } s < y.$$

Under these circumstances, we say that $\varphi(y, x_2, \ldots, x_n)$ is *primitive recursive uniformly in $\varphi(s, x_2, \ldots, x_n)$ for $s < y$ and Ψ.*

Like terminology is used for predicates (reading "P", "H", "$\equiv$" in place of "φ", "θ", "$=$").

In case we are considering the definition of φ from Ψ only for a restricted range of Ψ, then (7) as well as (6) need only hold on this range.

EXAMPLE 4. Let $\varphi(y, x)$ be defined by

(a) $$\varphi(y, x) = y \cdot \rho(\varphi(\sigma(y), x)) + \mu z_{z<y}[\varphi(z, x) \mid y]$$

where ρ, σ are given functions such that $\sigma(y) < y$ for $y > 0$. To see that $\varphi(y, x)$ is primitive recursive uniformly in $\varphi(s, x)$ for $s < y$ and ρ, σ, let us insert an unspecified function $\lambda s\, \theta(s)$ in place of $\lambda s\, \varphi(s, x)$ in the right member of (a), for convenience calling the resulting function $\chi_1(y, x)$:

(b) $$\chi_1(y, x) = y \cdot \rho(\theta(\sigma(y))) + \mu z_{z<y}[\theta(z) \mid y].$$

By ##A, C, E, 16 (using the second versions of A, C and E), $\chi_1(y, x)$ is primitive recursive uniformly in θ, ρ, σ; and changing values of $\theta(s)$ for $s \geq y$ only will not change the value of $\chi_1(y, x)$ under the restriction on σ.

EXAMPLE 5. We can see directly from (a) of Example 1 § 46 ((b) of Example 2 § 46) that $\varphi(y)$ is primitive recursive uniformly in $\varphi(s)$ for $s < y$ (in $\varphi(s)$ for $s < y$ and χ). Instead of first writing "θ" in place of "φ", we need merely to examine how the right member is constructed out of $\varphi(s)$ regarded momentarily as an unspecified function. Similarly from (a) of Example 3 § 46, $T(y)$ is primitive recursive uniformly in $T(s)$ for $s < y$ and V.

#G (third version). *If $\varphi(y, x_2, \ldots, x_n)$ is primitive recursive uniformly in $\varphi(s, x_2, \ldots, x_n)$ for $s < y$ and Ψ, then φ is primitive recursive uniformly in Ψ. Similarly for a predicate (reading "P" in place of "φ").*

PROOF, for a function φ. By (6), (7) and (2),

$$(8) \qquad \begin{aligned} \varphi(y, x_2, \ldots, x_n) &= \mathsf{F}(\lambda s\,(\tilde{\varphi}(y; x_2, \ldots, x_n))_s, \Psi; y, x_2, \ldots, x_n) \\ &= \chi(y, \tilde{\varphi}(y; x_2, \ldots, x_n), x_2, \ldots, x_n) \end{aligned}$$

where

$$(9) \qquad \chi(y, c, x_2, \ldots, x_n) = \mathsf{F}(\lambda s\,(c)_s, \Psi; y, x_2, \ldots, x_n).$$

By Lemma I, χ is primitive recursive uniformly in $\lambda sc\,(c)_s, \Psi$; and hence by #19, in Ψ. Now the second version of #G applies.

The result for a predicate P follows by going over from P to its representing function.

REMARK 1. Cf. Remark 1 end § 44. *If φ, Ψ are functions of $n, m_1, \ldots, m_l > 0$ variables, then φ is primitive recursive uniformly in Ψ under Basis* B, *if and only if under Basis* A. For any primitive recursive derivation schema of φ from Ψ under Basis A can be transformed into one under Basis B as above by supplying a description under Basis B of C^n_q (of C^0_q) for each application of (II) (of (Va)). Conversely, given a primitive recursive derivation schema $\varphi_1, \ldots, \varphi_k$ of φ from Ψ under Basis B, one under Basis A can be obtained by the following process. Say that $n = l = m_1 = 1$, i.e. that the derivation is of $\varphi(x)$ from $\psi(y)$. Let a parameter c be introduced into each of the functions $\varphi_1, \ldots, \varphi_k$. Similarly to the proof of Lemma I, we can then obtain a primitive recursive derivation schema of $\varphi(x, c)$ from $\psi(y, c)$ under Basis A. To this we prefix $\psi(y, c) = \psi(U^2_1(y, c))$ and suffix $\varphi(x) = \varphi(U^1_1(x), C^1_0(x))$. — For example, if $\varphi(0) = \psi(0)$, $\varphi(y') = \chi(y, \varphi(y))$, then φ is primitive recursive uniformly in ψ, χ under Basis B (using successively (II_B), (IV) with $n = 0$, (Vb) with $n = 1$). Hence it is also under Basis A.

§ 48. Gödel's β-function. The second problem of this chapter is to show that every primitive recursive predicate is numeralwise expressible in the formal system of Chapter IV, even though that system has function symbols only for the three functions $'$, $+$, $\cdot$. We shall prove this in the next section, following a method of Gödel (1931, 1934).

This proof is not essential to our program of formalizing number theory. If it did not succeed, we could have arranged instead that recursion equations for other functions besides $+$ and $\cdot$ should be axioms of the system. Indeed, by an enumerably infinite system of particular number-theoretic axioms, we could include recursion equations for all the primitive recursive functions. However it is of some interest that a finite system suffices, the more so that we can get along with the two chief functions $+$ and $\cdot$ of traditional arithmetic, when taken with the logical constants and the predicate $=$.

Gödel has called a predicate *arithmetical*, if it can be expressed explicitly in terms of constant and variable natural numbers, the functions $+$ and $\cdot$, equality $=$, the operations $\rightarrow$, &, $\vee$, $^{-}$ of the propositional calculus, and the quantifiers (x) and (Ex), combined according to the usual syntactical rules. (This uses the adjective 'arithmetical' in the narrower sense, § 9.)

The reader may readily give the definition more fully as an inductive definition, paralleling the definition of formula for the formal system. The arithmetical predicates are precisely those which can be expressed by name forms in the formal system under the usual interpretation of the symbols. (By comparison with the formal treatment in §§ 39 and 41, $a<b$ and $\text{rm}(c, d)=w$ are arithmetical.)

But, using the intuitive symbolism, we shall keep the discussion informal for the present. For the application to primitive recursive predicates, we shall require only constructive use of the quantifiers.

In the next section, we shall need a method of dealing with finite sequences $a_0, \ldots, a_n$ of natural numbers arithmetically; there we cannot use the functions a^b, p_i and $(a)_i$ of §§ 44, 45 with which we handled finite sequences primitive recursively in §§ 46, 47.

We know that the predicate $\text{rm}(c, d)=w$, where $\text{rm}(c, d)$ is the remainder when c is divided by d, is arithmetical.

A set of positive integers $d_0, \ldots, d_n$ are said to be *relatively prime*, if no two of them have a common positive integral factor except 1. For example, 3, 4, 5 are relatively prime.

Consider the $n+1$-tuples of the values of the function $\text{rm}(c, d)$, for a fixed $n+1$-tuple of relatively prime divisors $d_0, \ldots, d_n$, as c increases. For example (with $n = 1$), if $d_0 = 3$, $d_1 = 4$, they are as follows.

c	0	1	2	3	4	5	6	7	8	9	10	11	12	13 ...
rm$(c, 3)$	0	1	2	0	1	2	0	1	2	0	1	2	0	1 ...
rm$(c, 4)$	0	1	2	3	0	1	2	3	0	1	2	3	0	1 ...

We see that, as c ranges from 0 to 11, the pair of remainders rm$(c, 3)$, rm$(c, 4)$ assumes each of the 12 possible ordered pairs of numbers a_0, a_1 for $a_0 < 3$, $a_1 < 4$.

To establish this in general, let rm(c, d_0), rm(c, d_1), ..., rm(c, d_n) take the respective values $a_0, a_1, \ldots, a_n$ for $c = j$ and also later for $c = j+k$. Since j and $j+k$ give the same remainder a_i on dividing by d_i $(i = 0, \ldots, n)$, their difference k must contain d_i exactly; say that $k = b_i d_i$. Thus

$$k = b_0 d_0 = b_1 d_1 = \ldots = b_n d_n.$$

Here k has each of $d_0, d_1, \ldots, d_n$ as factor. Since by hypothesis $d_0, \ldots, d_n$ are relatively prime, by the fundamental theorem of arithmetic (§ 45) k must be a multiple of their product $d_0 \cdot d_1 \cdot \ldots \cdot d_n$.

Therefore the ordered $n+1$-tuple rm(c, d_0), rm(c, d_1), ..., rm(c, d_n) cannot return to a given sequence of numbers $a_0, a_1, \ldots, a_n$ after less than $d_0 \cdot d_1 \cdot \ldots \cdot d_n$ consecutive values of c. But there are exactly $d_0 \cdot d_1 \cdot \ldots \cdot d_n$ distinct sequences of numbers $a_0, a_1, \ldots, a_n$ for $a_0 < d_0$, $a_1 < d_1$, $\ldots, a_n < d_n$. Each sequence is therefore taken once in any $d_0 \cdot d_1 \cdot \ldots \cdot d_n$ consecutive values of c.

Following Gödel 1934, we use this fact to construct a function $\beta(c, d, i)$ with the two properties,

(1) *the predicate* $\beta(c, d, i) = w$ *is arithmetical, and*

(2) *for any finite sequence of natural numbers* $a_0, a_1, \ldots, a_n$, *there can be found a pair of natural numbers* c, d *such that*

$$\beta(c, d, i) = a_i \qquad (i = 0, 1, \ldots, n).$$

As we know, a number c $(c < d_0 \cdot d_1 \cdot \ldots \cdot d_n)$ can be chosen so that rm$(c, d_i) = a_i$ for $i = 0, 1, \ldots, n$, provided $d_0, d_1, \ldots, d_n$ is a set of numbers such that (a) $d_0, d_1, \ldots, d_n$ are relatively prime, and (b) $a_0 < d_0$, $a_1 < d_1, \ldots, a_n < d_n$. Our problem will be solved, if we can obtain the numbers $d_0, d_1, \ldots, d_n$ as the values of a function $\delta(d, i)$ for $i = 0, 1, \ldots, n$ and a suitable number d, so that

(i) $$\beta(c, d, i) = \text{rm}(c, \delta(d, i))$$

also satisfies (1).

Now (1) will be satisfied if we take

(ii) $$\delta(d, i) = 1+(i+1)d.$$

For rm$(c, d)=w$ is arithmetical, and $\delta(d, i)$, which we substitute for d to get $\beta(c, d, i)=w$, is defined explicitly from 1, + and ·.

For the given sequence of numbers $a_0, a_1, \ldots, a_n$, let s be the greatest of $n, a_0, a_1, \ldots, a_n$, and take $d = s!$.

Then, (a) the numbers $d_i = \delta(d, i)$ for $i = 0, 1, \ldots, n$ are relatively prime. For if two of them $1+(j+1)s!$ and $1+(j+k+1)s!$ had a factor other than 1 in common, they would have a prime factor p in common, and this factor p would divide the difference which is $k \cdot s!$. But p cannot divide $s!$, since then it would divide $(j+1)s!$, which is impossible since it divides $1+(j+1)s!$. Then also p cannot divide k, since $k \leq n \leq s$ and every number $\leq s$ divides $s!$. Hence p cannot divide $k \cdot s!$; so by reductio ad absurdum (a) is proved.

Moreover, (b) for each i $(i = 0, 1, \ldots, n)$, $a_i \leq s \leq s! < 1+(i+1)s! = \delta(d, i) = d_i$.

Julia Robinson 1949* shows that the predicate $|$ (#16) and function $'$ can be used in place of the two functions $+$ and $\cdot$ in defining the arithmetical predicates; and Church and Quine 1952 show that a suitably chosen symmetric 2-place predicate can be used instead.

§ 49. Primitive recursive functions and the number-theoretic formalism. THEOREM I. *If $\varphi(x_1, \ldots, x_n)$ is a primitive recursive function, then the predicate $\varphi(x_1, \ldots, x_n)=w$ is arithmetical.* (Gödel 1931.)

PROOF, by course-of-values induction on the length k of a given primitive recursive description $\varphi_1, \ldots, \varphi_k$ of φ (cf. § 43). The cases (I)—(V) correspond to the five schemata by which φ_k, i.e. φ, may occur in the description. (For a proof with a similar case structure, cf. that of Theorem 1 § 21.)

CASE (I): $\varphi(x) = x'$. Then $\varphi(x)=w \equiv w=x+1$, and $w=x+1$ is arithmetical.

CASE (II): $\varphi(x_1, \ldots, x_n) = q$. Then $\varphi(x_1, \ldots, x_n)=w \equiv w=q$.

CASE (IV): $\varphi(x_1, \ldots, x_n) = \psi(\chi_1(x_1, \ldots, x_n), \ldots, \chi_m(x_1, \ldots, x_n))$, where by the hypothesis of the induction, $\psi(y_1, \ldots, y_m)=w$, $\chi_1(x_1, \ldots, x_n)=y_1, \ldots, \chi_m(x_1, \ldots, x_n)=y_m$ are arithmetical. Then $\varphi(x_1, \ldots, x_n)=w \equiv (Ey_1) \ldots (Ey_m)[\chi_1(x_1, \ldots, x_n)=y_1 \,\&\, \ldots \,\&\, \chi_m(x_1, \ldots, x_n)=y_m \,\&\, \psi(y_1, \ldots, y_m)=w]$.

CASE (Vb): $\varphi(0, x_2, \ldots, x_n) = \psi(x_2, \ldots, x_n)$, $\varphi(y', x_2, \ldots, x_n) = \chi(y, \varphi(y, x_2, \ldots, x_n), x_2, \ldots, x_n)$, where $\psi(x_2, \ldots, x_n)=w$ and $\chi(y, z, x_2, \ldots, x_n)=w$ are arithmetical. Suppose that $y, x_2, \ldots, x_n, w$ are numbers such that $\varphi(y, x_2, \ldots, x_n)=w$ is true. Then there is a finite sequence of numbers

$$a_0, a_1, \ldots, a_y$$

(the values of $\varphi(i, x_2, \ldots, x_n)$ for $i = 0, 1, \ldots, y$) such that

$$\text{(A)} \quad \begin{aligned} a_0 &= \psi(x_2, \ldots, x_n), \\ a_1 &= \chi(0, a_0, x_2, \ldots, x_n), \\ a_2 &= \chi(1, a_1, x_2, \ldots, x_n), \\ &\ \ \cdots \\ a_y &= \chi(y-1, a_{y-1}, x_2, \ldots, x_n), \\ w &= a_y. \end{aligned}$$

But then there are numbers c, d for Gödel's β-function such that $\beta(c, d, i) = a_i$ $(i = 0, 1, \ldots, y)$, and the facts (A) can be expressed using the $\beta(c, d, i)$'s instead of the a_i's, thus:

$$\text{(B)} \quad \begin{aligned} &(Ec)(Ed)\{\beta(c, d, 0) = \psi(x_2, \ldots, x_n) \\ &\ \& \ (i)[i<y \rightarrow \beta(c, d, i+1) = \chi(i, \beta(c, d, i), x_2, \ldots, x_n)] \\ &\ \& \ w = \beta(c, d, y)\}. \end{aligned}$$

Conversely, if (B) is true, then for any c and d given by (B), the numbers $\beta(c, d, i)$ for $i = 0, 1, \ldots, y$ do constitute a sequence $a_0, a_1, \ldots, a_y$ satisfying (A); and (A) implies that $\varphi(y, x_2, \ldots, x_n)=w$. Thus $\varphi(y, x_2, \ldots, x_n)=w$ is equivalent to (B). But (B) is an arithmetical predicate of $y, x_2, \ldots, x_n, w$, as we see by rewriting it in the form

$$\text{(C)} \quad \begin{aligned} &(Ec)(Ed)\{(Eu)[\beta(c, d, 0)=u \ \& \ \psi(x_2, \ldots, x_n)=u] \ \& \ (i)[i<y \rightarrow \\ &(Eu)(Ev)[\beta(c, d, i+1)=u \ \& \ \beta(c, d, i)=v \ \& \ \chi(i, v, x_2, \ldots, x_n)=u]] \\ &\& \ \beta(c, d, y)=w\}, \end{aligned}$$

and taking into account the hypothesis of the induction and the arithmetical character of $\beta(c, d, i)=w$ and $i<y$.

The analysis of primitive recursion in terms of finite sequences of natural numbers used here is a number-theoretic adaptation of Dedekind's analysis of primitive recursion (1888).

COROLLARY. *Every primitive recursive predicate* $P(x_1, \ldots, x_n)$ *is arithmetical.*

For $P(x_1, \ldots, x_n) \equiv \varphi(x_1, \ldots, x_n)=0$, where φ is the representing function of P (§ 45). Conversely, the theorem follows from its corollary using ##14, C. The theorem however has the form necessary to the proof by induction on the length of the description $\varphi_1, \ldots, \varphi_k$.

By translating from the intuitive arithmetical symbolism into the formal symbolism, we obtain a formula $\mathrm{P}(\mathrm{x}_1, \ldots, \mathrm{x}_n, \mathrm{w})$ which expresses $\varphi(x_1, \ldots, x_n)=w$ under the interpretation of the formal system. By this means we shall now prove the following theorem.

THEOREM 27. *Every primitive recursive function* $\varphi(x_1, \ldots, x_n)$ *is numeralwise representable* (§ 41) *in the formal system of Chapter* IV; *i.e. there is a formula* $\mathrm{P}(\mathrm{x}_1, \ldots, \mathrm{x}_n, \mathrm{w})$, *containing no variables free other than the distinct variables* $\mathrm{x}_1, \ldots, \mathrm{x}_n, \mathrm{w}$, *such that, for each n-tuple of natural numbers* $x_1, \ldots, x_n$,

(v) *if* $\varphi(x_1, \ldots, x_n)=w$, *then* $\vdash \mathrm{P}(\boldsymbol{x}_1, \ldots, \boldsymbol{x}_n, \boldsymbol{w})$, *and*

(vi) $\vdash \exists!\mathrm{wP}(\boldsymbol{x}_1, \ldots, \boldsymbol{x}_n, \mathrm{w})$.

PROOF. The construction of $\mathrm{P}(\mathrm{x}_1, \ldots, \mathrm{x}_n, \mathrm{w})$, and the proof of the theorem, are by a course-of-values induction on k, with cases (I) — (V) corresponding to those in the proof of Theorem I.

CASE (Vb). By the hypothesis of the induction, there are formulas $\mathrm{Q}(\mathrm{x}_2, \ldots, \mathrm{x}_n, \mathrm{w})$ and $\mathrm{R}(\mathrm{y}, \mathrm{z}, \mathrm{x}_2, \ldots, \mathrm{x}_n, \mathrm{w})$ which numeralwise represent the respective functions $\psi(x_2, \ldots, x_n)$ and $\chi(y, z, x_2, \ldots, x_n)$, i.e. they have the properties for these functions corresponding to (v) and (vi) for $\varphi(x_1, \ldots, x_n)$.

According to *(180) § 41, Gödel's β-function $\beta(c, d, i)$ $[=\mathrm{rm}(c, 1+(i+1)d = \mathrm{rm}(c, (i' \cdot d)')]$ is numeralwise represented by a formula $\mathrm{B}(\mathrm{c}, \mathrm{d}, \mathrm{i}, \mathrm{w})$ having a further property *180a.

Thc formula

$$\exists \mathrm{c} \exists \mathrm{d}\{\exists \mathrm{u}[\mathrm{B}(\mathrm{c}, \mathrm{d}, 0, \mathrm{u}) \& \mathrm{Q}(\mathrm{x}_2, \ldots, \mathrm{x}_n, \mathrm{u})] \& \forall \mathrm{i}[\mathrm{i}<\mathrm{y} \supset \exists \mathrm{u} \exists \mathrm{v}[\mathrm{B}(\mathrm{c}, \mathrm{d}, \mathrm{i}', \mathrm{u}) \\ \& \mathrm{B}(\mathrm{c}, \mathrm{d}, \mathrm{i}, \mathrm{v}) \& \mathrm{R}(\mathrm{i}, \mathrm{v}, \mathrm{x}_2, \ldots, \mathrm{x}_n, \mathrm{u})]] \& \mathrm{B}(\mathrm{c}, \mathrm{d}, \mathrm{y}, \mathrm{w})\}$$

shall be the formula $\mathrm{P}(\mathrm{y}, \mathrm{x}_2, \ldots, \mathrm{x}_n, \mathrm{w})$ to represent $\varphi(y, x_2, \ldots, x_n)$. We must show that it has the properties (v) and (vi).

To establish (v), let $y, x_2, \ldots, x_n, w$ be numbers such that $\varphi(y, x_2, \ldots, x_n) = w$. Then there are numbers $a_0, a_1, \ldots, a_y$ as in the proof of Theorem I, and also numbers c and d for these $a_0, a_1, \ldots, a_y$ such that $\beta(c, d, i) = a_i$ $(i = 0, 1, \ldots, y)$. By the property (v) for B, Q and R, the following statements hold:

$$\begin{array}{ll} \vdash \mathrm{B}(\boldsymbol{c}, \boldsymbol{d}, 0, \boldsymbol{a}_0), & \vdash \mathrm{Q}(\boldsymbol{x}_2, \ldots, \boldsymbol{x}_n, \boldsymbol{a}_0), \\ \vdash \mathrm{B}(\boldsymbol{c}, \boldsymbol{d}, 1, \boldsymbol{a}_1), & \vdash \mathrm{R}(0, \boldsymbol{a}_0, \boldsymbol{x}_2, \ldots, \boldsymbol{x}_n, \boldsymbol{a}_1), \\ & \quad \ldots \\ \vdash \mathrm{B}(\boldsymbol{c}, \boldsymbol{d}, \boldsymbol{y}, \boldsymbol{a}_y), & \vdash \mathrm{R}(\boldsymbol{y}-1, \boldsymbol{a}_{y-1}, \boldsymbol{x}_2, \ldots, \boldsymbol{x}_n, \boldsymbol{a}_y), \\ \vdash \mathrm{B}(\boldsymbol{c}, \boldsymbol{d}, \boldsymbol{y}, \boldsymbol{w}). & \end{array}$$

We can thence show that $\vdash \mathrm{P}(\boldsymbol{y}, \boldsymbol{x}_2, \ldots, \boldsymbol{x}_n, \boldsymbol{w})$ by &-introd., ∃-introd. and *166 § 41.

To establish (vi), we use an intuitive induction on y. IND. STEP. Let $w = \varphi(y, x_2, \ldots, x_n)$ and $u = \varphi(y', x_2, \ldots, x_n) = \chi(y, w, x_2, \ldots, x_n)$.

By (v) and (vi) for R (and for brevity using the informal presentation, beginning § 38): (a) $\mathrm{R}(\boldsymbol{y}, \boldsymbol{w}, \boldsymbol{x}_2, \ldots, \boldsymbol{x}_n, \boldsymbol{u})$, and (b) $\exists!\mathrm{uR}(\boldsymbol{y}, \boldsymbol{w}, \boldsymbol{x}_2, \ldots, \boldsymbol{x}_n, \mathrm{u})$. By (v) (as already established for P): (c) $\mathrm{P}(\boldsymbol{y}, \boldsymbol{x}_2, \ldots, \boldsymbol{x}_n, \boldsymbol{w})$, and (d) $\mathrm{P}(\boldsymbol{y}', \boldsymbol{x}_2, \ldots, \boldsymbol{x}_n, \boldsymbol{u})$. By the hypothesis of the induction on y: (e) $\exists!\mathrm{wP}(\boldsymbol{y}, \boldsymbol{x}_2, \ldots, \boldsymbol{x}_n, \mathrm{w})$. We must prove $\exists!\mathrm{wP}(\boldsymbol{y}', \boldsymbol{x}_2, \ldots, \boldsymbol{x}_n, \mathrm{w})$. Assume: (f) $\mathrm{P}(\boldsymbol{y}', \boldsymbol{x}_2, \ldots, \boldsymbol{x}_n, \mathrm{w})$. By *170 with (d), it will suffice to deduce $\boldsymbol{u}=\mathrm{w}$ with w held constant. For &- and $\exists$-elim. from (f), assume: (g) $\exists\mathrm{u}[\mathrm{B}(\mathrm{c}, \mathrm{d}, 0, \mathrm{u}) \& \mathrm{Q}(\boldsymbol{x}_2, \ldots, \boldsymbol{x}_n, \mathrm{u})]$, (h) $\forall\mathrm{i}[\mathrm{i}<\boldsymbol{y}' \supset \exists\mathrm{u}\exists\mathrm{v}[\mathrm{B}(\mathrm{c}, \mathrm{d}, \mathrm{i}', \mathrm{u}) \& \mathrm{B}(\mathrm{c}, \mathrm{d}, \mathrm{i}, \mathrm{v}) \& \mathrm{R}(\mathrm{i}, \mathrm{v}, \boldsymbol{x}_2, \ldots, \boldsymbol{x}_n, \mathrm{u})]]$, and (i) $\mathrm{B}(\mathrm{c}, \mathrm{d}, \boldsymbol{y}', \mathrm{w})$. From (h) using *138a § 39 (or *167 and *166):
(j) $\forall\mathrm{i}[\mathrm{i}<\boldsymbol{y} \supset \exists\mathrm{u}\exists\mathrm{v}[\mathrm{B}(\mathrm{c}, \mathrm{d}, \mathrm{i}', \mathrm{u}) \& \mathrm{B}(\mathrm{c}, \mathrm{d}, \mathrm{i}, \mathrm{v}) \& \mathrm{R}(\mathrm{i}, \mathrm{v}, \boldsymbol{x}_2, \ldots, \boldsymbol{x}_n, \mathrm{u})]]$, and (k) $\exists\mathrm{u}\exists\mathrm{v}[\mathrm{B}(\mathrm{c}, \mathrm{d}, \boldsymbol{y}', \mathrm{u}) \& \mathrm{B}(\mathrm{c}, \mathrm{d}, \boldsymbol{y}, \mathrm{v}) \& \mathrm{R}(\boldsymbol{y}, \mathrm{v}, \boldsymbol{x}_2, \ldots, \boldsymbol{x}_n, \mathrm{u})]$. For &- and $\exists$-elim. from (k), assume: (l) $\mathrm{B}(\mathrm{c}, \mathrm{d}, \boldsymbol{y}', \mathrm{u})$, (m) $\mathrm{B}(\mathrm{c}, \mathrm{d}, \boldsymbol{y}, \mathrm{v})$, and (n) $\mathrm{R}(\boldsymbol{y}, \mathrm{v}, \boldsymbol{x}_2, \ldots, \boldsymbol{x}_n, \mathrm{u})$. From (g), (j) and (m) by &- and $\exists$-introd.: (o) $\mathrm{P}(\boldsymbol{y}, \boldsymbol{x}_2, \ldots, \boldsymbol{x}_n, \mathrm{v})$. From (o), (c) and (e) by *172, $\mathrm{v}=\boldsymbol{w}$, which with (n) gives: (p) $\mathrm{R}(\boldsymbol{y}, \boldsymbol{w}, \boldsymbol{x}_2, \ldots, \boldsymbol{x}_n, \mathrm{u})$. From (p), (a) and (b) by *172 $\mathrm{u}=\boldsymbol{u}$, which with (l) gives: (q) $\mathrm{B}(\mathrm{c}, \mathrm{d}, \boldsymbol{y}', \boldsymbol{u})$. From (q), (i), *180a and *172, $\boldsymbol{u}=\mathrm{w}$, as was to be deduced.

Corollary. *Every primitive recursive predicate* $P(x_1, \ldots, x_n)$ *is numeralwise expressible in the formal system.*

For if $\mathrm{P}(\mathrm{x}_1, \ldots, \mathrm{x}_n, \mathrm{w})$ numeralwise represents the representing function φ of P, then using (vii) § 41 (obtained there by *173, *(164)), $\mathrm{P}(\mathrm{x}_1, \ldots, \mathrm{x}_n, 0)$ numeralwise expresses P.

Lemma 18b. *Theorem 27 and Corollary hold for Raphael Robinson's formal system* (§§ 41, 76) *consisting of the predicate calculus with thirteen particular number-theoretic axioms as follows*: *Axioms* 14—21, *and* (*the formulas of*) *104 — *107 *and* *137 (*or* *136).

Using Lemma 18a § 41.

Remark 1. A more ambitious undertaking (relating to the full system, not to Robinson's) would be to establish the provability of formulas which express the recursion equations; e.g. for Case (Vb), to establish:

(1) $\vdash \mathrm{P}(0, \mathrm{x}_2, \ldots, \mathrm{x}_n, \mathrm{w}) \sim \mathrm{Q}(\mathrm{x}_2, \ldots, \mathrm{x}_n, \mathrm{w})$.

(2) $\vdash \mathrm{P}(\mathrm{y}', \mathrm{x}_2, \ldots, \mathrm{x}_n, \mathrm{w}) \sim$
$\exists\mathrm{z}[\mathrm{P}(\mathrm{y}, \mathrm{x}_2, \ldots, \mathrm{x}_n, \mathrm{z}) \& \mathrm{R}(\mathrm{y}, \mathrm{z}, \mathrm{x}_2, \ldots, \mathrm{x}_n, \mathrm{w})]$.

From (1) and (2) by formal induction on y (given by the hypothesis of an intuitive induction on k that $\vdash \exists!\mathrm{wQ}(\mathrm{x}_2, \ldots, \mathrm{x}_n, \mathrm{w})$ and

$\vdash \exists!wR(y, z, x_2, \ldots, x_n, w))$, then:

(3) $\vdash \exists!wP(y, x_2, \ldots, x_n, w)$.

To establish (1) and (2), we would begin by formalizing the theory of the β-function, which we gave informally in § 48. It would suffice to establish:

(α) $\vdash \exists c \exists d B(c, d, 0, w)$.

(β) $\vdash \exists c_2 \exists d_2 \{\forall i[i \leq y \supset \exists u[B(c_1, d_1, i, u) \,\&\, B(c_2, d_2, i, u)]] \,\&$
$B(c_2, d_2, y', w)\}$.

For then the four implications of (1) and (2) could all be proved, using *180c, (α) (for the second), and (β) (for the fourth). — We shall not take the space to carry out the formalization to establish (α) and (β). Hilbert and Bernays 1934 pp. 401—419 do practically this in another formal system, whence (in the manner to be indicated before Example 9 § 74) it can be inferred that (α) and (β) hold in our (classical or intuitionistic) system.

Chapter X

THE ARITHMETIZATION OF METAMATHEMATICS

§ 50. Metamathematics as a generalized arithmetic. As we remarked in § 42 (following Gödel 1931), by selecting a particular enumeration of the formal objects, or a particular correlation of distinct natural numbers to the distinct formal objects (not using every number), and then talking about the correlated numbers instead of the formal objects, metamathematics becomes a branch of the arithmetic of the natural numbers. In this chapter we shall carry out such an arithmetization of metamathematics, using a Gödel numbering similar to that of Hilbert and Bernays 1939.

However instead of carrying out the arithmetization directly, we shall first represent the formal system in an intermediate way as a generalized arithmetic, and then represent the generalized arithmetic in the ordinary arithmetic. This will bring out some analogies which are of heuristic value, and the representation of the system as a generalized arithmetic will be of interest on its own account.

The arithmetic of the natural numbers deals with the domain of objects which is generated by starting with one primitive object 0 and applying one primitive operation ′ or +1 (§ 6).

A generalized arithmetic (for the present purpose) is obtained by supposing one or more zeros, and one or more successor operations. We shall adhere to the convention (not the only useful one) that objects generated from the primitives in distinct ways are distinct. There are several possibilities for representing the formal system as a generalized arithmetic. Hermes 1938 considers an arithmetic with the empty expression as the zero, and the operations of suffixing one of the formal symbols as the successor operations.

The generalized arithmetic which we select has a more complicated structure as an arithmetic, but is designed to represent directly the grammatical and logical structure of the formal objects. There shall be $r+1$ zeros $0_0, 0_1, \ldots, 0_r$, where r is a natural number to be specified later; and there shall be one successor operation applying to an $s+1$-tuple of arguments, for each of the natural number values of *s* to be specified later. The result of the successor operation applied to $x_0, x_1, \ldots, x_s$ as arguments is written "$(x_0, x_1, \ldots, x_s)$" or also sometimes "$x_0(x_1, \ldots, x_s)$". We call the objects belonging to this generalized arithmetic *entities*.

We can express this by an inductive definition (analogous to that given for 'natural number' in § 6). 1. $0_0, 0_1, \ldots, 0_r$ are *entities*. 2. For each admitted *s*, if $x_0, x_1, \ldots, x_s$ are *entities*, then $(x_0, x_1, \ldots, x_s)$ is an *entity*. 3. The only *entities* are those given by 1 and 2.

As we have already indicated, two entities shall be equal, if and only if they are generated from the zeros by the successor operations in the same way. To say that x and y are equal we write "$x \asymp y$" (unequal, "$x \not\asymp y$"). We use "$\asymp$" rather than "$=$" merely to avoid confusion with the $=$ of the formal system.

Axioms characterizing the domain of entities can be stated, analogous to Peano's for the natural numbers (§§ 6, 7). In particular, they include the principle of proof by mathematical induction in the form corresponding to the mode of generation of the domain of entities (or to the inductive definition just given): If the entities $0_0, 0_1, \ldots, 0_r$ each possess a certain property, and if for each admitted *s*, whenever entities $x_0, x_1, \ldots, x_s$ possess the property, the entity $(x_0, x_1, \ldots, x_s)$ also possesses it. then all entities possess the property. The statement of the other Peano axioms for the generalized arithmetic is left to the reader.

The process of generating the entities partially orders them (end § 8); we write "$x \prec y$" to say that x is generated before y in the process of generating y. Expressed inductively: 1. For each admitted *s* and each $i \leq s$, $x_i \prec (x_0, x_1, \ldots, x_s)$. 2. For each admitted *s* and each $i \leq s$, if $x \prec x_i$, then $x \prec (x_0, x_1, \ldots, x_s)$. 3. $x \prec y$ only as required by 1 and 2.

We define a function of an entity x and a natural number *i*, which gives the predecessors of a successor entity, thus:

$$\{x\}_i \asymp \begin{cases} x_i, \text{ if } x \asymp (x_0, x_1, \ldots, x_s) \text{ and } i \leq s, \\ x, \text{ otherwise.} \end{cases}$$

We now specify for the rest of this chapter that the number $r+1$ of the zeros $0_0, 0_1, \ldots, 0_r$ shall be thirteen, and we name them as follows:

$$\supset, \quad \&, \quad \vee, \quad \neg, \quad \forall, \quad \exists, \quad =, \quad +, \quad \cdot, \quad ', \quad 0, \quad a, \quad |.$$

We further specify that *s* admit the values 0, 1 and 2. This completes the definition of our generalized arithmetic as a domain of abstract objects which can be recognized and distinguished from one another as individuals by the mode of their generation.

We now have to fix how our formal system (as originally introduced in

Chapter IV) is to be represented in the generalized arithmetic. This will consist in giving a correlation of entities to the objects of that formal system. Those formal objects were explained in § 16 as consisting of formal symbols, finite sequences of formal symbols (called 'formal expressions'), and finite sequences of formal expressions. It is not necessary to correlate an entity to every formal object, but only to those formal objects which are significant for the metamathematics. For example, an asyntactical expression such as ((0∀00= will have no entity correlated to it. Also there will be entities which are correlates of no formal object.

To the first eleven of the formal symbols listed in § 16 we correlate the respective entities ⊃, &, ∨, ¬, ∀, ∃, =, +, ·, ′, 0, which we are designating now by the same symbols, i.e. we correlate respectively the first eleven of the zeros of the generalized arithmetic.

To the variables a, b, c, d,... of the formal system, we correlate, respectively, the entities

$$a, \quad (_{|}, a), \quad (_{|}, (_{|}, a)), \quad (_{|}, (_{|}, (_{|}, a))), \ldots$$

(sometimes written a, $a_{|}$, $a_{||}$, $a_{|||}$, ...), i.e. the twelfth zero, and the further entities obtained thence by repeated applications of the successor operation of the generalized arithmetic with $s = 1$ and with the thirteenth zero as the first predecessor.

To terms and formulas such as r+s, r′, r=s, A & B, ¬A, ∀xA(x) we correlate the entities (+, r, s), (′, r), (=, r, s), (&, A, B), (¬, A), (∀,x,A(x)), respectively, where r, s, A, B, x, A(x) are now to be the entities correlated to the given r, s, A, B, x, A(x), i.e. we repeat the correlation procedure on the given r, s, A, B, x, A(x).

Example 1. The entity correlated to the formula ∃b(¬b=0) is (∃, ($_{|}$, a), (¬, (=, ($_{|}$, a), 0))).

But hereafter in designating these entities, except when we wish to emphasize their structure (i.e. mode of generation) as entities, we shall use the former expressions. For example, when ∀, x, A(x) are entities, we may write their successor (∀, x, A(x)) as "∀xA(x)"; and when +, r, s are entities, we may write (+, r, s) as "r+s". This way of designating entities correlated to objects of the formal system will make our statements about the entities read as our former statements about the objects of the formal system.

Furthermore, in dealing with the generalized arithmetic, it is convenient to call the entity ∀xA(x) correlated to a formula (i.e. the entity (∀, x, A(x))) simply a "formula", the entity r+s a "term", etc.; and the system of these entities "the formal system as a generalized arithmetic" in contrast to the formal system as originally described, which we can distinguish when necessary as the "formal linguistic system".

Proofs and deductions will be represented by entities corresponding to them in their tree form (end § 24) rather than to them as finite sequences of formulas. Thus, to get the entity corresponding to a deduction in sequence form with a given analysis, let that deduction first be put into tree form. In tree form it has one of the three forms

$$\mathrm{D}, \qquad \frac{\mathrm{P}}{\mathrm{D}}, \qquad \frac{\mathrm{P}\ \ \mathrm{Q}}{\mathrm{D}},$$

where D is a formula, and P and Q are deductions in tree form. In the generalized arithmetic, we construe these to be the entities (D), (D, P), (D, P, Q), respectively, at the same time of course construing D P, Q to be the entities correlated to the linguistic objects D, P, Q. (In particular, a formula D, and a deduction consisting of the single formula D, become different entities; the entity which the latter becomes is the successor with $s = 0$ of the entity which the former becomes.)

Example 2. The deduction (6) of § 21, after being rewritten in tree form as in Example 1 § 24, becomes an entity which we can write as (8, (7, (1), (6)), (5, (3, (1), (2)), (4))) where the numbers 1 — 8 abbreviate the formulas of (6) § 21 now considered as entities.

This completes the correlation of entities to the significant formal linguistic objects. Distinct entities are correlated to distinct formal linguistic objects (except in the case of two inessentially differing proofs or deductions in sequence form which become the same in tree form). The proof of this, for the case of terms and formulas, depends on the uniqueness of the scopes of the operators in the terms and formulas as formal linguistic expressions (§ 17).

In thus going over from the formal linguistic system to the generalized arithmetic, we have effected two changes, either of which could have been effected separately. The first of these is in the structure attributed to the formal objects. In the linguistic representation terms and formulas were finite sequences of formal symbols, in which the significant parts had to be recognized as subsequences, while in the generalized arithmetic they are constructed directly out of the significant parts by the generalized successor operation. In the latter the analysis of expressions into their significant parts (including the use of parentheses) is transferred from the formal level to the exposition of the metamathematics, where we do not let it worry us.

For example, consider (A) ⊃ (B) as a formula of the linguistic system, where A and B are formulas (i.e. "A" and "B" are metamathematical letters designating formulas). We are then talking explicitly about a finite sequence of symbols, with the four parentheses shown being symbols of the sequence, and the sequences designated by "A" and "B" occurring in the indicated position in the sequence (§ 16).

On the other hand, consider (A) ⊃ (B) as a formula in the system of entities, where A and B are likewise formulas. Then "(A) ⊃ (B)" means (⊃, A, B), which is the successor of the three entities ⊃, A, B. The parentheses in "(A) ⊃ (B)" and the parentheses and commas in "(⊃, A, B)" are not formal objects, but only part of our intuitive notation for naming the entity under consideration.

As the second change, we are now taking a different view of the role of the symbolism in presenting the formal system. In Chapter IV, the objects of the formal system were considered to be linguistic symbols or marks, and other linguistic objects constructed from such. In studying them we had in principle to watch the distinction between an *object* and a *name* or *designation* for the object, and between the *mention* of an expression (as itself the object under consideration) and the *use* of it (in designating another object or expressing a proposition). This has been emphasized by Frege (1893 p. 4), Carnap (1934 pp. 153—160) and Quine (1940 pp. 23—37). To make a statement about an object, ordinarily a name for the object is used. (Another method, sometimes applicable, is to point to the object, or to use a linguistic construction which amounts to pointing to the object, i.e. calls attention to it instead of naming it.) We do not speak our friend, but we speak the name of our friend. It is not likely that we shall mistake our friend John for a sequence of four letters, but in metamathematics as treated in the preceding chapters we did have to be careful because we were discussing objects which were themselves linguistic.

One method of obtaining names for linguistic objects is to place them in quotation marks. The name of John is "John", and the name of the name of John is " "John" ". The name of the name of John consists of four letters enclosed in one set of quotation marks; the second set of quotation marks used above is employed in naming that.

A second method is the use of separate metamathematical letters and expressions as names for the linguistic objects.

It need not be strictly forbidden that a specimen of a linguistic object be used as name of the object; then the object has two uses, its use as the object of study, and its use as name of itself. In the latter use, it is called *autonymous*.

The method we used in the preceding chapters was a combination of the second and third methods.

This problem of designation, which is troublesome to treat explicitly, is extraneous to the metamathematics as mathematics. The issue can be avoided by using only names of the formal objects, and not claiming to exhibit the objects themselves. We find it convenient to do this in the generalized arithmetic, considering now "$\supset$", "$\forall$", "$\forall x A(x)$" as names of certain objects (the names are the expressions inside the quotation marks), rather than as the objects themselves. We refrain from specifying what the objects are, other than that they belong to a domain of abstract objects arranged in a certain way in relation to one another, which we are calling entities (cf. § 8). The objects named could be formal symbols, formal expressions, etc. in the sense of Chapter IV, though we now leave this open as irrelevant for the metamathematics. (While we can thus avoid the problem of designation in our metamathematics, it would have to be faced in discussing the application of the metamathematics to a particular linguistic system.)

By going over from the conception of the formal system in terms of formal symbols, treated as if they were marks on paper, to an abstract system of objects, our metamathematics (i.e. the study of the formal system) becomes a branch of pure number theory entirely on a par conceptually with the arithmetic of the natural numbers and similar mathematical disciplines.

REMARK 1. The usual convention or practice in informal mathematical writing is to write all the symbols without quotes, so that when a symbol is being mentioned rather than used it is autonymous. In this book our practice is to employ quotes systematically in metamathematical passages to distinguish the mention of metamathematical expressions from their use in designating formal linguistic expressions, and elsewhere only for emphasis.

§ 51. Recursive metamathematical definitions. The arithmetization of metamathematics will be completed in § 52 by mapping the generalized arithmetic into the ordinary arithmetic of the natural numbers. Our main objectives are to complete the proof of the lemma for Gödel's theorem, and to prove Theorem 31. Both results will follow from the result that a certain succession of number-theoretic predicates, obtained by the mapping from metamathematical predicates, are all primitive recursive.

It is intuitively clear why these results hold, and would have to hold for any formal system of like structure, when we consider the nature of the definitions of the metamathematical predicates in the generalized arithmetic.

Because the entities are generated from zeros by successor operations, predicates and functions can be defined over the entities by recursion. We use this idea now, without stopping to state an accurate definition of 'primitive recursive' for the generalized arithmetic.

We give below a series of thirteen definitions of metamathematical predicates. Each definition is given by listing the cases in which the predicate is to be true. (A few clauses are starred for reference from § 52.)

Each definition is either explicit (the predicate being defined not appearing in any of the defining clauses), or constitutes a primitive recursion (the value of the predicate for a given entity depending on values of itself for immediately preceding entities, or similarly with parameters), except that in Dn5 and Dn11 the recursion is on two variables simultaneously (one a number variable in Dn11). For the discussion of a metamathematical definition not of this nature, cf. § 53.

The reader should verify that the definitions do define the predicates named, as we know them from earlier sections of the book (Chapter IV and §§ 41, 50).

Definitions of metamathematical predicates for the formal number-theoretic system as a generalized arithmetic

Dn1. y is a *numeral*. (Abbreviation: $\mathfrak{N}(y)$.)

1. $y \asymp 0$.
2. $y \asymp n'$ (i.e. $y \asymp (', n)$, cf. § 50), where n is a *numeral*.

Dn2. y is a *variable*. (Abbreviation: $\mathfrak{V}(y)$.)

1. $y \asymp a$.
2. $y \asymp x_{|}$ (i.e. $y \asymp (_{|}, x)$), where x is a *variable*.

Dn3. y is a *term*. (Abbreviation: $\mathfrak{T}(y)$.)

1. $y \asymp 0$.
2. y is a variable.

3—5. $y \asymp r+s$ or $r \cdot s$, where r and s are *terms*. $y \asymp r'$, where r is a *term*.

Dn4. D is a *formula*. (Abbreviation: $\mathfrak{F}(D)$.)

1. $D \asymp r=s$, where r and s are terms.

2—5. $D \asymp A \supset B$, $A \,\&\, B$ or $A \vee B$, where A and B are *formulas*. $D \asymp \neg A$, where A is a *formula*.

6—7. D $\asymp$ ∀xA(x) or ∃xA(x), where x is a variable, and A(x) is a *formula*.

Dn5. (t is a term, x is a variable, E is a term or formula, and) D comes from E by the *substitution* of t for (the free occurrences of) x. (Abbreviation: $\mathfrak{S}$(D, E, t, x).)

1. t is a term, x is a variable, E $\asymp$ x, and D $\asymp$ t.

2—3. t is a term, x is a variable, E is 0 or a variable $\not\asymp$ x, and D $\asymp$ E.

4—5. E is a term or formula, and E is (e_0, e_1) and D is (e_0, d_1), where $e_0 \not\asymp$ ' and $\mathfrak{S}$(d_1, e_1, t, x) (so t is a term, and x is a variable). E is a term or formula, and E is (e_0, e_1, e_2) and D is (e_0, d_1, d_2), where $e_0 \not\asymp$ ∀ or ∃, $\mathfrak{S}$(d_1, e_1, t, x) and $\mathfrak{S}$(d_2, e_2, t, x).

6—7. t is a term, and E is (∀, y, e_2) and D is (∀, y, d_2), where y is a variable, e_2 is a formula, and either y $\not\asymp$ x and $\mathfrak{S}$(d_2, e_2, t, x), or y $\asymp$ x and D $\asymp$ E. Similarly for ∃.

Dn6. (E is a term or formula, x is a variable, and) E *contains* x *free*. (Abbreviation: $\mathfrak{CF}$(E, x).)

1. E is a term or formula, x is a variable, and $\overline{\mathfrak{S}}$(E, E, 0, x).

Dn7. (t is a term, x is a variable, E is a formula, and) t is *free* for x in E. (Abbreviation: $\mathfrak{F}$(t, x, E)). By recursion on E, with seven clauses corresponding to 1—7Dn4. For example:

6. t is a term, x is a variable, and E $\asymp$ ∀yA(y), where y is a variable, A(y) is a formula, and either E does not contain x free, or t is *free* for x in A(y) and t does not contain y free.

Dn8. D is an *axiom*. (Abbreviation: $\mathfrak{A}$(D).)

1—10. D $\asymp$ A ⊃ (B ⊃ A), where A and B are formulas (Axiom Schema 1a). Similarly for Axiom Schemata 1b, 3, 4a, 4b, 5a, 5b, 6, 7, 8. (NOTE: We separate Axiom Schema 10 into two cases (Clauses 11 and 13), according as the A(x) contains the x free or not. Similarly for Axiom Schema 11.)

*11—12. There exists a t such that D $\asymp$ ∀xA(x) ⊃ A(t), where A(x) contains x free, t is free for x in A(x), and $\mathfrak{S}$(A(t), A(x), t, x). (NOTE: That x is a variable, A(x) is a formula, and t is a term, is included here in the stipulation "t is free for x in A(x)". Instead of presupposing the convention of § 18 by which A(t) stands for the result of substituting t for x in A(x), we make it explicit by "$\mathfrak{S}$(A(t), A(x), t, x)".) Similarly for Axiom Schema 11.

13—14. D $\asymp$ ∀xA ⊃ A, where x is a variable, A is a formula, and A does not contain x free. Similarly for Axiom Schema 11.

15. D $\asymp$ A(0) & ∀x(A(x) ⊃ A(x′)) ⊃ A(x), where A(x) is a formula, $\mathfrak{S}$(A(0), A(x), 0, x) and $\mathfrak{S}$(A(x′), A(x), x′, x).

16—23. D $\asymp$ $a'=b'$ ⊃ $a=b$ (Axiom 14). Similarly for Axioms 15—21.

Dn9. D is an *immediate consequence* of E. (Abbreviation: $\mathfrak{C}$(D, E).)

1—2. E $\asymp$ C ⊃ A(x) and D $\asymp$ C ⊃ ∀xA(x), where x is a variable, A(x) and C are formulas, and C does not contain x free (Rule 9). Similarly for Rule 12.

Dn10. D is an *immediate consequence* of E and F. (Abbreviation: $\mathfrak{C}$(D, E, F).)

1. D and E are formulas, and F $\asymp$ E ⊃ D (Rule 2).

Dn11. $\boldsymbol{x}$ is the *numeral for* the natural number x. (Abbreviation: $\mathfrak{Nu}(\boldsymbol{x}, x)$.)

1. $\boldsymbol{x} \asymp 0$ and $x = 0$.
2. $\boldsymbol{x} \asymp \boldsymbol{n}'$ and $x = n'$, where $\mathfrak{Nu}(\boldsymbol{n}, n)$.

Dn12. Y is a *proof*. (Abbreviation: $\mathfrak{Pf}$(Y).)

1. Y $\asymp$ (D), where D is an axiom.
2. Y $\asymp$ (D, P), where P is a *proof*, and D is an immediate consequence of $\{P\}_0$.
3. Y $\asymp$ (D, P, Q), where P and Q are *proofs*, and D is an immediate consequence of $\{P\}_0$ and $\{Q\}_0$.

Dn13. A(a) is a formula, x is a natural number, and Y is a *proof of* the formula A($\boldsymbol{x}$) (as a predicate of A(a), x, Y). (Abbreviation: $\mathfrak{Pf}$(A(a), x, Y).)

*1. A(a) contains a free, $\mathfrak{Pf}$(Y), and there is an $\boldsymbol{x}$ such that $\mathfrak{Nu}(\boldsymbol{x}, x)$ and $\mathfrak{S}(\{Y\}_0, A(a), \boldsymbol{x}, a)$.

2. A(a) does not contain a free, $\mathfrak{Pf}$(Y) and $\{Y\}_0 \asymp A(a)$.

Dn13a. For each n distinct variables $x_1, \ldots, x_n$ and formula $A(x_1, \ldots, x_n)$: Y is a *proof of* $A(\boldsymbol{x}_1, \ldots, \boldsymbol{x}_n)$. (Abbreviation: $\mathfrak{Pf}_{x_1,\ldots,x_n,A(x_1,\ldots,x_n)}(x_1, \ldots, x_n, Y)$ or $\mathfrak{Pf}_A(x_1, \ldots, x_n, Y)$.) Similarly.

§ 52. Gödel numbering. We now complete the arithmetization of metamathematics by representing the generalized arithmetic within the arithmetic of the natural numbers. First, we correlate distinct odd numbers to the zero entities, thus:

⊃	&	∨	¬	∀	∃	=	+	·	′	0	a	|
3	5	7	9	11	13	15	17	19	21	23	25	27

Then, whenever $\mathrm{x}_0, \ldots, \mathrm{x}_s$ are entities to which respective numbers $x_0, \ldots, x_s$ have already been correlated, we correlate to the successor entity $(\mathrm{x}_0, \ldots, \mathrm{x}_s)$ the number $p_0^{x_0} \cdot \ldots \cdot p_s^{x_s}$ (#18 § 45).

By a mathematical induction corresponding to the definition of entity a natural number > 0 is thereby correlated to each entity. This number we call the *Gödel number* of the entity, or say that it *represents* the entity (or formal linguistic object to which the entity in turn is correlated). Since only even numbers are correlated to successor entities (because $p_0 = 2$ and $x_0 \neq 0$), and because a given positive integer has the form $p_0^{x_0} \cdot \ldots \cdot p_s^{x_s}$ $(x_0, \ldots, x_s > 0)$ for at most one s and $x_0, \ldots, x_s$, distinct numbers are correlated to distinct entities.

Example 1. The Gödel number of $\exists b(\neg b=0)$, or as an entity $(\exists, (_{|}, a), (\neg, (=, (_{|}, a), 0)))$, is $2^{13} \cdot 3^{2^{27} \cdot 3^{25}} \cdot 5^{2^{9} \cdot 3^{2^{15} \cdot 3^{2^{27} \cdot 3^{25}} \cdot 5^{23}}}$

Since $x_i < p_0^{x_0} \cdot \ldots \cdot p_s^{x_s}$ for $0 \leq i \leq s$, entities x and y in the relationship $\mathrm{x} \prec \mathrm{y}$ are always represented by natural numbers x and y in the relationship $x < y$. (However $x < y$ may hold for pairs of numbers x and y correlated to entities x and y without $\mathrm{x} \prec \mathrm{y}$ holding; e.g. $3 < 5$ but not $\supset \prec \&$.)

If x is an entity of the successor form $(\mathrm{x}_0, \ldots, \mathrm{x}_s)$ with $s \geq i$, and x is the Gödel number of x, the Gödel number of the predecessor $\{\mathrm{x}\}_i$ is $(x)_i$ (#19 § 45).

When we pass from entities to their Gödel numbers, a predicate or function of entities becomes a predicate or function of Gödel numbers. A number-theoretic predicate or function obtained by extending the definition of the latter to all natural numbers we say *corresponds* to the original predicate. In particular, in the case of a predicate $\mathfrak{P}(\mathrm{x}_1, \ldots, \mathrm{x}_n)$, we shall understand by *the* corresponding number-theoretic predicate $P(x_1, \ldots, x_n)$ that one which is obtained by taking the value to be $\mathfrak{f}$ whenever not all of $x_1, \ldots, x_n$ are Gödel numbers; i.e.

$$P(x_1, \ldots, x_n) \equiv \{x_1, \ldots, x_n \text{ are Gödel numbers of entities } \mathrm{x}_1, \ldots, \mathrm{x}_n, \text{ and } \mathfrak{P}(\mathrm{x}_1, \ldots, \mathrm{x}_n)\}.$$

Similarly when some of the variables of the original predicate already range over natural numbers (e.g. Dn11 § 51).

Lemma 19. *For each of the predicates defined by* Dn1 — Dn13, Dn13a, *the corresponding number-theoretic predicate is primitive recursive.*

Proof. To illustrate the method, let us treat Dn3, assuming Dn2 already treated.

We can write Dn3 symbolically as follows.

$$\begin{aligned}
&\mathfrak{T}(\mathrm{y}) \equiv \mathrm{y} \asymp 0\\
&\qquad \vee\ \mathfrak{V}(\mathrm{y})\\
(1)\quad &\qquad \vee\ [\mathrm{y} \asymp (+, \{\mathrm{y}\}_1, \{\mathrm{y}\}_2) \ \&\ \mathfrak{T}(\{\mathrm{y}\}_1) \ \&\ \mathfrak{T}(\{\mathrm{y}\}_2)]\\
&\qquad \vee\ [\mathrm{y} \asymp (\cdot, \{\mathrm{y}\}_1, \{\mathrm{y}\}_2) \ \&\ \mathfrak{T}(\{\mathrm{y}\}_1) \ \&\ \mathfrak{T}(\{\mathrm{y}\}_2)]\\
&\qquad \vee\ [\mathrm{y} \asymp (\,', \{\mathrm{y}\}_1) \ \&\ \mathfrak{T}(\{\mathrm{y}\}_1)].
\end{aligned}$$

The five disjunctive members correspond to the five clauses of Dn3 as given in § 51. For the third clause we observe that if $\mathrm{y} \asymp \mathrm{r}+\mathrm{s}$, i.e. $\mathrm{y} \asymp (+, \mathrm{r}, \mathrm{s})$, for any entities r and s, then $\mathrm{r} \asymp \{\mathrm{y}\}_1$, $\mathrm{s} \asymp \{\mathrm{y}\}_2$. The fact that $\mathrm{y} \asymp (+, \mathrm{r}, \mathrm{s})$ for some entities r and s is then expressed by $\mathrm{y} \asymp (+, \{\mathrm{y}\}_1, \{\mathrm{y}\}_2)$.

In (1) let us replace the zero entities $+$, $\cdot$, $'$, 0 by their Gödel numbers 17, 19, 21, 23, the assumed predicate $\mathfrak{V}(\mathrm{y})$ by its corresponding number-theoretic predicate $V(y)$, $\asymp$ by $=$, successor entities $(\mathrm{x}_0, \ldots, \mathrm{x}_s)$ by $p_0^{x_0} \cdot \ldots \cdot p_s^{x_s}$, predecessors $\{\mathrm{y}\}_i$ by $(y)_i$, and write $T(y)$ instead of $\mathfrak{T}(\mathrm{y})$ for the predicate being defined. This leads formally to the following number-theoretic equivalence.

$$\begin{aligned}
&T(y) \equiv y=23\\
&\qquad \vee\ V(y)\\
(2)\quad &\qquad \vee\ [y=2^{17} \cdot 3^{(y)_1} \cdot 5^{(y)_2} \ \&\ T((y)_1) \ \&\ T((y)_2)]\\
&\qquad \vee\ [y=2^{19} \cdot 3^{(y)_1} \cdot 5^{(y)_2} \ \&\ T((y)_1) \ \&\ T((y)_2)]\\
&\qquad \vee\ [y=2^{21} \cdot 3^{(y)_1} \ \&\ T((y)_1)].
\end{aligned}$$

Now (2) defines a predicate $T(y)$ by course-of-values recursion in the arithmetic of the natural numbers, since $(y)_i < y$ for $y \neq 0$; and by #G with ##2, 3, 14, 19, A, C, D and our hypothesis that V is primitive recursive, $T(y)$ is primitive recursive (cf. Example 3 § 46).

It remains to prove that the predicate $T(y)$ defined by (2) is the number-theoretic predicate corresponding to $\mathfrak{T}(\mathrm{y})$. For this purpose, we prove two propositions by course-of-values induction on y:

(a) *If* $T(y)$ (by (2)), *then y is the Gödel number of an entity* y *such that* $\mathfrak{T}(\mathrm{y})$ (by (1)).

(b) *If* $\mathfrak{T}(\mathrm{y})$ (by (1)), *and y is the Gödel number of* y, *then* $T(y)$ (by (2)).

Proofs. (a) By (2), $T(y)$ is true only when one of the disjunctive members (or "clauses") on the right of (2) is true; so we have five cases to treat. Case 2: $V(y)$. Then, since V is the predicate corresponding to $\mathfrak{V}$, y is the Gödel number of a variable y, i.e. $\mathfrak{V}(\mathrm{y})$; and by the corresponding clause of (1), $\mathfrak{T}(\mathrm{y})$. Case 3: $y = 2^{17} \cdot 3^{(y)_1} \cdot 5^{(y)_2} \ \&\ T((y)_1) \ \&\ T((y)_2)$. Then $(y)_1, (y)_2 < y$; so from $T((y)_1) \ \&\ T((y)_2)$ by the hypothesis of the induction on y, $(y)_1$ and $(y)_2$ are Gödel numbers of entities r and s such that $\mathfrak{T}(\mathrm{r})$ and $\mathfrak{T}(\mathrm{s})$. Then y $(= 2^{17} \cdot 3^{(y)_1} \cdot 5^{(y)_2})$ is the Gödel number of $(+, \mathrm{r}, \mathrm{s})$.

Calling the latter y, then r $\asymp$ $\{y\}_1$, s $\asymp$ $\{y\}_2$; so y $\asymp$ (+, $\{y\}_1$, $\{y\}_2$) & $\mathfrak{T}(\{y\}_1)$ & $\mathfrak{T}(\{y\}_2)$, and by the respective clause of (1), $\mathfrak{T}$(y). The proof of (b) is similar, with cases from the disjunctive members (or "clauses") on the right of (1).

The other definitions of predicates in the list Dn1 — Dn13, Dn13a are handled similarly, except as noted below for the recursions on two variables and for the starred clauses. After translating (as from (1) to (2)), the number-theoretic predicate defined is true only for Gödel numbers as arguments, since in each clause of the original definition each variable entity is required to satisfy an earlier predicate of the list, or is a successor of entities which are fixed or must satisfy such predicates or the predicate being defined. For example, we translate Clause 1Dn9 as

$$e=2^3 \cdot 3^{(e)_1} \cdot 5^{(e)_2} \ \& \ d=2^3 \cdot 3^{(e)_1} \cdot 5^{2^{11} \cdot 3^{(d)_{2,1}} \cdot 5^{(e)_2}} \ \& \ V((d)_{2,1}) \\ \& \ F((e)_2) \ \& \ F((e)_1) \ \& \ \overline{CF}((e)_1, (d)_{2,1}),$$

where "$(d)_{2,1}$" abbreviates "$((d)_2)_1$". Note that $\overline{CF}(e, x)$ is not quite the number-theoretic predicate corresponding to $\overline{\mathfrak{CF}}$(E, x), since it is true when e or x is not a Gödel number. But this does not matter here, since $(e)_1$ occurs also in $F((e)_1)$ and $(d)_{2,1}$ also in $V((d)_{2,1})$, corresponding to the stipulations in 1Dn9 that C is a formula and x is a variable.

Dn5 and Dn11 are recursions (of a simple kind) on two variables. For Dn5, e.g., let $T(z, t, x) \equiv \{z = 2^d \cdot 3^e \text{ where } S(d, e, t, x)\}$. Then T satisfies a course-of-values recursion on the one variable z, and $S(d, e, t, x) \equiv T(2^d \cdot 3^e, t, x)$.

It remains to consider the starred clauses 11 and 12Dn8, and 1Dn13 and 1Dn13a. We translate 11Dn8 as

$$(Et)_{t<d}[d=2^3 \cdot 3^{2^{11} \cdot 3^{(d)_{1,1}} \cdot 5^{(d)_{1,2}}} \cdot 5^{(d)_2} \ \& \ CF((d)_{1,2}, (d)_{1,1}) \\ \& \ F(t, (d)_{1,1}, (d)_{1,2}) \ \& \ S((d)_2, (d)_{1,2}, t, (d)_{1,1})],$$

and use #E. The bound $t<d$ is justified, since when A(x) contains x free, t $\prec$ A(t) $\prec$ $\forall$xA(x) $\supset$ A(t) $\asymp$ D. We translate 1Dn13 as

$$CF(a, 25) \ \& \ Pf(y) \ \& \ (En)_{n<y}[Nu(n, x) \ \& \ S((y)_0, a, n, 25)].$$

This completes the proof of Lemma 19. The gist of this proof is that the primitive recursions in the generalized arithmetic become course-of-values recursions in the ordinary arithmetic, since the Gödel numbering preserves the order relationships although it destroys the relationships of immediate succession. It is necessary to verify that the range of each variable which we elected to introduce with a quantifier rather than as a function of the independent variables of the predicate being defined (e.g. t in 11Dn8 and x in 1Dn13) can be restricted.

LEMMA 20. *Under the Gödel numbering of this section, the predicates* $A(a, b)$ *and* $B(a, c)$ *of Lemma* 21 § 42 *are primitive recursive.*

PROOF. By Lemma 19, since we can express $A(a, b)$ and $B(a, c)$ in terms of the number-theoretic predicate $Pf(a, x, y)$ corresponding to the predicate $\mathfrak{Pf}(\mathrm{A}(a), x, \mathrm{Y})$ of Dn13 thus,

$$A(a, b) \equiv Pf(a, a, b), \qquad B(a, c) \equiv Pf(2^9 \cdot 3^a, a, c).$$

Lemma 21 § 42 follows now using Corollary Theorem 27 § 49.

THEOREM 31. *For any given formula* $\mathrm{A}(a)$ (*cf.* Dn13), *the predicate* '$\mathrm{A}(\boldsymbol{x})$ *is provable*' (*as predicate of* x, *where* $\boldsymbol{x}$ *is the numeral for* x) *is expressible in the form* $(Ey)R(x, y)$ *where* R *is primitive recursive; i.e. given a formula* $\mathrm{A}(a)$, *a primitive recursive predicate* $R(x, y)$ *can be found such that*

$$(Ey)R(x, y) \equiv \vdash \mathrm{A}(\boldsymbol{x}).$$

(*Similarly for* $\mathrm{A}(\mathrm{x}_1, \ldots, \mathrm{x}_n)$; *cf.* Dn13a.)

PROOF. A formula is provable, if and only if there exists a proof of it. Let a be the Gödel number of the particular formula $\mathrm{A}(a)$ of the hypothesis of the theorem, and set

$$R(x, y) \equiv Pf(a, x, y).$$

(For $\mathrm{A}(\mathrm{x}_1, \ldots, \mathrm{x}_n)$, set $R(x_1, \ldots, x_n, y) \equiv Pf_{\mathrm{A}}(x_1, \ldots, x_n, y)$.)

EXAMPLE 2. Let $\mathfrak{S}(\mathrm{E}, \mathrm{t}, \mathrm{x}) \asymp$ {the result of substituting t for x in E, if t is a term, x is a variable, and E is a term or formula; otherwise, E}; and let $\mathfrak{Nu}(x) \asymp$ {the numeral $\boldsymbol{x}$ for the natural number x}. These metamathematical functions $\mathfrak{S}(\mathrm{E}, \mathrm{t}, \mathrm{x})$ and $\mathfrak{Nu}(x)$ can be defined by recursion, similarly to the predicates $\mathfrak{S}(\mathrm{D}, \mathrm{E}, \mathrm{t}, \mathrm{x})$ (Dn5) and $\mathfrak{Nu}(\boldsymbol{x}, x)$ (Dn11); and the corresponding number-theoretic functions $S(e, t, x)$ ($= e$, when e, t, x are not all Gödel numbers) and $Nu(x)$ are primitive recursive.

***§ 53. Inductive and recursive definitions.** The definitions of 'term' and 'formula' were given originally in § 17 as inductive definitions. Other examples of inductive definitions are the definition of 'natural number' (§ 6), of 'provable formula' in the first version (§ 19), of 'primitive recursive function' if phrased similarly (§ 43), and of 'entity' (§ 50). The results of this chapter may be viewed in terms of the relationship between inductive and recursive definitions. We begin with a few remarks about inductive definitions generally.

Inductive definitions occur in two different roles, and we call them *fundamental* and *non-fundamental* accordingly. To which category a given inductive definition belongs may vary with the context or theory in which it is being used.

For the generalized arithmetic, the definition of 'entity' is the fundamental inductive definition. It establishes the domain of objects for the arithmetic. An entity is thereafter understood to be given, when and only when its mode of generation under the inductive definition of 'entity' is given.

Then the non-fundamental inductive definitions, such as those of 'term', 'formula' and 'provable formula', apply to objects already known in their status as entities. These definitions each define a class of entities, i.e. a subclass of the entities. We can ask in the arithmetic whether or not a given entity belongs to the subclass; and we can associate with the subclass a predicate taking the value t for an entity belonging to the subclass and f for an entity not belonging. We can regard the non-fundamental inductive definitions as definitions of these predicates.

Thus the fundamental inductive definition establishes the range of a variable, over which one may subsequently define predicates by non-fundamental inductive definitions (including as a special case the constant predicate t).

The manner in which a non-fundamental inductive definition defines a predicate is the following. The *direct clauses* tell us certain objects for which the predicate takes the value t. The *extremal clause* says that those are the only objects for which the value is t, so that we can attribute the value f whenever we are able to see that the direct clauses do not require the value to be t.

The direct clauses generally include *basic clauses*, each of which tells us outright (or under hypotheses involving only previously defined predicates) that the value is t for a certain object, and *inductive clauses*, each of which tells us that, if the value is t for certain objects (and possibly under hypotheses involving previously defined predicates), then the value is t for the object related to those in a given way. (If basic clauses are missing, then the predicate takes the value f for all arguments. If inductive clauses are missing, the definition is simply an explicit definition by cases.)

Non-fundamental inductive definitions can also be used to define predicates of more than one variable. Such a definition sometimes has the form of an inductive definition of a class depending on a parameter (e.g. that of '$<$' § 6), and in general it can be considered as the inductive definition of a class of ordered n-tuples.

Inductive definitions, both fundamental and non-fundamental, justify corresponding forms of 'proof by mathematical induction'. Those corresponding to the inductive definitions of 'natural number' and 'entity' have already been mentioned (§§ 7, 50). As another example, the principle of induction corresponding to the inductive definition of 'provable formula' is this: If every axiom has a certain property, and if whenever the premises for a formal inference have the property so does the conclusion, then every provable formula has the property. (This induction principle could have been invoked for the proof of Theorem 9 § 28, instead of course-of-values induction on the length of a proof. Then Lemmas 12a and 12b themselves constitute the basis and induction steps of the proof.)

In the same way, fundamental inductive definitions (under the convention that differently generated objects are distinct) justify 'definitions by induction' or 'recursive definitions' of a function over the domain established by the inductive definition. (But a recursive procedure corresponding to a non-fundamental inductive definition of a class which allows an object to be recognized as in the class by different successions of applications of the direct clauses may lead to more than one function value for such an object, e.g. "$\varphi(A) = 0$ if A is an axiom, $\varphi(A) = \varphi(B) + 1$ if A is an immediate consequence of B, and $\varphi(A) = \varphi(B) + \varphi(C) + 1$ if A is an immediate consequence of B and C" does not define a single-valued function φ from provable formulas to natural numbers.)

Predicates can be introduced from recursively defined functions serving as their representing functions, or often as we have seen in § 51 by recursive procedures directly.

In recursions (of such kinds as we have been considering for the simple arithmetic in Chapter IX) the value of a function or predicate, say of one variable, for any given non-zero argument is determined from the values of the same for only arguments preceding the given argument in terms of the order of generation of the domain by the fundamental inductive definition. This has the consequence that we can prove by a corresponding induction that a recursively defined predicate takes the value $\mathfrak{t}$ or $\mathfrak{f}$ for every argument. Thus the law of the excluded middle is proved intuitionistically to apply to every proposition taken as value of a recursively defined predicate.

This is not in general so for an inductively defined predicate, as the use of the extremal clause to assign the value $\mathfrak{f}$ whenever the direct clauses do not assign the value $\mathfrak{t}$ may leave us without the knowledge of effective means to determine which is the value for any given argument(s).

In a special case it is so, namely (e.g. for the inductive definition of a class) when the order in which the inductive clauses introduce members of the class agrees with the order of generation of the objects under the fundamental inductive definition. It is inductive definitions of this sort which we can recast as recursive definitions, as we did for those of 'term' and 'formula' in § 51.

An inductive definition not of this sort is that of 'provable formula' in the first version (§ 19). In the second version, the definition is set apart from the metamathematical definitions of § 51 by the fact that an existential quantifier "there exists a proof Y" is used without a bound being known for its variable Y (in contrast to 11—12Dn8 and 1Dn13). (Cf. § 30.) From this second version, we obtain as the corresponding number-theoretic predicate $(Ey)[Pf(y) \; \& \; (y)_0=d]$ (cf. Dn12), which is of the form $(Ey)R(d, y)$ where R is primitive recursive.

When the form of an inductive definition (with elementary direct clauses) is specified in a natural way, the predicates $P(x_1, \ldots, x_n)$ definable by use of inductive definitions in the natural number arithmetic are exactly those expressible in the form $(Ey)R(x_1, \ldots, x_n, y)$ with R primitive recursive. The proof can be given by an extension of the above methods, as was suggested in Kleene 1943 pp. 66—67; or by another method, indicated in Kleene 1944* p. 48.

CHAPTER XI

GENERAL RECURSIVE FUNCTIONS

§ 54. Formal calculation of primitive recursive functions. Each of the schemata (I) — (V) of § 43 considered intuitively is an operation defining a function φ from zero or more given functions. Actually we stated the schemata by means of equations.

Let us review the manner in which the equations define the function φ, to see whether we cannot analyze our use of them in determining particular values of φ into formal operations.

EXAMPLE 1. Let χ be a given function, two of whose values are:

1. $\chi(0, 4) = 7$. 2. $\chi(1, 7) = 7$.

Let φ be introduced by Schema (Va) with $q = 4$, thus:

3. $\varphi(0) = 4$. 4. $\varphi(y') = \chi(y, \varphi(y))$.

In § 43 we convinced ourselves that, for any number y, the recursion equations for φ determine the corresponding value $\varphi(y)$ of φ, if the values of χ are already determined. In particular, with the two values of χ just given, the reasoning of § 43 tells us that $\varphi(2) = 7$. We now ask: What sorts of formal inferences will enable us to deduce the equation "$\varphi(2) = 7$" from Equations 1 — 4?

Substituting "0" for "y" in Equation 4:

5. $\varphi(1) = \chi(0, \varphi(0))$.

Replacing "$\varphi(0)$" in the right member of Equation 5 by "4" from Equation 3:

6. $\varphi(1) = \chi(0, 4)$.

Four more steps of these two sorts complete the deduction:

7. $\varphi(1) = 7$ — Replacement, 6, 1.
8. $\varphi(2) = \chi(1, \varphi(1))$ — Substitution, 4.
9. $\varphi(2) = \chi(1, 7)$ — Replacement, 8, 7.
10. $\varphi(2) = 7$ — Replacement, 9, 2.

Thus a substitution and a replacement operation suffice for the deduction from the given equations 1 — 4 of the equation "$\varphi(2) = 7$" which states that the value of φ for the argument 2 is 7. Moreover, quite evidently, no succession of these two sorts of inferences can lead from Equations 1 — 4 to any other equation whose left member is "$\varphi(2)$" and whose right member is a numeral.

EXAMPLE 2. Suppose now more particularly that χ is the constant function (C_7^2) defined by the equation

—2. $$\chi(y, z) = 7,$$

while φ is defined from χ as in Example 1. (Then φ is primitive recursive, with χ, φ as a primitive recursive description.) Now we can deduce Equations 1 and 2 from Equation —2 by substitution, as follows:

—1. $\chi(0, z) = 7$ — Subst., —2. 0. $\chi(1, z) = 7$ — Subst., —2.

1. $\chi(0, 4) = 7$ — Subst., —1. 2. $\chi(1, 7) = 7$ — Subst., 0.

Combining these two deductions with that of Example 1, we obtain a deduction of "$\varphi(2) = 7$" from the three equations —2, 3, 4 defining φ ab initio.

In these examples we have been considering questions of a formal kind, without having explicitly set up a formal system in advance. We shall now establish a suitable formal system, and make our discussion rigorous as a metamathematical discussion referring to this system.

The new formal system we call the *formalism* (or *formal system*) *of recursive functions*. We describe it now in the linguistic manner, and later (§ 56) as a generalized arithmetic.

The *formal symbols* of the system are as follows: = (equals), ′(successor), 0 (zero), $a, b, c, \ldots, a_1, a_2, \ldots$ (variables for natural numbers), $f, g, h, \ldots, f_1, f_2, \ldots$ (function letters, i.e. symbols for unspecified number-theoretic functions), (,) (parentheses), and , (comma). A (potentially) infinite list of variables and of function letters are supposed to be given.

We call $f, g, h, \ldots, f_1, f_2, \ldots$ "function letters" rather than "function symbols" here to distinguish them from ′. Also the name is appropriate, because they will have a role similar to that of the predicate letters in the pure predicate calculus, i.e. they are to be interpreted as expressing different functions at different times, but there is no postulated rule of substitution for them. In discussions in which f, g, h, etc. express fixed functions, and are not being treated differently from e.g. ′, +, ·, we may call them "function symbols".

The formal expressions 0, 0′, 0″, ... we call *numerals*. As before (§ 41), we abbreviate them respectively by "0", "1", "2", ... ; and we continue to use the convention whereby "$\boldsymbol{x}$", "$\boldsymbol{y}$", etc. designate the numerals for the natural numbers designated respectively by "x", "y", etc.

The *terms* are 0, the variables, and expressions of the form r′ where r is a *term*, or $f(r_1, \ldots, r_n)$ where f is a function letter and $r_1, \ldots, r_n$ are *terms* ($n \geq 0$, omitting the parentheses when $n = 0$).

A formal expression r=s where r and s are terms is an *equation*. The equations are the only "formulas" for this system. By a *system of equations* we mean a finite sequence $e_0, \ldots, e_s$ of equations (not empty, unless otherwise stated).

No axioms will be provided; and we shall define only 'deducibility' but not 'provability'.

The rules of inference shall be a one-premise substitution rule R1 and a two-premise replacement rule R2, as follows.

R1: to pass from an equation d containing a variable y to the equation which results from d by substituting a numeral $\boldsymbol{y}$ for y.

R2: to pass from an equation r=s containing no variables (the *major premise*) and an equation $h(\boldsymbol{z}_1, \ldots, \boldsymbol{z}_p)=\boldsymbol{z}$ where h is a function letter and $\boldsymbol{z}_1, \ldots, \boldsymbol{z}_p, \boldsymbol{z}$ are numerals (the *minor premise*) to the equation which results from r=s by replacing an occurrence of $h(\boldsymbol{z}_1, \ldots, \boldsymbol{z}_p)$ in s (or several such occurrences simultaneously) by $\boldsymbol{z}$.

A *deduction of* an equation e (the *endequation* of the deduction) *from* a system (or set, possibly infinite) E of equations is to be one in tree form (end § 24); i.e. it shall have one of the three forms

c where c is one of the equations of E,

$\dfrac{\text{W}}{\text{c}}$ where W is a deduction from E, and c is an immediate consequence by R1 of the endequation of W, or

$\dfrac{\text{W X}}{\text{c}}$ where W and X are deductions from E, and c is an immediate consequence by R2 of the endequations of W and X respectively.

If there is a deduction of e from E, then e is *deducible from* E (in symbols, E ⊢ e).

EXAMPLE 2 (continued). Translating Equations —2 to 10 into the new formalism (using the formal function letters *f*, *h* for the intuitive function letters "φ", "χ", and *b*, *c* for the intuitive number variables "*y*", "*z*"), and going over from the sequence to the tree form, we obtain the following figure.

(a)

$$
\begin{array}{llll}
4_2.\ f(b')=h(b,f(b)) & & & \\
\hline
5.\ f(1)=h(0,f(0)) & 3.\ f(0)=4 & -2_1.\ h(b,c)=7 & \\
\hline
 & \quad | & -1.\ h(0,c)=7 & \\
\hline
4_1.\ f(b')=h(b,f(b)) & 6.\ f(1)=h(0,4) & 1.\ h(0,4)=7 & -2_2.\ h(b,c)=7 \\
\hline
8.\ f(2)=h(1,f(1)) & & 7.\ f(1)=7 & 0.\ h(1,c)=7 \\
\hline
 & 9.\ f(2)=h(1,7) & & 2.\ h(1,7)=7 \\
\hline
 & & 10.\ f(2)=7 &
\end{array}
$$

This is a deduction of the equation $f(2)=7$ from the system of equations

$$
\text{(b)} \quad \left\{\begin{array}{l} h(b,c)=7, \\ f(0)=4, \\ f(b')=h(b,f(b)). \end{array}\right. \quad \begin{array}{l} \} \ (\mathrm{b}_1) \\ \\ \} \ (\mathrm{b}_2) \end{array}
$$

Example 1 (continued). Consider the part of the tree (a) without the (occurrences of) equations -2_1, -1, -2_2, 0, call it (a_2). This is a deduction of $f(2)=7$ from $h(0,4)=7$, $h(1,7)=7$ and (b_2).

Remark 1. One may ask: Why take the trouble of translating? The reasons are of course the same as those which dictated our use of a special symbolism in the number-theoretic formal system of Chapter IV, distinct from the symbolism of intuitive number theory. Recapitulating: The translation now from "φ", "χ", "y", "z" to *f*, *h*, *b*, *c* is called for under the linguistic conception of a formalism, because the formal symbols must be from a fixed preassigned list of symbols considered in the metamathematics as mere marks. To use these autonymously (§§ 50, 16) without risk of confusion, most of them should be from a special alphabet. Under the conception of a formalism as a generalized arithmetic, we may if we wish consider that *f* is (i.e. that "*f*" is a name for) "φ" (but then it is a name for "φ" only, and not sometimes for "ψ", etc.). The "f" used e.g. in the definition of 'term', on the other hand, is a name for an unspecified one of *f*, *g*, *h*, etc. (and if we consider that "*f*" is a name for "φ", "*g*" for "ψ", "*h*" for "χ", etc., then "f" is a name for an unspecified one of "φ", "ψ", "χ", etc.). The net result of translating is to enable us to talk clearly about the symbols as distinguished from the functions, numbers, etc. without going to the trouble of continually using quotation marks and related devices (such as Quine's "corners" 1940).

Suppose that a function φ of *n* variables has been defined intuitively from l (≥ 0) functions $\psi_1, \ldots, \psi_l$ of $m_1, \ldots, m_l$ variables, respectively. Before we can discuss whether a given system E of equations "defines" φ from $\psi_1, \ldots, \psi_l$ in the formalism, we must say which function letters $\mathrm{f}, \mathrm{g}_1, \ldots, \mathrm{g}_l$ are to express $\varphi, \psi_1, \ldots, \psi_l$, respectively.

It is convenient to employ conventions which make these letters recognizable from E itself. It suffices to consider systems E in which the first (leftmost) symbol of the last equation is a function letter f; and we call this the *principal function letter* of E, and use it to express φ. The distinct function letters which occur in right members of equations of E but not in left members we call the *given function letters* of E. It suffices to consider systems E in which there are l of these; and we use them $g_1, \ldots, g_l$ in the order of their occurrence in the preassigned list of function letters to express $\psi_1, \ldots, \psi_l$, respectively. It suffices to use systems E in which f, $g_1, \ldots, g_l$ occur only in terms formed with $n, m_1, \ldots, m_l$ arguments, respectively (or we could for the present purpose count as distinct a function letter with each number of arguments, as we did predicate letters in § 31); we then call the other function letters (if any) occurring in equations of E the *auxiliary function letters* of E.

When $l > 0$, we shall need to have available as "assumption equations" not only the system E which we associate with the scheme defining φ from $\psi_1, \ldots, \psi_l$, but also equations giving the values of the functions $\psi_1, \ldots, \psi_l$. Let "$E^{\psi_1 \ldots \psi_l}_{g_1 \ldots g_l}$" denote the set of the equations $g_j(\boldsymbol{y}_1, \ldots, \boldsymbol{y}_{m_j}) = \boldsymbol{y}$ where $\psi_j(y_1, \ldots, y_{m_j}) = y$, for $j = 1, \ldots, l$ and all m_j-tuples $y_1, \ldots, y_{m_j}$ of natural numbers ($\boldsymbol{y}_1, \ldots, \boldsymbol{y}_{m_j}, \boldsymbol{y}$ being the numerals for the numbers $y_1, \ldots, y_{m_j}, y$). This set of equations is infinite, when $l > 0$ (unless $m_1 + \ldots + m_l = 0$); empty, when $l = 0$.

We bring these ideas together in the following metamathematical definition. A system E of equations *defines* φ *recursively in* (or *from*) $\psi_1, \ldots, \psi_l$, if for each n-tuple $x_1, \ldots, x_n$ of natural numbers: $E^{\psi_1 \ldots \psi_l}_{g_1 \ldots g_l}, E \vdash f(\boldsymbol{x}_1, \ldots, \boldsymbol{x}_n) = \boldsymbol{x}$, where f is the principal function letter of E, $g_1, \ldots, g_l$ are the given function letters of E in order of their occurrence in the preassigned list of function letters, and $\boldsymbol{x}$ is a numeral, if and only if $\varphi(x_1, \ldots, x_n) = x$.

In other words, E defines φ recursively from $\psi_1, \ldots, \psi_l$, if (for f, $g_1, \ldots, g_l$ as described): $E^{\psi_1 \ldots \psi_l}_{g_1 \ldots g_l}, E \vdash f(\boldsymbol{x}_1, \ldots, \boldsymbol{x}_n) = \boldsymbol{x}$ where $\boldsymbol{x}_1, \ldots, \boldsymbol{x}_n, \boldsymbol{x}$ are numerals, if (*completeness property*) and only if (*consistency property*) $f(\boldsymbol{x}_1, \ldots, \boldsymbol{x}_n) = \boldsymbol{x} \in E^{\varphi}_{f}$.

EXAMPLES 1 AND 2 (continued). The principal function letter of (b) is *f*; *h* is an auxiliary function letter; and quite evidently (b) defines recursively the function φ (where $\varphi(y) = 4$ if $y = 0$, and $\varphi(y) = 7$ if $y > 0$). The system (b_1) defines χ ($= C^2_7$) recursively; and (b_2) defines φ recursively from χ, with *h* as the given function letter.

THEOREM II. *If φ is primitive recursive in $\psi_1, \ldots, \psi_l$, then there is a system* E *of equations which defines φ recursively from $\psi_1, \ldots, \psi_l$.*

It is quite evident that we obtain such a system E by translating the schema applications for any primitive recursive derivation $\varphi_1, \ldots, \varphi_k$ of φ from $\psi_1, \ldots, \psi_l$ into the formalism, if we choose the function letters suitably, and if we first arrange (if necessary) to have each ψ_j used in some schema application (since our conventions provide that $\psi_1, \ldots, \psi_l$ be expressed by function letters $\mathrm{g}_1, \ldots, \mathrm{g}_l$, respectively, all occurring in E). However we shall give the metamathematical analysis in detail, with five lemmas, to lay the basis for brief treatment of similar matters later.

By the *principal branch* of a deduction, we mean the branch which, traced upward from the endequation, contains the major premise at each application of R2. The equation which stands at the top of the principal branch we call the *principal equation.* The deductions (occurring as parts of the given deduction) of the minor premises for the applications of R2 along the principal branch we call the *contributory deductions.*

EXAMPLE 2 (continued). The principal branch of (a), read downwards, consists of the equations numbered 4_1, 8, 9, 10. The principal equation is $f(b')=h(b, f(b))$. The two contributory deductions are the trees ending with 7 and with 2.

The principal branch of a deduction of an equation of the form $\mathrm{f}(\boldsymbol{x}_1, \ldots, \boldsymbol{x}_n)=\boldsymbol{x}$ where f is a function letter and $\boldsymbol{x}_1, \ldots, \boldsymbol{x}_n, \boldsymbol{x}$ are numerals, read downwards, consists of zero or more applications of R1, followed by zero or more applications of R2. The applications of R1 substitute respective numerals for the variables of the principal equation, until the left member becomes $\mathrm{f}(\boldsymbol{x}_1, \ldots, \boldsymbol{x}_n)$. The applications of R2 replace parts $\mathrm{h}(\boldsymbol{z}_1, \ldots, \boldsymbol{z}_p)$ in the right member (originally present or resulting in the course of these replacements) by respective numerals $\boldsymbol{z}$, until the right member becomes $\boldsymbol{x}$.

By the *identical schema,* we mean:

$$\varphi(x_1, \ldots, x_n) = \psi(x_1, \ldots, x_n).$$

LEMMA IIa. *If φ is an immediate dependent of $\psi_1, \ldots, \psi_l$ by one of Schemata* (I) — (V) *or the identical schema, then the system* E *of equations obtained by translating the informal equations of the schema application into the formalism (with any appropriate choice of the function letters) defines φ recursively from $\psi_1, \ldots, \psi_l$.*

PROOF OF LEMMA IIa. The proofs parallel the informal reasoning by which we recognized that the schema applications define the functions.

SCHEMA (Vb). The E is of the form $f(0, x_2, \ldots, x_n)=g(x_2, \ldots, x_n)$, $f(y', x_2, \ldots, x_n)=h(y, f(y, x_2, \ldots, x_n), x_2, \ldots, x_n)$. Choose any $n-1$ numbers $x_2, \ldots, x_n$. We use induction on x_1. BASIS: $x_1 = 0$. Then $\varphi(x_1, \ldots, x_n) = \psi(x_2, \ldots, x_n)$. Now $E^{\psi\chi}_{gh}, E \vdash f(\boldsymbol{x}_1, \ldots, \boldsymbol{x}_n)=\boldsymbol{x}$ for $x = \varphi(x_1, \ldots, x_n)$, using the first equation of E as the principal equation, and the equation $g(\boldsymbol{x}_2, \ldots, \boldsymbol{x}_n)=\boldsymbol{x}$ from $E^{\psi\chi}_{gh}$ as a minor premise for R2. Moreover, to deduce $f(\boldsymbol{x}_1, \ldots, \boldsymbol{x}_n)=\boldsymbol{x}$ for any numeral $\boldsymbol{x}$, we must use the same principal equation and the same substitutions of numerals by R1 (apart from their order), since from no other equation of $E^{\psi\chi}_{gh}$, E and by no other substitutions can we obtain an equation with $f(\boldsymbol{x}_1, \ldots, \boldsymbol{x}_n)$ (for $x_1 = 0$) as left member. Then the replacement step by R2 is also uniquely determined. So $E^{\psi\chi}_{gh}, E \vdash f(\boldsymbol{x}_1, \ldots, \boldsymbol{x}_n)=\boldsymbol{x}$ with $\boldsymbol{x}$ a numeral only for $x = \varphi(x_1, \ldots, x_n)$. INDUCTION STEP: $x_1 = y'$. Similarly.

LEMMA IIb. *Let* D *be a set of equations (finite or infinite),* F *be a system of equations whose left members contain no function letters which occur in (equations of)* D, *and* g *be a function letter occurring in* D. *Then* $D, F \vdash g(\boldsymbol{y}_1, \ldots, \boldsymbol{y}_m)=\boldsymbol{y}$ *where* $\boldsymbol{y}_1, \ldots, \boldsymbol{y}_m, \boldsymbol{y}$ *are numerals, only if* $D \vdash g(\boldsymbol{y}_1, \ldots, \boldsymbol{y}_m)=\boldsymbol{y}$.

PROOF OF LEMMA IIb. Consider any deduction from D, F of an equation of the described form $g(\boldsymbol{y}_1, \ldots, \boldsymbol{y}_m)=\boldsymbol{y}$. We prove by course-of-values induction on the height t of this deduction that only equations of D are used in it as assumption equations (i.e. occur in it at the tops of branches). The principal equation is an equation of D, since its first symbol is g, which occurs in D and hence not in the left member of an equation of F. Each contributory deduction is of height $< t$, and terminates in an equation $h(\boldsymbol{z}_1, \ldots, \boldsymbol{z}_p)=\boldsymbol{z}$, where h is a function letter occurring on the right side of the principal equation, and thus in D. Therefore, by the hypothesis of the induction, the contributory deductions use only assumption equations from D.

LEMMA IIc. *Let* D *and* F *be as in Lemma* IIb. *Let* G *be the set of the equations of the form* $g(\boldsymbol{y}_1, \ldots, \boldsymbol{y}_m)=\boldsymbol{y}$, *where* g *is a function letter occurring in both* D *and* F *and* $\boldsymbol{y}_1, \ldots, \boldsymbol{y}_m, \boldsymbol{y}$ *are numerals, which are deducible from* D. *Let* f *be a function letter not occurring in* D. *Then* $D, F \vdash f(\boldsymbol{x}_1, \ldots, \boldsymbol{x}_n)=\boldsymbol{x}$ *where* $\boldsymbol{x}_1, \ldots, \boldsymbol{x}_n, \boldsymbol{x}$ *are numerals, only if* $G, F \vdash f(\boldsymbol{x}_1, \ldots, \boldsymbol{x}_n)=\boldsymbol{x}$.

PROOF OF LEMMA IIc, by course-of-values induction on the height t of the given deduction of $f(\boldsymbol{x}_1, \ldots, \boldsymbol{x}_n)=\boldsymbol{x}$ from D, F. The principal equation is an equation of F, because its first symbol is f, which does not occur in any equation of D. Any minor premise along the principal branch is of the form $h(\boldsymbol{z}_1, \ldots, \boldsymbol{z}_p)=\boldsymbol{z}$ where h occurs in the right member of the principal equation and hence in F. If h occurs in D, then using Lemma IIb $h(\boldsymbol{z}_1, \ldots, \boldsymbol{z}_p)=\boldsymbol{z}$ is an equation of the form $g(\boldsymbol{y}_1, \ldots, \boldsymbol{y}_m)=\boldsymbol{y}$ which is deducible from D, i.e. $h(\boldsymbol{z}_1, \ldots, \boldsymbol{z}_p)=\boldsymbol{z} \in$ G. If h does not occur in D, then by the hypothesis of the induction on t, $h(\boldsymbol{z}_1, \ldots, \boldsymbol{z}_p)=\boldsymbol{z}$ is deducible from G, F.

LEMMA IId. (1) *Let* $f_1, \ldots, f_k$ *be distinct function letters in order of occurrence in the given list of function letters.* (2) *Let* $\varphi_1 = \psi_1, \ldots, \varphi_l = \psi_l$. (3) *For* $i = l+1, \ldots, k$ $(k \geq l)$, *let* E_i *define* φ_i *recursively from* $\varphi_{j_{i1}}, \ldots, \varphi_{j_{iq_i}}$ $(q_i \geq 0;\ j_{i1}, \ldots, j_{iq_i} < i)$, *with* f_i *as the principal function letter, and* $f_{j_{i1}}, \ldots, f_{j_{iq_i}}$ *as the given function letters.* (4) *Let the auxiliary function letters of* E_i *(if any) be distinct from those of each* E_j *for* $j \neq i$ *and from* $f_1, \ldots, f_k$. *Then for* $i=1, \ldots, k$: $E^{\psi_1 \ldots \psi_l}_{f_1 \ldots f_l}, E_{l+1} \ldots E_k \vdash f_i(\boldsymbol{x}_1, \ldots, \boldsymbol{x}_{n_i})=\boldsymbol{x}$ *where* $\boldsymbol{x}_1, \ldots, \boldsymbol{x}_{n_i}, \boldsymbol{x}$ *are numerals, if and only if* $f_i(\boldsymbol{x}_1, \ldots, \boldsymbol{x}_{n_i})=\boldsymbol{x} \in E^{\varphi_i}_{f_i}$.

EXAMPLE 2 (concluded). Let $k = 2$; $l = 0$; φ_1, φ_2 be the primitive recursive description χ, ψ; and E_1, E_2 be (b_1), (b_2) interchanging f and h.

EXAMPLE 3. Let $\varphi_1, \ldots, \varphi_k$ (with $k = 9$, $l = 3$) be the primitive recursive derivation $\zeta, \eta, \theta, U^3_1, \theta_1, U^3_3, \psi, C^3_2, \varphi$ of Examples 1 §§ 44 and 45, and E_i ($i = 4, \ldots, 9$) be the equation (c_i):

$$(c)\quad \begin{cases} f_4(a, c, b)=a, & (c_4)\\ f_5(a, c, b)=f_3(f_4(a, c, b)), & (c_5)\\ f_6(a, c, b)=b, & (c_6)\\ f_7(a, c, b)=f_2(f_6(a, c, b), f_5(a, c, b)), & (c_7)\\ f_8(a, c, b)=2, & (c_8)\\ f_9(a, c, b)=f_1(f_4(a,c,b), f_7(a,c,b), f_8(a,c,b)). & (c_9) \end{cases}$$

PROOF OF LEMMA IId. We easily see, by general properties of $\vdash$, that $E^{\psi_1 \ldots \psi_l}_{f_1 \ldots f_l}, E_{l+1} \ldots E_k \vdash f_i(\boldsymbol{x}_1, \ldots, \boldsymbol{x}_{n_i})=\boldsymbol{x}$, if $f_i(\boldsymbol{x}_1, \ldots, \boldsymbol{x}_{n_i})=\boldsymbol{x} \in E^{\varphi_i}_{f_i}$. We prove the converse by induction on k. BASIS: $k = l$. Then $E_{l+1} \ldots E_k$ is empty. The conclusion follows by the constitution of $E^{\psi_1 \ldots \psi_l}_{f_1 \ldots f_l}$ (noting that it contains no premise for R1 and no major premise for R2). INDUCTION STEP: $k > l$. By hypothesis of the induction, only those equations of the form $f_i(\boldsymbol{x}_1, \ldots, \boldsymbol{x}_{n_i})=\boldsymbol{x}$ for $i < k$ which $\in E^{\varphi_i}_{f_i}$ are deducible from $E^{\psi_1 \ldots \psi_l}_{f_1 \ldots f_l}, E_{l+1} \ldots E_{k-1}$. By Hypothesis (3) for $i = k$

(and writing "φ" for "φ_k", "φ_{j_s}" for "$\varphi_{j_{ks}}$", "f" for "f_k", etc.), only those equations of the form $f(\boldsymbol{x}_1, \ldots, \boldsymbol{x}_n) = \boldsymbol{x}$ which $\mathcal{E}\ E^{\varphi}_{f}$ are deducible from $E^{\varphi_{j_1} \ldots \varphi_{j_q}}_{f_{j_1} \ldots f_{j_q}}$, E_k; and by Lemma IIc no others become deducible when $E^{\varphi_{j_1} \ldots \varphi_{j_q}}_{f_{j_1} \ldots f_{j_q}}$ is replaced in the list of assumption equations by

$$E^{\psi_1 \ldots \psi_l}_{f_1 \ldots f_l},\ E_{l+1} \ldots E_{k-1}.$$

LEMMA IIe. *Let* $\varphi_1, \ldots, \varphi_k$ *be a finite sequence of functions such that* φ_k *is* φ *and for each* i $(i = 1, \ldots, k)$, *either* (A) φ_i *is one of the functions* $\psi_1, \ldots, \psi_l$, *or* (B) φ_i *is defined recursively by a system* E_i *of equations from* $\varphi_{j_{i1}}, \ldots, \varphi_{j_{iq_i}}$ $(q_i \geq 0;\ j_{i1}, \ldots, j_{iq_i} < i)$. *Then there is a system* E *of equations which defines* φ *recursively from* $\psi_1, \ldots, \psi_l$.

PROOF OF LEMMA IIe. If it is not already the case that each of the ψ's is introduced under (A) as one of the φ's and is thereafter used under (B) as one of the $\varphi_{j_{i1}}, \ldots, \varphi_{j_{iq_i}}$ for some φ_i, we can make it so (increasing k) by introducing some applications of the identical schema (cf. Lemma IIa). Then, by rearranging and renumbering the φ's and E_i's and changing the function letters in the latter (if necessary), we can bring about the situation described in Lemma IId, with $k > l$, $\varphi_k = \varphi$, and with $f_1, \ldots, f_l$ as the given function letters of $E_{l+1} \ldots E_k$. Let E be $E_{l+1} \ldots E_k$.

PROOF OF THEOREM II. By Lemma IIa and the hypothesis of the theorem, the hypotheses of Lemma IIe are satisfied.

§ 55. General recursive functions. The schemata (I)—(V) are not the only schemes of definition of a number-theoretic function, ab initio or from other number-theoretic functions, which can be expressed by systems of equations, using in the equations only function letters, ′, number variables and numerals.

Let us consider other examples, calling them all "recursions". We keep the equations in the informal language for the time being; and to keep them of the sort described now, we eliminate certain other modes of expression which were used in Chapter IX, e.g. $\prod_{y<z}$ (#B), $\mu y_{y<z}$ (#E), cases (#F).

Thus (a) of Example 1 § 46 we can write now

$$\text{(a)} \qquad \begin{cases} \pi(0, y) = 1, \\ \pi(z', y) = (y + \varphi(z)) \cdot \pi(z, y), \\ \varphi(y) = \pi(y, y) \end{cases}$$

(defining the auxiliary function π as well as φ), while (a) of Example 2 § 46 is already in the form under consideration. We showed in § 46 that these course-of-values recursions are reducible to primitive recursion, i.e. the same function can be defined by a series of applications of Schemata (I) — (V).

As another very simple example, consider the recursion

$$\text{(b)} \qquad \begin{cases} \varphi(0, z) = z, \\ \varphi(y', z) = \varphi(y, \sigma(y, z)). \end{cases}$$

This is not primitive, because the z, instead of being held fixed as a parameter, has $\sigma(y, z)$ substituted for it in the induction step of the definition. This recursion too can be reduced to primitive recursion. Expanding (b) for $y = 0, 1, 2, \ldots$ (as we expanded (1) in § 43), we find that the value $\varphi(y, z)$ is

$$\sigma(0, \sigma(1, \sigma(2, \ldots \sigma(y-3, \sigma(y-2, \sigma(y-1, z)))\ldots))).$$

Consider the sequence of the numbers z, $\sigma(y-1, z)$, $\sigma(y-2, \sigma(y-1, z))$, $\ldots$, $\sigma(0, \sigma(1, \sigma(2, \ldots \sigma(y-3, \sigma(y-2, \sigma(y-1, z)))\ldots)))$, which occur in building up this value from the inside instead of as (b) gives it to us. These are the values for $u = 0, 1, 2, \ldots, y$ of the function $\mu(u, y, z)$ defined by the primitive recursion

$$\text{(b}_1\text{)} \qquad \begin{cases} \mu(0, y, z) = z, \\ \mu(u', y, z) = \sigma(y \dot{-} u', \mu(u, y, z)). \end{cases}$$

Since the value for $u = y$ is the same as the value $\varphi(y, z)$,

$$\text{(b}_2\text{)} \qquad \varphi(y, z) = \mu(y, y, z);$$

as can also be seen by using induction on u to prove that

$$\text{(c)} \qquad \mu(u', y', z) = \mu(u, y, \sigma(y, z)),$$

and thence that the φ defined by (b_1) and (b_2) satisfies (b).

In a similar manner, Péter (1934, 1935a) showed that every recursion (called "nested") in which $\varphi(0, z)$ is a given function of z, and $\varphi(y', z)$ is expressed explicitly in terms of y, z, given functions (and constants), and $\varphi(y, t)$ as a function of t, is reducible to primitive recursion.

Are there recursions which are not reducible to primitive recursion; and in particular can recursion be used to define a function which is not primitive recursive?

This question arose from a conjecture of Hilbert 1926 on the continuum problem, and was answered by Ackermann 1928. Let $\xi_0(b, a) = a+b$, $\xi_1(b, a) = a \cdot b$, $\xi_2(b, a) = a^b$; and let this series of functions be extended by successive primitive recursions of the form $\xi_{n'}(0, a) = a$, $\xi_{n'}(b', a) = \xi_n(\xi_{n'}(b, a), a)$ $(n \geq 2)$, so that e.g. $\xi_3(b, a) = a^{a^{\cdot^{\cdot^{a}}}}$ with b exponents.

Now consider $\xi_n(b, a)$ as a function $\xi(n, b, a)$ of all three variables. Let α be the primitive recursive function defined thus,

(d) $$\alpha(n, a) = \begin{cases} 0 \text{ if } n = 0, \\ 1 \text{ if } n = 1, \\ a \text{ otherwise.} \end{cases}$$

Then the following recursion defines $\xi(n, b, a)$,

(e) $$\begin{cases} \xi(0, b, a) &= a+b, \\ \xi(n', 0, a) &= \alpha(n, a), \\ \xi(n', b', a) &= \xi(n, \xi(n', b, a), a). \end{cases}$$

This is an example of a "double recursion", i.e. one on two variables simultaneously. If the function $\xi(n, b, a)$ defined by (e) were primitive recursive, then the function $\xi(a)$ of one variable defined explicitly from it thus,

(f) $$\xi(a) = \xi(a, a, a),$$

would also be primitive recursive. Ackermann's investigation shows that $\xi(a)$ grows faster with increasing a than any primitive recursive function of a (just as 2^a grows faster than any polynomial in a), i.e. given any primitive recursive function $\varphi(a)$, a natural number c can be found such that $\xi(a) > \varphi(a)$ for all $a \geq c$. Thus $\xi(a)$, and hence also $\xi(n, b, a)$ (since $\xi(a)$ comes from it by the explicit definition (f)), are not primitive recursive. This example was simplified by Péter 1935 (cf. also Hilbert-Bernays 1934 pp. 330 ff.) and Raphael Robinson 1948.

A different method was followed by Péter 1935 in constructing another example. The class of the initial functions definable by Schemata (I) — (III) is enumerable. Then the class of the primitive recursive functions definable using Schema (IV) or (V) just once is enumerable, since the $m+1$-tuples $\psi, \chi_1, \ldots, \chi_m$ for (IV) or the pairs ψ, χ (or q, χ) for (V) formed from an enumerable class are enumerable (§ 1). Then the primitive recursive functions definable using Schema (IV) or (V) a second time are enumerable; and so on. Thus the class of all the primitive recursive functions is enumerable, as we could also see by enumerating the systems E for Theorem II § 54. In particular, the primitive recursive functions of one variable are enumerable. Hence by Cantor's diagonal method (§ 2) they cannot comprise all the number-theoretic functions of one variable; and if

$$\varphi_0(a), \varphi_1(a), \varphi_2(a), \ldots$$

is any enumeration of them allowing repetitions (i.e. any infinite list of them in which each occurs at least once), then $\varphi_a(a)+1$ is a number-theoretic function of one variable not in the enumeration, and so not primitive recursive. The enumerating function $\varphi(n, a)$ such that $\varphi(n, a) = \varphi_n(a)$ is a function of two variables which is not primitive recursive, since $\varphi_a(a)+1 = \varphi(a, a)+1$. This of course only establishes that number-theoretic functions $\varphi_a(a)+1$ and $\varphi(n, a)$ can be found which are not primitive recursive. What Péter did was to show that, for a suitable enumeration (with repetitions) of the primitive recursive functions of one variable, the enumerating function can be defined by a double recursion (besides applications of Schemata (I) — (V)).

Example 1. Do double recursions lead to any predicates which are not primitive recursive? Yes, for $1 \dot{-} \varphi(a, a)$ takes only 0 and 1 as values, and cannot occur in the above enumeration, so it is the representing function of a predicate not primitive recursive. (Skolem 1944.)

Péter 1936 studies k-fold recursions for every positive integer k. These comprise primitive recursions for $k = 1$, double recursions for $k = 2$, and so on. She shows that, for each successive k, new functions are obtained. Functions definable using (besides explicit definition) recursions up to order k she calls "k-recursive". She shows that every 2-recursive function is definable by a single double recursion of the form

$$\text{(g)} \qquad \begin{cases} \varphi(0, b) = \varphi(n, 0) = 1, \\ \varphi(n', b') = \alpha(n, b, \varphi(n, \beta(n, b, \varphi(n', b))), \varphi(n', b)) \end{cases}$$

besides applications of Schemata (I) — (V); and similarly (with a scheme reducing to (g) for $k = 2$) for each $k \geq 2$.

Example 2. To settle a point raised in § 45, suppose φ is 3-recursive but not 2-recursive, and ψ is 2-recursive but not 1-recursive, i.e. not primitive recursive. Then "if ψ is primitive recursive, then φ is primitive recursive" is vacuously true, but "φ is primitive recursive in ψ" is false, since that would make φ 2-recursive.

These subjects are treated in Péter's monograph 1951 (not available during the writing of the present book).

It is not to be expected that the k-fold recursions with finite k exhaust the possibilities for defining new functions by recursion. In 1950 Péter uses "transfinite recursions" (first employed by Ackermann 1940) to define new functions.

This brings us to the problem, whether we can characterize in any exact way the notion of any "recursion", or the class of all "recursive functions".

The examples (I) — (V), (a), (b), (e) (and others cited) of schemes of definition of a function which we have thus far agreed to call "recursions" possess two features: (i) They are expressed by equations in the manner which we analyzed formally (for (I) — (V) particularly) in § 54. (ii) They are definitions by mathematical induction, in one form or another, except in the trivial case when they are explicit definitions.

The characterization of all "recursive functions" was accomplished in the definition of 'general recursive function' by Gödel 1934, who built on a suggestion of Herbrand. This definition succeeds by a bold generalization, which consists in choosing Feature (i) by itself as the definition.

We say then that a function φ is *general recursive*, if there is a system E of equations which defines it recursively (§ 54, with $l = 0$).

This choice may seem unexpected, since the word "recursive" has its root in the verb "recur", and mathematical induction is our method for handling recurrent processes. The meaning of the choice is not that Feature (ii) will be absent from any particular recursion, but that it is transferred out of the definition itself to the application of the definition. To show by finitary means that a given scheme has Feature (i), except in trivial situations, one will presumably have to make use of mathematical induction somehow. But in defining the totality of general recursive functions, we forego the attempt to characterize in advance in what form the intuitive principle of induction must manifest itself. (By Gödel's theorem § 42 we know that the attempt at such a characterization by the formal number-theoretic system is incomplete.)

In stating the Herbrand-Gödel definition of general recursive function exactly, there is some latitude as to the details of the formalization, so that versions of the definition can be given which are equivalent to Gödel's but a bit simpler (cf. Kleene 1936, and 1943 § 8). The present version is that of Kleene 1943, except for inconsequential changes in R1 and R2 which simplify § 56 slightly, and the inclusion of functions of 0 variables in the treatment. (To relate the present treatment to Kleene 1943, we note: (1) The inclusion of functions of 0 variables does not alter the notion of general recursiveness for functions of $n > 0$ variables. For one can show that, if an auxiliary function letter h occurs as a term with 0 arguments in the assumption equations, all occurrences of this term may be changed to k(c), where k is a new function letter and c a new variable, without altering the class of the deducible equations containing only the principal function letter. After this: (2) One can show in a few lines that exactly the same equations of the form $\mathrm{f}(\boldsymbol{x}_1, \ldots, \boldsymbol{x}_n) = \boldsymbol{x}$, where f is a function letter and $\boldsymbol{x}_1, \ldots, \boldsymbol{x}_n, \boldsymbol{x}$ are numerals, are deducible from given assumption equations by the present

R1 and R2 as by the R1 and R2 of 1943; or with only a little more trouble one can carry out the treatment of §§ 54 and 56 with the R1 and R2 of 1943.)

A function φ is *general recursive in* functions $\psi_1, \ldots, \psi_l$, if there is a system E of equations which defines φ recursively from $\psi_1, \ldots, \psi_l$ (§ 54). This includes the definition of general recursive function as the case $l = 0$. For $l > 0$ (Kleene 1943), we are usually considering a scheme or functional $\varphi = \mathsf{F}(\psi_1, \ldots, \psi_l)$ (§ 47) which defines a number-theoretic function φ of n variables from $\psi_1, \ldots, \psi_l$, for any l number-theoretic functions $\psi_1, \ldots, \psi_l$ of $m_1, \ldots, m_l$ variables respectively, or any such functions subject to some stated restrictions. Then if the E can be given independently of $\psi_1, \ldots, \psi_l$ (for the fixed $n, l, m_1, \ldots, m_l$), we say that the scheme F is *general recursive*, or that φ is *general recursive uniformly in* $\psi_1, \ldots, \psi_l$. Since our treatment will always give uniformity in the ψ's (subject to any restrictions stated), we usually omit the word "uniformly" except for emphasis. (Unlike the primitive recursive case § 47, if the original scheme is for some restriction on $\psi_1, \ldots, \psi_l$, it is not implied that the scheme can necessarily be extended to a general recursive one defining a φ without restriction on the $\psi_1, \ldots, \psi_l$.)

Using the present terminology to restate the results of Lemmas IIa and IIe, we now have:

THEOREM II (second version). *If φ is defined from $\psi_1, \ldots, \psi_l$ by a succession of applications of general recursive schemes, then φ is general recursive in $\psi_1, \ldots, \psi_l$.*

In particular, Schemata (I) — (V) *are general recursive.* Hence: *If φ is primitive recursive in $\psi_1, \ldots, \psi_l$, it is general recursive in $\psi_1, \ldots, \psi_l$. Any primitive recursive scheme is general recursive. If φ is primitive recursive, it is general recursive.*

The definition of general recursiveness has been stated for the case that the function φ is already known, by intuitive use of the same equations which are formalized as the E, or by some other means. This anticipates our purpose of showing that various functions and schemes, known to us independently of the formalism of recursive functions, are general recursive (as we have just done for the primitive recursive functions and schemes). For the case that the φ is not previously known, we then have: A system E of equations defines recursively a function of n variables from $\psi_1, \ldots, \psi_l$, if for each n-tuple $x_1, \ldots, x_n$ of natural numbers, there is exactly one numeral $\boldsymbol{x}$ such that $E^{\psi_1 \ldots \psi_l}_{g_1 \ldots g_l}$, E $\vdash$ $f(\boldsymbol{x}_1, \ldots, \boldsymbol{x}_n) = \boldsymbol{x}$, where f is the principal function letter of E, and $g_1, \ldots, g_l$ are the given function letters in order of their occurrence in the given list of function letters. If so, the function φ which is defined recursively by E is the function whose value $\varphi(x_1, \ldots, x_n)$ for the natural numbers $x_1, \ldots, x_n$ as arguments is the natural number x for which that $\boldsymbol{x}$ is the numeral.

As with primitive recursiveness (§§ 45, 47), the notion of general recursiveness for functions extends to predicates and to mixed cases by use of the representing functions for the predicates.

§ 56. Arithmetization of the formalism of recursive functions. The formalism of recursive functions will be treated now as a generalized arithmetic of the sort described in § 50. We list below recursive definitions for this generalized arithmetic, as in § 51. Simultaneously, we indicate how to pass to the simple arithmetic by Gödel numbering, as in § 52.

The generalized arithmetic shall have six zeros, with respective Gödel numbers, as follows.

Zeros:	$=$	$'$	0	a	$_{\mathsf{I}}$	f
Correlated Gödel numbers:	15	21	23	25	27	29

We permit successors to be formed of any positive number of entities, i.e. all natural numbers are admitted now as values of s.

As our list $f, g, h, \ldots$ of function letters we use the entities f, $({}_{\mathsf{I}}, f)$, $({}_{\mathsf{I}}, ({}_{\mathsf{I}}, f))$, ... (sometimes written $f, f_{\mathsf{I}}, f_{\mathsf{II}}, \ldots$), constructed from the zero entity f in the same manner as the (number) variables from the zero entity a.

A term of the form $\mathrm{f}(\mathrm{r}_1, \ldots, \mathrm{r}_n)$ where f is a function letter and $\mathrm{r}_1, \ldots, \mathrm{r}_n$ are terms ($n \geq 0$) will be represented as the entity $(\mathrm{f}, \mathrm{r}_1, \ldots, \mathrm{r}_n)$. So in particular the function letter f and the term $\mathrm{f}(\mathrm{r}_1, \ldots, \mathrm{r}_n)$ for $n = 0$, although usually written alike linguistically, are not treated as the same entity; in the generalized arithmetic, if the former is f, the latter is (f). (We still have a unique entity correlated to each significant linguistic object, if we consider that the omission of parentheses, when $\mathrm{f}(\mathrm{r}_1, \ldots, \mathrm{r}_n)$ for $n = 0$ is written linguistically as "f", is merely an abbreviation.) For example, the equation $f=0$ is the entity $(=, (f), 0)$.

A system of equations $\mathrm{e}_0, \ldots, \mathrm{e}_s$ is represented as the entity $(\mathrm{e}_0, \ldots, \mathrm{e}_s)$.

In the passage from the generalized arithmetic to the natural number arithmetic by Gödel numbering, the clauses using a variable number $s+1$ of predecessors are handled with the help of $\#\#$E and 20 (§ 45). For these clauses (and a few other definitions), we append the corresponding number-theoretic clause (or definition).

Definitions of metamathematical predicates and functions for the formalism of recursive functions as a generalized arithmetic

Df1. y is a *numeral*. (Abbreviation: $\mathfrak{N}$(y).) Same as Dn1 § 51.

Df2. y is a *variable*. (Abbreviation: $\mathfrak{V}$(y).) Same as Dn2.

Df3. y is a *function letter*. (Abbreviation: $\mathfrak{FL}$(y).) Like Df2.

Df4. y is a *term*. (Abbreviation: $\mathfrak{Tm}$(y).)
1. y $\asymp$ 0.
2. y is a variable.
3. y $\asymp$ r′ (i.e. y $\asymp$ (′, r)), where r is a *term*.
4. y $\asymp$ f($r_1, \ldots, r_n$) (i.e. y $\asymp$ (f, $r_1, \ldots, r_n$), cf. § 50), where f is a function letter, and $r_1, \ldots, r_n$ are *terms* ($n \geq 0$).
$FL((y)_0) \;\&\; (i)_{0<i<\mathrm{lh}(y)} Tm((y)_i)$.

Df5. z is an *equation*. (Abbreviation: $\mathfrak{Eq}$(z).)
1. z $\asymp$ r=s, where r and s are terms.

Df6. Z is a *system of equations*. (Abbreviation: $\mathfrak{SE}$(Z).)
1. Z $\asymp$ ($z_0, \ldots, z_s$), where $z_0, \ldots, z_s$ are equations.
$\mathrm{lh}(z)>0 \;\&\; (i)_{i<\mathrm{lh}(z)} Eq((z)_i)$.

Df7. (t is a term, x is a variable, e is a term or equation, and) d comcs from e by the *substitution* of t for x. (Abbreviation: $\mathfrak{Sb}$(d, e, t, x).)
1. t is a term, x is a variable, e $\asymp$ x, and d $\asymp$ t.
2—3. t is a term, x is a variable, e is 0 or a variable $\not\asymp$ x, and d $\asymp$ e.
4. t is a term, x is a variable, and e is a term or equation of the form ($e_0, e_1, \ldots, e_n$) and d is ($d_0, d_1, \ldots, d_m$), where $m = n$, $e_0 \not\asymp$ ı, $d_0 \asymp e_0$, $\mathfrak{Sb}(d_1, e_1, t, x), \ldots, \mathfrak{Sb}(d_n, e_n, t, x)$.
$Tm(t) \;\&\; V(x) \;\&\; (Tm(e) \vee Eq(e)) \;\&\; \mathrm{lh}(e)>0 \;\&\; \mathrm{lh}(d)=\mathrm{lh}(e) \;\&$
$(e)_0 \neq 27 \;\&\; (d)_0=(e)_0 \;\&\; (i)_{0<i<\mathrm{lh}(e)} Sb((d)_i, (e)_i, t, x)$.

Df8. (e is a term or equation, x is a variable, and) e *contains* x. (Abbreviation: $\mathfrak{Ct}$(e, x).) Like Dn6.

Df9. c is an *immediate consequence* of d (by R1). (Abbreviation: $\mathfrak{Cn}$(c, d).)
*1. d is an equation, and there exist a (variable) y and a numeral n, such that d contains y, and $\mathfrak{Sb}$(c, d, n, y).
$Eq(d) \;\&\; (Ey)_{y<d}(En)_{n<c}[N(n) \;\&\; Ct(d, y) \;\&\; Sb(c, d, n, y)]$.
If d is an equation and $\mathfrak{Ct}$(d, y), then y is a variable $\prec$ d; and if also $\mathfrak{Sb}$(c, d, n, y), then n $\prec$ c.

Df10. c is an *immediate consequence* of d and e (by R2). (Abbreviation: $\mathfrak{Cn}$(c, d, e).)
*1. e $\asymp$ h($\boldsymbol{z}_1, \ldots, \boldsymbol{z}_p$)=$\boldsymbol{z}$, where h is a function letter, and

$\boldsymbol{z}_1, \ldots, \boldsymbol{z}_p, \boldsymbol{z}$ are numerals ($p \geq 0$); d is an equation, containing no variables, call it $\mathrm{d}_1=\mathrm{d}_2$; and c is of the form $\mathrm{d}_1=\mathrm{c}_2$, where, for some term u containing a, $\mathfrak{Sb}(\mathrm{d}_2, \mathrm{u}, \mathrm{h}(\boldsymbol{z}_1, \ldots, \boldsymbol{z}_p), a)$ and $\mathfrak{Sb}(\mathrm{c}_2, \mathrm{u}, \boldsymbol{z}, a)$.
$Eq(e)$ & $FL((e)_{1,0})$ & $(i)_{0<i<\mathrm{lh}((e)_1)}N((e)_{1,i})$ & $N((e)_2)$ & $Eq(d)$ & $(y)_{y<d}\overline{Ct}(d, y)$ & $c=2^{15}\cdot 3^{(d)_1}\cdot 5^{(c)_2}$ & $(Eu)_{u<d}[Tm(u)$ & $Ct(u, 25)$ & $Sb((d)_2, u, (e)_1, 25)$ & $Sb((c)_2, u, (e)_2, 25)]$.
Since a has a smaller Gödel number than any function letter, a has a smaller Gödel number than $\mathrm{h}(\boldsymbol{z}_1, \ldots, \boldsymbol{z}_p)$; and hence u has a smaller Gödel number than d.

Df11. $\boldsymbol{x}$ is the *numeral for* the natural number x. (Abbreviation: $\mathfrak{Nu}(\boldsymbol{x}, x)$.) Same as Dn11.

Df12. (Z is a system of equations, and) Y is a *deduction* from Z (by R1 and R2). (Abbreviation: $\mathfrak{D}$(Z, Y).)
1. Z is a system of equations $(\mathrm{z}_0, \ldots, \mathrm{z}_s)$, and $\mathrm{Y} \asymp (\mathrm{z}_i)$ $(i \leq s)$. $SE(z)$ & $(Ei)_{i<\mathrm{lh}(z)}[y=2^{(z)_i}]$.
2. $\mathrm{Y} \asymp (\mathrm{c}, \mathrm{Y}_1)$, where Y_1 is a *deduction* from Z, and c is an immediate consequence of $\{\mathrm{Y}_1\}_0$.
3. $\mathrm{Y} \asymp (\mathrm{c}, \mathrm{Y}_1, \mathrm{Y}_2)$, where Y_1 and Y_2 are *deductions* from Z, and c is an immediate consequence of $\{\mathrm{Y}_1\}_0$ and $\{\mathrm{Y}_2\}_0$.

Df13. Y is a deduction from Z of an equation of the form $\mathrm{f}(\boldsymbol{x}_1,\ldots,\boldsymbol{x}_n)=\boldsymbol{x}$, where f is the principal function letter of Z, $\boldsymbol{x}_1, \ldots, \boldsymbol{x}_n$ are the numerals for the natural numbers $x_1, \ldots, x_n$, respectively, and $\boldsymbol{x}$ is a numeral (as a predicate of Z, $x_1, \ldots, x_n$, Y, for each fixed $n \geq 0$). (Abbreviation: $\mathfrak{S}_n(\mathrm{Z}, x_1, \ldots, x_n, \mathrm{Y})$.)
1. Y is a deduction from Z, $\{\mathrm{Y}\}_0 \asymp \mathrm{f}(\boldsymbol{x}_1, \ldots, \boldsymbol{x}_n)=\boldsymbol{x}$, where f is a function letter, $\mathrm{f} \asymp \{\mathrm{z}_s\}_{1,0}$ if $\mathrm{Z} \asymp (\mathrm{z}_0, \ldots, \mathrm{z}_s)$, etc. $D(z, y)$ & $\mathrm{lh}((y)_{0,1})=n'$ & $FL((y)_{0,1,0})$ & $(y)_{0,1,0}=(z)_{\mathrm{lh}(z)\dot{-}1,1,0}$ & $Nu((y)_{0,1,1}, x_1)$ & $\ldots$ & $Nu((y)_{0,1,n}, x_n)$ & $N((y)_{0,2})$.

Df14. $\mathfrak{Nu}^{-1}(\mathrm{y}) = \begin{cases} x, \text{ if y is a numeral } \boldsymbol{x} \text{ (i.e. if } \mathfrak{Nu}(\mathrm{y}, x)), \\ \text{the Gödel number of y, otherwise.} \end{cases}$
$Nu^{-1}(y) = \mu x_{x<y} Nu(y, x)$.

Df15. $\mathfrak{U}(\mathrm{Y}) = \mathfrak{Nu}^{-1}(\{\mathrm{Y}\}_{0,2})$.
Then $\mathfrak{U}(\mathrm{Y}) = x$, whenever Y is a deduction of an equation of the form $\mathrm{r}=\boldsymbol{x}$ where $\boldsymbol{x}$ is a numeral.
$U(y) = Nu^{-1}((y)_{0,2})$.

By the methods illustrated in § 52, and the indications accompanying these definitions:

LEMMA III. *For each of the predicates and functions defined by* Df1 — Df15, *the corresponding number-theoretic predicate or a corresponding number-theoretic function is primitive recursive.*

§ 57. The μ-operator, enumeration, diagonal procedure. We shall now begin using the least number operator μy (§ 45) without a bound on the y. Thus for a number-theoretic predicate $R(y)$ such that $(Ey)R(y)$, $\mu y R(y) = \{$the least (natural number) y such that $R(y)\}$. For the time being, we use $\mu y R(y)$ only when the existence condition $(Ey)R(y)$ is fulfilled.

Thus we have a new schema

$$\text{(VIa)} \qquad \varphi(x_1, \ldots, x_n) = \mu y[\chi(x_1, \ldots, x_n, y)=0]$$

for the definition of a function φ of n variables ($n \geq 0$) from any function χ of $n+1$ variables such that

$$\text{(1a)} \qquad (x_1) \ldots (x_n)(Ey)[\chi(x_1, \ldots, x_n, y)=0].$$

By taking $R(x_1, \ldots, x_n, y) \equiv \chi(x_1, \ldots, x_n, y)=0$ if χ is given first, or if R is given first by taking χ to be the representing function of R, we can also write the schema thus,

$$\text{(VIb)} \qquad \varphi(x_1, \ldots, x_n) = \mu y R(x_1, \ldots, x_n, y)$$

as a definition of a function φ from a predicate R such that

$$\text{(1b)} \qquad (x_1) \ldots (x_n)(Ey)R(x_1, \ldots, x_n, y).$$

THEOREM III. *Schema* (VIa) *with* (1a) *holding* ((VIb) *with* (1b) *holding*) *is general recursive.* Hence by Theorem II: *A function* φ *defined from functions and predicates* Ψ *by applications of Schemata* (I) — (VI) *with* (1) *holding for the applications of* (VI) *is general recursive in* Ψ. (Church 1936, Kleene 1936.)

PROOF. We recast (VI) into a schema (VI′) suitable for translation into the formalism of recursive functions, as follows:

$$\text{(VI}'\text{)} \quad \begin{cases} \pi(x_1, \ldots, x_n, y) = \prod_{s<y} \chi(x_1, \ldots, x_n, s), & \text{(VI}_1'\text{)} \\ \tau(z', 0, y) = y, \\ \varphi(x_1, \ldots, x_n) = \tau(\pi(x_1, \ldots, x_n, y), \pi(x_1, \ldots, x_n, y'), y), & \text{(VI}_2'\text{)} \end{cases}$$

where $\tau(u, v, y)$ is an auxiliary function which is left undefined for $u = 0$ or $v > 0$. (For another simple method, see Kleene 1943.)

First let us convince ourselves informally that (VI′) is equivalent to (VI). Consider any fixed values of $x_1, \ldots, x_n$, and write simply "$\chi(y)$"

for "$\chi(x_1, \ldots, x_n, y)$", etc. To illustrate, suppose that for $y = 0, 1, 2, \ldots$ (first row below), $\chi(y)$ takes the values shown (second row).

y	0	1	2	3	4	5	6	7	...
$\chi(y)$	3	1	2	0	9	0	1	5	...
$\pi(y) = \prod_{s<y} \chi(s)$	1	3	3	6	0	0	0	0	...

According to (VI), $\varphi = \mu y R(y) = \mu y[\chi(y)=0]$, i.e. φ is the least value of y (first row) for which a 0 appears in the second row, namely 3 in this example. This number 3 is also identifiable as the unique y for which a successor (here 6) immediately precedes a 0 in the third row. Now (VI_2') gives this number and no other as value to φ, thus. Substituting 3 for y in the last equation and evaluating,

$$\varphi = \tau(\pi(3), \pi(4), 3) = \tau(6, 0, 3) = 3.$$

If we substitute any other number than 3 for y in the last equation, we are unable to evaluate τ. (If the example be changed so that $\overline{(Ey)}R(y)$, then we get no value for φ.)

Now let E_2 be the system of equations obtained by translating (VI_2') using say $p, t, f, a_1, \ldots, a_n, b$ for "π", "τ", "φ", "x_1", ..., "x_n", "y", respectively.

The following propositions (i) — (iv) treat the situation for any fixed n-tuple $x_1, \ldots, x_n$, without using (1). For (i) and (ii), π must be the function defined from χ or R by (VI_1').

(i) *If* $(Ey)R(x_1, \ldots, x_n, y)$, *then* $E_p^\pi, E_2 \vdash f(\mathbf{x}_1, \ldots, \mathbf{x}_n)=\mathbf{x}$ *when* $x = \mu y R(x_1, \ldots, x_n, y)$. (ii) *If* $E_p^\pi, E_2 \vdash f(\mathbf{x}_1, \ldots, \mathbf{x}_n)=\mathbf{x}$ *where* $\mathbf{x}$ *is a numeral, then* $(Ey)R(x_1, \ldots, x_n, y)$ *and* $x = \mu y R(x_1, \ldots, x_n, y)$.

The proofs closely parallel the informal explanation.

But π is primitive recursive in χ (#B § 45), so there is a system E_1 of equations which defines π recursively from χ (Theorem II § 54). We can choose E_1 so that p is the principal function letter, h is the given function letter, and the auxiliary function letters do not occur in E_2. Let E be E_1E_2. Then clearly $E_h^\chi, E \vdash f(\mathbf{x}_1, \ldots, \mathbf{x}_n)=\mathbf{x}$ if $E_p^\pi, E_2 \vdash f(\mathbf{x}_1, \ldots, \mathbf{x}_n)=\mathbf{x}$; and the converse follows from Lemma IIc § 54 as in the proof of Lemma IId. Using this in (i) and (ii), and combining the results into one statement:

(iii) $E_h^\chi, E \vdash f(\mathbf{x}_1, \ldots, \mathbf{x}_n)=\mathbf{x}$ *for some numeral* $\mathbf{x}$, *if and only if* $(Ey)R(x_1, \ldots, x_n, y)$, *in which case* $x = \mu y R(x_1, \ldots, x_n, y)$.

Now using (1) with (iii), for each n-tuple $x_1, \ldots, x_n$, $E_h^\chi, E \vdash f(\mathbf{x}_1, \ldots, \mathbf{x}_n)=\mathbf{x}$ where $\mathbf{x}$ is a numeral, if and only if $x = \mu y R(x_1, \ldots, x_n, y)$; i.e. E defines the function $\mu y R(x_1, \ldots, x_n, y)$ recursively from R.

PROOF OF THEOREM IV. Now suppose that $R(x_1, \ldots, x_n, y)$ is general recursive. Let D be a system of equations which defines recursively the representing function χ of R, with h as principal function letter, and with auxiliary function letters not occurring in E. Let F be DE. Now:

(iv) F $\vdash$ $f(\mathbf{x}_1, \ldots, \mathbf{x}_n) = \mathbf{x}$ *for some numeral* $\mathbf{x}$, *if and only if* $(Ey)R(x_1, \ldots, x_n, y)$, *in which case* $x = \mu y R(x_1, \ldots, x_n, y)$.

Using Df13 § 56, we state this result (omitting the final remark) in symbolic form, thus:

(2) $$(Ey)R(x_1, \ldots, x_n, y) \equiv (E\mathrm{Y})\mathfrak{S}_n(\mathrm{F}, x_1, \ldots, x_n, \mathrm{Y}).$$

Now let f be the Gödel number of F. By the definition of 'the corresponding number-theoretic predicate' § 52, $S_n(f, x_1, \ldots, x_n, y) \equiv \{y$ is the Gödel number of an entity Y such that $\mathfrak{S}_n(\mathrm{F}, x_1, \ldots, x_n, \mathrm{Y})\}$. Hence $(E\mathrm{Y})\mathfrak{S}_n(\mathrm{F}, x_1, \ldots, x_n, \mathrm{Y}) \equiv (Ey)S_n(f, x_1, \ldots, x_n, y)$. So (2) gives

(3) $$(Ey)R(x_1, \ldots, x_n, y) \equiv (Ey)S_n(f, x_1, \ldots, x_n, y).$$

By Lemma III, S_n is primitive recursive.

In stating the result in the theorem, we replace S_n by the predicate T_n defined from it thus,

$$T_n(z, x_1, \ldots, x_n, y) \equiv S_n(z, x_1, \ldots, x_n, y) \,\&\, (t)_{t<y}\overline{S}_n(z, x_1, \ldots, x_n, t).$$

For given $z, x_1, \ldots, x_n$, $T_n(z, x_1, \ldots, x_n, y)$ is true for at most one y (cf. *174 § 41). The advantage of using T_n instead of S_n as the basic predicate of the theory will appear in § 58. By ##D and E, T_n is also primitive recursive. By the informal counterparts of &-elim., *70 § 32 and *149a § 40 (noting that, since S_n is recursive,

$$S_n(z, x_1, \ldots, x_n, y) \vee \overline{S}_n(z, x_1, \ldots, x_n, y)$$

intuitionistically, as will be discussed in §§ 60 and 62),

(4) $$T_n(z, x_1, \ldots, x_n, y) \rightarrow S_n(z, x_1, \ldots, x_n, y),$$

(5) $$(Ey)T_n(z, x_1, \ldots, x_n, y) \equiv (Ey)S_n(z, x_1, \ldots, x_n, y).$$

THEOREM IV. *For each* $n \geq 0$: *Given any general recursive predicate* $R(x_1, \ldots, x_n, y)$, *numbers* f *and* g *can be found such that*

(6) $$(Ey)R(x_1, \ldots, x_n, y) \equiv (Ey)T_n(f, x_1, \ldots, x_n, y),$$

(7) $$(y)R(x_1, \ldots, x_n, y) \equiv (y)\overline{T}_n(g, x_1, \ldots, x_n, y),$$

where $T_n(z, x_1, \ldots, x_n, y)$ *is the particular primitive recursive predicate defined above. Similarly with more quantifiers; e.g. given a general recursive predicate* $R(a_1, \ldots, a_n, x, y)$, *there is a number* g *such that*

(8) $$(Ex)(y)R(a_1, \ldots, a_n, x, y) \equiv (Ex)(y)\overline{T}_{n+1}(g, a_1, \ldots, a_n, x, y).$$

(Enumeration theorem, Kleene 1943.)

Proof (completed). Formula (6) follows from (3) by (5). To infer (7), we apply (6) to the predicate $\overline{R}(x_1, \ldots, x_n, y)$, calling the f for this predicate "g", and transform the result by the informal counterparts of *30 § 26 and *86 § 35 to

$$(y)\overline{\overline{R}}(x_1, \ldots, x_n, y) \equiv (y)\overline{T}_n(g, x_1, \ldots, x_n, y).$$

Since R is general recursive, we have $R \vee \overline{R}$, and hence (cf. *49c § 27) $\overline{\overline{R}} \equiv R$. For (8), we apply (7) with $n+1$ as the n of (7), $a_1, \ldots, a_n, x$ as the $x_1, \ldots, x_n$, and y as the y, and use the informal counterpart of *72 § 33.

Discussion. By this theorem, we obtain an enumeration (with repetitions) of the n-variable predicates of the form $(Ey)R(x_1, \ldots, x_n, y)$ where R is general recursive by taking $z = 0, 1, 2, \ldots$ in the fixed $n+1$-variable predicate $(Ey)T_n(z, x_1, \ldots, x_n, y)$ of like form. Briefly, $(Ey)T_n(z, x_1, \ldots, x_n, y)$ 'enumerates' the predicates of the form $(Ey)R(x_1, \ldots, x_n, y)$ with a general recursive R. Similarly, $(y)\overline{T}_n(z, x_1, \ldots, x_n, y)$ enumerates the predicates of the form $(y)R(x_1, \ldots, x_n, y)$ with a general recursive R; etc. — Since T_n, $\overline{T}_n$, $\overline{T}_{n+1}$, etc. are primitive recursive:

Corollary. *The class of the predicates expressible in a given form consisting of a fixed succession of one or more quantifiers prefixed to a predicate R is the same whether a general recursive R or a primitive recursive R be allowed.* (Kleene 1943, generalizing a lemma of Rosser 1936 p. 87.)

We now use the above enumerations as the basis for an application of Cantor's diagonal method to prove the next theorem. Given a general recursive predicate $R(x, y)$, and using (6) for $n = 1$, there is a number f such that

$$(9) \qquad (Ey)R(x, y) \equiv (Ey)T_1(f, x, y).$$

Substituting f for x in this equivalence,

$$(10) \qquad (Ey)R(f, y) \equiv (Ey)T_1(f, f, y).$$

Thence, using the informal counterpart of *50a § 27,

$$(11) \qquad (Ey)R(f, y) \not\equiv \overline{(Ey)}T_1(f, f, y).$$

Formula (12) of the theorem follows, using the informal counterpart of *86 § 35. To prove (13), using (7) we have

$$(y)R(g, y) \equiv (y)\overline{T}_1(g, g, y) \equiv \overline{(Ey)}T_1(g, g, y) \not\equiv (Ey)T_1(g, g, y).$$

To infer (14) and (15), given any general recursive $R(x)$, let $R(x, y) \equiv R(x) \;\&\; y{=}y$ or $R(x, y) \equiv R(U_1^2(x, y))$ (§ 44), so that $R(x, y)$ is general recursive and $R(x) \equiv (Ey)R(x, y) \equiv (y)R(x, y)$.

THEOREM V (PART I). *Given any general recursive predicate $R(x, y)$, numbers f and g can be found such that*

(12) $$(Ey)R(f, y) \not\equiv (y)\overline{T}_1(f, f, y),$$

(13) $$(y)R(g, y) \not\equiv (Ey)T_1(g, g, y).$$

A fortiori, given any general recursive predicate $R(x)$, numbers f and g can be found such that

(14) $$R(f) \not\equiv (y)\overline{T}_1(f, f, y),$$

(15) $$R(g) \not\equiv (Ey)T_1(g, g, y).$$

DISCUSSION. By this theorem, $(y)\overline{T}_1(x, x, y)$ is an example of a predicate of the form $(y)R(x, y)$ with a recursive R which is not expressible in the dual form $(Ey)R(x, y)$ with a recursive R. That is,

$$(x)[(y)\overline{T}_1(x, x, y) \equiv (Ey)R(x, y)]$$

cannot hold for any general recursive predicate $R(x, y)$; and for a given $R(x, y)$, the f of (12) is a value of x which refutes it. A fortiori, $(y)\overline{T}_1(x, x, y)$ is also not general recursive (cf. (14)).

The proof (above) amounts simply to this: $(Ey)T_1(z, x, y)$ for $z = 0$, $1, 2, \ldots$ is an enumeration (with repetitions) of all predicates of the form $(Ey)R(x, y)$ with R recursive. By Cantor's diagonal method, $\overline{(Ey)}T_1(x, x, y)$ is a predicate not in the enumeration. The latter is equivalent to $(y)\overline{T}_1(x, x, y)$.

From the enumerability of all systems E of equations, we can conclude without the present theory that the general recursive predicates are enumerable, and so also the predicates of the form $(Ey)R(x, y)$ with R recursive. Hence by Cantor's results (§ 2), they cannot constitute all number-theoretic predicates. The additional content of the present theorem is that an example of a predicate neither general recursive nor expressible in the form $(Ey)R(x, y)$ with R recursive is given which is of the dual form $(y)R(x, y)$ with R recursive; and vice versa.

To save space, we write the next part of the theorem for predicates of one variable a; but it holds likewise for predicates of n variables $a_1, \ldots, a_n$ for each $n \geq 1$. In the proof of (b) we use a classical equivalence, not available to us intuitionistically. We accordingly label (b) with a "C" (cf. § 37). The results so labeled in this chapter are all on the number-theoretic level.

THEOREM V (PART II). *Consider the predicate forms*

$$R(a) \quad \begin{matrix} (Ex)R(a, x) & (x)(Ey)R(a, x, y) & (Ex)(y)(Ez)R(a, x, y, z) & \ldots \\ (x)R(a, x) & (Ex)(y)R(a, x, y) & (x)(Ey)(z)R(a, x, y, z) & \ldots \end{matrix}$$

where the R for each is general recursive. To each form with $k+1$ quantifiers ($k \geq 0$), *there is a predicate expressible* (a) *in the negation of the form* ((b)^{C} *in the other $k+1$-quantifier form*), *but not in the form itself nor in any of the forms with $\leq k$ quantifiers.* By Part I, the "^{C}" is unnecessary for $k = 0$. (Kleene 1943; Mostowski 1947.)

PROOF. For example, take $k = 1$. From (8) (for $n = 1$) we infer

(16) $$(Ex)(y)R(g, x, y) \not\equiv \overline{(Ex)}(y)\overline{T}_2(g, g, x, y),$$

just as from (6) we inferred (11). Thus $\overline{(Ex)}(y)\overline{T}_2(a, a, x, y)$ (equivalent classically to $(x)(Ey)T_2(a, a, x, y)$, cf. Theorem 18 § 35) is not expressible in the form $(Ex)(y)R(a, x, y)$. Similarly, $\overline{(x)}(Ey)T_2(a, a, x, y)$ (equivalent classically to $(Ex)(y)\overline{T}_2(a, a, x, y)$) is not expressible in the form $(x)(Ey)R(a, x, y)$. A fortiori, these predicates are not expressible in any of the three forms with one or no quantifier.

THEOREM VI. *For each $n \geq 0$*: (a) *Every general recursive predicate $P(x_1, \ldots, x_n)$ is expressible in both of the forms $(Ey)R(x_1, \ldots, x_n, y)$ and $(y)S(x_1, \ldots, x_n, y)$ where R and S are primitive recursive.* (b)^{C} *Conversely, every predicate expressible in both of these forms where R and S are general recursive is general recursive.* (c) *A predicate $P(x_1, \ldots, x_n)$ is general recursive, if and only if $P(x_1, \ldots, x_n)$ and $\overline{P}(x_1, \ldots, x_n)$ are each expressible in the form $(Ey)R(x_1, \ldots, x_n, y)$ with a general recursive R, and $(x_1) \ldots (x_n)[P(x_1, \ldots, x_n) \vee \overline{P}(x_1, \ldots, x_n)]$.* (Kleene 1943, Post 1944, Mostowski 1947.)

PROOFS. (a) Take $P(x_1, \ldots, x_n, y) \equiv P(x_1, \ldots, x_n) \,\&\, y=y$, so that $P(x_1, \ldots, x_n) \equiv (Ey)P(x_1, \ldots, x_n, y) \equiv (y)P(x_1, \ldots, x_n, y)$, and apply Corollary Theorem IV. (b) Suppose $P(x_1, \ldots, x_n) \equiv (Ey)R(x_1, \ldots, x_n, y) \equiv (y)S(x_1, \ldots, x_n, y)$. Then by classical logic (cf. *85 § 35), $\overline{P}(x_1, \ldots, x_n) \equiv (Ey)\overline{S}(x_1, \ldots, x_n, y)$. By the classical law of the excluded middle, $P(x_1, \ldots, x_n) \vee \overline{P}(x_1, \ldots, x_n)$. Hence

$$P(x_1, \ldots, x_n) \equiv R(x_1, \ldots, x_n, \mu y[R(x_1, \ldots, x_n, y) \vee \overline{S}(x_1, \ldots, x_n, y)]),$$

where the second member is general recursive by Theorem III. (c) The last hypothesis makes the statement valid intuitionistically.

In Kleene 1943, 1944, a predicate was called "elementary", if it can be expressed explicitly in terms of constant and variable natural numbers, general recursive predicates, the operators $\rightarrow$, &, $\vee$, $^{-}$ of the propositional calculus, and the quantifiers, combined according to the usual syntactical rules.

THEOREM VII. (a) *Every arithmetical predicate* (§ 48) *is "elementary", and* (b) *conversely.* (c) *Every predicate expressible by means of quantifiers prefixed to a general recursive predicate is expressible in one of the forms of Theorem* V *with a general recursive* R. (d)^{C} *Every arithmetical predicate is expressible in one of the forms of Theorem* V *with a general recursive* R.

PROOFS. (a) By ##1, 2, 14, C (§§ 44, 45), every predicate formed explicitly using $+$, $\cdot$, $=$ is primitive recursive, and hence general recursive. (b) By Theorem VI (a) and Corollary Theorem I § 49. (c) As x ranges over all natural numbers, the $m+1$-tuple of primitive recursive functions $(x)_0, \ldots, (x)_m$ (#19 § 45) ranges (with repetitions) over all $m+1$-tuples of natural numbers. Therefore

(17) $$(Ex_0) \ldots (Ex_m)A(x_0, \ldots, x_m) \equiv (Ex)A((x)_0, \ldots, (x)_m),$$

(18) $$(x_0) \ldots (x_m)A(x_0, \ldots, x_m) \equiv (x)A((x)_0, \ldots, (x)_m).$$

We use these to contract consecutive quantifiers of the same kind. (d) By (a), the informal counterpart of Theorem 19 § 35, and (c).

REMARK 1. For any predicate $A(i, x)$,

(19) $$(i)_{i<a}(Ex)A(i, x) \equiv (Ex)(i)_{i<a}A(i, (x)_i).$$

By substituting $\overline{A}(i, x)$ for $A(i, x)$ and using (the informal counterparts of) *30, *85, *86, *58 and *49 (cf. the proof of Corollary Theorems 8 and 18), we infer classically the dual

(20)^{C} $$(Ei)_{i<a}(x)A(i, x) \equiv (x)(Ei)_{i<a}A(i, (x)_i).$$

(But (20) does not hold in general intuitionistically, by Example 4 § 82.) — Simply by *95 and *77, $(i)_{i<a}(x)A(i, x) \equiv (x)(i)_{i<a}A(i, x)$; and similarly for $(Ei)_{i<a}(Ex)$, $(i)_{i<a}(x)_{x<b}$ and $(Ei)_{i<a}(Ex)_{x<b}$.

Although there is a substantial difference between the notions 'arithmetical' and 'elementary', which requires two basic theorems to bridge (Theorems I and IV), henceforth in the interest of unifying terminology we shall usually say "arithmetical" (even when primarily we have the other notion in mind).

EXAMPLE 1. "Elementary" is used by Kalmár 1943* in another sense, equivalent to the following. A function is "elementary", if it can be expressed explicitly in terms of variable natural numbers, the constant 1, the functions $+$, $\cdot$ and $[a/b]$, and the operations $\sum_{y<z}$ and $\prod_{y<z}$. Extending the notion to predicates, and to the case of assumed functions and predicates, in the familiar way, we can recognize successively that the following of our list ##1—21 of primitive recursive functions and predicates (§§ 44, 45) are elementary, and the following of our results ##A—G

hold reading "elementary" in place of "primitive recursive": #1, #2, #13, ##A—C, #3, #4, #9 ($\overline{\text{sg}}(a) = [1/(a+1)]$), #10, #D, #E ($\prod_{s \leq t}$ is $\prod_{s<t+1}$), #15 (the representing function is $\text{sg}[(a+1)/(b+1)]$), #6 ($a \dot{-} b = \mu c_{c \leq a}[\overline{b+c<a} \vee a<b]$), #5, #7, #8, #11, #12 ($\text{rm}(a, b) = a \dot{-} b[a/b]$), #14, #F, #16, #17, #19 as a function of a for each fixed i; also Gödel's β-function (§ 48). — Next we show that (A) *if* φ *comes from* ψ, χ *(from* χ*) by a primitive recursion (Schema* (V)*), and* $\varphi(y, x_2, \ldots, x_n) \leq \eta(y, x_2, \ldots, x_n)$, *then* φ *is elementary in* ψ, χ, η *(in* χ, η*)*. In the proof of Theorem I § 49 Case (Vb), (B) is of the form $(Ec)(Ed)R(y, x_2, \ldots, x_n, w, c, d)$, where R is elementary in ψ and χ, and $(c)(d)[R(y, x_2, \ldots, x_n, w, c, d) \rightarrow \varphi(y, x_2, \ldots, x_n)=w]$. Hence $\varphi(y, x_2, \ldots, x_n) = (\mu t R(y, x_2, \ldots, x_n, (t)_0, (t)_1, (t)_2))_0$. So by #E it will suffice to find a bound elementary in η on the t. But by § 48, we can choose $d = (\max(y, a_0, \ldots, a_y))!$ where $a_i = \varphi(i, x_2, \ldots, x_n)$, so that $d \leq D$ where $D = (y + \sum_{i \leq y} \eta(i, x_2, \ldots, x_n))!$, and $c < \prod_{i \leq y} \delta(d, i) = \prod_{i \leq y} (1+(i+1)d) \leq C$ where $C = \prod_{i \leq y} (1+(i+1)D)$. So we can take $t < 2^E \cdot 3^C \cdot 5^D$ where $E = \eta(y, x_2, \ldots, x_n)$. — Now p_i (#18) is elementary, for an elementary bound can be found, e.g. $p_i \leq 2^{2^i}$ (= only for $i = 0$), as we prove by course-of-values induction on i, thus. True for $i = 0, 1$. For $i \geq 2$, $p_i \leq p_0 \cdot p_1 \cdot \ldots \cdot p_{i-1} - 1$ (by reasoning as in the proof of Euclid's theorem § 40) $< 2^{2^0} \cdot 2^{2^1} \cdot \ldots \cdot 2^{2^{i-1}}$ (using the hyp. ind.) $= 2^{2^0+2^1+\ldots+2^{i-1}} = 2^{2^i-1} < 2^{2^i}$. — Then the following are elementary: #19, #20 ($\text{lh}(i, a) \leq a$), #21. Also (cf. #G) (B) *if* φ *comes from* χ *by the course-of-values recursion* (3) § 46, *and* $\varphi(y, x_2, \ldots, x_n) \leq \eta(y, x_2, \ldots, x_n)$, *then* φ *is elementary in* χ, η. For then $\prod_{i<y} p_i^{\eta(i, x_2, \ldots, x_n)}$ is a bound elementary in η for $\tilde{\varphi}(y; x_2, \ldots, x_n)$ in the primitive recursion (4) § 46. — It follows that the number-theoretic predicates and functions corresponding to the metamathematical ones defined by Dn1—Dn13a § 51 (cf. Lemma 19 § 52) and Df1—Df15 § 56 (cf. Lemma III) are elementary. For recursions are used in those metamathematical definitions in the generalized arithmetic only to introduce (the representing functions of) predicates, and so (B) applies to each corresponding recursion in the simple arithmetic with $\eta = 1$. In particular, S_n (Df13), and hence (C) T_n *(preceding Theorem* IV*), and* U (Df15) *are elementary*. This corresponds to the result of Ilona Bereczki (1949* unpublished) that (by means of devices used in Kalmár 1943) each of the predicates and functions shown in Kleene 1936 to be primitive recursive is either elementary or can be replaced by one which is elementary without deranging the

arguments of that paper. — So (D) *we can add "or an elementary R (in Kalmár's sense)" in Corollary Theorem* IV. — Kalmár (1943, 1948, 1950, 1950a) uses his elementary functions in presenting Gödel's theorem and other results which are presented in this book using primitive recursive functions. — Miss Bereczki (1952*) shows that the primitive recursive function ${}^{b}a$ defined by ${}^{0}a = 1$, ${}^{b'}a = a^{({}^{b}a)}$ (so that ${}^{b+1}a = \xi_3(b, a)$ § 55) is not elementary because ${}^{a}a$ grows too fast as a increases. She obtains another example of a non-elementary primitive recursive function by constructing a primitive recursive enumerating function $\varphi(n, a)$ for the elementary functions of one variable (cf. § 55). From this it follows that there are non-elementary primitive recursive predicates (similarly to Example 1 § 55).

THEOREM VIII^{C}. *For the primitive recursive V and* υ *defined below, the predicate M(a, k) defined by induction on k thus,*

$$\begin{cases} M(a, 0) \equiv V(a), \\ M(a, 2k+1) \equiv (Ex)M(\upsilon(a, x), 2k), \\ M(a, 2k+2) \equiv (x)M(\upsilon(a, x), 2k+1), \end{cases}$$

is not arithmetical. (Kleene 1943.)

Kalmár first obtained a result of this sort, which appears in Skolem 1936-7 pp. 86 ff. Also cf. Wang 1953, Mostowski 1951.

PROOF (optional). Let us in the expression for $S_n(z, x_1, \ldots, x_n, y)$ (Df13 § 56) replace "n'" by "$(x)_0'$", and "$Nu((y)_{0,1,1}, x_1)$ &...& $Nu((y)_{0,1,n}, x_n)$" by "$(i)_{1 \leq i \leq (x)_0} Nu((y)_{0,1,i}, (x)_i - 1)$". The result is a primitive recursive predicate $S(z, x, y)$ such that

(21) $$S(z, 2^n \cdot p_1^{x_1'} \cdot \ldots \cdot p_n^{x_n'} \cdot p_{n'}^{u}, y) \equiv S_n(z, x_1, \ldots, x_n, y).$$

Let $T(z, x, y) \equiv S(z, x, y)$ & $(t)_{t<y}\overline{S}(z, x, t)$. Then

(22) $$T(z, 2^n \cdot p_1^{x_1'} \cdot \ldots \cdot p_n^{x_n'} \cdot p_{n'}^{u}, y) \equiv T_n(z, x_1, \ldots, x_n, y).$$

Now let $V(a) \equiv T((a)_1 \dot{-} 1, a, (a)_{(a)_0'} \dot{-} 1)$. Then for $n \geq 1$,

(23) $$V(2^n \cdot p_1^{x_1'} \cdot \ldots \cdot p_n^{x_n'} \cdot p_{n'}^{y'}) \equiv T_n(x_1, x_1, \ldots, x_n, y).$$

Let $\upsilon(a, x) = a * 2^{x'}$ (cf. #21 § 45). Now $M(a, k)$ takes for $k = 0, 1, 2, \ldots$ the values $V(a)$, $(Ex)V(a*2^{x'})$, $(x)(Ey)V((a*2^{x'})*2^{y'})$, ... Suppose $M(a, k)$ were arithmetical. By Theorem VII (d), then it would be expressible in one of the forms of Theorem V. For illustration, suppose $M(a, k) \equiv (Ex)R(a, k, x)$ for a recursive R. Then $(Ex)R(2^2 \cdot 3^{a'}, 2, x) \equiv M(2^2 \cdot 3^{a'}, 2) \equiv (x)(Ey)V(((2^2 \cdot 3^{a'})*2^{x'})*2^{y'}) \equiv (x)(Ey)V(2^2 \cdot 3^{a'} \cdot 5^{x'} \cdot 7^{y'}) \equiv (x)(Ey)T_2(a, a, x, y)$. But $(Ex)R(2^2 \cdot 3^{a'}, 2, x)$ is of the form $(Ex)R(a, x)$ with R recursive; and in the proof of Theorem V Part II we saw that $(x)(Ey)T_2(a, a, x, y)$ is not expressible in this form.

The reader may pass if he wishes to §§ 60—62, which do not depend except incidentally on §§ 58 and 59. But § 58 contains a result which is fundamental for §§ 63—66 and later.

§ 58. Normal form, Post's theorem. Using Df13 and Df15 (§ 56), we can restate the definition of 'general recursive function' (§§ 55, 54) as follows. A function $\varphi(x_1, \ldots, x_n)$ is general recursive, if and only if there exists a system E of equations (without given function letters) such that

(24) $$(x_1) \ldots (x_n)(EY)\mathfrak{S}_n(\mathrm{E}, x_1, \ldots, x_n, \mathrm{Y}),$$

(25) $$(x_1) \ldots (x_n)(\mathrm{Y})[\mathfrak{S}_n(\mathrm{E}, x_1, \ldots, x_n, \mathrm{Y}) \rightarrow \mathfrak{U}(\mathrm{Y})=\varphi(x_1, \ldots, x_n)].$$

On passing over from the generalized arithmetic to the simple arithmetic by the Gödel numbering, $\mathfrak{S}_n$ becomes S_n, $\mathfrak{U}$ becomes U, E becomes its Gödel number e, and (24) and (25) give

(26) $$(x_1) \ldots (x_n)(Ey)S_n(e, x_1, \ldots, x_n, y),$$

(27) $$(x_1) \ldots (x_n)(y)[S_n(e, x_1, \ldots, x_n, y) \rightarrow U(y)=\varphi(x_1, \ldots, x_n)].$$

By Lemma III, U as well as S_n is primitive recursive.

It follows from (26) and (27) that the function $\varphi(x_1, \ldots, x_n)$ can be expressed in terms of the number e thus,

(28) $$\varphi(x_1, \ldots, x_n) = U(\mu y S_n(e, x_1, \ldots, x_n, y)).$$

By (5) and (4) § 57, now (26) and (27) and therefore also (28) remain valid when S_n is replaced by T_n.

THEOREM IX. *For each $n \geq 0$: Given any general recursive function $\varphi(x_1, \ldots, x_n)$, a number e can be found such that*

(29) $$(x_1) \ldots (x_n)(Ey)T_n(e, x_1, \ldots, x_n, y),$$

(30) $$\varphi(x_1, \ldots, x_n) = U(\mu y T_n(e, x_1, \ldots, x_n, y)),$$

(31) $$(x_1) \ldots (x_n)(y)[T_n(e, x_1, \ldots, x_n, y) \rightarrow U(y)=\varphi(x_1, \ldots, x_n)],$$

where $T_n(z, x_1, \ldots, x_n, y)$ and $U(y)$ are the particular primitive recursive predicate and function defined above. (Normal form theorem, Kleene 1936, 1943.)

The advantage of using T_n instead of S_n is that (31) holds for any number e such that (29) and (30) hold (whereas (26) and (28) might hold and (27) be false, when e is the Gödel number of a system E of equations which lacks the consistency property for defining φ recursively).

We now say, for any general recursive function φ, that any number e (whether or not it is the Gödel number of a system E of equations defining φ recursively) such that (29) and (30) (and hence (31)) hold *defines φ recursively* or is a *Gödel number of* φ.

A number e *defines recursively* (or is a *Gödel number of*) a general recursive predicate $P(x_1, \ldots, x_n)$, if it defines recursively the representing function of P. In this case,

$$(32) \qquad \begin{aligned} P(x_1, \ldots, x_n) &\equiv (Ey)[T_n(e, x_1, \ldots, x_n, y) \ \&\ U(y){=}0] \\ &\equiv (y)[T_n(e, x_1, \ldots, x_n, y) \rightarrow U(y){=}0]. \end{aligned}$$

To prove constructively that a function φ is general recursive, one must exhibit (or imply a method for obtaining) equations E which define φ recursively. Thus to give a general recursive function effectively means to give an E, or now a Gödel number e.

The theory of the Gödel numbers of recursive functions will be treated in the next chapter (§ 65).

Example 1. Is every general recursive function $\varphi(x_1, \ldots, x_n)$ expressible in the form $\mu y R(x_1, \ldots, x_n, y)$ where R is primitive recursive (and (1b) holds)? Hint: Use Example 1 § 55 and #E § 45. (A different method was used by Post 1946a.) — Call a function $\theta(y)$ "universal", if for each general recursive function $\varphi(x_1, \ldots, x_n)$ there exists a primitive recursive predicate $R(x_1, \ldots, x_n, y)$ with (1b) holding such that $\varphi(x_1, \ldots, x_n) = \theta(\mu y R(x_1, \ldots, x_n, y))$; and call $\theta(y)$ "of large oscillation", if $(x)(z)(Ey)_{y>z}\theta(y){=}x$. Markov 1947c, 1949 shows that a sufficient and classically necessary condition that a primitive recursive function θ be universal is that it be of large oscillation. Kuznécov 1950 announces further results concerning such functions θ.

Corollary. *Every general recursive function φ is definable by applications of Schemata* (I) — (VI) *with* (1) *holding for the applications of* (VI). (Converse of Theorem III, for Ψ empty.)

For simplicity, beginning with Theorem IV, we confined our attention to functions and predicates general recursive absolutely, i.e. recursive in $\psi_1, \ldots, \psi_l$ for $l = 0$. Now we shall extend the theory to relative general recursiveness, i.e. to $l > 0$.

We shall find that Theorem IX and the earlier results hold, if instead of a primitive recursive predicate T_n, we use one primitive recursive in $\psi_1, \ldots, \psi_l$. Let us work first with the case that $l = 1$ and ψ ($= \psi_1$) is a function of one variable ($m_1 = 1$).

By definition (§ 55), φ is general recursive in ψ, if there is a system E of equations which defines φ recursively from ψ (§ 54). If there is any such E, then we can choose one in which the given function letter g (with Gödel number g) is the first in the fixed enumeration of function letters.

Now we state appropriate modifications of Df12 and Df13 § 56.

Df12* (for $l = m_1 = 1$). (Z is a system of equations, and) Y is a *deduction* from E^{ψ}_{g}, Z (by R1 and R2). (Abbreviation: $\mathfrak{D}^{\psi}$(Z, Y).)

*0. Z is a system of equations; and for some natural number u_1, Y is $(\mathrm{g}(\boldsymbol{u}_1)=\boldsymbol{u})$ where $u = \psi(u_1)$.
$SE(z)$ & $y = 2 \exp 2^{15} \cdot (3 \exp 2^{g} \cdot 3^{(y)_{0,1,1}}) \cdot 5^{(y)_{0,2}}$ & $(Eu_1)_{u_1<y}[Nu((y)_{0,1,1}, u_1)$ & $Nu((y)_{0,2}, \psi(u_1))]$.

1—3. Like 1—3Df12, except reading "from E^{ψ}_{g}, Z" in place of "from Z".

Df13* (for $l = m_1 = 1$). Like Df13, reading "from E^{ψ}_{g}, Z" in place of "from Z", and "$D^{\psi}(z, y)$" in place of "$D(z, y)$".
(Abbreviation: $\mathfrak{S}^{\psi}_{n}(\mathrm{Z}, x_1, \ldots, x_n, \mathrm{Y})$.)

The reasoning used before to show that $D(z, y)$ and $S_n(z, x_1, \ldots, x_n, y)$ are primitive recursive (Lemma III § 56) shows now that $D^{\psi}(z, y)$ and $S^{\psi}_{n}(z, x_1, \ldots, x_n, y)$ are primitive recursive in ψ; and in place of (26) and (27) for a general recursive function $\varphi(x_1, \ldots, x_n)$, we now have for a function $\varphi(x_1, \ldots, x_n)$ general recursive in ψ,

(33) $$(x_1) \ldots (x_n)(Ey)S^{\psi}_{n}(e, x_1, \ldots, x_n, y),$$

(34) $$(x_1) \ldots (x_n)(y)[S^{\psi}_{n}(e, x_1, \ldots, x_n, y) \rightarrow U(y)=\varphi(x_1, \ldots, x_n)].$$

We could continue as before; but we shall show also that the dependence on ψ can be given a special form.

The course-of-values function $\tilde{\psi}(y)$ $(= \prod_{i<y} p_i^{\psi(i)}$, § 46 (1)) for ψ is primitive recursive in ψ (##A, B, 3, 18, §§ 44, 45).

Using § 46 (2), $\psi(u_1)$ in 0Df12* can be written as $(\tilde{\psi}(y))_{u_1}$, since $u_1 < y$, or even as $(\tilde{\psi}(v))_{u_1}$ for any $v \geq y$. Let $D^1(w, z, y)$ be the predicate obtained in place of $D^{\psi}(z, y)$ when we replace $\psi(u_1)$ in 0Df12* by $(w)_{u_1}$. Then D^1 is primitive recursive; and by course-of-values induction on y (with cases corresponding to the four clauses in the recursive definitions of D^1 and D^{ψ}, cf. § 52),

(35) $$(v)_{v \geq y}[D^1(\tilde{\psi}(v), z, y) \equiv D^{\psi}(z, y)].$$

Using $D^1(w, z, y)$ in place of $D^{\psi}(z, y)$ in Df13*, we obtain a primitive recursive predicate $S^1_n(w, z, x_1, \ldots, x_n, y)$ such that

(36) $$(v)_{v \geq y}[S^1_n(\tilde{\psi}(v), z, x_1, \ldots, x_n, y) \equiv S^{\psi}_{n}(z, x_1, \ldots, x_n, y)].$$

We define T_n^1 and T_n^ψ thus,

$$T_n^1(w, z, x_1, \ldots, x_n, y) \equiv S_n^1(w, z, x_1, \ldots, x_n, y) \ \&\ (t)_{t<y}\overline{S}_n^1(w, z, x_1, \ldots, x_n, t),$$

$$T_n^\psi(z, x_1, \ldots, x_n, y) \equiv T_n^1(\tilde{\psi}(y), z, x_1, \ldots, x_n, y).$$

Then T_n^1 is primitive recursive, and T_n^ψ is primitive recursive in ψ. Using (36) first with y, y and then with y, t as the v, y,

(37) $T_n^\psi(z, x_1, \ldots, x_n, y) \equiv S_n^\psi(z, x_1, \ldots, x_n, y) \ \&\ (t)_{t<y}\overline{S}_n^\psi(z, x_1, \ldots, x_n, t).$

Now we can continue from (33) and (34) with (37), as we did before from (26) and (27) with the definition of T_n (preceding (4) § 57).

Our statements here are to be understood intuitionistically as consequences of the hypothesis that particular values of ψ are available on demand. This hypothesis justifies e.g. expressing a given value $\psi(u_1)$ as $(\tilde{\psi}(v))_{u_1}$ for a given $v > u_1$, which requires the other values among $\psi(0), \ldots, \psi(v-1)$; and by it

$$(t)_{t<y}[S_n^\psi(z, x_1, \ldots, x_n, t) \vee \overline{S}_n^\psi(z, x_1, \ldots, x_n, t)]$$

for a given y, which requires the values $\psi(0), \ldots, \psi(y-1)$ (cf. the proof of (5)).

The results obtained in § 57 beginning with Theorem IV extend similarly.

The case of any l functions of $m_1, \ldots, m_l$ variables, respectively, can be reduced to the case $l = m_1 = 1$ (by taking $\psi_i^*(x) = \psi_i((x)_1, \ldots, (x)_{m_i})$, $\psi = p_1^{\psi_1^*} \cdot \ldots \cdot p_l^{\psi_l^*}$); but is also easily treated directly. For example, if $l = m_1 = 2$, $m_2 = 0$, we define the course-of-values function $\tilde{\psi}_1$ for ψ_1 (in both variables) thus, $\tilde{\psi}_1(y, z) = \prod_{i<y} p_i \exp (\prod_{j<z} p_j \exp \psi_1(i, j))$, so that $\psi_1(s, t) = (\tilde{\psi}_1(y, z))_{s, t}$ if $s<y$ & $t<z$. We define $\tilde{\psi}_2 = \psi_2$. Df12* and Df13* are formulated for $l = m_1 = 2$, $m_2 = 0$; and we introduce successively predicates D^{ψ_1, ψ_2}, $S_n^{\psi_1, \psi_2}$, $D^{2,0}$, $S_n^{2,0}$, $T_n^{2,0}$, and let

$$T_n^{\psi_1, \psi_2}(z, x_1, \ldots, x_n, y) \equiv T_n^{2,0}(\tilde{\psi}_1(y, y), \tilde{\psi}_2, z, x_1, \ldots, x_n, y).$$

In general, we come out with a primitive recursive predicate $T_n^{m_1, \ldots, m_l}$ of $n+l+2$ variables, and a predicate $T_n^{\psi_1, \ldots, \psi_l}$ of $n+2$ variables primitive recursive in $\psi_1, \ldots, \psi_l$.

When Ψ is a list of l functions and predicates, the foregoing applies by taking as $\psi_1, \ldots, \psi_l$ the list obtained from Ψ by replacing the predicates (if any) by their representing functions (cf. end § 55); and we then write $T_n^{\psi_1, \ldots, \psi_l}$ also as T_n^Ψ.

The definition of 'arithmetical predicate' (§ 48) is adapted to $l > 0$ by adding the functions $\psi_1, \ldots, \psi_l$ to the initial functions $+$ and $\cdot$; that of "elementary predicate" (§ 57 preceding Theorem VII) by substituting "general recursive in Ψ" for "general recursive". ('Uniformity' can be defined in the usual manner, and the resulting relationships in our theorems are uniform when the given ones are uniform.)

THEOREM X. *Let $l, m_1, \ldots, m_l$ be fixed numbers ≥ 0, and Ψ be l functions and predicates of $m_1, \ldots, m_l$ variables, respectively. Then Theorems* I, IV — IX *and corollaries hold good reading "general recursive in Ψ", "primitive recursive in Ψ", "arithmetical in Ψ", "elementary in Ψ", "T_n^{Ψ}", "V^{Ψ}", "M^{Ψ}", in place of "general recursive", "primitive recursive", "arithmetical", "elementary", "T_n", "V", "M", respectively (with U and υ unchanged).*

The theorems I, IV — IX thus extended we cite using stars. For example: THEOREM IX*. *For each $n \geq 0$: Given any function $\varphi(x_1, \ldots, x_n)$ general recursive in Ψ, a number e can be found such that*

$$(38) \qquad (x_1) \ldots (x_n)(Ey)T_n^{\Psi}(e, x_1, \ldots, x_n, y),$$

$$(39) \qquad \varphi(x_1, \ldots, x_n) = U(\mu y T_n^{\Psi}(e, x_1, \ldots, x_n, y)),$$

$$(40) \qquad (x_1) \ldots (x_n)(y)[T_n^{\Psi}(e, x_1, \ldots, x_n, y) \rightarrow U(y)=\varphi(x_1, \ldots, x_n)],$$

where $U(y)$ is the primitive recursive function, and $T_n^{\Psi}(z, x_1, \ldots, x_n, y)$ the predicate primitive recursive in Ψ, defined above; e.g. for $l = m_1 = 1$, $T_n^{\Psi}(z, x_1, \ldots, x_n, y) \equiv T_n^1(\tilde{\psi}(y), z, x_1, \ldots, x_n, y)$ where $T_n^1(w, z, x_1, \ldots, x_n, y)$ is the particular primitive recursive predicate defined above.

A number e such that (38) and (39) (and hence (40)) hold is said to *define φ recursively in* (or *from*) Ψ or to be a *Gödel number of φ from Ψ* or *of* the functional $\varphi = \mathsf{F}(\Psi)$. The notion extends to a predicate P with representing function φ as before.

COROLLARY. (a) *Every predicate P general recursive in arithmetical predicates Ψ is arithmetical. (Similarly, if P is general recursive in Ψ, Θ, and Ψ are arithmetical, then P is arithmetical in Θ.)* (b)[C] *The predicate $M(a, k)$ of Theorem* VIII *is not general recursive in any arithmetical predicates.*

PROOF OF (a). By Theorem VI* (a), P is expressible by a quantifier prefixed to a predicate R primitive recursive in Ψ. But by Corollary Theorem I*, R is then arithmetical in Ψ; so since Ψ are arithmetical, R and hence P is arithmetical. See Note 1 on p. 316.

Under the definition of "elementary predicate" (preceding Theorem VII § 57), the general recursions were applied only before the logical operations. The meaning of Corollary (a) is that permitting general recursive operations at all stages (i.e. interspersed with the logical operations in any manner) does not lead to a larger class of predicates.

It is natural to inquire just what happens to predicates falling in a given place in the scale of Theorem V Part II (cf. Theorem VII (d)) when general recursive schemes are applied to them.

The distinction (for $k > 0$) between the two k-quantifier forms is lost when primitive recursive operations are applied. For example, although $(Ex)T_1(a, a, x)$ is not expressible in the other one-quantifier form $(x)R(a, x)$, its negation $\overline{(Ex)}T_1(a, a, x)$ is primitive recursive in it (#D § 45), and assumes that other form (cf. *86 § 35). For any predicate $P(a)$, the representing predicate $P(a, w)$ (§ 41) of the representing function (§ 45) of $P(a)$ can be expressed thus,

(41) $$P(a, w) \equiv \{P(a) \mathbin{\&} w=0\} \vee \{\overline{P}(a) \mathbin{\&} w=1\}.$$

This is primitive recursive in $P(a)$. When $P(a) \equiv (Ex)T_1(a, a, x)$, $P(a, w)$ is expressible in neither of the one-quantifier forms: e.g. if $P(a, w) \equiv (x)R(a, w, x)$, then $(x)R(a, 0, x) \equiv P(a, 0) \equiv P(a) \equiv (Ex)T_1(a, a, x)$, which contradicts Theorem V if R is recursive.

Mostowski 1948a gives (classically) an example of a predicate, which (by (b) of the next theorem) is general recursive in predicates of the 1-quantifier forms, but which cannot be expressed in terms of predicates of the 1-quantifier forms by the operations of the propositional calculus.

The following theorem and corollary are Post's on the basis of an abstract (1948), as the author became aware after working out the present treatment (in 1949).

THEOREM XI^C. (a) *If a predicate P is general recursive in predicates $Q_1, \ldots, Q_l$ of the k-quantifier forms of Theorem* V, *then P is expressible in both the $k+1$-quantifier forms, and* (b) *conversely.*

The proof of Theorem VI (b) establishes the present (b), when reread taking the R and S now to be of appropriate k-quantifier forms. The proof of (a) will be completed following the lemmas.

LEMMA IV^C. *The representing predicate of the representing function of a predicate of either k-quantifier form is expressible in the $k+1$-quantifier form with existence first.*

PROOF OF LEMMA IV. For example, suppose $P(a) \equiv (x)(Ey)R(a, x, y)$ with recursive R. Then

$P(a,w) \equiv \{(x)(Ey)R(a,x,y) \ \&\ w=0\} \vee \{\overline{(x)}(Ey)R(a,x,y) \ \&\ w=1\}$ (by (41))
$\equiv \{(x_1)(Ey_1)R(a, x_1, y_1) \ \&\ w=0\} \vee \{(Ex_2)(y_2)\overline{R}(a, x_2, y_2) \ \&\ w=1\}$
(cf. *85, *86)
$\equiv (Ex_2)(x_1)(y_2)(Ey_1)[\{R(a, x_1, y_1) \ \&\ w=0\} \vee \{\overline{R}(a, x_2, y_2) \ \&\ w=1\}]$
(cf. *89—*92)
$\equiv (Ex)(y)(Ez)[\{R(a, (y)_0, z) \ \&\ w=0\} \vee \{\overline{R}(a, x, (y)_1) \ \&\ w=1\}]$ (by (18)).

The last expression is of the form $(Ex)(y)(Ez)R(a, w, x, y, z)$ with recursive R. (This and the next lemma could also be proved for generality first.)

Lemma V. *Let $\tilde{\psi}(a_1, \ldots, a_m)$ be the course-of-values function for $\psi(a_1, \ldots, a_m)$. If the representing predicate of $\psi(a_1, \ldots, a_m)$ is expressible in the $k+1$-quantifier form with existence first, so is the representing predicate of $\tilde{\psi}(a, \ldots, a)$.*

Proof of Lemma V. For example, take $m = k = 1$. By hypothesis, $\psi(a)=w \equiv (Ex)(y)Q(a, w, x, y)$ with recursive Q. Now

$$\tilde{\psi}(a)=w \equiv w = \prod_{i<a} p_i^{(w)_i} \ \&\ (i)_{i<a}\psi(i)=(w)_i$$

$$\equiv w = \prod_{i<a} p_i^{(w)_i} \ \&\ (i)_{i<a}(Ex)(y)Q(i, (w)_i, x, y)$$

$$\equiv w = \prod_{i<a} p_i^{(w)_i} \ \&\ (Ex)(y)(i)_{i<a}Q(i, (w)_i, (x)_i, y) \quad \text{(by Remark 1 § 57)}$$

$$\equiv (Ex)(y)\{w = \prod_{i<a} p_i^{(w)_i} \ \&\ (i)_{i<a}Q(i, (w)_i, (x)_i, y)\} \quad \text{(cf. *91, *89).}$$

The last expression is of the form $(Ex)(y)R(a, w, x, y)$ with recursive R.

Proof of Theorem XI (a). For example, take $l = m = k = 1$. The hypothesis that P is general recursive in Q means (§ 55) that P is general recursive in the representing function ψ of Q. By Lemmas IV and V, $\tilde{\psi}(a)=w \equiv (Ex)(y)R(a, w, x, y)$ with recursive R. We show first that $P(a)$ is expressible in the 2-quantifier form with generality first. Using Theorem VI* (a) with its proof from Theorem IV* (7),

$P(a) \equiv (t)\overline{T}_1^1(\tilde{\psi}(t), g, a, t) \equiv (t)(s)[\tilde{\psi}(t)=s \rightarrow \overline{T}_1^1(s, g, a, t)]$
$\equiv (t)(s)[(Ex)(y)R(t, s, x, y) \rightarrow \overline{T}_1^1(s, g, a, t)]$
$\equiv (t)(s)(x)(Ey)[R(t, s, x, y) \rightarrow \overline{T}_1^1(s, g, a, t)]$ (cf. *96, *98)
$\equiv (x)(Ey)[R((x)_0, (x)_1, (x)_2, y) \rightarrow \overline{T}_1^1((x)_1, g, a, (x)_0)]$ (by (18)),

which is of the desired form. To express $P(a)$ in the other 2-quantifier

form, we have similarly using Theorem IV* (6),
$P(a) \equiv (Et)T_1^1(\tilde{\Psi}(t), f, a, t) \equiv (Et)(Es)[\tilde{\Psi}(t)=s \,\&\, T_1^1(s, f, a, t)]$, etc.

COROLLARY^C. *For each of the* $k+1$*-quantifier forms, the predicate of Theorem* V (b) *which is expressible in the other* $k+1$*-quantifier form but not in the form itself is not recursive in predicates expressible in the forms with* k (*or fewer*) *quantifiers.*

We get a Theorem XI* (with corollary) by replacing "general recursive" for the forms of Theorem V (b) by "general recursive in Ψ".

***§ 59. General recursive functions and the number-theoretic formalism.** In this section, "(i)"—"(vii)" will refer to § 41.

We say that a number-theoretic predicate $P(x_1, \ldots, x_n)$ is *resolvable* in a formal system (or *decidable within* the system), if there is a numeralwise decidable formula $\mathrm{P}(\mathrm{x}_1, \ldots, \mathrm{x}_n)$ (cf. (iv)) with no free variables other than the distinct variables $\mathrm{x}_1, \ldots, \mathrm{x}_n$ such that, for each n-tuple $x_1, \ldots, x_n$ of natural numbers,

$$\text{(viii)} \qquad P(x_1, \ldots, x_n) \equiv \vdash \mathrm{P}(\boldsymbol{x}_1, \ldots, \boldsymbol{x}_n).$$

In this case, $\mathrm{P}(\mathrm{x}_1, \ldots, \mathrm{x}_n)$ *resolves* $P(x_1, \ldots, x_n)$ (with the obvious correspondence of formal to intuitive variables).

A number-theoretic function $\varphi(x_1, \ldots, x_n)$ is *reckonable* in a formal system (or *calculable within* the system), if there is a formula $\mathrm{P}(\mathrm{x}_1, \ldots, \mathrm{x}_n, \mathrm{w})$ with no free variables other than the distinct variables $\mathrm{x}_1, \ldots, \mathrm{x}_n, \mathrm{w}$ such that, for each $x_1, \ldots, x_n, w$,

$$\text{(ix)} \qquad \varphi(x_1, \ldots, x_n)=w \equiv \vdash \mathrm{P}(\boldsymbol{x}_1, \ldots, \boldsymbol{x}_n, \boldsymbol{w}).$$

In this case, $\mathrm{P}(\mathrm{x}_1, \ldots, \mathrm{x}_n, \mathrm{w})$ *reckons* $\varphi(x_1, \ldots, x_n)$.

THEOREM 32. *Let S be the number-theoretic formal system of Chapter* IV (*or Robinson's system described in Lemma* 18b § 49). *If S is simply consistent, then*: $\{\varphi$ *is general recursive*$\} \equiv \{\varphi$ *is numeralwise representable in S*$\} \equiv \{\varphi$ *is reckonable in S*$\}$.

PROOF. We establish three implications.

(a) *If* φ *is general recursive, then* φ *is numeralwise representable in S.*

By Theorem IX § 58, there is a number e for (29) and (30).

Using (29) and the definition of T_n preceding Theorem IV § 57,

$$\text{(42)} \qquad \mu y T_n(e, x_1, \ldots, x_n, y)=w \equiv \\ S_n(e, x_1, \ldots, x_n, w) \,\&\, (z)_{z<w} \overline{S}_n(e, x_1, \ldots, x_n, z).$$

By Corollary Theorem 27 § 49, since $S_n(z, x_1, \ldots, x_n, w)$ is primitive recursive, it is numeralwise expressed by a formula $S(z, x_1, \ldots, x_n, w)$. We shall prove that the formula

$$S(\boldsymbol{e}, x_1, \ldots, x_n, w) \mathbin{\&} \forall z(z<w \supset \neg S(\boldsymbol{e}, x_1, \ldots, x_n, z)),$$

call it "$M(x_1, \ldots, x_n, w)$", numeralwise represents $\mu y T_n(e, x_1, \ldots, x_n, y)$. Let $x_1, \ldots, x_n$ be any fixed n-tuple. To establish (v) for M, suppose that $\mu y T_n(e, x_1, \ldots, x_n, y) = w$. Then using (42), and (E) and (C) § 41 with (i) and (ii) for S, $\vdash M(\boldsymbol{x}_1, \ldots, \boldsymbol{x}_n, \boldsymbol{w})$. Thus we have (v) for M. But then we also have (vi) by *174a (with $\boldsymbol{w}$ as the t). So $\mu y T_n(e, x_1, \ldots, x_n, y)$ is numeralwise representable.

By Theorem 27, since $U(y)$ is primitive recursive, it is numeralwise representable.

By the reasoning for Case (IV) in the proof of Theorem 27, then the composite function $U(\mu y T_n(e, x_1, \ldots, x_n, y))$, i.e. (by (30)) $\varphi(x_1, \ldots, x_n)$, is numeralwise representable.

In this proof, besides the predicate calculus, Axioms 14 — 21, the replacement property of equality, and results already employed in obtaining Theorem 27, we have used only (E) and *174a (with the numeral $\boldsymbol{w}$ as the t). Hence, using Lemmas 18a § 41 and 18b § 49, the implication (a) holds also for Robinson's formal system.

(b) *If S is simply consistent, and φ is numeralwise representable in S, then φ is reckonable in S (and any formula* P *which numeralwise represents φ reckons φ (and* by § 41 *is numeralwise decidable)).*

Consider any fixed $x_1, \ldots, x_n$. We have (v) by hypothesis. To establish the converse, assume that $\vdash P(\boldsymbol{x}_1, \ldots, \boldsymbol{x}_n, \boldsymbol{w})$. Now $\varphi(x_1, \ldots, x_n)=w \vee \varphi(x_1, \ldots, x_n)\neq w$ (cf. *158 § 40). But if $\varphi(x_1, \ldots, x_n)\neq w$, then using (vii) we contradict the simple consistency.

(c) *If φ is reckonable in S, then φ is general recursive.*

Suppose $\varphi(x_1, \ldots, x_n)$ is reckoned by the formula $P(x_1, \ldots, x_n, w)$. If S is the full number-theoretic system, let Pf_P be the primitive recursive predicate corresponding by the Gödel numbering to $\mathfrak{P}\mathfrak{f}_P$ (cf. Dn13a § 51 and Lemma 19 § 52, or Theorem 31 § 52). If S is Robinson's system (Lemma 18b), we must first make the appropriate changes in Dn8. Now $(x_1) \ldots (x_n)(Ey)Pf_P(x_1, \ldots, x_n, (y)_0, (y)_1)$ and $\varphi(x_1, \ldots, x_n) = (\mu y Pf_P(x_1, \ldots, x_n, (y)_0, (y)_1))_0$. Hence using Theorem III § 57, φ is general recursive.

Corollary. *Under the hypotheses of the theorem, and if* $(x_1) \ldots (x_n)[P(x_1, \ldots, x_n) \vee \overline{P}(x_1, \ldots, x_n)]$: *{P is general recursive}* ≡ *{P is numeralwise expressible in S}* ≡ *{P is resolvable in S}.*

PROOF. Let φ be the representing function of P. We establish four implications,

$\{P$ *is general recursive*$\} \underset{(d)}{\rightarrow} \{\varphi$ *is numeralwise representable in* $S\}$
$\underset{(e)}{\rightarrow} \{P$ *is numeralwise expressible in* $S\}$
$\underset{(f)}{\rightarrow} \{P$ *is resolvable in* S *(and any formula* P *which numeralwise expresses* P *resolves* P)$\}$
$\underset{(g)}{\rightarrow} \{P$ *is general recursive*$\}$,

where the simple consistency of S *is a further hypothesis for* (f) *and* (g), *and also* $(x_1) \dots (x_n)[P(x_1, \dots, x_n) \vee \overline{P}(x_1, \dots, x_n)]$ *for* (f) (to make the proof of (f) valid intuitionistically).

(d) From (a) by the definition of general recursive predicate.

(e) As in the proof of Corollary Theorem 27 § 49.

(f) We obtain (iv) as in § 41. We have (i) by hypothesis. To establish the converse, assume that $\vdash \mathrm{P}(\boldsymbol{x}_1, \dots, \boldsymbol{x}_n)$. Now $P(x_1, \dots, x_n) \vee \overline{P}(x_1, \dots, x_n)$. But if $\overline{P}(x_1, \dots, x_n)$, then using (ii) we contradict the simple consistency.

(g) Suppose that the formula $\mathrm{P}(\mathrm{x}_1, \dots, \mathrm{x}_n)$ resolves $P(x_1, \dots, x_n)$. Similarly to (c), $(x_1) \dots (x_n)(Ey)[Pf_{\mathrm{P}}(x_1, \dots, x_n, y) \vee Pf_{\neg\mathrm{P}}(x_1, \dots, x_n, y)]$ (since P is numeralwise decidable) and $P(x_1, \dots, x_n) \equiv Pf_{\mathrm{P}}(x_1, \dots, x_n, \mu y[Pf_{\mathrm{P}}(x_1, \dots, x_n, y) \vee Pf_{\neg\mathrm{P}}(x_1, \dots, x_n, y)])$ (using (viii) and the simple consistency of S). (The simple consistency of S is implied by (viii), if $(Ex_1) \dots (Ex_n)\overline{P}(x_1, \dots, x_n)$.)

The equivalence of reckonability (resolvability) to general recursiveness was proved by Mostowski 1947 for any simply consistent S containing the usual number theory and such that (R_1) primitive recursive predicates are resolvable in S (cf. Corollary Theorem 27) and (R_2) the predicates Pf_{A} are primitive recursive (cf. Dn13a and Lemma 19). Other references will be given in § 62. Cf. R. M. Robinson 1950 abstract.

Let $\Psi^{\bullet}$ be a list $\psi_1, \dots, \psi_l$ of functions of $m_1, \dots, m_l$ variables, respectively. Choose distinct predicate letters $\mathrm{Q}_1, \dots, \mathrm{Q}_l$, and annex them to the stock of formal symbols for S. Extend the definition of formula for S by providing that $\mathrm{Q}_j(\mathrm{t}_1, \dots, \mathrm{t}_{m_j}, \mathrm{t})$ be a formula for each j $(j = 1, \dots, l)$ and terms $\mathrm{t}_1, \dots, \mathrm{t}_{m_j}, \mathrm{t}$. Let $\mathrm{F}^{\psi_1 \dots \psi_l}_{\mathrm{Q}_1 \dots \mathrm{Q}_l}$ be the set of the formulas $\mathrm{Q}_j(\boldsymbol{y}_1, \dots, \boldsymbol{y}_{m_j}, \boldsymbol{y})$ & $\forall \mathrm{z}(\mathrm{Q}_j(\boldsymbol{y}_1, \dots, \boldsymbol{y}_{m_j}, \mathrm{z}) \supset \boldsymbol{y}{=}\mathrm{z})$ where $\psi_j(y_1, \dots, y_{m_j}) = y$, for $j = 1, \dots, l$ and all m_j-tuples $y_1, \dots, y_{m_j}$ of natural numbers. Let notions *simply consistent* (*numeralwise decidable*, *numeralwise expressible, numeralwise representable, resolvable, reckonable*) *in* (or *from*) Ψ be obtained by changing "⊢" to "$F^{\psi_1 \dots \psi_l}_{Q_1 \dots Q_l}$ ⊢" (or in words, "provable" to "deducible from $F^{\psi_1 \dots \psi_l}_{Q_1 \dots Q_l}$") in the former definitions. Theorems 27, 31, 32 and corollaries (including (a) — (g)) hold with these notions and "$F^{\psi_1 \dots \psi_l}_{Q_1 \dots Q_l}$ ⊢", "primitive recursive in Ψ" and "general recursive in Ψ" in place of the respective former notions. (Also P is *numeralwise expressible uniformly in* (or *from*) Ψ, if a formula P can be given independently of Ψ which numeralwise expresses P from Ψ for each choice of Ψ under consideration; and similarly for numeralwise representability, resolvability and reckonability. The theorems hold when the notions for P or φ relative to Ψ are understood throughout as uniform.)

Equivalently, we may instead choose distinct function letters $g_1, \dots, g_l$, extend the definition of term to include $g_j(t_1, \dots, t_{m_j})$ when $t_1, \dots, t_{m_j}$ are terms, and substitute "$E^{\psi_1 \dots \psi_l}_{g_1 \dots g_l}$ ⊢" (§ 54) for "⊢" in the former definitions.

If we let Ψ include predicates, we may proceed in either of these ways, taking as ψ_j the representing function of Q_j when the j-th of the Ψ's is a predicate Q_j; or instead for each such j we may introduce a predicate letter Q_j to be used with m_j arguments, and let the assumption formula corresponding to this j and a given m_j-tuple $y_1, \dots, y_{m_j}$ be $Q_j(\mathbf{y}_1, \dots, \mathbf{y}_{m_j})$ or $\neg Q_j(\mathbf{y}_1, \dots, \mathbf{y}_{m_j})$ according as $Q_j(y_1, \dots, y_{m_j})$ or $\overline{Q}_j(y_1, \dots, y_{m_j})$.

§ 60. Church's theorem, the generalized Gödel theorem.

We now undertake to answer finally the question whether informal mathematics can be completely formalized (§ 15). We know by Gödel's theorem (§ 42) that the particular formal system of Chapter IV does not completely formalize intuitive number theory.

In informal number theory we consider propositions depending on parameters. Infinitely many particular propositions arise, according to the natural numbers taken as values by these parameters. We describe this situation by saying that the propositions are the values of predicates. Generally we have under consideration a number of predicates simultaneously. However, let us discuss the formalization in relation to one of them, say a predicate $P(x)$ of one variable x.

The formal number-theoretic system of earlier chapters provides one illustration of how formalization can be carried out. Let us put aside all the finer details, and consider only the bare skeleton of what a formal system must provide if it is to serve its purpose.

The formal system must have some domain of 'formal objects'. Among these, if the system is to constitute a formalization of the theory of the predicate $P(x)$, there must be particular distinct formal objects which we identify as expressing the propositions $P(0)$, $P(1)$, $P(2)$, ..., i.e. $P(x)$ for $x = 0, 1, 2, \ldots$. We may conveniently designate these formal objects by "A(0)", "A(1)", "A(2)", ..., respectively, i.e. "A(**x**)" for $x = 0, 1, 2, \ldots$; and call A(**x**) 'the formula expressing $P(x)$'. We do this without making any assumption as to whether there be such things as numerals **x**, a variable x, and a formula A(x) from which A(**x**) comes by substituting **x** for x.

Next, there must be a category of formal objects called 'proofs'. Each proof must be a proof 'of' a particular formal object, which may or may not be the object A(**x**) for a given natural number x. Let "$\mathfrak{R}(x, \mathrm{Y})$" stand for the metamathematical proposition that Y is a proof of A(**x**). The object A(**x**) is said to be 'provable', if there is a proof of it. Let "$\vdash$ A(**x**)" stand for the proposition that A(**x**) is provable; i.e.

$$(43) \qquad (E\mathrm{Y})\mathfrak{R}(x, \mathrm{Y}) \equiv \vdash \mathrm{A}(\mathbf{x}).$$

What is the nature of the predicate $\mathfrak{R}(x, \mathrm{Y})$? Our purpose in formalizing a theory is to make explicit the conditions which determine what propositions hold in the sense of being provable in the theory (§ 15), or in brief to give an explicit definition of what constitutes a proof. This purpose will be accomplished, for the theory of the predicate $P(x)$ as expressed by the formula A(**x**), only if there is a preassigned procedure, not requiring any mathematical invention on our part to apply, by which, whenever we are given a particular natural number x and formal object Y, we can tell whether Y is a proof of A(**x**) for that x. That is, there must be a decision procedure or algorithm for the question whether $\mathfrak{R}(x, \mathrm{Y})$ holds (§ 30). We shall also express this by saying that $\mathfrak{R}(x, \mathrm{Y})$ must be an "effectively decidable" metamathematical predicate.

We have not stipulated what kind of structure the domain of the formal objects should have. However each formal object Y must be capable of being given as a finite object, as otherwise it would make no sense to speak of a decision procedure for $\mathfrak{R}(x, \mathrm{Y})$. This may mean that each Y can be generated from a finite number of initial objects by a finite number of applications of recognized operations, as in our conception of a generalized arithmetic (§ 50); or that each Y can be given as a figure constituted out of a finite number of occurrences of symbols from a preassigned enumeration of symbols. By familiar methods (§§ 1, 50, 52) we can then give an effective enumeration of the formal objects, or perhaps more conveniently an effective Gödel numbering, i.e. a 1-1 correspondence between the formal objects and a subset of the natural numbers. The effectiveness means that, given any formal object Y we can always find the corresponding number y, and inversely given any natural number y we can always determine whether it corresponds to a formal object, and if so find that object Y. Thereby we correlate to the effectively decidable metamathematical predicate $\mathfrak{R}(x, \mathrm{Y})$ an effectively decidable number-theoretic predicate $R(x, y)$, where $R(x, y) \equiv \{y$ is the natural number correlated to a formal object Y such that $\mathfrak{R}(x, \mathrm{Y})\}$. Then $(E\mathrm{Y})\mathfrak{R}(x, \mathrm{Y}) \equiv (Ey)R(x, y)$; and by (43),

(44) $$(Ey)R(x, y) \equiv \vdash \mathrm{A}(\mathbf{x}).$$

What kind of a number-theoretic predicate can meet the condition on $R(x, y)$ of being effectively decidable? For the formal system of Chapter IV, and any formula $\mathrm{A}(a)$ in that system, this predicate $R(x, y)$ (corresponding by the Gödel numbering to 'Y is a proof of $\mathrm{A}(\mathbf{x})$') is primitive recursive, as we showed in proving Theorem 31 § 52.

Any general recursive predicate is effectively decidable. For any general recursive function φ is effectively calculable. Given a system E of equations defining φ recursively, an effective process for finding the value of φ for given arguments $x_1, \ldots, x_n$ is afforded by deducing equations from E until one $\mathrm{f}(\mathbf{x}_1, \ldots, \mathbf{x}_n)=\mathbf{x}$ expressing that this value is x is found. Such a system E always does exist and such an equation can always be deduced, according to the definitions of 'general recursive function' (§ 55) and 'E defines φ recursively' (§ 54). (We can also see that φ is effectively calculable, by considering Theorem IX (29) and (30) § 58, or Corollary Theorem IX.) Then if R is a general recursive predicate, we can decide whether it is true or false for given arguments $x_1, \ldots, x_n$, by calculating the value of the representing function for those arguments, and reading whether that value is 0 or 1.

The converse of this has seemed also to be true. Every example of a function (predicate) acknowledged to be effectively calculable (decidable), for which the question has been investigated, has turned out to be general recursive. This heuristic evidence and other considerations led Church 1936 to propose the following thesis.

THESIS I. *Every effectively calculable function (effectively decidable predicate) is general recursive.*

This thesis is also implicit in the conception of a computing machine formulated by Turing 1936-7 and Post 1936. We postpone the discussion of the evidence for the thesis to the next two chapters, and proceed at once to consider its implications.

The thesis and its converse provide the exact definition of the notion of a calculation (decision) procedure or algorithm, for the case of a function (predicate) of natural numbers, which we were not ready to provide in § 30. To give a decision procedure for a predicate $P(x)$ thus means to give a general recursive predicate $R(x)$ such that $P(x) \equiv R(x)$. By Theorem V (14) and (15) § 57, we have the following theorem, originally stated by Church 1936 with a different example of an "unsolvable" decision problem.

THEOREM XII. *There is no decision procedure (or algorithm) for either of the predicates* $(y)\overline{T}_1(x, x, y)$ *or* $(Ey)T_1(x, x, y)$.

From the considerations in the first part of this section, by applying Thesis I to the R of (44), we obtain a second thesis.

THESIS II. *For a given formal system S in which the values of a predicate* $P(x)$ *are expressed by designated distinct formulas* A($\mathbf{x}$) ($x = 0, 1, 2, \ldots$), *the predicate* 'A($\mathbf{x}$) *is provable in S' is expressible in the form* $(Ey)R(x, y)$ *where R is general recursive, i.e. there exists a general recursive predicate R such that* (44) *holds.* (*Similarly for a predicate* $P(x_1, \ldots, x_n)$ *of n variables.*)

REMARK 1. Here we have considered only the formulas A($\mathbf{x}$) in which we are interested. If we take other formulas into account, and the system satisfies our usual conceptions of what it should accomplish, we can analyze further. Let "$\mathfrak{P}$(A, Y)" denote 'Y is a proof of A' as a predicate of any two formal objects A, Y. This predicate $\mathfrak{P}$(A, Y) will be effectively decidable, A($\mathbf{x}$) will be an effectively calculable function of x, and the effective decidability of $\mathfrak{R}(x$, Y) will result by taking $\mathfrak{R}(x, \text{Y}) \equiv \mathfrak{P}(\text{A}(\mathbf{x}), \text{Y})$. For an effective Gödel numbering of the formal objects, let "A_a" stand for the object (if any) having a as its number; and let "$\vdash \text{A}_a$" express that this object is a provable formula ("$\vdash \text{A}_a$" being false when a is not a Gödel number). To $\mathfrak{P}$(A, Y) we correlate $P(a, y)$. Using Thesis I: (a) *There is a general recursive predicate P such that* $(Ey)P(a, y) \equiv \vdash \text{A}_a$. (b) *The Gödel number* $\alpha(x)$ *of* A($\mathbf{x}$) *is a general recursive function of* x. Thesis II follows by taking $R(x, y) \equiv P(\alpha(x), y)$.

Thesis II formulates the (minimum) structural requirement on a formal system S in order for it to serve as a formalization of the theory of a predicate P, with the propositions $P(x)$ for $x = 0, 1, 2, \ldots$ expressed by the respective formulas $A(\mathbf{x})$. As in the case of Thesis I, the converse holds (as stated below).

It remains to state the conditions on S relating provability of the formulas $A(\mathbf{x})$ with the propositions $P(x)$ which they are intended to express. For the formalization to be *correct* (or *consistent*) for $P(x)$, it is required that

(45) $$\vdash A(\mathbf{x}) \rightarrow P(x),$$

i.e. $A(\mathbf{x})$ is provable in S only when $P(x)$ is true. If the system S is also to constitute a *complete* formalization of the theory of the predicate, we must also have, conversely, that $P(x) \rightarrow \vdash A(\mathbf{x})$, i.e. $A(\mathbf{x})$ is provable whenever $P(x)$ is true. Combining this with (45),

(46) $$\vdash A(\mathbf{x}) \equiv P(x)$$

in the case that S is complete as well as correct for $P(x)$.

Combining this with the structural requirement given in Thesis II: To give a correct formal system for the predicate $P(x)$ entails finding a general recursive predicate R such that

(47) $$(Ey)R(x, y) \rightarrow P(x);$$

to set up one that is also complete, such that

(48) $$(Ey)R(x, y) \equiv P(x).$$

Now suppose $P(x)$ is the predicate $(y)\overline{T}_1(x, x, y)$. Then there is no general recursive R such that (48) holds for all x; for then by Theorem V (12), given any general recursive R, there is a number f such that (48) fails for $x = f$. Thus:

THEOREM XIII (PART I). *There is no correct and complete formal system for the predicate* $(y)\overline{T}_1(x, x, y)$. (A generalized form of Gödel's theorem, Kleene 1943.)

To examine the situation in more detail, consider any formal system S and choice of formulas $A(\mathbf{x})$ in S to express $(y)\overline{T}_1(x, x, y)$ for $x = 0, 1, 2, \ldots$. Let R be the general recursive predicate such that (44) holds (given by Thesis II); and consider the f of (9) for this R. Suppose S is correct for $(y)\overline{T}_1(x, x, y)$; then by (45),

(49) $$\vdash A(\mathbf{x}) \rightarrow (y)\overline{T}_1(x, x, y).$$

By the informal counterpart of *86 § 35, (9) and (44),

(50) $$(y)\overline{T}_1(f, f, y) \equiv \overline{(Ey)}T_1(f, f, y) \equiv \overline{(Ey)}R(f, y) \equiv \overline{\vdash A(\mathbf{f})}.$$

Assume $\vdash A(\mathbf{f})$. Then by (49), $(y)\overline{T}_1(f, f, y)$; and by (50), $\overline{\vdash A(\mathbf{f})}$. By reductio ad absurdum, $\overline{\vdash A(\mathbf{f})}$; and by (50), $(y)\overline{T}_1(f, f, y)$. Thus:

THEOREM XIII (PART II). *In particular, suppose S is a formal system with distinct formulas* A(**x**) *designated as expressing the propositions* $(y)\overline{T}_1(x, x, y)$ *for* $x = 0, 1, 2, \ldots$. *Then a number f can be found such that: If S is correct for* $(y)\overline{T}_1(x, x, y)$, *then* $(y)\overline{T}_1(f, f, y)$ & $\overline{\vdash \text{A}(\mathbf{f})}$; *i.e. the proposition* $(y)\overline{T}_1(f, f, y)$ *is true, but the formula* A(**f**) *expressing it is unprovable.*

Thus no formal system can be complete for the purpose of proving the true (and only the true) propositions taken as the values of a certain preassigned intuitive predicate $(y)\overline{T}_1(x, x, y)$. Nothing is assumed about the formal system, except that it fulfils the structural requirement expressed in Thesis II, and yields only results correct under the interpretation of the formulas A(**x**) as expressing the values of the predicate $(y)\overline{T}_1(x, x, y)$.

These assumptions constitute a very considerable abstraction from the particular formal systems we have studied. In those, a proof consisted in applications of listed postulates. We had grounds for belief in the correctness of each of these postulates separately, and hence in the system as a whole. The Gödel incompleteness, we now see, does not depend on the nature of this intuitive evidence.

To emphasize this, we can imagine an omniscient number-theorist. We should expect that his ability to see infinitely many facts at once would enable him to recognize as correct some principles of deduction which we could not discover ourselves. But any correct formal system for $(y)\overline{T}_1(x, x, y)$, which he could reveal to us, telling us how it works without telling us why, would still be incomplete.

To understand the meaning of the propositions $(y)\overline{T}_1(x, x, y)$, only the notion of a particular effectively calculable predicate (indeed, of one which is primitive recursive), and of the universal quantifier used constructively, are required. Lesser conceptual presuppositions, if any mathematical infinite is to be allowed, are hardly conceivable.

In using this predicate $(y)\overline{T}_1(x, x, y)$ on the metatheoretic level, as already meaningful to us, we have not assumed that each value of it is either true or false. What we can conclude by only finitary reasoning with this predicate is enough, taken with Thesis II, to rule out the possibility of our ever having a correct and complete formal system for it.

Here we have been dealing with the incompleteness of any (correct) formal system as a formalization of the existing intuitive theory of the predicate $(y)\overline{T}_1(x, x, y)$. Because this interpretation has been handled in a finitary way, the theorem can be considered as metamathematical in the broader sense of the term.

For formal systems having some ordinary formative and deductive properties, the theorem can also be formulated metamathematically in the narrower sense, replacing the reference to the interpretation of the formulas $\mathrm{A}(\boldsymbol{x})$ as expressing the values of the predicate $(y)\overline{T}_1(x, x, y)$ by consistency and completeness defined as intrinsic properties of the system; e.g. briefly thus:

THEOREM XIII (PART III). *Let S be a formal system having distinct formulas* $\mathrm{T}(\boldsymbol{x}, \boldsymbol{y})$, $\neg\mathrm{T}(\boldsymbol{x}, \boldsymbol{y})$, $\mathrm{A}(\boldsymbol{x})$ *(also written* "$\forall \mathrm{y} \neg \mathrm{T}(\boldsymbol{x}, \mathrm{y})$"*) and* $\neg\mathrm{A}(\boldsymbol{x})$ *(also written* "$\neg \forall \mathrm{y} \neg \mathrm{T}(\boldsymbol{x}, \mathrm{y})$"*)* $(x, y = 0, 1, 2, \ldots)$. *Suppose that* (A) $T_1(x, x, y) \rightarrow \vdash \mathrm{T}(\boldsymbol{x}, \boldsymbol{y})$ *and* $\overline{T}_1(x, x, y) \rightarrow \vdash \neg\mathrm{T}(\boldsymbol{x}, \boldsymbol{y})$, (B) $\vdash \forall \mathrm{y} \neg \mathrm{T}(\boldsymbol{x}, \mathrm{y}) \rightarrow (y)\{\vdash \neg\mathrm{T}(\boldsymbol{x}, \boldsymbol{y})\}$, *and* (C) *for some general recursive R,* (44) *holds. Then a number f can be found such that: If S is simply consistent in the sense that for no x, y both* $\vdash \mathrm{T}(\boldsymbol{x}, \boldsymbol{y})$ *and* $\vdash \neg\mathrm{T}(\boldsymbol{x}, \boldsymbol{y})$, *then* $\overline{\vdash \mathrm{A}(\boldsymbol{f})}$. *If S is also ω-consistent in the sense that for no x both* $(y)\{\vdash \neg\mathrm{T}(\boldsymbol{x}, \boldsymbol{y})\}$ *and* $\vdash \neg \forall \mathrm{y} \neg \mathrm{T}(\boldsymbol{x}, \mathrm{y})$, *then* $\overline{\vdash \neg\mathrm{A}(\boldsymbol{f})}$. *Thus if S is simply and ω-consistent, it is simply incomplete in the sense that for some x neither* $\vdash \mathrm{A}(\boldsymbol{x})$ *nor* $\vdash \neg\mathrm{A}(\boldsymbol{x})$.

PROOF. Assume that S is simply consistent, and (for reductio ad absurdum) that $\vdash \mathrm{A}(\boldsymbol{f})$. Then by (44), $(Ey)R(f, y)$; by (9), $(Ey)T_1(f, f, y)$; and by (A), $\vdash \mathrm{T}(\boldsymbol{f}, \boldsymbol{y})$ for some y. But also from $\vdash \mathrm{A}(\boldsymbol{f})$ by (B), $\vdash \neg\mathrm{T}(\boldsymbol{f}, \boldsymbol{y})$ for this y, contradicting the simple consistency. By reductio ad absurdum, $\overline{\vdash \mathrm{A}(\boldsymbol{f})}$. Now assume that S is also ω-consistent. From $\overline{\vdash \mathrm{A}(\boldsymbol{f})}$ by (50), $(y)\overline{T}_1(f, f, y)$; by (A), $(y)\{\vdash \neg\mathrm{T}(\boldsymbol{f}, \boldsymbol{y})\}$; and by the ω-consistency, $\overline{\vdash \neg \forall \mathrm{y} \neg \mathrm{T}(\boldsymbol{f}, \mathrm{y})}$, i.e. $\overline{\vdash \neg\mathrm{A}(\boldsymbol{f})}$.

Mostowski 1952, which was not available during the writing of the present book, compares various proofs of Gödel's theorem.

The incompleteness theorems XII and XIII appear in our presentation as applications of the cases of Theorem V for the respective predicate forms $R(x)$ and $(Ey)R(x, y)$. This theme is developed at length in Kleene 1943*. We conclude this section with some further remarks about the predicate form $(Ey)R(x, y)$.

CONVERSE OF THESIS II (PART I). *There is a correct and complete formal system for any predicate of the form* $(Ey)R(x, y)$ *with R general recursive. (Similarly for* $(Ey_1) \ldots (Ey_m)R(x_1, \ldots, x_n, y_1, \ldots, y_m)$ *with R general recursive* $(n, m \geq 0)$.*)*

In more detail (for $n = m = 1$): *Given any general recursive predicate* $R(x, y)$, *a formal system S with distinct formulas* $\mathrm{A}(\boldsymbol{x})$ *for* $x = 0, 1, 2, \ldots$ *can be found such that* (44) *holds.*

In Example 1 the correctness of the system remains a hypothesis.

However Example 3 provides a quick and unimpeachable demonstration. (Here (44) is the (viii) of § 59, but in general (iv) is lacking for resolvability.)

EXAMPLE 1. By Corollary Theorem IV § 57, there is no loss of generality in taking R to be primitive recursive. Let S be the number-theoretic formal system of Chapter IV, R(x, y) be a formula which numeralwise expresses $R(x, y)$ (Corollary Theorem 27 § 49), and A(**x**) be the formula ∃yR(**x**, y). Then clearly $(Ey)R(x, y) \rightarrow \vdash$ A(**x**). So (44) holds, if the system has the property that ⊢ ∃yR(**x**, y) only when $(Ey)R(x, y)$. This is a consistency property which (if $(Ex)(\overline{Ey})R(x, y)$) implies simple consistency, so by Gödel's second theorem (Theorem 30 § 42) we cannot expect to find an elementary proof of it; and in fact for the classical formal system it is not clear how any proof of it can be given without using classical logic in the metalanguage.

EXAMPLE 2. Similarly taking as S Robinson's system (Lemma 18b § 49) with only thirteen number-theoretic axioms. A lengthy but elementary proof of the required consistency property (for an R(x, y) constructed as in the proof of Corollary Theorem 27) will be given in §§ 77—79 (cf. Theorem 53 (b) § 79). — A fortiori (or directly, cf. Theorem 53 (a)), Robinson's system is simply consistent.

EXAMPLE 3. Let E be a system of equations in the formalism of recursive functions which defines recursively the representing function of R, with f as principal function letter. Let the predicate letter $\mathcal{A}$ be added to the stock of formal symbols. Let S be the system having the equations of E as its axioms, and having as its rules of inference R1, R2 and the following, where $\boldsymbol{x}$ and $\boldsymbol{y}$ are numerals:

$$\frac{f(\boldsymbol{x}, \boldsymbol{y})=0}{\mathcal{A}(\boldsymbol{x}).}$$

The consistency property (with $\mathcal{A}(\boldsymbol{x})$ as the A(**x**)) is immediate.

EXAMPLE 4. Let the formal symbols of S comprise only 0, ′, and the two predicate letters $\mathcal{R}$ and $\mathcal{A}$ (with comma and parentheses). The formulas shall be the expressions $\mathcal{R}(\boldsymbol{x}, \boldsymbol{y})$ and $\mathcal{A}(\boldsymbol{x})$ for $x, y = 0, 1, 2, \ldots$. The postulates shall be an axiom schema 1 and a rule of inference 2, as follows. For Axiom Schema 1, $\boldsymbol{x}$ and $\boldsymbol{y}$ are stipulated to be numerals such that $R(x, y)$.

1. $\mathcal{R}(\boldsymbol{x}, \boldsymbol{y})$.

2. $$\frac{\mathcal{R}(\boldsymbol{x}, \boldsymbol{y})}{\mathcal{A}(\boldsymbol{x}).}$$

This formal system may seem unorthodox. But the stipulation on the $\boldsymbol{x}$ and $\boldsymbol{y}$ for Axiom Schema 1 is an effective one (since R is general recursive), just as e.g. that on the t for Axiom Schemata 10 and 11 § 19.

A fifth example is given as Example 2 end § 73.

CONVERSE OF THESIS II (PART II). *There is a formal system S such that, given any general recursive predicate* $R(x, y)$, *distinct formulas* $\mathrm{A}(\boldsymbol{x})$ *for* $x = 0, 1, 2, \ldots$ *can be found such that* (44) *holds.* (*Similarly for any n, m; or for all n, m simultaneously.*)

PROOF. Let $\mathrm{A}(\boldsymbol{z}, \boldsymbol{x})$ $(z, x = 0, 1, 2, \ldots)$ be the formulas obtained by applying Part I (for $n = 2$, $m = 1$) to $T_1(z, x, y)$; and let $\mathrm{A}(\boldsymbol{x})$ $(x = 0, 1, 2, \ldots)$ be $\mathrm{A}(\boldsymbol{f}, \boldsymbol{x})$ for the f of (9) § 57.

REMARK 2. By adding new postulates to S (in Part I or II), we obtain systems S' such that $(Ey)R(x, y) \rightarrow\ \vdash \mathrm{A}(\boldsymbol{x})$, but not necessarily $\vdash \mathrm{A}(\boldsymbol{x}) \rightarrow (Ey)R(x, y)$.

By Thesis II and its converse, the same predicates are expressible in the form $(Ey)R(x, y)$ for some general recursive R as are expressible by $\vdash \mathrm{A}(\boldsymbol{x})$ for some formal system S and effective designation of formulas $\mathrm{A}(\boldsymbol{x})$ for $x = 0, 1, 2, \ldots$. Briefly, the predicate form $(Ey)R(x, y)$ coincides with the notion of provability in some formal system.

By the result mentioned at the end of § 53 (with Corollary Theorem IV) inductive definitions (with constructive direct clauses) lead to precisely the same class of predicates. This fact is closely related to the foregoing, in view of the role often given to inductive definitions in defining formal systems.

RECURSIVE ENUMERABILITY. A set or class C of natural numbers is *recursively enumerable*, if there is a general recursive function φ which enumerates it (allowing repetitions), i.e. such that $\varphi(0), \varphi(1), \varphi(2), \ldots$ is an enumeration (allowing repetitions) of the members of C. (Post 1944 includes also the empty class as recursively enumerable.)

THEOREM XIV. *A class C having a member is recursively enumerable, if and only if the predicate* $x \,\varepsilon\, C$ *is expressible in the form* $(Ey)R(x, y)$ *with a general recursive R.*

In more detail: (a) *If* φ *enumerates C, then* $x \,\varepsilon\, C \equiv (Ey)R(x, y)$ *with an R primitive recursive in* φ. (b) *If* $x \,\varepsilon\, C \equiv (Ey)R(x, y)$ *and C has a member m, then C is enumerated by a function* θ *primitive recursive in R* (Kleene 1936).

PROOFS. (a) $x \varepsilon C \equiv (Ey)[\varphi(y)=x]$ (cf. #14 § 45). (b) Let

$$\theta(y) = \begin{cases} (y)_0 & \text{if } R((y)_0, (y)_1), \\ m & \text{if } \bar{R}((y)_0, (y)_1) \end{cases}$$

(cf. ##D, F, 19).

Thus Thesis II is equivalent to saying that the class C of the numbers x for which A($\mathbf{x}$) is provable is recursively enumerable (if it has a member). We call a set or class C *general recursive*, if the predicate $x \varepsilon C$ is general recursive. Paraphrasing results of § 57: A general recursive class C is a fortiori recursively enumerable, if it has a member (Theorem VI (a)); likewise its complement $\bar{C}$ (#D § 45). Classically, a class C is general recursive, if both C and $\bar{C}$ are recursively enumerable (Theorem VI (b) or (c)). The class of the x's such that $(Ey)T_1(x, x, y)$ (in symbols, $\hat{x}(Ey)T_1(x, x, y)$) is recursively enumerable (by (29) § 58, $(Ey)T_1(e, e, y)$, so e is a member), but not general recursive (Theorem V (15)); its complement $\hat{x}(y)\bar{T}_1(x, x, y)$ is neither recursively enumerable nor general recursive (Theorem V (12) and (14)).

COROLLARY. *If a class can be enumerated (allowing repetitions) by a general recursive function, it can be enumerated (allowing repetitions) by a primitive recursive function.* (Rosser 1936.)

Using (a), then Corollary Theorem IV, then (b).

EXAMPLE 5. An infinite class C is general recursive, if and only if it is recursively enumerable without repetitions in order of magnitude (Kleene 1936). (HINT: Use Theorem III.) Every infinite recursively enumerable class contains an infinite general recursive subclass (Post 1944). If an infinite class is recursively enumerable allowing repetitions, it is recursively enumerable without repetitions (Kleene 1936).

EXAMPLE 6. PROBLEM: to define constructively (i.e. intuitionistically) 'general recursive function' from 'recursively enumerable class'. We must avoid the application of the law of the excluded middle which occurs in saying that a class is either empty or has a member, and the non-intuitionistic steps in the proof of Theorem VI (b). SOLUTION by combining the first of the following two propositions, Theorem VI (c), and the second (or Theorem XIV): A function $\varphi(x_1, \ldots, x_n)$ is general recursive, if and only if the class of the numbers $2^{\varphi(x_1, \ldots, x_n)} \cdot p_1^{x_1} \cdot \ldots \cdot p_n^{x_n}$ is general recursive. A predicate $x \varepsilon C$ is expressible in the form $(Ey)R(x, y)$ with general recursive R, if and only if the class (call it $\{0\}+C'$) consisting of 0 and the successors of the members of C is recursively enumerable.

We obtain a notion 'enumerable recursively in Ψ' by reading "function φ general recursive in Ψ" in place of "general recursive function φ" in the definition of recursive enumerability. The results extend to this.

§ 61. A symmetric form of Gödel's theorem. Theorem XIII § 60 generalizes Theorem 28 § 42 (Gödel's theorem in the original form), with A(**f**) corresponding to the $A_p(\boldsymbol{p})$. Part III of Theorem XIII was formulated metamathematically in the narrower sense. We shall now take up thus a generalization of Theorem 29 (the respective Rosser form of Gödel's theorem).

In place of $\overline{(y)\overline{T}_1(x, x, y)}$, we now use the slightly more complicated predicate $\overline{(y)[\overline{T}_1((x)_1, x, y) \vee (Ez)_{z \leq y} T_1((x)_0, x, z)]}$, or its equivalent $(\overline{Ey})[T_1((x)_1, x, y) \,\&\, (z)_{z \leq y}\overline{T}_1((x)_0, x, z)]$.

Let "$W_0(x, y)$" abbreviate $T_1((x)_1, x, y) \,\&\, (z)_{z \leq y}\overline{T}_1((x)_0, x, z)$ and "$W_1(x, y)$" abbreviate $T_1((x)_0, x, y) \,\&\, (z)_{z \leq y}\overline{T}_1((x)_1, x, z)$.

Let x be fixed. Suppose there is a number y_1 such that (i) $T_1((x)_0, x, y_1)$ and (ii) $(z)_{z \leq y_1}\overline{T}_1((x)_1, x, z)$. Then there can be no number y_0 such that (iii) $T_1((x)_1, x, y_0)$ and (iv) $(z)_{z \leq y_0}\overline{T}_1((x)_0, x, z)$. For (i) and (iv) imply $y_1 > y_0$, and (ii) and (iii) imply $y_0 > y_1$. Thus

(51) $$(Ey)W_1(x, y) \rightarrow (\overline{Ey})W_0(x, y).$$

Since the predicates $W_0(x, y)$ and $W_1(x, y)$ are primitive recursive (using ##A, C, D, E, 19 § 45), the theory of the predicate $(Ey)W_0(x, y)$ can be completely formalized, and likewise at least as much of the theory of $(\overline{Ey})W_0(x, y)$ as is given by the sufficient condition $(Ey)W_1(x, y)$ of (51) (by the Converse of Thesis II and Remark 2 § 60). We shall now show that a formal system S which formalizes at least this much, if consistent, cannot be complete.

Accordingly let S be any formal system in which there are formulas B(**x**) and ¬B(**x**) for $x = 0, 1, 2, \ldots$, all distinct. We shall not make any restrictive assumptions as to what kind of symbolism S has, or in particular that B(**x**) comes from a formula B(x) by substituting a numeral **x** for a variable x, or that ¬B(**x**) comes from B(**x**) by prefixing a certain symbol ¬. The deductive rules of S shall be such that

(52) $(Ey)W_0(x, y) \rightarrow\ \vdash$ B(**x**), (53) $(Ey)W_1(x, y) \rightarrow\ \vdash$ ¬B(**x**).

The system S is to serve the purpose of giving an explicit criterion of what constitutes proof for the formulas B(**x**) and ¬B(**x**), and hence (although we now avoid specifying that B(**x**) and ¬B(**x**) should express certain predicates) it is demanded as before by Thesis II that there exist general recursive predicates $R_0(x, y)$ and $R_1(x, y)$ such that

(54) $(Ey)R_0(x, y) \equiv\ \vdash \mathrm{B}(\mathbf{x})$, (55) $(Ey)R_1(x, y) \equiv\ \vdash \neg\mathrm{B}(\mathbf{x})$.

By the (*simple*) *consistency* of S we shall mean that for no natural number x, both $\vdash \mathrm{B}(\mathbf{x})$ and $\vdash \neg\mathrm{B}(\mathbf{x})$; and by the (*simple*) *completeness* that for every x, either $\vdash \mathrm{B}(\mathbf{x})$ or $\vdash \neg\mathrm{B}(\mathbf{x})$.

THEOREM XV. *There is no simply consistent and complete formal system satisfying* (52)—(55).

In more detail: *Given any formal system* S *with distinct formulas* $\mathrm{B}(\mathbf{x})$ *and* $\neg\mathrm{B}(\mathbf{x})$ $(x = 0, 1, 2, \ldots)$ *and general recursive predicates* $R_0(x, y)$ *and* $R_1(x, y)$ *such that* (52) — (55) *hold, a number* f *can be found such that, if* S *is simply consistent, then neither* $\vdash \mathrm{B}(\boldsymbol{f})$ *nor* $\vdash \neg\mathrm{B}(\boldsymbol{f})$. (Rosser's form of Gödel's theorem, in a generalized version.)

PROOF. Assume that S is simply consistent, or in symbols

(56) $$\overline{\vdash \mathrm{B}(\mathbf{x})\ \&\ \vdash \neg\mathrm{B}(\mathbf{x})}.$$

By Theorem IV (6) § 57, there are numbers f_0 and f_1 such that, if we put $f = 2^{f_0} \cdot 3^{f_1}$, then

(57) $$(Ey)R_0(x, y) \equiv (Ey)T_1(f_0, x, y) \equiv (Ey)T_1((f)_0, x, y),$$

(58) $$(Ey)R_1(x, y) \equiv (Ey)T_1(f_1, x, y) \equiv (Ey)T_1((f)_1, x, y).$$

In the rest of the proof, each time we use (52) — (58), we substitute the number f for the variable x. To show by reductio ad absurdum that $\overline{\vdash \mathrm{B}(\boldsymbol{f})}$, suppose that

(a) $$\vdash \mathrm{B}(\boldsymbol{f}).$$

Then by (54), $(Ey)R_0(f, y)$; and by (57),

(b) $$(Ey)T_1((f)_0, f, y).$$

Also by (a) and the simple consistency ((56)),

(c) $$\overline{\vdash \neg\mathrm{B}(\boldsymbol{f})}.$$

Hence by (55), $(\overline{Ey})R_1(f, y)$; by (58), $(\overline{Ey})T_1((f)_1, f, y)$; whence

(d) $$(y)\overline{T}_1((f)_1, f, y).$$

By (b) and (d), $(Ey)[T_1((f)_0, f, y)\ \&\ (z)_{z \leq y}\overline{T}_1((f)_1, f, z)]$, i.e. $(Ey)W_1(f, y)$; and by (53), $\vdash \neg\mathrm{B}(\boldsymbol{f})$, contradicting (c). Hence, rejecting the assumption (a) by reductio ad absurdum, $\overline{\vdash \mathrm{B}(\boldsymbol{f})}$.

By similar steps, or simply by observing the symmetry between (52), (54), (56), (57) and (53), (55), (56), (58): $\overline{\vdash \neg\mathrm{B}(\boldsymbol{f})}$.

Discussion. We motivated the conditions for S by suggesting that $\mathrm{B}(\boldsymbol{x})$ should express $(Ey)W_0(x, y)$ and $\neg\mathrm{B}(\boldsymbol{x})$ its negation. Let us call this, for convenience, the *preferred interpretation*. Under the preferred interpretation, $\neg\mathrm{B}(\boldsymbol{f})$ corresponds to the $\mathrm{A}_q(\boldsymbol{q})$ of § 42 and expresses a true proposition. However the preferred interpretation is not mentioned in the theorem itself. The conditions for S are entirely symmetrical. There is nothing to keep us equally well from interpreting $\neg\mathrm{B}(\boldsymbol{x})$ as expressing $(Ey)W_1(x, y)$ and $\mathrm{B}(\boldsymbol{x})$ the negation of that. Then $\mathrm{B}(\boldsymbol{f})$ corresponds to $\mathrm{A}_q(\boldsymbol{q})$ and expresses a true proposition, while $\neg\mathrm{B}(\boldsymbol{f})$ is false. Between these extremes, there are many intermediate possibilities for the interpretation. We shall illustrate this further in connection with the following examples of systems S for Theorem XV.

Example 1. In the number-theoretic formalism of Chapter IV, since $T_1((a)_1, a, b)$ and $T_1((a)_0, a, c)$ are primitive recursive, by Corollary Theorem 27 § 49 they are numeralwise expressed by formulas $\mathrm{A}(a, b)$ and $\mathrm{B}(a, c)$, respectively. Let $\mathrm{B}(\boldsymbol{x})$ be $\exists b[\mathrm{A}(\boldsymbol{x}, b) \,\&\, \forall c(c \leq b \supset \neg\mathrm{B}(\boldsymbol{x}, c))]$, and $\neg\mathrm{B}(\boldsymbol{x})$ be $\neg\exists b[\mathrm{A}(\boldsymbol{x}, b) \,\&\, \forall c(c \leq b \supset \neg\mathrm{B}(\boldsymbol{x}, c))]$. Then (52) can be shown to hold by methods used in the first part of the proof of Theorem 29 § 42. Also by steps shown there and $\supset$-introd.,
$\vdash \mathrm{B}(\boldsymbol{x}) \supset \neg\forall b[\neg\mathrm{A}(\boldsymbol{x}, b) \vee \exists c(c \leq b \,\&\, \mathrm{B}(\boldsymbol{x}, c))]$. Contraposing (by *13), $\vdash \forall b[\neg\mathrm{A}(\boldsymbol{x}, b) \vee \exists c(c \leq b \,\&\, \mathrm{B}(\boldsymbol{x}, c))] \supset \neg\mathrm{B}(\boldsymbol{x})$. This with the method of the second part of the proof of Theorem 29 gives (53). Note that this proof requires, besides the predicate calculus with equality, Axioms 14 — 21 and Corollary Theorem 27, only *166a, *168, *166 and *169 (with t a numeral). Hence by Lemma 18a (end § 41) and Lemma 18b (end § 49), it also holds good for the system of Robinson. For the number-theoretic system of Chapter IV, we have (54) and (55) for some recursive R_0 and R_1, by Theorem 31 § 52 (and for Robinson's system, by the method of the proof of Theorem 31). In this example, the $\neg$ of $\neg\mathrm{B}(\boldsymbol{x})$ for Theorem XV is actually the $\neg$ of the number-theoretic formalism; and under the usual interpretation of the number-theoretic symbolism, $\mathrm{B}(\boldsymbol{x})$ and $\neg\mathrm{B}(\boldsymbol{x})$ have the preferred interpretation. Now let S be the number-theoretic system of Chapter IV (or Robinson's), with this choice of $\mathrm{B}(\boldsymbol{x})$ and $\neg\mathrm{B}(\boldsymbol{x})$. By the theorem, S (if it is simply consistent) is simply incomplete, and so is every simply consistent enlargement of S obtained by adding more postulates (in such a way that (54) and (55) still hold for some recursive R_0 and R_1). Such an enlargement of S may even be at variance with the preferred interpretation of $\mathrm{B}(\boldsymbol{x})$ and $\neg\mathrm{B}(\boldsymbol{x})$ in S, provided only that the new postulates do not conflict

with the preferred interpretation in a sufficiently elementary way as to give rise to a simple inconsistency.

Example 2. Let the symbolism for a formal system S include the numerals and four predicate symbols $\mathcal{W}_0$, $\mathcal{W}_1$, $\mathcal{B}$ and $\neg\mathcal{B}$ (or in place of the last, an operator $\neg$). Let S have as its postulates two axiom schemata and two rules of inference, as follows. For Axiom Schema 1, $\boldsymbol{x}$ and $\boldsymbol{y}$ are numerals such that $W_0(x, y)$, and for Axiom Schema 2 such that $W_1(x, y)$.

1. $\mathcal{W}_0(\boldsymbol{x}, \boldsymbol{y})$.
2. $\mathcal{W}_1(\boldsymbol{x}, \boldsymbol{y})$.
3. $\dfrac{\mathcal{W}_0(\boldsymbol{x}, \boldsymbol{y})}{\mathcal{B}(\boldsymbol{x}).}$
4. $\dfrac{\mathcal{W}_1(\boldsymbol{x}, \boldsymbol{y})}{\neg\mathcal{B}(\boldsymbol{x}).}$

The simple consistency of this system is immediate from (51). This system S, or any simply consistent extension of it obtained by adding more postulates (with (54) and (55) remaining true for some recursive R_0 and R_1) is simply incomplete. In this S the formulas $\mathrm{B}(\boldsymbol{x})$ and $\neg\mathrm{B}(\boldsymbol{x})$ are provable only as required by (52) and (53). We are unrestricted by the interpretation in enlarging S.

Theorem XIII § 60 is the case of Theorem V § 57 for the predicate form $(Ey)R(x, y)$, in a metamathematical application. Likewise Theorem XV admits a version entirely in terms of predicate forms. Let us compare Theorems XIII and XV using the language of recursively enumerable classes (cf. Theorem XIV § 60).

Remark 1. Theorems XIII and XV make it absurd that any of the three classes $\hat{x}(Ey)T_1(x, x, y)$, $\hat{x}(Ey)W_0(x, y)$ and $\hat{x}(Ey)W_1(x, y)$ be empty. — Members can be found thus. Using (29) Theorem IX § 58, $(Ey)T_1(e, e, y)$. Choose any recursive R such that $(x)(Ey)R(x, y)$, and choose f for this R by (6) Theorem IV § 57; also choose any recursive R such that $(x)(y)R(x, y)$, and choose g for this R by (7). Let $e_0 = 2^g \cdot 3^f$ and $e_1 = 2^f \cdot 3^g$. Then $(Ey)W_0(e_0, y)$ and $(Ey)W_1(e_1, y)$.

In Theorem XIII we have a fixed recursively enumerable class C_0 of natural numbers (namely $\hat{x}(Ey)T_1(x, x, y)$) whose complement C_3 $(= \hat{x}(y)\overline{T}_1(x, x, y))$ is not recursively enumerable (Figure 1). In Theorem XV we have two fixed recursively enumerable classes C_0 and C_1 (namely, $\hat{x}(Ey)W_0(x, y)$ and $\hat{x}(Ey)W_1(x, y)$, respectively), which are disjoint (by (51)) and such that, for every separation of all natural numbers into two disjoint classes C_2 and C_3 with $C_0 \subset C_2$ and $C_1 \subset C_3$, the classes C_2 and C_3 are not both recursively enumerable (Figure 2). (Instead of $(x)(x \,\varepsilon\, C_2 \vee x \,\varepsilon\, C_3)$ it suffices to have $(x)\overline{\overline{(x \,\varepsilon\, C_2 \vee x \,\varepsilon\, C_3)}}$, which is weaker intuitionistically.) Only for the preferred interpretation is C_3 the complement of C_0. In proving Theorem XIII (Part II), we supposed given any recursively

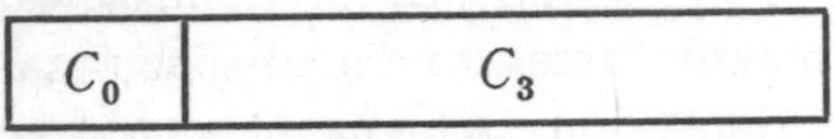

Figure 1.

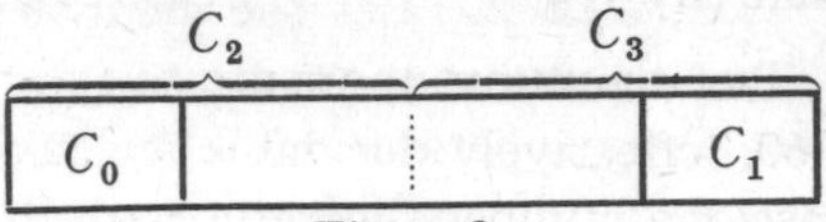

Figure 2.

enumerable class D_3 contained in C_3 (namely, $\hat{x}(Ey)R(x, y)$), and found a number f contained in neither C_0 nor D_3 (Figure 1a). In proving Theorem XV, we supposed given two disjoint recursively enumerable classes D_2 and D_3 containing C_0 and C_1, respectively (namely, $\hat{x}(Ey)R_0(x, y)$ and $\hat{x}(Ey)R_1(x, y)$), and found a number f contained in neither D_2 nor D_3 (Figure 2a). The metamathematical phraseology in the above proof can

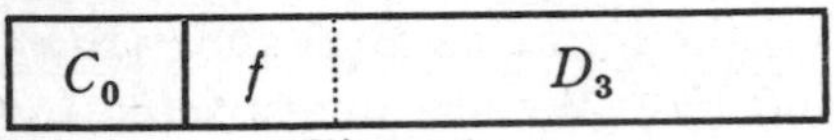

Figure 1a.

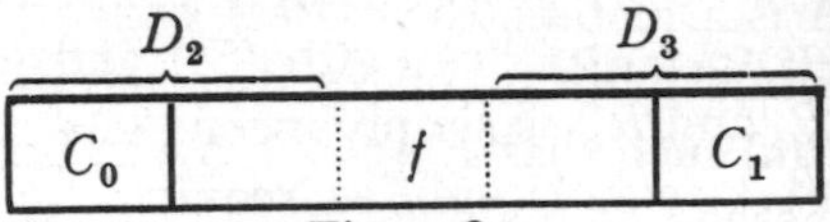

Figure 2a.

of course be bypassed, by first using (54) and (55) in (52), (53) and (56), so that the hypotheses become

(52a) $(Ey)W_0(x, y) \to (Ey)R_0(x, y)$, (53a) $(Ey)W_1(x, y) \to (Ey)R_1(x, y)$,

(56a) $\overline{(Ey)R_0(x, y) \;\&\; (Ey)R_1(x, y)}$

(Kleene 1950). These results extend to classes enumerable recursively in Ψ; cf. end § 60 and Theorem X § 58.

The numbers x for which $\mathrm{B}(\mathbf{x})$ is provable are recursively enumerable ((54), Theorem XIV; by (52) and Remark 1, $\vdash \mathrm{B}(\mathbf{e}_0)$).

THEOREM XVI. *If S as described in Theorem* XV *(omitting* (55)) *is simply consistent, the numbers x for which* $\mathrm{B}(\mathbf{x})$ *is unprovable in S are not recursively enumerable, or equivalently there is no general recursive predicate* $Q(x, y)$ *such that* $(Ey)Q(x, y) \equiv \overline{\vdash \mathrm{B}(\mathbf{x})}$. (After Rosser 1936.)

PROOF. For if $\hat{x}[\overline{\vdash \mathrm{B}(\mathbf{x})}]$ were recursively enumerable, then taking $C_2 = \hat{x}[\vdash \mathrm{B}(\mathbf{x})]$ and $C_3 = \hat{x}[\overline{\vdash \mathrm{B}(\mathbf{x})}]$, we would have the situation shown in Figure 2 with C_2 and C_3 both recursively enumerable. (Intuitionistically, $\overline{(x)(x \,\varepsilon\, C_2 \lor x \,\varepsilon\, C_3)}$; cf. *51a § 27.) The proof may also be given by observing that (52) — (56) would hold replacing "R_1" by "Q" and "$\vdash \neg \mathrm{B}(\mathbf{x})$" by "$\overline{\vdash \mathrm{B}(\mathbf{x})}$", whereupon the former proof that $\overline{\vdash \mathrm{B}(\boldsymbol{f})} \;\&\; \overline{\vdash \neg \mathrm{B}(\boldsymbol{f})}$ becomes a deduction of the logical contradiction $\overline{\vdash \mathrm{B}(\boldsymbol{f})}$ & $\overline{\overline{\vdash \mathrm{B}(\boldsymbol{f})}}$. (We use the hypotheses regarding $\neg \mathrm{B}(\boldsymbol{x})$ and the simple consistency only to infer that $(Ey)W_1(x, y) \rightarrow \overline{\vdash \mathrm{B}(\boldsymbol{x})}$.)

THE DECISION PROBLEM FOR A FORMAL SYSTEM (cf. § 30). By Thesis I § 60, 'effectively decidable (calculable)' means 'general recursive' in the case of a number-theoretic predicate (function). To give an exact sense to 'effectively decidable (calculable)' for a metamathematical predicate (function), we can require that the corresponding number-theoretic predicate (a corresponding number-theoretic function) be general recursive, in the case of any particular formal system S, the objects of which admit an effective Gödel numbering (as they must, if S is to serve our purpose in formalizing, beginning § 60). For example, to give a 'decision procedure' for provability in S, i.e. for the predicate $\vdash \mathrm{A}$ (where A is a metamathematical variable ranging over all formulas, or over all formal objects, of S), then means to give a general recursive predicate $R(a)$ such that $R(a) \equiv \vdash \mathrm{A}_a$, in the notation of Remark 1 § 60. (A second method of making 'effectively decidable (calculable)' exact for a metamathematical predicate (function) is indicated at the end of § 70.) The following can be read either in terms of our intuitive conception of a decision procedure applying to formulas of S, or in terms of this exact mathematical definition. The condition that $\mathrm{B}(\boldsymbol{x})$ be an effective metamathematical function of x (or that its Gödel number $\beta(x)$ be a general recursive number-theoretic function of x) must be met, if S is to serve the purpose of formalization for the formulas $\mathrm{B}(\boldsymbol{x})$.

COROLLARY. *Let S be as described in Theorem* XV (*omitting* (54) *and* (55)), *and such that* $\mathrm{B}(\boldsymbol{x})$ *can be effectively found from x* (*or that in some specified effective Gödel numbering, its Gödel number* $\beta(x)$ *is a general recursive function of x*). *If S is simply consistent, then its decision problem is unsolvable, i.e. there is no decision procedure for determining whether a formula is provable in S.*

PROOF. For if there were a method for determining effectively whether any given formula of the system is provable, one could, given any number x, find the corresponding formula $\mathrm{B}(\boldsymbol{x})$ and then apply the method to that formula. By Thesis I § 60, this would imply that the class $\hat{x}[\vdash \mathrm{B}(\boldsymbol{x})]$ is general recursive. Then a fortiori the classes $\hat{x}[\vdash \mathrm{B}(\boldsymbol{x})]$ and $\hat{x}[\overline{\vdash \mathrm{B}(\boldsymbol{x})}]$ would both be recursively enumerable, and hence there would be general recursive predicates R_0 and Q such that $(Ey)R_0(x, y) \equiv \vdash \mathrm{B}(\boldsymbol{x})$ (for (54)) and $(Ey)Q(x, y) \equiv \overline{\vdash \mathrm{B}(\boldsymbol{x})}$ (cf. end § 60, and Remark 1), contradicting the theorem. — Otherwise stated: Were there a general recursive R such that $R(a) \equiv \vdash \mathrm{A}_a$, then taking $R_0(x, y) \equiv R(\beta(x))$ and $Q(x, y) \equiv \overline{R}(\beta(x))$, we would contradict the theorem as above.

THEOREM 33. *If the number-theoretic formal system of Chapter* IV (*or Robinson's system described in Lemma* 18b §49) *is simply consistent, then its decision problem is unsolvable, and remains unsolvable when the system is extended by adding postulates in any way such that the system remains simply consistent.*

By the corollary with Example 1. Since in Example 1 the $\neg$ of $\neg\mathrm{B}(\boldsymbol{x})$ is the $\neg$ of the number-theoretic system, 'simple consistency' as used in Theorem XV coincides with 'simple consistency' as defined (in § 28) for the number-theoretic system. (For the definition of 'decidable' by use of a Gödel numbering, it may be understood that the numbering is that of §§ 50, 52. Using Example 2 § 52, then $\beta(x)$ is primitive recursive.)

REDUCIBILITY, DEGREES OF UNSOLVABILITY. Much of the work on decision problems is devoted not to outright solutions but to reductions of one decision problem to another.

To 'reduce' the decision problem for a predicate P (or the calculation problem for a function φ) of n variables to the respective problems for l functions and predicates $\psi_1, \ldots, \psi_{l_1}, Q_1, \ldots, Q_{l_2}$ (abbreviated Ψ) means intuitively to find a uniform method of procedure by which, given any n-tuple of arguments $x_1, \ldots, x_n$, one could decide whether or not $P(x_1, \ldots, x_n)$ is true (calculate the value $\varphi(x_1, \ldots, x_n)$), if, at each stage of the procedure, he had available the values of the functions $\psi_1, \ldots, \psi_{l_1}$ and the truth or falsity of the values of the predicates $Q_1, \ldots, Q_{l_2}$, for such arguments as he might then name; or briefly, to establish that P is effectively decidable (φ is effectively calculable) from Ψ.

To obtain a precise mathematical notion to correspond to this intuitive notion, we naturally extend Church's thesis (Thesis I § 60) to include the case of $l > 0$ assumed functions and predicates Ψ (calling it then Thesis I*). The evidence for Thesis I will also apply to Thesis I*. The converse of Thesis I* holds.

For example, to *reduce* the decision problem for a predicate $P(a)$ to that for another predicate $Q(a)$ now means to find a predicate $R(a)$ general recursive in $Q(a)$ and such that $P(a) \equiv R(a)$, or briefly to establish that $P(a)$ is general recursive in $Q(a)$. We infer this from our intuitive notion of reduction by Thesis I*; or if we take it as a definition, we appeal to Thesis I* in asserting that the defined notion agrees with our intuitive conception of reduction.

Post 1944 formulated several mathematical reducibility concepts. The most general of them, which Post takes from Turing 1939, is equivalent to the notion we obtain from Thesis I*. If the decision problem for $P(a)$ is reducible to that for $Q(a)$, and is unsolvable, Post says further that it is of *equal* or *lower degree of unsolvability* than that for $Q(a)$ according as the decision problem for $Q(a)$ is or is not reducible to that for $P(a)$ (cf. § 3). The degrees of unsolvability are at least partially ordered (cf. § 8). Each of the predicates $(Ex)T_1(a, a, x)$, $(x)(Ey)T_2(a, a, x, y)$, $(Ex)(y)(Ez)T_3(a, a, x, y, z)$, ... (cf. Theorem V Part II (b) § 57) has a decision problem of highest degree of unsolvability for predicates of the respective forms $(Ex)R(a, x)$, $(x)(Ey)R(a, x, y)$, $(Ex)(y)(Ez)R(a, x, y, z)$, ... with R recursive, as we shall prove later (Example 2 § 65; this holds intuitionistically, if taken to mean simply that each predicate of the respective one of the forms with a recursive R is recursive in that non-recursive predicate, which is what is directly proved). Classically then each of these predicates after the first has a decision problem of higher degree of unsolvability than the preceding (using also Corollary Theorem XI § 58), and the predicate $M(a, k)$ of Theorem VIII § 57 has one of still higher degree of unsolvability (by Theorem X Corollary (b) § 58 and the proof of Theorem VIII). Using T_n^M instead of T_n, we obtain degrees of unsolvability ascending from that (by Theorem XI* end § 58 and Example 2 § 65 for $l > 0$). Davis (1950 abstract) explores those degrees of unsolvability. Post 1944 raises, without answering, the question whether there exists a lower degree of unsolvability than that of the decision problem for $(Ex)T_1(a, a, x)$.

EXAMPLE 3. Let Theorem 33 be restated using the stronger consistency property of Example 1 (or 2) § 60 in place of simple consistency. In this weaker form Theorem 33 can be proved from Example 1 (or 2) § 60 by taking the $R(x, y)$ there $\equiv T_1(x, x, y)$ and using Theorem XII § 60. From this proof it follows, by the results of Example 2 § 65 just cited, that, under the stronger consistency hypothesis, the decision problem for the formal system of Chapter IV (or Robinson's, Lemma 18b), or for any extension having that consistency property for the same or some other R(x, y) which numeralwise expresses $R(x, y)$ ($\equiv T_1(x, x, y)$), is of the highest degree of unsolvability for 1-quantifier predicates. — For the system of Chapter IV (or Robinson's), we can also show this (with another choice of R(x, y) and $R(x, y)$ in the stronger consistency hypothesis) from the proof of Theorem 33 as given, thus. Let f be chosen by (6) with $T_1((x)_2, (x)_2, y)$ as the R, and g be chosen by (7) for any recursive R such that $(x)(y)R(x, y)$. Then $(Ey)T_1(x, x, y) \equiv (Ey)W_0(2^g \cdot 3^f \cdot 5^x, y)$. This reduces the decision problem for $(Ey)T_1(x, x, y)$ to that for $(Ey)W_0(x, y)$. So the decision problem for the system is of the highest degree for 1-quantifier predicates, if the system has the property that the converse of (52) holds for the B($\mathbf{x}$) of Example 1 (as Robinson's system does, by Theorem 53 (c) § 79). (This B($\mathbf{x}$) is of the form ∃yR($\mathbf{x}$, y) where R(x, y) numeralwise expresses $W_0(x, y)$, by § 41 (C) and (E).)

In the case Ψ are unspecified functions and predicates, one may discuss the reduction of the decision problem for P (the calculation problem for φ) to the respective problems for Ψ in the sense of obtaining a procedure uniform in Ψ as well as in $x_1, \ldots, x_n$; or briefly, of establishing that P is effectively decidable (φ is effectively calculable) uniformly from Ψ. Then Thesis I* and Converse are to be stated reading "uniformly" in hypothesis and conclusion.

Note 1. Proof of (a) bottom p. 292 should be amplified as follows. The application of Corollary Theorem I* leads to (I) an expression for the predicate R in terms of the logical operations of the predicate calculus with number variables, 0, ′, +, ·, = and the representing functions $\psi_1, \ldots, \psi_l$ of the predicates Ψ. By the method of proof of Theorem I* and Corollary, each of $\psi_1, \ldots, \psi_l$ enters into that expression only in parts of the form "$\psi(a_1, \ldots, a_m) = w$". Each such part can be replaced by "$\{Q(a_1, \ldots, a_m) \& w = 0\} \vee \{\bar{Q}(a_1, \ldots, a_m) \& w = 1\}$" where Q is the predicate represented by ψ. Thus we obtain (II) an expression for the predicate R in terms of the logical operations of the predicate calculus with number variables, 0, ′, +, ·, = and the predicates Ψ themselves. Now we are ready for the final step (p. 292). — Actually, an expression (I) exists (which is what 'R is arithmetical in Ψ' means for predicates Ψ, under our definition p. 239 with bottom p. 291) if and only if an expression (II) exists. Why?

Chapter XII

PARTIAL RECURSIVE FUNCTIONS

§ 62. Church's thesis. One of the main objectives of this and the next chapter is to present the evidence for Church's thesis (Thesis I § 60).

Since our original notion of effective calculability of a function (or of effective decidability of a predicate) is a somewhat vague intuitive one, the thesis cannot be proved.

The intuitive notion however is real, in that it vouchsafes as effectively calculable many particular functions (§ 30), and on the other hand enables us to recognize that our knowledge about many other functions is insufficient to place them in the category of effectively calculable functions.

For an example of the latter, let $R(x, y)$ be an effectively decidable predicate, and consider the function $\varepsilon y R(x, y)$ (Gödel 1931) defined classically thus,

$$\varepsilon y R(x, y) = \begin{cases} \text{the least } y \text{ such that } R(x, y), \text{ if } (Ey)R(x, y), \\ 0, \text{ otherwise.} \end{cases}$$

This definition does not (of itself) provide a calculation procedure. Given x, we can search through the propositions $R(x, 0)$, $R(x, 1)$, $R(x, 2)$, ... in succession, looking for one that is true, as far as we please; i.e. we can in principle complete the examination of the first n of them, for any finite n. If the given x is such that $(Ey)R(x, y)$, by persisting long enough we shall eventually encounter a first y for which $R(x, y)$ is true, which y is the value of the function $\varepsilon y R(x, y)$. But if x is such that $\overline{(Ey)}R(x, y)$, we shall never learn this by persisting in the search, which will remain forever uncompleted. The completion of the examination of all $\aleph_0$ propositions, which the classical definition envisages, is impossible for a human computer.

For some choices of $R(x, y)$, the function $\varepsilon y R(x, y)$ may nevertheless be effectively calculable, not "immediately" on the basis of its definition, but because of the existence of some other procedure for determining the value, which unlike the one suggested by the definition itself is effective.

For example, when $R(x, y) \equiv (x)_0(y)_0+(x)_1(y)_1=(x)_2$, there is known to be such a procedure (cf. Example 2 § 30).

The function $\varepsilon y R(x, y)$ is effectively calculable, if and only if the predicate $(Ey)R(x, y)$ is effectively decidable. For if $(Ey)R(x, y)$ is effectively decidable, then given x, to calculate $\varepsilon y R(x, y)$, we can first decide whether or not $(Ey)R(x, y)$ is true, and according to the answer either search for the least y such that $R(x, y)$ or take 0 as the value. Conversely, if $\varepsilon y R(x, y)$ is effectively calculable, then given x, we can decide whether or not $(Ey)R(x, y)$ is true, by first calculating $\varepsilon y R(x, y)$, and then ascertaining whether or not $R(x, \varepsilon y R(x, y))$ is true.

The intuitionist finds no justification for the belief that we can always tell, for a given predicate $P(y)$, whether or not $(Ey)P(y)$. This is his ground for not accepting the law of the excluded middle *A or not A* with his meaning of "or" (§ 13). His argument, applied to $R(x, y)$ as the $P(y)$, is an argument that we have no basis to suppose that, for any R, the predicate $(Ey)R(x, y)$ is effectively decidable.

Church's thesis, by supplying a precise delimitation of 'all effectively calculable functions', makes it possible to prove, for certain predicates $R(x, y)$, e.g. $T_1(x, x, y)$ (Theorem XII § 60), that there is no uniform method of solving the problem whether or not $(Ey)R(x, y)$. Thereby Brouwer's argument, that Hilbert's belief in the solvability of every mathematical problem is unproven, is now strengthened to an actual disproof, when solvability is taken to mean uniform solvability and Church's thesis is accepted. The relationship of Church's thesis to intuitionism will be discussed further below (§ 82).

The intuitionist does not regard the definition given above for $\varepsilon y R(x, y)$, lacking a proof of effective calculability, as properly defining a function. But our discussion of $\varepsilon y R(x, y)$ can refer intuitionistically to the predicate $\{R(x, w) \& (z)_{z<w}\overline{R}(x, z)\} \vee \{\overline{(Ey)}R(x, y) \& w=0\}$. Classically, this predicate, call it "$P(x, w)$", is the representing predicate of $\varepsilon y R(x, y)$. But intuitionistically, we may not be able to prove that $(x)(E!w)P(x, w)$, i.e. that $P(x, w)$ is a representing predicate of a function (cf. § 41; $(x)[(Ew)P(x, w) \equiv (E!w)P(x, w)]$, cf. *174b, *171).

While we cannot prove Church's thesis, since its role is to delimit precisely an hitherto vaguely conceived totality, we require evidence that it cannot conflict with the intuitive notion which it is supposed to complete; i.e. we require evidence that every particular function which our intuitive notion would authenticate as effectively calculable is general recursive. The thesis may be considered a hypothesis about the intuitive notion of effective calculability, or a mathematical definition of effective calculability; in the latter case, the evidence is required to give the theory based on the definition the intended significance.

The converse of Church's thesis, i.e. that every general recursive function φ is effectively calculable, we take to be already confirmed by the intuitive notion (cf. § 60). We use here the definition of 'E defines φ recursively' which says that, given $x_1, \ldots, x_n$, a deduction from E of an equation $f(\mathbf{x}_1, \ldots, \mathbf{x}_n)=\mathbf{x}$ expressing that the value $\varphi(x_1, \ldots, x_n)$ is x always exists (or if we base the computation procedure on Theorem IX (30), we use (29); or if we base it on Corollary Theorem IX, we use (1)). In concluding that we have an effective computation procedure, the existential quantifier which appears in the definition of 'E defines φ recursively' (or in (29), or in (1)) must be understood constructively (§ 13); and likewise the existential quantifier in the definition of 'φ is general recursive', which states that there exists an E defining φ recursively (or in Theorem IX, that a Gödel number e can be found; or in Corollary Theorem IX that a finite sequence of applications of (I) — (VI) can be found).

In other words, we should not claim that a function is effectively calculable on the ground that it has been shown to be general recursive, unless the demonstration that it is general recursive is effective (cf. Church 1936 Footnote 10).

We now summarize the evidence for Church's thesis (and Thesis I*, end § 61) under three main headings (A) — (C), and one other (D) which might be included under (A). Some of this evidence will be given in more detail in later sections.

(A) Heuristic evidence.

(A1) Every particular effectively calculable function, and every operation for defining a function effectively from other functions, for which the question has been investigated, has proved to be general recursive. A great variety of effectively calculable functions, of classes of effectively calculable functions, and of operations for defining functions effectively from other functions, selected with the intention of exhausting known types, have been investigated.

(A2) The methods for showing effectively calculable functions to be general recursive have been developed to a degree which virtually excludes doubt that one could describe an effective process for determining the values of a function which could not be transformed by these methods into a general recursive definition of the function.

(A3) The exploration of various methods which might be expected to lead to a function outside the class of the general recursive functions has in every case shown either that the method does not actually lead outside or that the new function obtained cannot be considered as effectively defined, i.e. its definition provides no effective process of calculation. In particular, the latter is the case for the Cantor diagonal method. (An illustration of the former will be given in Example 1 § 65.)

(B) Equivalence of diverse formulations.

(B1) Several other characterizations of a class of effectively calculable functions with the same heuristic property ((A)) exist. These have turned out to be equivalent to general recursiveness, i.e. the classes of functions which they describe are coextensive.

In fact three notions arose independently and almost simultaneously, namely ***general recursiveness***, ***λ-definability*** (successive steps toward which were taken by Church 1933 and Kleene 1935; cf. Church 1941) and ***computability*** (Turing 1936-7, Post 1936). The equivalence (i.e. coextensiveness) of the λ-definable functions with the general recursive functions was proved by Church 1936 and Kleene 1936a (also cf. the reference to work of Rosser in Church 1936 Footnote 16). The equivalence of the computable to the λ-definable functions (and hence to the general recursive functions) was proved by Turing 1937.

The notion of a function ***reckonable*** (§ 59) in a certain formal system S_1 described (very briefly) in Gödel 1936 is a fourth equivalent of general recursiveness, under the hypothesis that S_1 is simply consistent (as Rosser remarked in a review 1936a).

Still another approach is given by Post (1943, 1946) in terms of what he calls ***canonical*** and ***normal systems***. What this gives directly, as it is presented, is an equivalent of recursive enumerability, but then as in Example 6 § 60 we obtain an equivalent of recursiveness.

The fact that several notions which differ widely lead to the same class of functions is a strong indication that this class is fundamental.

(B2) Of less weight, but deserving mention, is the circumstance that several formulations of the main notions are equivalent; i.e. the notions possess a sort of "stability".

Thus, for general recursiveness, the formalism may be chosen in several ways (§ 55). Also one may give a formulation (***μ-recursiveness***) not based on any formalism but using instead Schemata (I) — (VI) (Theorem III § 57 and Corollary Theorem IX § 58), or one using Schemata (III), (IV) and (VI) with $x+y$, $x \cdot y$ and δ^x_y ($=1$ if $x=y$, $=0$ if $x \neq y$) as initial functions (Kleene 1936b). (Also cf. Julia Robinson 1950.)

The notion of λ-definability has the variants ***λ-K-definability*** (studied by Rosser, cf. Kleene 1936a Footnote 12) and ***λ-δ-definability*** (Church

1935). Also there is a parallel development, started by Schönfinkel 1924 and Curry (1929, 1930, 1932) and continued by Rosser (1935, 1942a*) (also cf. Curry 1948-9), which leads to a notion that we may call ***combinatory definability***, proved equivalent to λ-definability by Rosser.

The details of the definition of computability can also be varied, as we shall see later (Chapter XIII).

The system S_1 of Gödel 1936 is the first system in a hierarchy of systems S_i ($i = 1, 2, 3, \ldots$) using successively higher types of variables (cf. § 12). Gödel remarks, "It can be shown moreover, that a function which is reckonable in one of the systems S_i, or even in a system of transfinite order, is reckonable already in S_1, so that the concept 'reckonable' is in a certain sense 'absolute', while almost all hitherto known metamathematical concepts (e.g. provable, definable, etc.) depend very essentially on the system which is taken as the basis." Exactly the same functions are reckonable in our number-theoretic system of Chapter IV or Robinson's described in Lemma 18b § 49 (by Theorem 32 § 59 and the equivalence of reckonability in Gödel's S_1 to general recursiveness). The equivalence of reckonability in these systems is under the hypothesis of simple consistency for Gödel's systems and our system of Chapter IV. (The simple consistency of Robinson's system will be proved as Theorem 53 (a) § 79.) Two other systems (Z^0) and (Z_{00}) having the same class of reckonable formulas are given in Hilbert-Bernays 1939 Supplement II; these are formalizations of μ-recursiveness ((Z_{00}) utilizing also the normal form). (Mostowski 1947 bases his version of Theorem V § 57 on the notion of resolvability of a predicate P in a system S (§ 59), with S subject only to some quite general conditions. As we shall see below in connection with (D1) and Thesis II, only a general recursive function can be reckonable in an S which is a formal system with effective rules; but Mostowski considers also non-constructive generalizations of formal systems in our sense.)

(C) Turing's concept of a computing machine.

Turing's computable functions (1936-7) are those which can be computed by a machine of a kind which is designed, according to his analysis, to reproduce all the sorts of operations which a human computer could perform, working according to preassigned instructions. Turing's notion is thus the result of a direct attempt to formulate mathematically the notion of effective calculability, while the other notions arose differently and were afterwards identified with effective calculability. Turing's formulation hence constitutes an independent statement of Church's thesis (in equivalent terms). Post 1936 gave a similar formulation.

The work referred to under (A) (especially (A1)) was not all carried out originally for general recursiveness or the special notions of recursiveness subsumed under general recursiveness (§ 55), but much of it was done for λ-definability (in Kleene 1935) or computability (in Turing 1936-7). But by (B) the heuristic and other evidence accumulated in studying the various notions all applies to any one. The accumulation of methods shown to be general recursive under (A1) contributes to (A2).

The case under (A2) will be presented in this chapter in connection with the theory of partial recursive functions (cf. § 66). We shall take up computability in the next chapter, proving the equivalence of computability to general recursiveness in §§ 68, 69 (cf. (B1)) and incidentally the equivalence of some differing formulations of computability (cf. (B2)), and giving the evidence under (C) in § 70.

(D) Symbolic logics and symbolic algorithms.

Church 1936 gave the following arguments (in substance), as showing "that no more general definition of effective calculability than that proposed above can be obtained by either of two methods which naturally suggest themselves" (p. 358).

(D1) Suppose that we are dealing with a function $\varphi(x)$ and a formal system such that the following is true. The set of the axioms is finite or (if infinite) effectively enumerable, and likewise the set of the rules of inference; and each rule of inference is an effectively performable operation. We can effectively recognize a formula $\mathrm{P}(\boldsymbol{x}, \boldsymbol{w})$ which attributes a number w as value to φ for a given argument x, and effectively read from it this number. The formulas $\mathrm{P}(\boldsymbol{x}, \boldsymbol{w})$ attributing the correct and only the correct values to φ are provable in the system; i.e. φ is 'reckonable' § 59 (except that here we are not insisting that $\mathrm{P}(\boldsymbol{x}, \boldsymbol{w})$ come from some $\mathrm{P}(\mathrm{x}, \mathrm{w})$ by substituting $\boldsymbol{x}, \boldsymbol{w}$ for x, w). If the interpretation is allowed that the effectiveness of the metamathematical functions and predicate just mentioned implies that the number-theoretic functions and predicate corresponding to them under a suitable Gödel numbering are general recursive, then φ is general recursive. For by reasoning as in the proof of Theorem IX § 58 or (c) § 59, for some general recursive ψ and R, $(x)(Ey)R(x, y)$ and $\varphi(x) = \psi(\mu y R(x, y))$; whereupon Theorem III § 57 applies.

(D2) Consider a symbolic algorithm for the calculation of the values of a function $\varphi(x)$, which shall consist in a method by which, given any x, a finite sequence $\mathrm{E}_{x0}, \mathrm{E}_{x1}, \ldots, \mathrm{E}_{xr_x}$ of expressions (in some notation) can be obtained, in the following fashion. Given x, the first expression E_{x0} can be effectively found. Given x and the expressions E_{xi} for $i \leq j$, it can be effectively recognized whether the algorithm has terminated (i.e. whether $j = r_x$), and if so, the value $\varphi(x)$ can be effectively found; while in the contrary case, the next expression $E_{x,j+1}$ can be effectively found. Again, if the effective functions and predicate described become general recursive under some Gödel numbering, then φ is general recursive. For we can reason as in (D1), regarding (x, E_{x0}) now as analogous to an axiom, and the operation of passing from $(x, E_{x0}, \ldots, E_{xj})$ to $(x, E_{x0}, \ldots, E_{xj}, E_{x,j+1})$ as analogous to a rule of inference.

In brief, (D1) and (D2) show that if the individual operations or rules of a formal system or symbolic algorithm used to define a function are general recursive, then the whole is general recursive. So we could include (D1) and (D2) as particular examples of operations or methods of definition under (A1).

Note that (D1) and (D2) refer to formal systems and symbolic algorithms having a special kind of structure, exemplified by particular formal systems and algorithms we know. We have elsewhere (§§ 30, 60, 61) used "algorithm" more broadly to mean any calculation (or decision) procedure; and we generalized the notion of a formal system likewise in connection with Thesis II and Theorem XIII (§ 60). There is of course no circularity in adding the evidence provided by algorithms and formal systems of the special sorts to the case for Church's thesis, and afterwards applying the thesis (as in §§ 60, 61) to the discussion of algorithms and formal systems in the broader sense.

If we consider only systems satisfying Thesis II (for $n+1$ variables), the functions (of n variables) which are reckonable in various formal systems (i.e. each one in some system) are all general recursive, and hence all are reckonable in one system (e.g. any one of the systems mentioned under (B2)).

§ 63. Partial recursive functions. As at the beginning of § 62, let $R(x, y)$ be an effectively decidable predicate. Consider the procedure which consists, for a given x, in deciding as to the truth or falsity of each of the propositions $R(x, 0)$, $R(x, 1)$, $R(x, 2)$, ..., successively, until one is found to be true, and taking the second argument y of that one $R(x, y)$. This procedure leads to a natural number y in a finite number of steps, if $(Ey)R(x, y)$ and only then. Therefore it can be considered as an algorithm for calculating a mathematical function of x defined over the subset $\hat{x}(Ey)R(x, y)$ of the natural numbers. The function calculated is 'the least y such that $R(x, y)$' or in symbols '$\mu y R(x, y)$'.

It may be impossible to extend the definition of this function $\mu y R(x, y)$

to all natural numbers, in such a way that there will be an algorithm for calculating the resulting completely defined number-theoretic function. We noted in § 62 that the particular extension $\varepsilon y R(x, y)$ is effectively calculable, if and only if the predicate $(Ey)R(x, y)$ is effectively decidable; and the method shows that no extension of $\mu y R(x, y)$ to all natural numbers is effectively calculable, unless $(Ey)R(x, y)$ is effectively decidable.

This can be stated in terms of the theory of general recursive functions. Church 1936 called a function $\varphi(x_1, \ldots, x_n)$ defined over a subset of the n-tuples of natural numbers *potentially recursive*, if there exists a general recursive function $\varphi'(x_1, \ldots, x_n)$ such that $\varphi'(x_1, \ldots, x_n) = \varphi(x_1, \ldots, x_n)$ for each n-tuple $x_1, \ldots, x_n$ for which $\varphi(x_1, \ldots, x_n)$ is defined. Now if $R(x, y)$ is general recursive, then $\mu y R(x, y)$ is potentially recursive if and only if $(Ey)R(x, y)$ is general recursive. For

$$(59) \qquad \varepsilon y R(x, y) = \mu w[R(x, w) \vee \{\overline{(Ey)}R(x, y) \;\&\; w=0\}];$$

and therefore by #D § 45 and Theorem III § 57, if $(Ey)R(x, y)$ is general recursive, then $\varepsilon y R(x, y)$ is a general recursive extension $\varphi'(x)$ of $\mu y R(x, y)$. Conversely, if $\mu y R(x, y)$ is potentially recursive with $\varphi'(x)$ as a general recursive extension, then $(Ey)R(x, y) \equiv R(x, \varphi'(x))$, and therefore $(Ey)R(x, y)$ is general recursive.

Example 1. Hence by Theorem V (15) § 57, $\mu y T_1(x, x, y)$ is not potentially recursive (Kleene 1938, 1943*), and $\varepsilon y T_1(x, x, y)$ is not general recursive (Kleene 1936).

An algorithm for calculating a function φ may, for a given x, fail to lead to a number as value of $\varphi(x)$ either by not terminating (so that no matter how many steps have already been performed, the rules of the algorithm call for a next step), or by terminating but without giving a number as value. We can modify any given algorithm so that whenever, for a given x, the given algorithm terminates without producing a number as value, the new algorithm gives 0 as value. The new algorithm calculates an extension φ' of φ defined exactly when the original (and the new) algorithm terminate.

Example 1 (continued). Hence any algorithm which will lead to the number $\mu y T_1(x, x, y)$ for every x such that $(Ey)T_1(x, x, y)$ cannot terminate for every x (using Thesis I § 60).

If there is an algorithm for deciding, given x, whether the function $\varphi(x)$ calculated by a given algorithm is defined or not, then a new algorithm can be set up which calculates an extension $\varphi'(x)$ of $\varphi(x)$ to all natural numbers. (Also cf. Example 5 § 64.)

EXAMPLE 1 (continued). Hence there is no algorithm for deciding, given x, whether $\mu y T_1(x, x, y)$ is defined or not, as we can also see directly from its condition of definition $(Ey)T_1(x, x, y)$ (cf. Theorem XII § 60).

We can also modify a given algorithm without extending the function $\varphi(x)$ so that, for a given x, the algorithm will always fail to terminate whenever $\varphi(x)$ is undefined (as is already the case for the algorithm for $\mu y R(x, y)$ described above). To do so, we arrange that, when the given algorithm terminates without giving a number as value of $\varphi(x)$, the new algorithm calls for additional steps which will continue ad infinitum. In discussing algorithms in the rest of this chapter, we shall often tacitly assume that the algorithms are of this kind.

Suppose that $\chi(x)$ is defined over all natural numbers, and $\psi(x)$ over a proper subset of them containing all the numbers taken as values by $\chi(x)$, and that both functions are effectively calculable. Then $\psi(\chi(x))$ is completely defined and effectively calculable. The function $\psi(x)$ might be $\mu y T_1(x, x, y)$. Thus an effectively calculable function restricted to a proper subset of the natural numbers may be useful in constructing another effectively calculable function defined over all natural numbers.

Also there are problems in foundations which call for a function, needed only on a proper subset of the natural numbers, to be effectively calculable. This occurs in the theory of constructive ordinals (Church-Kleene 1936, Kleene 1938, Church 1938), and in studies of the intuitionistic logic (cf. § 82).

These considerations indicate the desirability of including partially defined functions under our treatment of effective calculability. We shall accordingly extend the class of the general recursive functions to take in certain incompletely defined functions, calling the resulting class of functions the 'partial recursive functions'. The technical advantages of thus extending the class of the general recursive functions, even if our purpose were only to support Church's thesis for the case of completely defined functions (Theses I and I*), will become fully apparent in §§ 65 and 66. At the end of the present section, we use the partial recursive functions in stating Church's thesis for the case of partially defined functions (Theses I† and I*†).

To fix our terminology, let us now call a function from any subset (proper or improper) of the n-tuples of the natural numbers to the natural numbers a *partial function*. In other words, a partial function φ is a function which for each n-tuple $x_1, \ldots, x_n$ of natural numbers as arguments takes at most one natural number $\varphi(x_1, \ldots, x_n)$ as value. For an n-tuple $x_1, \ldots, x_n$ for which φ has a natural number as value, we say φ (or

$\varphi(x_1, \ldots, x_n)$) is *defined*; for an n-tuple $x_1, \ldots, x_n$ for which φ has no natural number as value, we say φ (or $\varphi(x_1, \ldots, x_n)$) is *undefined* (sometimes written "u"). The *range of definition* of a partial function is the set of the n-tuples $x_1, \ldots, x_n$ for which $\varphi(x_1, \ldots, x_n)$ is defined. When this consists of all n-tuples, we have an ordinary (*completely defined*) number-theoretic function; otherwise an *incompletely defined* function. When it is empty, we have the *completely undefined* function.

To obtain the definition of 'partial recursive function' (Kleene 1938), we adapt the Herbrand-Gödel definition of 'general recursive function' to partial functions, as follows.

For the case that $\psi_1, \ldots, \psi_l$ are partial functions (of $m_1, \ldots, m_l$ variables, respectively) we now understand naturally that $E^{\psi_1 \ldots \psi_l}_{g_1 \ldots g_l}$ (cf. § 54) is the set of the equations $g_j(\mathbf{y}_1, \ldots, \mathbf{y}_{m_j}) = \mathbf{y}$ where $\psi_j(y_1, \ldots, y_{m_j}) = y$, for all $j = 1, \ldots, l$ and in the case of each j for those m_j-tuples $y_1, \ldots, y_{m_j}$ for which ψ_j is defined. Then for a partial function φ the definition of E *defines* φ *recursively in* (or *from*) $\psi_1, \ldots, \psi_l$ given in § 54 reads correctly, if (for emphasis) we now replace "if and only if $\varphi(x_1, \ldots, x_n) = x$" by "if and only if $\varphi(x_1, \ldots, x_n)$ is defined and $\varphi(x_1, \ldots, x_n) = x$". The second phrasing of the definition there (with a completeness and a consistency property) can be used, if we now understand E^{φ}_{f} for a partial function φ in like sense to that just explained for $E^{\psi_1 \ldots \psi_l}_{g_1 \ldots g_l}$. Finally we say (corresponding to the definition in § 55) that a partial function φ is *partial recursive in* $\psi_1, \ldots, \psi_l$, if there is a system E of equations which defines φ recursively from $\psi_1, \ldots, \psi_l$.

In the case of a scheme $\varphi = \mathsf{F}(\psi_1, \ldots, \psi_l)$ where $\psi_1, \ldots, \psi_l$ range over partial functions (subject to any stated restrictions), we say that F is *partial recursive*, or that φ is *partial recursive uniformly in* $\psi_1, \ldots, \psi_l$, if (for fixed $n, l, m_1, \ldots, m_l$) there is such an E independent of $\psi_1, \ldots, \psi_l$. As before, we omit the word "uniformly" except for emphasis.

We now have, for the case the φ is not previously known (as at the end of § 55): A system E of equations defines recursively a partial recursive function of n variables from partial functions $\psi_1, \ldots, \psi_l$, if for each n-tuple $x_1, \ldots, x_n$ of natural numbers there is at most one numeral $\mathbf{x}$ such that $E^{\psi_1 \ldots \psi_l}_{g_1 \ldots g_l}, E \vdash f(\mathbf{x}_1, \ldots, \mathbf{x}_n) = \mathbf{x}$ (where $f, g_1, \ldots, g_l$ are as before). Here no completeness property is required. The function which is defined recursively by E is the function φ such that $\varphi(x_1, \ldots, x_n)$ is defined for a given n-tuple $x_1, \ldots, x_n$, if and only if there is an $\mathbf{x}$ for this $x_1, \ldots, x_n$, in which case $\varphi(x_1, \ldots, x_n) = x$ where x is the number for which the $\mathbf{x}$ is the numeral.

The partial recursive functions include the general recursive functions as those for which the range of definition consists of all the n-tuples $x_1, \ldots, x_n$ of natural numbers.

When $R(x_1, \ldots, x_n, y)$ is a general recursive predicate, the partial function $\mu y R(x_1, \ldots, x_n, y)$ (defined if and only if $(Ey)R(x_1, \ldots, x_n, y)$, in which case its value is the least y such that $R(x_1, \ldots, x_n, y)$) is partial recursive. We have already shown this (without the present terminology) as (iv) in the first part of the proof of Theorem IV § 57. (Then $\mu y R(x_1, \ldots, x_n, y)$ is general recursive exactly when (1b) § 57 holds.)

EXAMPLE 1 (concluded). $\mu y T_1(x, x, y)$ is partial recursive.

For partial functions $\chi_1, \ldots, \chi_m, \psi$, we take $\psi(\chi_1(x_1, \ldots, x_n), \ldots, \chi_m(x_1, \ldots, x_n))$ to be defined when and only when $\chi_1(x_1, \ldots, x_n), \ldots, \chi_m(x_1, \ldots, x_n)$ are all defined and their values constitute an m-tuple for which ψ is defined, except when we have otherwise specified. We call this the *weak sense* of $\psi(\chi_1(x_1, \ldots, x_n), \ldots, \chi_m(x_1, \ldots, x_n))$. This convention shall apply likewise to definitions by substitution not in this standard form (cf. § 44). The ambiguity which the convention removes arises when ψ is a constant function, or becomes such in one variable for some substitution for the other variables. For example, shall $0 \cdot \chi(x)$ have the value 0 or be undefined, for an x which makes $\chi(x)$ undefined? According to our convention, it shall be undefined.

We also employ *partial predicates* with the same convention. For example, by substituting partial functions $\psi(x_1, \ldots, x_n)$ and $\chi(x_1, \ldots, x_n)$ into the completely defined predicate $y_1 = y_2$, we obtain a partial predicate $\psi(x_1, \ldots, x_n) = \chi(x_1, \ldots, x_n)$. This predicate, for given $x_1, \ldots, x_n$, is defined if and only if ψ and χ are both defined, in which case it takes a true proposition as value if ψ and χ have the same value, and a false proposition as value if ψ and χ have different values.

Similarly, by substituting partial predicates $Q(x_1, \ldots, x_n)$ and $R(x_1, \ldots, x_n)$ into the truth-value function $Y_1 \equiv Y_2$ ('equivalence', § 45), we obtain a partial predicate $Q(x_1, \ldots, x_n) \equiv R(x_1, \ldots, x_n)$, defined if and only if $Q(x_1, \ldots, x_n)$ and $R(x_1, \ldots, x_n)$ are both defined, in which case it asserts the equivalence of those two propositions, being true or false according as the two are equivalent or not.

We now introduce "$\psi(x_1, \ldots, x_n) \simeq \chi(x_1, \ldots, x_n)$" to express, for particular $x_1, \ldots, x_n$, that if either of $\psi(x_1, \ldots, x_n)$ and $\chi(x_1, \ldots, x_n)$ is defined, so is the other and the values are the same (and hence if either of $\psi(x_1, \ldots, x_n)$ and $\chi(x_1, \ldots, x_n)$ is undefined, so is the other). The difference in the meaning of (i) "$\psi(x_1, \ldots, x_n) = \chi(x_1, \ldots, x_n)$" and

(ii) "$\psi(x_1, \ldots, x_n) \simeq \chi(x_1, \ldots, x_n)$" comes when one of $\psi(x_1, \ldots, x_n)$ and $\chi(x_1, \ldots, x_n)$ is undefined. Then (i) is undefined, while (ii) is true or false according as the other is or is not undefined. We distinguish $=$ and $\simeq$ as *weak* and *complete equality*, respectively. Our use of $\simeq$ constitutes an exception to the convention stated above.

Similarly "$Q(x_1, \ldots, x_n) \cong R(x_1, \ldots, x_n)$" shall express, for particular $x_1, \ldots, x_n$, that if either of $Q(x_1, \ldots, x_n)$ and $R(x_1, \ldots, x_n)$ is defined, so is the other and the two values are equivalent propositions (and hence if either is undefined, so is the other). We distinguish $\equiv$ and $\cong$ as *weak* and *complete equivalence*.

Now $(x_1) \ldots (x_n)[\psi(x_1, \ldots, x_n) \simeq \chi(x_1, \ldots, x_n)]$, or $\psi(x_1, \ldots, x_n) \simeq \chi(x_1, \ldots, x_n)$ when $x_1, \ldots, x_n$ have the generality interpretation, expresses that ψ and χ are equal as functions, i.e. they have the same range of definition, and over this common range they agree in value. Similarly $(x_1) \ldots (x_n)[Q(x_1, \ldots, x_n) \cong R(x_1, \ldots, x_n)]$, or $Q(x_1, \ldots, x_n) \cong R(x_1, \ldots, x_n)$ under the generality interpretation of $x_1, \ldots, x_n$, expresses that Q and R are equal as predicates.

We say that a partial function $\varphi(x_1, \ldots, x_n)$ is the *representing function* of a predicate $P(x_1, \ldots, x_n)$, if $\varphi(x_1, \ldots, x_n)$ takes only 0 and 1 as values, and

$$P(x_1, \ldots, x_n) \cong \varphi(x_1, \ldots, x_n)=0;$$

or in other words, if according as the value of $P(x_1, \ldots, x_n)$ is $\mathfrak{t}$, $\mathfrak{f}$ or $\mathfrak{u}$, that of $\varphi(x_1, \ldots, x_n)$ is 0, 1 or $\mathfrak{u}$.

We say that a partial function φ or partial predicate P is *partial recursive in* partial predicates and functions Ψ, if the corresponding statement holds replacing the predicates among P, Ψ by their representing functions.

The role of the two equality predicates $=$ and $\simeq$ will be different. The weak equality $=$ will serve as an operation in building partial recursive predicates. We shall see in a moment (Theorem XVII ##14, C†) that $\psi(x_1, \ldots, x_n)=\chi(x_1, \ldots, x_n)$ is partial recursive in ψ and χ. The complete equality $\simeq$ will be used in expressing our theory about partial recursive functions. The predicate $\psi(x_1, \ldots, x_n) \simeq \chi(x_1, \ldots, x_n)$ is not always partial recursive when ψ and χ are partial recursive (cf. Example 7 § 64).

Similar remarks apply to the two equivalences $\equiv$ and $\cong$ (cf. Theorem XVII #D† and Example 8 § 64).

The particular functions and predicates of ##1—21 (§§ 44, 45), being primitive recursive, are general recursive (Theorem II § 55) and therefore partial recursive. Rewriting Schemata (IV) and (V) (§ 43) with

"$\simeq$" in place of "$=$", and using our convention to read the expressions on the right in the weak sense, the notion 'φ is primitive recursive in Ψ' takes on a meaning for the case that the assumed functions and predicates are partially defined. For example, in a primitive recursion (Va), for a given y, $\varphi(y')$ is defined, if and only if $\varphi(y)$ is defined and $\chi(y, z)$ is defined when z is the value of $\varphi(y)$ (hence by induction, only if all of $\varphi(0), \varphi(1), \ldots, \varphi(y)$ are defined). The notion extends from functions to predicates via representing functions. Now the former proofs of ##A—G (§§ 44—47) apply, provided we understand the resulting functions and predicates in the suitable weak senses, e.g. $\sum_{y<z} \psi(y)$ is defined when and only when all of $\psi(0), \ldots, \psi(z-1)$ are defined, $Q \vee R$ when and only when both Q and R are defined, $(Ey)_{y<z}R(y)$ when and only when $R(0), \ldots, R(z-1)$ are, etc. In each case the appropriate weak sense is easily inferred from the proof. But also, with these senses for (IV) and (V), the proof of Theorem II (§§ 54, 55) carries over. Hence:

THEOREM XVII. (a) *Any function* φ *definable from partial functions* Ψ *by a succession of applications of partial recursive schemes is partial recursive in* Ψ. *Schemata* (I) — (V) *are partial recursive.* (b) *The functions and predicates of* ##1 — 21 *are partial recursive*; *and* ##A — G *hold reading "partial recursive" for "primitive recursive" and using the weak senses of the resulting functions and predicates* (call them then ##A†—G†).

We used the μ-operator above to form $\mu yR(x_1, \ldots, x_n, y)$ as a partial function from a completely defined predicate $R(x_1, \ldots, x_n, y)$. Now when $R(x_1, \ldots, x_n, y)$ is any partial predicate, we take $\mu yR(x_1, \ldots, x_n, y)$ to be defined when and only when there is a y such that $R(x_1, \ldots, x_n, y)$ is true and $R(x_1, \ldots, x_n, 0), \ldots, R(x_1, \ldots, x_n, y{-}1)$ are all defined, in which case its value is the least such y. For example, if $R(0) \cong R(1) \cong \mathfrak{f}$, $R(2) \cong \mathfrak{t}$, then $\mu yR(y) \simeq 2$, but if $R(0) \cong \mathfrak{f}$, $R(1) \cong \mathfrak{u}$, $R(2) \cong \mathfrak{t}$, then $\mu yR(y) \simeq \mathfrak{u}$.

Now we can consider (VI) § 57 reading "$\simeq \mu y$" for "$= \mu y$" as a schema for any given partial function $\chi(x_1, \ldots, x_n, y)$ or partial predicate $R(x_1, \ldots, x_n, y)$. Let the equations E be set up as in the proof of Theorem III. If $\mu yR(x_1, \ldots, x_n, y)$ is defined, then E_h^χ, E $\vdash$ f$(\mathbf{x}_1, \ldots, \mathbf{x}_n)=\mathbf{x}$ when $x = \mu yR(x_1, \ldots, x_n, y)$ and for no other numeral $\mathbf{x}$, just as before ((iii) § 57). Conversely, if E_h^χ, E $\vdash$ f$(\mathbf{x}_1, \ldots, \mathbf{x}_n)=\mathbf{x}$ where $\mathbf{x}$ is a numeral, then the present conditions for $\mu yR(x_1, \ldots, x_n, y)$ to be defined are met (noting that for #B† $\prod_{s<y} \chi(x_1, \ldots, x_n, s)$ is defined only if $\chi(x_1, \ldots, x_n, s)$ for $s = 0, 1, \ldots, y{-}1$ are all defined). Thus:

THEOREM XVIII (= Theorem III†). *Schema* (VI) *is partial recursive.* Hence by Theorem XVII: *Every function* φ *definable from partial functions and predicates* Ψ *by applications of* (I) — (VI) *is partial recursive in* Ψ.

Now let us see what happens to the proof of the normal form theorem (Theorem IX § 58) when we take $\varphi(x_1, \ldots, x_n)$ to be a partial recursive function. Let E define φ recursively. Now (24) and (26) do not necessarily hold, but instead, omitting the universal quantifiers, we obtain (from (26)) $(Ey)S_n(e, x_1, \ldots, x_n, y)$ as the condition on $x_1, \ldots, x_n$ that $\varphi(x_1, \ldots, x_n)$ be defined. Also (25) and hence (27) hold with "$\simeq$" in place of "$=$"; and (28) holds, not with the generality interpretation, but for each n-tuple $x_1, \ldots, x_n$ for which $\varphi(x_1, \ldots, x_n)$ is defined. But under our meaning of the μ-operator applied to a completely defined predicate, $U(\mu y S_n(e, x_1, \ldots, x_n, y))$ is defined exactly when $(Ey)S_n(e, x_1, \ldots, x_n, y)$. Hence both members of (28) have the same range of definition, so (28) with "$=$" replaced by "$\simeq$" holds for all $x_1, \ldots, x_n$. The proof given for Theorem IX* (under Theorem X) goes through with the same modifications, provided the assumed functions $\psi_1, \ldots, \psi_l$ are completely defined (otherwise e.g. $(Eu_1)_{u_1<y}[Nu((y)_{0,1,1}, u_1) \;\&\; Nu((y)_{0,2}, \psi(u_1))]$ in 0Df12*, likewise $\tilde{\psi}(y)$, might be undefined in some case in which for the proof we would need it to be defined). Thus:

THEOREM XIX. (a) (= Theorem IX†). *Given any partial recursive function* $\varphi(x_1, \ldots, x_n)$, *a number* e *can be found such that*

$$(60) \qquad \varphi(x_1, \ldots, x_n) \simeq U(\mu y T_n(e, x_1, \ldots, x_n, y))$$

(so that $(Ey)T_n(e, x_1, \ldots, x_n, y)$ *is the condition of definition of the function* $\varphi(x_1, \ldots, x_n)$*), and*

$$(61a) \quad (x_1) \ldots (x_n)(y)[T_n(e, x_1, \ldots, x_n, y) \rightarrow U(y) \simeq \varphi(x_1, \ldots, x_n)].$$

(b) (= Theorem IX*†). *Similarly reading "partial recursive in* Ψ*",* "T_n^{Ψ}" *in place of "partial recursive",* "T_n"*, respectively, where* "Ψ" *stands for any* l (≥ 0) *completely defined functions and predicates of* $m_1, \ldots, m_l$ *variables, respectively.*

Extending the definitions given in § 58, we say that any number e such that (60) (and hence (61a)) holds *defines* φ *recursively* or is a *Gödel number of* φ; and similarly in the case of a function φ partial recursive in completely defined functions Ψ. The notions extend to a predicate P with representing function φ as before.

By the proof of Theorem XIX, if E is a system of equations defining φ recursively (recursively from completely defined Ψ, with suitable given function letters), and e is the Gödel number of E, then e defines φ recursively (recursively from Ψ).

EXAMPLE 2. Let f and g be Gödel numbers of partial recursive functions ψ and χ, respectively. Then the predicate $\psi(x) \simeq \chi(x)$ is expressed by

$$(y)[\{T_1(f, x, y) \rightarrow (Ez)(T_1(g, x, z) \,\&\, U(y)=U(z))\} \\ \&\, \{T_1(g, x, y) \rightarrow (Ez)(T_1(f, x, z) \,\&\, U(y)=U(z))\}].$$

COROLLARY. *Every partial recursive function φ (function φ partial recursive in completely defined functions and predicates Ψ) is definable (definable from Ψ) by applications of Schemata* (I) — (VI).

The algorithm given by (60) for calculating a partial recursive function φ is of the kind which does not terminate when $\varphi(x_1, \ldots, x_n)$ is undefined. By the theorem, a partial recursive function $\varphi(x_1, \ldots, x_n)$ has a range of definition of the form $\hat{x}(Ey)R(x_1, \ldots, x_n, y)$ where R is primitive recursive, or in other words for $n = 1$, the range of definition (if it has a member) is recursively enumerable (Theorem XIV § 60).

EXAMPLE 3. Hence by Theorem V (12) § 57, no partial function with $\hat{x}(y)\overline{T}_1(x, x, y)$ as its range of definition is partial recursive. It is impossible to devise any algorithm which will lead to some natural number for exactly those x's such that $(y)\overline{T}_1(x, x, y)$ and no others (by Thesis I† (a) below). In particular, the function φ defined thus,

$$\varphi(x) \simeq \begin{cases} 0 & \text{if} \quad (y)\overline{T}_1(x\ x, y), \\ u & \text{otherwise}, \end{cases}$$

is not partial recursive. This function is effectively calculable for x's in its range of definition, and is potentially recursive.

Now we state Church's thesis for the case of partial functions, keeping in mind Examples 1 and 3. We call a partial function $\varphi(x_1, \ldots, x_n)$ *potentially partial recursive*, if there is a partial recursive function $\varphi'(x_1, \ldots, x_n)$ such that $\varphi'(x_1, \ldots, x_n) = \varphi(x_1, \ldots, x_n)$ on the range of definition of φ. The thesis will be stated in two parts, according as we require that the effective calculation procedure lead to no function value off the range of definition of the function in question, or merely disregard what happens off this range.

EXAMPLE 4. Show that: If $\varphi(x)$ is potentially partial recursive and has a range of definition of the form $\hat{x}(Ey)R(x, y)$ where R is general recursive, then $\varphi(x)$ is partial recursive.

THESIS I†. (a) *The function which any algorithm calculates (the function being undefined for each n-tuple of arguments for which the algorithm leads to no natural number as value) is partial recursive.* (b) *Every partial function which is effectively calculable (in the sense that there is an algorithm by which its value can be calculated for every n-tuple belonging to its range of definition) is potentially partial recursive.*

The thesis can also be phrased to apply to predicates.

For l (≥ 0) assumed functions and predicates Ψ, we have a corresponding Thesis I*†, including the case of uniformity.

Much of our treatment of functions partial recursive in l assumed functions and predicates Ψ will be limited (for $l > 0$) to the case each of the functions and predicates Ψ is completely defined, or is incompletely defined but partial recursive or partial recursive in completely defined functions. These kinds of incompletely defined functions have been introduced to meet the requirements of the theory of algorithms (including reductions of decision problems), because it may be impossible to complete the definition of such a function and still have an algorithm for it. Outside the theory of algorithms, a like reason for not completing the definitions of incompletely defined number-theoretic functions is not readily apparent (cf. Example 4 § 64).

EXAMPLE 5. If $\psi(x)$ is a partial function with the range of definition $\hat{x}(Ey)R(x, y)$ (or $\hat{x}R(x)$) where R is a completely defined predicate, then there is a completely defined function $\psi^c(x)$ primitive recursive in ψ, R such that ψ is partial recursive in ψ^c. For let $C = \hat{x}(Ey)R(x, y)$; let θ enumerate recursively $\{0\}+C'$ (cf. Example 6 § 60); and let

$$\psi^c(y) = 2^{\theta(y)} \cdot 3^{\eta(\theta(y))} \text{ where } \eta(0) = 0,\ \eta(x') \simeq \psi(x).$$

Now $\psi(x) \simeq (\psi^c(\mu y[(\psi^c(y))_0 = x']))_1$.

EXAMPLE 6. $W_0(x, \mu y[W_0(x, y) \vee W_1(x, y)])$ is a partial, but not potentially, recursive predicate (cf. § 61).

§ 64. The 3-valued logic. In this section we shall introduce new senses of the propositional connectives, in which, e.g. $Q(x) \vee R(x)$ will be defined in some cases when $Q(x)$ or $R(x)$ is undefined.

It will be convenient to use truth tables, with three "truth values" $\mathfrak{t}$ ('true'), $\mathfrak{f}$ ('false') and $\mathfrak{u}$ ('undefined'), in describing the senses which the connectives shall now have.

Some remarks are appropriate to justify our use of truth tables here from the finitary standpoint, and to explain how we are led to choose the particular tables given below.

We were justified intuitionistically in using the classical 2-valued logic, when we were using the connectives in building primitive and general recursive predicates, since there is a decision procedure for each general recursive predicate; i.e. the law of the excluded middle is proved intuitionistically to apply to general recursive predicates.

Now if $Q(x)$ is a partial recursive predicate, there is a decision procedure for $Q(x)$ on its range of definition, so the law of the excluded middle or excluded "third" (saying that, for each x, $Q(x)$ is either $\mathfrak{t}$ or $\mathfrak{f}$) applies intuitionistically on the range of definition. But there may be no algorithm for deciding, given x, whether $Q(x)$ is defined or not (e.g. there is none when $Q(x)$ is $\mu y T_1(x, x, y){=}0$). Hence it is only classically and not intuitionistically that we have a law of the excluded fourth (saying that, for each x, $Q(x)$ is either $\mathfrak{t}$, $\mathfrak{f}$ or $\mathfrak{u}$).

The third "truth value" $\mathfrak{u}$ is thus not on a par with the other two $\mathfrak{t}$ and $\mathfrak{f}$ in our theory. Consideration of its status will show that we are limited to a special kind of truth table.

In asserting e.g. that $Q(x) \vee R(x)$ is primitive or partial recursive (uniformly) in Q and R, we assert the existence of an algorithm for obtaining the truth value of $Q(x) \vee R(x)$ from those of $Q(x)$ and $R(x)$. Again, in the partial case, $\mathfrak{u}$ will have a different status from $\mathfrak{t}$ and $\mathfrak{f}$.

Suppose we are to pick a truth table for $Q \vee R$, so that $Q(x) \vee R(x)$ will be partial recursive (uniformly) in Q and R. Let us discuss this heuristically, for the moment, identifying partial recursiveness with effective decidability. We ask to be able to decide by an algorithm, given x, whether $Q(x) \vee R(x)$ is $\mathfrak{t}$ or $\mathfrak{f}$ (if it is defined) from information that $Q(x)$ is $\mathfrak{t}$ or is $\mathfrak{f}$ (if it is defined) and like information about $R(x)$. Information that $Q(x)$ is $\mathfrak{u}$ is not utilizable by the algorithm; $\mathfrak{u}$ means only the absence of information that $Q(x)$ is $\mathfrak{t}$ or is $\mathfrak{f}$. If in case $Q(x)$ is $\mathfrak{u}$, the algorithm gives e.g. $\mathfrak{t}$ as value to $Q(x) \vee R(x)$, the decision to do so (for the given x and $R(x)$) must not have depended on information about $Q(x)$ (since none was available). In particular, if without changing the value of $R(x)$, that of $Q(x)$ were changed to $\mathfrak{t}$ or $\mathfrak{f}$, the same decision would still be made.

We reach the same conclusion, if we ask instead merely that $Q(x) \vee R(x)$ be partial recursive, whenever Q and R are partial recursive. In general, an algorithm for $Q(x) \vee R(x)$ (ab initio) will have access to information about $Q(x)$ and $R(x)$ only by utilizing algorithms for $Q(x)$ and $R(x)$ which are incorporated into it. A decision reached in pursuing the algorithm for $Q(x) \vee R(x)$ that e.g. $\mathfrak{t}$ is the value must have been based on information about $Q(x)$ and about $R(x)$ which had been produced at some finite stages in pursuing the algorithms for $Q(x)$ and $R(x)$. At any stage in the algorithm for $Q(x)$, we shall either have found out that $Q(x)$ is $\mathfrak{t}$, or that $Q(x)$ is $\mathfrak{f}$, or we shall not have learned the truth value of $Q(x)$. If $Q(x)$ is actually $\mathfrak{u}$, we cannot learn this by pursuing the algorithm, but if at all only in some other way, as by some metatheoretic reasoning about the algorithm. For special Q's we might substitute another algorithm which would also tell us when $Q(x)$ is $\mathfrak{u}$, but we cannot do this in general. Thus, if when $Q(x)$ is $\mathfrak{u}$, $Q(x) \vee R(x)$ receives the value $\mathfrak{t}$, the decision must (in the general case) have been made in ignorance about $Q(x)$, and in the face of the possibility that, at some stage in the pursuit of the algorithm for $Q(x)$ later than the last one examined, $Q(x)$ might be found to be $\mathfrak{t}$ or to be $\mathfrak{f}$.

Proofs in terms of the theory of partial recursive functions confirming these heuristic arguments (and extending them to other operators besides the propositional connectives) will be given at the end of the section (Theorem XXI and Examples 6 — 8).

We conclude that, in order for the propositional connectives to be partial recursive operations (or at least to produce partial recursive predicates when applied to partial recursive predicates), we must choose tables for them which are *regular*, in the following sense: A given column (row) contains $\mathfrak{t}$ in the $\mathfrak{u}$ row (column), only if the column (row) consists entirely of $\mathfrak{t}$'s; and likewise for $\mathfrak{f}$.

When we extended #D from primitive to partial recursiveness by taking over substantially the former proofs (#D† of Theorem XVII § 63), we were using the propositional connectives in the *weak senses*, which are described by the 3-valued tables (the *weak tables*) obtained from the classical 2-valued tables by supplying $\mathfrak{u}$ throughout the row and column headed by $\mathfrak{u}$. These are regular tables (trivially).

Now we introduce *strong senses* of the propositional connectives, described by the following *strong tables*.

Q	$\bar{Q}$
$\mathfrak{t}$	$\mathfrak{f}$
$\mathfrak{f}$	$\mathfrak{t}$
$\mathfrak{u}$	$\mathfrak{u}$

$Q \vee R$

Q \ R	$\mathfrak{t}$	$\mathfrak{f}$	$\mathfrak{u}$
$\mathfrak{t}$	$\mathfrak{t}$	$\mathfrak{t}$	$\mathfrak{t}$
$\mathfrak{f}$	$\mathfrak{t}$	$\mathfrak{f}$	$\mathfrak{u}$
$\mathfrak{u}$	$\mathfrak{t}$	$\mathfrak{u}$	$\mathfrak{u}$

$Q \,\&\, R$

Q \ R	$\mathfrak{t}$	$\mathfrak{f}$	$\mathfrak{u}$
$\mathfrak{t}$	$\mathfrak{t}$	$\mathfrak{f}$	$\mathfrak{u}$
$\mathfrak{f}$	$\mathfrak{f}$	$\mathfrak{f}$	$\mathfrak{f}$
$\mathfrak{u}$	$\mathfrak{u}$	$\mathfrak{f}$	$\mathfrak{u}$

$Q \rightarrow R$

Q \ R	$\mathfrak{t}$	$\mathfrak{f}$	$\mathfrak{u}$
$\mathfrak{t}$	$\mathfrak{t}$	$\mathfrak{f}$	$\mathfrak{u}$
$\mathfrak{f}$	$\mathfrak{t}$	$\mathfrak{t}$	$\mathfrak{t}$
$\mathfrak{u}$	$\mathfrak{t}$	$\mathfrak{u}$	$\mathfrak{u}$

$Q \equiv R$

Q \ R	$\mathfrak{t}$	$\mathfrak{f}$	$\mathfrak{u}$
$\mathfrak{t}$	$\mathfrak{t}$	$\mathfrak{f}$	$\mathfrak{u}$
$\mathfrak{f}$	$\mathfrak{f}$	$\mathfrak{t}$	$\mathfrak{u}$
$\mathfrak{u}$	$\mathfrak{u}$	$\mathfrak{u}$	$\mathfrak{u}$

Of these tables, only those for $\vee$, & and $\rightarrow$ differ from the respective weak tables. Henceforth $^{-}$, $\vee$, &, $\rightarrow$ and $\equiv$ applied to partial predicates shall be understood in these strong senses, except when otherwise stated.

EXAMPLE 1. Now (61a) can be restated thus:

(61b) $\quad (x_1) \ldots (x_n)(y)[T_n(e, x_1, \ldots, x_n, y) \rightarrow U(y)=\varphi(x_1, \ldots, x_n)].$

Statements of the form "If $\varphi(x_1, \ldots, x_n)$ is defined, then ...", where the conclusion is meaningless when $\varphi(x_1, \ldots, x_n)$ is undefined, can be understood then as uses of the strong $\rightarrow$. (Such statements occur already in § 63.)

These strong tables are uniquely determined as the strongest possible regular extensions of the classical 2-valued tables, i.e. they are regular, and have a $\mathfrak{t}$ or an $\mathfrak{f}$ in each position where any regular extension of the 2-valued tables can have a $\mathfrak{t}$ or an $\mathfrak{f}$ (whether $\mathfrak{t}$ or $\mathfrak{f}$ being uniquely determined).

We give the following three tables as examples of irregular tables. The present strong 3-valued logic (Kleene 1938) is not the same as the original 3-valued logic of Łukasiewicz (1920; cf. Lewis and Langford 1932 pp. 213 ff.), which differs from it by having $\mathfrak{t}$ instead of $\mathfrak{u}$ in Row 3 Column 3 of the tables for $\rightarrow$ and $\equiv$ (labeled here as $\rightarrow_{\L}$ and $\equiv_{\L}$).

$Q \rightarrow_{\L} R$

Q \ R	$\mathfrak{t}$	$\mathfrak{f}$	$\mathfrak{u}$
$\mathfrak{t}$	$\mathfrak{t}$	$\mathfrak{f}$	$\mathfrak{u}$
$\mathfrak{f}$	$\mathfrak{t}$	$\mathfrak{t}$	$\mathfrak{t}$
$\mathfrak{u}$	$\mathfrak{t}$	$\mathfrak{u}$	$\mathfrak{t}$

$Q \equiv_{\L} R$

Q \ R	$\mathfrak{t}$	$\mathfrak{f}$	$\mathfrak{u}$
$\mathfrak{t}$	$\mathfrak{t}$	$\mathfrak{f}$	$\mathfrak{u}$
$\mathfrak{f}$	$\mathfrak{f}$	$\mathfrak{t}$	$\mathfrak{u}$
$\mathfrak{u}$	$\mathfrak{u}$	$\mathfrak{u}$	$\mathfrak{t}$

$Q \simeq R$

Q \ R	$\mathfrak{t}$	$\mathfrak{f}$	$\mathfrak{u}$
$\mathfrak{t}$	$\mathfrak{t}$	$\mathfrak{f}$	$\mathfrak{f}$
$\mathfrak{f}$	$\mathfrak{f}$	$\mathfrak{t}$	$\mathfrak{f}$
$\mathfrak{u}$	$\mathfrak{f}$	$\mathfrak{f}$	$\mathfrak{t}$

We further conclude from the introductory discussion that, for the definitions of partial recursive operations, $\mathfrak{t}$, $\mathfrak{f}$, $\mathfrak{u}$ must be susceptible of another meaning besides (i) 'true', 'false', 'undefined', namely (ii) 'true', 'false', 'unknown (or value immaterial)'. Here 'unknown' is a category into which we can regard any proposition as falling, whose value we either do not know or choose for the moment to disregard; and it does not then exclude the other two possibilities 'true' and 'false'.

EXAMPLE 2. Suppose that, for a given x, we know $Q(x)$ to be undefined and $R(x)$ to be false. Then using $\mathfrak{t}$, $\mathfrak{f}$, $\mathfrak{u}$ as 'true', 'false', 'undefined' ((i)), we can conclude by the entry of Row 3 Column 2 in the table for $\vee$ that $Q(x) \vee R(x)$ is undefined.

EXAMPLE 3. Suppose that, for a given x, we know $Q(x)$ to be true. Then, using $\mathfrak{t}$, $\mathfrak{f}$, $\mathfrak{u}$ as 'true', 'false', 'unknown' ((ii)), we can conclude by the entry of Row 1 Column 3 that $Q(x) \vee R(x)$ is true. To draw this conclusion by using the tables with Meaning (i), we would need to use the classical law of the excluded fourth, thus: Either $R(x)$ is $\mathfrak{t}$, $\mathfrak{f}$ or $\mathfrak{u}$; and in each of Row 1 Column 1, Row 1 Column 2 and Row 1 Column 3 a $\mathfrak{t}$ appears.

From this standpoint, the meaning of $Q \vee R$ is brought out clearly by the statement in words: $Q \vee R$ is true, if Q is true (here nothing is said about R) or if R is true (similarly); false, if Q and R are both false; defined, only in these cases (and hence undefined, otherwise).

The strong 3-valued logic can be applied to completely defined predicates $Q(x)$ and $R(x)$, from which composite predicates are formed using $^{-}$, $\vee$, &, $\rightarrow$, $\equiv$ in the usual 2-valued meanings, thus. (iii) Suppose that there are fixed algorithms which decide the truth or falsity of $Q(x)$ and of $R(x)$, each on a subset of the natural numbers (as occurs e.g. after completing the definitions of any two partial recursive predicates classically). Let $\mathfrak{t}$, $\mathfrak{f}$, $\mathfrak{u}$ mean 'decidable by the algorithms (i.e. by use of only such information about $Q(x)$ and $R(x)$ as can be obtained by the algorithms) to be true', 'decidable by the algorithms to be false', 'undecidable by the algorithms whether true or false'. (iv) Assume a fixed state of knowledge about $Q(x)$ and $R(x)$ (as occurs e.g. after pursuing algorithms for each of them up to a given stage). Let $\mathfrak{t}$, $\mathfrak{f}$, $\mathfrak{u}$ mean 'known to be true', 'known to be false', 'unknown whether true or false'.

The following three classical equivalences

(62) $Q \,\&\, R \simeq \overline{\bar{Q} \vee \bar{R}}$, (63) $Q \rightarrow R \simeq \bar{Q} \vee R$,

(64) $$Q \equiv R \simeq (Q \rightarrow R) \,\&\, (R \rightarrow Q)$$

hold, as the reader may verify by constructing the tables for the right members, and comparing them with the given tables for the left members. But e.g. $Q \,\&\, (R \vee \bar{R}) \simeq Q$ (cf. *52 § 27) does not (when Q is $\mathfrak{t}$ and R is $\mathfrak{u}$, the left member is $\mathfrak{u}$ and the right is $\mathfrak{t}$).

The proofs of (62) — (64) by use of the 3-valued tables can be construed as showing that if either member is defined the other is and has the same value (as $\simeq$ asserts), using the law of the excluded third on the ranges of definition. This law we have given when Q and R are partial recursive; and the equivalences in the general case are subject to it intuitionistically as an hypothesis. Similar remarks apply to (65).

Strong senses are given to the bounded quantifiers, thus. For each $z > 0$, $(Ey)_{y<z}R(y) \simeq R(0) \vee \ldots \vee R(z-1)$; and $(Ey)_{y<0}R(y) \simeq \mathfrak{f}$. Expressed in words, $(Ey)_{y<z}R(y)$ is true, if $R(y)$ is true for some $y < z$; false, if $R(y)$ is false for all $y < z$; defined, only in these cases.

Similarly, for each $z > 0$, $(y)_{y<z}R(y) \simeq R(0) \,\&\, \ldots \,\&\, R(z-1)$; and $(y)_{y<0}R(y) \simeq \mathfrak{t}$.

We then have

(65) $$(y)_{y<z}R(y) \simeq \overline{(Ey)}_{y<z}\overline{R}(y).$$

Similarly, we give strong senses to the unbounded quantifiers, by thinking of $(Ey)R(y)$ as the strong disjunction of $R(y)$ for $y = 0, 1, 2, \ldots$, and of $(y)R(y)$ as the strong conjunction.

In words, $(Ey)R(y)$ is true, if $R(y)$ is true for some natural number y; false, if $R(y)$ is false for every y; defined, only in these cases. (Then $(y)R(y) \simeq \overline{(Ey)}\overline{R}(y)$.) Unlike the bounded quantifiers (Theorem XX (b)), the unbounded quantifiers are of course not partial recursive operations (Theorem V § 57).

Example 4. Consider the class of the predicates expressible in the form $(Ey)R(x, y)$ with R partial recursive. The definitions of all incompletely defined predicates of this class can be completed without going outside the class (in fact, with a primitive recursive R). For if r is a Gödel number of $R(x, y)$, then $(Ey)[T_2(r, x, (y)_0, (y)_1) \& U((y)_1){=}0]$ is completely defined and $\equiv (Ey)R(x, y)$ on the range of definition of the latter. Similarly for the form $(y)R(x, y)$. (Cf. Kleene 1943 p. 57 Theorem VI.)

Theorem XX. (a) *The (strong) predicate* $\overline{Q}(x_1, \ldots, x_n)$ *is partial recursive in the predicate* Q. *The (strong) predicates* $Q(x_1, \ldots, x_n) \vee R(x_1, \ldots, x_n)$, $Q(x_1, \ldots, x_n) \& R(x_1, \ldots, x_n)$, $Q(x_1, \ldots, x_n) \rightarrow R(x_1, \ldots, x_n)$ *and* $Q(x_1, \ldots, x_n) \equiv R(x_1, \ldots, x_n)$ *are partial recursive in the predicates* Q *and* R.

(b) *The (strong) predicates* $(Ey)_{y<z}R(x_1, \ldots, x_n, y)$ *and* $(y)_{y<z}R(x_1, \ldots, x_n, y)$ *are partial recursive in the predicate* R.

(c) (Strong) definition by cases. *The function* φ *defined by*

$$\varphi(x_1, \ldots, x_n) \simeq \begin{cases} \varphi_1(x_1, \ldots, x_n) & \text{if } Q_1(x_1, \ldots, x_n), \\ \quad\cdot \quad \cdot \quad \cdot \\ \varphi_m(x_1, \ldots, x_n) & \text{if } Q_m(x_1, \ldots, x_n), \end{cases}$$

where $Q_1, \ldots, Q_m$ *are mutually exclusive (under the interpretation that* $\varphi(x_1, \ldots, x_n)$ *shall* $\simeq \varphi_i(x_1, \ldots, x_n)$ *if* $Q_i(x_1, \ldots, x_n)$ *is true, disregarding* $\varphi_j(x_1, \ldots, x_n)$ *and* $Q_j(x_1, \ldots, x_n)$ *for all* $j \neq i$), *is partial recursive in* $\varphi_1, \ldots, \varphi_m, Q_1, \ldots, Q_m$.

Proofs. (a) To treat $Q \vee R$ for example, let $\psi(x_1, \ldots, x_n)$, $\chi(x_1, \ldots, x_n)$ and $\varphi(x_1, \ldots, x_n)$ be the representing functions of $Q(x_1, \ldots, x_n)$, $R(x_1, \ldots, x_n)$ and $Q(x_1, \ldots, x_n) \vee R(x_1, \ldots, x_n)$, respectively. Consider the equations

$$\text{(A)} \quad \begin{cases} \sigma(0) = 0, \qquad \tau(1,1) = 1, \\ \varphi(x_1, \ldots, x_n) = \sigma(\psi(x_1, \ldots, x_n)), \\ \varphi(x_1, \ldots, x_n) = \sigma(\chi(x_1, \ldots, x_n)), \\ \varphi(x_1, \ldots, x_n) = \tau(\psi(x_1, \ldots, x_n), \chi(x_1, \ldots, x_n)), \end{cases}$$

where σ and τ are partially defined auxiliary functions. By translating these equations (A) into the formal symbolism of recursive functions (§ 54), we obtain a system E defining φ recursively from ψ, χ. — The method illustrated applies to any regular table. (Alternatively, one can treat the other connectives thence, noting that $\bar{Q}$ has already been treated in D† of Theorem XVII, since the strong table for $\bar{Q}$ agrees with the weak one, and using (62) — (64).)

(b) By (65) it will suffice to treat $(Ey)_{y<z}$. Let $\chi(x_1, \ldots, x_n, y)$ and $\varphi(x_1, \ldots, x_n, z)$ be the representing functions of $R(x_1, \ldots, x_n, y)$ and $(Ey)_{y<z}R(x_1, \ldots, x_n, y)$, respectively. Then (using ##6, B†) the equations

$$\text{(B)} \quad \begin{cases} \sigma(0) = 0, \qquad \tau(1) = 1, \\ \varphi(x_1, \ldots, x_n, z') = \sigma(\chi(x_1, \ldots, x_n, z \dot{-} y)), \\ \varphi(x_1, \ldots, x_n, z) = \tau(\prod_{y<z} \chi(x_1, \ldots, x_n, y)) \end{cases}$$

translate into a system E defining φ recursively from χ.

(c) First method. Like (a); e.g. for $m = 2$ and $n = 1$,

$$\text{(C)} \quad \begin{cases} \sigma_1(0, x) = \varphi_1(x), \qquad \sigma_2(0, x) = \varphi_2(x), \\ \varphi(x) = \sigma_1(\psi_1(x), x), \quad \varphi(x) = \sigma_2(\psi_2(x), x). \end{cases}$$

Second method, for $Q_1, \ldots, Q_m$ simultaneously defined,

$$\varphi \simeq \mu y[(Q_1 \,\&\, y=\varphi_1) \vee \ldots \vee (Q_m \,\&\, y=\varphi_m)].$$

Remark 1. For consistency with our usage in (VI′) § 57, and at the beginning of § 54 where we first handle "=" quasi-formally before translating, we write (A) — (C) here with "=". But considered intuitively, as laws obeyed by the partial functions appearing in them, (VI′) and (A) — (C) should be written with "$\simeq$".

Example 5. If $\varphi(x)$ is partial recursive, and '$\varphi(x)$ is defined' is general recursive, then $\varphi(x)$ is potentially recursive. For let

$$\varphi'(x) \simeq \mu y[y=\varphi(x) \vee (\overline{\varphi(x) \text{ is defined}} \,\&\, y=0)].$$

Let Ψ be a sequence of partial functions $\psi_1, \ldots, \psi_l$. By an *extension* Ψ' of Ψ we mean a sequence $\psi_1', \ldots, \psi_l'$ of partial functions which are extensions respectively of $\psi_1, \ldots, \psi_l$, i.e. such that for $i = 1, \ldots, l$, $\psi_i'(y_1, \ldots, y_{m_i}) = \psi_i(y_1, \ldots, y_{m_i})$ on the range of definition of ψ_i. Similarly if Ψ include predicates.

The reader wishing to advance rapidly to the main results of the chapter in § 66 may omit Part (b) of the following theorem.

THEOREM XXI. (a) *If* $\varphi \simeq \mathsf{F}(\Psi)$ *or* $\varphi(x) \simeq \mathsf{F}(\Psi; x)$ *is a partial recursive functional, and* $\mathsf{F}(\Psi_1; x_1) \simeq k$, *where* Ψ_1 *are particular functions and* x_1, k *are particular natural numbers, then for every extension* Ψ_1' *of* Ψ_1, $\mathsf{F}(\Psi_1'; x_1) \simeq k$.

(b) *Let a function* φ *be defined from a function* ψ *by an operation of the form* $\varphi(x) \simeq \mathsf{F}(\psi(x))$, *where* $\mathsf{F}(\alpha)$ *is a function from* $\{\mathfrak{u}, 0, 1, 2, \ldots\}$ *to* $\{\mathfrak{u}, 0, 1, 2, \ldots\}$. *If* $\mathsf{F}(\mathfrak{u}) \simeq k$, *where* k *is a natural number, but for some natural number* m, *not* $\mathsf{F}(m) \simeq k$, *then there is a partial recursive function* ψ *(taking only* m *as values) for which the resulting function* φ *is not partial recursive.*

We can read "$x_1, \ldots, x_n$", "$x_{11}, \ldots, x_{1n}$" in place of "x", "x_1", respectively (where $n \geq 0$ for (a), ≥ 1 for (b)); and the theorem can be stated for predicates, with $\mathfrak{t}$ and $\mathfrak{f}$ taking the place of 0, 1, 2, ... as defined values.

PROOFS. (a) By hypothesis, there is a system E of equations with given function letters G and principal function letter f, such that, for any natural number x and partial functions Ψ: $\mathrm{E}_{\mathrm{G}}^{\Psi}, \mathrm{E} \vdash \mathrm{f}(\boldsymbol{x})=\boldsymbol{y}$ where $\boldsymbol{y}$ is a numeral, if and only if $\mathsf{F}(\Psi; x) = y$. But $\mathsf{F}(\Psi_1; x_1) = k$, where k is a natural number; so $\mathrm{E}_{\mathrm{G}}^{\Psi_1}, \mathrm{E} \vdash \mathrm{f}(\boldsymbol{x}_1)=\boldsymbol{k}$. Now if Ψ_1' is any extension of Ψ_1, then $\mathrm{E}_{\mathrm{G}}^{\Psi_1} \subset \mathrm{E}_{\mathrm{G}}^{\Psi_1'}$; hence also $\mathrm{E}_{\mathrm{G}}^{\Psi_1'}, \mathrm{E} \vdash \mathrm{f}(\boldsymbol{x}_1)=\boldsymbol{k}$; and therefore $\mathsf{F}(\Psi_1'; x_1) = k$. (If the functional $\mathsf{F}(\Psi)$ is defined only under some restriction on the range of Ψ, the theorem applies only to extensions Ψ_1' satisfying the restriction.)

(b) Let $\psi(x) \simeq m + 0 \cdot \mu y T_1(x, x, y)$ and $\rho(x) \simeq \mu y[\varphi(x)=k \;\&\; y=0]$. By Theorem XVIII, $\psi(x)$ is partial recursive, and $\rho(x)$ is partial recursive if $\varphi(x)$ is. We show now that $\rho(x)$ is not partial recursive. If $\overline{(Ey)}T_1(x, x, y)$, then $\mu y T_1(x, x, y)$ is undefined, hence $\psi(x)$ is undefined, hence by hypothesis $\varphi(x) = k$, hence $\rho(x)$ is defined. Thus $\overline{(Ey)}T_1(x, x, y) \rightarrow \{\rho(x)$ is defined$\}$. Similarly, $(Ey)T_1(x, x, y) \rightarrow \{\rho(x)$ is undefined$\}$; or by contraposition (cf. *13 § 26), $\{\rho(x)$ is defined$\} \rightarrow \overline{(Ey)}T_1(x, x, y)$. Thus $\{\rho(x)$ is defined$\} \equiv \overline{(Ey)}T_1(x, x, y) \equiv (y)\overline{T}_1(x, x, y)$. By Example 3 § 63, $\rho(x)$ is therefore not partial recursive.

In Examples 6 — 8, we give (a) and (b) parts separately, so as to illustrate both parts of the theorem, although the conclusion of the (b) part implies that of the (a) part.

Example 6. Can we improve upon Theorem XVIII by strengthening $\mu y R(x, y)$ to be the least y such that $R(x, y)$ is true irrespective of whether $R(x, 0), \ldots, R(x, y-1)$ are all defined (write it then $\mu' y R(x, y)$)? (a) No, since when $R(x, 1)$ is t, then $\mu' y R(x, y)$ changes from 1 to 0 when $R(x, 0)$ is changed from u to t. In more detail: Let $\chi(x, y)$ be the representing function of $R(x, y)$ and let $\varphi(x) \simeq \mu' y R(x, y) \simeq \mathsf{F}(\chi; x)$. Let χ_1, x_1 be choices of χ, x such that $\chi_1(x_1, 0) \simeq \mathfrak{u}$, $\chi_1(x_1, 1) \simeq 0$. Then $\mathsf{F}(\chi_1; x_1) \simeq 1$. Now by (a) of the theorem, if φ is partial recursive in χ, then $\mathsf{F}(\chi_1'; x_1) \simeq 1$ for every extension χ_1' of χ_1. But $\mathsf{F}(\chi_1'; x_1) \simeq 0$ for an extension χ_1' such that $\chi_1'(x_1, 0) \simeq 0$. Therefore φ is not partial recursive in χ. (b) We can even find a particular partial recursive R for which $\mu' y R(x, y)$ is not partial recursive. To see this, let $R(x, y)$ be of the form $y = \psi(x) \vee y = 1$. Then $\mu' y R(x, y)$ changes from 1 to 0 when $\psi(x)$ is changed from u to 0. In detail: Let $\varphi(x) \simeq \mu' y R(x, y) \simeq \mathsf{F}(\psi(x))$. Then $\mathsf{F}(\mathfrak{u}) \simeq 1$, but $\mathsf{F}(0) \simeq 0$. Hence by (b) of the theorem a partial recursive ψ can be chosen so that φ is not partial recursive.

Example 7. When $\chi(x) \simeq 0$, then $\psi(x) \simeq \chi(x)$ changes from f to t when $\psi(x)$ is changed from u to 0. Hence (a) $\psi(x) \simeq \chi(x)$ is not partial recursive in ψ, χ. Also (b) for some partial recursive ψ and χ, $\psi(x) \simeq \chi(x)$ is not partial recursive. (First take χ to be C_0^1 § 44; then choose a ψ to go with this χ by (b) of the theorem.)

Example 8. The table for $Q \cong R$ is irregular; e.g. when $R \cong$ t, then $Q \cong R$ changes from f to t when Q is changed from u to t. Hence (a) $Q(x) \cong R(x)$ is not partial recursive in Q and R, and (b) for some partial recursive Q and R, $Q(x) \cong R(x)$ is not partial recursive. — Any irregular table can be dealt with similarly.

§ 65. Gödel numbers. We now abbreviate $U(\mu y T_n(z, x_1, \ldots, x_n, y))$ as "$\Phi_n(z, x_1, \ldots, x_n)$" or even as "$\{z\}(x_1, \ldots, x_n)$" or "$z(x_1, \ldots, x_n)$". By Theorem XVIII, Φ_n is a partial recursive function of $n+1$ variables (and hence, for each fixed z, $\Phi_n(z, x_1, \ldots, x_n)$ is a partial recursive function of the n variables $x_1, \ldots, x_n$). Rewriting Theorem XIX (60), any partial recursive function $\varphi(x_1, \ldots, x_n)$ of n variables can be obtained from Φ_n, thus,

(66) $$\varphi(x_1, \ldots, x_n) \simeq \Phi_n(e, x_1, \ldots, x_n) \simeq e(x_1, \ldots, x_n),$$

where e is any Gödel number of φ. Similarly, $U(\mu y T_n^{\Psi}(z, x_1, \ldots, x_n, y))$

will be written "$\Phi_n^{\Psi}(z, x_1, \ldots, x_n)$", "$\{z\}^{\Psi}(x_1, \ldots, x_n)$" or "$z^{\Psi}(x_1, \ldots, x_n)$" for completely defined functions Ψ, with corresponding remarks. Summarizing:

THEOREM XXII (= Theorems XVIII + XIX). *The function $\Phi_n(z, x_1, \ldots, x_n)$ is partial recursive, and $\Phi_n(z, x_1, \ldots, x_n)$ for $z = 0, 1, 2, \ldots$ is an enumeration (with repetitions) of the partial recursive functions of n variables. Similarly, for completely defined Ψ, Φ_n^{Ψ} is partial recursive in Ψ and enumerates (with repetitions) the functions of n variables which are partial recursive in Ψ.* (Enumeration theorem for partial recursive functions.)

This theorem is only possible because a partial recursive function may be undefined for some sets of arguments.

Let us recapitulate the usual Cantor diagonal argument for completely defined functions. Suppose C is a class of such functions of various numbers of variables; and that $\Phi(z, x_1, \ldots, x_n)$ enumerates (with repetitions) the n-variable functions of C (for some fixed $n \geq 1$). Then $\Phi(x_1, x_1, x_2, \ldots, x_n)+1$ cannot ε C, because otherwise we would have

$$\Phi(q, q, x_2, \ldots, x_n)+1 = \Phi(q, q, x_2, \ldots, x_n)$$

for some number q, which is impossible. If C is closed under the operation of passing from a function $\varphi(z, x_1, \ldots, x_n)$ to $\varphi(x_1, x_1, x_2, \ldots, x_n)+1$, then $\Phi(z, x_1, \ldots, x_n)$ cannot ε C. In particular, this shows that there is no corresponding enumeration theorem for the general recursive functions.

But with partial functions, we would have instead

$$\Phi(q, q, x_2, \ldots, x_n)+1 \simeq \Phi(q, q, x_2, \ldots, x_n),$$

which is not impossible, but simply means that $\Phi(q, q, x_2, \ldots, x_n)$ must be undefined. In particular, we thus prove that the partial recursive function $\Phi_n(z, x_1, \ldots, x_n)$ is undefined, when $z = x_1 = q$ where q is any Gödel number of $\Phi_n(x_1, x_1, x_2, \ldots, x_n)+1$.

The Richard paradox (§ 11) arose by attempting to maintain simultaneously that $\Phi(z, x_1, \ldots, x_n)$ is in the class and is completely defined. (In § 11, $n = 1$.)

Diagonal reasoning with partial functions will be exploited further in establishing Theorem XXVII § 66.

EXAMPLE 1. Let $\eta(z_1, \ldots, z_r)$ be a given partial recursive function. For each $z_1, \ldots, z_r$, let $\varphi_{z_1,\ldots,z_r}(x_1, \ldots, x_n)$ be the partial recursive function which is defined for an n-tuple $x_1, \ldots, x_n$ only if $\eta(z_1, \ldots, z_r)$ is defined, and of which in this case $\eta(z_1, \ldots, z_r)$ is a Gödel number.

Then $\varphi_{z_1,\ldots,z_r}(x_1, \ldots, x_n)$ considered as a function $\varphi(z_1, \ldots, z_r, x_1, \ldots, x_n)$ of all $r+n$ variables is partial recursive. For

(67) $$\varphi(z_1, \ldots, z_r, x_1, \ldots, x_n) \simeq \Phi_n(\eta(z_1, \ldots, z_r), x_1, \ldots, x_n).$$

(This is an example for the first alternative under (A3) § 62.)

THEOREM XXIII. *For each m, $n \geq 0$, there is a primitive recursive function $S_n^m(z, y_1, \ldots, y_m)$ (defined below) such that, if e defines recursively $\varphi(y_1, \ldots, y_m, x_1, \ldots, x_n)$ as a function of the $m+n$ variables $y_1, \ldots, y_m$, $x_1, \ldots, x_n$, then for each fixed m-tuple $y_1, \ldots, y_m$ of natural numbers, $S_n^m(e, y_1, \ldots, y_m)$ defines recursively $\varphi(y_1, \ldots, y_m, x_1, \ldots, x_n)$ as a function of the remaining n variables $x_1, \ldots, x_n$.* Stated in the λ-notation (§ 10): *If e defines $\lambda y_1 \ldots y_m x_1 \ldots x_n\, \varphi(y_1, \ldots, y_m, x_1, \ldots, x_n)$ recursively, then $S_n^m(e, y_1, \ldots, y_m)$ defines $\lambda x_1 \ldots x_n\, \varphi(y_1, \ldots, y_m, x_1, \ldots, x_n)$ recursively.*

Similarly reading "primitive recursive function $S_n^{m,m_1,\ldots,m_l}(z, y_1, \ldots, y_m)$", "defines recursively from Ψ" in place of "primitive recursive function $S_n^m(z, y_1, \ldots, y_m)$", "defines recursively", respectively, where Ψ are l completely defined functions and predicates of $m_1, \ldots, m_l$ variables, respectively.

PROOF (for $l = 0$). Let $S_n^0(z) = z$. For $m > 0$, choose numbers $y_1, \ldots, y_m$. With these fixed, let $\varphi(y_1, \ldots, y_m, x_1, \ldots, x_n)$ be written "$\varphi(x_1, \ldots, x_n)$" Now

(68) $$\varphi(x_1, \ldots, x_n) \simeq \Phi_{m+n}(e, y_1, \ldots, y_m, x_1, \ldots, x_n).$$

Let D be a system of equations defining Φ_{m+n} recursively, with g as principal function letter, and not containing f. Let C consist of the equations of D followed by the equation

$$f(a_1, \ldots, a_n) = g(\mathbf{e}, \mathbf{y}_1, \ldots, \mathbf{y}_m, a_1, \ldots, a_n)$$

which we obtain by translating (68). This system C defines $\varphi(x_1, \ldots, x_n)$ recursively. Let $d, f, g, a_1, \ldots, a_n$ be the Gödel numbers of D, f, g, $a_1, \ldots, a_n$, respectively. Let $S_n^m(z, y_1, \ldots, y_m) =$

$$d * [2 \exp 2^{15} \cdot 3^{2^{f} \cdot p_1^{a_1} \cdot \ldots \cdot p_n^{a_n}} \cdot 5^{2^{g} \cdot 3^{Nu(z)} \cdot p_2^{Nu(y_1)} \cdot \ldots \cdot p_{m+1}^{Nu(y_m)} \cdot p_{m+2}^{a_1} \cdot \ldots \cdot p_{m+n+1}^{a_n}}]$$

(cf. § 56, #21 § 45, Example 2 § 52). Then $S_n^m(z, y_1, \ldots, y_m)$ is primitive recursive as a function of $z, y_1, \ldots, y_m$; and for the fixed $y_1, \ldots, y_m$, $S_n^m(e, y_1, \ldots, y_m)$ is the Gödel number of C, and hence defines $\varphi(x_1, \ldots, x_n)$ recursively.

EXAMPLE 1 (concluded). We do not get a larger class of functions $\varphi(z_1, \ldots, z_r, x_1, \ldots, x_n)$ by starting with a partial recursive η (as above) than with a primitive recursive η. For let the $\varphi(z_1, \ldots, z_r, x, \ldots, x_n)$ of (67) have e as Gödel number. Then $S^r_n(e, z_1, \ldots, z_r)$ is a Gödel number of $\varphi_{z_1,\ldots,z_r}(x_1, \ldots, x_n)$, i.e. $S^r_n(e, z_1, \ldots, z_r)$ is a primitive recursive "$\eta(z_1, \ldots, z_r)$" for the same $\varphi_{z_1,\ldots,z_r}(x_1, \ldots, x_n)$.

Example 2. For any general recursive predicate $R(x_1, \ldots, x_n, y)$ (with $n \geq 1$), let e be a Gödel number of the partial recursive function $\lambda x_1 z x_2 \ldots x_n\, \mu y R(x_1, \ldots, x_n, y)$. For any fixed x_1, then $S^1_n(e, x_1)$ is a Gödel number of $\lambda z x_2 \ldots x_n\, \mu y R(x_1, \ldots, x_n, y)$. This function is defined for a given n-tuple $z, x_2, \ldots, x_n$, if and only if $(Ey)R(x_1, \ldots, x_n, y)$. Hence by Theorem XIX,

(69) $$(Ey)R(x_1, \ldots, x_n, y) \equiv (Ey)T_n(S^1_n(e, x_1), z, x_2, \ldots, x_n, y).$$

Substituting $S^1_n(e, x_1)$ for z,

(70) $$(Ey)R(x_1, \ldots, x_n, y) \equiv (Ey)T_n(S^1_n(e, x_1), S^1_n(e, x_1), x_2, \ldots, x_n, y).$$

Taking $n = 1$ and writing "a" for "x_1" and "x" for "y", this shows that $(Ex)R(a, x)$ is primitive recursive in $(Ex)T_1(a, a, x)$. Thus the decision problem for $(Ex)T_1(a, a, x)$ is of highest degree of unsolvability for predicates of the form $(Ex)R(a, x)$ with general recursive R (cf. end § 61). Furthermore, by the definition of S^1_1, $a_1 \neq a_2 \rightarrow S^1_1(e, a_1) \neq S^1_1(e, a_2)$. Thus there is a general recursive function $\psi(a)$ such that $\{a_1 \neq a_2 \rightarrow \psi(a_1) \neq \psi(a_2)\}$ & $\{(Ex)R(a, x) \equiv (Ex)T_1(\psi(a), \psi(a), x)\}$; in Post's terminology (1944), the decision problem for the set $\hat{a}(Ex)R(a, x)$ is 1-1 *reducible* to that for $\hat{a}(Ex)T_1(a, a, x)$. That this is so for every set $\hat{a}(Ex)R(a, x)$ with general recursive R is a property of the present set $\hat{a}(Ex)T_1(a, a, x)$ which Post showed is possessed by another recursively enumerable set "K" called by him "the complete set" (1944 p. 295 and Theorem p. 297). We obtain like results for the forms with more quantifiers and for $l > 0$. For example, from (70) with $n = 3$ ($l = 0$), we infer that

$$(Ex)(y)(Ez)R(a, x, y, z) \equiv (Ex)(y)(Ez)T_3(S^1_3(e, a), S^1_3(e, a), x, y, z)$$

(cf. *71, *72 § 33). Thus $(Ex)(y)(Ez)T_3(a, a, x, y, z)$ has a decision problem of highest degree of unsolvability for predicates of the form $(Ex)(y)(Ez)R(a, x, y, z)$ with R recursive, and the decision problem for any predicate of this form is 1-1 reducible to its decision problem.

Example 3. Omitting the z in Example 2, we obtain that the decision problem for $\hat{a}(Ex)R(a, x)$ is 1-1 reducible to that for $\hat{a}(Ex)T_0(a, x)$ (and hence by Example 2, the predicates $(Ex)T_1(a, a, x)$ and $(Ex)T_0(a, x)$

have decision problems of the same degree of unsolvability); and similarly with more quantifiers, e.g.

$$(Ex)(y)(Ez)R(a, x, y, z) \equiv (Ex)(y)(Ez)T_2(S_2^1(e, a), x, y, z),$$

where e is a Gödel number of $\mu z R(a, x, y, z)$.

The major part of § 66 can be understood without the rest of this section.

THE Λ-NOTATION (to be used in § 82). When

$$\lambda y_1 \ldots y_m x_1 \ldots x_n\, \varphi(y_1, \ldots, y_m, x_1, \ldots, x_n)$$

is partial recursive and e defines it recursively, we shall use

$$\text{“}\Lambda_{(e)} x_1 \ldots x_n\, \varphi(y_1, \ldots, y_m, x_1, \ldots, x_n)\text{”}$$

as an abbreviation for $S_n^m(e, y_1, \ldots, y_m)$. Usually we omit the subscript "$_{(e)}$". Thus (for $m = 0$) "$\Lambda x_1 \ldots x_n\, \varphi(x_1, \ldots, x_n)$" will stand for some Gödel number of the function $\lambda x_1 \ldots x_n\, \varphi(x_1, \ldots, x_n)$; and (for $m > 0$) "$\Lambda x_1 \ldots x_n\, \varphi(y_1, \ldots, y_m, x_1, \ldots, x_n)$" will stand for some primitive recursive function, whose value for each m-tuple $y_1, \ldots, y_m$ of natural numbers as arguments is some Gödel number of the function

$$\lambda x_1 \ldots x_n\, \varphi(y_1, \ldots, y_m, x_1, \ldots, x_n).$$

Using this abbreviation with the abbreviation

$$\text{“}\{z\}(x_1, \ldots, x_n)\text{” for } \Phi_n(z, x_1, \ldots, x_n),$$

we have, for any n-tuple $t_1, \ldots, t_n$ of natural numbers,

(71)
$$\{\Lambda x_1 \ldots x_n\, \varphi(y_1, \ldots, y_m, x_1, \ldots, x_n)\}(t_1, \ldots, t_n) \simeq \varphi(y_1, \ldots, y_m, t_1, \ldots, t_n).$$

Like notation with "$\Lambda^{m_1, \ldots, m_l}$" may be used, when Ψ are l completely defined functions and predicates of $m_1, \ldots, m_l$ variables, respectively.

LEMMA VI. *Lemma* I § 47 *holds reading "partial recursive" in place of "primitive recursive"*. Thus (for $p = 1$): *If* $\varphi(x_1, \ldots, x_n)$ *is partial recursive uniformly in functions* θ, Ψ, *and* $\varphi^*(x_1, \ldots, x_n, c)$ *is the function obtained when* θ *in the definition of* φ *is taken to be a function* θ^* *depending on a parameter* c, *then* φ^* *is partial recursive uniformly in* θ^*, Ψ.

PROOF. By hypothesis there is a system E of equations such that, for each choice of θ, Ψ, the system E defines the resulting function φ recursively from θ, Ψ. Let Ψ be $\psi_1, \ldots, \psi_l$; and say that the given function letters of E (expressing θ, Ψ, respectively) are t, $g_1, \ldots, g_l$, and the principal function letter is f. Let c be a variable not occurring in E. Let

E_2^* result from E by changing simultaneously each part $h(r_1, \ldots, r_s)$ where h is a function letter and $r_1, \ldots, r_s$ are terms to $h(r_1, \ldots, r_s, c)$. Let E_1^* be the system of equations
$g_1(a_1, \ldots, a_{m_1}, c)=\bar{g}_1(a_1, \ldots, a_{m_1}), \ldots, g_l(a_1, \ldots, a_{m_l}, c)=\bar{g}_l(a_1, \ldots, a_{m_l})$, where $\bar{g}_1, \ldots, \bar{g}_l$ are distinct function letters not occurring in E. Let E^* be $E_1^*E_2^*$. We show that, for each choice of θ^*, Ψ, the system E^* defines φ^* recursively from θ^*, Ψ.

Consider any fixed choice of θ^*, Ψ and c. Let $(E_t^{\theta^*})_c$ be the set of the equations $t(\boldsymbol{s}_1, \ldots, \boldsymbol{s}_q, \boldsymbol{c})=\boldsymbol{u}$ which $\varepsilon\, E_t^{\theta^*}$. Let $(E_t^{\theta})_c$ be the set of the respective equations $t(\boldsymbol{s}_1, \ldots, \boldsymbol{s}_q)=\boldsymbol{u}$, i.e. the set of the equations expressing the values of the function θ when we take $\theta(s_1, \ldots, s_q) = \theta^*(s_1, \ldots, s_q, c)$ for the fixed c.

We easily see that if $(E_t^{\theta})_c, E_{g_1 \ldots g_l}^{\psi_1 \ldots \psi_l}, E \vdash f(\boldsymbol{x}_1, \ldots, \boldsymbol{x}_n)=\boldsymbol{x}$, then $(E_t^{\theta^*})_c, E_{\bar{g}_1 \ldots \bar{g}_l}^{\psi_1 \ldots \psi_l}, E^* \vdash f(\boldsymbol{x}_1, \ldots, \boldsymbol{x}_n, \boldsymbol{c})=\boldsymbol{x}$, a fortiori $E_t^{\theta^*}{}_{\bar{g}_1 \ldots \bar{g}_l}^{\psi_1 \ldots \psi_l}, E^* \vdash f(\boldsymbol{x}_1, \ldots, \boldsymbol{x}_n, \boldsymbol{c})=\boldsymbol{x}$.

We now demonstrate the converse. Let $(E_{g_1 \ldots g_l}^{\psi_1 \ldots \psi_l})_c$ be the set of the equations $g_i(\boldsymbol{y}_1, \ldots, \boldsymbol{y}_{m_i}, \boldsymbol{c})=\boldsymbol{y}$ where $g_i(\boldsymbol{y}_1, \ldots, \boldsymbol{y}_{m_i})=\boldsymbol{y}\ \varepsilon\ E_{g_1 \ldots g_l}^{\psi_1 \ldots \psi_l}$. Let $(E^*)_c$ be the system of equations which results by substituting $\boldsymbol{c}$ for c throughout E_2^*. We say that an equation e is a *c-equation*, if there is a deduction of e from $E_t^{\theta^*}{}_{\bar{g}_1 \ldots \bar{g}_l}^{\psi_1 \ldots \psi_l}, E^*$ and either e ε $(E_t^{\theta^*})_c$, or e ε $(E_{g_1 \ldots g_l}^{\psi_1 \ldots \psi_l})_c$, or the principal equation (§ 54) of that deduction of e ε E_2^* and the principal branch contains an application of R1 which substitutes $\boldsymbol{c}$ for c. We can prove (by induction on the height of a given such deduction of e) that, if e is a c-equation, then $(E_t^{\theta^*})_c, (E_{g_1 \ldots g_l}^{\psi_1 \ldots \psi_l})_c, (E^*)_c \vdash$ e. In this resulting deduction, every occurrence of a function symbol h is in a part of the form $h(r_1, \ldots, r_s, \boldsymbol{c})$. Any equation of the form $f(\boldsymbol{x}_1, \ldots, \boldsymbol{x}_n, \boldsymbol{c})=\boldsymbol{x}$ deducible from $E_t^{\theta^*}{}_{\bar{g}_1 \ldots \bar{g}_l}^{\psi_1 \ldots \psi_l}, E^*$ is a c-equation. If in the resulting deduction just described we change simultaneously each part $h(r_1, \ldots, r_s, \boldsymbol{c})$ to $h(r_1, \ldots, r_s)$, we obtain a deduction of $f(\boldsymbol{x}_1, \ldots, \boldsymbol{x}_n)=\boldsymbol{x}$ from $(E_t^{\theta})_c, E_{g_1 \ldots g_l}^{\psi_1 \ldots \psi_l}, E$.

THEOREM XXIV. (a) *If $\varphi(x_1, \ldots, x_n)$ is partial recursive uniformly in partial recursive functions $\theta_1, \ldots, \theta_r$, then there is a partial recursive function $\varphi(z_1, \ldots, z_r, x_1, \ldots, x_n)$ such that, when $t_1, \ldots, t_r$ are any Gödel numbers of $\theta_1, \ldots, \theta_r$, respectively, $\varphi(x_1, \ldots, x_n) \simeq \varphi(t_1, \ldots, t_r, x_1, \ldots, x_n)$.*

(b) *If φ is partial recursive uniformly in partial recursive functions $\theta_1, \ldots, \theta_r$, then there is a primitive recursive function $\eta(z_1, \ldots, z_r)$ such* *that, when* $t_1, \ldots, t_r$ *are any Gödel numbers of* $\theta_1, \ldots, \theta_r$, *respectively,* $\eta(t_1, \ldots, t_r)$ *is a Gödel number of* φ.

Also both parts hold reading "partial recursive in $\theta_1, \ldots, \theta_r, \Psi$", *"partial recursive in* Ψ", *"Gödel number from* Ψ" *in place of "partial recursive in* $\theta_1, \ldots, \theta_r$", *"partial recursive", "Gödel number", respectively, where* Ψ *are l completely defined functions.*

PROOFS (for $l = 0$). (a) By use of Lemma VI, the result of replacing $\theta_i(s_1, \ldots, s_{q_i})$ by $\Phi_{q_i}(z_i, s_1, \ldots, s_{q_i})$ $(i = 1, \ldots, r)$ in the definition of $\varphi(x_1, \ldots, x_n)$ from $\theta_1, \ldots, \theta_r$ is a function $\varphi(z_1, \ldots, z_r, x_1, \ldots, x_n)$ partial recursive in $\Phi_{q_1}, \ldots, \Phi_{q_r}$. But $\Phi_{q_1}, \ldots, \Phi_{q_r}$ are partial recursive, so $\varphi(z_1, \ldots, z_r, x_1, \ldots, x_n)$ is partial recursive. Also
$\theta_i(s_1, \ldots, s_{q_i}) \simeq \Phi_{q_i}(t_i, s_1, \ldots, s_{q_i})$, so $\varphi(x_1, \ldots, x_n) \simeq \varphi(t_1, \ldots, t_r, x_1, \ldots, x_n)$.

(b) Let e be a Gödel number of $\varphi(z_1, \ldots, z_r, x_1, \ldots, x_n)$, and take $\eta(z_1, \ldots, z_r) = S^r_n(e, z_1, \ldots, z_r)$.

EXAMPLE 4. By our proof of Theorem XIII § 60 (going back upon that of Theorem IV § 57), the f of Figure 1a § 61 can be any Gödel number of the partial recursive function $\mu y R(x, y)$. As $\mu y R(x, y)$ is partial recursive uniformly in R, by Theorem XXIV (b) (applied to the representing function of R) there is a general recursive (actually, primitive recursive) function $\eta(z)$ such that, for any Gödel number r of $R(x, y)$, $\eta(r)$ is an f for Figure 1a. This shows that the recursively enumerable set C_0 (namely, $\hat{x}(Ey)T_1(x, x, y)$) is what Post 1944 calls a *creative set*. (The Gödel number r of $R(x, y)$ takes the place here of Post's "basis B" for the recursively enumerable set $\hat{x}(Ey)R(x, y)$.)

EXAMPLE 5. Our examples of predicates not general recursive given in Theorem V § 57 were of $n \geq 1$ variables. — The predicate $(Ex)R(x)$ of 0 variables is not general recursive uniformly in the predicate R. For suppose it were. Then by Theorem XXIV (a) for $n = 0$ (applied to the representing functions), there would be a partial recursive predicate $Q(z)$ such that $(Ex)R(x) \equiv Q(t)$ for any Gödel number t of $R(x)$. Now let e be a Gödel number of the predicate $T_1(a, a, x)$. Then $Q(S^1_1(e, a))$ would be a general recursive predicate of a, and $(Ex)T_1(a, a, x) \equiv Q(S^1_1(e, a))$. But $(Ex)T_1(a, a, x)$ is not general recursive (Theorem V (15)).

INDEFINITE DESCRIPTION. THEOREM XXV. *For each* $n \geq 0$, *there is a partial recursive function* $\nu_n(z, x_1, \ldots, x_n)$ *with the following property. Suppose* r *is a Gödel number of a partial recursive predicate* $R(x_1, \ldots, x_n, y)$. *Then* $\nu_n(r, x_1, \ldots, x_n)$ *is defined if and only if* $(Ey)R(x_1, \ldots, x_n, y)$, *in which case its value is a number* y *such that* $R(x_1, \ldots, x_n, y)$. We usually abbreviate $\nu_n(r, x_1, \ldots, x_n)$ as "$\nu y_{(r)} R(x_1, \ldots, x_n, y)$" or even "$\nu y R(x_1, \ldots, x_n, y)$", and read it "a y (depending on r) such that $R(x_1, \ldots, x_n, y)$".

Similarly for l *completely defined functions and predicates* Ψ, *reading "partial recursive in* Ψ*", "Gödel number from* Ψ*", "*ν_n^{Ψ}*", "*$\nu y_{(r)}^{\Psi}$*" in place of "partial recursive", "Gödel number", "*ν_n*", "*$\nu y_{(r)}$*", respectively.*

Proof (for $l = 0$). We define
$\nu_n(z, x_1, \ldots, x_n) \simeq (\mu y[T_{n+1}(z, x_1, \ldots, x_n, (y)_0, (y)_1) \,\&\, U((y)_1)=0])_0$.

Discussion. The least number operator μy and the indefinite description νy correspond to two different effective procedures for calculating a y such that $R(x_1, \ldots, x_n, y)$, each with respective limitations.

Let R be effectively decidable. To calculate $\mu y R(x_1, \ldots, x_n, y)$, we first try to settle by the algorithm for R whether $R(x_1, \ldots, x_n, 0)$ is true or false. If it is true, we take 0 as the number sought; if false, we then try next to settle whether $R(x_1, \ldots, x_n, 1)$ is true or false; and so on. If before finding a y for which $R(x_1, \ldots, x_n, y)$ is true, we come to one for which $R(x_1, \ldots, x_n, y)$ is undefined, we are unable to get past this y, but must (in obedience to the rules of our calculation procedure) continue ad infinitum in the futile effort to settle whether $R(x_1, \ldots, x_n, y)$ is true or false for it. For a particular R, we might find another procedure which would get around this obstacle, but we cannot in general (cf. Example 6 § 64).

To calculate $\nu y R(x_1, \ldots, x_n, y)$, we distribute our efforts to settle whether $R(x_1, \ldots, x_n, y)$ is true or false for various y's, so that, while our efforts to settle whether $R(x_1, \ldots, x_n, 0)$ is true or false are in progress, if after a certain number of steps they have not led to a decision, we then set to work also on $R(x_1, \ldots, x_n, 1)$, and so on. The search, if not terminated, will for each y eventually carry the algorithm for determining the truth or falsity of $R(x_1, \ldots, x_n, y)$ for that y arbitrarily far. As soon as $R(x_1, \ldots, x_n, y)$ is found to be true for any y, we accept that y without attempting to settle whether it is the least. The y obtained by this procedure may vary with the algorithm for R (or the Gödel number r) which is used. According to the following example (stated for $n = 0$), this is unavoidable in general.

Example 6. Suppose $\nu'(z)$ is a partial function with the two properties: (a) If r is a Gödel number of a partial recursive predicate $R(y)$, then $(Ey)R(y) \rightarrow R(\nu'(r))$. (b) If r and s are Gödel numbers of the same predicate, then $\nu'(r) \simeq \nu'(s)$. We shall show that then ν' is not partial recursive. For each k, let partial recursive predicates R_k and S_k be defined thus:

$$R_k(y) \simeq y=0 \vee y=1+0\cdot\mu z T_1(k, k, z), \quad S_k(y) \simeq y=0\cdot\mu z T_1(k, k, z) \vee y=1.$$

Let r_k and s_k be any Gödel numbers of R_k and S_k, respectively. Given k, $R_k(0)$ and $S_k(1)$ are true; so by (a), $\nu'(r_k)$ and $\nu'(s_k)$ are both defined. If $(Ez)T_1(k, k, z)$, then $(y)[R_k(y) \simeq S_k(y)]$, i.e. R_k and S_k are the same predicate; and hence using (b), $\nu'(r_k)=\nu'(s_k)$. Thus $(Ez)T_1(k, k, z) \rightarrow \nu'(r_k)=\nu'(s_k)$, or contraposing (cf. *12 § 26), $\nu'(r_k) \neq \nu'(s_k) \rightarrow \overline{(Ez)}T_1(k, k, z)$. Conversely, if $\overline{(Ez)}T_1(k, k, z)$, then $R_k(y)$ is true only for $y = 0$ and $S_k(y)$ only for $y = 1$, so by (a), $\nu'(r_k) \neq \nu'(s_k)$. Thus $\nu'(r_k) \neq \nu'(s_k) \equiv \overline{(Ez)}T_1(k, k, z) \equiv (z)\overline{T}_1(k, k, z)$. The expressions defining $R_k(y)$ and $S_k(y)$ are partial recursive predicates of the two variables k, y; say those predicates have Gödel numbers r and s, respectively. We can take $r_k = S^1_1(r, k)$ and $s_k = S^1_1(s, k)$ in the above, obtaining the equivalence $\nu'(S^1_1(r, k)) \neq \nu'(S^1_1(s, k)) \equiv (z)\overline{T}_1(k, k, z)$. If ν' were partial recursive, the left member would be a general recursive predicate of k; but the right is not (Theorem V (14)).

§ 66. The recursion theorem. THEOREM XXVI. *For any $n \geq 0$, let $\mathsf{F}(\zeta; x_1, \ldots, x_n)$ be a partial recursive functional, in which the function variable ζ ranges over partial functions of n variables. Then the equation*

$$\zeta(x_1, \ldots, x_n) \simeq \mathsf{F}(\zeta; x_1, \ldots, x_n)$$

has a solution φ for ζ such that any solution φ' for ζ is an extension of φ, and this solution φ is partial recursive.

Similarly, when Ψ are l partial functions and predicates,

$$\zeta(x_1, \ldots, x_n) \simeq \mathsf{F}(\zeta, \Psi; x_1, \ldots, x_n)$$

has a solution φ for ζ such that any solution φ' for ζ is an extension of φ, and this solution φ is partial recursive in Ψ. (The first recursion theorem.)

PROOF (for $l = 0$, $n = 1$). Let φ_0 be the completely undefined function. Then introduce $\varphi_1, \varphi_2, \varphi_3, \ldots$ successively by

$$\varphi_1(x) \simeq \mathsf{F}(\varphi_0; x), \quad \varphi_2(x) \simeq \mathsf{F}(\varphi_1; x), \quad \varphi_3(x) \simeq \mathsf{F}(\varphi_2; x), \ldots$$

Since φ_0 is completely undefined, φ_1 is an extension of φ_0; then by Theorem XXI (a), φ_2 is an extension of φ_1, φ_3 of φ_2, etc. Let φ be the "limit function" of $\varphi_0, \varphi_1, \varphi_2, \ldots$; i.e. for each x, let $\varphi(x)$ be defined if and only if $\varphi_s(x)$ is defined for some s, in which case its value is the common value of $\varphi_s(x)$ for all $s \geq$ the least such s. Now:

(i) *For each* x, $\varphi(x) \simeq \mathsf{F}(\varphi; x)$. For consider any x. Suppose $\varphi(x)$ is defined. Then for some s, $\varphi(x) \simeq \varphi_{s+1}(x)$ [by definition of φ] $\simeq \mathsf{F}(\varphi_s; x)$ [by definition of φ_{s+1}] $\simeq \mathsf{F}(\varphi; x)$ [by Theorem XXI (a), since φ is an extension of φ_s]. Conversely, suppose $\mathsf{F}(\varphi; x)$ is defined; call its value k. Since F is partial recursive, there is a system F of equations defining $\mathsf{F}(\zeta; x)$ recursively from ζ, say with f as principal and g as given function letter; so now there is a deduction of $\mathrm{f}(\boldsymbol{x})=\boldsymbol{k}$ from $\mathrm{E}_{\mathrm{g}}^{\varphi}$, F. Let $\mathrm{g}(\boldsymbol{y}_1)=\boldsymbol{z}_1, \ldots, \mathrm{g}(\boldsymbol{y}_p)=\boldsymbol{z}_p$ (where $z_i = \varphi(y_i)$) be the equations of $\mathrm{E}_{\mathrm{g}}^{\varphi}$ occurring in this deduction. But $\varphi(y_1) = \varphi_{s_1}(y_1), \ldots, \varphi(y_p) = \varphi_{s_p}(y_p)$ for some $s_1, \ldots, s_p$. Let $s = \max(s_1, \ldots, s_p)$. Then $\varphi(y_1) = \varphi_s(y_1), \ldots, \varphi(y_p) = \varphi_s(y_p)$. So $\mathrm{g}(\boldsymbol{y}_1)=\boldsymbol{z}_1, \ldots, \mathrm{g}(\boldsymbol{y}_p)=\boldsymbol{z}_p \in \mathrm{E}_{\mathrm{g}}^{\varphi_s}$. Thus $\mathrm{E}_{\mathrm{g}}^{\varphi_s}, \mathrm{F} \vdash \mathrm{f}(\boldsymbol{x})=\boldsymbol{k}$. Hence $k \simeq \mathsf{F}(\varphi_s; x) \simeq \varphi_{s+1}(x) \simeq \varphi(x)$.

(ii) *If for each* x, $\varphi'(x) \simeq \mathsf{F}(\varphi'; x)$, *then* φ' *is an extension of* φ. It will suffice to show by induction on s that, for each x, if $\varphi_s(x)$ is defined, then $\varphi'(x) \simeq \varphi_s(x)$. Basis: $s=0$. True vacuously. Ind. step. Suppose for a given x that $\varphi_{s+1}(x)$ is defined. Then $\varphi_{s+1}(x) \simeq \mathsf{F}(\varphi_s; x) \simeq \mathsf{F}(\varphi'; x)$ [by Theorem XXI (a), since by hyp. ind. φ' is an extension of φ_s] $\simeq \varphi'(x)$.

(iii) *If* F *defines* $\mathsf{F}(\zeta; x)$ *recursively from* ζ, *and* E *comes from* F *by substituting the principal function symbol* f *for the given function symbol* g, *then* E *defines* φ *recursively*. It will suffice to show that $\mathrm{E} \vdash \mathrm{f}(\boldsymbol{x})=\boldsymbol{k}$, if and only if $\varphi_s(x) \simeq k$ for some s. We easily see that if $\varphi_s(x) = k$, then $\mathrm{E} \vdash \mathrm{f}(\boldsymbol{x})=\boldsymbol{k}$. For the converse, we show by induction on h that if there is a deduction of $\mathrm{f}(\boldsymbol{x})=\boldsymbol{k}$ from E of height h, then $\varphi_s(x) = k$ for some s. The deduction can be altered if necessary, so that in each inference by R2 with a minor premise of the form $\mathrm{f}(\boldsymbol{y})=\boldsymbol{z}$ only one occurrence of $\mathrm{f}(\boldsymbol{y})$ in the major premise is replaced by $\boldsymbol{z}$ (Act 1). The occurrences of f in equations of the deduction can be classified in an evident manner into those which come from an occurrence of f in F, and those which come via the substitution of f for g from an occurrence of g in F. Now consider the inferences by R2 with minor premise of the form $\mathrm{f}(\boldsymbol{y})=\boldsymbol{z}$ in which the f of the part $\mathrm{f}(\boldsymbol{y})$ replaced comes from a g in F. Say there are p such inferences, the minor premises $\mathrm{f}(\boldsymbol{y}_1)=\boldsymbol{z}_1, \ldots, \mathrm{f}(\boldsymbol{y}_p)=\boldsymbol{z}_p$ of which do not stand above other such premises. Each of these p premises occurred above the endequation of the given deduction before Act 1; so using the hypothesis of the induction, $z_1 \simeq \varphi_{s_1}(y_1) \simeq \varphi_s(y_1), \ldots, z_p \simeq \varphi_{s_p}(y_p) \simeq \varphi_s(y_p)$ where $s = \max(s_1, \ldots, s_p)$. Now consider the tree remaining from the deduction after Act 1, when all the equations above $\mathrm{f}(\boldsymbol{y}_1)=\boldsymbol{z}_1, \ldots, \mathrm{f}(\boldsymbol{y}_p)=\boldsymbol{z}_p$ are removed (Act 2). In this tree, let each occurrence of f which (before Act 2) came from a g of F be changed back to g (Act 3). The f's in question all occurred in the right members of equations, since g being the given function symbol of F occurs in F only on the right; so no f is changed by Act 3 in what was a minor premise for R2 before Act 3 or in the end-equation $\mathrm{f}(\boldsymbol{x})=\boldsymbol{k}$. Finally, let the f's of $\mathrm{f}(\boldsymbol{y}_1)=\boldsymbol{z}_1, \ldots, \mathrm{f}(\boldsymbol{y}_p)=\boldsymbol{z}_p$ be changed to g (ACT 4), which restores the inferences by R2 which Act 3 spoiled. The resulting tree is a deduction of $\mathrm{f}(\boldsymbol{x})=\boldsymbol{k}$ from $\mathrm{E}_{\mathrm{g}}^{\varphi_s}$, F. Hence

$$k \simeq \mathsf{F}(\varphi_s; x) \simeq \varphi_{s+1}(x).$$

EXAMPLE 1. Consider the problem: to find a partial recursive function φ such that

(a) $$\varphi(x) \simeq \varphi(x);$$

i.e. to solve the equation $\zeta(x) \simeq \zeta(x)$ for ζ. Obviously any partial function satisfies this equation. The partial function with the least range of definition which satisfies is the completely undefined function. This is the solution φ given by the theorem (with $\mathsf{F}(\zeta; x) \simeq \zeta(x)$).

EXAMPLE 2. To find a partial recursive function φ such that

(a) $$\varphi(x) \simeq \varphi(x)+1;$$

i.e. to solve $\zeta(x) \simeq \zeta(x)+1$ for ζ. Only the completely undefined partial function satisfies. This of course is the solution φ given by the theorem (with $\mathsf{F}(\zeta; x) \simeq \zeta(x)+1$).

EXAMPLE 3. To find a function φ partial recursive in χ such that

(a) $$\begin{cases} \varphi(0) \simeq q, \\ \varphi(y') \simeq \chi(y, \varphi(y)) \end{cases}$$

(Schema (Va) § 43). Only one function φ satisfies for a given χ, and we already know by Theorem XVII (a) that it is partial recursive in χ. However to see how the theorem applies, we rewrite (a) as

(b) $\varphi(x) \simeq \mathsf{F}(\varphi, \chi; x)$ where $\mathsf{F}(\zeta, \chi; x) \simeq \begin{cases} q \text{ if } x=0, \\ \chi(x \dot{-} 1, \zeta(x \dot{-} 1)) \text{ if } x>0 \end{cases}$

(equivalently,

$$\mathsf{F}(\zeta, \chi; x) \simeq \mu w[\{x=0 \;\&\; w=q\} \vee \{x>0 \;\&\; w=\chi(x \dot{-} 1, \zeta(x \dot{-} 1))\}]).$$

Since $\mathsf{F}(\zeta, \chi; x)$ is partial recursive (using Theorems XVII, XX (c); or XVII, XVIII, XX (a)), by the theorem φ is partial recursive in χ.

EXAMPLE 4. We give a new proof of Theorem XVIII (which proof in various guises appeared in Kleene 1935, 1936, 1943). Let $\varphi(x) \sim \mu y[\chi(x, y)=0]$. Then $\varphi(x) \simeq \varphi(x, 0)$ where

(a) $$\varphi(x, y) \simeq \mu t_{t \geq y}[\chi(x, t)=0].$$

But $\varphi(x, y)$ is the partial function φ with the least range of definition such that

$$\text{(b)} \qquad \varphi(x, y) \simeq \begin{cases} y \text{ if } \chi(x, y) = 0, \\ \varphi(x, y') \text{ if } \chi(x, y) \neq 0. \end{cases}$$

By Theorem XX (c) (with the first proof), the right side of (b) is of the form $\mathsf{F}(\varphi, \chi; x, y)$ where $\mathsf{F}(\zeta, \chi; x, y)$ is partial recursive; so by the present theorem $\varphi(x, y)$, and hence $\varphi(x)$, is partial recursive in χ.

DISCUSSION. The theorem for $l = 0$ asserts that we can impose any relationship of the form

$$\text{(72)} \qquad \varphi(x_1, \ldots, x_n) \simeq \mathsf{F}(\varphi; x_1, \ldots, x_n)$$

expressing the ambiguous value $\varphi(x_1, \ldots, x_n)$ of a function φ in terms of φ itself and $x_1, \ldots, x_n$ by methods already treated in the theory of partial recursive functions; and conclude that the partial function with the least range of definition which satisfies the relationship is partial recursive.

Moreover the case of the theorem for $l > 0$, in which

$$\text{(73)} \qquad \varphi(x_1, \ldots, x_n) \simeq \mathsf{F}(\varphi, \Psi; x_1, \ldots, x_n)$$

is the relationship imposed, can be used to extend the body of the methods available for use in further applications.

In our examples of special kinds of "recursion" (§§ 43, 46 and beginning § 55) the ambiguous function value $\varphi(x_1, \ldots, x_n)$ was expressed in terms of values of the same function for sets of arguments preceding the given n-tuple $x_1, \ldots, x_n$ in terms of some special ordering of the n-tuples. We now have a general kind of "recursion", in which the value $\varphi(x_1, \ldots, x_n)$ can be expressed as depending on other values of the same function in a quite arbitrary manner, provided only that the rule of dependence is describable by previously treated effective methods.

The given "recursion" may now be ambiguous as a definition of an ordinary (i.e. completely defined) number-theoretic function φ, in the sense that it is satisfied by more than one such function (Example 1, or (b) in Example 4 when $\chi(x, y)$ does not vanish for infinitely many values of y). But now we choose as the solution which interests us that partial function which is defined only when the recursion requires it to be. The given "recursion" may be inconsistent as a definition of an ordinary function (Example 2); again the difficulty is escaped now through the fact that it is only a partial function which we are seeking as the solution. Both these situations can arise when the F is general recursive (Examples 1 and 2). When F is incompletely defined, the recursion may also directly demand under our usual convention (§ 63) that φ be undefined for some arguments (e.g. Example 3 when χ is given to be the completely undefined function), as well as indirectly through an inconsistency (not necessarily as obvious as in Example 2).

Given a particular relationship of the form (72) or (73), it may be a difficult problem to recognize for what arguments $x_1, \ldots, x_n$ the function value $\varphi(x_1, \ldots, x_n)$ must be defined. This problem is separate from the problem, which the first recursion theorem solves, of recognizing the partial recursiveness of the solution φ having the least range of definition.

We can use the theorem in presenting the case under (A2) § 62. Our methods for showing given effectively calculable functions to be partial recursive (and hence when completely defined, general recursive) are now developed to the point where they seem adequate for handling any effective definition of a function which might be proposed. To describe in ordinary language a process for calculating a new function φ, we would have to explain effectively how any function value $\varphi(x_1, \ldots, x_n)$ is to be obtained from values of φ already calculated. In this explanation, we would normally employ effectively calculable functions previously studied, the connectives of the propositional calculus, also possibly bounded quantifiers (unbounded quantifiers would not be effective), and descriptions of the form 'the least number such that'. This vocabulary translates into operations already treated in our theory (cf. particularly Theorems XVIII and XX). The explanation as a whole would then come under the first recursion theorem; namely we could express it as a statement that φ is to satisfy (72) for a certain F, and is to be defined only when the explanation leads to a value, i.e. φ is to be the function of least range of definition satisfying (72). Then by the theorem we can conclude that φ is partial recursive.

Some other operations besides those just noted can be handled by methods already considered, e.g. the definition of several functions simultaneously (cf. Example 4 § 46). Still other notions we might employ we would expect to be able to explain first in terms of the above vocabulary. Our results are formulated so as to constitute, not only methods for showing particular functions to be partial (or general) recursive, but also tools for enlarging our stock of methods as the need may appear.

THEOREM XXVII. *For each* $n > 0$: *Given any partial recursive function* $\psi(z, x_1, \ldots, x_n)$, *a number* e *can be found which defines* $\psi(e, x_1, \ldots, x_n)$ *recursively, i.e. such that*

$$\{e\}(x_1, \ldots, x_n) \simeq \psi(e, x_1, \ldots, x_n). \tag{74a}$$

Similarly, for l completely defined functions and predicates Ψ, reading "partial recursive in Ψ", "defines recursively from Ψ", "$\{\ \}^{\Psi}$" in place of "partial recursive", "defines recursively", "$\{\ \}$", respectively. (The recursion theorem, Kleene 1938.)

PROOF (for $l = 0$). The function $\psi(S^1_n(y, y), x_1, \ldots, x_n)$ is partial recursive (cf. Theorem XXIII). Let f define it recursively, and take $e = S^1_n(f, f)$. Then e defines recursively the function of n variables obtained by substituting the number f for the variable y in $\psi(S^1_n(y, y), x_1, \ldots, x_n)$; i.e. e defines recursively $\psi(S^1_n(f, f), x_1, \ldots, x_n)$; i.e. e defines recursively $\psi(e, x_1, \ldots, x_n)$, as was to be shown.

DISCUSSION. The theorem can be read as saying that for any partial recursive function ψ the equation

$$z(x_1, \ldots, x_n) \simeq \psi(z, x_1, \ldots, x_n)$$

can be solved for z. For the notation, cf. § 65 especially (66). If we write $\varphi(x_1, \ldots, x_n)$ for the function $e(x_1, \ldots, x_n)$ defined recursively by the solution e of this equation, (74a) can be written

(74b) $$\varphi(x_1, \ldots, x_n) \simeq \psi(e, x_1, \ldots, x_n).$$

But $\psi(z, x_1, \ldots, x_n)$ can be any partial recursive function of $n+1$ variables. Thus the theorem says that a partial recursive function φ can be found whose ambiguous value $\varphi(x_1, \ldots, x_n)$ is given from a Gödel number e of itself and the numbers $x_1, \ldots, x_n$ by any preassigned partial recursive function ψ. Then φ can be used in constructing its own ambiguous value, since in building $\psi(e, x_1, \ldots, x_n)$ we can use e in parts of the form $\Phi_n(e, u_1, \ldots, u_n)$ (briefly $e(u_1, \ldots, u_n)$), and $\Phi_n(e, u_1, \ldots, u_n)$ is $\varphi(u_1, \ldots, u_n)$. This can be emphasized by stating a corollary. (The version of the corollary for $l > 0$ is left to the reader.)

COROLLARY. *Given a partial recursive functional $\mathsf{F}(\zeta; z, x_1, \ldots, x_n)$, where ζ ranges over partial recursive functions of n variables, there can be found a partial recursive function φ and a Gödel number e of φ such that*

(75) $$\varphi(x_1, \ldots, x_n) \simeq \mathsf{F}(\varphi; e, x_1, \ldots, x_n).$$

Given a partial recursive functional $\mathsf{F}(\zeta, \theta_1, \ldots, \theta_r; z, w_1, \ldots, w_r, x_1, \ldots, x_n)$, where ζ ranges over partial recursive functions of n variables, and $\theta_1, \ldots, \theta_r$ over partial recursive functions of specified numbers of variables, there can be found a partial recursive function $\varphi(w_1, \ldots, w_r, x_1, \ldots, x_n)$ and a Gödel number e of φ such that, when $t_1, \ldots, t_r$ are any Gödel numbers of $\theta_1, \ldots, \theta_r$, respectively,

(76) $$\varphi(t_1, \ldots, t_r, x_1, \ldots, x_n) \simeq \mathsf{F}(\varphi, \theta_1, \ldots, \theta_r; e, t_1, \ldots, t_r, x_1, \ldots, x_n).$$

PROOF (for $r = 0$). By Theorem XXIV (a), we can find a partial recursive function ψ of $n+2$ variables such that

$$\mathsf{F}(\zeta; z, x_1, \ldots, x_n) \simeq \psi(s, z, x_1, \ldots, x_n)$$

when s is any Gödel number of ζ. Now let $\psi(z, x_1, \ldots, x_n) \simeq \psi(z, z, x_1, \ldots, x_n)$. Then by the theorem we find a number e for (74). Writing $\varphi(x_1, \ldots, x_n)$ for the function defined recursively by e, we have
$\varphi(x_1, \ldots, x_n) \simeq \psi(e, x_1, \ldots, x_n) \simeq \psi(e, e, x_1, \ldots, x_n) \simeq \mathsf{F}(\varphi; e, x_1, \ldots, x_n)$.

DISCUSSION (concluded). When φ is partial recursive uniformly in ζ, we may consider that φ depends partial recursively on ζ as a function; when $\varphi(x_1, \ldots, x_n)$ is a partial recursive function of $x_1, \ldots, x_n$ and a Gödel number of ζ, that φ depends partial recursively on ζ as an object. The gain in Theorem XXVII over XXVI is that now in imposing a relationship expressing the ambiguous value $\varphi(x_1, \ldots, x_n)$ partial recursively in terms of φ itself and $x_1, \ldots, x_n$, we can let φ enter not only as a function but also as an object. Our conclusion then is that some partial recursive function φ satisfies the relationship; but in general different solutions φ will be obtained from different selections of the Gödel number f of $\psi(S^1_n(y, y), x_1, \ldots, x_n)$ in the proof of Theorem XXVII.

Theorem XXVII does not quite include XXVI as the case φ enters into the "recursion" only as a function (so that the $\mathsf{F}(\zeta; z, x_1, \ldots, x_n)$ of the corollary reduces to $\mathsf{F}(\zeta; x_1, \ldots, x_n)$), because the method of proof of Theorem XXVII does not (at least without some further argument) show that the partial recursive solution φ obtained is necessarily the one having the least range of definition. So Theorem XXVII via its corollary can take the place of Theorem XXVI in supporting Theses I, I*, I† (b) and I*† (b), but not I† (a) and I*† (a).

Of course it is only after we have Church's thesis that we have the means of regarding every effectively calculable function as a number-theoretic object. That then an effectively calculable function can be found to satisfy any "recursion" in which it enters as an object besides as a function is a consequence of the thesis which proves useful in further developments.

EXAMPLE 2 (concluded). To treat this by Theorem XXVII instead of XXVI, take the $\psi(z, x)$ for Theorem XXVII $\simeq \Phi_1(z, x)+1$.

EXAMPLE 3 (concluded). Similarly taking $\psi(z, x) \simeq$
$\mathsf{F}(\lambda x\, \Phi_1(z, x), \chi; x) \simeq \mu w[\{x=0 \,\&\, w=q\} \vee \{x>0 \,\&\, w=\chi(x \dot{-} 1, \Phi_1(z, x \dot{-} 1))\}]$.

EXAMPLE 5. Given fixed partial recursive functions $\theta_1, \ldots, \theta_5$, to find a partial recursive function φ with the following properties. If

$\theta_1(x) = 0$, $\varphi(x) = 1$. If $\theta_1(x) = 1$, $\varphi(x) \simeq \theta_2(\varphi(\theta_3(x)))$. If $\theta_1(x) = 2$, $\varphi(x) \simeq \theta_4(a_{\varphi,x})$ where $a_{\varphi,x}$ is some number which defines $\lambda y\, \varphi(\theta_5(x, y))$ recursively. Note first that if e is any Gödel number of φ, then $\varphi(\theta_5(x, y)) \simeq \Phi_1(e, \theta_5(x, y))$. Now $\lambda zxy\, \Phi_1(z, \theta_5(x, y))$ is a fixed partial recursive function. If g be a Gödel number of it, then $S^2_1(g, e, x)$ is a Gödel number of $\lambda y\, \Phi_1(e, \theta_5(x, y))$, i.e. of $\lambda y\, \varphi(\theta_5(x, y))$. Now the above three properties are imposed on φ by the equation

$$\text{(a)} \quad \begin{aligned} \varphi(x) \simeq \mu w[\{\theta_1(x)=0 \ \&\ w=1\} \\ \vee \{\theta_1(x)=1 \ \&\ w=\theta_2(\varphi(\theta_3(x)))\} \vee \{\theta_1(x)=2 \ \&\ w=\theta_4(S^2_1(g, e, x))\}]. \end{aligned}$$

This is of the form (75) for the corollary, since (using Theorems XVII, XVIII, XX, XXIII) the right side is of the form $\mathrm{F}(\varphi; e, x)$ where $\mathrm{F}(\zeta; z, x)$ is a fixed partial recursive scheme function, and e may be any Gödel number of φ. For the theorem

$$\begin{aligned} \psi(z, x) \simeq \mu w[\{\theta_1(x)=0 \ \&\ w=1\} \\ \vee \{\theta_1(x)=1 \ \&\ w=\theta_2(\Phi_1(z, \theta_3(x)))\} \vee \{\theta_1(x)=2 \ \&\ w=\theta_4(S^2_1(g, z, x))\}]. \end{aligned}$$

The problem arose as above with particular functions $\theta_1, \ldots, \theta_5$ in Kleene 1938. We can generalize it by considering $\theta_1, \ldots, \theta_5$ as unspecified partial recursive functions. Let $t_1, \ldots, t_5$ be any Gödel numbers of them. If h is a Gödel number of $\lambda zwxy\, \Phi_1(z, \Phi_2(w, x, y))$, then $S^3_1(h, e, t_5, x)$ is a Gödel number of $\lambda y\, \Phi_1(e, \Phi_2(t_5, x, y))$, i.e. of $\lambda y\, \varphi(\theta_5(x, y))$. Now the properties are imposed on φ by

$$\text{(b)} \quad \begin{aligned} \varphi(x) \simeq \varphi(t_1, \ldots, t_5, x) \simeq \mu w[\{\theta_1(x)=0 \ \&\ w=1\} \\ \vee \{\theta_1(x)=1 \ \&\ w=\theta_2(\varphi(\theta_3(x)))\} \vee \{\theta_1(x)=2 \ \&\ w=\theta_4(S^3_1(h, e, t_5, x))\}]. \end{aligned}$$

By the second part of the corollary, we can find a partial recursive $\varphi(w_1, \ldots, w_5, x)$ and a Gödel number e of φ to satisfy (b).

CHAPTER XIII

COMPUTABLE FUNCTIONS

§ 67. Turing machines. Suppose that a person is to compute the value of a function for a given set of arguments by following preassigned effective instructions. In performing the computation he will use a finite number of distinct symbols or tokens of some sort. He can have only a finite number of occurrences of symbols under observation at one time. He can also remember others previously observed, but again only a finite number. The preassigned instructions must also be finite. Applying the instructions to the finite number of observed and remembered symbols or tokens, he can perform an act that changes the situation in a finite way, e.g. he adds or erases some occurrences of symbols, shifts his observation to others, registers in his memory those just observed. A succession of such acts must lead him from a symbolic expression representing the arguments to another symbolic expression representing the function value.

We now inquire whether it is not possible to analyze the acts the computer can perform into certain "atomic" acts, such that any performable act will be equivalent to some succession of atomic acts. The atomic acts would be combinations of the following: recognizing a single observed occurrence of a given symbol, erasing this occurrence, marking down a single occurrence of a symbol, displacing the point of observation of a given array of symbols to an adjacent point, and altering the remembered information.

Such an analysis was undertaken by Turing (1936-7, received for publication 28 May 1936) in the form of a definition of a kind of computing machine. A similar analysis was proposed briefly by Post (1936, received for publication 7 October 1936).

The evidence that the analysis is complete, i.e. that to any function which is effectively calculable a Turing machine can be found which computes it, will be reviewed after we have become familiar with the Turing machines (§ 70).

We begin by formulating the idea of a Turing machine, as follows.

The machine is supplied with a linear *tape*, (potentially) infinite in both directions (say to the *left* and *right*). The tape is divided into *squares*. Each square is capable of being *blank*, or of having *printed* upon it any one of a finite list $s_1, \ldots, s_j$ $(j \geq 1)$ of *symbols*, fixed for a particular machine. If we write "s_0" to stand for "blank", a given square can thus have any one of $j+1$ *conditions* $s_0, \ldots, s_j$. The tape will be so employed that in any "situation" only a finite number (≥ 0) of squares will be printed.

The tape will pass through the machine so that in a given "situation" the machine *scans* just one square (the *scanned square*). The symbol on this square, or s_0 if it is blank, we call the *scanned symbol* (even though s_0 is not properly a symbol).

The machine is capable of being in any one of a finite list $q_0, \ldots, q_k$ $(k \geq 1)$ of (*machine*) *states* (called by Turing "machine configurations" or "*m*-configurations"). We call q_0 the *passive* (or *terminal*) *state*; and $q_1, \ldots, q_k$ we call *active states*. The list $q_0, \ldots, q_k$ is fixed for a particular machine.

A (*tape vs. machine*) *situation* (called by Turing "complete configuration") consists in a particular printing on the tape (i.e. which squares are printed, and each with which of the j symbols), a particular position of the tape in the machine (i.e. which square is scanned), and a particular state (i.e. which of the $k+1$ states the machine is in). If the state is active, we call the situation *active*; otherwise, *passive*.

Given an active situation, the machine performs an (*atomic*) *act* (called a "move" by Turing). The act performed is determined by the scanned symbol s_a and the machine state q_c in the given situation. This pair (s_a, q_c) we call the *configuration*. (It is *active* in the present case that q_c is active; otherwise *passive*.) The act alters the three parts of the situation to produce a resulting situation, thus. First, the scanned symbol s_a is changed to s_b. (But $a = b$ is permitted, in which case the "change" is identical.) Second, the tape is shifted in the machine (or the machine shifts along the tape) so that the square scanned in the resulting situation is either one square to the left of, or the same square as, or one square to the right of, the square scanned in the given situation. Third, the machine state q_c is changed to q_d. (But $c = d$ is permitted.)

No act is performed, if the given situation is passive.

The machine is used in the following way. We choose some active situation in which to start the machine. We call this the *initial situation* or *input*. Our notation will be chosen so that the state in this situation (the *initial state*) is q_1. The machine then performs an atomic act. If the situation resulting from this act is active, the machine acts again. The machine continues in this manner, clicking off successive acts, as long and only as long as active situations result. If eventually a passive situation is reached, the machine is said then to *stop*. The situation in which it stops we call the *terminal situation* or *output*.

The change from the initial situation to the terminal situation (when there is one) may be called the *operation* performed by the machine.

To describe an atomic act, we use an expression of one of the three following forms:

$$s_b L q_d, \qquad s_b C q_d, \qquad s_b R q_d.$$

The "L", "C", "R" indicate that the resulting scanned square is to the left of, the same as ("center"), or to the right of, respectively, the given scanned square.

The first part of the act (i.e. the change of s_a to s_b) falls into four cases: when $a=0$ and $b>0$, it is "prints s_b"; when $a>0$ and $b=0$, "erases s_a"; when $a, b>0$ and $a \neq b$, "erases s_a and prints s_b" or briefly "overprints s_b"; when $a = b$, "no change". We often describe this part of the act as "prints s_b" without regard to the case.

To define a particular machine, we must list the symbols $s_1, \ldots, s_j$ and the active states $q_1, \ldots, q_k$, and for each active configuration (s_a, q_c) we must specify the atomic act to be performed. These specifications may be given by displaying the descriptions of the required acts in the form of a (*machine*) *table* with k rows for the active states and $j+1$ columns for the square conditions.

EXAMPLE 1. The following table defines a machine ("Machine $\mathfrak{A}$") having only one symbol s_1 and only one active state q_1.

Name of machine	Machine state	Scanned symbol s_0	s_1
$\mathfrak{A}$	q_1	$s_1 C q_0$	$s_1 R q_1$

Suppose the symbol s_1 is actually a tally mark "|". Let us see what the machine does, if a tape of the following appearance is placed initially in the machine so that the square which we identify by writing the machine state q_1 over it is the scanned square. The conditions of all squares not shown will be immaterial, and will not be changed during the action.

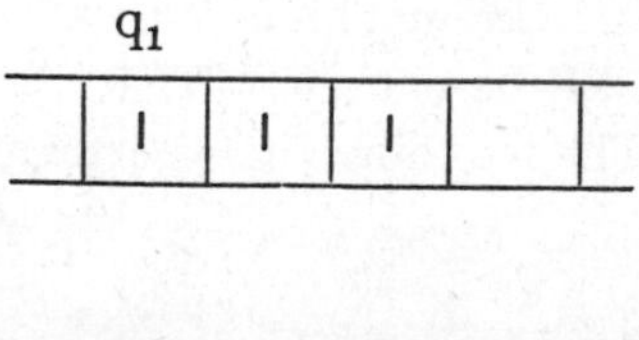

The machine is in state q_1, and is scanning a square on which the symbol s_1 is printed. In this configuration, the atomic act ordered by the table is $s_1 R q_1$; i.e. no change is made in the condition of the scanned square, the machine shifts right, and again assumes state q_1. The resulting situation appears as follows.

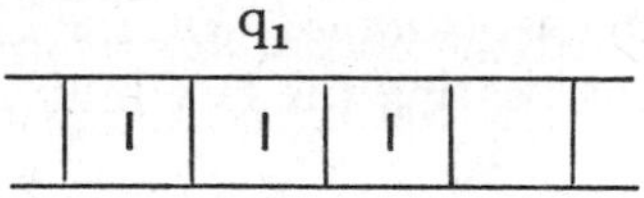

The next three acts lead successively to the following situations, in the last of which the machine stops.

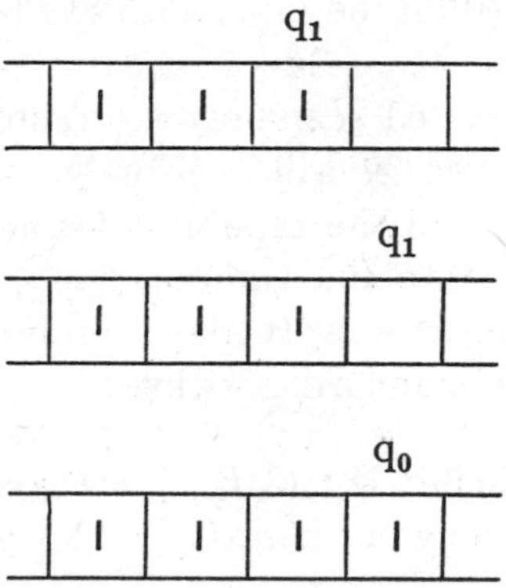

Machine $\mathfrak{A}$ performs the following operation: It seeks the first blank square at or to the right of the scanned square, prints a I there, and stops scanning that square.

Now we define how a machine shall 'compute' a partial number-theoretic function φ of n variables (cf. § 63). The definition for an ordinary (i.e. completely defined) number-theoretic function is obtained by omitting the reference to the possibility that $\varphi(x_1, \ldots, x_n)$ may be undefined.

We begin by agreeing to represent the natural numbers 0, 1, 2, ... by the sequences of tallies I, II, III, ..., respectively, the tally "I" being the symbol s_1. There are $y+1$ tallies in the representation of the natural number y.

Then to represent an m-tuple $y_1, \ldots, y_m$ $(m \geq 1)$ of natural numbers on the tape, we print the corresponding numbers of tallies, leaving a single blank between each two groups of tallies and before the first and after the last.

EXAMPLE 2. The triple 3, 0, 2 is represented thus:

We say that (the representation of) a number y (or of an m-tuple $y_1, \ldots, y_m$) on the tape is *(scanned) in standard position*, when the scanned square is the one bearing the last tally in the representation of y (or of y_m).

Now we say that a given machine $\mathfrak{M}$ *computes* a given partial function φ of n variables ($n \geq 1$), if the following holds for each n-tuple $x_1, \ldots, x_n$ of natural numbers. (For the case $n = 0$, cf. Remark 1 below.) Let $x_1, \ldots, x_n$ be represented on the tape, with the tape blank elsewhere, i.e. outside of the $x_1 + \ldots + x_n + 2n + 1$ squares required for the representation. Let $\mathfrak{M}$ be started scanning the representation of $x_1, \ldots, x_n$ in standard position. Then $\mathfrak{M}$ will eventually stop with the $n+1$-tuple $x_1, \ldots, x_n, x$ represented on the tape and scanned in standard position, if and only if $\varphi(x_1, \ldots, x_n)$ is defined and $\varphi(x_1, \ldots, x_n) = x$. (If $\varphi(x_1, \ldots, x_n)$ is undefined, $\mathfrak{M}$ may fail to stop. It may stop but without an $n+1$-tuple $x_1, \ldots, x_n, x$ scanned in standard position.)

Example 2 (concluded). If $\varphi(3, 0, 2) = 1$ and $\mathfrak{M}$ computes φ, then when $\mathfrak{M}$ is started in the situation

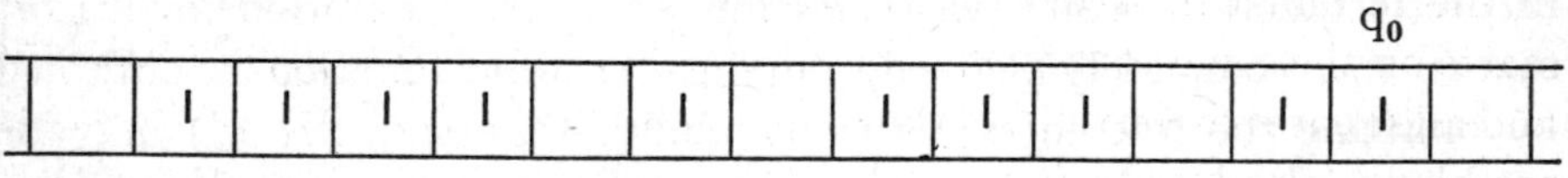

with all squares other than those shown blank, it must eventually stop in the situation

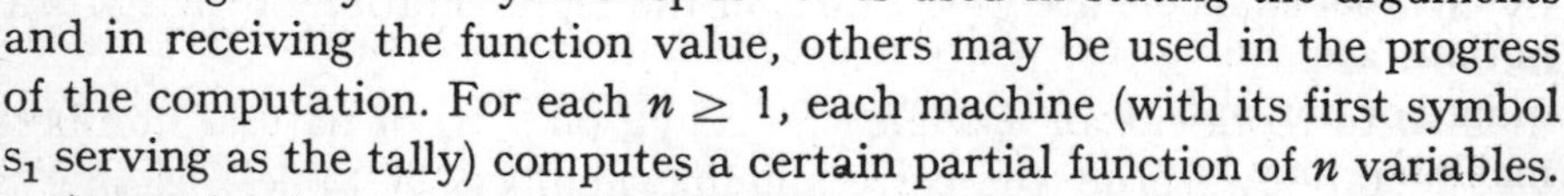

where the condition of the squares other than those shown is immaterial.

Although only one symbol s_1 or "I" is used in stating the arguments and in receiving the function value, others may be used in the progress of the computation. For each $n \geq 1$, each machine (with its first symbol s_1 serving as the tally) computes a certain partial function of n variables.

A partial function φ is *computable*, if there is a machine $\mathfrak{M}$ which computes it.

We have not attempted here to reproduce the detailed formulation of Turing 1936-7, but only his general conception of the behavior of the machines. Although he noted a variety of applications of his machines, he confined his detailed development to machines for computing dual expansions of real numbers x $(0 \leq x \leq 1)$. The successive digits were to be printed ad infinitum on alternate squares of a 1-way infinite tape, while the intervening squares were reserved for temporary notes serving as scratch work in the continuing computation. It should be an easy exercise, after §§ 68 and 69, to show that a machine exists which does this, if and only if the n-th digit in the dual expansion is a computable function of n. A critique, of help to one who would study Turing's paper in detail, is given in the appendix to Post 1947. Our treatment here is closer in some respects to Post 1936. Post 1936 considered computation with a 2-way infinite tape and only 1 symbol.

Our main objective next is to prove the equivalence of computability with partial recursiveness, or, when only completely defined functions are considered, with general recursiveness (§§ 68, 69).

It is of some interest to see at the same time whether a 1-way infinite tape and 1 symbol will not suffice. We say that a machine $\mathfrak{M}$ 1/1 *computes* φ, if it computes φ subject to the following restrictions, and we say that φ is 1/1 *computable*, if it is 1/1 computed by some machine $\mathfrak{M}$: (i) The machine $\mathfrak{M}$ has only one symbol s_1. Moreover, when $\mathfrak{M}$ has been started as described for any n-tuple $x_1, \ldots, x_n$, it behaves so that the following ((ii) — (iv)) are the case. (ii) A square which in the initial situation is to the left of the representation of $x_1, \ldots, x_n$ (i.e. to the left of the blank preceding the first tally of x_1) will not be scanned in any subsequent situation. Hence the computation can equally well be performed on a 1-way infinite tape (infinite to the right). (iii) If $\varphi(x_1, \ldots, x_n)$ is defined, then in the terminal situation the representation of $x_1, \ldots, x_n, \varphi(x_1, \ldots, x_n)$ starts on the same square as did that of $x_1, \ldots, x_n$ in the initial situation, and all squares to the right of the representation of $x_1, \ldots, x_n, \varphi(x_1, \ldots, x_n)$ are blank (also by (ii), those to the left). (iv) The machine $\mathfrak{M}$ eventually stops, only if $\varphi(x_1, \ldots, x_n)$ is defined.

It will follow from the results of §§ 68 and 69 that 1/1 computability is equivalent to computability; and hence that all w/s computability notions are equivalent, where w is 1 or 2 according as (ii) — (iv) are required or not, and s is an upper bound for the numbers of symbols different machines may have (∞, if there is no finite upper bound). (In this scale, our original notion of computability is $2/\infty$ computability.)

Other variants of 'computability' can be formulated, e.g. we might omit (iii) and (iv) while retaining (ii), or instead of (ii) we might assume that the machine is supplied with only a 1-way infinite tape, and require it to stop if a situation is reached from which the machine table orders a motion leftward from the leftmost square. Instead of representing the numbers on the tape by tallies, we might use dual notation or decimal notation. It should not be hard to show, after §§ 68 and 69, that each of these other computability notions is equivalent to ours (cf. § 70).

Now we extend our notions to the case of computation from l completely defined functions $\psi_1, \ldots, \psi_l$ (briefly Ψ) of $m_1, \ldots, m_l$ variables, respectively. Here the idea is modified by assuming that any value of one of the functions Ψ, if demanded in the course of the computation, will thereupon be supplied (cf. end § 61).

A machine for this purpose may have among its active states $q_1, \ldots, q_k$ ones from which a new kind of act (not atomic in character) is performed. Let q_c be one of these states. When the state is q_c, and (for a certain i depending on c) an m_i-tuple $y_1, \ldots, y_{m_i}$ is scanned in standard position, the act performed by the machine shall consist in supplying next to the right of this m_i-tuple $\psi_i(y_1, \ldots, y_{m_i})+1$ tallies and a blank, at the same time displacing by $\psi_i(y_1, \ldots, y_{m_i})+2$ squares to the right all printing which previously existed to the right of the scanned square, and then assuming state q_d (depending on c) with the resulting m_i+1-tuple $y_1, \ldots, y_{m_i}, \psi_i(y_1, \ldots, y_{m_i})$ scanned in standard position. When the state is q_c but an m_i-tuple is not scanned in standard position, we shall consider that the machine performs an identical act (with resulting situation the same as the original situation). In the machine table, corresponding to each such state q_c, we specify only the pair iq_d, as in other respects the act is determined from the situation by the definitions just given and the functions Ψ.

Modifying our machine notion in this way, we obtain the three notions: *machine from* Ψ, $\mathfrak{M}$ *computes* φ *from* Ψ, φ is *computable from* Ψ. If (for fixed $n, l, m_1, \ldots, m_l$) φ is computable from Ψ by a machine $\mathfrak{M}$, the table for which is independent of Ψ, we say that φ is *computable uniformly from* Ψ, or that the functional $\varphi \simeq \mathsf{F}(\Psi)$ is *computable*. (The theorems of §§ 68 and 69 establish uniformity, whenever uniformity is assumed.)

In defining $\mathfrak{M}$ 1/1 *computes* φ *from* Ψ, and φ is 1/1 *computable from* Ψ, we add the following to our former list (i) — (iv) of restrictions: (v) For each state q_c for which the table entry is of the form iq_d, the state q_c is reached only when some m_i-tuple $y_1, \ldots, y_{m_i}$ is scanned in standard position and all squares to the right of the scanned representation of $y_1, \ldots, y_{m_i}$ are blank.

We can easily formulate the definition of 'computability' from assumed functions, say from ψ (with $l = m_1 = 1$), in an equivalent way, in which the machine performs only acts atomic in character, but is supplied with a tape having a (potentially) infinite printing representing the sequence of the values of ψ. This printing may be on a second tape, or on alternate squares of the one tape.

REMARK 1. In this chapter, outside the present remark and passages referring to it, we shall understand that we are dealing with functions of $n \geq 1$ variables. Since we have not provided for representing n-tuples of natural numbers on the tape for $n = 0$, we say a machine *computes* a function φ of 0 variables, if it computes the function $\varphi(x)$ of 1 variable such that $\varphi(x) \simeq \varphi$. For an assumed function ψ_i of 0 variables, the non-identical act from a state q_c with table entry iq_d is to be performed when any 1-tuple x is represented on the tape. With these definitions, it will follow, as soon as we have proved Theorems XXVIII—XXX for functions of > 0 variables, that they also hold for functions of 0 variables.

§ 68. Computability of recursive functions. THEOREM XXVIII. *Every partial recursive function φ is 1/1 computable. Every function φ partial recursive in l completely defined functions Ψ is 1/1 computable from Ψ.*

The proof, given at the end of this section, will be based on Corollary Theorem XIX § 63 (for $l = 0$ and a general recursive φ, on Corollary Theorem IX § 58). An intuitive calculation by Schemata (I) — (VI) is accomplished by repetitions of a few simple operations, such as copying a number previously written (at a determinate earlier position), adding or subtracting one, deciding whether a given number is 0 or not 0. We shall first construct some machines to perform such operations as these.

We begin by introducing some notations which will be convenient here, including modifications of notations used in § 67.

A given square of the tape must now have one of two conditions s_0 and s_1, or blank and printed with a tally "|", or white and black. In the illustrations in this section, it will be convenient to show these two conditions as "0" and "1", respectively.

To identify the scanned symbol in our illustrations, we now usually write simply a bar "‾" over it, instead of the machine state as in § 67. Sometimes a small numeral "¹" or "²" will be written with the bar to indicate a certain machine state (the same in all occurrences of that numeral), to which we wish to call attention without indicating at the moment which of $q_0, \ldots, q_k$ it is.

In describing an atomic act, we now write "P" ("prints") for changing 0 to 1 (i.e. s_0 to s_1), "E" ("erases") for changing 1 to 0 (i.e. s_1 to s_0), and nothing for the change s_a to s_b when $a = b$. We omit the "C" which we used in § 67 to signify no change in the scanned square. We now write simply "0", "1", . . ., "k" for the machine states $q_0, \ldots, q_k$. For example, the act written "s_1Cq_0" in § 67 is now written as "$P0$" when s_0 was the scanned symbol initially, and as "0" when s_1 was the scanned symbol initially.

As a further example, we repeat the table for Machine $\mathfrak{A}$ (Example 1 § 67), and the former illustration of the operation it performs (showing now only the initial and final situations).

Name of machine	Machine state	Scanned symbol 0	1
$\mathfrak{A}$	1	$P0$	$R1$

Starting from the initial situation

$$\bar{1}\ 1\ 1\ 0,$$

Machine $\mathfrak{A}$ reaches the terminal situation

$$1\ 1\ 1\ \bar{1}.$$

Machine $\mathfrak{A}$ prints on the first blank square at or to the right of the scanned square, and stops there.

In our illustrations prior to "Proof of Theorem XXVIII", none of the squares to the left or right of those shown is scanned in any intermediate situation during the machine action. Thus their condition is immaterial.

For each machine constructed prior to "Proof of Theorem XXVIII", we shall state what is the leftmost square scanned in any intermediate situation, in each case when it falls outside the interval between the initially and terminally scanned squares inclusive. This information will be used in concluding that the machines we build in the proof of the theorem satisfy the restriction (ii) § 67.

In this section we shall generally think of a sequence of $y+1$ consecutive printed squares preceded and followed by a blank square as representing the natural number y. The same blank square may be regarded simultaneously as the last square in the representation of one number and the first in the representation of another. This enables us to think of any printing on the (2-way infinite) tape as consisting of a finite succession of representations of natural numbers. More than one consecutive blank squares (say $z+1$ of them) between two groups of consecutive printed squares we call a *gap* (of z squares) between the numbers represented. The blank portion of the tape before the first, or after the last, printed square we also call a *gap* (of ∞ *squares*). As in § 67, we do not think of m successive representations of natural numbers on the tape as representing an m-tuple, unless there are no gaps between them.

Similar remarks apply to a 1-way infinite tape, provided the first (leftmost) square is blank. There may or may not be a (finite) gap before the first number.

Now consider the problem of constructing a machine $\mathfrak{B}$ to perform the following operation: Given a number on the tape, not the leftmost, to move this number to the left so as to close the gap (if any) between it and the preceding number. The given number is to be scanned in standard position before and after the operation. The leftmost square scanned in any situation during the action shall be the rightmost printed square of the preceding number.

We begin with an illustration, showing a typical initial situation (Situation 1), some proposed intermediate situations not necessarily consecutive (Situations 2 — 16), and the desired terminal situation (Situation 17), for one plan for mechanizing the operation. Explanations, and the table of a machine which will perform the operation according to this plan, will follow. The "$\mathfrak{B}_1$", "$\mathfrak{B}_2$", "$\mathfrak{B}_3$", "$\mathfrak{A}$" at the right refer to an analysis of this machine as a combination of simpler machines, given afterwards.

1.	1	0	0	0	1	1	$\bar{1}$	0		
2.	1	0	0	0	1	$\bar{1}$	0	0		
3.	1	0	0	$\bar{0}$	1	1	0	0	$\mathfrak{B}_1$	
4.	1	0	$\bar{0}$	1	1	1	0	0		
5.	1	0	0	$\bar{1}^1$	1	1	0	0		
6.	1	0	0	1	1	$\bar{1}$	0	0		$\mathfrak{B}_2$
7.	1	0	0	1	$\bar{1}$	0	0	0		
8.	1	0	$\bar{0}$	1	1	0	0	0	$\mathfrak{B}_1$	
9.	1	$\bar{0}$	1	1	1	0	0	0		
10.	1	0	$\bar{1}^1$	1	1	0	0	0		
11.	1	0	1	1	$\bar{1}$	0	0	0		$\mathfrak{B}_2$
12.	1	0	1	$\bar{1}$	0	0	0	0		
13.	1	$\bar{0}$	1	1	0	0	0	0	$\mathfrak{B}_1$	
14.	$\bar{1}$	1	1	1	0	0	0	0		
15.	1	$\bar{1}^2$	1	1	0	0	0	0		
16.	1	0	$\bar{1}$	1	0	0	0	0		$\mathfrak{B}_3$
17.	1	0	1	1	$\bar{1}$	0	0	0	$\mathfrak{A}$	

The step from Situation 1 to Situation 2 is an erasure of the scanned 1, and a motion once to the left. Then (2 — 3) the machine seeks the first blank square at or to the left of the scanned square; (3 — 4) it prints there, and goes one more square to the left; (4 — 5) it recognizes (in this illustration) and registers that it is now on a blank square, and goes one square to the right; (5 — 6) it goes to standard position over the number now being scanned. Altogether 1 — 6 move the number as a whole one square to the left. Then 6 — 11 repeat this operation. The same cycle of steps is started again (11 — 14), but is concluded differently (14 — 17) after 1 instead of 0 is discovered on the leftmost square examined (at Situation 14).

The reader may verify that the machine defined by the following table will carry out the operation in this illustration, passing through Situations 1 — 17 and other intermediate situations; and he may convince himself now (or after the next discussion) that it will always perform the operation described, starting from any initial situation of the kind described. We leave a dash "—" in place of the atomic act order at those places in the table where the act ordered is immaterial to us, because the configuration is one which will not arise in our use of the machine, i.e. when it is started from an initial situation of the kind described. However the definition of the machine may be understood to be completed by supplying "0" at those places.

Name of machine	Machine state	Scanned symbol 0	1
$\mathfrak{B}$	1	—	*EL*2
	2	*PL*3	*L*2
	3	*R*4	*R*5
	4	*L*1	*R*4
	5	—	*ER*6
	6	*P*0	*R*6

In discovering this machine, we first analyzed the whole operation we wish it to perform into simpler (not necessarily atomic) acts, and then further analyzed these into the atomic acts to be performed by the machine. We can think of the machine as obtained by connecting together several simpler machines which perform one or a succession of the steps in the preliminary analysis. We now introduce notations which will be useful in describing a machine as a combination of simpler machines.

If two operations are to be performed successively, and a machine $\mathfrak{X}$ performs the first of them, and a machine $\mathfrak{Y}$ the other, then the combined operation will be performed by the machine we get by identifying the passive (or terminal) state of $\mathfrak{X}$ with the first active (or initial) state of $\mathfrak{Y}$. The output of $\mathfrak{X}$ thus becomes the input of $\mathfrak{Y}$. The resulting machine we denote by "$\mathfrak{X}\mathfrak{Y}$". (Then $(\mathfrak{X}\mathfrak{Y})\mathfrak{Z} = \mathfrak{X}(\mathfrak{Y}\mathfrak{Z})$.)

We use "$\mathfrak{X}^n$" for $n > 0$ to mean $\mathfrak{X} \dots \mathfrak{X}$ (n factors); and "$\mathfrak{X}^0$" for a machine whose table has only 0 as entries, so that $\mathfrak{X}^0\mathfrak{Y}$ and $\mathfrak{Y}\mathfrak{X}^0$ both perform the same operation as $\mathfrak{Y}$.

We may also wish the output of one machine $\mathfrak{X}$ to become the input of either a machine $\mathfrak{Y}$ or a machine $\mathfrak{Z}$, depending on some circumstance arising during the action of $\mathfrak{X}$. We can provide for this by extending our notion of a Turing machine to allow two terminal states 0_1 and 0_2. Here such *2-terminal machines* will be used only as components in the construction ultimately of machines as defined in § 67 with one terminal state. Upon identifying the state 0_1 of $\mathfrak{X}$ with the initial state of $\mathfrak{Y}$ and the state 0_2 of $\mathfrak{X}$ with the initial state of $\mathfrak{Z}$, we obtain a machine which we denote by "$\mathfrak{X}\begin{cases}\mathfrak{Y}\\ \mathfrak{Z}\end{cases}$".

We shall now express Machine $\mathfrak{B}$ as a combination of several machines. First, we define a machine $\mathfrak{B}_1$ which performs the operation illustrated by 1 — 5 or by 6 — 10 or by 11 — 15; i.e. such that, when started scanning a number in standard position, it erases the scanned square, prints on the first blank square to the left, and goes to state 0_1 or 0_2 scanning that square, according as the square next left of that is blank or printed. The leftmost square scanned during the operation is the square next left of the terminally scanned square. This machine has the following table (cf. Lines 1 — 3 of the table for Machine $\mathfrak{B}$).

Name of machine	Machine state	Scanned symbol 0	Scanned symbol 1
$\mathfrak{B}_1$	1	—	$EL2$
	2	$PL3$	$L2$
	3	$R0_1$	$R0_2$

The operation illustrated by 5 — 6 or 10 — 11 is performed by the machine with the table (cf. Line 4 of the table for Machine $\mathfrak{B}$):

$\mathfrak{B}_2$	1	$L0$	$R1$

To perform 15 — 16, similarly we have (cf. Line 5 for Machine $\mathfrak{B}$):

$\mathfrak{B}_3$	1	—	$ER0$

The operation illustrated by 16 — 17 is performed by Machine $\mathfrak{A}$.

The action of Machine $\mathfrak{B}$ can be described in terms of $\mathfrak{A}$, $\mathfrak{B}_1$, $\mathfrak{B}_2$ and $\mathfrak{B}_3$, thus. We first use $\mathfrak{B}_1$, then according as the terminal state is 0_1 or 0_2, we use $\mathfrak{B}_2$ or $\mathfrak{B}_3$. In the case that $\mathfrak{B}_2$ is used, its output is fed back into $\mathfrak{B}_1$. In the case that $\mathfrak{B}_3$ is used, its output is fed into $\mathfrak{A}$. We express this by the formula

$$\text{(a)} \qquad \mathfrak{B} = \dot{\mathfrak{B}}_1 \begin{cases} \dot{\mathfrak{B}}_2 \\ \mathfrak{B}_3\mathfrak{A}, \end{cases}$$

where the dots express that the output of $\mathfrak{B}_2$ is fed back as input for $\mathfrak{B}_1$. The notation is suggested by that for repeating decimals. If the operation performed by $\mathfrak{B}_1$ each time produced an output with state 0_1, the operation performed by $\mathfrak{B}_1\mathfrak{B}_2$ would be repeated ad infinitum. This would actually happen if Machine $\mathfrak{B}$ were started scanning the leftmost number on the tape in standard position; Machine $\mathfrak{B}$ would then keep moving this number square after square to the left.

Formula (a) indicates how to construct the table for Machine $\mathfrak{B}$ from those for $\mathfrak{A}$, $\mathfrak{B}_1$, $\mathfrak{B}_2$ and $\mathfrak{B}_3$. In the table for $\mathfrak{B}_1$, we replace the terminal states 0_1 and 0_2 by the initial states for $\mathfrak{B}_2$ and $\mathfrak{B}_3$, respectively, renumbering these suitably as 4 and 5; etc. (cf. the table for $\mathfrak{B}$ as first given).

Now let us build a machine $\mathfrak{J}_m$ (for each fixed $m \geq 1$) such that: Machine $\mathfrak{J}_m$, when started scanning in standard position the representation of an m-tuple $y_1, \ldots, y_m$ of numbers, with all squares (or at least the first y_1+2 of them) to the right of the m-tuple blank, copies y_1 following the m-tuple without a gap, and stops scanning the copy in standard position. The leftmost square scanned during the action is the first (blank) square of the given m-tuple.

For example, from the initial situation shown next (Situation 1), $\mathfrak{J}_4$ shall reach the situation shown last (Situation 16). A plan for the action is indicated by the intervening situations shown.

1.	0 1 1 1 0 1 0 1 1 1 1 0 1 $\bar{1}$ 0 0 0 0 0	$\mathfrak{C}$ (1–2)
2.	0 1 1 1 0 1 0 1 1 1 1 0 1 1 0 $\bar{1}$ 0 0 0	$\mathfrak{D}^4$ (2–3)
3.	0 1 1 $\bar{1}$ 0 1 0 1 1 1 1 0 1 1 0 1 0 0 0	$\mathfrak{E}$ (3–4)
4.	0 1 1 $\bar{1}^2$ 0 1 0 1 1 1 1 0 1 1 0 1 0 0 0	$\mathfrak{F}$ (4–5)
5.	0 1 $\bar{1}$ 0 0 1 0 1 1 1 1 0 1 1 0 1 0 0 0	$\mathfrak{G}^4$ (5–6)
6.	0 1 1 0 0 1 0 1 1 1 1 0 1 1 0 $\bar{1}$ 0 0 0	$\mathfrak{A}$ (6–7)
7.	0 1 1 0 0 1 0 1 1 1 1 0 1 1 0 1 $\bar{1}$ 0 0	$\mathfrak{D}^4$ (7–8)
8.	0 1 $\bar{1}$ 0 0 1 0 1 1 1 1 0 1 1 0 1 1 0 0	$\mathfrak{E}$ (8–9)
9.	0 1 $\bar{1}^2$ 0 0 1 0 1 1 1 1 0 1 1 0 1 1 0 0	$\mathfrak{F}$ (9–10)
10.	0 $\bar{1}$ 0 0 0 1 0 1 1 1 1 0 1 1 0 1 1 0 0	$\mathfrak{G}^4$ (10–11)
11.	0 1 0 0 0 1 0 1 1 1 1 0 1 1 0 1 $\bar{1}$ 0 0	$\mathfrak{A}$ (11–12)
12.	0 1 0 0 0 1 0 1 1 1 1 0 1 1 0 1 1 $\bar{1}$ 0	$\mathfrak{D}^4$ (12–13)
13.	0 $\bar{1}$ 0 0 0 1 0 1 1 1 1 0 1 1 0 1 1 1 0	$\mathfrak{E}$ (13–14)
14.	0 $\bar{1}^1$ 0 0 0 1 0 1 1 1 1 0 1 1 0 1 1 1 0	$\mathfrak{H}$ (14–15)
15.	0 1 1 $\bar{1}$ 0 1 0 1 1 1 1 0 1 1 0 1 1 1 0	$\mathfrak{G}^4$ (15–16)
16.	0 1 1 1 0 1 0 1 1 1 1 0 1 1 0 1 1 $\bar{1}$ 0	

Machine $\mathfrak{C}$, according to the plan, when started scanning in standard position a number which is followed by a gap, goes right two squares, prints and stops there.

Machine $\mathfrak{D}$, when started scanning in standard position a number which is not the leftmost on the tape, goes left to standard position on the next number to the left. Hence $\mathfrak{D}^m$, when started scanning in standard position a number to the left of which at least m numbers occur, goes left passing over $m-1$ intervening numbers to standard position on the m-th number to the left.

Machine $\mathfrak{E}$, when started in standard position on a number, decides whether that number is 0 or greater than 0, and assumes state 0_1 or 0_2 according to which is the case, with the number still scanned in standard position. The leftmost square scanned during the operation is the square next left of the scanned square.

Machine $\mathfrak{F}$, when started scanning a printed square, erases and goes left one square.

Machine $\mathfrak{G}$ goes one number ($\mathfrak{G}^m$ goes m numbers) to the right, just as $\mathfrak{D}$ goes one number ($\mathfrak{D}^m$ goes m numbers) to the left.

Machine $\mathfrak{H}$, when started scanning in standard position a number which is not the rightmost on the tape, fills up the gap (if any) between that number and the next one to the right, increasing the first number by the number of squares that constituted the gap, and stops scanning the resulting number in standard position.

If we can find machines $\mathfrak{C}$, $\mathfrak{D}$, $\mathfrak{E}$, $\mathfrak{F}$, $\mathfrak{G}$, $\mathfrak{H}$ as described, then Machine $\mathfrak{I}_m$ will be given by the formula

(b) $$\mathfrak{I}_m = \mathfrak{C}\dot{\mathfrak{D}}^m\mathfrak{E}\begin{cases}\mathfrak{H}\mathfrak{G}^m. \\ \mathfrak{F}\mathfrak{G}^m\dot{\mathfrak{A}}\end{cases}$$

The operation performed by $\mathfrak{D}^m\mathfrak{E}\mathfrak{F}\mathfrak{G}^m\mathfrak{A}$ is repeated, so long as the application of $\mathfrak{E}$ gives state 0_2; but when it gives 0_1, the action is terminated by $\mathfrak{H}\mathfrak{G}^m$.

We give tables for $\mathfrak{D}$, $\mathfrak{E}$ and $\mathfrak{H}$, leaving those for $\mathfrak{C}$, $\mathfrak{F}$ and $\mathfrak{G}$ to the reader.

Name of machine	Machine state	Scanned symbol 0	1
$\mathfrak{D}$	1	$L2$	$L1$
	2	$L2$	0
$\mathfrak{E}$	1	—	$L2$
	2	$R0_1$	$R0_2$
$\mathfrak{H}$	1	—	$R2$
	2	$PR2$	$L3$
	3	—	$EL0$

By several applications of $\mathfrak{I}_m$ with suitable values of m, we can copy without gaps any permutation (allowing repetitions) of the numbers represented rightmost on the tape without gaps between. For example, from the initial situation

$0\ 1\ 1\ 1\ 0\ 1\ 0\ 1\ 1\ 1\ 1\ 0\ 1\ \bar{1}\ 0\ 0\ 0\ 0\ 0\ 0\ 0\ 0\ 0\ 0\ 0\ 0\ 0\ 0\ 0\ 0,$

the machine $\mathfrak{I}_4^4$ $(= (\mathfrak{I}_4)^4)$ reaches the terminal situation

$0\ 1\ 1\ 1\ 0\ 1\ 0\ 1\ 1\ 1\ 1\ 0\ 1\ 1\ 0\ 1\ 1\ 1\ 0\ 1\ 0\ 1\ 1\ 1\ 1\ 0\ 1\ \bar{1}\ 0\ 0,$

the whole quadruple being copied; and $\mathfrak{I}_4\mathfrak{I}_2$ reaches

$0\ 1\ 1\ 1\ 0\ 1\ 0\ 1\ 1\ 1\ 1\ 0\ 1\ 1\ 0\ 1\ 1\ 1\ 0\ 1\ \bar{1}\ 0\ 0\ 0\ 0\ 0\ 0\ 0\ 0\ 0,$

the first and fourth numbers being copied.

The machine $\mathfrak{K}_m$ defined thus

(c) $$\mathfrak{K}_m = \mathfrak{A}\mathfrak{I}_m^m\mathfrak{F}\mathfrak{D}^m\mathfrak{F}\mathfrak{G}^m,$$

when started in standard position on an m-tuple $y_1, \ldots, y_m$, with all squares (or at least the first $y_1 + \ldots + y_m + 2m + 1$) to the right blank, copies the m-tuple to the right after leaving a one-square gap, and stops scanning the copy in standard position. The leftmost square scanned during the action is the first (blank) square of the given m-tuple. For example, from the above initial situation, $\mathfrak{K}_4$ reaches the terminal situation

$0\ 1\ 1\ 1\ 0\ 1\ 0\ 1\ 1\ 1\ 1\ 0\ 1\ 1\ 0\ 0\ 1\ 1\ 1\ 0\ 1\ 0\ 1\ 1\ 1\ 1\ 0\ 1\ \bar{1}\ 0.$

We now wish a machine $\mathfrak{L}$ which, started scanning a number in standard position, will erase all numbers (if any) to the left of this up to the first gap encountered, and return to standard position on the number originally scanned. The leftmost square scanned in the operation shall be the square next rightmost in the group of consecutive blank squares constituting the gap. For example, from the situation

$$0\ 0\ 1\ 1\ 1\ 0\ 1\ 1\ 1\ 1\ 0\ 1\ 1\ 0\ 1\ 0\ 1\ 1\ \bar{1}\ 0,$$

Machine $\mathfrak{L}$ reaches the terminal situation

$$0\ 0\ 0\ 0\ 0\ 0\ 0\ 0\ 0\ 0\ 0\ 0\ 0\ 0\ 0\ 0\ 1\ 1\ \bar{1}\ 0.$$

The construction of $\mathfrak{L}$ is left to the reader.

Proof of Theorem XXVIII for $l = 0$. The proof is by an induction based on Corollary Theorem XIX § 63. There are six cases, according to which one of the schemata (I) — (VI) is applied last in the given definition of φ by these schemata. For each case, we must show how to construct a machine $\mathfrak{M}_\varphi$ which 1/1 computes φ.

To describe the initial situation in the computation of $\varphi(x_1, \ldots, x_n)$ for a given n-tuple $x_1, \ldots, x_n$ we now write:

1. $\quad , x_1, \ldots, \bar{x}_n,$

Here each "x_i" stands for x_i+1 consecutive printed squares, the commas stand for blanks forming part of the representation of the n-tuple, and the bar indicates that the representation of x_n is scanned in standard position. Under the definition of computability (§ 67), all other squares to the left and right are also blank. The terminal situation, which $\mathfrak{M}_\varphi$ must reach if $\varphi(x_1, \ldots, x_n)$ is defined, we may write similarly:

$$, x_1, \ldots, x_n, \overline{\varphi(x_1, \ldots, x_n)},$$

The first comma here and in the abbreviation for the initial situation (Situation 1) refer to the same square of the tape, and here again all squares not indicated are blank (for (iii) § 67). When started from Situation 1, $\mathfrak{M}_\varphi$ shall stop eventually, only if $\varphi(x_1, \ldots, x_n)$ is defined (for (iv)). From Situation 1, $\mathfrak{M}_\varphi$ may go arbitrarily far to the right, but must never scan a square to the left of the one represented here by the first comma (for (ii)).

Case (I) (Schema (I)): $\varphi(x) = x'$. Let $\mathfrak{M}_\varphi = \mathfrak{J}_1\mathfrak{A}$.

Case (II): $\varphi(x_1, \ldots, x_n) = q$. Let $\mathfrak{M}_\varphi = \mathfrak{C}\mathfrak{A}^q$.

Case (III): $\varphi(x_1, \ldots, x_n) = x_i$. Let $\mathfrak{M}_\varphi = \mathfrak{J}_{n-i+1}$.

Case (IV): $\varphi(x_1, \ldots, x_n) = \psi(\chi_1(x_1, \ldots, x_n), \ldots, \chi_m(x_1, \ldots, x_n))$.

By the hypothesis of the induction, there are machines $\mathfrak{M}_{\chi_1}, \ldots, \mathfrak{M}_{\chi_m}, \mathfrak{M}_\psi$

which 1/1 compute $\chi_1, \ldots, \chi_m, \psi$, respectively. The plan of the computation of $\varphi(x_1, \ldots, x_n)$ is as follows. Starting from Situation 1, we copy the n-tuple $x_1, \ldots, x_n$ with a one-square gap (shown by the double comma):

2. $\quad , x_1, \ldots, x_n, , x_1, \ldots, \bar{x}_n,$

The gap marks the beginning of a temporary record, to be erased later. Machine $\mathfrak{K}_n$ performs this copying operation. Machine $\mathfrak{M}_{\chi_1}$, if started from the situation $\quad , x_1, \ldots, \bar{x}_n, \quad$, will go to the situation $\quad , x_1, \ldots, x_n, \overline{\chi_1(x_1, \ldots, x_n)}, \quad$, provided $\chi_1(x_1, \ldots, x_n)$ is defined. In performing this operation, $\mathfrak{M}_{\chi_1}$ does not in any intermediate situation scan a square to the left of the first square in $\quad , x_1, \ldots, \bar{x}_n, \quad$. Hence if $\mathfrak{M}_{\chi_1}$ is started from Situation 2, the presence of the additional printing $\quad , x_1, \ldots, x_n, \quad$ to the left will not affect its action. So from Situation 2, $\mathfrak{M}_{\chi_1}$ will go to the following, provided $\chi_1(x_1, \ldots, x_n)$ is defined:

3. $\quad , x_1, \ldots, x_n, , x_1, \ldots, x_n, \overline{\chi_1(x_1, \ldots, x_n)}, \quad .$

Next we copy $x_1, \ldots, x_n$, without a gap, by Machine $\mathfrak{J}^n_{n+1}$, obtaining:

4. $\quad , x_1, \ldots, x_n, , x_1, \ldots, x_n, \chi_1(x_1, \ldots, x_n), x_1, \ldots, \bar{x}_n, \quad .$

Applying $\mathfrak{M}_{\chi_2}$, if $\chi_2(x_1, \ldots, x_n)$ is defined, we obtain:

5. $\quad , x_1, \ldots, x_n, , x_1, \ldots, x_n, \chi_1(x_1, \ldots, x_n), x_1, \ldots, x_n, \overline{\chi_2(x_1, \ldots, x_n)}, \quad .$

Continuing in this manner, we eventually obtain the following, provided all the function values appearing are defined:

6. $\quad , x_1, \ldots, x_n, , x_1, \ldots, x_n, \chi_1(x_1, \ldots, x_n), \ldots, x_1, \ldots, x_n, \chi_m(x_1, \ldots, x_n),$
$\chi_1(x_1, \ldots, x_n), \ldots, \chi_m(x_1, \ldots, x_n), \overline{\psi(\chi_1(x_1, \ldots, x_n), \ldots, \chi_m(x_1, \ldots, x_n))}, \quad .$

By Machine $\mathfrak{L}$ we can then erase every number between the scanned number $\psi(\chi_1(x_1, \ldots, x_n), \ldots, \chi_m(x_1, \ldots, x_n))$ (non-inclusive) and the gap (represented by the double comma), after which we can close up the gap by Machine $\mathfrak{B}$ to obtain:

7. $\quad , x_1, \ldots, x_n, \overline{\psi(\chi_1(x_1, \ldots, x_n), \ldots, \chi_m(x_1, \ldots, x_n))}, \quad$, i.e.
$\quad , x_1, \ldots, x_n, \overline{\varphi(x_1, \ldots, x_n)}, \quad .$

The entire operation, when $\varphi(x_1, \ldots, x_n)$ is defined, is performed by the machine $\mathfrak{M}_\varphi$ defined thus:

$$\mathfrak{M}_\varphi = \mathfrak{K}_n \mathfrak{M}_{\chi_1} \mathfrak{J}^n_{n+1} \mathfrak{M}_{\chi_2} \cdots \mathfrak{J}^n_{n+1} \mathfrak{M}_{\chi_m} \mathfrak{J}_{(m-1)(n+1)+1} \mathfrak{J}_{(m-2)(n+1)+2} \cdots$$
$$\mathfrak{J}_{1\cdot(n+1)+(m-1)} \mathfrak{J}_{0\cdot(n+1)+m} \mathfrak{M}_\psi \mathfrak{L} \mathfrak{B}.$$

Conversely, using the property (iv) of the machines $\mathfrak{M}_{\chi_1}, \ldots, \mathfrak{M}_{\chi_m}$ and $\mathfrak{M}_\psi$, Machine $\mathfrak{M}_\varphi$ applied to Situation 1 will eventually stop, only if all of $\chi_1(x_1, \ldots, x_n), \ldots, \chi_m(x_1, \ldots, x_n), \psi(\chi_1(x_1, \ldots, x_n), \ldots, \chi_m(x_1, \ldots, x_n))$ are defined, i.e. only if $\varphi(x_1, \ldots, x_n)$ is defined.

Case (V): For $n > 1$ (Schema (Vb)), $\varphi(0, x_2, \ldots, x_n) = \psi(x_2, \ldots, x_n)$, $\varphi(y', x_2, \ldots, x_n) = \chi(y, \varphi(y, x_2, \ldots, x_n), x_2, \ldots, x_n)$. By the hypothesis of the induction, there are machines $\mathfrak{M}_\psi$ and $\mathfrak{M}_\chi$ which 1/1 compute ψ and χ, respectively. We carry out a series of operations to obtain the following situation (corresponding to Situation 6 for Case (IV)), if the required function values are defined. At each place where a choice is indicated, the upper alternative applies under the condition stated, the lower otherwise; i.e. for a given y, the lower alternative is taken on the first y choices, and the upper on the $y+1$-st choice.

$$, y, x_2, \ldots, x_n, , y, x_2, \ldots, x_n, \psi(x_2, \ldots, x_n),$$

$$y, \begin{cases} \overline{\psi(x_2, \ldots, x_n),} & \text{if } y = 0. \\ 0, \psi(x_2, \ldots, x_n), x_2, \ldots, x_n, \chi(0, \psi(x_2, \ldots, x_n), x_2, \ldots, x_n), \end{cases}$$

$$y{-}1, \begin{cases} \overline{\chi(0, \psi(x_2, \ldots, x_n), x_2, \ldots, x_n),} & \text{if } y{-}1 = 0. \\ 1, \chi(0, \psi(x_2, \ldots, x_n), x_2, \ldots, x_n), x_2, \ldots, x_n, \end{cases}$$

$$\chi(1, \chi(0, \psi(x_2, \ldots, x_n), x_2, \ldots, x_n), x_2, \ldots, x_n),$$

$$y{-}2, \begin{cases} \overline{\chi(1, \chi(0, \psi(x_2, \ldots, x_n), x_2, \ldots, x_n), x_2, \ldots, x_n),} & \text{if } y{-}2 = 0. \\ 2, \ldots . \end{cases}$$

Then everything between the last number and the gap is erased, and the gap is closed up. The entire operation is performed by the machine $\mathfrak{M}_\varphi$ defined thus:

$$\mathfrak{M}_\varphi = \mathfrak{K}_n \mathfrak{M}_\psi \mathfrak{J}_{n+1} \mathfrak{E} \begin{cases} \mathfrak{J}_2 \mathfrak{L} \mathfrak{B}. \\ \mathfrak{C} \dot{\mathfrak{J}}_3 \mathfrak{J}_{n+3}^{n-1} \mathfrak{M}_\chi \mathfrak{J}_{n+3} \mathfrak{F} \mathfrak{E} \begin{cases} \mathfrak{J}_2 \mathfrak{L} \mathfrak{B}. \\ \mathfrak{J}_{n+3} \dot{\mathfrak{A}} \end{cases} \end{cases}$$

Slight changes adapt the treatment to the case $n = 1$ (Schema (Va)).

Case (VI): $\varphi(x_1, \ldots, x_n) = \mu y[\chi(x_1, \ldots, x_n, y) = 0]$ (for $n \geq 1$; cf. Remark 1 end § 67). Handled like Case (V) (but more simply).

Proof of Theorem XXVIII for $l > 0$. We now have as an additional case that φ is one, say ψ_i, of the assumed functions Ψ. In this case φ is 1/1 computed from Ψ by the machine $\mathfrak{M}_\varphi$ having a single active state q_1 with the table entry $i q_0$.

§ 69. Recursiveness of computable functions. In this section the notations will be those of § 67 rather than § 68.

Theorem XXIX. *Every computable partial function* φ *is partial* *recursive. Every partial function φ computable from l completely defined functions Ψ is partial recursive in Ψ.*

PROOF FOR $l = 0$. It is possible to represent the tape vs. machine situations of a given machine $\mathfrak{M}$ by formal expressions (as indeed we shall do for another purpose in § 71, where the expressions will be called "Post words"). The theorem can then be considered as an application of (D2) § 62 (extended to partial functions; here $E_{x,j+1}$ depends only on E_{xj}).

If details are to be supplied, the following proof is a little more direct. Gödel numbers are assigned directly to the tape vs. machine situations; and instead of giving Gödel numbers to deductions or proofs (as for Theorem IX § 58 and (D1) § 62), we simply number the successive situations reached from a given situation by a given machine as the 0-th, 1-st, . . . , z-th, ... Then if one will read "function" for "partial function" and "general recursive" for "partial recursive", he need not use Chapter XII. The proof can be shortened slightly by using Theorem XXVI § 66.

In establishing the Gödel numbering of situations, we describe the condition of the tape only relative to the scanned square, instead of relative to some fixed square. This suffices for our purpose here, since absolute position on the tape does not enter into the definition of computability. (For $1/s$ computability, absolute position or at least position relative to the first square of the representation of $x_1, \ldots, x_n$ in the initial situation does matter, by (ii) and (iii).)

We begin by assigning a Gödel number to the (condition of the) tape to the left of any particular square. Let the conditions of the successive squares to the left of that square be $s_{u_0}, s_{u_1}, s_{u_2}, \ldots$. Since only a finite number of squares are printed, all but a finite number of the subscripts u_i are 0. The Gödel number u of the tape to the left of the square shall be $\prod_i p_i^{u_i}$, i.e. $\prod_{i<t} p_i^{u_i}$ where t is any number which exceeds every i for which $u_i \neq 0$. Then u itself is such a number; so $u = \prod_{i<u} p_i^{u_i} = \prod_{i<u} p_i^{(u)_i}$.

A Gödel number is assigned similarly to represent the condition of the tape to the right of a given square.

If in a given situation, the Gödel number of the tape to the left of the scanned square is u, the scanned symbol is s_a, the machine state is q_c, and the Gödel number of the tape to the right of the scanned square is v, then the Gödel number of the situation shall be $2^u \cdot 3^a \cdot 5^c \cdot 7^v$.

EXAMPLE 1. The Gödel number of the situation

q$_4$

s$_1$	s$_1$	s$_3$	s$_1$	s$_0$	s$_1$

where all squares not shown are blank is $2^{5^1 \cdot 3^1 \cdot 2^3} \cdot 3^1 \cdot 5^4 \cdot 7^{2^0 \cdot 3^1}$.

If the Gödel number of the situation is $2^u \cdot 3^a \cdot 5^c \cdot 7^v$, the configuration is $(\mathrm{s}_a, \mathrm{q}_c)$. If $c > 0$, and the act which the machine performs from this configuration is of the form $\mathrm{s}_b L \mathrm{q}_d$, the Gödel number $\rho_{a,c}(u, v)$ of the resulting situation is

$$[2 \exp \prod_{i<u} p_i^{(u)_{i'}}] \cdot 3^{(u)_0} \cdot 5^d \cdot [7 \exp \{2^b \cdot \prod_{i<v} p_{i'}^{(v)_i}\}];$$

and similarly if the act is $\mathrm{s}_b R \mathrm{q}_d$. If the act is $\mathrm{s}_b C \mathrm{q}_d$, then $\rho_{a,c}(u, v)$ is $2^u \cdot 3^b \cdot 5^d \cdot 7^v$. Each of these functions $\rho_{a,c}$ is primitive recursive.

Now ρ defined as follows is primitive recursive (#F § 45), and has the property that, if w is the Gödel number of an active (passive) situation, then $\rho(w)$ is the Gödel number of the next (same) situation:

$$\rho(w) = \begin{cases} \rho_{a,c}((w)_0, (w)_3) \quad \text{if} \quad (w)_1 = a \ \& \ (w)_2 = c \\ \qquad\qquad (a = 0, \ldots, j; \ c = 1, \ldots, k), \\ w \ \text{otherwise.} \end{cases}$$

Thence we define a primitive recursive function θ thus:

$$\begin{cases} \theta(w, 0) = w, \\ \theta(w, z') = \rho(\theta(w, z)). \end{cases}$$

If w is the Gödel number of any situation, then $\theta(w, z)$ is the Gödel number of the situation after the next z acts, if the machine performs at least z acts from the given situation; and $\theta(w, z)$ is the Gödel number of the terminal situation reached from the given situation, if the machine performs $< z$ acts from the given situation.

Next, for each $n \geq 1$ (cf. Remark 1 end § 67), we define a primitive recursive function τ_n with the following property. If the n-tuple $x_1, \ldots, x_n$ is scanned in standard position, the state is q_c, the Gödel number of the tape to the left of the representation of $x_1, \ldots, x_n$ is u, and the Gödel number of the tape to the right of that representation is v, then $\tau_n(x_1, \ldots, x_n, c, u, v)$ is the Gödel number of the situation. First we define τ_1 thus:

$\tau_1(x_1, c, u, v) =$

$$[2 \exp \{(\prod_{i<x_1} p_i^1) \cdot p_{x_1}^0 \cdot \prod_{i<u} p_{x_1'+i}^{(u)_i}\}] \cdot 3^1 \cdot 5^c \cdot [7 \exp \{2^0 \cdot \prod_{i<v} p_{i'}^{(v)_i}\}].$$

Then, for $n = 1, 2, 3, \ldots$:

$$\tau_{n+1}(x_1, \ldots, x_n, x_{n+1}, c, u, v) = \tau_1(x_{n+1}, c, (\tau_n(x_1, \ldots, x_{n-1}, x_n', c, u, v))_0, v).$$

When $x_1, \ldots, x_n$ is scanned in standard position with state q_1, and the tape is blank elsewhere, the Gödel number of the situation is $\tau_n(x_1, \ldots, x_n, 1, 1, 1)$. When $x_1, \ldots, x_n, x$ is scanned in standard position with state q_0, the Gödel number of the situation is $\tau_{n+1}(x_1, \ldots, x_n, x, 0, u, v)$ for some u and v; and conversely.

Now, if φ is the partial function of n variables computed by the given machine $\mathfrak{M}$, and $x_1, \ldots, x_n$ is a given n-tuple, then $\varphi(x_1, \ldots, x_n)$ is defined, if and only if there exists a quadruple (z, x, u, v) of numbers such that $\theta(\tau_n(x_1, \ldots, x_n, 1, 1, 1), z) = \tau_{n+1}(x_1, \ldots, x_n, x, 0, u, v)$, in which case x is the value of $\varphi(x_1, \ldots, x_n)$. Accordingly,

$$\varphi(x_1, \ldots, x_n) \simeq$$
$$(\mu t[\theta(\tau_n(x_1, \ldots, x_n, 1, 1, 1), (t)_0) = \tau_{n+1}(x_1, \ldots, x_n, (t)_1, 0, (t)_2, (t)_3)])_1.$$

Therefore, by Theorem XVIII § 63, φ is partial recursive (or if φ is completely defined, by Theorem III § 57, φ is general recursive).

Proof for $l > 0$. Say e.g. there is one assumed function ψ of one variable (i.e. $l = m_1 = 1$). Now, for each c for which the table entry corresponding to q_c is of the form $1q_d$, we replace "$\rho_{a,c}((w)_0, (w)_3)$ if $(w)_1 = a$ & $(w)_2 = c$ $(a = 0, \ldots, j)$" in the definition of $\rho(w)$ by "$\rho_c(w)$ if $Q_c(w)$", where Q_c is the primitive recursive predicate and ρ_c the function primitive recursive in ψ defined thus:

$$\begin{aligned}
Q_c(w) &\equiv (Ey)_{y<w}(Eu)_{u<w}(Ev)_{v<w}[w=\tau_1(y, c, u, v)],\\
\rho_c(w) &= \tau_2(Y, \psi(Y), d, U, V) \text{ where}\\
Y &= \mu y_{y<w}(Eu)_{u<w}(Ev)_{v<w}[w=\tau_1(y, c, u, v)],\\
U &= \mu u_{u<w}(Ey)_{y<w}(Ev)_{v<w}[w=\tau_1(y, c, u, v)], \text{ etc.}
\end{aligned}$$

Theorem XXX (= Theorems XXVIII + XXIX). *The following classes of partial functions are coextensive, i.e. have the same members:* (a) *the partial recursive functions,* (b) *the computable functions,* (c) *the* 1/1 *computable functions. Similarly with l completely defined assumed functions* Ψ.

§ 70. Turing's thesis. Turing's thesis that every function which would naturally be regarded as computable is computable under his definition, i.e. by one of his machines, is equivalent to Church's thesis by Theorem XXX. We shall now examine the part of the evidence for it which pertains to the machine concept, i.e. what we listed as (C) in § 62. What we must do is to convince ourselves that any acts a human computer could carry out are analyzable into successions of atomic acts of some Turing machine.

"The behavior of the computer at any moment is determined by the symbols which he is observing, and his 'state of mind' at that moment." The number of symbols which he can recognize is finite. "If we were to allow an infinity of symbols, then there would be symbols differing to an arbitrarily small extent." (Turing 1936-7 pp. 249—250.) The work leading from the problem statement to the answer must be carried out in some "symbol space" (Post 1936), i.e. some systematic arrangement of cells or boxes, each of which may bear (an occurrence of) a symbol. There is a finite bound to the number of occurrences of symbols (or of boxes where a symbol may occur) which he can observe at one moment. He can also remember symbols previously observed, by altering his state of mind. However "the number of states of mind which need to be taken into account is finite. ... If we admitted an infinity of states of mind, some of them will be 'arbitrarily close' and will be confused." (Turing 1936-7 p. 250.) But the computer's action must lead from a quite discrete object, namely the symbol array representing some natural number (or n-tuple of natural numbers) as argument(s), to another such object, namely the symbol array representing the corresponding function value. The possible states of mind are fixed in advance of naming the particular argument(s), as we are considering computation by a preassigned method, and do not allow mathematical invention in the midst of the computer's performance. Each act he performs must constitute a discrete change in the finite system consisting of the occurrences of symbols in the symbol space, the distribution of observed squares in this space, and his state of mind.

These limitations on the behavior of the human computer in computing the value of a number-theoretic function for given arguments, by following only preassigned rules, are of the same kind as enter in the construction of a Turing machine. The tape is the symbol space for the machine, and the machine state corresponds to the computer's state of mind.

The human computer is less restricted in behavior than the machine, as follows: (a) He can observe more than one symbol occurrence at a time. (b) He can perform more complicated atomic acts than the machine. (c) His symbol space need not be a one-dimensional tape. (d) He can choose some other symbolic representation of the arguments and function values than that used in our definition of computability.

We shall examine various possibilities under (a) — (d), and see briefly how each can be reduced to an equivalent in terms of Turing machines. We shall usually speak as though only one were being reduced, but our methods would serve to reduce any combination of them successively.

Under (a), we remark that e.g. 17 and 21 and 100 can each be observed in a single act. But a long sequence of symbols can only be observed by a succession of acts. For example, we cannot tell at a glance whether 157767733443477 and 157767733443477 are the same; "we should have to compare the two numbers figure by figure, possibly ticking the figures off in pencil to make sure of their not being counted twice." (Turing 1936-7 p. 251.)

If 17 and 21 and 100 are not only observed as units but manipulated as though each occupies a single cell of the symbol space, we need only redefine the symbols so that each of these constitutes a single symbol, in order to reduce the compound observation to a simple observation of the kind used by a Turing machine.

In actual computing we sometimes use certain marks (accent, check, movable physical pointer, etc.), which may be placed on a given square in addition to an ordinary symbol. If there are j of the ordinary symbols, and n of these special marks, any subset of which may be placed on a given square, the number of the square conditions is merely increased from $j+1$ to $(j+1) \cdot 2^n$.

As another example of behavior involving compound observation, suppose that the following sequence of symbols is printed,

$$\ldots 4401385789264 \ldots,$$

that the observer's attention is centered at the figure 7 near the middle, and that he observes clearly at most five figures centered at this 7; thus the sequence of the five digits 85789 together with his state of mind determine his next act. Some digits further off may be vaguely observed, but without affecting his act. The act shall be of one of the kinds performed by Turing machines, with each separate symbol occurrence (not groups of five) occupying a square. For example, if the next act is $0L\mathrm{q}_d$, the printing becomes

$$\ldots 4401385089264 \ldots,$$

with 38508 observed. Such behavior can be reduced to Turing machine behavior as follows. Say that the symbols are the ten Arabic digits. The behavior can be considered as that of a generalized Turing machine, in which the configuration (determining the act) is $(e, f, a, g, h, \mathrm{q}_c)$ where e, f, a, g, h are the digits occupying the five squares centered at the scanned square. Corresponding to each state q_c of this generalized machine, we introduce a set of 10^4 states q_{cefgh} $(e, f, g, h = 0, \ldots, 9)$; and we modify the table so that upon reaching state q_c, a series of Turing machine acts is performed, consisting of inspections of the two adjacent squares on each side, leading to state q_{cefgh} when the four squares in question are occupied by the respective digits e, f, g, h. Not only the states q_{cefgh} must be added, but also some states to be assumed during the action leading from q_c to q_{cefgh}. Details are left to the reader. Now the act the generalized machine performed from the configuration (e, f, a, g, h, q_c) shall be performed from the configuration (a, q_{cefgh}). This reduction is an illustration of the remark that one can remember a finite number of previously observed symbols by having changed one's state of mind when they were observed.

It might be thought that the printing on still other squares may constitute part of the observation, e.g. that on certain specially marked squares (finite in number). If these squares are so located in the symbol space that the computer can find them and return by acts of the kinds performed by Turing machines (cf. the discussion of (c) to follow), this kind of compound observation can be reduced in a similar fashion to the preceding.

Under (b), the computer can alter other squares besides the scanned square. The new observed square need not be adjacent to the original. However there is a finite bound to the complexity of the act, if it is to constitute a single act of the computer. More complicated acts will require renewed motivation by reference to the observed data and the state of mind at intermediate situations between the given and resulting ones. (Indeed it can be argued that the Turing machine act is already compound; and consists psychologically in a printing and change in state of mind, followed by a motion and another change of mind. Post 1947 does thus separate the Turing act into two; we have not here, primarily because it saves space in the machine tables not to do so.)

All simple alterations of the situation, not in the Turing machine form, which are readily proposed, e.g. printing after motion instead of before, are easily expressed as successions of the atomic acts of a Turing machine. (Much more complicated operations, which could hardly be regarded as single acts, have already been so treated in § 68.)

Turning to (c), computing is commonly performed on 2-dimensional paper, and the 2-dimensional character of the paper is sometimes used in elementary arithmetic. Theoretically, we must also consider the possibility of still other kinds of symbol space. The symbol space must be sufficiently regular in structure so that the computer will not become lost in it during the computation.

From a given square or cell of the space, there will be a finite number $m+1$ of ways of moving to the same or an adjacent cell, call them $M_0, \ldots, M_m$ where M_0 is the identical motion. For example, in the plane ruled into squares, $m = 4$ (no motion, left, up, right, down), or if diagonal motions are also allowed, $m = 8$. The computer, whose act from a given situation must be determined by which one of a finite number of configurations is existing, could not use more. We lose no generality in supposing that there are the same number of directions of motion from every cell; in case there are fewer from some cells, the terminus of the rest of the $m+1$ motions may be defined to be the given cell, i.e. these as well as M_0 may be taken to be identical.

The number of cells which can ultimately be reached is therefore countable. The same cell may be reached by different successions of motions, e.g. in the plane, down and then right leads to the same square as right and then down.

We shall suppose that an enumeration without repetitions can be given of all the cells, such that the following is the case. To each of the ways of moving M_i ($i = 0, \ldots, m$), there is a computable function μ_i such that, if x is the index in the enumeration of the given cell, then $\mu_i(x)$ is the index of the cell reached by the motion M_i. This supposition is realized by any readily imagined symbol space.

Using this enumeration, let the cell numbered x in the enumeration ($x = 0, 1, 2, \ldots$) correspond to the x-th square counting rightward from a certain square (called the 0-th) on a linear tape.

Using methods from § 68, we can set up a Turing machine which will find the $\mu_i(x)$-th square, when started on the x-th square, if a distinguishing mark is kept on the 0-th (or -1-st) square. The computation for this purpose can be done by marking squares with accents, afterwards erased, without interfering with the printing already on them. This enables us to reduce computation in the given symbol space to computation on the linear tape of a Turing machine.

For this reduction, we did not assume that from any cell adjacent to a given cell one of the motions returns us to the given cell, i.e. that every motion in the space has an inverse. This would be the case in any ordinary symbol space. An exception is represented by the computer who receives a signal at intervals by ear.

The symbol space may consist of several disconnected subspaces, each having its own scanned cell, as e.g. in the case of a computer who simultaneously reads a symbol on a paper by eye, reads another in braille on a tape by hand, and receives a signal by ear. If there are r such subspaces, we can reconstrue the cells to be the r-tuples consisting of a cell from each of those respective subspaces.

In regard to (d), we may argue that a natural number y is given in the original sense (§ 6), only if some sequence of $y+1$ objects, say $y+1$ tallies, is given; and hence that a procedure for computing a function φ from its argument(s), when both are expressed in some other notation, would not solve the computation problem for φ, unless the computer can also proceed from the other notation for a number y to the sequence of $y+1$ tallies, and vice versa.

According to our other arguments, Turing machines could then be built which, given the other notation for y would supply the $y+1$ tallies, and vice versa. Details can be arranged as in the definition of computation within one system of notation. Thus for decimal notation, the first machine started in the first of the following situations would go to the second.

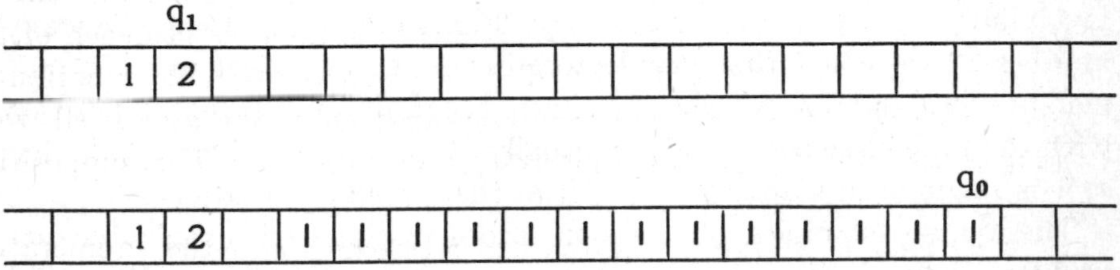

For the familiar systems of notation, such as the dual or decimal, the existence of such a pair of machines can be established.

We have been defending Turing's thesis for number-theoretic functions; but Turing machines apply equally well to expressions in any language having a finite list of symbols. By using them as just illustrated for the case of converting one notation for a natural number into another, we get a direct way of characterizing 'effective' operations on expressions in such languages, as an alternative to requiring a corresponding number-theoretic function under a particular effective Gödel numbering to be general recursive or computable (§ 61). The method extends to languages having an enumerable infinity of symbols, whenever the symbols can be considered effectively as composed in turn from the symbols of some finite list; e.g. to the formal number-theoretic symbolism, by regarding the variables $a, b, c, \ldots$ as $a, a_{|}, a_{||}, \ldots$ (§§ 16, 50).

***§ 71. The word problem for semi-groups.** Church's original example of a decision problem which, on the basis of his thesis, is unsolvable was constructed in terms of λ-definability (1936). The corresponding example given above (Theorem XII § 60) is constructed in terms of general recursiveness (following Kleene 1936, 1943). Turing 1936-7 gave examples constructed in terms of computability. This can be done e.g. as follows. A machine $\mathfrak{M}$ is determined by its table, containing $(j+1)k$ entries. We can set up a Gödel numbering of the tables, and thus of the machines. Then the function ξ defined as follows is not computable: $\xi(x) = 0$, if x is the Gödel number of a machine $\mathfrak{M}_x$, and the partial function φ_x of one variable which $\mathfrak{M}_x$ computes has 1 as value for x as argument, and $\xi(x) = 1$ otherwise. So by Turing's thesis (or via the equivalence of general recursiveness and computability, by Church's thesis) there is no algorithm for deciding whether any given number x is the Gödel number of a machine which, when started scanning x in standard position with the tape elsewhere blank, eventually stops scanning $x, 1$ in standard position. As another example, there is no algorithm for deciding whether any given machine, when started from any given initial situation, eventually stops. For if there were, then, given any number x, we could first decide whether x is the Gödel number of a machine $\mathfrak{M}_x$, and if so whether $\mathfrak{M}_x$ started scanning x in standard position with the tape elsewhere blank eventually stops, and if so finally whether $x, 1$ is scanned in standard position in the terminal situation.

These first examples of decision problems proved unsolvable are problems arising directly in connection with one of the mathematical notions (λ-definability, general recursiveness, or computability) originally identified with effectiveness by the Church-Turing thesis.

A second class of examples, a step removed from these, are the decision problems for certain formal systems, e.g. Theorem 33 § 61 (also cf. § 76, Church 1936 p. 363).

A decision problem proved unsolvable by Post 1947 and Markov 1947 is of interest as constituting the first example in which an existing problem from outside the field of logic and foundations has been treated.

The problem which Post and Markov prove unsolvable was proposed by Thue 1914. Suppose that a finite list $a_1, \ldots, a_m$ $(m \geq 1)$ of distinct symbols is given; let us call them *letters*, and the list of them the *alphabet*. A finite sequence of zero or more (occurrences of) the letters, we call a *word* (in, or formed from, that alphabet); in the language of Chapter IV (§ 16), a word is simply a formal expression, when $a_1, \ldots, a_m$ are the formal symbols, except that now we always include the empty expression.

A word C is *part* of another word D, if D is of the form UCV where U and V are words (possibly empty).

Now suppose further that a finite list $(A_1, B_1), \ldots, (A_n, B_n)$ $(n \geq 1)$ of pairs of words is given; we call this list the *dictionary*. We say that two words R and S are *immediately equivalent* (by the given dictionary), if R and S are of the respective forms UA_iV and UB_iV, or of the respective forms UB_iV and UA_iV, for some words U and V and pair (A_i, B_i) $(1 \leq i \leq n)$; in other words, if R is transformable into S by replacing a part A_i by its correspondent B_i in the dictionary, or inversely. We call two words P and Q *equivalent* (by the given dictionary), if there is a finite sequence $R_1, \ldots, R_l$ $(l \geq 1)$ of words such that R_1 is P, and R_l is Q, and R_{t-1} is immediately equivalent to R_t $(t = 2, \ldots, l)$.

Thue's (general) problem is to find an algorithm for deciding, for any given alphabet and dictionary, whether any two given words are equivalent. The problem is also known as the *word problem for semi-groups*.

THEOREM XXXI. *The word problem for semi-groups is unsolvable; in fact, there is a particular alphabet and dictionary, such that there is no algorithm for deciding whether any two words (formed from that alphabet) are equivalent (by that dictionary).* (Post 1947, Markov 1947.)

PROOF. Our method of proof will consist in picking an alphabet and a dictionary, such that, if we had a decision procedure for the equivalence of any two words, we could thence obtain a decision procedure for the predicate $(Ey)T_1(x, x, y)$, contradicting Theorem XII § 60 (based on Church's thesis). The unsolvability of Thue's problem for the case of this particular alphabet and dictionary of course implies the unsolvability of the general problem.

It is convenient now to consider the equivalence relationship between two words in terms of the possibility of formally deducing the second word from the first by use of $2n$ rules of inference, as follows $(i = 1, \ldots, n)$:

$$\text{(a)} \quad \frac{UA_iV}{UB_iV,} \qquad\qquad \text{(b)} \quad \frac{UB_iV}{UA_iV,}$$

where U and V are any words (possibly empty) in the alphabet $a_1, \ldots, a_m$.

We shall first study *semi-Thue systems* in which only the n rules of inference (a) are admitted, but not their inverses (b).

We shall describe a method by which, given any particular Turing machine, we can set up a semi-Thue system such that the tape vs. machine situations are represented by words of the semi-Thue system, and the atomic acts of the machine correspond to applications of the rules (a).

The alphabet of the semi-Thue system shall consist of $s_0, \ldots, s_j$ (representing the square conditions for the machine), $q_0, \ldots, q_k$ (representing the machine states), and an additional symbol h ($j+k+3$ letters altogether).

In a given tape vs. machine situation, say that the smallest unbroken piece of tape containing all printed squares and the scanned square consists of r squares ($r \geq 1$). Let the conditions of these squares from left to right be $s_{g_1}, \ldots, s_{g_r}$. Let the p-th of these squares be the scanned square ($1 \leq p \leq r$). Let the machine state be q_c. Then the situation shall be represented by the word

$$hs_{g_1} \ldots s_{g_p} q_c s_{g_{p+1}} \ldots s_{g_r} h,$$

which we call the *Post word* for it. (When is a word a Post word?)

EXAMPLE 1. The Post word for the situation of Example 1 § 69 is $hs_1s_1s_3s_1q_4s_0s_1h$.

The n rules of inference (a) of the semi-Thue system shall comprise one or more rules corresponding to each of the $(j+1)k$ active configurations of the Turing machine. If the table entry for an active configuration (s_a, q_c) is of the form $s_b Lq_d$ with $b \neq 0$, there shall be $j+2$ corresponding rules as follows ($e = 0, \ldots, j$),

$$\frac{Us_e s_a q_c V}{Us_e q_d s_b V,} \qquad \frac{Uhs_a q_c V}{Uhs_0 q_d s_b V;}$$

if the table entry is $s_0 Lq_d$, there shall be $(j+2)^2$ rules as follows ($e, f = 0, \ldots, j$),

$$\frac{Us_e s_a q_c s_f V}{Us_e q_d s_0 s_f V,} \qquad \frac{Uhs_a q_c s_f V}{Uhs_0 q_d s_0 s_f V,} \qquad \frac{Us_e s_a q_c hV}{Us_e q_d hV,} \qquad \frac{Uhs_a q_c hV}{Uhs_0 q_d hV.}$$

Similarly there shall be $j+2$ rules, if the table entry is of the form $s_b Rq_d$ with $b \neq 0$; and $(j+2)^2$, if of the form $s_0 Rq_d$. If the entry is of the form $s_b Cq_d$, there shall be one rule, as follows,

$$\frac{Us_a q_c V}{Us_b q_d V.}$$

In these n rules the A_i's are all distinct. Given the Post word for an active situation, exactly one of these n rules (a) is applicable to it as premise, namely the rule or one of the rules corresponding to the configuration (s_a, q_c) in that situation, and in only one way, i.e. with only one choice of the U and V. (For a rule in which the first symbol of the A_i is h, the U will always be empty.) The application of the rule gives as conclusion the Post word for the situation resulting by the atomic act of the machine from the given situation. Given the Post word for a passive situation, none of the n rules is applicable.

Hence a given word Q is deducible from a given Post word P in the semi-Thue system, if and only if Q is the Post word for a situation which the Turing machine will reach from the situation represented by the Post word P.

The partial recursive function $0 \cdot \mu y T_1(x, x, y)$ is defined and has the value 0, if and only if $(Ey)T_1(x, x, y)$ (cf. § 63). By Theorem XXVIII, there is a Turing machine which 1/1 computes $0 \cdot \mu y T_1(x, x, y)$. We set up the semi-Thue system corresponding to this machine. In this semi-Thue system, from the Post word for the situation in which a number x is scanned in standard position with state q_1 and the tape is blank elsewhere (i.e. the Post word $hs_1 \ldots s_1q_1h$ with $x+1$ occurrences of s_1), we can deduce the Post word for the situation in which the number pair $x, 0$ is scanned in standard position with state q_0 and the tape blank elsewhere (i.e. the Post word $hs_1 \ldots s_1s_0s_1q_0h$ with $x+1$ occurrences of s_1 preceding the s_0), if and only if $(Ey)T_1(x, x, y)$. Since by use of Church's thesis there is no algorithm for deciding whether $(Ey)T_1(x, x, y)$ (Theorem XII), there can be no algorithm for deciding, for any two given words P and Q in the semi-Thue system, whether Q is deducible from P, i.e. whether Q follows from P by the rules (a).

To establish the theorem, it remains to extend this result to the full Thue system in which the inverse rules (b) are admitted. This is accomplished by the following lemma.

Lemma VII. *For the rules* (a) *corresponding to a given Turing machine as described above: If* P *is a Post word,* Q *is deducible from* P *by the rules* (a) *and* (b), *and* Q *contains* q_0, *then* Q *is deducible from* P *by the rules* (a) *only.*

Proof of Lemma VII, by course-of-values induction on the length l of a given deduction of Q from P by the rules (a) and (b). Let the deduction be $R_1, \ldots, R_l$, where R_1 is P and R_l is Q. The case for $l = 1$ is trivial, and we now suppose $l > 1$. Since P is a Post word, and the rules (a) and (b) each preserve this property, each of $R_1, \ldots, R_l$ is a Post word, and hence contains exactly one occurrence of a q, i.e. of one of $q_0, \ldots, q_k$. Now R_l, i.e. Q, contains q_0; and by the choice of the rules (a) to correspond to the active configurations of the Turing machine, each of the A_i's contains q_c for some $c \neq 0$. Hence R_l must come from R_{l-1} by one of the rules (a). So if there are any applications of the rules (b) in the given deduction, the last will be in the step from R_{t-1} to R_t

for some $t < l$. Then R_{t+1} comes from R_t by one of the rules (a); but also since the rules (b) are the inverses of the rules (a), R_{t-1} comes from R_t by one of the rules (a). But R_t is a Post word, and to such a word at most one of the rules (a) is applicable and in at most one way. Hence R_{t-1} and R_{t+1} are the same word. Hence we can shorten the given deduction of Q from P by omitting $R_t R_{t+1}$. Applying the hypothesis of the induction to the shortened deduction of Q from P by the rules (a) and (b), we conclude that there is a deduction of Q from P by the rules (a) only.

It is easily seen that the word problem for semi-groups is equivalent via Gödel numbering to a problem of the form whether $(Ey)R(x, y)$ is true for given x, where R is general recursive. Since our proof of Theorem XXXI is by reducing the problem whether $(Ey)T_1(x, x, y)$ to the word problem, the word problem is of highest degree of unsolvability for decision problems of predicates of the form $(Ey)R(x, y)$ (cf. end § 61 and Example 2 § 65).

Some further results along the same line as Theorem XXXI are contained in Markov's papers 1947, 1947a, 1947b, 1951, 1951a, 1951b. Also cf. Hall 1949 and Boone 1951 abstract.

The definition of equivalence of two words P and Q (in symbols, $P \sim Q$) which we used above in the word problem for semi-groups can be expressed inductively thus, where (extremal clause) $P \sim Q$ only as required by the following (direct clauses): 1. $A_i \sim B_i$ ($i = 1, \ldots, n$). 2. $U \sim U$. 3. If $U \sim V$, then $V \sim U$. 4. If $U \sim V$ and $V \sim W$, then $U \sim W$. 5—6. If $U \sim V$, then $Ua_i \sim Va_i$ and $a_iU \sim a_iV$ ($i = 1, \ldots, m$). Turing 1950* shows that the *word problem for semi-groups with cancellation*, which we obtain by adding the two following clauses, is likewise unsolvable: 7—8. If $Ua_i \sim Va_i$ or $a_iU \sim a_iV$, then $U \sim V$ ($i = 1, \ldots, m$).

PART IV

MATHEMATICAL LOGIC (ADDITIONAL TOPICS)

CHAPTER XIV

THE PREDICATE CALCULUS AND AXIOM SYSTEMS

§ 72. Gödel's completeness theorem. We resume the study of the predicate calculus, continuing from the point reached in § 37. Say that F is a predicate letter formula containing free only the distinct variables $z_1, \ldots, z_q$ ($q \geq 0$) and containing only the distinct predicate letters $P_1, \ldots, P_s$ ($s \geq 1$). An assignment of objects $z_1, \ldots, z_q$ from some non-empty domain D as values to $z_1, \ldots, z_q$ and of logical functions $P_1, \ldots, P_s$ over D as values to $P_1, \ldots, P_s$ we say *satisfies* F (or is a *satisfying assignment to* $z_1, \ldots, z_q, P_1, \ldots, P_s$ *for* F), if under the valuation rules given in §§ 28, 36 and 37 F then takes the value $\mathfrak{t}$. As defined in § 37, F is *satisfiable* (*valid*) in a non-empty domain D, if some (every) assignment to $z_1, \ldots, z_q, P_1, \ldots, P_s$ in D satisfies F. As to the notation, we are now writing the logical functions "$P_j(a_1, \ldots, a_{n_j})$", "$A(a, b)$", etc., instead of "$\mathfrak{l}_j(a_1, \ldots, a_{n_j})$", "$\mathfrak{l}(a, b)$", etc. as we did in §§ 36, 37. In the case that the domain is the natural numbers, logical functions are simply number-theoretic predicates, when we do not make a distinction between propositions and truth values $\mathfrak{t}$ or $\mathfrak{f}$ (cf. (b) § 45 and remarks there); and indeed we shall sometimes call them now predicates.

THEOREM $34^{\circ C}$. *If a predicate letter formula* F *is irrefutable* (i.e. if $\neg$F is unprovable, § 41) *in the predicate calculus, then* F *is satisfiable in the domain of the natural numbers.* (Gödel's completeness theorem for the predicate calculus, 1930.)

Modifications of Gödel's proof appeared in the 2nd (1938) edition of Hilbert-Ackermann 1928 and in Hilbert-Bernays 1939. Henkin 1949 gave a proof employing a minimum of knowledge of the deductive properties of the predicate calculus. We give a proof which is intermediate in this respect between Hilbert-Bernays' and Henkin's. There is also a proof by Rasiowa and Sikorski 1950 using algebra and topology.

PROOF OF THEOREM 34 (preliminaries). By Theorem 19 § 35, any predicate letter formula F is equivalent to a prenex predicate letter formula, which (by the method of proof) has the same distinct free variables $z_1, \ldots, z_q$ and predicate letters $P_1, \ldots, P_s$ as F. By Theorem 21 § 37 and the valuation table for $\sim$ § 28, or by paralleling the proof of Theorem 19 set-theoretically, the prenex form of F is satisfied by a given assignment $z_1, \ldots, z_q, P_1, \ldots, P_s$, if and only if F is satisfied by it.

For the remainder of the proof (including Lemmas 22 and 23), we shall assume that F is prenex. For illustration, suppose that F is $\forall x_1 \exists y_1 \forall x_2 \forall x_3 \exists y_2 \forall x_4 B(z_1, z_2, x_1, y_1, x_2, x_3, y_2, x_4)$ where $B(z_1, z_2, x_1, y_1, x_2, x_3, y_2, x_4)$ contains no quantifiers and only the distinct variables shown (so $q = 2$).

Instead of speaking of the value which a predicate letter formula $A(u_1, \ldots, u_p)$ takes when its free variables and predicate letters $u_1, \ldots, u_p, P_1, \ldots, P_s$ take respectively the values $u_1, \ldots, u_p, P_1, \ldots, P_s$, it will usually be more convenient notationally to permit the substitution of numerals for the free variables of predicate letter formulas, and then to speak of the value taken by $A(\boldsymbol{u}_1, \ldots, \boldsymbol{u}_p)$ (where $\boldsymbol{u}_1, \ldots, \boldsymbol{u}_p$ are the numerals for the natural numbers $u_1, \ldots, u_p$) when $P_1, \ldots, P_s$ take the values $P_1, \ldots, P_s$. (Here $A(\boldsymbol{u}_1, \ldots, \boldsymbol{u}_p)$ is a *predicate letter formula with numerals* in the sense obtained by extending the notion of 'k-predicate letter formula' § 37 to allow all numerals and not simply $1, \ldots, \boldsymbol{k}$ (and variables) as terms. A predicate letter formula with numerals containing no variables free or bound is a *proposition letter formula with numerals.*)

We can then treat the problem of choosing the logical functions $P_1, \ldots, P_s$ as a problem of choosing a value (t or f) for each of the formulas $P_j(\boldsymbol{a}_1, \ldots, \boldsymbol{a}_{n_j})$ where $j = 1, \ldots, s$ and $a_1, \ldots, a_{n_j}$ range over all n_j-tuples of natural numbers. Let these formulas be enumerated in some manner without repetitions as $Q_0, Q_1, Q_2, \ldots$.

By the valuation rules for $\forall$ and $\exists$, F is satisfied by $z_1, z_2, P_1, \ldots, P_s$, if for each natural number x_1, there is some natural number y_1 depending on x_1 (write it "$y_1(x_1)$"), such that for each x_2 and x_3, there is some y_2 depending on x_1, x_2, x_3 (write it "$y_2(x_1, x_2, x_3)$"), such that for each x_4,

$$\text{(I)} \qquad B(\boldsymbol{z}_1, \boldsymbol{z}_2, \boldsymbol{x}_1, \boldsymbol{y}_1(x_1), \boldsymbol{x}_2, \boldsymbol{x}_3, \boldsymbol{y}_2(x_1, x_2, x_3), \boldsymbol{x}_4)$$

(where $\boldsymbol{y}_1(x_1)$ is the numeral for the natural number $y_1(x_1)$, etc.) has the value t. We now take $z_1, z_2, y_1(x_1), y_2(x_1, x_2, x_3)$ to be $2^0 \cdot 3^1$, $2^0 \cdot 3^2$, $2^1 \cdot 3^{x_1}$, $2^2 \cdot 3^{x_1} \cdot 5^{x_2} \cdot 7^{x_3}$, respectively. Thus we determine an infinite class F_0 of proposition letter formulas with numerals (namely the formulas (I) when x_1, x_2, x_3, x_4 range over all quadruples of natural numbers, and $z_1, z_2, y_1(x_1), y_2(x_1, x_2, x_3)$ are as just specified) such that if $P_1, \ldots, P_s$ *jointly satisfy* these formulas, i.e. give them all the value t, then $z_1, z_2, P_1, \ldots, P_s$ satisfy F.

We say that a class of formulas is *consistent in* a formal system S, if the formal system obtained by adjoining the formulas of the class as axioms to the postulates of S is simply consistent (§ 28), i.e. if for no formula A are both A and $\neg$A deducible in S from formulas of the class.

The proof of Theorem 34 will be completed by Lemmas 22 and 23, which relate to any prenex predicate letter formula F and the class F_0 obtained from it as illustrated.

LEMMA 22^{C}. *If* F_0 *is consistent in the propositional calculus, then* F *is satisfiable in the domain of the natural numbers.*

PROOF. By the preliminaries, it will suffice to show that the formulas of F_0 can be jointly satisfied under the valuation procedure of the propositional calculus by an assignment of truth values ($\mathfrak{t}$ or $\mathfrak{f}$) to each of $Q_0, Q_1, Q_2, \ldots$. (Our method now will show this for any class F_0 of formulas consistent in the propositional calculus and list $Q_0, Q_1, Q_2, \ldots$ of distinct formulas prime for the propositional calculus including all components of F_0 prime for the propositional calculus, § 25.)

Let R_0 be Q_0 or $\neg Q_0$ according as $\mathsf{F}_0 \vdash Q_0$ or not $\mathsf{F}_0 \vdash Q_0$ in the propositional calculus (where "$\mathsf{F}_0 \vdash$" means deducible from formulas of F_0), and adjoin R_0 to F_0 to obtain a new class F_1. Then F_1 is also consistent in the propositional calculus. For in the first case (i.e. when $\mathsf{F}_0 \vdash Q_0$ and R_0 is Q_0), the addition of R_0 does not increase the class of the formulas which can be deduced; and in the second case (i.e. when $\overline{\mathsf{F}_0 \vdash Q_0}$ and R_0 is $\neg Q_0$), if $\mathsf{F}_1 \vdash$ A and $\mathsf{F}_1 \vdash \neg$A for some A, then $\mathsf{F}_0, \neg Q_0 \vdash$ A and $\mathsf{F}_0, \neg Q_0 \vdash \neg$A, and thence by $\neg$-introd. and elim., $\mathsf{F}_0 \vdash \neg\neg Q_0 \vdash Q_0$, contradicting the case hypothesis.

Similarly for each natural number i, let R_i be Q_i or $\neg Q_i$ according as $\mathsf{F}_i \vdash Q_i$ or $\overline{\mathsf{F}_i \vdash Q_i}$, and adjoin R_i to F_i to obtain F_{i+1}; then the consistency of F_{i+1} follows from that of F_i.

We now assign to Q_i the value $\mathfrak{t}$ or $\mathfrak{f}$ according as R_i is Q_i or R_i is $\neg Q_i$.

For this assignment, not only $R_0, R_1, R_2, \ldots$ but also the formulas of F_0 take the value $\mathfrak{t}$. For let H be a formula of F_0. The distinct parts of H prime for the propositional calculus belong to the list $Q_0, Q_1, Q_2, \ldots$; say they are $Q_{i_1}, \ldots, Q_{i_l}$. Consider the formula H & R_{i_1} & ... & R_{i_l}; call it "A". Let $i = 1+\max(i_1, \ldots, i_l)$; then $\mathsf{F}_i \vdash$ A, since H, $R_{i_1}, \ldots, R_{i_l}$ all belong to F_i. The assigned values are the only ones for which $R_{i_1}, \ldots, R_{i_l}$ are all $\mathfrak{t}$. Hence if H were not $\mathfrak{t}$ for this assignment, then A would be identically false, and $\neg$A would be identically true (§ 28); so by Theorem 10 § 29 $\neg$A would be provable in the propositional calculus, a fortiori $\mathsf{F}_i \vdash \neg$A, which with $\mathsf{F}_i \vdash$ A would contradict the consistency of F_i.

LEMMA 23. *If* F *is irrefutable in the predicate calculus, then* F_0 *is consistent in the propositional calculus.*

PROOF. Note that by our choice of the numbers z_1, z_2 and functions $y_1(x_1)$ and $y_2(x_1, x_2, x_3)$: (A) The numbers z_1 and z_2, $y_1(x_1)$ for $x_1 = 0, 1, 2, \ldots$, and $y_2(x_1, x_2, x_3)$ for $x_1, x_2, x_3 = 0, 1, 2, \ldots$ are all distinct. (B) $x_1 < y_1(x_1)$ and $x_1, y_1(x_1), x_2, x_3 < y_2(x_1, x_2, x_3)$.

To show by reductio ad absurdum that F_0 is consistent, suppose that for some A, both A and $\neg$A are deducible in the propositional calculus (using predicate letter formulas with numerals) from formulas of F_0. Then using weak $\neg$-elim., there is a deduction of the formula $\mathcal{A} \& \neg \mathcal{A}$ from the same formulas, i.e. from a finite set of formulas of the form (I).

Let "$\bar{0}$", "$\bar{1}$", "$\bar{2}$", ... denote variables distinct from each other and from $\mathrm{x}_1, \mathrm{y}_1, \mathrm{x}_2, \mathrm{x}_3, \mathrm{y}_2, \mathrm{x}_4$, but such that $\bar{z}_1$ is z_1 and $\bar{z}_2$ is z_2. By changing each numeral $\boldsymbol{u}$ where it occurs in this deduction not as a part of another numeral to the corresponding variable $\bar{u}$, we obtain a deduction of $\mathcal{A} \& \neg \mathcal{A}$ in the (predicate letter) propositional calculus, a fortiori in the (pure) predicate calculus with all variables held constant, from a finite set of formulas of the form $\mathrm{B}(\mathrm{z}_1, \mathrm{z}_2, \bar{x}_1, \bar{y}_1(x_1), \bar{x}_2, \bar{x}_3, \bar{y}_2(x_1, x_2, x_3), \bar{x}_4)$; and thence by use of $\forall$-elim. (noting that x_4 is distinct from the other variables shown), from formulas of the form

$$\forall \mathrm{x}_4 \mathrm{B}(\mathrm{z}_1, \mathrm{z}_2, \bar{x}_1, \bar{y}_1(x_1), \bar{x}_2, \bar{x}_3, \bar{y}_2(x_1, x_2, x_3), \mathrm{x}_4).$$

Thus writing out the distinct assumption formulas (say there are l of them),

$$(1) \quad \begin{array}{l} \forall \mathrm{x}_4 \mathrm{B}(\mathrm{z}_1, \mathrm{z}_2, \bar{x}_1^1, \bar{y}_1(x_1^1), \bar{x}_2^1, \bar{x}_3^1, \bar{y}_2(x_1^1, x_2^1, x_3^1), \mathrm{x}_4), \\ \forall \mathrm{x}_4 \mathrm{B}(\mathrm{z}_1, \mathrm{z}_2, \bar{x}_1^2, \bar{y}_1(x_1^2), \bar{x}_2^2, \bar{x}_3^2, \bar{y}_2(x_1^2, x_2^2, x_3^2), \mathrm{x}_4), \\ \quad \cdot \quad \cdot \quad \cdot \\ \forall \mathrm{x}_4 \mathrm{B}(\mathrm{z}_1, \mathrm{z}_2, \bar{x}_1^l, \bar{y}_1(x_1^l), \bar{x}_2^l, \bar{x}_3^l, \bar{y}_2(x_1^l, x_2^l, x_3^l), \mathrm{x}_4) \vdash \mathcal{A} \& \neg \mathcal{A}. \end{array}$$

The formula $\mathcal{A} \& \neg \mathcal{A}$ contains no variables. The variables which appear free rightmost in the assumption formulas of (1) are $\bar{y}_2(x_1^1, x_2^1, x_3^1), \ldots, \bar{y}_2(x_1^l, x_2^l, x_3^l)$. Since the l assumption formulas are distinct, i.e. x_1^j, x_2^j, x_3^j for $j = 1, \ldots, l$ are distinct triples of natural numbers, by (A) these l variables are distinct from each other as well as from $\mathrm{z}_1, \mathrm{z}_2$. By (B), we can choose one of them, say $\bar{y}_2(x_1^1, x_2^1, x_3^1)$, which is of greater index (i.e. comes later in the list $\bar{0}, \bar{1}, \bar{2}, \ldots$) than any of the variables which appear free elsewhere in (1) (i.e. not rightmost) except perhaps z_1 or z_2, and hence is distinct from those variables also. By $\exists$-elim., followed by a change of bound variables (*74 § 33, noting that y_2 is distinct from the other variables shown) and two $\forall$-eliminations (noting that x_2, x_3 are distinct from each other and the other variables shown),

$$\forall x_2 \forall x_3 \exists y_2 \forall x_4 B(z_1, z_2, \bar{x}_1^1, \bar{y}_1(x_1^1), x_2, x_3, y_2, x_4),$$

(2)
$$\forall x_4 B(z_1, z_2, \bar{x}_1^2, \bar{y}_1(x_1^2), \bar{x}_2^2, \bar{x}_3^2, \bar{y}_2(x_1^2, x_2^2, x_3^2), x_4),$$
$$\cdots$$
$$\forall x_4 B(z_1, z_2, \bar{x}_1^l, \bar{y}_1(x_1^l), \bar{x}_2^l, \bar{x}_3^l, \bar{y}_2(x_1^l, x_2^l, x_3^l), x_4) \vdash \mathcal{A} \,\&\, \neg \mathcal{A}.$$

No variables are varied, since the variable $\bar{y}_2(x_1^1, x_2^1, x_3^1)$ of the $\exists$-elim. does not occur in any of the other assumption formulas (cf. Lemma 7b § 24).

Again by (A) the variables $\bar{y}_1(x_1^1)$, $\bar{y}_2(x_1^2, x_2^2, x_3^2)$, ..., $\bar{y}_2(x_1^l, x_2^l, x_3^l)$ which appear free rightmost are distinct from each other as well as from z_1 and z_2. By (B) we can choose one of them which is of greater index than any of the variables appearing free elsewhere in (2) except z_1 and z_2, and so must be distinct from those also. This variable may be $\bar{y}_1(x_1^1)$ or say $\bar{y}_2(x_1^2, x_2^2, x_3^2)$. If it is $\bar{y}_1(x_1^1)$, by $\exists$-elim., *74 and $\forall$-elim. we replace the first assumption formula by $\forall x_1 \exists y_1 \forall x_2 \forall x_3 \exists y_2 \forall x_4 B(z_1, z_2, x_1, y_1, x_2, x_3, y_2, x_4)$, i.e. by F. If it is $\bar{y}_2(x_1^2, x_2^2, x_3^2)$, we instead replace the second assumption formula by $\forall x_2 \forall x_3 \exists y_2 \forall x_4 B(z_1, z_2, \bar{x}_1^2, \bar{y}_1(x_1^2), x_2, x_3, y_2, x_4)$, and if this is a duplicate of the first (i.e. if $x_1^1 = x_1^2$) we omit it.

We continue in this manner. After each use of $\exists$-elim. (applied to a $\bar{y}$ appearing rightmost and distinct from all the other variables shown) and *74, we apply $\forall$-elim. to the $\bar{x}$'s which are "uncovered" by the $\exists$-elim., and then omit the resulting assumption formula, if it is a duplicate of another, so that the $\bar{y}$'s which appear rightmost at the next stage will again be distinct from each other. Eventually we obtain simply

(3)
$$F \vdash \mathcal{A} \,\&\, \neg \mathcal{A}.$$

From (3) by &-elim. and $\neg$-introd.,

(4)
$$\vdash \neg F,$$

contradicting the hypothesis of the lemma that F is irrefutable.

Corollary 1°C. *Every predicate letter formula* G *which is valid in the domain of the natural numbers is provable in the predicate calculus* (*and hence,* by Theorem 21 § 37, *is valid in every non-empty domain*). (Another version of Gödel's completeness theorem, 1930.)

Proof. {G is valid in the domain of the natural numbers} $\rightarrow$ {$\neg$G is not satisfiable in that domain} $\rightarrow$ {$\neg$G is refutable, i.e. $\neg\neg$G is provable, in the predicate calculus} [by the theorem, applied with ¬G as the F, and contraposed (cf. *14 § 26)] → {G is provable in the same} [by ¬-elim].

COROLLARY 2^C. *If a predicate letter formula* F *is satisfiable in some (non-empty) domain, then* F *is satisfiable in the domain of the natural numbers.* (Löwenheim's theorem, 1915, also called the Löwenheim-Skolem theorem.)

PROOF. By contraposing Corollary 1; or thus: {F is satisfiable in some domain} → {¬F is not valid in that domain} → {¬F is not provable, i.e. F is irrefutable, in the predicate calculus} [by Theorem 21 contraposed] → {F is satisfiable in the domain of the natural numbers} [by the theorem].

Löwenheim's proof of his theorem, and the simpler proof given by Skolem 1920, employ the set-theoretic axiom of choice (Zermelo 1904, cf. § 13). The proof via Gödel's theorem is non-constructive to a lesser degree. The non-intuitionistic step (in the present treatment) occurs in the proof of Lemma 22, where we assume that $\mathsf{F}_i \vdash \mathrm{Q}_i$ or $\overline{\mathsf{F}_i \vdash \mathrm{Q}_i}$. By formalizing a part of their proof of Gödel's completeness theorem which contains the non-constructive step, Hilbert and Bernays obtain a metamathematical completeness theorem for the predicate calculus (1939 pp. 252—253), which we shall formulate as Theorem 36.

THEOREM 35$^{\circ C}$. *The satisfying predicates* $P_1, \dots, P_s$ *for* F *in Theorem* 34 *can be chosen so that* $P_j(a_1, \dots, a_{n_j}) \equiv (Ex)(y)R_j(a_1, \dots, a_{n_j}, x, y) \equiv (x)(Ey)S_j(a_1, \dots, a_{n_j}, x, y)$ *where* R_j *and* S_j *are primitive recursive* $(j = 1, \dots, s)$.

PROOF. In the following, "recursive" can mean general recursive (though actually the statements hold in the meaning primitive recursive); then by Corollary Theorem IV § 57, we can take R_j and S_j in the conclusion to be primitive recursive.

Suppose we have set up a Gödel numbering of the proposition letter formulas with numerals by the methods of §§ 52 and 56. Then if a and b are the Gödel numbers of formulas A and B, respectively, that of A ⊃ B is $\mu(a, b)$ and of ¬A is $\nu(a)$, for certain recursive functions μ and ν. Let $H(a) \equiv$ {a is the Gödel number of a formula belonging to F_0}; then H is recursive. If the enumeration $\mathrm{Q}_0, \mathrm{Q}_1, \mathrm{Q}_2, \dots$ was chosen suitably, the following functions will be recursive: $\varkappa(i) =$ {the Gödel number of Q_i}, $\alpha_j(a_1, \dots, a_{n_j}) =$ {the i such that $\mathrm{P}_j(\boldsymbol{a}_1, \dots, \boldsymbol{a}_{n_j})$ is Q_i}.

By the definition of the satisfying predicates P_j as given in the proof of Lemma 22, if $P_j(\boldsymbol{a}_1, \ldots, \boldsymbol{a}_{n_j})$ is Q_i, then $P_j(a_1, \ldots, a_{n_j}) \equiv \{R_i \text{ is } Q_i\} \equiv \{\mathsf{F}_i \vdash Q_i\}$. Let $F(i, a) \equiv \{a$ is the Gödel number of a formula A such that $\mathsf{F}_i \vdash A\}$. Then

(a) $$P_j(a_1, \ldots, a_{n_j}) \equiv F(\alpha_j(a_1, \ldots, a_{n_j}), \varkappa(\alpha_j(a_1, \ldots, a_{n_j}))).$$

Now we shall investigate the predicate $F(i, a)$.

To say that $\mathsf{F}_0 \vdash A$ in the propositional calculus means the same as that A is provable in the formal system obtained by adjoining F_0 as axioms to the propositional calculus. Let $F_0(a) \equiv \{a$ is the Gödel number of a provable formula of this system$\}$. By the methods of §§ 51, 52 (cf. Dn12), since H is recursive, $F_0(a) \equiv (Ey)R(a, y)$ with a (primitive) recursive R; i.e. $F_0(a)$ is expressible in the existential 1-quantifier form of Theorem V Part II § 57.

By the definition of F_{i+1} from F_i and the $\supset$-rules, $\{\mathsf{F}_{i+1} \vdash A\} \equiv \{\mathsf{F}_i, R_i \vdash A\} \equiv \{\mathsf{F}_i \vdash R_i \supset A\}$. Taking into account the definition of R_i by cases, we thus have

$$\begin{cases} F(0, a) \equiv F_0(a), \\ F(i', a) \equiv [F(i, \varkappa(i)) \mathbin{\&} F(i, \mu(\varkappa(i), a))] \vee [\overline{F}(i, \varkappa(i)) \mathbin{\&} F(i, \mu(\nu(\varkappa(i)), a))]. \end{cases}$$

This shows that F is recursive in F_0; for applying #D § 45, and going over from the predicates F and F_0 to their representing functions φ and φ_0, we have a "nested recursion" (§ 55),

$$\begin{cases} \varphi(0, a) = \varphi_0(a), \\ \varphi(i', a) = \chi(\varphi(i, \varkappa(i)), \varphi(i, \mu(\varkappa(i), a)), \varphi(i, \mu(\nu(\varkappa(i)), a))), \end{cases}$$

where χ, $\varkappa$, μ and ν are (primitive) recursive. (In fact by the result of Péter 1934 cited in § 55, F is primitive recursive in F_0.)

By (a), P_j is recursive in F, α_j, $\varkappa$; hence since α_j and $\varkappa$ are recursive, in F; and hence in F_0, which is expressible in the existential 1-quantifier form. Therefore, by a theorem of Post (Theorem XI § 58), P_j is expressible in both the 2-quantifier forms of Theorem V, as was to be shown.

THEOREM 36°. *The addition to the postulate list for the predicate calculus of an unprovable predicate letter formula* G *for use as an axiom schema would cause the number-theoretic system as based on the predicate calculus and Postulate Group* B (§ 19) *to become* ω*-inconsistent* (§ 42). (*In fact, a certain formula would become refutable which expresses a true proposition of the form* $(y)D(y)$ *where* $D(y)$ *is an effectively decidable predicate.*) (Hilbert-Bernays completeness theorem, 1939.)

Note the partial analogy to Corollary 2 Theorem 10 § 29 for the propositional calculus.

METHOD OF PROOF. Without loss of generality, we can take G to be closed, so that $q = 0$ (cf. end § 32). Let F be a prenex form of $\neg$G, so that by Theorem 19 with *30 and *49,

(i) $\vdash$ G $\sim \neg$F in the predicate calculus.

By (i), since G is unprovable, so is $\neg$F, i.e. F is irrefutable.

Hence by Lemma 23 (the proof of which was finitary),

(ii) F_0 is consistent in the propositional calculus.

The consistency of F_0 is equivalent to the proposition that $\overline{\mathsf{F}_0 \vdash \mathcal{A} \& \neg \mathcal{A}}$. If r be the Gödel number of $\mathcal{A} \& \neg \mathcal{A}$, then $\overline{\mathsf{F}_0 \vdash \mathcal{A} \& \neg \mathcal{A}} \equiv \overline{(Ey)}R(r, y) \equiv (y)\overline{R}(r, y)$ for the primitive recursive $R(a, y)$ used in the proof of Theorem 35. Let $D(y) \equiv \overline{R}(r, y)$. Then $D(y)$ is primitive recursive, and (ii) is equivalent to

(ii$_a$) $(y)D(y)$.

By Corollary Theorem 27 § 49, $D(y)$ is numeralwise expressed in the number-theoretic formalism by a formula D(y). Then from (ii$_a$),

(iii) $(y)[\vdash \mathrm{D}(\boldsymbol{y})]$

in the number-theoretic formalism.

According to Lemma 22, classically,

(iv) {F_0 is consistent in the propositional calculus}$\rightarrow$
{F is satisfied by certain predicates $P_1, \ldots, P_s$}.

The premise of the implication (iv) can be expressed in the symbolism of the number-theoretic system by the formula $\forall$yD(y). The conclusion can also be expressed in the number-theoretic symbolism, when we use the expressions for $P_1, \ldots, P_s$ given in Theorem 35. Let $\mathrm{R}_j(\mathrm{a}_1, \ldots, \mathrm{a}_{n_j}, \mathrm{x}, \mathrm{y})$ numeralwise express $R_j(a_1, \ldots, a_{n_j}, x, y)$. Then $\exists\mathrm{x}\forall\mathrm{y}\mathrm{R}_j(\mathrm{a}_1, \ldots, \mathrm{a}_{n_j}, \mathrm{x}, \mathrm{y})$ expresses $P_j(a_1, \ldots, a_{n_j})$ in the symbolism. The proposition that F is satisfied by $P_1, \ldots, P_s$ is then expressed by the formula F* which we obtain from F by substituting the formulas $\exists\mathrm{x}\forall\mathrm{y}\mathrm{R}_j(\mathrm{a}_1, \ldots, \mathrm{a}_{n_j}, \mathrm{x}, \mathrm{y})$ $(j = 1, \ldots, s)$ for the respective predicate letters $\mathrm{P}_j(\mathrm{a}_1, \ldots, \mathrm{a}_{n_j})$ (assuming that the bound variables have been suitably chosen). Then the implication (iv) is expressed by the formula $\forall$yD(y) $\supset$ F*.

We now propose that the informal classical demonstration of (iv) should be formalized in the classical number-theoretic system as a proof of this formula, so that we should then have

(v) $\vdash \forall$yD(y) $\supset$ F*

in that system. By contraposition (*12 § 26),

(vi) $\vdash \neg F^* \supset \neg \forall y D(y)$.

From (i) by substitution (Theorem 15 § 34),

(vii) $\vdash G^* \sim \neg F^*$.

Using (vii) in (vi),

(viii) $\vdash G^* \supset \neg \forall y D(y)$.

In (iii) and (viii), the "$\vdash$" refers to the unaugmented number-theoretic formalism. Now if G be added to this system as an axiom schema, then G* becomes an axiom (by the new schema), and then (since (iii) and (viii) still hold) $D(\boldsymbol{y})$ for $y = 0, 1, 2, \ldots$ and $\neg \forall y D(y)$ are provable simultaneously, i.e. the augmented system is ω-inconsistent. (Thus $\forall y D(y)$ becomes refutable, although it expresses the true proposition $(y)D(y)$.)

We shall not take the space to carry out the formalization of a given informal demonstration called for here in the step from (iv) to (v), just as we did not for the step from (I) to (II) in the proof of Theorem 30 § 42.

Hilbert and Bernays 1939 (pp. 205 ff., especially pp. 243—252) carry out the formalization of the corresponding part of their proof of Gödel's completeness theorem in another formal system, whence it can be inferred that Theorem 36 holds for ours (cf. the remarks on that system preceding Example 9 § 74).

THEOREM 37°C. *Given an enumerably infinite (or finite) class of predicate letter formulas* $F_0, F_1, F_2, \ldots$, *if every conjunction of a finite number of them is irrefutable in the predicate calculus, then they are jointly satisfiable in the domain of the natural numbers*, by a satisfying assignment of natural numbers $z_0, z_1, z_2, \ldots$ to the distinct variables $z_0, z_1, z_2, \ldots$ which occur free, and of predicates $P_0, P_1, P_2, \ldots$ to the distinct predicate letters $P_0, P_1, P_2, \ldots$ which occur, in formulas of the class. The lists $z_0, z_1, z_2, \ldots$ and $P_0, P_1, P_2, \ldots$ may be finite or infinite. (Gödel's completeness theorem for infinitely many formulas, 1930.)

PROOF. For example, suppose now that for some k, F_k is $\forall x_{k1} \exists y_{k1} \forall x_{k2} \forall x_{k3} \exists y_{k2} \forall x_{k4} B(z_{e_{k1}}, z_{e_{k2}}, x_{k1}, y_{k1}, x_{k2}, x_{k3}, y_{k2}, x_{k4})$. Then we take $z_{e_{k1}}, z_{e_{k2}}, y_{k1}(x_{k1}), y_{k2}(x_{k1}, x_{k2}, x_{k3})$ to be $2^0 \cdot 3^{e_{k1}}$, $2^0 \cdot 3^{e_{k2}}$, $2^1 \cdot 3^k \cdot 5^{x_{k1}}$, $2^2 \cdot 3^k \cdot 5^{x_{k1}} \cdot 7^{x_{k2}} \cdot 11^{x_{k3}}$. The set F_0 is to be the sum of the sets $\mathsf{F}_{00}, \mathsf{F}_{10}, \mathsf{F}_{20}, \ldots$ formed as was illustrated.

COROLLARY 1°C. *If for each assignment in the domain of the natural numbers to the free variables and predicate letters of the formulas* $G_0, G_1, G_2, \ldots$, *one of those formulas takes the value* t, *then some disjunction of a finite number of them is provable in the predicate calculus.*

COROLLARY 2^C. *If* $F_0, F_1, F_2, \ldots$ *are jointly satisfiable in some non-empty domain (or even if each conjunction of a finite number of* $F_0, F_1, F_2, \ldots$ *is satisfiable in a respective non-empty domain* (Gödel 1930)), *then* $F_0, F_1, F_2, \ldots$ *are jointly satisfiable in the domain of the natural numbers.* (A generalization of Löwenheim's theorem, Skolem 1920.)

PROOF OF COROLLARY 2. {Each conjunction of a finite number of $F_0, F_1, F_2, \ldots$ is satisfiable in a respective non-empty domain} $\rightarrow$ {the negation of each such conjunction is not valid in every domain} $\rightarrow$ {each such conjunction is irrefutable} (by Theorem 21 § 37) $\rightarrow$ {$F_0, F_1, F_2, \ldots$ are jointly satisfiable in the domain of the natural numbers} (by the theorem).

THEOREM $38^{\circ C}$. *If the enumeration* $F_0, F_1, F_2, \ldots$ *of formulas in Theorem* 37 *is effective (if infinite), the jointly satisfying predicates* $P_0, P_1, P_2, \ldots$ *can be chosen so that* $P_j(a_1, \ldots, a_{n_j}) \equiv (Ex)(y)R_j(a_1, \ldots, a_{n_j}, x, y) \equiv (x)(Ey)S_j(a_1, \ldots, a_{n_j}, x, y)$ *where* R_j *and* S_j *are primitive recursive* ($j = 0, 1, 2, \ldots$). The hypothesis that the enumeration $F_0, F_1, F_2, \ldots$ is effective can be made exact by requiring, for a suitable Gödel numbering, that the Gödel number of F_k be a general recursive function of k (cf. § 61), or by use of Turing machines in the manner suggested at the end of § 70.

PROOF. Now the class $\hat{a}H(a)$ (cf. the proof of Theorem 35) is recursively enumerable (but not necessarily recursive). However by taking $F_0(a) \equiv (En)F_0(a, n)$ where $F_0(a, n) \equiv$ {a is the Gödel number of a provable formula of the system obtained by adjoining the first n of the formulas F_0 as axioms to the propositional calculus}, and using (17) § 57 (or end § 53), we still have $F_0(a) \equiv (Ey)R(a, y)$ with a recursive R.

The significance of Gödel's completeness theorem and Löwenheim's theorem (including the versions given in § 73) will be discussed in § 75, which may be read without the starred § 74, provided the reader will accept a few plausible statements referring to § 74. In § 76 somewhat more use is made of § 74.

If F is deducible from G in the predicate calculus with a postulated substitution rule (end § 37), then F is valid in every domain in which G is; and hence interdeducible formulas are valid in the same domains. The converse is true when only 0- and 1-place predicate variables occur, by use of theory cited in § 76; but not in general, by Hasenjaeger 1950.

§ 73. The predicate calculus with equality. A treatment of equality may be combined with the predicate calculus by adding to the postulates the following axiom and axiom schema, where x is a variable, A(x) is a formula, and a and b are distinct variables free for x in A(x):

22. $a=a$. 23. $a=b \supset (A(a) \supset A(b))$.

For the *pure predicate calculus with equality*, 'term' shall mean variable, and 'formula' shall have the sense of *equality and predicate letter formula*, which we obtain from 'predicate letter formula' (§ 31) by adding to the definition a clause which states that, if s and t are terms, s=t is a formula. An equality and predicate letter formula containing no predicate letters other than the distinct letters $P_1, \ldots, P_s$ we call a *letter formula in* $=$, $P_1, \ldots, P_s$.

(A) Axiom 22 (which is *100 § 38) and $a=b \supset (a=c \supset b=c)$ (Axiom 16 § 19, which is now an axiom by Axiom Schema 23) we call the *open equality axioms for* $=$. The n following axioms by Schema 23, $a=b \supset (P(a_1, \ldots, a_{i-1}, a, a_{i+1}, \ldots, a_n) \supset P(a_1, \ldots, a_{i-1}, b, a_{i+1}, \ldots, a_n))$ $(i = 1, \ldots, n)$, where P is an n-place predicate letter and $a_1, \ldots, a_{i-1}, a, b, a_{i+1}, \ldots, a_n$ are some $n+1$ distinct variables, we call the *open equality axioms for* P. The *closed equality axioms* are the closures of the respective open equality axioms (with which they are interdeducible, end § 32). By "Eq($=$, $P_1, \ldots, P_s$)" we denote the conjunction of the closed equality axioms for $=$, $P_1, \ldots, P_s$.

EXAMPLE 1. If $\mathcal{A}$ takes two arguments, Eq($=$, $\mathcal{A}$) is the formula

$$\forall a[a=a] \& \forall a\forall b\forall c[a=b \supset (a=c \supset b=c)] \& \forall a\forall b\forall c[a=b \supset (\mathcal{A}(a,c) \supset \mathcal{A}(b,c))] \& \forall a\forall b\forall c[a=b \supset (\mathcal{A}(c,a) \supset \mathcal{A}(c,b))].$$

(B) From the equality axioms for $=$ (Axioms 22 and 16), we can deduce in the predicate calculus the reflexive (*100), symmetric (*101) and transitive (*102) properties of equality, and both the special replacement properties (*108, *109) as in § 38. From any axiom $a=b \supset (A(a) \supset A(b))$ by Schema 23 with A(x) not containing a or b free (in particular, *108, *109 or an equality axiom for a predicate letter P) and *101 we can deduce $a=b \supset (A(a) \sim A(b))$ (as we did in a slightly different format when we inferred *115 and *116 from *108, *109 and *101).

Now and in § 75, when we are dealing with a class of equality and predicate letter formulas containing predicate letters only from a given list, we shall use "Q" to stand for some particular 2-place predicate letter not in the list. Given a formula of the class, call it "E" or "E($=$)", by "E^Q" or "E(Q)" we shall mean the predicate letter formula obtained from it by replacing simultaneously each part of the form s=t where s and t are terms by Q(s, t).

The notions of k-identity and k-equality (§ 36), and of satisfiability and validity in a given non-empty domain, are extended to equality and predicate letter formulas by providing that $a=b$ shall have $\mathfrak{t}$ as value ($\mathfrak{f}$ as value) when a and b assume the same (different) objects from the domain as their values; or if we have first substituted numerals, that $\boldsymbol{a}=\boldsymbol{b}$ have the value $\mathfrak{t}$ or $\mathfrak{f}$ according as $a = b$ or $a \neq b$. Thus a letter formula F in =, $P_1, \ldots, P_s$ will be satisfied by $z_1, \ldots, z_q$, $P_1, \ldots, P_s$, if and only if F^Q is satisfied by $z_1, \ldots, z_q, Q, P_1, \ldots, P_s$ with $Q(a, b) \equiv a=b$.

In Gödel's extension of his completeness theorem to the predicate calculus with equality (1930), it is necessary to allow the alternative that the domain be finite, since e.g. $a \neq b \;\&\; \forall c\,(c=a \vee c=b)$ is satisfiable in and only in a domain of two objects.

THEOREM $39^{(\circ C)}$. *Theorems* 20 (§ 36), 21^C (§ 37), $34^{\circ C}$ *and* $37^{\circ C}$ (§ 72) *and their corollaries hold reading "equality and predicate letter formula", "predicate calculus with equality", "satisfiable (valid, each assignment) in the domain of the natural numbers or a (and every, or a) non-empty finite domain" in place of "predicate letter formula", "predicate calculus", "satisfiable (valid, each assignment) in the domain of the natural numbers", respectively.* (The theorems thus extended we cite using a star "*"; the marks "$^\circ$" and "^{C}" apply to the starred theorem when they apply to the unstarred.)

PROOFS. Theorem 34*. Let F be a letter formula in =, $P_1, \ldots, P_s$ which is irrefutable in the predicate calculus with equality. By (A), $Eq(=, P_1, \ldots, P_s)$ is provable in the predicate calculus with equality. Hence by *45 § 27, F & $Eq(=, P_1, \ldots, P_s)$ is irrefutable in the predicate calculus with equality, a fortiori in the predicate calculus (using equality and predicate letter formulas). Then by Theorem 15 § 34, F^Q & $Eq(Q, P_1, \ldots, P_s)$ is irrefutable in the pure predicate calculus. Hence by Theorem 34, F^Q & $Eq(Q, P_1, \ldots, P_s)$ is satisfiable in the domain of the natural numbers. The proof is completed by (a) of the following lemma.

LEMMA 24^C. (a) *If* F^Q & $Eq(Q, P_1, \ldots, P_s)$ *is satisfiable in a given non-empty domain D, then* F *is satisfiable in a non-empty domain D* with the same or a lesser cardinal number.*

(b) *If* F^Q_k & $Eq(Q, P_{k1}, \ldots, P_{ks_k})$ *where* $P_{k1}, \ldots, P_{ks_k}$ *are the predicate letters of* F_k $(k = 0, 1, 2, \ldots)$ *are jointly satisfiable in a non-empty domain D, then* $F_0, F_1, F_2, \ldots$ *are jointly satisfiable in a domain* D^* *with* $0 < \bar{\bar{D}}^* \leq \bar{\bar{D}}$.

PROOFS. (a) Suppose given a satisfying assignment $z_1, \ldots, z_q, Q, P_1, \ldots, P_s$ for F^Q & $Eq(Q, P_1, \ldots, P_s)$. Then $Q, P_1, \ldots, P_s$ must satisfy the following formulas: (i) $\forall a Q(a, a)$, (ii) $\forall a \forall b[Q(a, b) \supset Q(b, a)]$, (iii) $\forall a \forall b \forall c[Q(a, b) \ \& \ Q(b, c) \supset Q(a, c)]$, (iv) $\forall[Q(a, b) \supset (P_j(a_1, \ldots, a_{i-1}, a, a_{i+1}, \ldots, a_{n_j}) \sim P_j(a_1, \ldots, a_{i-1}, b, a_{i+1}, \ldots, a_{n_j}))]$ $(j = 1, \ldots, s;\ i = 1, \ldots, n_j)$. We see this by paralleling set-theoretically the reasoning given proof-theoretically under (B); or by noting that the conjunction of these formulas is implied by (in fact, is equivalent to) $Eq(Q, P_1, \ldots, P_s)$ in the pure predicate calculus, and using Theorem 21 § 37 and the valuation tables for & and $\supset$ (or $\sim$). (For proving Theorem 34*, this step can be avoided by using this conjunction in place of $Eq(Q, P_1, \ldots, P_s)$.)

From the form of (i) — (iii) and the valuation procedures for $\forall$, $\supset$ and &, we see that the logical function $Q(a, b)$ which fulfils them must be reflexive, symmetric and transitive. (A relation $Q(a, b)$ with these three properties we call an *equivalence relation*.) Hence the domain D falls into *equivalence classes* with respect to the relation Q, i.e. mutually exclusive non-empty classes such that any two members a and b of D belong to the same class, if and only if $Q(a, b)$. Then since the formulas (iv) are satisfied, the value of $P_j(a_1, \ldots, a_{n_j})$ for any j $(j = 1, \ldots, s)$ is unchanged by changing any one of its arguments to another in the same equivalence class.

Now let us take the equivalence classes as a new domain D^* (with $0 < \bar{\bar{D}}^* \leq \bar{\bar{D}}$); and define objects $z_1^*, \ldots, z_q^*$ from D^* and logical functions $Q^*, P_1^*, \ldots, P_s^*$ over D^* thus: z_j^* is the equivalence class to which z_j belongs, i.e. $z_j^* = \hat{b}Q(z_j, b)$; and $Q^*(a^*, b^*)$ $(P_j^*(a_1^*, \ldots, a_{n_j}^*))$ shall have the value which $Q(a, b)$ $(P_j(a_1, \ldots, a_{n_j}))$ takes for any a which $\varepsilon\ a^*$ and $b \ \varepsilon\ b^*$ (for any $a_1 \ \varepsilon\ a_1^*, \ldots, a_{n_j} \ \varepsilon\ a_{n_j}^*$). Then $z_1^*, \ldots, z_q^*, Q^*, P_1^*, \ldots, P_s^*$ satisfy in D^* any formula which $z_1, \ldots, z_q, Q, P_1, \ldots, P_s$ satisfy in D; in particular they satisfy F^Q in D^*. But $Q^*(a^*, b^*) \equiv a^* = b^*$. Hence $z_1^*, \ldots, z_q^*, P_1^*, \ldots, P_s^*$ satisfy F in D^*.

THEOREM $40^{\circ C}$ (= Theorem 38*). *Let one of the predicate letters* $P_0, P_1, P_2, \ldots$ *occurring in* $F_0, F_1, F_2, \ldots$, *say* P_0, *be a 2-place predicate letter. If the enumeration* $F_0, F_1, F_2, \ldots$ *is effective (if infinite), then there are a domain* D^* *and jointly satisfying predicates* $P_0^*, P_1^*, P_2^*, \ldots$ *for Theorem 37* such that: If* D^* *is infinite, and for a suitable enumeration* $s_0, s_1, s_2, \ldots$ *of it* $P_0^*(s_a, s_b) \equiv a' = b$, *then* $P_j^*(s_{a_1}, \ldots, s_{a_{n_j}}) \equiv$

$(Ex)(y)R_j^*(a_1, \ldots, a_{n_j}, x, y) \equiv (x)(Ey)S_j^*(a_1, \ldots, a_{n_j}, x, y)$ *where* R_j^* *and* S_j^* *are primitive recursive* ($j = 1, 2, 3, \ldots$).

PROOF. By Theorem 38, jointly satisfying predicates Q, P_0, P_j for the formulas $\mathrm{F}_k^{\mathrm{Q}}$ & $\mathrm{Eq}(\mathrm{Q}, \mathrm{P}_{k1}, \ldots, \mathrm{P}_{ks_k})$ ($k = 0, 1, 2, \ldots$) can be chosen which are expressible in both the 2-quantifier forms of Theorem V § 57, and hence by Theorem XI § 58 are general recursive in 1-quantifier predicates.

By the definition of the predicates P_j^* in the proof of Lemma 24,

(1) $P_j^*(s_{a_1}, \ldots, s_{a_{n_j}}) \equiv (Ec_1) \ldots (Ec_{n_j})[c_1 \mathcal{E}\, s_{a_1} \;\&\; \ldots \;\&\; c_{n_j} \mathcal{E}\, s_{a_{n_j}} \;\&$ $P_j(c_1, \ldots, c_{n_j})] \equiv (c_1) \ldots (c_{n_j})[c_1 \mathcal{E}\, s_{a_1} \;\&\; \ldots \;\&\; c_{n_j} \mathcal{E}\, s_{a_{n_j}} \rightarrow P_j(c_1, \ldots, c_{n_j})]$.

Let z be some member of s_0 (which is not empty); then $s_0 = \hat{c}Q(z, c)$. By the definition of P_0^*, $P_0(d, c)$ holds if and only if $P_0^*(d^*, c^*)$ where d^* and c^* are the equivalence classes to which d and c, respectively, belong. But by hypothesis, $P_0^*(s_a, s_b) \equiv a'=b$. Hence if $d \mathcal{E}\, s_a$, then $c \mathcal{E}\, s_{a'}$ if and only if $P_0(d, c)$. Since no s_a is empty, $(a)(Ed)[d \mathcal{E}\, s_a]$. Thus

$$(2) \quad \begin{cases} c \mathcal{E}\, s_0 \equiv Q(z, c), \\ c \mathcal{E}\, s_{a'} \equiv (Ed)[d \mathcal{E}\, s_a \;\&\; P_0(d, c)] \equiv (d)[d \mathcal{E}\, s_a \rightarrow P_0(d, c)]. \end{cases}$$

Applying Theorem VI* § 57 or XI* § 58 to the second line, this shows that the predicate $c \mathcal{E}\, s_a$ is general recursive in Q, P_0. In more detail: Consider the second line of (2) as of the form

$$H(c) \equiv (Ed)[K(d) \;\&\; P_0(d, c)] \equiv (d)[K(d) \rightarrow P_0(d, c)].$$

Let q, k, p, h, f be function letters expressing the representing functions of $Q, K, P_0, H, c \mathcal{E}\, s_a$, respectively. By Theorem VI* or XI*, $H(c)$ is general recursive (uniformly) in $K(d)$, $P_0(d, c)$, i.e. there is a system of equations (containing k, p, h) defining recursively (the representing function of) $H(c)$ from (those of) $K(d)$, $P_0(d, c)$. By Lemma VI § 65, we can introduce a parameter to obtain equations E defining recursively $H(c, a)$ from $K(d, a)$, $P_0(d, c)$. Then E with the three equations $\mathrm{f(c, 0)=q}(\boldsymbol{z}, \mathrm{c})$, $\mathrm{k(d, a)=f(d, a)}$, $\mathrm{f(c, a')=h(c, a)}$ defines $c \mathcal{E}\, s_a$ recursively from Q, P_0, as we see with the help of induction on a.

Since Q, P_0 are in turn general recursive in 1-quantifier predicates, so is $c \mathcal{E}\, s_a$; and hence by Theorem XI, $c \mathcal{E}\, s_a$ is expressible in both the 2-quantifier forms.

Using the $(Ex)(y)$-expressions for $c \mathcal{E}\, s_a$ and $P_j(c_1, \ldots, c_{n_j})$ in the middle expression of (1), advancing the quantifiers (by the informal analogs of *91 and *87 § 35), and contracting (by (17) § 57), we obtain an $(Ex)(y)$-expression for $P_j^*(s_{a_1}, \ldots, s_{a_{n_j}})$. An $(x)(Ey)$-expression is obtained similarly, using instead the $(x)(Ey)$-expression for $P_j(c_1, \ldots, c_{n_j})$ and the right member of (1) (and applying *91, *96, *95 *87, *98, *97, (17), (18)).

We now consider also *applied predicate calculi with equality*, in which the terms and formulas are constructed using the logical symbolism of the predicate calculus with certain individual symbols $e_1, \ldots, e_q$, function symbols $f_1, \ldots, f_r$ and predicate symbols $=$, $P_1, \ldots, P_s$ (but no predicate letters). The number-theoretic definitions of 'term' and 'formula' (§ 17) provide an example (with $q = 1$, $r = 3$, $s = 0$). Although commonly each function or predicate symbol takes a number $n \geq 1$ of arguments, we may allow $n \geq 0$, in which case individual symbols may be included among the function symbols, and proposition symbols among the predicate symbols. We shall write e.g. "f(s, t)" for the term constructed by placing terms s and t in the respective argument positions of a 2-place function symbol f, even though in a given system some other manner of combining the symbols may be used, e.g. "f" may stand for $+$ and "f(s, t)" for s+t.

The predicate calculus with equality is dealt with at length in Hilbert-Bernays 1934 pp. 164 ff.

We shall see (Theorem 41 (b)) that in an applied predicate calculus with equality, Axiom Schema 23 is replaceable by a finite list of particular axioms without changing the provability and deducibility notions. The idea has already been used in setting up the number-theoretic system without Axiom Schema 23; in that case the particular axioms which replace Schema 23 did not appear as postulates except Axioms 16 and 17, since the rest were deducible from the other number-theoretic axioms.

(C) For the applied case, we read "predicate symbol P other than =" in place of "predicate letter" in (A). The *open equality axioms for* an n-place function symbol f shall be the n formulas
$a=b \supset f(a_1, \ldots, a_{i-1}, a, a_{i+1}, \ldots, a_n)=f(a_1, \ldots, a_{i-1}, b, a_{i+1}, \ldots, a_n)$ $(i = 1, \ldots, n)$. These are deducible in the predicate calculus from Axiom 22 and axioms by Axiom Schema 23; e.g. (with $n = 2$), $a=b \supset f(a, c)=f(b, c)$ is deducible by *3 and $\supset$-elim. from
$a=b \supset (f(a, c)=f(a, c) \supset f(a, c)=f(b, c))$, which is an axiom by Axiom Schema 23, and $f(a, c)=f(a, c)$, which is deducible by substitution from Axiom 22. Except in the case of $=$, the open equality axioms for a symbol are what we previously called the special replacement properties (cf. Theorem 23 § 38). We use "$Eq(=, P_1, \ldots, P_s, f_1, \ldots, f_r)$" for the conjunction of the closed equality axioms for $=$, $P_1, \ldots, P_s, f_1, \ldots, f_r$.

(D) Given the equality axioms for $=$, $P_1, \ldots, P_s$, $f_1, \ldots, f_r$, we can use the results of (B) and the former method of proof to establish Theorem 24 and its corollaries for the case the part r which is replaced does not stand within the scope of any predicate symbol or letter, or function symbol, other than $=$, $P_1, \ldots, P_s$, $f_1, \ldots, f_r$.

(E) In any system in which Theorem 24 holds under the restriction just stated, every axiom by Axiom Schema 23 containing only the predicate symbols or letters $=$, $P_1, \ldots, P_s$ and the function symbols $f_1, \ldots, f_r$ is provable. For under the stipulations for the schema, by applications of Theorem 24 which replace by b each occurrence of a in A(a) which entered by substitution for x in A(x), we obtain $a=b \vdash A(a) \sim A(b)$ with no variables varied. Thence by *17a and $\supset$-introd., $\vdash a=b \supset (A(a) \supset A(b))$.

THEOREM 41. (a) *In the predicate calculus with equality, the reflexive* (*100), *symmetric* (*101), *transitive* (*102) *and replacement* (*Theorem* 24 *and corollaries*) *properties of equality hold.*

(b) $\Gamma \vdash E$ *in the applied predicate calculus with equality having* $=, P_1, \ldots, P_s, f_1, \ldots, f_r$ *as its predicate and function symbols, if and only if* Γ, Eq($=, P_1, \ldots, P_s, f_1, \ldots, f_r$) $\vdash E$ *in the predicate calculus.*

(c) $\Gamma \vdash E$ *in the pure predicate calculus with equality, when* Γ, E *are letter formulas in* $=, P_1, \ldots, P_s$; *if and only if* Γ, Eq($=, P_1, \ldots, P_s$) $\vdash E$ *in the predicate calculus.*

PROOFS. (a) By (A) — (D).

(b) By (A) — (E).

(c) Similarly, if we can first exclude the possibility that the deduction $\Gamma \vdash E$ requires axioms by Axiom Schema 23 containing other predicate letters $P_{s+1}, \ldots, P_{s+t}$ besides $P_1, \ldots, P_s$. The deduction $\Gamma \vdash E$ is a deduction in the predicate calculus of E from Γ, $a=a$ and axioms by Axiom Schema 23. By the method of Remark 1 § 34, we can thence obtain a deduction of E from Γ, $a=a$ and axioms by Axiom Schema 23 which contain only the predicate letters $P_1, \ldots, P_s$.

EXAMPLE 2. As a fifth example for the Converse of Thesis II § 60, for a primitive recursive $R(x, y)$ (cf. Example 1 § 60), let $\varphi_1, \ldots, \varphi_k$ be a primitive recursive description of the representing function φ ($= \varphi_k$) of R. Let $f_1, \ldots, f_k$ be distinct function symbols (to express $\varphi_1, \ldots, \varphi_k$, respectively). Let the terms and formulas of S be constructed using the logical symbolism of the predicate calculus with the individual symbol 0, the function symbols $'$, $f_1, \ldots, f_k$ and the predicate symbol $=$. Let S

have the postulates of the predicate calculus and as particular axioms the equations obtained by translating the schema applications for the description $\varphi_1, \ldots, \varphi_k$ (as Example 1 § 44 was translated to get Example 3 § 54, but with $l = 0$), together with the open equality axioms for $=$, $'$, $f_1, \ldots, f_k$. Let $A(\mathbf{x})$ be the formula $\exists y f_k(\mathbf{x}, y)=0$. In S the substitution rule R1 of § 54 holds as a derived rule (by § 23), and likewise the replacement rule R2 (by Theorem 41 (a) and (b)). Hence if, for some y, $R(x, y)$ is true, i.e. $\varphi_k(x, y) = 0$, then $f_k(\mathbf{x}, \mathbf{y})=0$ is provable in S, and by $\exists$-introd., so is $A(\mathbf{x})$. Conversely, $A(\mathbf{x})$ is provable in S only if $(Ey)R(x, y)$, as will be shown in Theorem 52 § 79.

***§ 74. Eliminability of descriptive definitions.** At various stages in the informal development of a mathematical theory additions may be made to the stock of concepts and notations. If the development is formalized, at the corresponding stages new formation rules and postulates are added to a given formal system S_1 to obtain another S_2. Thus the formulas (provable formulas) of S_1 become a subset of those of S_2. The new formation rules introduce new formal symbols or notations, and the new postulates provide for their use deductively. We shall write "$\vdash_1$" ("$\vdash_2$") for the deducibility relation in S_1 (in S_2).

Under such circumstances, we say that the new notations or symbols (with their postulates) are *eliminable* (*from S_2 in S_1*), if there is an effective process by which, given any formula E of S_2, a formula E′ of S_1 can be found, such that:

(I) *If* E *is a formula of* S_1, *then* E′ *is* E.

(II) $\vdash_2 E \sim E'$.

(III) *If* $\Gamma \vdash_2 E$, *then* $\Gamma' \vdash_1 E'$.

Here Γ' is $D_1', \ldots, D_l'$, if Γ is $D_1, \ldots, D_l$. We call (I) — (III) the *elimination relations*. (In Example 13, slight modifications are called for in our formulation of "eliminability".)

When the elimination relations hold, then furthermore:

(IV) $\Gamma \vdash_2 E$, *if and only if* $\Gamma' \vdash_1 E'$.

(V) *If* Γ, E *are formulas of* S_1, *then* $\Gamma \vdash_2 E$ *if and only if* $\Gamma \vdash_1 E$.

PROOFS. (IV) For conversely to (III): If $\Gamma' \vdash_1 E'$, then a fortiori $\Gamma' \vdash_2 E'$; thence by (II), $\Gamma \vdash_2 E$.

(V) By (I) with (III) or (IV).

Thus an eliminable extension of S_1 to obtain S_2 is inessential, in that by (V) it gives no enlargement of the class of the original formulas which are provable, while by (II) any new formula is equivalent in the enlarged system to one of the original formulas.

EXAMPLE 1. ELIMINABILITY OF EXPLICIT DEFINITIONS. In studying our formal system, we regarded $\sim$, 1, $<$, $\exists!$x, x^2, etc. as merely abbreviations in the presentation of the metamathematics (cf. end § 17). Alternatively, we could have treated them as successive additions to the formal symbolism. In this case, each time we should have added a new formation rule (if A and B are *formulas*, so is A $\sim$ B; 1 is a *term*; if s and t are terms, s$<$t is a *formula*; if x is a variable and A(x) is a *formula*, $\exists!$xA(x) is a *formula*; if s is a *term*, s^2 is a *term*; respectively), and a defining axiom or axiom schema
$(\{(A \sim B) \supset (A \supset B) \& (B \supset A)\} \& \{(A \supset B) \& (B \supset A) \supset (A \sim B)\}$, $1=0'$, $a<b \sim \exists c(c'+a=b)$, $\exists!xA(x) \sim \exists x[A(x) \& \forall y(A(y) \supset x=y)]$, $a^2=a \cdot a$, respectively, with appropriate stipulations about A, B, x, A(x), y). These additions are eliminable, with ′ the operation previously regarded as unabbreviation. Generally this is the case under the following conditions (briefly stated). The defining axiom or schema is an equivalence (an equation). Then S_1 shall be the predicate calculus (the predicate calculus with equality) and possibly additional particular axioms and axiom schemata. Theorem 14 § 33 (Theorem 24 (b) § 38) is used in proving (II). The two conventions for "permanent abbreviations" end § 33 shall apply; the first of these is used in treating the case for Rules 9 and 12 in proving (III), and the second for Axiom Schemata 10 and 11, and an additional convention can be adopted to fix which bound varables are used in the E′ for each E. For each additional axiom schema, whenever A is an axiom of S_2 by it, A′ must be provable in S_1.

EXAMPLE 2. Let S_2 be our system of the classical predicate calculus with the addition of Axiom Schema 9a of Lemma 11 § 24, which by *95 § 35 is redundant in S_2. (An axiom or axiom schema or several such are ***redundant*** in a formal system S, if the axioms involved are all provable in the system left after omitting those axiom(s) or axiom schema(ta) as postulates.) Let S_1 be what remains from S_2 when &, $\vee$, $\exists$ and their postulates are omitted. Then the elimination relations hold, when ′ is the replacement of &, $\vee$ and $\exists$ by the equivalents given by *60 and *61 § 27 and *83 § 35. (In treating the case for Axiom Schema 6 in the proof of (III), assume $A \supset C$, $B \supset C$, $\neg A \supset B$ and $\neg C$, and deduce both B and $\neg B$ with the help of *12. Then use $\neg$-introd. and elim., and $\supset$-introd.)

EXAMPLE 3. In our number-theoretic system, $\vdash \neg A \sim A \supset 1=0$. This enables $\neg$ to be eliminated, if (redundant) postulates 8′ (or $8^{I\prime}$) and 15′ are first added, where 8′ is $((A \supset 1=0) \supset 1=0) \supset A$, etc. (But 1b includes 7′.)

An elimination theorem can be looked upon as a new sort of derived rule (§ 20) for the study of the original system S_1. It enables us, when our purpose is to establish the provability of a formula E in S_1, to undertake instead to prove E in a suitable system S_2 having more machinery than S_1. Also by it any formula E not of S_1 which we prove in S_2 can be construed as an abbreviation for a provable formula E′ of S_1.

An elimination theorem has as corollaries that the simple consistency of S_2 is implied by that of S_1 (using (V), cf. § 28) and the decision problem for S_2 is reduced to that for S_1 (by (IV), cf. § 30, end § 61).

EXAMPLE 4. NON-ELIMINABILITY OF THE RECURSIVE DEFINITION OF $\cdot$. The function symbol $\cdot$ with its recursion equations (Axioms 20 and 21) is not eliminable from the formalism of Chapter IV, call that S_2. For by Presburger's result (beginning § 42) the remaining system S_1 is simply consistent and its decision problem is solvable. If $\cdot$ were eliminable, the same would be true of S_2, contradicting Theorem 33 § 61.

ELIMINABILITY OF DESCRIPTIVE DEFINITIONS. In a descriptive definition, an object f is defined as the w such that $F(w)$ (in symbols, $\iota w F(w)$), where F is a predicate for which it is known that there is a unique w such that $F(w)$ (in symbols, $(E!w)F(w)$). If w is the only independent variable for F, then $\iota w F(w)$ is an individual f. If F depends on n other individual variables, write it "$F(x_1, \ldots, x_n, w)$", then $\iota w F(x_1, \ldots, x_n, w)$ is a function $f(x_1, \ldots, x_n)$. We shall include the first case in the second by considering an individual as a function of 0 variables (accordingly, we take 'function symbol' to include 'individual symbol' in this section).

The logic of descriptive definitions was treated by Whitehead and Russell 1910 (pp. 30—32, 66—71, 173—186 in the 2nd ed. 1925).

Their eliminability was established by Hilbert and Bernays 1934 pp. 422—457. Another proof was indicated by Rosser 1939. These proofs establish the eliminability of ιw as a formal operator, the admission of which into a given formalism introduces all the possibilities for descriptive definitions at once. Notationally it is simpler to use function symbols. A mathematician developing a theory will ordinarily introduce new function symbols successively as the need for them arises. We shall establish the eliminability of function symbols introduced in this manner.

It suffices to consider the introduction of one new function symbol at a time.

THEOREM 42. *Let S_1 have the formation rules of an applied predicate calculus with equality* (§ 73), *and let the postulates of S_1 be those of the predicate calculus with additional particular axioms and axiom schemata such that the equality axioms for the function and predicate symbols of S_1 are provable (or let S_1 be simply an applied predicate calculus with equality and possibly additional particular axioms and axiom schemata).*

Let $x_1, \ldots, x_n, w$ $(n \geq 0)$ *be distinct variables, and* $F(x_1, \ldots, x_n, w)$ *be a formula which contains free only* $x_1, \ldots, x_n, w$, *and in which* $x_1, \ldots, x_n$ *are free for* w. *Suppose that*

(i) $$\exists! w F(x_1, \ldots, x_n, w)$$

is provable in S_1.

Let S_2 be obtained from S_1 by adjoining a new n-place function symbol f *and the new axiom*

(ii) $$F(x_1, \ldots, x_n, f(x_1, \ldots, x_n)).$$

Then the new function symbol f *and its axiom are eliminable, i.e.* (I) — (III) (and hence (IV) and (V)) *hold for a certain effective correlation* ′ (which will be specified in the proof), *provided each of the additional axiom schemata has the property that, if* E *is an axiom of S_2 by it, then* E′ *is provable in S_1.*

PROOF is provided by Lemmas 25 — 31. By Theorem 41 (b), it is immaterial whether we consider the logic to be the predicate calculus or the predicate calculus with equality, when we know the equality axioms for the function and predicate symbols to be provable. Hence from the outset this is immaterial in the case of S_1, and it will be in the case of S_2 as soon as we learn (in Lemma 27) that the equality axioms for the new function symbol f are provable in S_2.

LEMMA 25. *In the predicate calculus with equality, if* u, v *and* x *are distinct variables,* F(v), C(v), C(u, v), A, B, A(v), B(v) *and* A(x, v) *are formulas,* u *is free for* v *in* F(v) *and* C(u, v), A *and* B *do not contain* v *free, and* F(v) *does not contain* u *or* x *free*:

*181. $\exists! v F(v) \vdash \exists v[F(v) \& C(v)] \sim \forall v[F(v) \supset C(v)]$.

*182. $\exists! v F(v),\ C(v) \vdash^{v} \exists v[F(v) \& C(v)]$.

*183. $\exists! v F(v) \vdash \exists u[F(u) \& C(u, u)] \sim \exists u[F(u) \& \exists v[F(v) \& C(u, v)]]$.

*184. $\exists! v F(v) \vdash \exists v[F(v) \& (A \supset B(v))] \sim A \supset \exists v[F(v) \& B(v)]$.

*185. $\exists! v F(v) \vdash \exists v[F(v) \& (A(v) \supset B)] \sim \exists v[F(v) \& A(v)] \supset B$.

$*186.$ $\quad\vdash \exists v[F(v) \& A \& B(v)] \sim A \& \exists v[F(v) \& B(v)].$

$*187.$ $\quad\exists!vF(v) \vdash \exists v[F(v) \& (A \vee B(v))] \sim A \vee \exists v[F(v) \& B(v)].$

$*188.$ $\quad\exists!vF(v) \vdash \exists v[F(v) \& \neg A(v)] \sim \neg\exists v[F(v) \& A(v)].$

$*189.$ $\quad\exists!vF(v) \vdash \exists v[F(v) \& \forall xA(x, v)] \sim \forall x\exists v[F(v) \& A(x, v)].$

$*190.$ $\quad\vdash \exists v[F(v) \& \exists xA(x, v)] \sim \exists x\exists v[F(v) \& A(x, v)].$

(Cf. David Nelson 1947 Lemma 23 pp. 347—348.)

PROOFS. *181. Assume $\exists!vF(v)$, $F(v) \& C(v)$ (for $\exists$-elim.) and $F(t)$ where t is a new variable (for $\supset$-introd.). Then using *172 § 41, $v=t$; and hence by replacement, $C(t)$. By $\supset$- and $\forall$-introd. and change of bound variables, $\forall v[F(v) \supset C(v)]$. The variable of the $\forall$-introd. was t, so no variable has been varied. By $\exists$-elim. and $\supset$-introd., $\exists v[F(v) \& C(v)] \supset \forall v[F(v) \supset C(v)]$. For the converse, assume $\exists!vF(v)$ and $\forall v[F(v) \supset C(v)]$. From $\exists!vF(v)$, we get $\exists vF(v)$. Preparatory to $\exists$-elim., assume $F(v)$.

*183. $\exists u[F(u) \& C(u, u)] \vdash \exists u[F(u) \& F(u) \& C(u, u)]$ (*37 § 27) $\vdash \exists u\exists v[F(u) \& F(v) \& C(u, v)]$ (*80 § 35) $\vdash \exists u[F(u) \& \exists y[F(v) \& C(u, v)]]$ (*91). The converse can be based similarly on *79, with help from *181, *4 § 26 (with *69 § 32), etc.

*184. $\exists!vF(v) \vdash \exists v[F(v) \& (A \supset B(v))] \sim \forall v[F(v) \supset (A \supset B(v))]$ (*181) $\sim \forall v[A \supset (F(v) \supset B(v))]$ (since using *3, $\vdash B \supset (A \supset C) \sim A \supset (B \supset C)$) $\sim A \supset \forall v[F(v) \supset B(v)]$ (*95) $\sim A \supset \exists v[F(v) \& B(v)]$ (*181).

*187. $\exists!vF(v) \vdash \exists vF(v) \vdash \exists v[F(v) \& (A \vee B(v))] \sim \exists v[(F(v) \& A) \vee (F(v) \& B(v))]$ (*35) $\sim (A \& \exists vF(v)) \vee \exists v[F(v) \& B(v)]$ (*88, *91 with *33) $\sim A \vee \exists v[F(v) \& B(v)]$ (*45).

*188. Use successively *181, *58b, *86.

LEMMA 26. *In the predicate calculus with the equality axioms for the function and predicate symbols of S_1 only but with* f *admitted to the symbolism (a fortiori, in the predicate calculus with equality), the conjunction of* (i) *and* (ii) *is interdeducible with*

$$\text{(iii)} \qquad f(x_1, \ldots, x_n)=w \sim F(x_1, \ldots, x_n, w).$$

Hence (iii) *is provable in S_2.*

PROOF. From (ii) and $f(x_1, \ldots, x_n)=w$, we deduce $F(x_1, \ldots, x_n, w)$ by the replacement property of equality, which by (D) § 73 requires only the predicate calculus with the equality axioms for $=$ and the function and predicate symbols of $F(x_1, \ldots, x_n, w)$. From (i), (ii) and $F(x_1, \ldots, x_n, w)$, we deduce $f(x_1, \ldots, x_n)=w$ by *172. From (iii), we deduce (i) with the help of *171, and (ii) by substituting $f(x_1, \ldots, x_n)$ for w in (iii) and using Axiom 22 § 73.

For the rest of the proof of Theorem 42, we shall use "$F(x_1, \ldots, x_n, w)$" under the convention which applies to permanent abbreviations (cf. end § 33) that, for any terms $t_1, \ldots, t_n$, s, "$F(t_1, \ldots, t_n, s)$" shall denote the result of substituting $t_1, \ldots, t_n$, s for $x_1, \ldots, x_n$, w in $F(x_1, \ldots, x_n, w)$ after any legitimate change of bound variables in $F(x_1, \ldots, x_n, w)$ which makes the substitution free.

LEMMA 27. *In the system of Lemma* 26, *the equality axioms for* f *are deducible from* (iii). *Hence they are provable in* S_2.

Were this not so, adding only (ii) to the axioms of S_1 would not give effective use of f in S_2 (cf. Theorem 41 (a) and (b)).

PROOF. For example, if $n = 2$ (and writing a, c for x_1, x_2), we can prove $a=b \supset f(a, c)=f(b, c)$ thus. Assume $a=b$. By replacement, $F(a, c, f(b, c)) \sim F(b, c, f(b, c))$. Thence using (iii), $f(a, c)=f(b, c) \sim f(b, c)=f(b, c)$; whence (Axiom 22 and *18b), $f(a, c)=f(b, c)$.

LEMMA 28. *Let* $t_1, \ldots, t_n$ *be terms,* v *be a variable not occurring in* $t_1, \ldots, t_n$, *and* C(v) *be a formula in which* $f(t_1, \ldots, t_n)$ *is free for* v. *Then* $C(f(t_1, \ldots, t_n)) \sim \exists v[F(t_1, \ldots, t_n, v) \,\&\, C(v)]$ *is deducible from* (iii) *in the predicate calculus with equality, and hence is provable in* S_2.

PROOF. Assume $C(f(t_1, \ldots, t_n))$. Substituting in (ii) (cf. Lemma 26), $F(t_1, \ldots, t_n, f(t_1, \ldots, t_n))$. Now use &-, ∃- and ⊃-introd. Conversely, assume (for ∃-elim.) $F(t_1, \ldots, t_n, v) \,\&\, C(v)$. Using (iii), $f(t_1, \ldots, t_n)=v$. By replacement in C(v), $C(f(t_1, \ldots, t_n))$.

A *prime* formula is one containing no logical symbol, i.e. here it is a predicate symbol with terms as arguments. A term or formula of S_1, i.e. one not containing f, we call f-*less*. A term of the form $f(t_1, \ldots, t_n)$ where $t_1, \ldots, t_n$ are terms we call an f-*term*; and if $t_1, \ldots, t_n$ are f-less, we say it is a *plain* f-term. An occurrence of a term in a formula is *bound* (*free*), if it is (is not) within the scope of some (any) quantifier ∀y or ∃y where y is a variable of the term.

EXAMPLE 5. Let P and Q be predicate symbols, g be a function symbol distinct from f, and x and y be distinct variables. In the following formula, the second occurrence of an f-term is bound; the other six are free.

1. $\forall x\{P(f(y), f(g(x))) \,\&\, Q(x, x)\}$
$\supset P(f(y), f(g(f(y)))) \,\&\, Q(f(y), f(y))$.

The f-terms f(y) and f(g(x)) are plain, but f(g(f(y))) is not, as the f-term f(y) is nested within it.

LEMMA 29. *There can be correlated effectively to each formula* E *of* S_2 *a formula* E′ *of* S_1 (called the *principal* f-*less transform of* E) *in such a way that* (I) *and* (II) *hold, no free variables are introduced or removed, and the operators of the predicate calculus are preserved, i.e.* (A ⊃ B)′ *is* A′ ⊃ B′, (A & B)′ *is* A′ & B′, (A ∨ B)′ *is* A′ ∨ B′, (¬A)′ *is* ¬A′, (∀xA(x))′ *is* ∀xA′(x) (*where* A′(x) *is* (A(x))′) *and* (∃xA(x))′ *is* ∃xA′(x).

PROOF. The condition that the operators are preserved defines E′ by recursion on the number g of occurrences of logical symbols in E, provided we supply as basis a definition of E′ for the case E is prime. We do this by induction on the number q of occurrences of f-terms in E, thus.

If $g = q = 0$, E′ shall be E.

If $g = 0$ and $q > 0$, select the first occurrence of a plain f-term in E, say it is $f(t_1, \ldots, t_n)$. Let v be a variable which does not occur in E. Let C(v) result from E by changing the occurrence of $f(t_1, \ldots, t_n)$ under consideration to v. Then E′ shall be $\exists v[F(t_1, \ldots, t_n, v) \& C'(v)]$. (By *181, we could equally well use $\forall v[F(t_1, \ldots, t_n, v) \supset C'(v)]$.) There is an ambiguity here regarding the choice of the bound variable v and the manner in which the bound variables of $F(x_1, \ldots, x_n, w)$ are changed when necessary to make the substitution of $t_1, \ldots, t_n$, v for $x_1, \ldots, x_n$, w free. But different legitimate choices lead to congruent formulas (§ 33). We may suppose some convention supplied to fix which one is E′ itself. In our illustrations, it will suffice to use any congruent of E′. Note that C(v) is prime and contains just q—1 occurrences of f-terms.

The properties of ′ mentioned in the lemma follow by a corresponding induction on g (using Theorem 14 § 33 for (II)), with induction on q within the basis (using Lemma 28).

A suggestive abbreviation is to write "$F_v^{t_1,\ldots,t_n} C(v)$" for

$$\exists v[F(t_1, \ldots, t_n, v) \& C(v)].$$

EXAMPLE 5 (continued). Formula 1 is reduced to a congruent of its principal f-less transform thus.

2. $\forall x\{F_{v_2}^{y} P(v_2, f(g(x))) \& Q(x, x)\}$
$\supset F_{v_2}^{y} P(v_2, f(g(f(y)))) \& F_{v_{12}}^{y} Q(v_{12}, f(y))$.

3. $\forall x\{F_{v_2}^{y} F_{v_3}^{g(x)} P(v_2, v_3) \& Q(x, x)\}$
$\supset F_{v_2}^{y} F_{v_{11}}^{y} P(v_2, f(g(v_{11}))) \& F_{v_{12}}^{y} F_{v_{13}}^{y} Q(v_{12}, v_{13})$.

4. $\forall x\{F_{v_2}^{y} F_{v_3}^{g(x)} P(v_2, v_3) \& Q(x, x)\}$
$\supset F_{v_2}^{y} F_{v_{11}}^{y} F_{v_3}^{g(v_{11})} P(v_2, v_3) \& F_{v_{12}}^{y} F_{v_{13}}^{y} Q(v_{12}, v_{13})$.

Let us call the prefixes $F_v^{t_1,\ldots,t_n}$ "F-quantifiers". By *184—*190 (since (i) gives us the assumption formulas $\exists!vF(v)$), F-quantifiers can be permuted in S_1 with the operators of the predicate calculus and with each other (changing bound variables as necessary), subject to the restriction that $F_v^{t_1,\ldots,t_n}$ may not be advanced (leftward) over an ordinary or F-quantifier which binds any variable of $t_1, \ldots, t_n$ (since for *189 and *190 the F(v) must not contain the x free). This restriction as between two F-quantifiers means simply that two F-quantifiers which result from eliminating f-terms one nested within the other must be kept always in the same relative order (the one corresponding to the inner f-term being to the left). As between an F- and an ordinary quantifier, it means that an F-quantifier resulting from the elimination of a bound occurrence of an f-term may be advanced leftward only up to the rightmost of the ordinary quantifiers which bound the occurrence.

Moreover by *183, adjacent like F-quantifiers $F_u^{t_1,\ldots,t_n}$ and $F_v^{t_1,\ldots,t_n}$ can be contracted.

Also *182 constitutes an introduction rule for F-quantifiers.

Example 5 (concluded). Formula 1 is an axiom $\forall xA(x) \supset A(t)$ of S_2 by Axiom Schema 10, with f(y) as the t; and we chose the same bound variables in eliminating corresponding f-terms of A(x) and A(t) in the reduction to Formula 4. Now by *186, *190, *186 (with *33), *184 and *183 (with a change of bound variables), we can advance the three F-quantifiers $F_{v_{11}}^y$, $F_{v_{12}}^y$, $F_{v_{13}}^y$ resulting from the elimination of the three occurrences of f(y) as the t of the schema application to the front, and contract them to one F-quantifier $F_{v_1}^y$. This gives us the following formula, as an equivalent in S_1 of Formula 4 and hence of the principal f-less transform of Formula 1.

$$5. \quad F_{v_1}^y[\forall x\{F_{v_2}^y F_{v_3}^{g(x)} P(v_2, v_3) \& Q(x, x)\} \\ \supset F_{v_2}^y F_{v_3}^{g(v_1)} P(v_2, v_3) \& Q(v_1, v_1)].$$

Now the scope of $F_{v_1}^y$ in 5 is an axiom of S_1 by Axiom Schema 10, with v_1 as the t. So by F-introd. (*182), Formula 5 is provable in S_1, and hence also the principal f-less transform of Formula 1.

Lemma 30. *If* E *is an axiom of* S_2, *then* $\vdash_1$ E′.

Proof. If E is an axiom of S_2 by any axiom schema of the propositional calculus, then E′ is an axiom of S_1 by the same schema, since ′ preserves the operators of the calculus (Lemma 29).

Axiom Schema 10: E is $\forall xA(x) \supset A(t)$, where t is free for x in A(x).

CASE 1: t is f-less. Then by choosing the same bound variables for corresponding steps in the reductions of A(x) and A(t), we can obtain a congruent of E′ which is of the form $\forall x B(x) \supset B(t)$ where t is free for x in B(x). This is an axiom of S_1 by Axiom Schema 10, with the same t. Hence $\vdash_1$ E′.

EXAMPLE 6. Let E be

$$\forall x\{P(f(y), f(g(x))) \;\&\; Q(x, x)\} \supset P(f(y), f(g(t))) \;\&\; Q(t, t),$$

where t is f-less. Then

$$\forall x\{F^{y}_{v_1} F^{g(x)}_{v_2} P(v_1, v_2) \;\&\; Q(x, x)\} \supset F^{y}_{v_1} F^{g(t)}_{v_2} P(v_1, v_2) \;\&\; Q(t, t)$$

is congruent to E′, and is an axiom of S_1 by Axiom Schema 10.

CASE 2: the general case. Say that A(x) contains k occurrences of f-terms and l free occurrences of x, and that t contains m occurrences of f-terms. (Illustrated with $k = 2$, $l = 3$, $m = 1$ by Example 5.) Then A(t) contains k occurrences of f-terms which originate from A(x) and thus correspond to the f-terms of A(x), and lm others consisting of m in each of the l occurrences of t which take the place of the free occurrences of x in A(x). In the reduction of E to a congruent of E′, we can use F-quantifiers with the same bound variable in eliminating each of the k pairs of corresponding f-term occurrences from A(x) and A(t), and F-quantifiers with other distinct bound variables in eliminating from A(t) the lm f-term occurrences in the t's. Say that in the elimination, these l occurrences of t become $t^*_1, \ldots, t^*_l$ (v_{11}, v_{12}, v_{13} in the example). Since none of the k f-term occurrences in A(t) which originate from A(x) can be nested within any of the lm which enter by the substitution of t for x, and since the substitution is free, the lm F-quantifiers used in eliminating the latter can be advanced to the front, and in such an order that each group of l of them belonging to corresponding f-term occurrences in the l occurrences of t are adjacent, after which each group can be contracted. We thus obtain as an equivalent in S_1 of E′ a formula of the form

$$\text{(A)} \qquad F^{s_{11}, \ldots, s_{1n}}_{v_1} \ldots F^{s_{m1}, \ldots, s_{mn}}_{v_m}[\forall x B(x) \supset B(t^*)],$$

where t^* results from each of $t^*_1, \ldots, t^*_l$ by the identification of variables in the contraction, and is free for x in B(x). Now $\forall x B(x) \supset B(t^*)$ is an axiom of S_1 by Axiom Schema 10, and (A) is provable thence by m applications of F-introd. (*182).

AXIOM (ii): E is $F(x_1, \ldots, x_n, f(x_1, \ldots, x_n))$. Suppose w occurs free l times in $F(x_1, \ldots, x_n, w)$. Then E′ contains l F-quantifiers. These can be advanced and contracted to give $F^{x_1, \ldots, x_n}_{v} F(x_1, \ldots, x_n, v)$, i.e. $\exists v\{F(x_1, \ldots, x_n, v) \;\&\; F(x_1, \ldots, x_n, v)\}$, which is provable from (i).

LEMMA 31. *If* E *is an immediate consequence of* F (*of* F *and* G) *in* S_2, *then* E′ *is an immediate consequence of* F′ (*of* F′ *and* G′) *in* S_1.

For each of Rules 2, 9 and 12, because ′ preserves the operators, and does not introduce free variables (so that the C of Rule 9 or 12 is not transformed into a formula C′ containing x free).

REMARK 1. If f is not 0 or ′, the induction schema satisfies the proviso of the theorem for additional axiom schemata, as is seen by the reasoning used for Axiom Schema 10 Case 1.

EXAMPLE 7. Let S_1 be the number-theoretic system of Chapter IV. Let S_2 result from S_1 by adjoining the function symbol rm (to express the remainder function) with the axiom

$$\exists q(a=bq+\mathrm{rm}(a, b) \ \& \ \mathrm{rm}(a, b)<b) \vee (b=0 \ \& \ \mathrm{rm}(a, b)=a)$$

(cf. *179b, c § 41). Then by the theorem (together with Remark 1), rm and its axiom are eliminable. — Let the notation $[a/b]$ for the quotient and the axiom $\exists r(a=b[a/b]+r \ \& \ r<b) \vee b=[a/b]=0$ (cf. *178b, c) also be adjoined. By successive applications of the theorem, both rm and $[a/b]$ can be eliminated.

EXAMPLE 8. Let S_1 be the number-theoretic formal system, R(x, y) be a formula containing free only x and y, and $R(x, y)$ be the predicate which R(x, y) expresses under the interpretation. (a) Consider the classical system S_1, and suppose R is such that: (A) $\vdash_1$ ∃yR(x, y). Then using *149 and *174b, a function symbol f introduced with the axiom R(x, f(x)) & ∀z(z<f(x) ⊃ ¬R(x, z)), so that under the (classical) interpretation (at least) f(x) expresses the function $\mu y R(x, y)$ (beginning § 57, assuming about S_1 that (A) implies (1b) § 57 (with $n = 1$)), will be eliminable, i.e. the elimination relations hold from the system S_2 thus obtained. Using *149a instead of *149, the same holds in the intuitionistic S_1, when besides (A) also: (α) $\vdash_1$ R(x, y) ∨ ¬R(x, y). (b) Now consider the classical S_1, without supposing (A). Let $\mathrm{R}^{\dagger}$(x, w) be R(x, w) ∨ {¬∃yR(x, y) & w=0}, and $\mathrm{R}^{\ddagger}$(x, w) be $\mathrm{R}^{\dagger}$(x, w) & ∀z(z<w ⊃ ¬$\mathrm{R}^{\dagger}$(x, z)). By *51, $\vdash_1$ ∃yR(x, y) ∨ ¬∃yR(x, y). Thence using cases (∨-elim.), $\vdash_1$ ∃w$\mathrm{R}^{\dagger}$(x, w); and by *149 and *174b: (1) $\vdash_1$ ∃!w$\mathrm{R}^{\ddagger}$(x, w). So a function symbol f introduced with the axiom $\mathrm{R}^{\ddagger}$(x, f(x)) will always be eliminable classically. Under the (classical) interpretation, now f(x) expresses $\varepsilon y R(x, y)$ (beginning § 62; cf. (59) § 63). The eliminability holds in the intuitionistic S_1, when R is such that (α) holds and also: (β) $\vdash_1$ ∃yR(x, y) ∨ ¬∃yR(x, y). For (β) enables us to dispense with *51, and (α) and (β) with *158 and Remark 1 (b) § 29 give $\vdash_1$ $\mathrm{R}^{\dagger}$(x, w) ∨

$\neg$R†(x, w), which enables us to use *149a instead of *149. (c) Let $\varphi(x)$ be any function of which the representing predicate $\varphi(x)=w$ is arithmetical (§ 48). Let R(x, w) be a formula expressing $\varphi(x)=w$. Then the f(x) of (b) expresses $\varepsilon w[\varphi(x)=w]$, i.e. $\varphi(x)$. Thus *in the classical number-theoretic system, for any function* $\varphi(x)$ *such that* $\varphi(x)=w$ *is arithmetical, a formula* F(x, w) *containing free only* x *and* w *can be found such that* F($\boldsymbol{x}, \boldsymbol{w}$) *is true under the interpretation exactly when* $w=\varphi(x)$, *and a new function symbol* f *expressing* φ *with the axiom* F(x, f(x)) *is eliminable.* In particular, *such a formula* F(x, w) *can be found for any general recursive function* $\varphi(x)$ (by Theorem VII (b) § 57); *and for many functions (under classical interpretation) which are not general recursive,* e.g. $\varepsilon y T_1(x, x, y)$ (cf. (b) or beginning § 62, and Example 1 § 63). (d) Conversely, if an axiom of the form F(x, f(x)) characterizes f(x) as expressing a function $\varphi(x)$ (i.e. if for each x, F($\boldsymbol{x}, \boldsymbol{w}$) is true under the interpretation exactly when $w=\varphi(x)$), then $\varphi(x)=w$ is arithmetical. — The situation for the intuitionistic system will be considered further in § 82 (Examples 1 and 2).

For the next two examples, we shall suppose that (1) — (3) of Remark 1 § 49 have been established, either by formalizing § 48 directly, or by borrowing from Hilbert-Bernays 1934 pp. 401—419. The Hilbert-Bernays treatment is in a formal system which (disregarding obviously inessential differences, including their use of predicate variables, cf. end § 37) results from our classical number-theoretic system by adding an operator (with appropriate postulates) which, applied to a formula R(x, y), gives a term expressing the function $\varepsilon y R(x, y)$ where $R(x, y)$ is the predicate expressed by R(x, y). By Example 8 (b), each use of this operator can be eliminated. Applying the process to the formulas displayed fifth on p. 416 and seventh on p. 419, taking the $\mathfrak{a}$ and $\mathfrak{b}(n, \rho(m, n' \cdot l+1))$ to be simply a variable w, we are led to (α) and (β) of Remark 1 § 49. This treatment can be adapted to the intuitionistic system. (Hilbert and Bernays write the operator μ_x; their ε_x has another meaning, cf. 1939 pp. 9 ff., Hilbert 1928.)

Example 9. Eliminability of further primitive recursive definitions, having those for + and · (cf. Example 4). Suppose $\varphi_1, \ldots, \varphi_k$ is the primitive recursive description of a function φ ($=\varphi_k$). Let S_1 be the number-theoretic system with additional function symbols $\mathrm{f}_1, \ldots, \mathrm{f}_{k-1}$ (expressing $\varphi_1, \ldots, \varphi_{k-1}$, respectively), and with equations obtained by translating the schema applications for $\varphi_1, \ldots, \varphi_{k-1}$ (as in § 54) adjoined as axioms. Say e.g. that φ comes from ψ, χ (where ψ, χ are from the list $\varphi_1, \ldots, \varphi_{k-1}$) by Schema (Vb) § 43 with $n=2$. Applying

Remark 1 § 49: (1) $\vdash_1$ P(0, x, w) $\sim$ Q(x, w), (2) $\vdash_1$ P(y', x, w) $\sim$ $\exists$z[P(y, x, z) & R(y, z, x, w)], (3) $\vdash_1$ $\exists$!wP(y, x, w). We also assume (as hypothesis of an induction on k): (4) $\vdash_1$ g(x)=w $\sim$ Q(x, w), (5) $\vdash_1$ h(y, z, x)=w $\sim$ R(y, z, x, w) (where g, h express ψ, χ, respectively). The theorem (with (3)) tells us that the addition of f to S_1 with P(y, x, f(y, x)) as the additional axiom is eliminable. But in S_1 with f added to the symbolism, P(y, x, f(y, x)) is interdeducible with f(0, x)=g(x) & f(y', x)=h(y, f(y, x), x), as we easily see (using (1) — (5), and in one direction, induction on y). Hence the pair of equations f(0, x)=g(x), f(y', x)=h(y, f(y, x), x) may be used instead of the formula P(y, x, f(y, x)) as the additional axioms, with the same results. (This pair of equations is obtained slightly differently in Hilbert-Bernays 1934 on p. 421.)

EXAMPLE 10. Let S_1 be the number-theoretic formalism. By the proof of Theorem 32 (a) § 59, there is a formula P(z, x, w) such that, if e is a Gödel number of a general recursive function $\varphi(x)$, then P(**e**, x, w) numeralwise represents $\varphi(x)$. Then $\exists$!wP(**e**, **x**, w) is provable for each natural number x. Must $\exists$!wP(**e**, x, w) be provable? (It certainly is for some choices of φ and e, e.g. by formalizing via § 56 reasoning given in § 54.) By Theorem 31 § 52, $\{\vdash_1 \exists!\text{wP}(\boldsymbol{z}, \text{x}, \text{w})\} \equiv (Ey)R(z, y)$ for some primitive recursive R. Let θ be obtained from this R by Theorem XIV (b) § 60. Then θ is primitive recursive, and $\theta(y)$ for $y = 0, 1, 2, \ldots$ is an enumeration of the numbers z for which $\exists$!wP(**z**, x, w) is provable. Under the interpretation, $\exists$!wP(**z**, x, w) is true only when z is the Gödel number of a general recursive function of one variable. Suppose that S_1 has the consistency property that $\exists$!wP(**z**, x, w) is provable only then. Now for each y, $\theta(y)$ is the Gödel number of a general recursive function, which can be written $\Phi_1(\theta(y), x)$ (beginning § 65); and so $\Phi_1(\theta(x), x)+1$ is a general recursive function $\varphi(x)$, for any Gödel number e of which $\exists$!wP(**e**, x, w) is unprovable in S_1. — For such an e, let S_2 be obtained from S_1 by adjoining a new function symbol f with the axiom P(**e**, x, f(x)). Then f (and its axiom) are not eliminable. For, using *174a and the result (3) of Remark 1 § 49 for the primitive recursive function U (cf. the proof of Theorem 32), we easily show that P(**e**, x, t) $\vdash_1$ $\exists$!wP(**e**, x, w). Hence, using the new axiom, $\vdash_2$ $\exists$!wP(**e**, x, w). If f were eliminable, then $\exists$!wP(**e**, x, w) would be provable in S_1, which is not the case. Thus *in the number-theoretic system, there is a formula* P(x, w) *containing free only* x *and* w *such that, under a consistency assumption*: P(x, w) *numeralwise represents a general recursive function* φ, *but a new function symbol* f (*expressing* φ) *with the axiom* P(x, f(x)) *is not eliminable.*

For a given F, f and formation rules (here those of S_2), we shall mean by a *transform* of a formula E any formula D such that $E \sim D$ is deducible in the predicate calculus with equality from the formula (iii).

REMARK 2. (a) The transforms of E include its principal f-less transform E′ (by Lemma 28 and the proof of Lemma 29) and all formulas obtainable thence by manipulations of F-quantifiers based on Lemma 25 (by Lemma 26). (b) Any two f-less transforms E^1 and E^2 of a formula E of S_2, since equivalent in S_2 (by Lemmas 26 and 27), are equivalent in S_1 (by (V)). This holds for any S_1 for Theorem 42 with the given formation rules (without the proviso for additional axiom schemata, since the proof of $E^1 \sim E^2$ in S_2 uses axioms by these only of S_1), and in particular when S_1 is simply the predicate calculus with equality and (i) as an axiom.

REPLACEABILITY OF UNDEFINED FUNCTIONS BY PREDICATES. THEOREM 43. (a) *Let S_2 be an applied predicate calculus with equality which has a symbol* f *for a function of n variables* ($n \geq 0$); *and let S_1 come from S_2 by omitting* f *and supplying instead a symbol* F *for a predicate of* $n+1$ *variables with the axiom* $\exists!wF(x_1, \ldots, x_n, w)$ (*or the postulates of S_2 may be those of the predicate calculus with the equality axioms for the function and predicate symbols of S_2, in which case in forming S_1 we also omit the n equality axioms for* f *and supply instead the* $n+1$ *equality axioms for* F).

For any formula E *of S_2, let* E′ *be any particular* f*-less transform of* E (*with the present* f *and* F, *under formation rules allowing both in the symbolism*). *For any formula* E *of S_1, let* E° *be the formula of S_2 obtained from* E *by replacing simultaneously each part of the form* $F(t_1, \ldots, t_n, s)$ *where* $t_1, \ldots, t_n, s$ *are terms by* $f(t_1, \ldots, t_n)=s$. *Then*:

(VIa) $\vdash_1 E \sim E^{\circ\prime}$. (VIb) $\vdash_2 E \sim E'^{\circ}$.

(VIIa) $\{\Gamma \vdash_2 E\} \rightarrow \{\Gamma' \vdash_1 E'\}$. (VIIb) $\{\Gamma \vdash_1 E\} \rightarrow \{\Gamma^\circ \vdash_2 E^\circ\}$.

(b) *Likewise when S_2 has additional particular axioms* $B_1, \ldots, B_k$ *and axiom schemata* $\mathfrak{B}_1, \ldots, \mathfrak{B}_l$, *and S_1 has as additional particular axioms* $B_1', \ldots, B_k'$ *and additional axiom schemata* $\mathfrak{A}_1, \ldots, \mathfrak{A}_l$ *such that, if* E *is an axiom of S_2 by* $\mathfrak{B}_i$ (*of S_1 by* $\mathfrak{A}_i$), *then* $\vdash_1 E'$ ($\vdash_2 E^\circ$). (Cf. Hilbert-Bernays 1934 pp. 460 ff.)

From (VIa) — (VIIb) it follows that:

(VIIIa) $\{\Gamma \vdash_2 E\} \equiv \{\Gamma' \vdash_1 E'\}$. (VIIIb) $\{\Gamma \vdash_1 E\} \equiv \{\Gamma^\circ \vdash_2 E^\circ\}$.

PROOFS. (VIIIa). For conversely to (VIIa): If $\Gamma' \vdash_1 E'$, then by (VIIb), $\Gamma'^\circ \vdash_2 E'^\circ$; and thence by (VIb), $\Gamma \vdash_2 E$.

PROOF OF THEOREM 43. (a) We begin with the version in which

the logic is the predicate calculus with equality. Let S_{3a} come from S_2 by adding F to the symbolism with $f(x_1, \ldots, x_n)=w \sim F(x_1, \ldots, x_n, w)$ as axiom. Regarding this axiom as an explicit definition of F, the additions are eliminable with $^\circ$ as the correlation, by Example 1. But by Lemma 26, the axiom $f(x_1, \ldots, x_n)=w \sim F(x_1, \ldots, x_n, w)$ can be replaced in S_{3a} by the pair of axioms $\exists!wF(x_1, \ldots, x_n, w)$ and $F(x_1, \ldots, x_n, f(x_1, \ldots, x_n))$ without changing the deducibility relationship. So the elimination relations hold also from the resulting system S_3, i.e.:

(Ib) If E is a formula of S_2, E° is E.

(IIb) $\vdash_3 E \sim E^\circ$. (IIIb) $\{\Gamma \vdash_3 E\} \rightarrow \{\Gamma^\circ \vdash_2 E^\circ\}$.

But Theorem 42 applies to S_3 (as its S_2), and the result of the elimination of f from S_3 is S_1. Thus, using Remark 2 (b) if $'$ indicates some other than the principal f-less transform:

(Ia) If E is a formula of S_1, $\vdash_1 E' \sim E$.

(IIa) $\vdash_3 E \sim E'$. (IIIa) $\{\Gamma \vdash_3 E\} \rightarrow \{\Gamma' \vdash_1 E'\}$.

Now (VIa) — (VIIb) follow, e.g.:

(VIa) By (IIb) and (IIa), $\vdash_3 E \sim E^\circ \sim E^{\circ\prime}$. But $E \sim E^{\circ\prime}$ is a formula of S_1. Hence by (Va), $\vdash_1 E \sim E^{\circ\prime}$.

(VIIa) $\{\Gamma \vdash_2 E\} \rightarrow \{\Gamma \vdash_3 E\}$ (a fortiori) $\rightarrow \{\Gamma' \vdash_1 E'\}$ (by (IIIa)). The version with equality axioms follows by Theorem 41 (b), or can be treated directly thus. The equality axioms for F are provable in S_{3a}. To pass to S_3, we first add them as axioms, then replace (iii) by (i) and (ii), and finally omit the equality axioms for f (using Lemma 27).

Remark 3. Any two f-less transforms E^1 and E^2 of E are equivalent in S_1, by the proof. Since this equivalence is already established in the system S_1 of (a) of the theorem, it suffices to satisfy the conditions of (b) for any one convenient way of choosing the transforms.

Remark 4. For the version with equality axioms, and for F a predicate symbol: The entire discussion beginning with Theorem 42 and including the definition of 'transform' holds good, when, for certain values of i, we exclude the formation of terms $f(t_1, \ldots, t_n)$ and formulas $F(t_1, \ldots, t_n, s)$ with t_i for any of these values of i containing f, and omit the equality axioms for f and F for these values of i.

Remark 5. With equality axioms, in Theorem 43 (b) the additional postulates may make some of the n equality axioms for f redundant in S_2. Are the corresponding equality axioms for F redundant in S_1? Suppose more particularly that for certain values of i there exist proofs of the i-th equality axioms for f from the remaining postulates of S_2 in which proofs no f-terms $f(t_1, \ldots, t_n)$ occur with t_i for any of these values of i containing f. Then the equality axioms for F for these values of i are redundant in S_1, provided that (b) is satisfied when $'$ means principal f-less transform, or any other f-less transform in the altered sense of Remark 4. For then by Remark 4, using (VII) the principal f-less transforms of the equality axioms in question for f are provable in the altered S_1, and thence the corresponding equality axioms for F.

EXAMPLE 11. (a) Let S_2 be the full number-theoretic system or Robinson's (Lemma 18b § 49). By (b) of the theorem, we can replace the function symbol $\cdot$ by a predicate symbol, in the following manner. Say the new predicate symbol is $\cdot$, written preceding its three arguments. We adjoin as new axioms

$$a=b \supset (\cdot(c, d, a) \supset \cdot(c, d, b)), \quad \exists! c \cdot(a, b, c);$$

and if we use principal $\cdot$-less transforms, we change Axioms 20 and 21 to

$$\exists b[\cdot(a, 0, b) \,\&\, b=0], \quad \exists c[\cdot(a, b', c) \,\&\, \exists d[\cdot(a, b, d) \,\&\, c=d+a]],$$

respectively, but these may be simplified to

$$\cdot(a, 0, 0), \qquad \exists d[\cdot(a, b', d+a) \,\&\, \cdot(a, b, d)].$$

The other two equality axioms

$$a=b \supset (\cdot(a, c, d) \supset \cdot(b, c, d)), \quad a=b \supset (\cdot(c, a, d) \supset \cdot(c, b, d))$$

for $\cdot$ as a predicate symbol need not be adjoined, if S_2 is the full number-theoretic system, since they are in fact provable in the system described (by Remark 5 with the proofs of the equality axioms for $\cdot$ as a function symbol § 38); but if S_2 is Robinson's system, we adjoin them in place of the formulas of *106 and *107 as axioms. By a second application of the theorem we can further replace $+$. In doing so, if Axiom 18 is changed to its principal $+$-less transform or to $+(a, 0, a)$, $a=a$ will still be provable (and will remain so if 0 is replaced similarly under (b) below). By a third application we can further replace $'$. In doing so, we change the induction schema say to $A(0) \,\&\, \forall x(A(x) \supset \exists y[{}'(x, y) \,\&\, A(y)]) \supset A(x)$. Thus we obtain a system S_1 without function symbols in the ordinary sense, i.e. for $n > 0$, related to S_2 by (VIa) — (VIIIb), where now $'$ and $^\circ$ denote successive eliminations of several symbols. (b) If we wish a system lacking also individual symbols, we can still further replace 0 by an application with $n = 0$, or we can eliminate 0 before replacing $'$ (next example).

EXAMPLE 12. Using *137 and Axiom 15, $0=b \sim \forall a(a' \neq b)$ (which is of the form (iii)) is provable. This fact can be utilized to eliminate 0 by Theorem 42 after some preliminary transformations.

EXAMPLE 13. ELIMINABILITY OF A DEFINED SORT OF VARIABLES. Let S_1 be the predicate calculus (say under formation rules using individual, function and predicate symbols) with additional particular axioms and axiom schemata. Suppose that for a certain formula M(w) containing free only w, the formula $\exists$wM(w) is provable in S_1. Let S_2 come from S_1 by adjoining a new sort of variables $\bar{a}, \bar{b}, \bar{c}, \ldots$, admitting these in constructing terms and formulas and for Rules 9 and 12, restricting the x for Axiom Schemata 10 and 11 to be a variable of the original sort, and adding the following three axiom schemata, where $\bar{\mathrm{x}}$ is a variable of the new sort, $\mathrm{A}(\bar{\mathrm{x}})$ is a formula, and t is a term free for $\bar{\mathrm{x}}$ in $\mathrm{A}(\bar{\mathrm{x}})$ and for w in M(w).

$\bar{0}$. $\mathrm{M}(\bar{\mathrm{x}})$. $\overline{10}$. $\mathrm{M(t)} \supset (\forall\bar{\mathrm{x}}\mathrm{A}(\bar{\mathrm{x}}) \supset \mathrm{A(t)})$. $\overline{11}$. $\mathrm{M(t)} \supset (\mathrm{A(t)} \supset \exists\bar{\mathrm{x}}\mathrm{A}(\bar{\mathrm{x}}))$.

Given any formula E of S_2, let $\mathrm{E}^\dagger$ result from E by replacing each part of the form $\forall\bar{\mathrm{x}}\mathrm{A}(\bar{\mathrm{x}})$ by one of the form $\forall\mathrm{x}[\mathrm{M(x)} \supset \mathrm{A(x)}]$, and of $\exists\bar{\mathrm{x}}\mathrm{A}(\bar{\mathrm{x}})$ by $\exists\mathrm{x}[\mathrm{M(x)} \,\&\, \mathrm{A(x)}]$, where x is a variable of the original sort not occurring in $\mathrm{A}(\bar{\mathrm{x}})$ or M(w); then let $\mathrm{E}^\ddagger$ come from $\mathrm{E}^\dagger$ by prefixing $\mathrm{M}(\bar{\mathrm{y}}_1) \,\&\, \ldots \,\&\, \mathrm{M}(\bar{\mathrm{y}}_m) \supset$ where $\bar{\mathrm{y}}_1, \ldots, \bar{\mathrm{y}}_m$ are exactly the distinct variables of the new sort which occur free in E (and hence in $\mathrm{E}^\dagger$); and let E′ come from $\mathrm{E}^\ddagger$ by substituting for $\bar{\mathrm{y}}_1, \ldots, \bar{\mathrm{y}}_m$ distinct variables $\mathrm{y}_1, \ldots, \mathrm{y}_m$ of the original sort not occurring in $\mathrm{E}^\ddagger$ (and hence not in E). Then (I) — (III) hold with the following modifications, provided that for each additional axiom schema of S_1, to each axiom A of S_2 by it, A′ is provable in S_1. For $m > 0$, (II) becomes: $\mathrm{E} \;{}^{\mathrm{y}_1 \ldots \mathrm{y}_m}\!\!\underset{2}{\dashv} \underset{2}{\vdash}^{\bar{\mathrm{y}}_1 \ldots \bar{\mathrm{y}}_m} \mathrm{E}'$. In (III), if corresponding variables are to be held constant for corresponding assumption formulas, for each $\bar{\mathrm{y}}$ the same y should be substituted in E and each of Γ for which $\bar{\mathrm{y}}$ is held constant (so in this case the operation ′ is not specified for each single formula by itself). Before treating (II), Theorems 1, 2 and 14 can be extended appropriately to S_2. We can use Lemma 8a § 24 to reduce (III) to the case of it with Γ empty. To treat this, write $\mathrm{E}^\dagger$ as "$\mathrm{E}^\dagger(\bar{\mathrm{y}}_1, \ldots, \bar{\mathrm{y}}_m)$". We can show by induction that, if $\vdash_2$ E, then $\mathrm{M}(\mathrm{y}_1), \ldots, \mathrm{M}(\mathrm{y}_m) \vdash_1 \mathrm{E}^\dagger(\mathrm{y}_1, \ldots, \mathrm{y}_m)$ holding $\mathrm{y}_1, \ldots, \mathrm{y}_m$ constant. (For Rule 2, say e.g. $\mathrm{A}^\dagger$ contains only one new variable $\bar{\mathrm{y}}$, write it "$\mathrm{A}^\dagger(\bar{\mathrm{y}})$", and $\mathrm{B}^\dagger$ none. By hyp. ind., $\mathrm{M(y)} \vdash_1 \mathrm{A}^\dagger(\mathrm{y})$ and $\mathrm{M(y)} \vdash_1 \mathrm{A}^\dagger(\mathrm{y}) \supset \mathrm{B}^\dagger$. By Rule 2, $\mathrm{M(y)} \vdash_1 \mathrm{B}^\dagger$. By $\exists$-elim. and *74, $\exists\mathrm{wM(w)} \vdash_1 \mathrm{B}^\dagger$. But $\vdash_1 \exists\mathrm{wM(w)}$. Hence $\vdash_1 \mathrm{B}^\dagger$.) — Similarly introducing several sorts of variables successively.

§ 75. Axiom systems, Skolem's paradox, the natural number sequence. Suppose we are dealing with an axiom system (§ 8) having as its primitive or undefined notions a set or domain D of individuals, certain individuals $z_1, \ldots, z_q$ from D, and certain predicates $P_1, \ldots, P_s$ over D. An axiom of the system which can be expressed by a formula in the symbolism of the predicate calculus (i.e. the restricted or first order predicate calculus, cf. § 37) with individual symbols $\mathrm{e}_1, \ldots, \mathrm{e}_q$ to express $z_1, \ldots, z_q$ and predicate symbols $\mathrm{Pr}_1, \ldots, \mathrm{Pr}_s$ to express $P_1, \ldots, P_s$, respectively, we call *elementary*. If each axiom is elementary, and the axioms are finite in number, we call the axiom system *elementary* or *of first order*.

Now we can always choose closed formulas to express elementary axioms, since under the generality interpretation any formula is synonymous with its closure (cf. end § 32). Moreover, since the axioms of an elementary system are finite in number, we can form the conjunction $\mathrm{F}(\mathrm{e}_1, \ldots, \mathrm{e}_q, \mathrm{Pr}_1, \ldots, \mathrm{Pr}_s)$ of the closed formulas expressing the axioms. Finally, by changing the individual symbols $\mathrm{e}_1, \ldots, \mathrm{e}_q$ to respective distinct variables $\mathrm{z}_1, \ldots, \mathrm{z}_q$ not occurring in $\mathrm{F}(\mathrm{e}_1, \ldots, \mathrm{e}_q, \mathrm{Pr}_1, \ldots, \mathrm{Pr}_s)$ and the predicate symbols $\mathrm{Pr}_1, \ldots, \mathrm{Pr}_s$ to distinct predicate letters $\mathrm{P}_1, \ldots, \mathrm{P}_s$, we obtain a predicate letter formula $\mathrm{F}(\mathrm{z}_1, \ldots, \mathrm{z}_q, \mathrm{P}_1, \ldots, \mathrm{P}_s)$ or briefly F. A simple illustration (with $q = 0$, $s = 1$) has already been given in § 37.

Expressing the axiom system thus by a predicate letter formula F helps to emphasize the standpoint of formal axiomatics (§ 8), from which the set D, the individuals $z_1, \ldots, z_q$ and the predicates $P_1, \ldots, P_s$ of the axiomatic theory are undetermined except as the axioms characterize them. Every predicate letter formula can be considered as expressing an axiom system with the free variables and predicate letters occurring in it representing the undefined individuals and predicates.

When we interpret the logical symbols classically, and treat the predicates "extensionally" as simply logical functions, the notions of set-theoretic predicate logic (§ 37) become applicable to the discussion of axiomatic systems. To say that the axioms are satisfied (in the intuitive sense, § 8) by some non-empty system of objects (which we also expressed in § 8 by saying that the axioms are 'non-vacuous') now means exactly that the formula F is satisfiable (in the set-theoretic sense) in some non-empty domain. Predicate letter formulas which are satisfiable but not valid are the ones which are of interest as axiom systems. A valid predicate letter formula does not restrict or characterize the individuals and predicates expressed by its free variables and predicate letters; but rather expresses a law of logic applicable to all choices of those individuals and predicates in any non-empty domain.

In formal axiomatics, without the further step of formalizing the processes of logical deduction so as to obtain a formal system (§ 15), theorems are deduced from the axioms on the basis of the meanings of the logical symbols. What it means on this basis for a proposition to be a theorem can be expressed in set-theoretic predicate logic as follows. Consider any proposition of the axiomatic theory which is expressible by a predicate letter formula in $P_1, \ldots, P_s$. We can always choose that formula to contain no variables free other than $z_1, \ldots, z_q$, and to contain these only free. Now any such formula $B(z_1, \ldots, z_q, P_1, \ldots, P_s)$ or briefly B expresses a true proposition or theorem of the axiomatic theory, precisely if every assignment of individuals $z_1, \ldots, z_q$ from some non-empty domain D to $z_1, \ldots, z_q$ and of predicates $P_1, \ldots, P_s$ over D to $P_1, \ldots, P_s$ which satisfies F also satisfies B. In view of the valuation table for $\supset$ § 28, this is equivalent to saying that the formula $F \supset B$ should be valid in every non-empty domain.

Now suppose that the axiomatic theory is formalized (§ 15) by adopting the deductive rules of the predicate calculus as the means of deducing theorems, under the proviso that the variables $z_1, \ldots, z_q$ be held constant; i.e. we now say proof-theoretically that B expresses a theorem, if in the predicate calculus $F \vdash B$ with $z_1, \ldots, z_q$ held constant. (By Remarks 1 and 2 (a) § 34, we can then always find a deduction of B from F in which no predicate letters other than $P_1, \ldots, P_s$ occur and $z_1, \ldots, z_q$ occur only free.)

By the $\supset$-rules, noting that, since F contains no variables free except $z_1, \ldots, z_q$, no variables are varied, this is equivalent to saying that $\vdash F \supset B$ in the predicate calculus.

We are now in a position to establish that the formalization of deduction for elementary axiomatic theories by the predicate calculus is both correct (or consistent) and adequate (or complete), i.e. the predicate calculus enables only and all those formulas to be deduced from F which express propositions that are true of any system satisfying the axioms. For $\{\vdash F \supset B\} \equiv \{F \supset B$ is valid in every non-empty domain$\}$, by Theorem 21 § 37 and Corollary 1 Theorem 34 § 72.

The question whether the theorems are consistent with the axioms (just answered affirmatively) is of course quite separate from the question whether the axioms themselves are consistent. Prior to Hilbert's proof theory or metamathematics, proofs of consistency of an axiomatic system or theory were by exhibiting a model for the theory (§ 14). The consistency property proved immediately in this case is the satisfiability of F in some non-empty domain.

We gave a heuristic argument in § 14 that this property implies consistency in the sense of non-existence of a contradiction (one theorem denying another) in the theory deducible from the axioms. The converse that from any unsatisfiable system of axioms a contradiction must necessarily follow by a finite number of logical steps was then by no means clear.

It is only with the step taken by the modern formalists of formalizing deduction that consistency in the sense of non-deducibility of a contradiction becomes amenable to exact discussion. We now have as the consistency property that for no formula A, both $F \vdash A$ and $F \vdash \neg A$ with $z_1, \ldots, z_q$ held constant.

By the $\neg$-rules § 23 (since F contains only $z_1, \ldots, z_q$ free), this property is equivalent to 'not $\vdash \neg F$', i.e. to 'F is irrefutable'. The formalist's transformation of the consistency problem may thus be described (for the case of elementary axiom systems) as the replacement of satisfiability by irrefutability.

By Theorem 21 (which takes the place now of the reasoning given in § 14) and Gödel's completeness theorem (Theorem 34), satisfiability and irrefutability are equivalent.

The purpose of the formalistic transformation in the notions of deducibility and consistency is to obtain notions which are finitary. A reduction from the non-enumerably to the enumerably infinite is achieved, as validity and satisfiability refer to the totality of logical functions, which is non-enumerable, while the proof-theoretic equivalents provability and irrefutability refer only to the enumerable infinity of formal proofs. In metamathematics, the reasoning with the notions is also finitary. Although the equivalence proof, as given by Gödel's completeness theorem, cannot belong to metamathematics, it is significant for metamathematics that the set-theoretic notions are actually equivalent to the proof-theoretic ones when one reasons on the non-finitary plane to which the set-theoretic notions belong.

We see now that the decision problem for provability in the pure predicate calculus includes the decision problem for provability in every axiomatic theory having an elementary axiom system (by asking whether a certain predicate letter formula $F \supset B$ is provable), and also the decision problem whether any given elementary axiom system is consistent (by asking whether $\neg F$ is unprovable).

Axiom systems used in mathematics often employ $=$ in the role of an ordinary or logical term which must be understood in advance rather than as one of the undefined predicates which the axioms characterize. The foregoing remarks will apply, if we first supply some additional axioms for equality, formalized as $\mathrm{Eq}(=, \mathrm{Pr}_1, \ldots, \mathrm{Pr}_s)$ or $\mathrm{Eq}(Q, \mathrm{P}_1, \ldots, \mathrm{P}_s)$; or we can instead formalize the axioms as they stand by an equality and predicate letter formula, and deduction from the axioms by the predicate calculus with equality, and then use the extension of Gödel's completeness theorem to that. The two methods give results which are equivalent via Lemma 24 (a) and Theorem 41 (c) § 73, though set-theoretically the former does not narrow the interpretations which satisfy the axioms to those in which Q is equality but allows Q also to be an equivalence relation.

EXAMPLE 1. The axiom system L1—L3 for linear order (end § 8) is expressed by the following equality and predicate letter formula (call it "$\mathrm{F}(=, \mathcal{A})$"), with $\mathcal{A}$ expressing $<$:

$$\forall a \forall b \forall c[\mathcal{A}(a,b) \,\&\, \mathcal{A}(b,c) \supset \mathcal{A}(a,c)] \,\&\, \forall a \forall b[\neg(\mathcal{A}(a,b) \,\&\, a=b) \,\&\, \neg(\mathcal{A}(a,b) \,\&\, \mathcal{A}(b,a)) \,\&\, \neg(a=b \,\&\, \mathcal{A}(b,a))] \,\&\, \forall a \forall b[\mathcal{A}(a,b) \vee a=b \vee \mathcal{A}(b,a)].$$

The same axiom system is expressed by the predicate letter formula $\mathrm{Eq}(\mathcal{B}, \mathcal{A}) \,\&\, \mathrm{F}(\mathcal{B}, \mathcal{A})$, with $\mathcal{B}$ expressing $=$ (cf. Example 1 § 73).

Our remarks also apply indirectly to axiom systems having functions $f_1, \ldots, f_r$ among their primitive notions, as with the help of $=$ these can be replaced by the representing predicates of the functions, as was discussed from the proof-theoretic standpoint in Theorem 43 § 74.

Elementary axiom systems occur frequently in mathematics, if we use the term 'elementary' more widely to include systems which can be transformed by well-known devices so as to become elementary in the sense formulated at the beginning of the section. For example the axioms for groups, and Hilbert's axioms for geometry with the continuity axiom omitted, are elementary in the wider sense. (In the first, the group operation can be replaced by its representing predicate, using $=$; and in both, axioms for $=$ can be supplied. An example is worked out in Hilbert-Bernays 1934 pp. 3—8, 380—381.)

The foregoing discussion for the case of an elementary axiom system can be paralleled for the case of an enumerable infinity of elementary axioms as follows. Let $\mathrm{F}_0, \mathrm{F}_1, \mathrm{F}_2, \ldots$ be predicate letter formulas expressing the respective axioms and containing free only the variables $z_0, z_1, z_2, \ldots$ which stand for the undefined individuals of the axiomatic theory. Now {B is a "theorem" set-theoretically} $\equiv$ {every assignment which satisfies all of $\mathrm{F}_0, \mathrm{F}_1, \mathrm{F}_2, \ldots$ satisfies B} $\equiv$ {for every assignment, one of $\mathrm{B}, \neg\mathrm{F}_0, \neg\mathrm{F}_1, \neg\mathrm{F}_2, \ldots$ is t} $\equiv$ {some disjunction of a finite number of $\mathrm{B}, \neg\mathrm{F}_0, \neg\mathrm{F}_1, \neg\mathrm{F}_2, \ldots$ is provable} (by Theorem 21 and Corollary 1 Theorem 37) $\equiv$ {$\vdash \mathrm{F} \supset \mathrm{B}$ for some conjunction F of a finite number of $F_0, F_1, F_2, \ldots\}$ (using *62, *59) $\equiv \{F_0, F_1, F_2, \ldots \vdash$ B with $z_0, z_1, z_2, \ldots$ held constant$\} \equiv \{$B is a "theorem" proof-theoretically$\}$. Similarly {the axioms are "consistent" set-theoretically} $\equiv$ $\{F_0, F_1, F_2, \ldots$ are jointly satisfiable$\} \equiv \{$every conjunction F of a finite number of $F_0, F_1, F_2, \ldots$ is irrefutable$\}$ (by Theorems 21 and 37) $\equiv$ {for every A, not both $F_0, F_1, F_2, \ldots \vdash$ A and $F_0, F_1, F_2, \ldots \vdash \neg$A, with $z_0, z_1, z_2, \ldots$ held constant$\} \equiv \{$the axioms are "consistent" proof-theoretically}. Thus as before the set-theoretic and proof-theoretic notions are equivalent. But the former method of reducing the decision problems for deducibility from the axioms and for consistency of the axioms to that for provability in the predicate calculus fails, since now there are quantifications with respect to the finite conjunctions F of $F_0, F_1, F_2, \ldots$ (however cf. Remark 3 § 76).

Using the starred forms of Theorems 21 and 37 (cf. Theorem 39 § 73), these results extend to the case = is used as a logical notion, and the axioms are expressed by equality and predicate letter formulas.

AXIOMATIC SET THEORY. The axiom systems for set theory of von Neumann 1925, of Bernays 1937-48 and of Gödel 1940* are elementary (in the wider sense).

As Gödel's axioms are stated, there are three primitive notions, $\mathfrak{Cls}$ (to be a class), $\mathfrak{M}$ (to be a set) and $\mathcal{E}$ (to belong to), besides which = is used as a logical notion. All sets are classes, and no other objects are considered; so that the classes constitute the domain. The axiom system can then be expressed by an equality and predicate letter formula $F(=, \mathcal{A}, \mathcal{B})$ where $\mathcal{A}(a)$ and $\mathcal{B}(a, b)$ express $\mathfrak{M}(a)$ and $a \mathcal{E} b$, respectively, or by a predicate letter formula $Eq(C, \mathcal{A}, \mathcal{B})$ & $F(C, \mathcal{A}, \mathcal{B})$ where $C(a, b)$ expresses $a=b$.

This axiom system is extremely powerful. From it with appropriate definitions the usual classical analysis and much of general set theory can be deduced. In particular, the existence of an infinite set is postulated (by the axiom of infinity), and also the existence to any set of a set which includes the subsets of that set; so it is deducible via Cantor's theorem (Theorem C § 5) that there exists a non-enumerably infinite set of sets.

But by Löwenheim's theorem (Corollary 2 Theorem 34*, cf. Theorem 39), if the formula $F(=, \mathcal{A}, \mathcal{B})$ expressing the axioms is satisfiable at all, as it appears to be from its presumed interpretation by set theory, it is satisfiable in a finite or enumerably infinite domain. (Examination of the axioms rules out the case of a finite domain.) Thus we can interpret the primitive notions so that there are only enumerably many sets and the axioms are all true (i.e. an enumerable model exists for axiomatic set theory, with $=$ in its usual meaning), even though a theorem in the theory asserts that there are non-enumerably many sets. This is the Skolem "paradox" (1922-3).

By the Skolem extension of Löwenheim's theorem to the case of joint satisfiability of an enumerable infinity of formulas F_0, F_1, F_2, ... (Corollary 2 Theorem 37*), the "paradox" applies equally to axiomatizations of set theory using infinitely many axioms, such as those of Fraenkel 1922 and of Skolem 1922-3.

Light is shed on the "paradox" by two observations. Only those particular subsets of a given set are definable within the axiomatic theory which can be constructed by operations, or separated out from the set by properties (i.e. predicates), available in the theory. The basic operations for building sets (or processes for constructing predicates) provided by the axioms are finite or at most enumerably infinite in number. The iteration of them then give the means for defining only enumerably many subsets of a given set. This explains the possibility of interpreting the axiom system, i.e. of satisfying the formula(s) expressing the axioms, in an enumerable domain.

On the other hand, to enumerate a set is to give a 1-1 correspondence of the set with a particular enumerable set, say the set of the natural numbers (§ 1). A 1-1 correspondence can be considered as the set of the corresponding pairs.

Thus it may be possible for the subsets of a given infinite set definable within the theory to be enumerable from without the theory, and yet be non-enumerable within the theory, because no enumerating set of corresponding pairs is among the sets definable within the theory. The construction of the enumerating set of pairs is accomplished by taking into account the structure of the axiom system as a whole, and this construction is not possible within the theory, i.e. using only the operations provided by the axioms.

The situation is similar to that in Gödel's incompleteness or undecidability theorem (Theorem 28 § 42), where, if we suppose the number-theoretic formal system to be consistent, we can recognize that $A_p(\boldsymbol{p})$ is true by taking into view the structure of that system as a whole, though we cannot recognize the truth of $A_p(\boldsymbol{p})$ by use only of the principles of inference formalized within that system, i.e. not $\vdash A_p(\boldsymbol{p})$.

Although there is this "explanation", the "paradox" still confronts us with the following alternative. Either we must maintain that the concepts of an arbitrary subset of a given set, and of a non-enumerable set, are a priori concepts which elude characterization by any finite or enumerably infinite system of elementary axioms; or else (if we stick to what can be explicitly characterized by elementary axioms, as we may well wish to in consequence of the set-theoretic paradoxes § 11) we must accept the set-theoretic concepts, in particular that of non-enumerability, as being relative, so that a set which is non-enumerable in a given axiomatization may become enumerable in another, and no absolute non-enumerability exists. This relativization of set theory was proposed by Skolem (1922-3, 1929, 1929-30).

The Löwenheim theorem, since it leads to Skolem's "paradox", can be regarded as the first of the modern incompleteness theorems. For further discussion, see Skolem 1938.

AXIOMATIC ARITHMETIC. Postulate Group B of our formal number-theoretic system provides an example of an axiom system for the theory of the natural numbers consisting of an effectively enumerable infinity of elementary axioms, i.e. the formulas expressing the axioms are effectively enumerable (cf. Theorem 38 § 72). The functions are of course replaceable by their representing predicates. Ryll-Nardzewski 1952* shows that no finite subset of these axioms would suffice for the deduction of the same class of theorems.

Another question is whether these axioms do completely characterize the natural number sequence. Gödel's completeness theory for the predicate calculus provides us with a proof of the following theorem, which was originally obtained in another way by Skolem (1933, 1934; cf. 1938).

We shall consider axioms for the sequence of the natural numbers (call the set of them N), using as primitive notions the individual 0 and the predicate $a'=b$, i.e. in the λ-notation (§ 10) $\lambda ab\ a'=b$, and perhaps other primitive notions. The axioms shall be expressible by equality and predicate letter formulas, with z expressing 0 and $\mathrm{P}_0(\mathrm{a}, \mathrm{b})$ expressing $a'=b$.

In discussing assignments to the free variables and predicate letters of any such formula, we let "D" stand for the domain, "z" for the individual assigned to z, and "$P_0(a, b)$" for the predicate assigned to $\mathrm{P}_0(\mathrm{a}, \mathrm{b})$. Then $(D, z, P_0(a, b))$ is a mathematical system in the sense of § 8, consisting of a set or domain, a member of the set, and a binary predicate over the set.

THEOREM 44^{C}. *Any finite or effectively enumerable infinite class of equality and predicate letter formulas which can be jointly satisfied so that*

$(D, z, P_0(a, b))$ is $(N, 0, a'=b)$ can also be jointly satisfied (with $0 < \overline{\overline{D}} \leq \aleph_0$) so that $(D, z, P_0(a, b))$ is not isomorphic to $(N, 0, a'=b)$.

PROOF. By hypothesis, there is a satisfying assignment for the given formulas jointly in which the domain D is N, z has the value 0, and $P_0(a, b)$ has the value $a'=b$.

Let P_1, P_2 and P_3 be other distinct predicate letters, which either do not occur in the given formulas, or have the respective values $a+b=c$, $a \cdot b=c$ and $(x)(Ey)T_2(a, a, x, y)$ in the given assignment. We shall extend the given class of formulas by adding seven formulas (if not already included) which are satisfied when the given assignment is extended (if necessary) by assigning P_1, P_2 and P_3 the values just mentioned.

We add four closed formulas, say

(a) $\forall a \mathrm{P}_1(a,z,a)$, $\forall a \forall b \exists c \exists d \exists e[\mathrm{P}_0(b,c) \;\&\; \mathrm{P}_1(a,c,d) \;\&\; \mathrm{P}_1(a,b,e) \;\&\; \mathrm{P}_0(e,d)]$,
$\forall a \mathrm{P}_2(a,z,z)$, $\forall a \forall b \exists c \exists d \exists e[\mathrm{P}_0(b,c) \;\&\; \mathrm{P}_2(a,c,d) \;\&\; \mathrm{P}_2(a,b,e) \;\&\; \mathrm{P}_1(e,a,d)]$

(cf. Example 11 (a) § 74), which under the described assignment express the recursion equations for $a+b$ and $a \cdot b$ as paraphrased in terms of the representing predicates $a+b=c$ and $a \cdot b=c$, together with the two formulas

(b) $\forall a \forall b \exists ! c \mathrm{P}_1(a, b, c)$, $\forall a \forall b \exists ! c \mathrm{P}_2(a, b, c)$,

which express that $a+b=c$ and $a \cdot b=c$ are representing predicates. Since $T_2(a, b, x, y)$ is primitive recursive, by Corollary Theorem I § 49 it is arithmetical (§ 48), and so (replacing $'$, $+$ and $\cdot$ by their representing predicates) we can find a letter formula $\mathrm{T}_2(a, b, x, y)$ in $=$, P_0, P_1, P_2 which expresses it under the described assignment. We then add the formula

(c) $\forall a(\mathrm{P}_3(a) \sim \forall x \exists y \mathrm{T}_2(a, a, x, y))$.

Let the formulas of the resulting (enlarged) class be F_0, F_1, F_2, ... As in the proof of Löwenheim's theorem (Corollary 2 Theorem 37*), the hypothesis of Theorem 37* is satisfied; and we use Theorems 37* and 40 to obtain another satisfying assignment for F_0, F_1, F_2, ... jointly. Let D^*, z^*, P_0^*, P_1^*, P_2^*, P_3^* be respectively the domain and the values of z, P_0, P_1, P_2, P_3 in this.

Suppose (for reductio ad absurdum) that $(D^*, z^*, P_0^*(a^*, b^*))$ is isomorphic (§ 8) to $(N, 0, a'=b)$, i.e. D^* is infinite and can be enumerated as $s_0, s_1, s_2, \ldots$ so that $z^* = s_0$ and $P_0^*(s_a, s_b) \equiv a'=b$.

Then by Theorem 40,

(i) $P_3^*(s_a) \equiv (Ex)(y)R_3^*(a, x, y)$

for some primitive recursive R_3^*.

In § 43 we reasoned that when the variables range over the natural numbers, and 0 and ′ have their usual meanings, the recursion equations for + and · have the usual functions + and · as their unique solution. Since the formulas (a) and (b) are satisfied, that reasoning (with minor rearrangements to fit the use of the representing predicates instead of the functions) applies now to show that $P_1^*(s_a, s_b, s_c) \equiv a+b=c$ and $P_2^*(s_a, s_b, s_c) \equiv a \cdot b=c$. Then similarly our proof of Theorem I § 49 shows that the formula $\mathrm{T}_2(\mathrm{a, b, x, y})$ now expresses a predicate $T_2^*(a^*, b^*, x^*, y^*)$ such that $T_2^*(s_a, s_b, s_x, s_y) \equiv T_2(a, b, x, y)$. Hence $\forall \mathrm{x} \exists \mathrm{y} \mathrm{T}_2(\mathrm{a, a, x, y})$ expresses a predicate $T^*(a^*)$ such that

(ii) $$T^*(s_a) \equiv (x)(Ey)T_2(a, a, x, y).$$

By the valuation rules for $\sim$ (Example 1 § 28) and $\forall$, since (c) is satisfied,

(iii) $$P_3^*(a^*) \equiv T^*(a^*).$$

Combining (i) — (iii), $(Ex)(y)R_3^*(a, x, y) \equiv (x)(Ey)T_2(a, a, x, y)$. But by Theorem V (16) § 57, the predicate $(x)(Ey)T_2(a, a, x, y)$ is not expressible in the other 2-quantifier form; for a certain number g,

$$(Ex)(y)R_3^*(g, x, y) \not\equiv (x)(Ey)T_2(g, g, x, y).$$

By reductio ad absurdum, $(D^*, z^*, P_0^*(a^*, b^*))$ is not isomorphic to $(N, 0, a'=b)$.

Discussion. By the theorem, no finite or effectively enumerable infinite set of elementary axioms can characterize the natural number sequence $0, 1, 2, \ldots, a, a', \ldots$. Any such set which are true of the natural number sequence must also be true under another interpretation. We stated the theorem for the natural number sequence as a system of the form $(N, 0, a'=b)$, but by the replaceability of a' by $a'=b$ it applies also to the natural number sequence as a system of the form $(N, 0, ')$. In particular, the axioms of Postulate Group B of our formal number-theoretic system (§ 19) admit an interpretation (using the logical symbols and = in their usual meanings) other than the intended one.

This incompleteness of Postulate Group B as a characterization of the natural number sequence is understandable when we compare Peano's fifth axiom (the principle of mathematical induction, § 7) with Axiom Schema 13. Peano's fifth axiom asserts that

(I) $$A(0) \;\&\; (x)(A(x) \rightarrow A(x')) \rightarrow (x)A(x)$$

holds for all number-theoretic predicates $A(x)$. These predicates constitute a non-enumerable totality. But the bundle of axioms given by Axiom Schema 13 only express that (I) holds for those predicates $A(x)$ which are expressible by formulas A(x) of the system, i.e. only for enumerably many predicates. Peano's fifth axiom is not elementary. We can express it in the symbolism of the second order predicate calculus (§ 37), by using a generality quantifier with a predicate variable $\mathcal{A}$, thus:

$$\forall \mathcal{A}[\mathcal{A}(0) \;\&\; \forall x(\mathcal{A}(x) \supset \mathcal{A}(x')) \supset \forall x \mathcal{A}(x)].$$

These ideas have a connection with Gödel's theorem on formally undecidable propositions (Theorem 28 or 29 § 42).

One may think of the formula $A_p(\boldsymbol{p})$ or $A_q(\boldsymbol{q})$ (which is true but unprovable, if the number-theoretic system is simply consistent) as expressing a proposition which can be "proved" from Peano's axioms, but only by making use of induction with some induction predicate $A(x)$ which is not expressible in the system under the intended interpretation. (This suggestion will receive confirmation later; cf. end § 79, noting (II) § 42.)

The unprovability of $A_p(\boldsymbol{p})$ becomes understandable also from Skolem's result (Theorem 44), on the ground that $A_p(\boldsymbol{p})$, although true of the natural numbers, is false under one of the other interpretations which satisfy the axioms. Then the undecidability of $A_p(\boldsymbol{p})$ in the number-theoretic formalism appears as a phenomenon of the same kind as the impossibility of proving either Euclid's parallel postulate or its negation from the other axioms of geometry (§ 8). The given axioms are not categorical.

Indeed conversely, as remarked above (using Corollary 1 Theorem 37*), a formula is provable, if it is true under all interpretations which make the axioms true. So the known unprovability of $A_p(\boldsymbol{p})$ makes it absurd that $A_p(\boldsymbol{p})$ should be true under all the interpretations which satisfy the axioms. Thus Gödel's theorems 28 and 37* afford another proof of Theorem 44 for the case the class of formulas for Theorem 44 is Postulate Group B of our formal system (restated as equality and predicate letter formulas). But (as remarked above, using Theorem 21*), if any enumerable class of equality and predicate letter formulas are jointly satisfiable, the formal system obtained by adjoining them as axioms to the predicate calculus with equality is (simply) consistent. So given any class of formulas for Theorem 44, by adjoining Postulate Group B, and carrying out the proof of Theorem 28 in the resulting system (or using Theorem XIII Part III § 60), we get Theorem 44 in general.

Mostowski 1949 gives an interesting example (suggested by Skolem's "paradox") of a proposition in axiomatic set theory, which he demonstrates to be undecidable by showing it to be true under one interpretation and false under another. Kreisel 1950 deals with similar problems.

The proof of Theorem 44 we gave first, and that based on Theorem 28 (or XIII), are stated for the case of an elementary axiom system or one having an effectively enumerable infinity of elementary axioms. Skolem's proof does not restrict the enumeration of the axioms to be effective. The additional generality is not essential, when we are considering the theorem as an incompleteness theorem for formal axiomatics from the standpoint that the aim of axiomatization is to make the assumptions of the theory explicit.

Remark 1. Our (first) proof of Theorem 44 can be modified to secure additional generality. Suppose now the class of the formulas for Theorem 44 is merely *arithmetical*, in the sense that, under a Gödel numbering established by the methods of §§ 52 and 56, the predicate 'x is the Gödel number of a formula of the class', call it "$C(x)$", is arithmetical. Then by Theorem VII (d) § 57, $C(x)$ is expressible in one of the forms of Theorem V, say a q-quantifier form. Let $B(x)$ refer similarly to the given class of formulas extended by adding some finite list (as above we added the seven (a) — (c)); then, however that list is chosen, $B(x)$ is expressible in the same q-quantifier form. By Theorem XIV (b) § 60 (taking $R(x, y) \equiv B(x)$), the class $\hat{x}B(x)$ is enumerated by a function $\theta(k)$ recursive in q-quantifier predicates (in the case of the q-quantifier form with existence first, even in $q-1$-quantifier predicates). But the proofs of Theorems 38 and 40 hold good, when the hypothesis that the enumeration $F_0, F_1, F_2, \ldots$ is effective is omitted, and the conclusion is altered by changing "primitive recursive" to "primitive recursive in θ" where $\theta(k)$ is the Gödel number of F_k; and hence (using Theorem XI § 58, and (17) and (18) § 57) if θ is recursive in q-quantifier predicates, when the alteration in the conclusion consists in substituting the $q+2$- for the 2-quantifier forms. So the proof of Theorem 44 goes through now, by using a case of Theorem V for a $q+2$- instead of a 2-quantifier form. — We can still further generalize the $C(x)$ for Theorem 44 to be arithmetical in the predicate M of Theorem VIII § 57, including among the added formulas three to express the definition of M, and using Theorems I*, V*, VII*, XI* (with M as the Ψ) instead of I, V, VII, XI. (The second proof of Theorem 44 can also be carried out under more general hypotheses, by using generalizations of Theorem 28 or XIII to "non-constructive logics".)

Gödel's undecidability theorem however is not restricted to the case the axioms are elementary (Theorem XIII § 60). But we can characterize the natural number sequence completely by Peano's axioms, the fifth of which is non-elementary, if we grant the notion of all predicates over the domain. Suppose we have a consistent formal system containing these categorical axioms for the natural numbers. Under the conception of a formal system which we are entertaining, a formal system may have only an enumerable infinity of formal objects. So only an enumerable infinity of formulas can be substituted in the system for the predicate variable $\mathcal{A}$ of the fifth Peano axiom. Thus for deductive purposes within the system, just as before, (I) is available only for an enumerable infinity of predicates. In fact, by Gödel's theorem (Theorem XIII), there is a consequence of the axioms under the interpretation which is not provable, i.e. not deducible from the axioms by the logic formalized in the system. So when we have non-elementary axioms, not all formulas need be provable which are true under all interpretations which satisfy the axioms. (In our example, there is essentially just one such interpretation.) The incompleteness which appeared in the axiom system in the case of elementary axioms is transferred to the deductive apparatus, if we undertake to avoid it by using non-elementary axioms.

As Skolem expresses it (1934 p. 160), "... the [natural number] series is completely characterized, for example, by the Peano axioms, if one regards the notion 'set' or 'propositional function' as something given in advance with an absolute meaning independent of all principles of generation or axioms. But if one would make the axiomatics consequent, so that also the reasoning with the sets or propositional functions is axiomatized, then, as we have seen, the unique or complete characterization of the number series is impossible."

This situation is discussed in Henkin 1950, which came to the author's attention after this section was written (the first draft in 1947). Other papers are e.g. Mostowski 1947a (cf. Kemeny's review 1948) and Rosser and Wang 1950 (cf. Skolem's review 1951).

§ 76. The decision problem.

THEOREM 54. *The decision problem for the pure predicate calculus (pure predicate calculus with equality) is unsolvable, i.e. there is no decision procedure for determining whether a predicate letter formula (an equality and predicate letter formula) is provable in the calculus.* (Church 1936a, Turing 1936-7.)

PROOF, for the predicate calculus. We saw in § 75 that the decision problem for provability in any axiomatic theory having an elementary axiom system reduces to that for provability in the pure predicate calculus. Thus to prove this theorem of Church, it will suffice to find an elementary axiomatic theory for which, on the basis of Church's thesis (§ 60), there can be no decision procedure.

According to Theorem 33 § 61, an example of such an axiomatic theory is provided by the formal system of Robinson described in Lemma 18b § 49, if that system is simply consistent. A proof of its simple consistency, which the present theorem is numbered to follow, will be given in § 79 (Theorem 53 (a)).

We repeat the reasoning in detail (already outlined in § 75). Let S_2 be the system of Lemma 18b with thirteen particular axioms.

(A) By applications of Theorem 43 (see Example 11 (a) § 74), we find another system S_1 in which the function symbols $'$, $+$, $\cdot$ are replaced by respective predicate symbols, the number of the axioms being increased to nineteen. By (VIIIa), a formula E of S_2 is provable in S_2, if and only if the formula E′ of S_1 is provable in S_1.

(B) We can then replace the axioms by their closures, without changing the provability notion (end § 32).

(C) Moreover, by the &-rules, since the axioms are finite in number, we can likewise replace them by their conjunction as a single axiom.

(D) We can furthermore change the notation to employ a variable z not occurring in the axiom(s) in place of the individual symbol 0, with the understanding that then provability shall mean deducibility from the axiom(s) in the predicate calculus with z held constant. If C be the result of making this change in a formula D of S_1 not containing z, then by Remark 2 (b) § 34, C is provable now, if and only if D was provable before. (This treatment of 0 separately from the function symbols can be avoided by using instead Example 11 (b) § 74 in (A).)

(E) We may further change the notation to employ predicate letters in place of the predicate symbols. If B results from a formula C by this change of notation, then by trivial applications of Theorems 15 and 16 § 34, B is now provable, if and only if C was before. (In § 75 we took B to contain no variables free except z, but that was done to make the set-theoretic notions apply properly, and is unnecessary now.)

(F) Finally, by the ⊃-rules, B is provable in the last described system, i.e. F $\vdash$ B in the predicate calculus with z held constant, where F is the formula (containing only z free) expressing the axioms now, if and only if F ⊃ B is provable in the predicate calculus.

The whole process by which from the formula E of S_2 we find a predicate letter formula F ⊃ B such that {⊢ E in S_2} ≡ {⊢ F ⊃ B in the predicate calculus} is effective. (It could be represented via Gödel numbering by a general recursive function as discussed in § 61, and it could be effected by a Turing machine as at end § 70.) Therefore, if there were a decision procedure for provability in the pure predicate calculus, there would be one for S_2, which would consist, given a formula E of S_2, in finding the corresponding predicate letter formula F ⊃ B, and applying the procedure for the predicate calculus to the latter. But by Theorem 33, if S_2 is simply consistent, there is no decision procedure for provability in S_2.

The argument applies also to the predicate calculus with equality, since by Theorem 41 (b) provability in the system of Lemma 18b is equivalent to provability in a system consisting of the predicate calculus with equality and seven particular axioms.

REMARK 1. The order in which the reduction steps (A) — (F) are performed is immaterial, so long as (B) and (C) precede (F), (A) precedes (B), (C) and (E), and if (D) precedes (B) the variable z is exempted from the closure operation of (B). (Or (C) may be omitted, and (F) performed once for each axiom; cf. *4 and *5 § 26.)

REMARK 2. The proof of Theorem 54 may be based on Theorem XII § 60 instead of Theorem 33, thus. By the foregoing reductions (A) — (F) on the system of Lemma 18b with Example 2 § 60, or by (the method of) those reductions on the system of Example 2 § 73, and using the consistency property to be established in § 79 (Theorem 53 (b) or Theorem 52): *For any fixed primitive (or general) recursive predicate $R(x, y)$, there is an effective procedure by which, given any number x, a predicate letter formula* K_x *can be found such that*

(1) $$(Ey)R(x, y) \equiv \{\vdash K_x \textit{ in the predicate calculus}\}.$$

Theorem 54 then follows from Theorem XII by taking $R(x, y) \equiv T_1(x, x, y)$. This proof from Theorem XII with Example 2 § 73 is essentially Church's original proof; that from Theorem 33 essentially Mostowski and Tarski's (1949 abstract).

REMARK 3. Our conception of a formal system S implies that the formulas of S should be effectively enumerable, or admit a Gödel numbering, so that given any formula A we can effectively find its number x, and inversely given any number x we can effectively decide whether it is the Gödel number of a formula and if so find that formula A_x. Then (cf. Remark 1 (a) § 60): *There is a general recursive predicate R such that*

(2) $$\{\vdash \mathrm{A}_x \text{ in } S\} \equiv (Ey)R(x, y).$$

So the decision problem for provability in any system S is equivalent to that for a predicate of the form $(Ey)R(x, y)$. By Remark 2, or by the (first) proof of Theorem 54 with the latter part of Example 3 § 61, the decision problem for the predicate calculus is of the highest degree of unsolvability for predicates of this form (cf. preceding Example 3 § 61). Thus (combining (1) and (2)), the decision problem for provability in any formal system is reduced to that for the predicate calculus (either classical or intuitionistic). This generalizes our remark (§ 75) that the problem for any axiomatic theory with an elementary axiom system reduces to it; but of course the reductions by going out of the system to a Gödel numbering via (2), and thence into the predicate calculus via (1) are very indirect.

By §§ 37, 72, 73, 75, provability in the predicate calculus with equality is equivalent to validity in every non-empty domain; so now there is no decision procedure for the latter property of an equality and predicate letter formula. Trahténbrot 1950 proves the analogous theorem for validity in every non-empty finite domain.

Reductions and special cases. Because so many particular questions (e.g. Fermat's "last theorem" § 13) and decision problems reduce to the decision problem for the predicate calculus, much work has been done on it, leading to positive results of two sorts: (α) reductions of the general problem, and (β) solutions of special cases. The results are often presented in a dual set-theoretic form, in which the problem is to decide as to the satisfiability of a predicate letter formula in some non-empty domain (§§ 72, 75), rather than as to its provability.

An early example of (α) is Skolem's normal form (Skolem 1920, Hilbert-Bernays 1934 pp. 158 ff). The Skolem proof-theoretic (satisfaction-theoretic) normal form is a prenex formula (Theorem 19 § 35) in which all the existential (generality) quantifiers come first. Given a predicate letter formula G, there can be found effectively a predicate letter formula M (N) of this form, such that M is provable in the predicate calculus (N is satisfiable in a given domain), if and only if G is. Thus the decision problem for provability (satisfiability) for predicate letter formulas generally is reduced to the same problem for Skolem normal forms (cf. the latter part of § 61). The normal form M (N) is not in general equivalent to G, but M (¬N) is interdeducible with G (¬G) in the predicate calculus with a postulated substitution rule (§ 37). Skolem used his satisfaction-theoretic normal form in simplifying the proof of Löwenheim's theorem and generalizing it, and Hilbert and Bernays 1939 employ it in proving Gödel's completeness theorem in a way which makes the formalization referred to in the proof of Theorem 36 § 72 reasonably simple.

An example of (β) is the solution of the decision problem by Löwenheim 1915 (simplified by Skolem 1919), and independently by Behmann 1922, for the case of predicate letter formulas containing only predicate letters with 0 or 1 argument. Equivalently, by Remark 1 § 34, the decision problem is solved for the *1-place predicate calculus*, i.e. the calculus with only 0- and 1-place predicate letters. (Cf. end § 72, Hilbert-Bernays 1934 pp. 179—209.)

Reductions and special cases of the decision problem have remained an active field of research, since Church showed that there can be no general solution (Theorem 54). The literature is too extensive to be cited here, and the reader is referred to Church's bibliography and the review sections of the Journal of Symbolic Logic (cf. the preface to the bibliography of this book). Quite a number of the results are described in Hilbert-Bernays 1934 and 1939. Church 1951 discusses special cases.

AXIOMATIC THEORIES. We take up now a method of Tarski (1949 abstract) for investigating the decision problems for axiomatic theories. We shall consider theories formalized on the basis of a logical calculus, which may be either the predicate calculus or the predicate calculus with equality. (Tarski uses the latter.) We shall usually say "formal system S" for uniformity with our previous terminology, where Tarski says "theory $\mathfrak{T}$" which emphasizes the mathematical application.

By the *logical constants* we shall mean the six logical symbols $\supset$, &, $\vee$, $\neg$, $\forall$, $\exists$, if the logical calculus is the predicate calculus; these and also $=$, if it is the predicate calculus with equality. The terms and formulas of a system are to be constructed using besides these logical constants a finite number of individual, function and predicate symbols, called the *non-logical constants* (but no predicate letters). The postulates besides those of the logical calculus shall be a finite or infinite set of *non-logical axioms*.

Following Tarski, we call such a system *finitely axiomatizable*, if the non-logical axioms are finite in number or all but some finite set of them are redundant (Example 2 § 74). We say of such systems that S_2 is an *extension* of S_1 (or S_1 is a *subsystem* of S_2), if each formula provable in S_1 is provable in S_2; S_2 must then have all the non-logical constants of S_1, but it may have others in addition. An extension S_2 of S_1 is a *finite extension*, if all but a finite number of the axioms of S_2 are provable in S_1. We say briefly that S_1 is *undecidable* to mean that the decision problem for provability in S_1 is unsolvable.

Following Tarski, we say that S is *essentially undecidable*, if S is (simply) consistent, and every (simply) consistent extension of S is undecidable.

Rosser 1936 showed that systems like our number-theoretic system of Chapter IV (if they are consistent) have this property (cf. Theorem 33 § 61). Then the formalized systems of axiomatic set theory of von Neumann 1925, of Bernays 1937-48 and of Gödel 1940 (if consistent) are examples of systems S which are both essentially undecidable (since they include the usual number-theory) and finitely axiomatizable. Mostowski and Tarski (1949 abstract) were the first to note the existence of a system S which is both essentially undecidable and finitely axiomatizable, and also simple enough to be easily interpretable in various other theories, in the sense to be defined next. This provides the basis for the application of the method of Tarski which is given in Theorem 45 (b) and (c). A still simpler example of an essentially undecidable and finitely axiomatizable system is that of Raphael Robinson (1950 abstract), which has thirteen non-logical axioms as described in Lemma 18b § 49 on the basis of the predicate calculus, or seven only (Axs. 14, 15, 18—21, and the formula of *137, or equivalently of *136) as it was described by Robinson on the basis of the predicate calculus with equality. Robinson states that none of these seven can be omitted without sacrificing the essential undecidability.

Tarski says that two systems S_1 and S_2 are *compatible*, if they have the same non-logical constants and a (simply) consistent common extension. Now consider any two systems S_1 and S_2 which in general do not have the same non-logical constants. First we take the case the logic is the predicate calculus with equality. Then S_2 is *consistently interpretable* in S_1, if S_1 and S_2 have a consistent common extension S_3, in which there is provable, for each n-place predicate symbol P (function symbol f) of S_2 which S_1 lacks, a formula having the form $P(x_1, \ldots, x_n) \sim F(x_1, \ldots, x_n)$ of an explicit definition of P (the form $f(x_1, \ldots, x_n) = w \sim F(x_1, \ldots, x_n, w)$, i.e. (iii) of Lemma 26 § 74) where the variables shown are distinct and $F(x_1, \ldots, x_n)$ $(F(x_1, \ldots, x_n, w))$ contains only these variables free and as non-logical constants only ones of S_1 and possibly additional individual symbols. For the case the logical calculus is the predicate calculus and S_2 has function symbols which S_1 lacks, furthermore S_1 shall have $=$ among its constants, and in S_3 there shall be provable the equality axioms for the predicate and function symbols of S_1. The situation is illustrated (rather trivially) by the S_1, S_2 and S_3 in the proof of Theorem 43 § 74 (but either for (a), or for (b) assuming consistency).

THEOREM 45. (a) *If S is undecidable, then every system S_1 which lacks none of the constants of S except possibly individual symbols and of which S is a finite extension is undecidable.*

(b) *If S is essentially undecidable and finitely axiomatizable, then every system S_1 which lacks none of the constants of S except possibly individual symbols and which has a consistent common extension S_3 with S (in particular every system S_1 compatible with S) is undecidable.*

(c) *If S is essentially undecidable and finitely axiomatizable, then every system S_1 in which S is consistently interpretable is undecidable.* (Tarski 1949 abstract.)

PROOFS. (a) By the reductions (B), (C), (D) applied only to the individual symbols of S which S_1 lacks, and (F). (Tarski takes the axioms to be closed ab initio, and deals with the case that S_1 and S have the same constants; then (B) and (D) are not required.)

(b) Let S_2 be the system having the axioms (and constants) of both S_1 and S. Then S_2 is a subsystem of S_3; and hence, since S_3 is consistent, so is S_2. Also S_2 is an extension of S; and hence, since S is essentially undecidable and S_2 is consistent, S_2 is undecidable. But S_2 is a finite extension of S_1. Now (a) applies with S_2 as its S.

(c) We shall treat in detail the case S has a function symbol f as its only constant (except perhaps individual symbols) which S_1 lacks, for the predicate calculus as the logic. If S has more such function symbols, we merely iterate the application of Theorem 42 and its lemmas; and if S has such predicate symbols, we use Example 1 § 74 likewise. The results will then hold also for the predicate calculus with equality, as (by Theorem 41 (b)) extending the logic to that is equivalent to assuming that the equality axioms for all the function and predicate symbols are present in all the systems considered (which only makes the argument easier).

Let S_3 be the common extension of S_1 and S described in the definition of consistent interpretability (with S as the S_2).

Let S_{4a} be the subsystem of S_3 having as its constants those of S_1, f, and the additional individual symbols (if any) belonging to S or occurring in $F(x_1, \ldots, x_n, w)$, and having as its non-logical axioms those of S_1 and of S, the equality axioms for the predicate and function symbols of S_1, and (iii).

Since S_{4a} is a subsystem of S_3 and S_3 is consistent, S_{4a} is consistent. Hence, since S_{4a} is an extension of S and S is essentially undecidable, S_{4a} is undecidable.

Using Lemmas 26 and 27 and Remark 2 (a) § 74, in the list of non-logical axioms for S_{4a} we can replace each one A of the non-logical axioms of S by its principal f-less transform A′, and (iii) by (i) and (ii), without changing the class of the provable formulas; call the resulting undecidable system S_4.

By Theorem 42 § 74, the function symbol f and its axiom (ii) can be eliminated from S_4, leaving a system S_5 which (by (IV) § 74) is also undecidable.

But S_5 has as its constants only those of S_1 and possibly individual symbols, and S_5 is a finite extension of S_1. So by (a) (with S_5 as its S), S_1 is undecidable.

Remark 4. For the conditions on S_3 in the definition of consistent interpretability, instead of (iii) we may have provable in S_3 a formula having the form $f(x_1, \ldots, x_n) = t(x_1, \ldots, x_n)$ of an explicit definition of f, where $t(x_1, \ldots, x_n)$ is a term containing only the variables shown and as non-logical constants only function symbols of S_1 except possibly individual symbols. For then $t(x_1, \ldots, x_n) = w$ is an $F(x_1, \ldots, x_n, w)$.

Example 1. By (b), since Robinson's system, call it S, is essentially undecidable and finitely axiomatizable, every formal system S_1 with the constants $=$, $'$, $+$, $\cdot$ (and perhaps others, e.g. 0), the provable sentences of which express true propositions about natural numbers, is undecidable, if we accept the simple consistency of a common extension S_3 (say that one which has the axioms and constants of bo.h S_1 and S) as guaranteed by the truth. To make the undecidability of such a system S_1 a metamathematical result, it remains to supply a metamathematical consistency proof for the S_3. — By (c) and Remark 4, since $'$ is definable explicitly from 1 as an individual symbol and $+$, the same holds for such systems with the constants $=$, $+$, $\cdot$ (at least).

Starting from Mostowski and Tarski's example of a finitely axiomatizable and essentially undecidable system, Mostowski and Tarski (1949 abstract), Tarski (1949a, 1949b abstracts), Julia Robinson (1949 abstract, 1949) and Raphael Robinson (1949 abstract) obtain in rapid succession the undecidability of a variety of mathematical theories in the arithmetic of integers and rationals, rings, groups, fields, lattices and projective geometries.

CHAPTER XV

CONSISTENCY, CLASSICAL AND INTUITIONISTIC SYSTEMS

§ 77. Gentzen's formal system. In Example 2 § 73 we found what may be described as a direct way of deducing A(**x**) from the axioms of S in the predicate calculus when $(Ey)R(x, y)$. This direct way can lead from the axioms to A(**x**) only when $(Ey)R(x, y)$. To establish the consistency property, i.e. that A(**x**) is deducible only when $(Ey)R(x, y)$, what we must do is to show that a roundabout way of proceeding in the predicate calculus can lead from the axioms to A(**x**) only when the direct way does. In the formalism of recursive functions, the corresponding consistency problem was trivial (§ 54, Example 3 § 60), precisely because no other than the direct way of proceeding from the assumption formulas was allowed by the rules of the system. This leads us to inquire whether there may not be a theorem about the predicate calculus asserting that, if a formula is provable (or deducible from other formulas), it is provable (or deducible) in a certain direct fashion; in other words, a theorem giving a normal form for proofs and deductions, the proofs and deductions in normal form being in some sense direct.

A theorem of this sort was obtained by Gentzen 1934-5*. We shall present it in § 78, and apply it in § 79 to obtain the consistency results referred to in Example 2 § 60 and Example 2 § 73 (and used in § 76), as well as the consistency of number theory with the restricted rule of induction (mentioned at the beginning of § 42). These consistency proofs can be given by other methods, as by Ackermann 1924-5, von Neumann 1927 and Herbrand 1930, 1931-2. All are somewhat long. Gentzen's is one of the easiest to follow, as the proof of his "Hauptsatz" or normal form theorem (of which it mainly consists) breaks down into a list of cases, each of which is simple to handle. Another application of this theorem is given in § 80. Except incidentally, §§ 81 and 82 are independent of §§ 77—80.

Gentzen's normal form for proofs in the predicate calculus requires a different classification of the deductive steps than is given by the postulates of the formal system of predicate calculus of Chapter IV

(§ 19). The implication symbol ⊃ has to be separated in its role of mediating inferences from its role as a component symbol of the formula being proved. In the former role it will be replaced by a new formal symbol → (read "gives" or "entails"), to which properties will be assigned similar to those of the informal symbol "⊢" in our former derived rules.

Gentzen's classification of the deductive operations is made explicit by setting up a new formal system of the predicate calculus. The formal system of propositional and predicate calculus studied previously (Chapters IV ff.) we call now a *Hilbert-type system*, and denote by *H*. Precisely, *H* denotes any one or a particular one of several systems, according to whether we are considering propositional calculus or predicate calculus, in the classical or the intuitionistic version (§ 23), and according to the sense in which we are using 'term' and 'formula' (§§ 17, 25, 31, 37, 72—76). The same respective choices will apply to the *Gentzen-type system G*1 which we introduce now and the *G*2, *G*3 and *G*3a later.

The transformation or deductive rules of *G*1 will apply to objects which are not formulas of the system *H*, but are built from them by an additional formation rule, so we use a new term 'sequent' for these objects. (Gentzen says "Sequenz", which we translate as "sequent", because we have already used "sequence" for any succession of objects, where the German is "Folge".) A *sequent* is a formal expression of the form $A_1, \ldots, A_l \rightarrow B_1, \ldots, B_m$ where $l, m \geq 0$ and $A_1, \ldots, A_l, B_1, \ldots, B_m$ are formulas. The part $A_1, \ldots, A_l$ is the *antecedent*, and $B_1, \ldots, B_m$ the *succedent* of the sequent $A_1, \ldots, A_l \rightarrow B_1, \ldots, B_m$.

When $l, m \geq 1$, the sequent $A_1, \ldots, A_l \rightarrow B_1, \ldots, B_m$ has the same interpretation for *G*1 as the formula $A_1 \,\&\, \ldots \,\&\, A_l \supset B_1 \vee \ldots \vee B_m$ for *H*. The interpretation extends to the cases with $l = 0$ or $m = 0$ by regarding $A_1 \,\&\, \ldots \,\&\, A_l$ for $l = 0$ (the "empty conjunction") as true and $B_1 \vee \ldots \vee B_m$ for $m = 0$ (the "empty disjunction") as false.

A formula *occurs* in (or *belongs* to) a sequent $A_1, \ldots, A_l \rightarrow B_1, \ldots, B_m$, if it is one of the $l+m$ occurrences of formulas $A_1, \ldots, A_l, B_1, \ldots, B_m$; and similarly for occurrence of a formula in antecedent or succedent. For example, $\mathcal{A}$ and $\mathcal{A} \,\&\, \mathcal{B}$ but not $\mathcal{B}$ occur in the sequent $\mathcal{A}, \mathcal{A} \,\&\, \mathcal{B} \rightarrow \mathcal{A}$. A variable (symbol, quantifier, etc.) *occurs* in a sequent, etc., if it occurs in some formula of the same.

As in Chapter V, we use Greek capitals "Γ", "Δ", "Θ", "Λ", etc. to stand for finite sequences of zero or more formulas, but now also as antecedent (succedent), or parts of antecedent (succedent), with separating formal commas included.

Postulates for the formal system $G1$

Stipulations: A, B, C, D are formulas; Γ, Δ, Θ, Λ are finite sequences of zero or more formulas; x is a variable; A(x) is a formula; t is a term free for x in A(x); and b is a variable free for x in A(x) and (unless b is x) not occurring free in A(x).

Restriction on variables (for two of the postulates as indicated): The variable b of the postulate shall not occur free in its conclusion. (When the A(x) does not contain the x free, then A(b) is A(x) no matter what variable b is; we agree in such a case to choose for the analysis a b not occurring free in the conclusion, so that the restriction is met.)

The difference between the classical and intuitionistic systems $G1$ is secured by the intuitionistic restriction stated for two of the postulates.

Axiom schema.

$$C \to C.$$

Logical rules of inference for the propositional calculus.

Introduction of	in succedent.	in antecedent.
$\supset$	$\dfrac{A, \Gamma \to \Theta, B}{\Gamma \to \Theta, A \supset B.}$	$\dfrac{\Delta \to \Lambda, A \qquad B, \Gamma \to \Theta}{A \supset B, \Delta, \Gamma \to \Lambda, \Theta.}$
&	$\dfrac{\Gamma \to \Theta, A \qquad \Gamma \to \Theta, B}{\Gamma \to \Theta, A \,\&\, B.}$	$\dfrac{A, \Gamma \to \Theta}{A \,\&\, B, \Gamma \to \Theta.}$ $\dfrac{B, \Gamma \to \Theta}{A \,\&\, B, \Gamma \to \Theta.}$
$\vee$	$\dfrac{\Gamma \to \Theta, A}{\Gamma \to \Theta, A \vee B.}$ $\dfrac{\Gamma \to \Theta, B}{\Gamma \to \Theta, A \vee B.}$	$\dfrac{A, \Gamma \to \Theta \qquad B, \Gamma \to \Theta}{A \vee B, \Gamma \to \Theta.}$
$\neg$	$\dfrac{A, \Gamma \to \Theta}{\Gamma \to \Theta, \neg A,}$ with Θ empty for the intuitionistic system.	$\dfrac{\Gamma \to \Theta, A}{\neg A, \Gamma \to \Theta.}$

Additional logical rules of inference for the predicate calculus.

Introduction of	in succedent.	in antecedent.
$\forall$	$\dfrac{\Gamma \to \Theta, A(b)}{\Gamma \to \Theta, \forall x A(x),}$ subject to the restriction on variables.	$\dfrac{A(t), \Gamma \to \Theta}{\forall x A(x), \Gamma \to \Theta.}$

$$\exists \qquad \frac{\Gamma \rightarrow \Theta, A(t)}{\Gamma \rightarrow \Theta, \exists x A(x).} \qquad \frac{A(b), \Gamma \rightarrow \Theta}{\exists x A(x), \Gamma \rightarrow \Theta,}$$

subject to the restriction on variables.

Structural rules of inference.

in succedent. in antecedent.

Thinning
$$\frac{\Gamma \rightarrow \Theta}{\Gamma \rightarrow \Theta, C,} \qquad \frac{\Gamma \rightarrow \Theta}{C, \Gamma \rightarrow \Theta.}$$
with Θ empty for the intuitionistic system.

Contraction
$$\frac{\Gamma \rightarrow \Theta, C, C}{\Gamma \rightarrow \Theta, C.} \qquad \frac{C, C, \Gamma \rightarrow \Theta}{C, \Gamma \rightarrow \Theta.}$$

Interchange
$$\frac{\Gamma \rightarrow \Lambda, C, D, \Theta}{\Gamma \rightarrow \Lambda, D, C, \Theta.} \qquad \frac{\Delta, D, C, \Gamma \rightarrow \Theta}{\Delta, C, D, \Gamma \rightarrow \Theta.}$$

Cut.
$$\frac{\Delta \rightarrow \Lambda, C \qquad C, \Gamma \rightarrow \Theta}{\Delta, \Gamma \rightarrow \Lambda, \Theta.}$$

For the classical system *G*1, the postulates except the two ⊃-rules fall into a dual-symmetric arrangement, thus. The rules for & and ∨ are dual to each other, the one set being transformed into the other by the interchange of & with ∨ and → with ←. Similarly, the ∀- and ∃-rules are dual. The axiom schema, the ¬-rules, and the structural rules of the four kinds, are each self-dual.

The rules in the left column we call *succedent rules*; and we denote them briefly by "→⊃", "→ &", "→∨", "→¬", "→∀", "→∃", "→*T*", "→ *C*", "→ *I*", respectively. The rules in the right column we call *antecedent rules*, and denote by "⊃ →", "& →", etc.

The logical rules constitute introductions of a logical symbol, but sometimes in the succedent (left column), and sometimes in the antecedent (right column). The formula in which the logical symbol is introduced is called the *principal formula*; and the one or two formulas shown explicitly in the premise(s) the *side formula*(*s*).

Example 1. The uppermost rule in the right column is "⊃-introduction in the antecedent", or "the ⊃-antecedent rule", or briefly "⊃ →". The principal formula is A ⊃ B, the first premise has A as side formula, and the second B.

The logical rules of $G1$ are more or less similar in form to the respective derived rules of Theorem 2 § 23, with the undefined formal symbol $\rightarrow$ appearing now in place of the defined metamathematical symbol "$\vdash$". An introduction in the succedent corresponds to an introduction in Theorem 2, and in the antecedent to an elimination in Theorem 2. The present axiom schema and structural rules correspond to general properties of the former $\vdash$ as listed in Lemma 5 § 20.

The tree form (end § 24) is used in the construction of proofs in $G1$; and "$\vdash$ S", where S is a sequent, is used to express that the sequent S is provable.

In exhibiting proofs (or parts thereof), it is tedious to show separately all the applications of the one-premise structural rules. We shall adopt the convention that a double line (with or without citation of another rule) stands for a sequence of zero or more thinnings ("*T*"), contractions ("*C*") and interchanges ("*I*") (following the application of the other rule when another is cited).

EXAMPLE 2. For any formulas A, B and C, (a) and (b) are proofs in $G1$ intuitionistically, (c) only classically.

(a)

$$\dfrac{\dfrac{\dfrac{\dfrac{A \rightarrow A \qquad \dfrac{A \rightarrow A \qquad \dfrac{B \rightarrow B \qquad C \rightarrow C}{B \supset C, B \rightarrow C}\supset\rightarrow}{B, A \supset (B \supset C), A \rightarrow C}\supset\rightarrow}{A, A \supset (B \supset C), A \supset B \rightarrow C}\supset\rightarrow}{A \supset (B \supset C), A \supset B \rightarrow A \supset C}\rightarrow\supset}{A \supset B \rightarrow (A \supset (B \supset C)) \supset (A \supset C)}\rightarrow\supset}{\rightarrow (A \supset B) \supset ((A \supset (B \supset C)) \supset (A \supset C)).}\rightarrow\supset$$

(b)

$$\dfrac{\dfrac{\dfrac{A \rightarrow A}{A, \neg A \rightarrow B}\neg\rightarrow}{\neg A \rightarrow A \supset B}\rightarrow\supset}{\rightarrow \neg A \supset (A \supset B).}\rightarrow\supset$$

(c)

$$\dfrac{\dfrac{\dfrac{A \rightarrow A}{\rightarrow A, \neg A}\rightarrow\neg}{\neg\neg A \rightarrow A}\neg\rightarrow}{\rightarrow \neg\neg A \supset A.}\rightarrow\supset$$

From the postulate list for $G1$, we verify by induction:

LEMMA 32a. *If* $\vdash \Gamma \rightarrow B_1, \ldots, B_m$ *in the intuitionistic system* $G1$, *then* $m = 0$ *or* $m = 1$.

LEMMA 32b. *If* $\vdash \Gamma \rightarrow B_1, \ldots, B_m$ *in the intuitionistic system* $G1$ *without using the rule* $\neg\rightarrow$, *then* $m = 1$.

Lemma 32a expresses the whole difference between the intuitionistic and the classical system $G1$; but it is useful to observe that we needed to restrict only two of the postulates for the intuitionistic system $G1$ to secure this difference.

Our first objective is to show (as did Gentzen) that system $G1$ is equivalent to our former system H, in the sense that, for any formula E, $\vdash \rightarrow$ E in $G1$, if and only if $\vdash$ E in H. This result will be contained in the next two theorems for Γ empty.

THEOREM 46. *If* $\Gamma \vdash$ E *in H with all variables held constant, then* $\vdash \Gamma \rightarrow$ E *in* $G1$. *When the given deduction in H uses the postulates only for certain of the symbols* $\supset$, &, $\vee$, $\neg$, $\forall$, $\exists$, *then the resulting proof in* $G1$ *uses the logical rules only for* $\supset$ *and for the same symbols.*

PROOF, by course-of-values induction on the length of the given deduction in H of E from Γ. Sixteen cases arise, as follows, according to the analysis for E in the given deduction.

CASE 0: E is one of the formulas Γ. Then the following is a proof in $G1$ of $\Gamma \rightarrow$ E.

$$\frac{E \rightarrow E}{\Gamma \rightarrow E.}$$

The other cases will be numbered as the respective postulates 1a, 1b, 2, 3, 4a, 4b, 5a, 5b, 6, 7, 8 or 8^{I}, 9 — 12 of H.

CASE 1b: E is an axiom by Axiom Schema 1b, i.e. E is $(A \supset B) \supset ((A \supset (B \supset C)) \supset (A \supset C))$ for some formulas A, B and C. Writing Γ before the $\rightarrow$ in the endsequent of Example 2 (a), and doubling the line over it (to represent thinnings), makes that tree into a proof in $G1$ of $\Gamma \rightarrow$ E.

CASE 2: E is an immediate consequence of two preceding formulas by Rule 2, i.e. for some pair of formulas A and B, E is B and the two preceding formulas are A and $A \supset B$. By the hypothesis of the induction, there are proofs in $G1$ of $\Gamma \rightarrow A$ and $\Gamma \rightarrow A \supset B$. Grafting these two proofs onto the following tree, we obtain a proof of $\Gamma \rightarrow B$.

$$\dfrac{\Gamma \rightarrow A \qquad \dfrac{\Gamma \rightarrow A \supset B \qquad \dfrac{A \rightarrow A \qquad B \rightarrow B}{A \supset B, A \rightarrow B}\supset\rightarrow}{A, \Gamma \rightarrow B}\text{Cut}}{\Gamma \rightarrow B.}\text{Cut}$$

CASE 8 OR 8^{I}. See Example 2 (c) or (b), respectively.

CASE 9: E is an immediate consequence of a preceding formula by Rule 9. Then E is $C \supset \forall x A(x)$, and the preceding formula is $C \supset A(x)$, where C does not contain x free. Let Γ_1 be the subsequence of Γ comprising those of the formulas Γ on which that preceding formula $C \supset A(x)$ depends in the given deduction of E from Γ. By omitting from the given deduction all formulas below the formula $C \supset A(x)$ and those above which depend on other assumption formulas than Γ_1, we obtain a deduction of $C \supset A(x)$ from Γ_1. Applying the hypothesis of the induction to this deduction, there is a proof in *G*1 of $\Gamma_1 \to C \supset A(x)$. Since the variables are held constant in the given deduction of $C \supset \forall x A(x)$ from Γ, none of the formulas Γ_1 contains free the variable x of the application of Rule 9. This and the fact that C does not contain x free are used in verifying that the restriction on variables is satisfied for the $\to\forall$ in the following.

$$\dfrac{\dfrac{\dfrac{\Gamma_1 \to C \supset A(x) \qquad \dfrac{C \to C \qquad A(x) \to A(x)}{C \supset A(x), C \to A(x)}\supset\to}{C, \Gamma_1 \to A(x)}\text{Cut}}{C, \Gamma_1 \to \forall x A(x)}\to\forall}{\Gamma \to C \supset \forall x A(x).}\to\supset$$

CASE 12: E is an immediate consequence of a preceding formula by Rule 12. Dual to Case 9.

We introduce the notation to be used in Theorem 47. Let F be some particular closed formula. Say that Θ is $B_1, \ldots, B_m$ $(m \geq 0)$. Then let Θ' be $B_1, \ldots, B_{m-1}$ (empty if $m \leq 1$), Θ'' be B_m if $m \geq 1$ and $\neg(F \supset F)$ if $m = 0$, $\neg\Theta$ be $\neg B_1, \ldots, \neg B_m$, and $\neg\Theta'$ be $\neg B_1, \ldots, \neg B_{m-1}$ (empty if $m \leq 1$).

COROLLARY 1. *If* $\Gamma, \neg\Theta' \vdash \Theta''$ *in H with all variables held constant, and provided for the intuitionistic systems that* $m \leq 1$, *then* $\vdash \Gamma \to \Theta$ *in G*1.

Use cases according as $m = 1$, $m = 0$ or $m > 1$.

COROLLARY 2. *For the classical (intuitionistic) systems when* $l, m \geq 1$ $(l \geq 1,\ m = 1)$: *If* $\vdash A_1 \& \ldots \& A_l \supset B_1 \vee \ldots \vee B_m$ *in H, then* $\vdash A_1, \ldots, A_l \to B_1, \ldots, B_m$ *in G*1.

THEOREM 47. *If* $\vdash \Gamma \to \Theta$ *in G*1, *then* $\Gamma, \neg\Theta' \vdash \Theta''$ *in H with all variables held constant.* (In particular: *If* $\vdash \Gamma \to E$ *in G*1, *then* $\Gamma \vdash E$ *in H with all variables held constant.*)

*Moreover, for the intuitionistic (classical) systems, when the given proof in G*1 *uses the logical rules only for certain of the symbols* $\supset$, &, $\vee$, $\neg$, $\forall$, $\exists$, *then the resulting deduction in H uses only the* $\supset$*-postulates (the* $\supset$*- and* $\neg$*-postulates) and the postulates for the same symbols, provided in case the symbols include* $\forall$ *but not* & *the* $\forall$*-postulates include Axiom Schema* 9a *of Lemma* 11 § 24.

Proof. We prove the first statement of the theorem by course-of-values induction on the height (i.e. number of levels) of the given proof in *G*1 of $\Gamma \rightarrow \Theta$, using cases according to the postulate of *G*1 applied last in this proof.

The additional details given in the second part of the theorem will be verified after we have gone through the cases. In all but the cases and subcases indicated by a single or double star, the demonstration of the existence of the resulting deduction is almost immediate by use of general properties of $\vdash$ and, in the case of a logical rule of *G*1, an application of the corresponding derived rule (other than a $\neg$-rule) of Theorem 2 § 23, or in the case of $\rightarrow\forall$ and $\exists\rightarrow$ of the corresponding strong rule of Lemma 10 § 24. In the cases marked by a single star, we use also the intuitionistic $\neg$-rules ($\neg$-introd. and weak $\neg$-elim. § 23) and sometimes *1 § 26. In the cases marked by a double star, we further use the classical (strong) $\neg$-elimination rule (Theorem 2). None of the nine cases not mentioned below requires either subcases or starring.

Case 1: the axiom schema. By general properties of $\vdash$, $C \vdash C$ in *H*.

Case 2: $\rightarrow\supset$. We have by the hypothesis of the induction that $A, \Gamma, \neg\Theta \vdash B$ in *H* with all variables held constant, and we must infer that $\Gamma, \neg\Theta \vdash A \supset B$ likewise. This we can do by $\supset$-introd.

Case 3: $\supset\rightarrow$. Subcase 1: Λ empty or Θ not empty. Then $(\Lambda, \Theta)''$ is Θ''. By hyp. ind., $\Delta, \neg\Lambda \vdash A$ and $B, \Gamma, \neg\Theta' \vdash \Theta''$. Thence, using $\supset$-elim., $A \supset B, \Delta, \Gamma, \neg\Lambda, \neg\Theta' \vdash \Theta''$. Subcase 2**: Λ not empty and Θ empty. By hyp. ind., $\Delta, \neg\Lambda \vdash A$ and $B, \Gamma \vdash \neg(F \supset F)$. By $\supset$-elim., $A \supset B, \Delta, \Gamma, \neg\Lambda \vdash \neg(F \supset F)$. Using *1, $A \supset B, \Delta, \Gamma, \neg\Lambda \vdash F \supset F$. Hence, by $\neg$-introd. and $\neg$-elim., $A \supset B, \Delta, \Gamma, \neg\Lambda' \vdash \neg\neg\Lambda'' \vdash \Lambda''$.

Case 10*: $\rightarrow\neg$. Subcase 1: Θ empty. From $A, \Gamma \vdash \neg(F \supset F)$, we infer $\Gamma \vdash \neg A$ by *1 and $\neg$-introd. Subcase 2: Θ not empty. From $A, \Gamma, \neg\Theta' \vdash \Theta''$, we infer $\Gamma, \neg\Theta', \neg\Theta'' \vdash \neg A$ by $\neg$-introd.

Case 11: $\neg\rightarrow$. Subcase 1*: Θ empty. Use weak $\neg$-elim. Subcase 2**: Θ not empty. Use $\neg$-introd. and $\neg$-elim.

CASE 12: $\rightarrow\forall$. By hyp. ind., $\Gamma, \neg\Theta \vdash A(b)$ with all variables held constant. By strong $\forall$-introd., $A(b) \vdash^{b} \forall x A(x)$. Hence $\Gamma, \neg\Theta \vdash \forall x A(x)$, with all variables including b held constant, since by the restriction on variables for $\rightarrow\forall$, Γ and Θ do not contain b free.

CASE 16: any one-premise structural rule. Let the premise be $\Gamma \rightarrow \Theta$, and the conclusion be $\Gamma^{\dagger} \rightarrow \Theta^{\dagger}$. Then $\Gamma^{\dagger}$ ($\Theta^{\dagger}$) comes from Γ (Θ) by permuting formulas, suppressing repetitions of formulas, or introducing new formulas. SUBCASE 1: $\Theta^{\dagger}$ is Θ. From $\Gamma, \neg\Theta' \vdash \Theta''$, we infer $\Gamma^{\dagger}$, $\neg\Theta' \vdash \Theta''$ by general properties of $\vdash$. SUBCASE 2*: $\Theta^{\dagger}$ is not Θ, and Θ is empty. By hyp. ind., $\Gamma \vdash \neg(F \supset F)$. Thence by general properties of $\vdash$, $\Gamma^{\dagger}, \neg\Theta^{\dagger\prime} \vdash \neg(F \supset F)$. Thence by *1 and weak $\neg$-elim., $\Gamma^{\dagger}$, $\neg\Theta^{\dagger\prime}$ $\vdash \Theta^{\dagger\prime\prime}$. SUBCASE 3**: $\Theta^{\dagger}$ is not Θ, and Θ is not empty. Then $\Theta^{\dagger}$ is not empty, and at least one of Θ and $\Theta^{\dagger}$ consists of more than one formula. By hyp. ind., $\Gamma, \neg\Theta' \vdash \Theta''$. By weak $\neg$-elim., $\Gamma, \neg\Theta', \neg\Theta'' \vdash \neg(F \supset F)$, i.e. Γ, $\neg\Theta \vdash \neg(F \supset F)$. Thence by general properties of $\vdash$, $\Gamma^{\dagger}$, $\neg\Theta^{\dagger}$ $\vdash \neg(F \supset F)$, i.e. $\Gamma^{\dagger}, \neg\Theta^{\dagger\prime}, \neg\Theta^{\dagger\prime\prime} \vdash \neg(F \supset F)$. Thence by *1, $\neg$-introd. and $\neg$-elim., $\Gamma^{\dagger}$, $\neg\Theta^{\dagger\prime} \vdash \Theta^{\dagger\prime\prime}$.

CASE 17: Cut. Treated as Case 3, except without using $\supset$-elim. SUBCASE 1: Λ empty or Θ not empty. SUBCASE 2**: Λ not empty and Θ empty.

To verify the second statement of the theorem, first suppose that the given proof in *G*1 of $\Gamma \rightarrow \Theta$ where Θ is $B_1, \ldots, B_m$ is intuitionistic and does not use the $\neg$-rules. Then using Lemma 32b, we see that none of the singly or doubly starred cases or subcases can occur. The statement then follows from the manner of treatment of the unstarred cases, by Lemma 11 § 24.

If the proof does use the $\neg$-rules but is intuitionistic, the statement permits the intuitionistic $\neg$-postulates of *H* to be used in the resulting deduction, and we need only verify, using Lemma 32a, that none of the doubly starred cases or subcases can occur.

COROLLARY. *When l, $m \geq 1$ (and hence for the intuitionistic systems, $m = 1$): If* $\vdash A_1, \ldots, A_l \rightarrow B_1, \ldots, B_m$ *in G*1, *then* $\vdash A_1 \,\&\, \ldots \,\&\, A_l \supset B_1 \vee \ldots \vee B_m$ *in H.*

§ 78. Gentzen's normal form theorem. EXAMPLE 1. The proof (a) contains a cut, while (b) is a proof without cut of the same sequent.

(a)

$$\dfrac{\dfrac{\mathcal{A}(b) \to \mathcal{A}(b)}{\mathcal{A}(b) \to \exists x\mathcal{A}(x)}\,{\scriptstyle \to\exists} \qquad \dfrac{\exists x\mathcal{A}(x) \to \exists x\mathcal{A}(x)}{\exists x\mathcal{A}(x), \neg\exists x\mathcal{A}(x) \to}\,{\scriptstyle \neg\to}}{\dfrac{\dfrac{\dfrac{\mathcal{A}(b), \neg\exists x\mathcal{A}(x) \to}{\neg\exists x\mathcal{A}(x) \to \neg\mathcal{A}(b)}\,{\scriptstyle \to\neg}}{\neg\exists x\mathcal{A}(x) \to \forall x\neg\mathcal{A}(x)}\,{\scriptstyle \to\forall}}{\to \neg\exists x\mathcal{A}(x) \supset \forall x\neg\mathcal{A}(x).}\,{\scriptstyle \to\supset}}\,\text{Cut}$$

(b)

$$\dfrac{\dfrac{\dfrac{\dfrac{\dfrac{\mathcal{A}(b) \to \mathcal{A}(b)}{\mathcal{A}(b) \to \exists x\mathcal{A}(x)}\,{\scriptstyle \to\exists}}{\mathcal{A}(b), \neg\exists x\mathcal{A}(x) \to}\,{\scriptstyle \neg\to}}{\neg\exists x\mathcal{A}(x) \to \neg\mathcal{A}(b)}\,{\scriptstyle \to\neg}}{\neg\exists x\mathcal{A}(x) \to \forall x\neg\mathcal{A}(x)}\,{\scriptstyle \to\forall}}{\to \neg\exists x\mathcal{A}(x) \supset \forall x\neg\mathcal{A}(x).}\,{\scriptstyle \to\supset}$$

The first proof uses an unnecessarily complicated formula $\exists x\mathcal{A}(x)$ in the antecedents of the right branch. This complication is unravelled by means of the cut. The second proof proceeds directly, without introducing complications that are subsequently unravelled.

The significance of proofs without cut, as in a sense proofs in normal form, is further emphasized by the subformula property (Lemma 33a below).

We define 'subformula' of a given formula thus.

1. If A is a formula, A is a *subformula* of A. 2 — 4. If A and B are formulas, the *subformulas* of A and the *subformulas* of B are *subformulas* of A ⊃ B, A & B and A ∨ B. 5. If A is a formula, the *subformulas* of A are *subformulas* of ¬A. 6 — 7. If x is a variable, A(x) is a formula, and t is a term free for x in A(x), the *subformulas* of A(t) are *subformulas* of ∀xA(x) and ∃xA(x). 8. A formula has only the *subformulas* required by 1 — 7.

Example 2. The subformulas of $\mathcal{A} \supset (\neg\mathcal{A} \supset \mathcal{B})$ are the five formulas $\mathcal{A} \supset (\neg\mathcal{A} \supset \mathcal{B})$, $\mathcal{A}$, $\neg\mathcal{A} \supset \mathcal{B}$, $\neg\mathcal{A}$, $\mathcal{B}$.

Example 3. (a) The subformulas of $\forall b\forall c(\mathcal{B}(c) \,\&\, \mathcal{A}(b))$ are the formulas $\forall b\forall c(\mathcal{B}(c) \,\&\, \mathcal{A}(b))$, $\forall c(\mathcal{B}(c) \,\&\, \mathcal{A}(\mathrm{t}))$, $\mathcal{B}(\mathrm{u}) \,\&\, \mathcal{A}(\mathrm{t})$, $\mathcal{B}(\mathrm{u})$, $\mathcal{A}(\mathrm{t})$, for every term t not containing c free and every term u. (b) The only subformula of $\mathcal{A}(c)$ is $\mathcal{A}(c)$.

From the postulate list for *G*1, we verify by induction:

LEMMA 33a. *Each formula occurring in any sequent of a proof in G1 without a cut is a subformula of some formula occurring in the endsequent.* (Subformula property.)

LEMMA 33b. *Each formula occurring in the antecedent (succedent) of any sequent of a proof in G1 without a cut or application of the* $\supset$*- or* $\neg$*-rules is a subformula of some formula occurring in the antecedent (succedent) of the endsequent.*

Gentzen's "Hauptsatz" or normal form theorem (Theorem 48 below) asserts that the cuts can always be eliminated from the proof of any sequent in which no variable both occurs free and occurs bound.

The restriction that no variable occur both free and bound in the endsequent does not detract from the usefulness of the theorem. For when variables do occur both free and bound in a given sequent, by replacing the formulas by others congruent to them we can obtain a sequent satisfying the restriction and provable if and only if the given one is provable (by Theorem 47, Lemma 15b § 33, *18a and *18b § 26, and Corollary 1 Theorem 46). The restriction is necessary, as we illustrate now.

EXAMPLE 4. Consider the proof

$$\dfrac{\dfrac{\dfrac{\dfrac{\dfrac{\mathcal{A}(b)\rightarrow\mathcal{A}(b)}{\mathcal{B}(c)\ \&\ \mathcal{A}(b)\rightarrow\mathcal{A}(b)}\ \&\!\rightarrow}{\forall c(\mathcal{B}(c)\ \&\ \mathcal{A}(b))\rightarrow\mathcal{A}(b)}\ \forall\!\rightarrow}{\forall b\forall c(\mathcal{B}(c)\ \&\ \mathcal{A}(b))\rightarrow\mathcal{A}(b)}\ \forall\!\rightarrow}{\forall b\forall c(\mathcal{B}(c)\ \&\ \mathcal{A}(b))\rightarrow\forall b\mathcal{A}(b)}\ \rightarrow\!\forall \qquad \dfrac{\mathcal{A}(c)\rightarrow\mathcal{A}(c)}{\forall b\mathcal{A}(b)\rightarrow\mathcal{A}(c)}\ \forall\!\rightarrow}{\forall b\forall c(\mathcal{B}(c)\ \&\ \mathcal{A}(b))\rightarrow\mathcal{A}(c).}\ \text{Cut}$$

The cut cannot be eliminated. For by Lemma 33a, no sequent in a proof without cut of $\forall b\forall c(\mathcal{B}(c)\ \&\ \mathcal{A}(b))\rightarrow\mathcal{A}(c)$ can contain the symbols $\supset$ and $\neg$; so the $\supset$- and $\neg$-rules cannot be used. Hence Lemma 33b applies. But the two lists of subformulas in Example 3 have no formula in common, so that no axiom satisfies the requirement of Lemma 33b. (The method of this example will be developed further in § 80.)

In proving the normal form theorem, we use a formal system *G2* obtained from *G1* by changing two of the postulates, as follows.

The cut is replaced by the following rule, called "mix". Here M is a formula (the *mix formula*); Π, Φ, Σ, Ω are sequences of zero or more formulas such that both Φ and Σ contain M; and Φ_M and Σ_M are the results of suppressing all occurrences of M in Φ and Σ, respectively.

$$\frac{\Pi \to \Phi \qquad \Sigma \to \Omega}{\Pi, \Sigma_M \to \Phi_M, \Omega.}\ \text{Mix}$$

EXAMPLE 5. The following is a mix.

$$\frac{\mathcal{A} \to \mathcal{B} \qquad \mathcal{B} \vee \mathcal{C}, \mathcal{B}, \mathcal{D}, \mathcal{B} \to}{\mathcal{A}, \mathcal{B} \vee \mathcal{C}, \mathcal{D} \to.}\ \text{Mix}$$

The $\supset \to$ of G1 (distinguished as $\supset \to_1$) is replaced by a new one ($\supset \to_2$), due for the classical system to Ketonen 1944. Here A, B, Γ, Θ are as above; and Θ° is Θ for the classical system and empty for the intuitionistic.

$$\frac{\Gamma \to \Theta^\circ, A \qquad B, \Gamma \to \Theta}{A \supset B, \Gamma \to \Theta.}\ \supset \to_2$$

Any cut can be accomplished by a mix (below left), and vice versa (right), with the help of *TCI* steps.

$$\cfrac{\cfrac{\Delta \to \Lambda, C \qquad C, \Gamma \to \Theta}{\Delta, \Gamma_C \to \Lambda_C, \Theta}\ \text{Mix}}{\Delta, \Gamma \to \Lambda, \Theta.} \qquad \cfrac{\cfrac{\Pi \to \Phi}{\Pi \to \Phi_M, M} \qquad \cfrac{\Sigma \to \Omega}{M, \Sigma_M \to \Omega}}{\Pi, \Sigma_M \to \Phi_M, \Omega.}\ \text{Cut}$$

Similarly, any $\supset \to_1$ can be accomplished by a $\supset \to_2$ (below), noting that for the intuitionistic case Λ is empty by Lemma 32a; and vice versa (left to the reader).

$$\cfrac{\cfrac{\Delta \to \Lambda, A}{\Delta, \Gamma \to \Lambda, \Theta^\circ, A} \qquad \cfrac{B, \Gamma \to \Theta}{B, \Delta, \Gamma \to \Lambda, \Theta}}{A \supset B, \Delta, \Gamma \to \Lambda, \Theta.}\ \supset \to_2$$

This shows that the two changes do not alter the class of the provable sequents, as we state with additional details in Lemma 34.

A proof in G1 or in G2 is said to have the *pure variable property*, or to be a *pure variable proof*, if no variable both occurs free and occurs bound in the proof, and for each application of $\to \forall$ or $\exists \to$ the variable b of the application occurs only in sequents above the conclusion of the application (where if the A(x) does not contain the x free, we choose for the analysis a b occurring only thus).

LEMMA 34. *If* $\vdash \Gamma \to \Theta$ *in* G1, *then* $\vdash \Gamma \to \Theta$ *in* G2; *and conversely. The proof in* G2 *contains a mix, only if the proof in* G1 *contains a cut; and conversely. Either proof contains applications of exactly the same-named logical rules as the other. If either proof has the pure variable property, so does the other. Lemmas* 32a—33b (*stated above for* G1 *and the cut*) *hold good also for* G2 *and the mix.*

LEMMA 35. *A given postulate application of G1 or G2 remains an application of the same postulate when, in the sequent(s) of the application (namely, the axiom in the case of the axiom schema, and the premise(s) and conclusion in the case of a rule of inference), a variable is changed in exactly its free occurrences (or in exactly its bound occurrences) to another variable not occurring either free or bound in the sequent(s) in question.*

Lemma 35, in the case of an application of $\rightarrow\forall$ or $\exists\rightarrow$, depends on the fact that the b and the x do not need to be the same variable (as they did for the corresponding rules 9 and 12 of the system *H*).

LEMMA 36. *A given postulate application of G1 or G2 remains an application of the same postulate when, in the sequent(s) of the application, a given term is substituted for (the free occurrences of) a given variable, provided in the case of an $\rightarrow\forall$ or $\exists\rightarrow$ that* (i) *the term does not contain the* b *of the application and* (ii) *the variable is not the* b *of the application, and also provided in every case that* (iii) *the term is free for the variable in each formula of the sequent(s).*

Condition (i) insures that the restriction on variables remains satisfied for an $\rightarrow\forall$ or $\exists\rightarrow$.

LEMMA 37. *Given a proof in G1 or G2 of a sequent in which no variable both occurs free and occurs bound, by changes in free and bound occurrences of variables in sequents of the proof (each postulate application remaining an application of the same postulate), we can obtain a proof of the same sequent in which proof no variable both occurs free and occurs bound.*

PROOF. Let $x_1, \ldots, x_n$ be the distinct variables which occur free in the endsequent and occur bound (elsewhere) in the proof, and $a_1, \ldots, a_p$ be the other distinct variables which occur both free and bound in the proof. Let $y_1, \ldots, y_n, b_1, \ldots, b_p$ be distinct variables not occurring in the proof. Change $x_1, \ldots, x_n$ in their bound occurrences only to $y_1, \ldots, y_n$, respectively, and $a_1, \ldots, a_p$ in their free occurences only to $b_1, \ldots, b_p$. By Lemma 35, the figure remains a proof; and by the hypothesis that the endsequent contains no variable both free and bound, the endsequent is unchanged.

LEMMA 38. *Given a proof in G1 or G2 in which no variable occurs both free and bound, by changes only in free occurrences of variables in it (each postulate application remaining an application of the same postulate), we can obtain a pure variable proof of the same sequent.*

PROOF. Suppose that in the given proof in $G1$ or $G2$ there are exactly q applications of the rules $\rightarrow \forall$ and $\exists \rightarrow$ with respective variables $c_1, \ldots, c_q$ (not necessarily distinct) as the b's of the applications. Select any q distinct variables $d_1, \ldots, d_q$ not occurring in the given proof. Choose one of the applications which is uppermost (i.e. has no other over it), say its b is c_1. Substitute d_1 for c_1 throughout all sequents above the conclusion of the application, but nowhere else. Under the restriction on variables for $\rightarrow \forall$ and $\exists \rightarrow$, c_1 cannot occur free in the conclusion of the application, so using Lemma 35 all postulate applications remain valid. Repeat the procedure, each time working on one of the applications of $\rightarrow \forall$ or $\exists \rightarrow$ which is uppermost amongst those not yet treated, until the b's of all q of the applications have been changed from c's to d's. Because each substitution alters only sequents above the conclusion of an application of $\rightarrow \forall$ or $\exists \rightarrow$, the endsequent is unaltered.

THEOREM 48. *Given a proof in* $G1$ (*in* $G2$) *of a sequent in which no variable occurs both free and bound, another proof in* $G1$ (*in* $G2$) *of the same sequent can be found which contains no cut* (*no mix*). *This proof is a pure variable proof. The only logical rules applied in it are ones which were applied in the given proof.* (Gentzen's Hauptsatz or normal form theorem, 1934-5.)

PROOF, reducing the theorem to a lemma. By Lemmas 34, 37 and 38, it suffices to prove the theorem for $G2$ assuming the given proof already to have the pure variable property. We do so by induction on the number m of mixes in this 'given proof'. If $m > 0$, there must occur in it a mix which has no other mix over it. Consider the part of the given proof which terminates with the conclusion $\Pi, \Sigma_M \rightarrow \Phi_M, \Omega$ of this mix; call it the 'given part'. Suppose that we can transform this given part so as to obtain another proof in $G2$ of $\Pi, \Sigma_M \rightarrow \Phi_M, \Omega$ without mix; call it the 'resulting part'. Then the replacement of the given part by the resulting part in the given proof gives us a new proof in $G2$ of the same sequent with only $m-1$ mixes. Suppose further that the resulting part can be constructed so that it has the pure variable property by itself, and also contains no variable free (bound; as the b of an $\rightarrow \forall$ or $\exists \rightarrow$) that did not so occur in the given part. Then the new proof as a whole will have the pure variable property. Hence we can apply the hypothesis of the induction to conclude that there is a pure variable proof with no mix. To prove the theorem it thus remains to establish the following lemma.

EXAMPLE 1 (continued). The given part for (a) (restated with a mix instead of a cut) is as follows.

$$\dfrac{\dfrac{\mathcal{A}(b) \rightarrow \mathcal{A}(b)}{\mathcal{A}(b) \rightarrow \exists x\mathcal{A}(x)} \rightarrow\exists \qquad \dfrac{\exists x\mathcal{A}(x) \rightarrow \exists x\mathcal{A}(x)}{\neg\exists x\mathcal{A}(x), \exists x\mathcal{A}(x) \rightarrow} \neg\rightarrow}{\mathcal{A}(b), \neg\exists x\mathcal{A}(x) \rightarrow.} \text{Mix}$$

LEMMA 39. *Given a proof in G2 of* $\Pi, \Sigma_M \rightarrow \Phi_M, \Omega$ *with a mix as the final step, and no other mix, and with the pure variable property, a proof in G2 of* $\Pi, \Sigma_M \rightarrow \Phi_M, \Omega$ *can be found with no mix, with the pure variable property, and with no variable occurring free (bound; as the* b *of an* $\rightarrow\forall$ *or* $\exists\rightarrow$*) which did not so occur in the given proof. Only logical rules are applied in the resulting proof which are applied in the given proof.* (Principal lemma.)

PROOF OF THE PRINCIPAL LEMMA. We define the *left rank a* of a mix as the greatest number of sequents, located consecutively one above another at the bottom of any branch terminating with the left premise of the mix, which contain the mix formula M in the succedent. The *right rank b* is defined similarly. The *rank* $r = a+b$. (The least possible rank is 2.) The *grade g* of the mix is the number (≥ 0) of occurrences of logical symbols ($\supset$, &, $\vee$, $\neg$, $\forall$, $\exists$) in the mix formula M.

EXAMPLE 1 (concluded). The left rank is 1, the right rank 2, the rank 3, and the grade 1.

The lemma is proved by course-of-values induction on the grade *g* of the mix. Within both the basis and the induction step of this induction, a course-of-values induction is used on the rank *r*. We give a treatment by cases, so that by drawing upon the results of the cases the bases and induction steps of the inductions can all be carried through.

We write the mix to be eliminated thus,

$$\frac{\Pi \rightarrow \Phi \qquad \Sigma \rightarrow \Omega}{\Pi, \Sigma_M \rightarrow \Phi_M, \Omega,} \qquad \text{or briefly} \qquad \frac{S_1 \qquad S_2}{S_3,}$$

where M ε Φ and M ε Σ.

The letters "A", "B", "C", "D", "Γ", "Θ", "x", "A(x)", "t", "b" will refer to the statements of the other postulates in question.

A. PRELIMINARY CASES.

CASE 1a: S_1 has M in the antecedent, i.e. M ε Π. Then the conclusion $\Pi, \Sigma_M \rightarrow \Phi_M, \Omega$ of the mix comes from its second premise $\Sigma \rightarrow \Omega$ by *TCI*, and is hence provable without mix. The intuitionistic restriction on the $\rightarrow T$'s can be satisfied, as the *TCI* steps terminate with the original endsequent, which by Lemma 32a can have intuitionistically at most one formula in its succedent.

CASE 2a: the left rank is 1, and S_1 is by a structural rule. Since $M \in \Phi$, but not to the succedent of the premise for the inference of S_1, the inference can only be a $\rightarrow T$ with M as the C. Thus the bottom of the given proof is as at the left below with $M \notin \Theta$. We alter this to the figure at the right, to obtain a proof of the original endsequent without mix.

$$\dfrac{\dfrac{\Gamma \rightarrow \Theta}{\Gamma \rightarrow \Theta, M}\rightarrow T \qquad \Sigma \rightarrow \Omega}{\Gamma, \Sigma_M \rightarrow \Theta, \Omega.}\text{Mix} \qquad\qquad \dfrac{\Gamma \rightarrow \Theta}{\Gamma, \Sigma_M \rightarrow \Theta, \Omega.}$$

CASES 1b, 2b: similarly, reading "S_2", "succedent", "Ω", "right" in place of "S_1", "antecedent", "Π", "left", respectively. Treated symmetrically to Cases 1a, 2a.

B. OTHER CASES. For each of these cases, it is part of the case hypothesis that none of the four preliminary cases applies.

B1: the rank is 2. Since Cases 1a, 1b are excluded, S_1 and S_2 must both be conclusions of inferences. Since the rank is 2 and Cases 2a and 2b are excluded, both inferences must be logical. Moreover, since the rank is only 2, M must be the principal formula of both inferences. Therefore M contains a logical symbol, and the mix is of grade ≥ 1. Thus these cases can arise only under the induction step for the induction on grade, and the hypothesis of the induction on the grade is available in treating them. The rules used in inferring S_1 and S_2 can only be, respectively, the rule introducing the outermost logical symbol of M in succedent, and the rule introducing the same symbol in antecedent. Thus under B1 we have only the following six cases.

CASE 3: S_1 is by $\rightarrow \supset$, and S_2 by $\supset \rightarrow$, with M as the principal formula $A \supset B$. Then the bottom of the given proof is as follows, where $A \supset B \notin \Theta, \Gamma$ since the rank is only 2.

$$\dfrac{\dfrac{A, \Pi \rightarrow \Theta, B}{\Pi \rightarrow \Theta, A \supset B}\rightarrow\supset \qquad \dfrac{\Gamma \rightarrow \Omega^\circ, A \qquad B, \Gamma \rightarrow \Omega}{A \supset B, \Gamma \rightarrow \Omega}\supset\rightarrow}{\Pi, \Gamma \rightarrow \Theta, \Omega.}\text{Mix}$$

We alter this to the following.

$$\dfrac{\dfrac{\dfrac{\Gamma \rightarrow \Omega^\circ, A \qquad A, \Pi \rightarrow \Theta, B}{\Gamma, \Pi_A \rightarrow \Omega^\circ_A, \Theta, B}\text{Mix} \qquad B, \Gamma \rightarrow \Omega}{\Gamma, \Pi_A, \Gamma_B \rightarrow \Omega^\circ_{AB}, \Theta_B, \Omega}\text{Mix}}{\Pi, \Gamma \rightarrow \Theta, \Omega.}$$

The upper mix is of grade lower than the original, so by the hypothesis of the induction on the grade, it can be eliminated, i.e. a proof without mix of its conclusion can be found. Then the lower mix will have no mix over it, and can likewise be eliminated. Thus we obtain a proof without mix of the original endsequent $\Pi, \Gamma \rightarrow \Theta, \Omega$.

CASE 4: S_1 is by $\rightarrow \&$, and S_2 by $\& \rightarrow$, with M as the principal formula A & B.

CASE 5: S_1 is by $\rightarrow \vee$, and S_2 by $\vee \rightarrow$, with M as the principal formula $A \vee B$. Treatment is dual to that of Case 4.

CASE 6: S_1 is by $\rightarrow \neg$, and S_2 by $\neg \rightarrow$, with M as the principal formula $\neg A$.

CASE 7: S_1 is by $\rightarrow \forall$, and S_2 by $\forall \rightarrow$, with M as the principal formula $\forall x A(x)$. We have as the given figure, where $\forall x A(x) \notin \Theta, \Gamma$,

$$\dfrac{\dfrac{\Pi \rightarrow \Theta, A(b)}{\Pi \rightarrow \Theta, \forall x A(x)} \rightarrow\forall \qquad \dfrac{A(t), \Gamma \rightarrow \Omega}{\forall x A(x), \Gamma \rightarrow \Omega} \forall\rightarrow}{\Pi, \Gamma \rightarrow \Theta, \Omega.} \text{Mix}$$

In constructing the altered figure, we shall need a proof of $\Pi \rightarrow \Theta, A(t)$. If A(x) does not contain x free, then A(b) and A(t) are the same formula, and we already have it. Suppose then that A(x) does contain x free. Then A(t) contains t, and so, since t is free for x in A(x), the variables of t occur free in A(t). Now we can conclude from the pure variable property of the given proof of $\Pi, \Gamma \rightarrow \Theta, \Omega$ that (i) no variable of t is the b of an $\rightarrow \forall$ or $\exists \rightarrow$ in the proof of $\Pi \rightarrow \Theta, A(b)$ in the left branch of our figure, (ii) our b is not the b of an $\rightarrow \forall$ or $\exists \rightarrow$ in the same, and (iii) t is free for b in all formulas of the same (since the pure variable property allows no variable to occur both free and bound). Moreover, in view of the restriction on variables for the exhibited $\rightarrow \forall$, (iv) b does not occur in Π, Θ. Therefore, using Lemma 36, by substituting t for b throughout the proof of $\Pi \rightarrow \Theta, A(b)$ we obtain a proof of $\Pi \rightarrow \Theta, A(t)$. When this proof is used in the altered figure as follows, the new proof of $\Pi, \Gamma \rightarrow \Theta, \Omega$ thus obtained will have the pure variable property and will contain free (bound; as the b of an $\rightarrow \forall$ or $\exists \rightarrow$) no variable not previously so occurring.

$$\dfrac{\dfrac{\Pi \rightarrow \Theta, A(t) \qquad A(t), \Gamma \rightarrow \Omega}{\Pi, \Gamma_{A(t)} \rightarrow \Theta_{A(t)}, \Omega} \text{Mix}}{\Pi, \Gamma \rightarrow \Theta, \Omega.}$$

CASE 8: S_1 is by $\rightarrow\exists$, and S_2 by $\exists\rightarrow$, with M as the principal formula $\exists xA(x)$. Dual to Case 7.

B2: the rank is > 2. These cases can only occur in the induction step of an induction on the rank (either within the basis, or the induction step, of the induction on the grade). Hence the hypothesis of the induction on rank is available in treating them.

B2.1: the left rank is ≥ 2. Then M occurs in the succedent of at least one of the premises for the inference of S_1.

CASE 9a: S_1 is by a succedent structural rule S with M not the C and not the D, or S_1 is by an antecedent structural rule S. Let the given figure be as shown at the left. We alter this as shown at the right (explanation follows).

$$\dfrac{\dfrac{\Pi_1 \rightarrow \Phi_1}{\Pi \rightarrow \Phi}\, S \qquad \Sigma \rightarrow \Omega}{\Pi, \Sigma_M \rightarrow \Phi_M, \Omega.}\,\text{Mix} \qquad\qquad \dfrac{\dfrac{\dfrac{\Pi_1 \rightarrow \Phi_1 \qquad \Sigma \rightarrow \Omega}{\Pi_1, \Sigma_M \rightarrow \Phi_{1M}, \Omega}\,\text{Mix}}{\dfrac{\Pi_1, \Sigma_M \rightarrow \Omega, \Phi_{1M}}{\Pi, \Sigma_M \rightarrow \Omega, \Phi_M}\, S}}{\Pi, \Sigma_M \rightarrow \Phi_M, \Omega.}$$

Because $M \in \Phi_1$ (by B2.1), we can take $\Pi_1 \rightarrow \Phi_1$ as first premise for the new mix. Then from the case hypothesis and the form of the one-premise structural rules, we verify that the new S is correct. In the altered figure, the rank of the mix is one less than in the original. Hence by the hypothesis of the induction on the rank, we can find a proof of its conclusion, and hence of the original endsequent, without mix.

CASE 10a: S_1 is by a succedent structural rule S with M as the C or the D. Let the premise be $\Pi \rightarrow \Phi_1$. From the form of the succedent structural rules, we verify that then Φ_{1M} and Φ_M are identical.

$$\dfrac{\dfrac{\Pi \rightarrow \Phi_1}{\Pi \rightarrow \Phi}\, S \qquad \Sigma \rightarrow \Omega}{\Pi, \Sigma_M \rightarrow \Phi_M, \Omega.}\,\text{Mix} \qquad\qquad \dfrac{\Pi \rightarrow \Phi_1 \qquad \Sigma \rightarrow \Omega}{\Pi, \Sigma_M \rightarrow \Phi_M, \Omega.}\,\text{Mix}$$

CASE 11a: S_1 is by a one-premise logical rule L. The inference by any one of these rules which gives S_1 has the form

$$\dfrac{\Lambda_1, \Gamma \rightarrow \Theta, \Lambda_2}{\Xi_1, \Gamma \rightarrow \Theta, \Xi_2}\, L$$

where each of Λ_1, Λ_2 is either a side formula or empty, and one of Ξ_1, Ξ_2 is the principal formula while the other is empty.

SUBCASE 1: Ξ_2 is not M. Then $M \in \Theta$, since $M \in \Theta, \Xi_2$. We write the given figure thus.

$$\dfrac{\dfrac{\Lambda_1, \Gamma \rightarrow \Theta, \Lambda_2}{\Xi_1, \Gamma \rightarrow \Theta, \Xi_2}\,L \qquad \Sigma \rightarrow \Omega}{\Xi_1, \Gamma, \Sigma_M \rightarrow \Theta_M, \Xi_2, \Omega.}\,\text{Mix}$$

We alter to this (explanation follows).

$$\dfrac{\dfrac{\dfrac{\dfrac{\Lambda_1, \Gamma \rightarrow \Theta, \Lambda_2 \qquad \Sigma \rightarrow \Omega}{\Lambda_1, \Gamma, \Sigma_M \rightarrow \Theta_M, \Lambda_{2M}, \Omega}\,\text{Mix}}{\Lambda_1, \Gamma, \Sigma_M \rightarrow \Theta_M, \Omega, \Lambda_2}}{\Xi_1, \Gamma, \Sigma_M \rightarrow \Theta_M, \Omega, \Xi_2}\,L}{\Xi_1, \Gamma, \Sigma_M \rightarrow \Theta_M, \Xi_2, \Omega.}$$

The new L has Γ, Σ_M as its Γ and Θ_M, Ω as its Θ. The conclusion of the new L is the original endsequent, except for the order of formulas within the succedent. This enables us to infer that, if L is $\rightarrow \forall$ or $\exists \rightarrow$, the restriction on variables is satisfied for the new application, since by the pure variable property of the given proof, the b cannot occur in the original endsequent. If the given proof is intuitionistic, then (by Lemma 32a) Θ, Λ_2 consists of at most one formula. But $M \in \Theta$; hence Λ_2 is empty. Therefore the *TCI* steps preceding the new L require no violation of the intuitionistic restriction on $\rightarrow T$. (The possibility that the new L is a $\rightarrow \neg$ violating the intuitionistic restriction is ruled out a priori, by comparison of its conclusion with the given endsequent; but in fact L cannot be $\rightarrow \neg$.) The new mix is of rank one less than the original.

SUBCASE 2: Ξ_2 is M. Then Ξ_1 is empty, and we omit it in writing the given figure thus.

$$\dfrac{\dfrac{\Lambda_1, \Gamma \rightarrow \Theta, \Lambda_2}{\Gamma \rightarrow \Theta, M}\,L \qquad \Sigma \rightarrow \Omega}{\Gamma, \Sigma_M \rightarrow \Theta_M, \Omega.}\,\text{Mix}$$

Since Ξ_2 is M, then Λ_2 is not M (and hence $M \in \Theta$, since $M \in \Theta, \Lambda_2$ by B2.1). Because Case 1b is excluded, $M \notin \Omega$. We use these facts in writing the mixes in the altered figure thus.

$$\dfrac{\dfrac{\dfrac{\dfrac{\Lambda_1, \Gamma \rightarrow \Theta, \Lambda_2 \qquad \Sigma \rightarrow \Omega}{\Lambda_1, \Gamma, \Sigma_M \rightarrow \Theta_M, \Lambda_2, \Omega}\,\text{Mix}}{\Lambda_1, \Gamma, \Sigma_M \rightarrow \Theta_M, \Omega, \Lambda_2}}{\Gamma, \Sigma_M \rightarrow \Theta_M, \Omega, M}\,L \qquad \Sigma \rightarrow \Omega}{\dfrac{\Gamma, \Sigma_M, \Sigma_M \rightarrow \Theta_M, \Omega, \Omega}{\Gamma, \Sigma_M \rightarrow \Theta_M, \Omega.}}\,\text{Mix}$$

If L is $\rightarrow\forall$ or $\exists\rightarrow$, the restriction on variables is satisfied because Γ, Σ_M, Θ_M, Ω, M all occur in the given pure variable proof elsewhere than above the conclusion of the original L. (But L cannot be $\exists\rightarrow$.) This subcase cannot occur intuitionistically, since the sequent $\Gamma \rightarrow \Theta$, M occurring in the given proof has more than one M in its succedent. Now the upper mix in the altered figure is of rank one lower than the original mix; so by the hypothesis of the induction on rank, it can be eliminated. Then the lower mix will have no mix over it. Since M $\not\mathcal{E}$ Ω, Λ_2, the left rank will be only 1, while the right rank will be the same as in the original mix. Since by hypothesis the left rank was originally ≥ 2, the rank of this mix is less than that of the original; and hence by the hypothesis of the induction on rank, it too can be eliminated.

CASE 12a: S_1 is by a two-premise logical rule L, except the intuitionistic $\supset\rightarrow$. The inference which gives S_1 may be written

$$\frac{\Lambda_{11}, \Gamma \rightarrow \Theta, \Lambda_{12} \qquad \Lambda_{21}, \Gamma \rightarrow \Theta, \Lambda_{22}}{\Xi_1, \Gamma \rightarrow \Theta, \Xi_2.} L$$

Treatment is similar to Case 11a. Both premises are mixed with $\Sigma \rightarrow \Omega$ (noting that M $\mathcal{E}$ Θ), prior to the L in the altered figure.

CASE 13: S_1 is by the intuitionistic $\supset\rightarrow$. Since M $\mathcal{E}$ Θ, and Θ is at most one formula, Θ is M. Only the second premise B, $\Gamma \rightarrow$ M is mixed with $\Sigma \rightarrow \Omega$ in the altered figure.

B2.2. CASES 9b—12b. Statement and treatment symmetric to Cases 9a — 12a, except as follows. The intuitionistic verifications for Case 11b are immediate. (Subcase 2 can arise intuitionistically.) The treatment of the intuitionistic $\supset\rightarrow$ can be included in Case 12b by writing Θ° in the first premise; the verification that the new $\supset\rightarrow$ has an empty sequent for its Θ° is obtained by observing that intuitionistically the Φ of the given mix is simply M.

The following application of Theorem 48 was given for the intuitionistic system by Curry 1939.

THEOREM 49. *If a formula* E *is provable in the intuitionistic (classical) system H, it is provable using only the $\supset$-postulates (the $\supset$- and $\neg$-postulates) and the postulates for the logical symbols occurring in the formula, provided that in case $\forall$ occurs but not & the $\forall$-postulates include Axiom Schema* 9a *of Lemma* 11 § 24.

PROOF. Using Lemma 33a, no logical rules can be applied in a proof in $G1$ without cut, except rules for logical symbols occurring in the endsequent. The theorem follows by Theorems 46 (using the first part only), 48 and 47 (both parts), if no variable occurs in E both free and bound; otherwise, use also Remark 1 (c) § 33.

Curry's book 1950 (not available during the writing of the present §§ 77—80) contains contributions to the theory of Gentzen-type systems, and a full bibliography. Curry uses the name "elimination theorem" for the Hauptsatz. Our name "normal form theorem" is intended to suggest the intent of the theorem, when it is merely explained, without giving details of Gentzen's system, that the normal form is one for proofs; and we have kept "elimination theorem" for cases when a symbol or notation is being eliminated as in § 74. (But "normal form" has the similar disadvantage that it commonly refers to one for formulas as in §§ 29, 76.)

The next two sections, in which two applications of the theorem are presented, may be read independently of each other.

***§ 79. Consistency proofs.** For $G1$ or $G2$, we call an application of one of the structural rules a *structural inference*; of one of the logical rules of the propositional calculus, a *propositional inference*; of one of the additional logical rules of the predicate calculus, a *predicate inference.*

Under special assumptions as to the form of the endsequent, a still further normalization of proofs can be achieved, as in the following "extended Hauptsatz" given by Gentzen 1934-5 for his classical system. (It is closely related to Herbrand's theorem, 1930.) As Gentzen remarked, the proof is an illustration of the possibilities for permuting inferences in his systems. These possibilities are discussed further in Curry 1952 for the classical system of his 1950, and in Kleene 1952 for the classical and intuitionistic systems described here. For example:

THEOREM 50. *Given a sequent containing only prenex formulas and in which no variable occurs both free and bound, and given a proof of this sequent in the classical system* $G1$ (*the intuitionistic system* $G1$ *without* $\vee\rightarrow$), *another proof in the same system of the same sequent can be found which contains no cut and in which there is an* (*occurrence of*) *a sequent* S (called the *midsequent*) *such that no quantifiers occur in* S, *and the part of the proof from* S *to the endsequent consists solely of predicate and structural inferences. The new proof is a pure variable proof. Similarly reading "*$G2$*", "mix" for "*$G1$*", "cut", respectively.*

PROOF, reducing the theorem to a lemma. We suppose Theorem 48 already applied, so that we are dealing with a given pure variable proof in *G*1 without cut (or *G*2 without mix). By the subformula property, only prenex formulas can occur in sequents of this proof.

Consider any axiom in the given proof containing quantifiers, say that ∀ comes first. We can replace the axiom (left) by the following figure (right),

$$\forall x A(x) \rightarrow \forall x A(x), \qquad \dfrac{\dfrac{A(b) \rightarrow A(b)}{\forall x A(x) \rightarrow A(b)}\ \forall\rightarrow}{\forall x A(x) \rightarrow \forall x A(x),}\ \rightarrow\forall$$

where b is a variable not previously occurring in the proof. The formula A(b) of the new axiom has one less quantifier than the formula ∀xA(x) of the original axiom. Similarly, if ∃ comes first. By induction on the sum of the numbers of quantifiers in the formulas of all the axioms, we can thus eliminate axioms containing quantifiers altogether from the given proof (retaining its other mentioned features).

Now suppose, as we state in the following lemma, that we can rearrange the logical inferences in this proof (retaining its other features) so that each predicate inference follows all the propositional inferences. Then there will be (an occurrence of) a sequent S_1 below which the proof contains only predicate and structural inferences (with no branchings, as the rules considered are all one premise rules) and above which only propositional and structural inferences. There may be occurrences of formulas with quantifiers in S_1 and above. However none of them is as side formula for a propositional inference, since the resulting principal formula would not be prenex. None of them is as principal formula, since there are no predicate inferences in this part of the proof. None of them is in an axiom, as previously arranged. Hence each postulate application in the part of the proof down to S_1 inclusive will remain correct, if we alter this part of the proof by suppressing every occurrence in it of a formula containing a quantifier, except that some of the structural inferences may thereby become identical inferences (with premise and conclusion the same) and can be omitted. This alteration will replace S_1 by a sequent S containing no quantifiers, but from S we can pass to S_1 by zero or more *T* and *I* steps, and thence by the unaltered part of the proof using only predicate and structural inferences to the original endsequent. Thus we obtain the new proof as described in the theorem, with S as the midsequent.

LEMMA 40. *Given a pure variable proof in the classical system G*1 (*the intuitionistic system G*1 *without* ∨ →) *without cut of a sequent containing* *only prenex formulas, another such proof of the same sequent can be found in which each predicate inference follows every propositional inference. The same sequents occur as axioms in the new proof as in the given proof. Similarly reading "G2", "mix" for "G1", "cut", respectively.*

PROOF OF THE LEMMA. Consider any predicate inference in the given proof, and count the number of propositional inferences occurring in the branch leading from its conclusion down to the endsequent of the entire proof. The sum of these numbers, for all the predicate inferences in the proof, we call the *order* of the proof. We establish the lemma by induction on the order.

If the order is not 0, there is some predicate inference such that a propositional inference occurs below it with no intervening logical inference.

CASE 1: the predicate inference is an $\to \forall$, and the first propositional inference below it is a one-premise inference L. As noted above, using the subformula property, the $\forall x A(x)$ of the $\to \forall$ cannot be the side formula of the inference L. Hence the given figure is as shown at the left. Classically we alter this to the figure shown at the right.

$$\begin{array}{cl} \Gamma_1 \to \Theta_1, A(b) & \\ \hline \Gamma_1 \to \Theta_1, \forall x A(x) & \to \forall \\ \hline\hline \Gamma_2 \to \Phi, \forall x A(x), \Theta_2 & \\ \hline \Gamma_3 \to \Phi, \forall x A(x), \Theta_3. & L \end{array} \qquad\qquad \begin{array}{cl} \Gamma_1 \to \Theta_1, A(b) & \\ \hline \Gamma_1 \to \Theta_1, A(b), \forall x A(x) & \to T \\ \hline\hline \Gamma_2 \to \Phi, A(b), \forall x A(x), \Theta_2 & \\ \hline \Gamma_3 \to \Phi, \forall x A(x), \Theta_3, A(b) & L \\ \hline\hline \Gamma_3 \to \Phi, \forall x A(x), \Theta_3. & \to \forall \end{array}$$

The $\to T$ is to take care of the possibility that the *TCI* steps in the given figure include a $\to C$ with $\forall x A(x)$ as the C. The pure variable property of the given proof ensures that the restriction on variables is satisfied for the $\to \forall$ in the altered figure. Intuitionistically Θ_1, Φ, Θ_2 and Θ_3 are all empty, and then we omit the $\to T$ in constructing the altered figure. The alteration decreases the order of the proof by 1.

CASE 2: $\to \forall$ followed by a two-premise propositional inference L. Classically the treatment has only to be changed to show an extra premise (either left or right) above the L, preceded in the altered figure (except when L is $\supset \to_1$) by a $\to T$. Intuitionistically L can only be $\supset \to$ with the extra premise on the left.

CASES 3 — 8. The classical and intuitionistic treatment of the cases for $\forall \to$ followed by either a one- or a two-premise propositional inference is essentially symmetric to the classical treatment for $\rightarrow \forall$. The four cases for $\rightarrow \exists$ and $\exists \rightarrow$ follow dually.

EXAMPLE 1. Theorem 50 does not hold for the intuitionistic system $G1$ with $\vee \rightarrow$. For consider the following proof.

$$\dfrac{\dfrac{\mathcal{A}(a) \rightarrow \mathcal{A}(a)}{\mathcal{A}(a) \rightarrow \exists x \mathcal{A}(x)} \rightarrow \exists \qquad \dfrac{\mathcal{A}(b) \rightarrow \mathcal{A}(b)}{\mathcal{A}(b) \rightarrow \exists x \mathcal{A}(x)} \rightarrow \exists}{\mathcal{A}(a) \vee \mathcal{A}(b) \rightarrow \exists x \mathcal{A}(x).} \vee \rightarrow$$

Suppose there were another proof as described in the theorem. Then the midsequent S would be of the form $\Pi \rightarrow \Phi$ where Π consists of zero or more occurrences of $\mathcal{A}(a) \vee \mathcal{A}(b)$ and Φ either is empty or is $\mathcal{A}(\mathrm{t})$ for some term t, since reading upward from the endsequent to S, the *TCI* steps (if any) can only suppress, duplicate or permute formulas but not introduce new formulas, and the predicate inferences (if any) can only be an $\rightarrow \exists$ which (reading upward) changes $\exists x \mathcal{A}(x)$ to $\mathcal{A}(\mathrm{t})$. But then if Π or Φ were empty, $\Pi \rightarrow \Phi$ could not be provable in $G1$ without cut, by Lemmas 33a and 33b used as in Example 4 § 78. So consider e.g. the case $\Pi \rightarrow \Phi$ is $\mathcal{A}(a) \vee \mathcal{A}(b) \rightarrow \mathcal{A}(\mathrm{t})$. The term t may be a or b or neither. Consider e.g. the case t is a. Then by Corollary Theorem 47, $\mathcal{A}(a) \vee \mathcal{A}(b) \supset \mathcal{A}(a)$ would be provable in the propositional calculus H; and by Theorem 4 § 25, so would be $\mathcal{A} \vee \mathcal{B} \supset \mathcal{A}$, contradicting Theorem 9 § 28.

THE CONSISTENCY THEOREM. Gentzen illustrated the use of his extended Hauptsatz in establishing consistency results such as had previously been obtained by Ackermann, von Neumann and Herbrand. Bernays 1936 and Hilbert and Bernays 1939 stated a general consistency theorem for axiomatic theories, which they based on the Ackermann treatment. We state such a theorem now.

The theorem can be used to infer metamathematically the consistency of an axiomatic theory from number theory, geometry or algebra, when a model for the theory, i.e. more precisely for its notions and axioms (§ 14), can be established constructively, i.e. in finitary terms.

The theory is to be formalized as a formal system, the terms and formulas of which are constructed using the logical symbolism of the predicate calculus H with certain individual symbols $\mathrm{e}_1, \ldots, \mathrm{e}_q$, function symbols $\mathrm{f}_1, \ldots, \mathrm{f}_r$ and predicate symbols $\mathrm{P}_1, \ldots, \mathrm{P}_s$. The system may have a finite or infinite number of axioms in addition to the postulates of the predicate calculus H.

To establish a constructive model, we must start with a domain D of objects which is either finite (and non-empty) or enumerably infinite. We could take D to be the natural numbers N in every case, by selecting some fixed effective enumeration of it when it is not already (with repetitions if it is finite), and thereafter dealing with the indices in this enumeration in place of the original objects. But in practice it is convenient to deal with other domains directly. The case of a finite domain admits a simpler treatment from Theorem 20 § 36 extended to include individual and function symbols in the valuation procedure.

In establishing a model, the next step is to interpret the individual, function and predicate symbols in the domain D, i.e. to chose objects $e_1, \ldots, e_q$ from D as values of $\mathrm{e}_1, \ldots, \mathrm{e}_q$, functions $f_1, \ldots, f_r$ with independent variables ranging over D and values in D as values of $\mathrm{f}_1, \ldots, \mathrm{f}_r$, and logical functions or predicates $P_1, \ldots, P_s$ with independent variables ranging over D as values of $\mathrm{P}_1, \ldots, \mathrm{P}_s$. For the model to be constructive, $f_1, \ldots, f_r$ must be effectively calculable functions and $P_1, \ldots, P_s$ effectively decidable predicates. We say in this case that $e_1, \ldots, e_q, f_1, \ldots, f_r, P_1, \ldots, P_s$ is an *effective interpretation* of $\mathrm{e}_1, \ldots, \mathrm{e}_q, \mathrm{f}_1, \ldots, \mathrm{f}_r, \mathrm{P}_1, \ldots, \mathrm{P}_s$ in D. (When D is N, by Church's thesis §§ 60, 62 we can expect $f_1, \ldots, f_r, P_1, \ldots, P_s$ to be general recursive, in which case we have a *general recursive interpretation*. However the consistency theory does not need to be connected with Church's thesis, since we merely need to recognize at each application of the consistency theorem that the particular $f_1, \ldots, f_r, P_1, \ldots, P_s$ which we use are effective.)

Given an effective interpretation, and using the 2-valued truth tables for $\supset$, &, $\vee$, $\neg$ (§ 28), we have a valuation procedure by which, given any formula $\mathrm{A}(\mathrm{x}_1, \ldots, \mathrm{x}_n)$ containing no quantifiers and only the distinct variables $\mathrm{x}_1, \ldots, \mathrm{x}_n$, we can, for each n-tuple $x_1, \ldots, x_n$ of objects from D as values of $\mathrm{x}_1, \ldots, \mathrm{x}_n$, effectively determine the value of $\mathrm{A}(\mathrm{x}_1, \ldots, \mathrm{x}_n)$ to be $\mathfrak{t}$ (true) or $\mathfrak{f}$ (false). (When D is N, by ##A, C, D § 45, the predicate $A(x_1, \ldots, x_n)$ which the formula thus expresses is primitive recursive in $f_1, \ldots, f_r, P_1, \ldots, P_s$.)

For N as the domain D, instead of speaking of the value of $\mathrm{A}(\mathrm{x}_1, \ldots, \mathrm{x}_n)$ when $\mathrm{x}_1, \ldots, \mathrm{x}_n$ take the natural numbers $x_1, \ldots, x_n$ as values, it is usually more convenient to speak of the value of $\mathrm{A}(\boldsymbol{x}_1, \ldots, \boldsymbol{x}_n)$ (where $\boldsymbol{x}_1, \ldots, \boldsymbol{x}_n$ are the numerals for the natural numbers $x_1, \ldots, x_n$, respectively). When we do this, $\mathrm{A}(\boldsymbol{x}_1, \ldots, \boldsymbol{x}_n)$ is a formula in the symbolism extended if necessary to include 0 as an individual symbol and $'$ as a function symbol, and the interpretation is extended to give 0 and $'$ their usual values. We can suppose the original symbols not to have included 0 or $'$, unless in the original interpretation it receives the usual value.

We can do similarly when D is not N. There must be provided a particular variable-less term $\boldsymbol{x}$ (the analog of a numeral) for each object x of D; and the symbolism and interpretation are extended (if necessary) to include these terms (consistently with the original interpretation). In both cases, we shall now say simply "number" for member x of D, and "numeral" for the variable-less term $\boldsymbol{x}$ which expresses x. The extension of the symbolism (when necessary) is to assist in describing the valuation process, and need not apply to the formal system under consideration, except when we say so.

In the model, i.e. after selecting the domain and the interpretation of the non-logical constants, the axioms must be true. As the axioms will (in general) contain variables, we need a more general sense of 'true' than that given by the valuation procedure. We shall formulate it here only for prenex formulas (Theorem 19 § 35). Consider first a closed prenex formula, e.g. for illustration $\exists y_1 \forall x_1 \exists y_2 \forall x_2 \exists y_3 A(y_1, x_1, y_2, x_2, y_3)$ where $A(y_1, x_1, y_2, x_2, y_3)$ contains no quantifiers and only the distinct variables shown; call this formula "G". Under the interpretation of $e_1, \ldots, e_q$, $f_1, \ldots, f_r$, $P_1, \ldots, P_s$ and the usual meanings of the quantifiers, G is true if and only if there is a number y_1, such that for each number x_1, there is a number y_2 depending on x_1 (write it "$y_2(x_1)$"), such that for each number x_2, there is a number y_3 depending on x_1 and x_2 (write it "$y_3(x_1, x_2)$"), such that

$$\text{(I)} \qquad A(\boldsymbol{y}_1, \boldsymbol{x}_1, \boldsymbol{y}_2(x_1), \boldsymbol{x}_2, \boldsymbol{y}_3(x_1, x_2))$$

(where $\boldsymbol{y}_2(x_1)$ is the numeral for the number $y_2(x_1)$, etc.) has the value t. For metamathematical purposes, moreover we wish the existence to be understood constructively, i.e. to mean that the y_1, the $y_2(x_1)$ (for any given x_1) and the $y_3(x_1, x_2)$ (for any given x_1, x_2) can be found. This implies that $y_2(x_1)$ and $y_3(x_1, x_2)$ are effectively calculable functions. We say then that G is *effectively true*, if there are a number y_1 and effectively calculable functions $y_2(x_1)$ and $y_3(x_1, x_2)$ such that for every x_1 and x_2, (I) is t. (When D is N, by Church's thesis we can expect $y_2(x_1)$ and $y_3(x_1, x_2)$ to be general recursive, in which case we say that G is *general recursively true*.) An open prenex formula shall be *effectively* (*general recursively*) *true*, if its closure is. The name *verifiable* is given to a formula without quantifiers, when for each substitution of numerals for its variables the resulting formula takes the value t by the valuation procedure, i.e. in the present terminology, to an effectively true formula without quantifiers.

Actually our requirement that $y_2(x_1)$ and $y_3(x_1, x_2)$ be effectively calculable only emphasizes what would in any case be implied in the constructive use of the existential quantifier; and in other respects also (left implicit) the hypothesis of the theorem must be satisfied in a constructive way to conclude consistency metamathematically, e.g. the number y_1 and the description of the functions $y_2(x_1)$ and $y_3(x_1, x_2)$ must be given effectively, and the demonstration that (I) is t for all x_1 and x_2 must be by finitary reasoning (cf. the remarks on the converse of Church's thesis § 62).

A prenex formula in which no $\forall$-quantifier follows an $\exists$-quantifier we shall call an *$\forall\exists$-prenex formula.*

THEOREM 51. *Let the terms and formulas be constructed using the logical symbolism of the predicate calculus H with* $e_1, \ldots, e_q, f_1, \ldots, f_r, P_1, \ldots, P_s$ *as non-logical constants. For any given domain D and effective evaluation of these constants in D*:

(a) *If* Γ *are effectively true closed prenex formulas,* E *is a closed* $\forall\exists$*-prenex formula, and* $\Gamma \vdash$ E *in the predicate calculus H, then* E *is effectively true.*

(b) *For any formal system S, the postulates of which are those of the predicate calculus H and axioms each of which is (or is equivalent in H to) an effectively true prenex formula: If* E *is an* $\forall\exists$*-prenex formula, and* $\vdash$ E *in S, then* E *is effectively true.* In particular: *S is simply consistent.*

PROOF OF (b) FROM (a). $\{\vdash$ E in $S\} \rightarrow \{\Gamma \vdash$ E in H, where Γ is some finite list of non-logical axioms of $S\} \rightarrow \{\Gamma_1 \vdash E_1$ in H, where Γ_1 are the closures of the effectively true prenex equivalents of Γ, which are likewise effectively true, and E_1 is the closure of E$\} \rightarrow \{E_1$ is effectively true$\}$ (by (a) with Γ_1, E_1 as its Γ, E) $\rightarrow$ {E is effectively true}. In particular, 1=0 (in the case of the number-theoretic symbolism with the usual interpretation), or A & $\neg$A where A contains no quantifiers, is not effectively true, and hence is unprovable in S. So S is simply consistent, by the second form of the definition in § 28.

PROOF OF (a). If it is in the intuitionistic H that $\Gamma \vdash$ E is given, then a fortiori $\Gamma \vdash$ E in the classical H, since the intuitionistic postulate 8^I is provable classically (§ 23).

Since Γ, E are closed, all variables are held constant in the deduction $\Gamma \vdash$ E, and no variable occurs both free and bound in the sequent $\Gamma \rightarrow$ E. So by Theorems 46 and 50 there is in the classical predicate calculus $G1$ a proof of $\Gamma \rightarrow$ E with the features described in Theorem 50. Let h be the level at which the midsequent occurs.

Continuing the illustration, say that Γ is the single formula G above and E is $\forall v_1 \forall v_2 \exists w B(v_1, v_2, w)$ where $B(v_1, v_2, w)$ contains no quantifiers and only the distinct variables shown.

Select any pair v_1, v_2 of numbers.

Now we shall carry out a series of acts, one to each predicate inference in this *G*1 proof, beginning with the lowest and working upward. Each act will consist in substituting a certain numeral (specified below) for every occurrence throughout the tree of each variable occurring free in the premise of the inference. When the act is performed on an inference by $\rightarrow\forall$ or $\exists\rightarrow$, the inference is of course destroyed. The given proof is a pure variable proof, so the b of an application of $\rightarrow\forall$ or $\exists\rightarrow$ does not occur below its premise. Hence by Lemma 36, at the stage (call it *stage g*) when the acts have been performed for the inferences the premises of which are at or below level g ($\leq h$), each of the original postulate applications the premises of which are above level g will have been transformed into an application of the same postulate, but in the system *G*1 with the symbolism extended (if necessary) to include the numerals.

We now specify the choice of the numerals for the substitutions, at the same time proving by induction on g that, if $g \leq h$, then at the g-th stage all sequents up to level g inclusive have the following property (call it P): the antecedents (succedents) contain only formulas of the forms shown in the left (right) column

$\exists y_1 \forall x_1 \exists y_2 \forall x_2 \exists y_3 A(y_1, x_1, y_2, x_2, y_3)$	$\forall v_1 \forall v_2 \exists w B(v_1, v_2, w)$
$\forall x_1 \exists y_2 \forall x_2 \exists y_3 A(\boldsymbol{y}_1, x_1, y_2, x_2, y_3)$	$\forall v_2 \exists w B(\boldsymbol{v}_1, v_2, w)$
$\exists y_2 \forall x_2 \exists y_3 A(\boldsymbol{y}_1, t_1, y_2, x_2, y_3)$	$\exists w B(\boldsymbol{v}_1, \boldsymbol{v}_2, w)$
$\forall x_2 \exists y_3 A(\boldsymbol{y}_1, t_1, \boldsymbol{y}_2(t_1), x_2, y_3)$	$B(\boldsymbol{v}_1, \boldsymbol{v}_2, s)$
$\exists y_3 A(\boldsymbol{y}_1, t_1, \boldsymbol{y}_2(t_1), t_2, y_3)$	
$A(\boldsymbol{y}_1, t_1, \boldsymbol{y}_2(t_1), t_2, \boldsymbol{y}_3(t_1, t_2))$	

where t_1, t_2 and s are variable-less terms, t_1 and t_2 are the numbers expressed under the given effective interpretation by t_1 and t_2, respectively, and $\boldsymbol{y}_1$, $\boldsymbol{y}_2(t_1)$, $\boldsymbol{y}_3(t_1, t_2)$, $\boldsymbol{v}_1$ and $\boldsymbol{v}_2$ are the numerals for the numbers $y_1, y_2(t_1), y_3(t_1, t_2), v_1$ and v_2 respectively, where y_1, $y_2(x_1)$ and $y_3(x_1, x_2)$ are the number and effectively calculable functions given by the hypothesis that G is effectively true.

BASIS: $g = 1$. Only the endsequent is at or below level g, and it has property P.

IND. STEP: $g > 1$. For $g > h$ the induction proposition holds vacuously. For $g \leq h$ by the hypothesis of the induction, as the tree figure now stands, the sequents below level g have property P. We distinguish cases according to the kind of inference which applies from level g to level $g-1$.

CASE 1: $\rightarrow\forall$. In our illustration, the principal formula must have one of two forms, e.g. (using the second) $\forall v_2 \exists w B(\boldsymbol{v}_1, v_2, w)$. The side formula is then $\exists w B(\boldsymbol{v}_1, b, w)$ where b is the b of the original $\rightarrow\forall$. We substitute $\boldsymbol{v}_2$ for b wherever it occurs, i.e. only in the side formula of the premise (at level g) and in sequents above level g. By this act, property P is established at level g, since the side formula becomes $\exists w B(\boldsymbol{v}_1, \boldsymbol{v}_2, w)$ which is one of the allowed succedent forms for property P, and all the other formulas in the sequent are duplicates of respective formulas in the conclusion, which by hyp. ind. were already of allowed forms.

CASE 2: $\forall\rightarrow$. In our illustration, the principal formula must be of one of two forms, e.g. (taking the second) $\forall x_2 \exists y_3 A(\boldsymbol{y}_1, t_1, \boldsymbol{y}_2(t_1), x_2, y_3)$; and the side formula is then of the form $\exists y_3 A(\boldsymbol{y}_1, t_1, \boldsymbol{y}_2(t_1), t^*, y_3)$ where t^* is a term resulting by previous substitutions from the t of the original inference. By the hyp. ind., no variable occurs free in sequents below level g, and so only the variables of t^* occur free in the premise. We substitute 0 for each of these (if any), if the domain D is N, and otherwise some specified numeral, wherever they occur, i.e. only in the side formula (at level g) and above level g. The side formula becomes $\exists y_3 A(\boldsymbol{y}_1, t_1, \boldsymbol{y}_2(t_1), t_2, y_3)$ where t_2 is the result of this substitution on t^*, and the other formulas at level g are unchanged and were already of allowed forms for property P.

CASE 3: $\rightarrow\exists$. Similar to Case 2 (with one possibility for the form of the principal formula in our illustration).

CASE 4: $\exists\rightarrow$. In our illustration the principal formula may have one of three forms, e.g. $\exists y_2 \forall x_2 \exists y_3 A(\boldsymbol{y}_1, t_1, y_2, x_2, y_3)$; and the side formula is then of the form $\forall x_2 \exists y_3 A(\boldsymbol{y}_1, t_1, b, x_2, y_3)$ with the original b. We substitute the numeral $\boldsymbol{y}_2(t_1)$ for b.

CASE 5: T, C or I. The premise already has property P, because it contains no formula not occurring in the conclusion; and no act is performed to change the situation.

This completes the specification of the acts, and the proof that at stage g ($\leq h$) sequents up to level g inclusive have property P. So at stage h, when the whole alteration of the given proof in the classical predicate calculus $G1$ has been completed, the original midsequent, since it contained no quantifiers, has become of the form

$$A(\boldsymbol{y}_1, t_{11}, \boldsymbol{y}_2(t_{11}), t_{12}, \boldsymbol{y}_3(t_{11}, t_{12})), \ldots, A(\boldsymbol{y}_1, t_{l1}, \boldsymbol{y}_2(t_{l1}), t_{l2}, \boldsymbol{y}_3(t_{l1}, t_{l2})) \\ \rightarrow B(\boldsymbol{v}_1, \boldsymbol{v}_2, s_1), \ldots, B(\boldsymbol{v}_1, \boldsymbol{v}_2, s_m).$$

The tree figure down to the midsequent has become a proof of this sequent in the propositional calculus $G1$ with numerals added to the symbolism. So by Corollary Theorem 47,

$$A(\boldsymbol{y}_1, t_{11}, \boldsymbol{y}_2(t_{11}), t_{12}, \boldsymbol{y}_3(t_{11}, t_{12})) \ \& \ \ldots \ \& \ A(\boldsymbol{y}_1, t_{l1}, \boldsymbol{y}_2(t_{l1}), t_{l2}, \boldsymbol{y}_3(t_{l1}, t_{l2})) \\ \supset B(\boldsymbol{v}_1, \boldsymbol{v}_2, s_1) \vee \ldots \vee B(\boldsymbol{v}_1, \boldsymbol{v}_2, s_m)$$

is provable in the propositional calculus H, and hence by Theorem 9 § 28 (and Theorem 4 § 25) is identically true when its distinct prime parts are treated as distinct proposition letters for the valuation procedure of the propositional calculus. In particular, it takes the value $\mathfrak{t}$ when we assign to the distinct prime parts (which contain no variables) the values $\mathfrak{t}$ or $\mathfrak{f}$ which they take under the given effective interpretation of the non-logical constants. By hypothesis, (I) takes the value $\mathfrak{t}$ for every pair x_1, x_2 of numbers. Hence by the valuation tables for &, $\supset$ and $\vee$, one of $B(\boldsymbol{v}_1, \boldsymbol{v}_2, s_1), \ldots, B(\boldsymbol{v}_1, \boldsymbol{v}_2, s_m)$ must be $\mathfrak{t}$. Let the first which is be $B(\boldsymbol{v}_1, \boldsymbol{v}_2, s_a)$. The variable-less term s_a then expresses a number s_a such that $B(\boldsymbol{v}_1, \boldsymbol{v}_2, \boldsymbol{s}_a)$ is $\mathfrak{t}$.

The whole process by which, after choosing the numbers v_1, v_2, we obtain this number s_a is effective; so $s_a = w(v_1, v_2)$, where $w(v_1, v_2)$ is an effectively calculable function. Then for every v_1, v_2,

(II) $$B(\boldsymbol{v}_1, \boldsymbol{v}_2, \boldsymbol{w}(v_1, v_2))$$

is $\mathfrak{t}$, i.e. E is effectively true, as was to be shown.

Remark 1. The above construction enables us to say something about how the function $w(v_1, v_2)$ is related to the functions and predicates $f_1, \ldots, f_r, P_1, \ldots, P_s, y_2(x_1), y_3(x_1, x_2)$, irrespective of the nature of the latter. Thus, with or without the hypotheses of effectiveness in the theorem, we have when D is N: (a) *w is primitive recursive in $f_1, \ldots, f_r, P_1, \ldots, P_s, y_2, y_3$.* For we can show by induction on g that, if $g \leq h$, at stage g each term t occurring free in the tree and containing exactly p distinct variables expresses, as v_1, v_2 vary, a function $t(v_1, v_2, u_1, \ldots, u_p)$ explicit in $f_1, \ldots, f_r, y_2, y_3$ and constants. Hence (for $i = 1, \ldots, m$) s_i expresses a function $s_i(v_1, v_2)$ explicit in the same; and each prime part of $B(\boldsymbol{v}_1, \boldsymbol{v}_2, s_i)$ expresses a predicate explicit in the same and $P_1, \ldots, P_s$, whence using ## A, C, D § 45 $B(\boldsymbol{v}_1, \boldsymbol{v}_2, s_i)$ expresses a predicate $B_i(v_1, v_2)$ primitive recursive in $f_1, \ldots, f_r, P_1, \ldots, P_s, y_2, y_3$. Thence (a) follows by applying #F with B_i as the Q_i and s_i as the φ_i (no φ_{m+1} being required). More specifically: (b) *w is explicit* in $f_1, \ldots, f_r, y_2, y_3, +, \cdot, \overline{\mathrm{sg}}$, ***the representing functions of*** $P_1, \ldots, P_s$, ***and constants*** (# # 1, 2, 9).

APPLICATIONS. THEOREM 52. *For the primitive recursive predicate* $R(x, y)$, *formal system* S, *and formulas* $\mathrm{A}(x)$ $(x = 0, 1, 2, \ldots)$ *described in Example* 2 § 73: $\mathrm{A}(\boldsymbol{x})$ *is provable in* S, *only if* $(Ey)R(x, y)$. (In fact: *Every* ∀∃*-prenex formula provable in* S *is effectively true under the intended interpretation.*)

PROOF. The axioms of S are all verifiable (hence effectively true), when the domain is the natural numbers and the non-logical constants $0, ', \mathrm{f}_1, \ldots, \mathrm{f}_k, =$ are interpreted in the intended way (which is effective), i.e. by $0, ', \varphi_1, \ldots, \varphi_k, =$, respectively. So (b) applies. Using it with $\mathrm{A}(\boldsymbol{x})$, i.e. $\exists y \mathrm{f}_k(\boldsymbol{x}, \mathrm{y})=0$, as the E: If $\vdash \mathrm{A}(\boldsymbol{x})$ in S, then $\mathrm{A}(\boldsymbol{x})$ is effectively true under this interpretation, i.e. there is a y for which $f_k(\boldsymbol{x}, \boldsymbol{y})=0$ is t (i.e. for which $\varphi_k(x, y) = 0$), i.e. $(Ey)R(x, y)$.

THEOREM 53. (a) *Robinson's system* (*Lemma* 18b § 49), *call it* S, *is simply consistent* (*and every* ∀∃*-prenex formula provable in* S *is effectively true*). (b) *In* S, *for a given primitive recursive predicate* $R(x, y)$, *and a formula* $\mathrm{R}(\mathrm{x}, \mathrm{y})$ *which numeralwise expresses it obtained by the method of proof of Corollary Theorem* 27 § 49: $\vdash \exists y \mathrm{R}(\boldsymbol{x}, \mathrm{y})$ *only if* $(Ey)R(x, y)$. (c) *In* S, *if the formulas* $\mathrm{A}(a, b)$ *and* $\mathrm{B}(a, c)$ *of Example* 1 § 61 *are obtained by the method of proof of Corollary Theorem* 27, *then* (*conversely to* (52)): $\{\vdash \mathrm{B}(\boldsymbol{x})\} \rightarrow (Ey)W_0(x, y)$.

PROOF. It will suffice to prove the theorem for the classical systems, as $1=0$ or $\exists y \mathrm{R}(\boldsymbol{x}, \mathrm{y})$ or $\mathrm{B}(\boldsymbol{x})$ is provable in the intuitionistic system only if provable in the classical.

(a) Each of the thirteen axioms except *137 (or *136) is verifiable under the usual (effective) interpretation. Employing *90 § 35, we obtain $\exists b(a=0 \vee a=b')$ as an ∀∃-prenex equivalent of *137. This is effectively true, with $b(a) = a \dot{-} 1$, since then for each natural number a, $\boldsymbol{a}=0 \vee \boldsymbol{a}=(\boldsymbol{b}(a))'$ is t.

(b) The consistency theorem does not apply immediately, because $\exists y \mathrm{R}(\boldsymbol{x}, \mathrm{y})$ is not an ∀∃-prenex formula. However we shall show (following the lemma) that we can add new axioms to S containing new predicate symbols, and extend the interpretation effectively to the latter, in such a way that each of the new axioms is equivalent in the predicate calculus to an effectively true prenex formula, and $\vdash \mathrm{S}(\mathrm{x}, \mathrm{y}) \sim \mathrm{R}(\mathrm{x}, \mathrm{y})$ in the resulting system S' where $\mathrm{S}(\mathrm{x}, \mathrm{y})$ contains no quantifiers and expresses $R(x, y)$ under the interpretation. Then (b) will follow thus:

$\{\vdash \exists y R(\mathbf{x}, y)$ in $S\} \to \{\vdash \exists y R(\mathbf{x}, y)$ in $S'\} \to \{\vdash \exists y S(\mathbf{x}, y)$ in $S'\}$
$\to (Ey)R(x, y)$.

LEMMA 41°. *Let* A(x, y) *be a formula containing no quantifiers and only the distinct variables shown, suppose given an effective interpretation of its non-logical constants, and let* $A(x, y)$ *be the predicate which it expresses under this interpretation. Let* $\dot{A}(x)$ *be a new predicate letter.* (a) *Suppose that*

(1) $$(Ey)A(x, y) \to (Ey)_{y \leq \upsilon(x)} A(x, y)$$

where $\upsilon(x)$ *is an effectively calculable function. Let*

(2) $$\dot{A}(x) \equiv (Ey)A(x, y).$$

Let $\dot{A}(x)$ *be interpreted by* $\dot{A}(x)$ *(which by* (1) *and* (2) *is effective). Then the formula*

(i) $$\dot{A}(x) \sim \exists y A(x, y)$$

is equivalent in the predicate calculus to an effectively true prenex formula. Similarly with "$x_1, \ldots, x_n, y_1, \ldots, y_m$" *in place of* "x, y". (b) *Similarly with universal instead of existential quantifiers (and* "$\leftarrow$" *in place of* "$\to$" *in* (1)).

PROOF OF LEMMA 41. (a) Unabbreviating $\sim$ in (i), and using *96, *89, *97 and *91, we obtain as an $\forall\exists$-prenex equivalent

(ii) $$\forall y \exists z[\{\dot{A}(x) \supset A(x, z)\} \& \{A(x, y) \supset \dot{A}(x)\}].$$

This formula is effectively true with $z(x, y) = \mu z_{z \leq \upsilon(x)} A(x, z)$.

(b) Similarly using *95, *89, *98 and *91, we obtain

$$\forall y \exists z[\{\dot{A}(x) \supset A(x, y)\} \& \{A(x, z) \supset \dot{A}(x)\}],$$

which is effectively true with $z(x, y) = \mu z_{z \leq \upsilon(x)} \bar{A}(x, z)$.

PROOF OF THEOREM 53 (b) (concluded). By the proof of Corollary Theorem 27 § 49 from Theorem 27, it will suffice now to show, for the proof of Theorem 27, that S can be extended so that $\vdash \dot{P}(x_1, \ldots, x_n, w) \sim P(x_1, \ldots, x_n, w)$ with $P(x_1, \ldots, x_n, w)$ interpreted by $\varphi(x_1, \ldots, x_n) = w$.

CASE (Vb). By hyp. ind., S is already extended to include a predicate symbol $\dot{Q}(x_2, \ldots, x_n, w)$ interpreted by $\psi(x_2, \ldots, x_n) = w$ such that $\vdash \dot{Q}(x_2, \ldots, x_n, w) \sim Q(x_2, \ldots, x_n, w)$, and $\dot{R}(y, z, x_2, \ldots, x_n, w)$ interpreted by $\chi(y, z, x_2, \ldots, x_n) = w$ such that $\vdash \dot{R}(y, z, x_2, \ldots, x_n, w) \sim R(y, z, x_2, \ldots, x_n, w)$. We introduce (if we have not already) $a \dot{<} b$, to be interpreted by $a < b$, with the axiom $a \dot{<} b \sim a < b$, i.e. $a \dot{<} b \sim \exists c(c' + a = b)$, using $c \leq b$ as the bound $y \leq \upsilon(x_1, x_2)$ for Lemma 41. We further extend S (if we have not already) to include a predicate symbol

$\dot{\mathrm{B}}(\mathrm{c, d, i, w})$, to be interpreted by $\beta(c, d, i)=w$, such that $\vdash \dot{\mathrm{B}}(\mathrm{c, d, i, w}) \sim \mathrm{B}(\mathrm{c, d, i, w})$; referring to the definition of $\mathrm{B}(\mathrm{c, d, i, w})$ accompanying *(180) § 41, this can be done by several steps (left to the reader) similar to those we perform next. Now we introduce $\dot{\mathrm{D}}(\mathrm{c, d, i, x_2, \ldots, x}_n)$, interpreted by $(Eu)(Ev)[\beta(c, d, i')=u \;\&\; \beta(c, d, i)=v \;\&\; \chi(i, v, x_2, \ldots, x_n)=u]$, with the axiom $\dot{\mathrm{D}}(\mathrm{c, d, i, x_2, \ldots, x}_n) \sim \exists\mathrm{u}\exists\mathrm{v}[\dot{\mathrm{B}}(\mathrm{c, d, i', u}) \;\&\; \dot{\mathrm{B}}(\mathrm{c, d, i, v}) \;\&\; \dot{\mathrm{R}}(\mathrm{i, v, x_2, \ldots, x}_n, \mathrm{u})]$, using the bounds $u \leq \beta(c, d, i')$, $v \leq \beta(c, d, i)$. Next we introduce $\dot{\mathrm{E}}(\mathrm{c, d, y, x_2, \ldots, x}_n)$, interpreted by $(i)[i<y \rightarrow (Eu)(Ev)[\beta(c, d, i')=u \;\&\; \beta(c, d, i)=v \;\&\; \chi(i, v, x_2, \ldots, x_n)=u]]$, with the axiom $\dot{\mathrm{E}}(\mathrm{c, d, y, x_2, \ldots, x}_n) \sim \forall\mathrm{i}[\mathrm{i} \dot{<} \mathrm{y} \supset \dot{\mathrm{D}}(\mathrm{c, d, i, x_2, \ldots, x}_n)]$, using the bound $i \leq y$. Then we introduce $\dot{\mathrm{F}}$ to eliminate the first $\exists\mathrm{u}$ of $\mathrm{P}(\mathrm{y, x_2, \ldots, x}_n, \mathrm{w})$, using $u \leq \beta(c, d, 0)$; and finally $\dot{\mathrm{P}}$ to eliminate the $\exists\mathrm{c}\exists\mathrm{d}$, using as bounds $c \leq C$ and $d \leq D$ with C and D as described in Example 1 (A) § 57 when $\eta(y, x_2, \ldots, x_n) = \varphi(y, x_2, \ldots, x_n)$. By Theorem I Case (Vb) (C) § 49, the predicate $\dot{P}(y, x_2, \ldots, x_n, w)$ assigned to interpret $\dot{\mathrm{P}}(\mathrm{y, x_2, \ldots, x}_n, \mathrm{w})$ is indeed $\varphi(y, x_2, \ldots, x_n)=w$; and by the equivalences introduced as axioms or already established,

$$\vdash \dot{\mathrm{P}}(\mathrm{y, x_2, \ldots, x}_n, \mathrm{w}) \sim \mathrm{P}(\mathrm{y, x_2, \ldots, x}_n, \mathrm{w}).$$

PROOF OF THEOREM 53 (c). Similarly, with a quantifier elimination of $\forall c$ following those for Theorem 27.

Theorem 53 (a) gives the consistency property required for the first proof of Theorem 54 in § 76 (and Theorems 53 (b) and 52 for the proofs in Remark 2 § 76).

THEOREM 55. *The formal number-theoretic system of Chapter* IV, *under the restriction on the induction schema that in the* A(x) *the* x *should not occur free within the scope of a quantifier, is simply consistent.* (Ackermann 1924-5, von Neumann 1927; cf. Hilbert and Bernays 1939 pp. 121, 122 and 127.)

Moreover: *Every* $\forall\exists$*-prenex formula provable in it is effectively true, and this remains the case upon adjoining to it Robinson's axioms* (*Lemma* 18b) *and the axioms used in the proof of Parts* (b) *and* (c) *of Theorem* 53, *which parts apply to this system also.*

PROOF, reducing the theorem to a lemma. It suffices to prove the theorem for the classical system. We shall first treat the case the A(x) is restricted to contain no quantifier at all. Then Lemma 42 will complete the proof.

Consider an axiom by Postulate 13 in this system, say its A(x) is $\mathrm{A}(\mathrm{x, x_1, \ldots, x}_n)$ with exactly the distinct variables shown and no quantifiers. Let $A(x, x_1, \ldots, x_n)$ be the (primitive recursive) predicate expressed by $\mathrm{A}(\mathrm{x}, \mathrm{x}_1, \ldots, \mathrm{x}_n)$ under the usual interpretation. Using *89 and *98, the axiom is equivalent to

$$\exists \mathrm{y}[\mathrm{A}(0, \mathrm{x}_1, \ldots, \mathrm{x}_n) \,\&\, (\mathrm{A}(\mathrm{y}, \mathrm{x}_1, \ldots, \mathrm{x}_n) \supset \mathrm{A}(\mathrm{y}', \mathrm{x}_1, \ldots, \mathrm{x}_n)) \\ \supset \mathrm{A}(\mathrm{x}, \mathrm{x}_1, \ldots, \mathrm{x}_n)].$$

This formula is effectively true, with

$$y(x, x_1, \ldots, x_n) = \begin{cases} 0 \text{ if } A(x, x_1, \ldots, x_n) \vee \bar{A}(0, x_1, \ldots, x_n), \\ \mu y_{y \leq x} A(y, x_1, \ldots, x_n) \,\&\, \bar{A}(y', x_1, \ldots, x_n) \text{ otherwise.} \end{cases}$$

LEMMA 42°. *The class of the provable formulas (or of those deducible from given assumption formulas) in the system of Theorem* 55 *is not diminished by further restricting the* A(x) *for the induction schema to contain no quantifier at all.*

PROOF. Any formula A(x) not containing x free within the scope of a quantifier must be composed by operations of the propositional calculus from formulas $\mathrm{A}_1, \ldots, \mathrm{A}_{m_1}$, each of which contains no quantifiers but may contain x, and formulas $\mathrm{A}_{m_1+1}, \ldots, \mathrm{A}_{m_1+m_2}$, each of which contains quantifiers but does not contain x free ($m_1, m_2 \geq 0$; $m = m_1+m_2 \geq 1$). By Theorem 11 § 29 on principal disjunctive normal form (with Theorem 3 § 25), A(x) is equivalent to a disjunction of formulas $\mathrm{A}_{i1} \,\&\, \ldots \,\&\, \mathrm{A}_{im}$ ($i = 1, \ldots, n$) where each A_{ij} is either A_j or $\neg \mathrm{A}_j$ depending on i, if the first case of the normal form applies. For the moment suppose $m_1, m_2 \geq 1$. Write "$\mathrm{B}_i(\mathrm{x})$" for $\mathrm{A}_{i1} \,\&\, \ldots \,\&\, \mathrm{A}_{im_1}$, "$\mathrm{C}_i$" for $\mathrm{A}_{i,m_1+1} \,\&\, \ldots \,\&\, \mathrm{A}_{im}$, and "B(x)" for some refutable formula without quantifiers. Then using *48 and *34 § 27, A(x) is equivalent to

(a) $$\mathrm{B}(\mathrm{x}) \vee (\mathrm{B}_1(\mathrm{x}) \,\&\, \mathrm{C}_1) \vee \ldots \vee (\mathrm{B}_n(\mathrm{x}) \,\&\, \mathrm{C}_n).$$

Now consider any formula of the form (a) with $n \geq 0$ where (as above) the B's contain no quantifiers and the C's contain quantifiers but no free x's; call n its *degree*. We prove by induction on the degree that any axiom by Postulate 13 with A(x) of this form is provable using Postulate 13 only with A(x)'s containing no quantifiers.

IND. STEP: $n > 0$. Write (a) as

(b) $$\mathrm{D}(\mathrm{x}) \vee (\mathrm{B}_n(\mathrm{x}) \,\&\, \mathrm{C}_n).$$

The axiom under consideration is then

(c) $$[\mathrm{D}(0) \vee (\mathrm{B}_n(0) \,\&\, \mathrm{C}_n)] \,\&\, \forall \mathrm{x}[\mathrm{D}(\mathrm{x}) \vee (\mathrm{B}_n(\mathrm{x}) \,\&\, \mathrm{C}_n) \supset \mathrm{D}(\mathrm{x}') \vee (\mathrm{B}_n(\mathrm{x}') \,\&\, \mathrm{C}_n)] \\ \supset \mathrm{D}(\mathrm{x}) \vee (\mathrm{B}_n(\mathrm{x}) \,\&\, \mathrm{C}_n).$$

We shall show that (c) is deducible in the predicate calculus from the two following axioms,

(d) $[\mathrm{B}_n(0) \vee \mathrm{D}(0)] \,\&\, \forall x[\mathrm{B}_n(x) \vee \mathrm{D}(x) \supset \mathrm{B}_n(x') \vee \mathrm{D}(x')] \supset \mathrm{B}_n(x) \vee \mathrm{D}(x)$,

(e) $\mathrm{D}(0) \,\&\, \forall x[\mathrm{D}(x) \supset \mathrm{D}(x')] \supset \mathrm{D}(x)$;

i.e. we are to show: (d), (e) $\vdash$ (c). By Theorem 14 § 33 with *45 and *34 § 27: $\mathrm{C}_n \vdash$ (c) $\sim$ (d); and with *47 and *48: $\neg\mathrm{C}_n \vdash$ (c) $\sim$ (e). No variables are varied since C_n does not contain free the variable x of the quantifier $\forall$x within which replacements are performed. So, using $\vee$-elim.: (d), (e), $\mathrm{C}_n \vee \neg\mathrm{C}_n \vdash$ (c); and hence using *51: (d), (e) $\vdash$ (c).

But in (e) the A(x) is of the form (a) with degree $n-1$, and likewise in (d), when $\mathrm{B}_n(x) \vee \mathrm{B}(x)$ is taken as a new B(x).

When $m_1 = 0$, the method applies construing "$\mathrm{B}_i(x)$" and "$\mathrm{B}_i(x)$ &" as the empty expression, with the following differences. Consider

(f) $\mathrm{C}_n \,\&\, \forall x[\mathrm{C}_n \supset \mathrm{C}_n] \supset \mathrm{C}_n$.

Using *46: $\mathrm{C}_n \vdash$ (c) $\sim$ (f); and using *48: $\neg\mathrm{C}_n \vdash$ (c) $\sim$ (e). But using *1 § 26, *75 § 35, *45, and *1 again: $\vdash$ (f).

When $m_2 = 0$, the A(x) already lacks quantifiers.

If the second case of the normal form applies, then using *53, *34 and *53, A(x) is equivalent to $\mathrm{B}(x) \,\&\, \neg\mathrm{B}(x)$.

Remark 2. In the systems of Theorems 52, 53 and 55, every provable $\forall\exists$-prenex formula is *primitive recursively true*. For $R(x, y)$ and R(x, y) as in Theorem 53 (b), $\{\vdash \exists y\mathrm{R}(x, y)\} \rightarrow$ {there is a primitive recursive function φ such that $(x)R(x, \varphi(x))$}. Proofs. By Remark 1, and our constructions of the functions and predicates for the effective interpretation and effective truth in Theorems 52, 53 and 55.

Example 2. Let S be the number-theoretic formal system with omitted. What the adaptation of Presburger 1930 cited at the beginning of § 42 gives directly is an effective correlation, to each closed formula A of S, of another B, with properties (1) — (4) as follows. (To consider an open formula, let A be its closure.) (1) $\vdash$ A $\sim$ B in S. (2) B is either true or false, under an obvious extension of the valuation procedure (preceding Theorem 51). Now say A is *true* (*false*), if B is. (This special definition of truth for closed formulas of S is equivalent to the one called for under the general definition of truth which will be taken up at the end of § 81, by (3).) (3) Truth and falsity in this sense obey the 2-valued truth tables; $\{\exists x\mathrm{A}(x)$ is true$\} \equiv (Ex)\{\mathrm{A}(\mathbf{x})$ is true$\}$; and $\{\forall x\mathrm{A}(x)$ is true$\} \equiv (x)\{\mathrm{A}(\mathbf{x})$ is true$\}$. (4) According as B is true or false, B is provable or refutable in S. Thus: (5) S is simply complete, and complete with respect to the interpretation (§§ 41, 29). (6) There is a decision procedure for the question whether A is true. (7) If S is simply consistent, there is a decision procedure for *S*, i.e. for the question whether $\vdash$ A in *S*. Now we show: (8) If $\vdash$ A in *S*, then A is true; so *S* is simply consistent. Suppose $\vdash$ A in *S*. Then for some finite collection Γ of non-logical axioms of *S*, $\Gamma \vdash$ A in *H*. We can use Lemma 41 to eliminate the quantifiers from A and from the induction formula A(x) of each induction axiom among Γ, taking e.g. for a part $\exists$yA(x, y)

$$\upsilon(x) = \mu y[(\{\exists y\mathrm{A}(\mathbf{x}, \mathrm{y}) \text{ is false}\} \,\&\, y{=}0) \vee A(x, y)].$$

We thus obtain $\Gamma', \Theta \vdash$ A′ where Θ are the formulas (i) of Lemma 41 with $\exists$ or $\forall$ for the predicate symbols introduced in the elimination. Then A′ (and hence A) is true, by Theorem 55 (or the first part of its proof) for the system with Θ adjoined as axioms.

Discussion. In these applications of the consistency theorem, the domain *D* is the natural numbers, the numerals are already a part of the symbolism, and the effective interpretation is the intended one. Hilbert and Bernays 1939 pp. 38 — 48 give two applications of their consistency theorem to geometrical axiom systems. There certain enumerable systems of complex numbers are used as the domains *D*.

These consistency proofs all depend on having a model for the axioms, as did those given before the advent of Hilbert's proof theory (cf. § 14). But giving a model for the axioms in intuitive arithmetical terms does not establish beyond all doubt that no contradiction can arise in the theory deduced from the axioms, unless it can also be demonstrated that the reasonings in the theory can be translated into intuitive arithmetical reasonings in terms of the objects used in the model. This demonstration is what the present consistency theorem (Theorem 51) adds to the earlier treatment. (Cf. Bernays 1936 pp. 115—116 and Hilbert-Bernays 1939 p. 48.)

We did take the deduction of the theory from its axioms into account in the discussion of consistency in the first part of § 75, but there we were using non-finitary set-theoretic methods.

The consistency theorem depends, via the extended Hauptsatz (Theorem 50), on the Hauptsatz (Theorem 48) and the reduction of *H* to *G*1 (Theorem 46). By these, given a proof of a formal theorem in a system based on the predicate calculus with mathematical axioms, it is possible to alter the system and proof until we have a proof which contains no formulas more complicated than the axioms and theorem themselves, i.e. only subformulas of them. In this situation there is no excursion through "ideal" statements in proving a "real" theorem from "real" axioms (§ 14).

Our metamathematical consistency result of Theorem 55 for a part of number theory of course holds good upon extending the system by further effectively true prenex axioms, e.g. one could add symbols for further primitive recursive functions with their recursion equations. These were eliminable in the full system (Example 9 § 74), but presumably are not in general in the system with the restricted induction schema.

One may also consider some new induction postulates, which would hold as derived rules in the full system, but presumably do not when Postulate 13 is restricted as for Theorem 55, and which are susceptible of like treatment under corresponding restrictions. Examples of such are given in Hilbert and Bernays 1934 pp. 343 — 346, which however appear from Skolem 1939 and Péter 1940 to be derivable when suitable primitive recursive functions with their recursion equations are adjoined.

All such consistency results obtained by strictly elementary methods must stop short of giving the consistency of the number-theoretic formalism with the unrestricted induction schema, as we know from the famous second Gödel 1931 theorem (Theorem 30 § 42), according to which the consistency of that system cannot be established by methods formalizable in the system itself.

GENTZEN'S CONSISTENCY PROOF FOR NUMBER THEORY. We shall now give a brief heuristic account of the method used by Gentzen (1936, 1938) in a proof of the consistency of classical pure number theory with the unrestricted induction postulate.

In the proof of Gentzen's 1934-5 Hauptsatz (Theorem 48 § 78), we used a triple induction, consisting of an induction on the number of mixes, within the induction step of which (in establishing the principal lemma) we used an induction on the grade, within the basis and induction step of which we used an induction on the rank. This triple induction can be regarded as a single "transfinite induction", if our system of ordinal numbers, hitherto consisting simply of the natural numbers, is extended sufficiently into the transfinite.

Beyond the natural numbers or "finite ordinals" a next number or "first transfinite ordinal" called ω is supplied. Then new numbers $\omega+1$, $\omega+2$, ... are obtained by use of the successor operation, after the infinity of which still another called 2ω shall follow. Repeating this process, after all these infinite sequences of numbers, each isomorphic to the natural number sequence, and starting respectively with $0, \omega, 2\omega, \ldots,$ still another number called ω^2 shall follow; and so on, thus.

$0, 1, 2, \ldots; \omega, \omega+1, \omega+2, \ldots; 2\omega, 2\omega+1, 2\omega+2, \ldots; \ldots;;$
$\omega^2, \omega^2+1, \omega^2+2, \ldots; \omega^2+\omega, \omega^2+\omega+1, \omega^2+\omega+2, \ldots;$
$\omega^2+2\omega, \omega^2+2\omega+1, \omega^2+2\omega+2, \ldots; \ldots;;$
$2\omega^2, 2\omega^2+1, 2\omega^2+2, \ldots; 2\omega^2+\omega, 2\omega^2+\omega+1, 2\omega^2+\omega+2, \ldots;$
$2\omega^2+2\omega, 2\omega^2+2\omega+1, 2\omega^2+2\omega+2, \ldots; \ldots;; \ldots;;; \omega^3, \ldots.$

This figure is intended only to suggest the manner of generation and the notations, up to a certain pcint. The general theory of transfinite ordinals forms a part of Cantor's abstract set theory (cf. 1897). A set linearly ordered (§ 8) so that each non-empty subset has a first element is called *well-ordered*. Two ordered sets M and N are *similar* ($M \simeq N$), if they can be put into a 1-1 correspondence preserving the order. Cantor's ordinal numbers arise by abstracting from well-ordered sets with respect to similarity, in the same way as his cardinals arise by abstracting from sets with respect to equivalence (§ 3). However, while the whole system of Cantor's transfinite ordinals requires a set-theoretic approach, the theory of initial segments (at least of not too great ones) can be handled in a finitary way.

For example, the system of the ordinals $< \omega^3$ can be represented as the triples of natural numbers, in a certain ordering. Let $\alpha = (a, b, c) = a\omega^2+b\omega+c$ be any such triple; the last notation is the one customary in the theory of ordinal numbers $< \omega^3$. The order relation between two such triples (as ordinals $< \omega^3$) is defined thus:

$$\alpha_1 < \alpha_2 \equiv (a_1 < a_2) \vee (a_1 = a_2 \;\&\; b_1 < b_2) \vee (a_1 = a_2 \;\&\; b_1 = b_2 \;\&\; c_1 < c_2).$$

In other words, the ordering of the triples (a, b, c) is alphabetical, with an infinite alphabet consisting of the natural numbers.

Now the triple ordinary induction on number of mixes a, grade b and rank c can be considered as a single transfinite induction with $(a, b, c) = a\omega^2+b\omega+c$ as the induction number, thus. In a transfinite induction up to ω^3, to prove that all ordinals $< \omega^3$ have a property, one shows that, for any ordinal $\alpha < \omega^3$, if all ordinals $\beta < \alpha$ have the property, then α has the property also. We are using the more compact statement, in which basis and induction step are combined (cf. *162b § 40 for this form of the statement of ordinary induction). The case $\alpha = 0$, for which the set of the β's is empty, can be treated separately as the basis, if one wishes. The induction is of the course-of-values type, where now whenever $\alpha \geq \omega$, there are an infinitude of preceding β's. For the Gentzen Hauptsatz, the reasoning is that, if the theorem is true for all proofs with induction number $(a, b, c) = \beta < \alpha \, (< \omega^3)$, it is true for a proof with $(a, b, c) = \alpha$.

The induction number $\alpha = (a, b, c)$ now well-orders the cases of the theorem in an order in which they are being proved, just as the natural number used as induction number does in an ordinary induction.

Conversely, using the definition of ordinals $< \omega^3$ as triples (a, b, c), every transfinite induction up to ω^3 can be accomplished by ordinary inductions.

One can define in a finitary manner somewhat higher ordinals. Clearly we can go up to ω^n for any finite n. After all these ordinals as next we take ω^ω; eventually ω^{ω^ω}; and so on.

Gentzen's discovery is that the Gödel obstacle to proving the consistency of number theory can be overcome by using transfinite induction up to a sufficiently great ordinal. His transfinite induction is up to the ordinal called ε_0 by Cantor, which is the first ordinal greater than all the ordinals in the infinite sequence $\omega, \omega^\omega, \omega^{\omega^\omega}, \ldots$. It figures in Cantor's theory as the least of the solutions (called ε-numbers) for ξ of the equation $\omega^\xi = \xi$.

Gentzen works with systems of his type with sequents, but they have Hilbert-type equivalents. In the 1938 version of his consistency proof, the simple consistency of the system is identified with the unprovability of the sequent $\rightarrow$. For from $\rightarrow$ any sequent can be deduced by thinnings, while conversely from $\rightarrow A \& \neg A$ and the provable sequent $A \& \neg A \rightarrow$ one can infer $\rightarrow$ by a cut. He begins by correlating to each proof in his system an ordinal number $< \varepsilon_0$. Taking the induction in the form of an infinite descent (cf. *163 § 40), he shows that, given any proof of the sequent $\rightarrow$, another proof of $\rightarrow$ with a lesser ordinal can be found. So his system (and hence ours) is simply consistent.

In the 1936* version, his sequents each have exactly one succedent formula. He shows, by transfinite induction on the ordinal ($< \varepsilon_0$) of a proof, that a certain kind of reduction can be carried out on any provable sequent. It is absurd that this reduction should be performable on $\rightarrow 1=0$. The performability of this reduction is offered as a finitary meaning which can be attributed to the ideal statements of classical number theory (§ 14).

Ackermann 1940 uses transfinite induction up to ε_0 to carry through a proof of the consistency of elementary number theory in another manner using Hilbert's ε-symbol (originally proposed by Hilbert, and carried by Ackermann in 1924-5 as far as showing the consistency with the restricted induction schema).

Just as transfinite induction up to ω^3 can be reduced to ordinary induction, so can induction up to ε_0, as is done formally by Hilbert and Bernays 1939 pp. 360 ff. But there is the difference that in reducing the latter a predicate is used as the induction predicate (the $A(x)$ of (I) § 75, or the $P(n)$ of § 7) into which there enters explicitly a predicate Q defined by an induction similar in nature to that defining M in Theorem VIII § 57 and hence probably not arithmetical (§ 48) or equivalently not "elementary" (Theorem VII § 57). It can in fact be anticipated from the second Gödel theorem (Theorem 30) that transfinite induction up to ε_0 cannot be reduced to ordinary induction within the system, since the reasonings used in Gentzen's consistency proof other than this transfinite induction are of sorts that are formalizable in the system (whence in particular no formula of the system can satisfy the equivalences defining Q). In his last paper 1943, Gentzen proves the non-reducibility of induction up to ε_0 directly, instead of indirectly from Gödel's theorem with his consistency proof.

The original proposals of the formalists to make classical mathematics secure by a consistency proof (§§ 14, 15) did not contemplate that such a method as transfinite induction up to ε_0 would have to be used. To what extent the Gentzen proof can be accepted as securing classical number theory in the sense of that problem formulation is in the present state of affairs a matter for individual judgement, depending on how ready one is to accept induction up to ε_0 as a finitary method. (Cf. end § 81.)

Gentzen in 1938a speculates that the use of transfinite induction up to some ordinal greater than ε_0 may enable the consistency of analysis to be proved. By a result of Schütte 1951, stronger forms of induction are obtainable thus; in fact for any ordinal α, induction up to the least Cantor ε-number greater than α cannot be reduced to induction up to α (but induction up to any intermediate ordinal can be).

§ 80. Decision procedure, intuitionistic unprovability. Given the conclusion B of an inference by the modus ponens rule (Rule 2) of the formal system H, we cannot determine the premises A and A $\supset$ B, because the A will be unknown. Similarly, given the conclusion $\Delta, \Gamma \rightarrow \Lambda, \Theta$ of a cut in $G1$, and the analysis of the conclusion specifying how its antecedent is separated into the Δ and the Γ and its succedent into the Λ and the Θ, we cannot determine the premises $\Delta \rightarrow \Lambda$, C and C, $\Gamma \rightarrow \Theta$, because the C will be unknown.

However, for each of the rules of the propositional calculus $G1$ except the cut (or of $G2$ except the mix), given the conclusion of an inference by the rule and the analysis of the conclusion, the premise(s) for the inference are ascertainable. Using this fact with Gentzen's normal form theorem (Theorem 48), we shall obtain a decision procedure for the propositional calculus, which unlike the truth-table procedure (§§ 28—30, Theorem 12) works also for the intuitionistic system as well as for the classical.

The steps in the procedure will consist in listing the choices of the premise(s) for the inference of a given conclusion. In doing this, it is tedious to have to distinguish all the ways of applying the structural rules *TCI*. Therefore, for use in our version of Gentzen's decision procedure, we shall introduce a new Gentzen-type system *G*3, in which the structural alterations *TCI* are not counted as separate inferences. We define *G*3 for the predicate calculus also, although it is only for the propositional calculus that we shall have a decision procedure.

In order in *G*3 to dispense with the *TCI* rules, we must construe the postulates of *G*3 to apply irrespective of the order and number of repetitions of formulas in the antecedents, and classically in the succedents. In other words, for *G*3 any postulate application shall remain an application of the same postulate when any sequent is replaced by a sequent 'cognate' to it in the following sense: Two sequents $\Gamma \rightarrow \Theta$ and $\Gamma' \rightarrow \Theta'$ are *cognate*, if exactly the same formulas occur in Γ (in Θ) as in Γ' (in Θ'), provided intuitionistically that Θ and Θ' neither consist of more than one occurrence of a formula and are hence the same.

EXAMPLE 1. The sequents $C, \mathcal{A}, \mathcal{B} \,\&\, \mathcal{A}, \mathcal{A} \rightarrow \mathcal{B}$ and $\mathcal{B} \,\&\, \mathcal{A}, \mathcal{A}, C \rightarrow \mathcal{B}, \mathcal{B}$ are cognate classically, but the latter sequent is not employed intuitionistically.

For the classical system *G*3, the postulate list differs from the list given for *G*2 thus. The axiom schema is replaced by

$$C, \Gamma \rightarrow \Theta, C.$$

There are no structural rules of inference; and each logical rule of inference is modified by retaining the principal formula in the premise(s). For example, $\rightarrow \neg$, $\supset \rightarrow$, $\rightarrow \vee$ and $\neg \rightarrow$ become:

$$\frac{A, \Gamma \rightarrow \Theta, \neg A}{\Gamma \rightarrow \Theta, \neg A.} \qquad \frac{A \supset B, \Gamma \rightarrow \Theta, A \text{ and } B, A \supset B, \Gamma \rightarrow \Theta}{A \supset B, \Gamma \rightarrow \Theta.}$$

$$\frac{\Gamma \rightarrow \Theta, A \vee B, A \text{ or } \Gamma \rightarrow \Theta, A \vee B, B}{\Gamma \rightarrow \Theta, A \vee B.} \qquad \frac{\neg A, \Gamma \rightarrow \Theta, A}{\neg A, \Gamma \rightarrow \Theta.}$$

(For $\supset \rightarrow$, both premises are to be used; for $\rightarrow \vee$, written now combining the two rules into one statement, one or the other.)

For the intuitionistic *G*3 the postulate list is as follows.

POSTULATES FOR THE INTUITIONISTIC FORMAL SYSTEM *G*3

Axiom schema.

$$C, \Gamma \to C.$$

Rules of inference for the propositional calculus.

$$\frac{A, \Gamma \to B}{\Gamma \to A \supset B.} \qquad \frac{A \supset B, \Gamma \to A \quad \text{and} \quad B, A \supset B, \Gamma \to \Theta}{A \supset B, \Gamma \to \Theta.}$$

$$\frac{\Gamma \to A \quad \text{and} \quad \Gamma \to B}{\Gamma \to A \,\&\, B.} \qquad \frac{A, A \,\&\, B, \Gamma \to \Theta \quad \text{or} \quad B, A \,\&\, B, \Gamma \to \Theta}{A \,\&\, B, \Gamma \to \Theta.}$$

$$\frac{\Gamma \to A \quad \text{or} \quad \Gamma \to B}{\Gamma \to A \vee B.} \qquad \frac{A, A \vee B, \Gamma \to \Theta \text{ and } B, A \vee B, \Gamma \to \Theta}{A \vee B, \Gamma \to \Theta.}$$

$$\frac{A, \Gamma \to}{\Gamma \to \neg A.} \qquad \frac{\neg A, \Gamma \to A}{\neg A, \Gamma \to \Theta,}$$

with Θ empty or consisting of one formula.

Additional rules of inference for the predicate calculus.

$$\frac{\Gamma \to A(b)}{\Gamma \to \forall x A(x),} \qquad \frac{A(t), \forall x A(x), \Gamma \to \Theta}{\forall x A(x), \Gamma \to \Theta.}$$

subject to the restriction on variables.

$$\frac{\Gamma \to A(t)}{\Gamma \to \exists x A(x).} \qquad \frac{A(b), \exists x A(x), \Gamma \to \Theta}{\exists x A(x), \Gamma \to \Theta,}$$

subject to the restriction on variables.

We also define classical and intuitionistic systems *G*3a. These differ from the systems *G*3 in that we permit arbitrary omissions of formulas in the antecedent and succedent of the premise(s) for an inference by any one of the rules.

The system *G*3 is designed to minimize the number of choices of premise(s) for a given conclusion, when we are attempting to exhaust the possibilities for proving a given endsequent, especially in showing the endsequent to be unprovable. When the endsequent is provable, the use of *G*3a usually permits shortening the sequents used in the proof.

A proof in $G3$ is *irredundant*, if it contains no pair of cognate sequents one occurring above the other in the same branch.

THEOREM 56. (a) *If* $\vdash \Gamma \to \Theta$ *in* $G3$a (*a fortiori if* $\vdash \Gamma \to \Theta$ *in* $G3$), *then* $\vdash \Gamma \to \Theta$ *in* $G2$ (*or* $G1$), *using exactly the same-named logical rules as in the given proof in* $G3$a *and no mix* (*or cut*).

(b) *Conversely, if* $\vdash \Gamma \to \Theta$ *in* $G2$ (*or* $G1$), *and no variable occurs both free and bound in* $\Gamma \to \Theta$, *then* $\vdash \Gamma \to \Theta$ *in* $G3$ (*a fortiori in* $G3$a), *using only rules the same-named as logical rules used in the given proof in* $G2$ (*or* $G1$). *Lemmas* 32a—33b (*stated above for* $G1$ *and the cut, and for* $G2$ *and the mix*) *hold also for* $G3$ (*and* $G3$a).

(c) *A formula* E *containing no variable both free and bound is provable in* H, *if and only if there is an irredundant proof in* $G3$ *of the sequent* $\to$ E.

(d) *A decision procedure* (*or algorithm*) *for determining whether or not a proposition letter formula* E *is provable in the propositional calculus* H *is afforded by the process of attempting to construct an irredundant proof of* $\to$ E *in* $G3$. *According as such a proof is found or is determined not to exist,* E *is provable in* H *or is not provable in* H.

PROOFS. (a) An axiom of $G3$a is provable by TI steps from an axiom of $G2$. Given any inference in $G3$a, by TCI steps we can bring its premises to the standard form shown in the postulate list for $G3$. Then the corresponding rule of $G2$ applies, with the given conclusion or a conclusion which leads to it by TCI steps.

EXAMPLE 2. The inference in the intuitionistic $G3$a shown at the left is then accomplished in $G2$ as shown at the right.

$$\frac{\mathcal{B}, \mathcal{B} \to \mathcal{A}}{\mathcal{B}, \neg\mathcal{A} \to C.}\ \neg\!\to_{3a} \qquad\qquad \cfrac{\cfrac{\cfrac{\mathcal{B}, \mathcal{B} \to \mathcal{A}}{\neg\mathcal{A}, \mathcal{B} \to \mathcal{A}}}{\neg\mathcal{A}, \neg\mathcal{A}, \mathcal{B} \to}\ \neg\!\to_2}{\mathcal{B}, \neg\mathcal{A} \to C.}$$

(b) By Theorem 48 (and Lemma 34), we can take the given proof to be in $G2$ without mix. An axiom of $G2$ is an axiom of $G3$; and we easily verify that any inference in $G2$ without mix can be performed (by one or more steps) in the system obtained from $G3$ by adding the six TCI rules. Hence it will suffice to show that these additions to $G3$ do not increase its class of provable sequents. For this purpose, we first show by induction that, if $\vdash \Gamma \to \Theta$ in $G3$, then $\vdash \Gamma \to \Theta$, C in $G3$, provided intuitionistically that Θ is empty, i.e. we establish that $\to T$ holds as a derived rule for *G*3. In this induction, the restriction on variables for an $\rightarrow \forall$ or $\exists \rightarrow$ is met by first using Lemma 35 (which holds for *G*3 as well as for *G*1 and *G*2) to change the b in its free occurrences in the given proof of the old premise to a new variable not occurring free in C. The rule $T \rightarrow$ is handled similarly; and $\rightarrow C$, $C \rightarrow$, $\rightarrow I$, $I \rightarrow$ immediately by the convention under which the rules of *G*3 are used.

(c) By (a), (b) and Theorems 46 and 47, E is provable in *H*, if and only if there is a proof of $\rightarrow$ E in *G*3. But given any proof of $\rightarrow$ E in *G*3, we can find an irredundant one, as we show by induction on the number of pairs of cognate sequents one above the other in the same branch. Given such a pair, the lower sequent of the pair and the intervening sequents, together with all branches contributing to either, can be suppressed.

Proof of (d) is postponed until after the following example illustrating the decision procedure.

Example 3. (a) Is $\mathcal{A} \vee \neg \mathcal{A}$ provable in the intuitionistic propositional calculus *H*? By (c), it is if and only if there is an irredundant proof of $\rightarrow \mathcal{A} \vee \neg \mathcal{A}$ in the intuitionistic *G*3. We attempt to find such a proof thus. The sequent $\rightarrow \mathcal{A} \vee \neg \mathcal{A}$, as we see by inspection, is not an axiom of *G*3. The only rule of inference of *G*3 applicable with $\rightarrow \mathcal{A} \vee \neg \mathcal{A}$ as conclusion is $\rightarrow \vee$. Intuitionistically the inference of $\rightarrow \mathcal{A} \vee \neg \mathcal{A}$ by this rule can have as premise only $\rightarrow \mathcal{A}$ or $\rightarrow \neg \mathcal{A}$. Neither is an axiom, the first $\rightarrow \mathcal{A}$ can be the conclusion of no inference in *G*3, while the second $\rightarrow \neg \mathcal{A}$ can only come by $\rightarrow \neg$ from the premise $\mathcal{A} \rightarrow$ or a premise such as $\mathcal{A}, \mathcal{A} \rightarrow$ cognate to $\mathcal{A} \rightarrow$. However since two cognate sequents are interchangible for proofs in *G*3, it suffices to consider $\mathcal{A} \rightarrow$. This sequent is not an axiom, and no inference of *G*3 is possible with it as conclusion. The entire construction is shown below in the figure, on three lines or levels numbered upward from the given endsequent $\rightarrow \mathcal{A} \vee \neg \mathcal{A}$. Briefly, we apply the rules of *G*3 upward from conclusion to premises, in all possible ways not distinguishing between cognate sequents.

$$\begin{array}{ll} 3. & \mathcal{A} \rightarrow \\ \hline 2. & \rightarrow \mathcal{A} \text{ or } \rightarrow \neg \mathcal{A} \\ \hline 1. & \rightarrow \mathcal{A} \vee \neg \mathcal{A}. \end{array}$$

In this construction, we have exhausted all the possibilities for finding a proof of $\rightarrow \mathcal{A} \vee \neg \mathcal{A}$ in the intuitionistic *G*3, without finding one. Hence $\mathcal{A} \vee \neg \mathcal{A}$ is not provable in the intuitionistic *H*.

(b) We already know that $\mathcal{A} \vee \neg \mathcal{A}$ is provable in the classical propositional calculus H (*51 § 27). However it is of interest to see how the decision procedure leads us to a proof of $\to \mathcal{A} \vee \neg \mathcal{A}$ in the classical system $G3$, whence if we followed out the proofs of Theorem 56 (a), Theorem 47, and of results in Chapter V on which the latter depends, we should be led to one of $\mathcal{A} \vee \neg \mathcal{A}$ in the classical H. At Line 2, the formula $\mathcal{A} \vee \neg \mathcal{A}$ is now retained in the succeedent (owing to the difference between the classical and intutionistic $\to \vee$ rule of $G3$). This gives us more possibilities at Line 3. The "2" written there signifies that the sequent listed below it at Line 2 is one of the possible premises at Line 3 (by $\to \vee$). As we are seeking an irredundant proof, we need consider further only the new premise $\to \mathcal{A} \vee \neg \mathcal{A}, \mathcal{A}, \neg \mathcal{A}$ or $\mathcal{A} \to \mathcal{A} \vee \neg \mathcal{A}, \neg \mathcal{A}$. The construction is shown below up to Line 4.

$$\dfrac{\dfrac{\dfrac{3 \text{ or } \mathcal{A}\to\mathcal{A}\vee\neg\mathcal{A}, \mathcal{A}, \neg\mathcal{A}}{2 \text{ or} \to\mathcal{A}\vee\neg\mathcal{A}, \mathcal{A}, \neg\mathcal{A}}}{\to\mathcal{A}\vee\neg\mathcal{A}, \mathcal{A}} \quad \text{or} \quad \dfrac{\dfrac{3 \text{ or } \mathcal{A}\to\mathcal{A}\vee\neg\mathcal{A}, \mathcal{A}, \neg\mathcal{A}}{2 \text{ or} \to\mathcal{A}\vee\neg\mathcal{A}, \mathcal{A}, \neg\mathcal{A}} \ \text{or} \ \dfrac{3 \text{ or } \mathcal{A}\to\mathcal{A}\vee\neg\mathcal{A}, \mathcal{A}, \neg}{\mathcal{A}\to\mathcal{A}\vee\neg\mathcal{A}, \neg\mathcal{A}}}{\to\mathcal{A}\vee\neg\mathcal{A}, \neg\mathcal{A}}}{\to\mathcal{A}\vee\neg\mathcal{A}.}$$

At Line 4, three of our series of choices have ended above in an axiom; i.e. we have discovered proofs of $\to \mathcal{A} \vee \neg \mathcal{A}$ in $G3$. Say using the left choice at Line 2 (and the new choices above that), we have in particular the following proof in $G3$ (left). The sequents of this can be simplified in $G3$a (right).

$$\begin{array}{ll} 4. & \mathcal{A}\to\mathcal{A}\vee\neg\mathcal{A}, \mathcal{A}, \neg\mathcal{A} \\ \hline 3. & \to\mathcal{A}\vee\neg\mathcal{A}, \mathcal{A}, \neg\mathcal{A} \quad \to\neg \\ \hline 2. & \to\mathcal{A}\vee\neg\mathcal{A}, \mathcal{A} \quad \to\vee \\ \hline 1. & \to\mathcal{A}\vee\neg\mathcal{A}. \quad \to\vee \end{array} \qquad \begin{array}{ll} 4. & \mathcal{A}\to\mathcal{A} \\ \hline 3. & \to\mathcal{A}, \neg\mathcal{A} \quad \to\neg \\ \hline 2. & \to\mathcal{A}\vee\neg\mathcal{A}, \mathcal{A} \quad \to\vee \\ \hline 1. & \to\mathcal{A}\vee\neg\mathcal{A}. \quad \to\vee \end{array}$$

In terms of $G2$ (or $G1$) the latter becomes:

$$\begin{array}{ll} & \text{etc.} \\ 3. & \to\mathcal{A}\vee\neg\mathcal{A}, \mathcal{A} \\ \hline 2. & \to\mathcal{A}\vee\neg\mathcal{A}, \mathcal{A}\vee\neg\mathcal{A} \quad \to\vee \\ \hline 1. & \to\mathcal{A}\vee\neg\mathcal{A}. \quad \to C \end{array}$$

(c) We already know that $\neg\neg(\mathcal{A} \vee \neg \mathcal{A})$ is provable intuitionistically in H (*51a). A proof of $\to \neg\neg(\mathcal{A} \vee \neg \mathcal{A})$ in $G3$a follows which is discovered by use of the decision procedure. In terms of $G2$, the contraction which we could not perform in (a), because of the intuitionistic restriction to not more than one formula in the succedent, is possible now as it is performed in the antecedent.

7. $\mathcal{A} \to \mathcal{A}$

$\to\vee$

6. $\mathcal{A} \to \mathcal{A} \vee \neg\mathcal{A}$

$\neg\to$

5. $\mathcal{A}, \neg(\mathcal{A} \vee \neg\mathcal{A}) \to$

$\to\neg$

4. $\neg(\mathcal{A} \vee \neg\mathcal{A}) \to \neg\mathcal{A}$

$\to\vee$

3. $\neg(\mathcal{A} \vee \neg\mathcal{A}) \to \mathcal{A} \vee \neg\mathcal{A}$

$\neg\to$

2. $\neg(\mathcal{A} \vee \neg\mathcal{A}) \to$

$\to\neg$

1. $\to \neg\neg(\mathcal{A} \vee \neg\mathcal{A})$.

Proof of Theorem 56 (d). It is clear that the procedure, as illustrated in Example 3, can be completed up to any desired level, noting the following fact. Given any sequent $\Gamma \to \Theta$ composed of proposition letter formulas, to each choice from Γ or from Θ of a formula containing a logical symbol to serve as the principal formula, there are exactly one or two incognate choices of premise(s) for the inference of $\Gamma \to \Theta$ in $G3$.

It remains to prove that the whole procedure must terminate. By the subformula property of $G3$, every sequent in a proof of $\to$ E in $G3$ must be composed of subformulas of E. But a proposition letter formula E has only a finite class of subformulas; and from these there are only a finite number k of ways of choosing formulas to occur in antecedent and to occur in succedent, i.e. at most k incognate sequents can be written down formed of subformulas of E. Therefore an irredundant proof of $\to$ E cannot exist having more than k levels; so we can exhaust the possibilities for finding such a proof by completing the procedure up to (at most) the k-th level.

Example 4. Is $\neg\neg(\mathcal{A}_1 \vee \mathcal{A}_2) \supset \neg\neg\mathcal{A}_1 \vee \neg\neg\mathcal{A}_2$ provable in the intuitionistic propositional calculus? We start out as follows.

3. $\neg\neg(\mathcal{A}_1 \vee \mathcal{A}_2) \to \neg(\mathcal{A}_1 \vee \mathcal{A}_2)$ or $\neg\neg(\mathcal{A}_1 \vee \mathcal{A}_2) \to \neg\neg\mathcal{A}_1$ or $\neg\neg(\mathcal{A}_1 \vee \mathcal{A}_2) \to \neg$-

2. $\neg\neg(\mathcal{A}_1 \vee \mathcal{A}_2) \to \neg\neg\mathcal{A}_1 \vee \neg\neg\mathcal{A}_2$

1. $\to \neg\neg(\mathcal{A}_1 \vee \mathcal{A}_2) \supset \neg\neg\mathcal{A}_1 \vee \neg\neg\mathcal{A}_2$.

Without carrying this procedure further, we can now answer the question in the negative. For we can quickly verify by 2-valued truth table methods that none of the sequents at Line 3 is provable. Thus the first of them $\neg\neg(\mathcal{A}_1 \vee \mathcal{A}_2) \to \neg(\mathcal{A}_1 \vee \mathcal{A}_2)$ is only provable in $G3$ and hence (Theorem 56 (a)) in $G1$, if $\neg\neg(\mathcal{A}_1 \vee \mathcal{A}_2) \supset \neg(\mathcal{A}_1 \vee \mathcal{A}_2)$ is provable in H (Corollary Theorem 47). But $\neg\neg(\mathcal{A}_1 \vee \mathcal{A}_2) \supset \neg(\mathcal{A}_1 \vee \mathcal{A}_2)$ is not provable in H, since it assumes the value $\mathfrak{f}$ when $\mathcal{A}_1$, $\mathcal{A}_2$ take the values $\mathfrak{t}$, $\mathfrak{t}$ (Theorem 9 § 28).

THEOREM 57. (a) *In the intuitionistic propositional calculus H, for any formulas* A *and* B: $\vdash$ A $\vee$ B, *only if* $\vdash$ A *or* $\vdash$ B. (Gödel 1932.)

(b) *Each of the numbered results* *14, *15, *49, *51, *52, *55—*62, *which were established in Chapter* VI *only for the classical propositional calculus, does actually fail to hold for the intuitionistic propositional calculus (and likewise the converse of each implication among* *49a—*62a).

PROOFS. Part (a) is immediate from the form of $\rightarrow \vee$ in *G*3. For (b) we can show by the decision procedure that each formula in question is unprovable when A and B are simple proposition letters $\mathcal{A}$ and $\mathcal{B}$, as we have already done for *51 in Example 3 (a). (For *51 the unprovability also follows from Part (a) with Theorem 9.) However for the others it is more expeditious to take advantage of deductions in the intuitionistic propositional calculus. For example, if *49 held, by Remark 1 § 27 so would *51, contradicting our result for *51. The others we consider in their numerical order.

*14. Suppose $\neg$A $\supset$ B $\vdash$ $\neg$B $\supset$ A did hold in the intuitionistic propositional calculus for all formulas A and B. Then in particular we would have $\neg\mathcal{A} \supset \neg\mathcal{A} \vdash \neg\neg\mathcal{A} \supset \mathcal{A}$, whence using *1 we would get $\vdash \neg\neg\mathcal{A} \supset \mathcal{A}$, contradicting our result for *49.

*56. (Cf. *56a.) If $\vdash \neg(\neg \text{A} \,\&\, \neg \text{B}) \supset \text{A} \vee \text{B}$ intuitionistically for all A and B, then in particular $\vdash \neg(\neg\mathcal{A} \,\&\, \neg\mathcal{A}) \supset \mathcal{A} \vee \mathcal{A}$, whence by *37 and *38 again $\vdash \neg\neg\mathcal{A} \supset \mathcal{A}$. A fortiori by &-elim., not $\vdash \text{A} \vee \text{B} \sim \neg(\neg \text{A} \,\&\, \neg \text{B})$ intuitionistically for all A and B.

*62. (Cf. *62a.) If $\vdash \neg(\text{A} \,\&\, \text{B}) \supset \neg \text{A} \vee \neg \text{B}$ intuitionistically for all A and B, then in particular $\vdash \neg(\mathcal{A} \,\&\, \neg\mathcal{A}) \supset \neg\mathcal{A} \vee \neg\neg\mathcal{A}$, whence by *50, $\vdash \neg\mathcal{A} \vee \neg\neg\mathcal{A}$. By (a) of the theorem, then either $\vdash \neg\mathcal{A}$ or $\vdash \neg\neg\mathcal{A}$, contradicting Theorem 9.

REMARK 1. Likewise the theorems and corollaries of Chapter VI marked with ° as being established only classically can (with one exception) be inferred by the present methods to fail intuitionistically. Thus Theorem 8 would give *49; its corollary would give *55 from *54; Theorem 11 would give the equivalence of $\neg\neg\mathcal{A}$ to one of $\mathcal{A} \vee \neg\mathcal{A}$, $\mathcal{A}$, $\neg\mathcal{A}$ and $\mathcal{A} \,\&\, \neg\mathcal{A}$; etc. EXCEPTION: Theorem 12 is obviously false for the intuitionistic propositional calculus in the sense that the indicated procedure does not apply. That no other truth table procedure with finitely many values applies was shown by Gödel 1932. There does exist a decision procedure of another kind (Theorem 56 (d)).

Predicate calculus. By Theorem 54 § 76, there is no decision procedure for the predicate calculus. (At what point does the proof of Theorem 56 (d) fail, when we attempt to apply it to the predicate calculus? Contrast Examples 2 and 3 (a) § 78.) Although Theorem 56 (c) thus does not afford a decision procedure in the case of the predicate calculus, nevertheless it is useful in investigating provability in the predicate calculus. Given a predicate letter formula E, by attempting to find an irredundant proof in $G3$ of $\rightarrow$ E, we may actually find one, or we may discover some feature of the situation which shows that there cannot be any.

Theorem 58. *In the intuitionistic predicate calculus H*:

(a) $\neg\neg\forall x(\mathcal{A}(x) \vee \neg\mathcal{A}(x))$ *is unprovable.* (Heyting 1930a; Kleene 1945 with Nelson 1947.)

(b) (i) $\forall x(\mathcal{A} \vee \mathcal{B}(x)) \supset \mathcal{A} \vee \forall x\mathcal{B}(x)$ *is unprovable,*

(ii) $\neg\neg\{\forall x(\mathcal{A} \vee \mathcal{B}(x)) \supset \mathcal{A} \vee \forall x\mathcal{B}(x)\}$ *is provable, but*

(iii) $\neg\neg\forall y\{\forall x(\mathcal{A}(y) \vee \mathcal{B}(x)) \supset \mathcal{A}(y) \vee \forall x\mathcal{B}(x)\}$ *is unprovable.*

(c) *In each table of Corollary Theorem* 17 § 35, *when* A(x) *is the simple predicate letter* $\mathcal{A}(x)$, *the implication (and hence the equivalence) of a formula above a line by (to) one below the line is unprovable, and likewise the double negation of that implication (and hence,* by *25, *of that equivalence) when a double line separates the formulas.* (Heyting 1946.)

(d) *Each of the numbered results* *83—*85, *92, *97—*99 (*Theorem* 17), *which were established in Chapter* VII *only for the classical predicate calculus, does fail to hold. Of them,* *83, *92 *and* *97 *hold, but* *84, *85, *98 *and* *99 *fail to hold, when double negation is applied to the formula.*

Proofs. (a) We attempt to construct an irredundant proof of $\rightarrow\neg\neg\forall x(\mathcal{A}(x) \vee \neg\mathcal{A}(x))$ in the intuitionistic system $G3$ as follows. For abbreviation, we let "B" stand for $\forall x(\mathcal{A}(x) \vee \neg\mathcal{A}(x))$ at certain places. From Line 3 to 4, either $\neg$B or B can be the principal formula of the inference. If $\neg$B (using $\neg\rightarrow$), the premise is what is already obtained at 3 (the original B disappearing as the Θ and a new occurrence of it appearing as the side formula). For the definition of what constitutes a proof of a given sequent in $G3$, all variables not occurring in the sequent are on a par; hence at Line 4 it suffices to list the premise for the $\rightarrow\forall$ with the particular variable b_1. Then similarly at Line 8 we choose another particular variable b_2, which must be distinct from b_1 to satisfy the restriction on variables for the $\rightarrow\forall$; etc.

*11.	$\neg B, \mathcal{A}(b_1), \mathcal{A}(b_2) \rightarrow B$
10.	$7 \qquad\qquad 7$ or $\neg B, \mathcal{A}(b_1), \mathcal{A}(b_2) \rightarrow$
9.	7 or $\neg B, \mathcal{A}(b_1) \rightarrow \mathcal{A}(b_2)$ or $\neg B, \mathcal{A}(b_1) \rightarrow \neg\mathcal{A}(b_2)$
8.	7 or $\neg B, \mathcal{A}(b_1) \rightarrow \mathcal{A}(b_2) \vee \neg\mathcal{A}(b_2)$
*7.	$\neg B, \mathcal{A}(b_1) \rightarrow B$
6.	$3 \qquad\qquad 3$ or $\neg B, \mathcal{A}(b_1) \rightarrow$
5.	3 or $\neg B \rightarrow \mathcal{A}(b_1)$ or $\neg B \rightarrow \neg\mathcal{A}(b_1)$
4.	3 or $\neg B \rightarrow \mathcal{A}(b_1) \vee \neg\mathcal{A}(b_1)$
*3.	$\neg B \rightarrow B$
2.	$\neg B \rightarrow$
1.	$\rightarrow \neg\neg B.$

From the portion of the structure shown, the general pattern is clear. We fail to have an axiom in the first new sequent $\neg B, \mathcal{A}(b_1) \rightarrow \mathcal{A}(b_2)$ of Line 9 because b_1 and b_2 are distinct variables; similarly in the first new sequent $\neg B, \mathcal{A}(b_1), \mathcal{A}(b_2) \rightarrow \mathcal{A}(b_3)$ of Line 13; and so on. All other sequents occurring are even more obviously not axioms. Note the form of Lines 3, 7, 11, . . . ; at Line $3+4n$ for $n = 0, 1, 2, \ldots$ we have closed out all the possibilities for finding an irredundant proof of $\rightarrow \neg\neg B$ other than by finding one of $\neg B, \mathcal{A}(b_1), \ldots, \mathcal{A}(b_n) \rightarrow B$ with distinct variables $b_1, \ldots, b_n$. Thus the search for an irredundant proof of $\rightarrow \neg\neg B$ in $G3$ will never terminate successfully, but will only lead us upward through an infinite regression of increasingly complicated sequents. Otherwise expressed, we establish that there is an irredundant proof of $\rightarrow \neg\neg B$ in $G3$, only if there is a shorter one of $\neg B \rightarrow B$, a still shorter one of $\neg B, \mathcal{A}(b_1) \rightarrow B$, a still shorter one again of $\neg B, \mathcal{A}(b_1), \mathcal{A}(b_2) \rightarrow B$, ad infinitum. Since it is absurd that there should exist an infinite succession of successively shorter proofs starting with a first proof, we conclude that there is no proof of $\rightarrow \neg\neg B$ in the intuitionistic system $G3$; and hence by Theorem 56 (c), none of $\neg\neg B$ in the intuitionistic predicate calculus H.

(b) (i) We attempt to construct a proof in $G3$, with the first step uniquely determined thus:

2.	$\forall x(\mathcal{A} \vee \mathcal{B}(x)) \rightarrow \mathcal{A} \vee \forall x\mathcal{B}(x)$
1.	$\rightarrow \forall x(\mathcal{A} \vee \mathcal{B}(x)) \supset \mathcal{A} \vee \forall x\mathcal{B}(x).$

From the form of the sequent at Line 2, and of the rules of $G3$, we see that in any sequent above the bottom one only formulas of the four forms $\forall x(\mathcal{A} \vee \mathcal{B}(x))$, $\mathcal{A} \vee \mathcal{B}(t)$ (t a term, i.e. for the pure predicate calculus, a variable), $\mathcal{A}$ and $\mathcal{B}(t)$ can occur in the antecedent, and only a formula of one of the four forms $\mathcal{A} \vee \forall x\mathcal{B}(x)$, $\mathcal{A}$, $\forall x\mathcal{B}(x)$ and $\mathcal{B}(b)$ (b a variable) as the succedent. The only chances for such a sequent to be an axiom are for it to have the form $\mathcal{A}, \Gamma \rightarrow \mathcal{A}$ or the form $\mathcal{B}(t), \Gamma \rightarrow \mathcal{B}(b)$ where t is b. Whenever the two-premise rule $\vee \rightarrow$ is applied, the tree we are constructing will branch. The other rules which there is a possibility of applying after the first step are the one-premise rules $\forall \rightarrow$, $\rightarrow \vee$ and $\rightarrow \forall$. In order to have found a proof, for some succession of choices, every branch must be terminated above in an axiom. We shall now show that, no matter what succession of steps has been performed, an axiom will not have been reached along one of the branches. For this purpose, we define the *designated branch* (along which we are to show that an axiom cannot be reached) by specifying which premise belongs to it at each $\vee \rightarrow$, thus. Let the principal formula for the $\vee \rightarrow$ be $\mathcal{A} \vee \mathcal{B}(t)$. If the formula of the succedent contains $\mathcal{A}$ as whole or part, the premise in the designated branch (or *designated premise*) shall be the one with $\mathcal{B}(t)$ as the side formula; otherwise the one with $\mathcal{A}$ as the side formula. Now consider the following *property P* of a sequent, namely that (1) $\mathcal{A}$ does not occur as one of the antecedent formulas, if the succedent formula contains $\mathcal{A}$ as whole or part, and (2) for every variable b, $\mathcal{B}(b)$ does not occur as one of the antecedent formulas, if $\mathcal{B}(b)$ (for the same b) is the succedent formula. Neither kind of axiom described above has property P. Hence, to prove that an axiom cannot be reached along the designated branch, it suffices to show that every sequent in the designated branch has property P. This we do by induction. For, first, the sequents at Lines 1 and 2 have property P. Thereafter, as we shall verify next, each inference will preserve property P along the designated branch, i.e. if the conclusion of the inference has property P, so does the premise, or in the case of an $\vee \rightarrow$ the designated premise. To verify this, we must examine four cases, according to the form of the principal formula of the inference. CASE 1: $\forall x(\mathcal{A} \vee \mathcal{B}(x))$ in the antecedent. Property P is obviously preserved, since the side formula introduced into the antecedent by the $\forall \rightarrow$ is of the form $\mathcal{A} \vee \mathcal{B}(t)$ and the succedent is unchanged. CASE 2: $\mathcal{A} \vee \mathcal{B}(t)$ in the antecedent. If the succedent contains $\mathcal{A}$ as whole or part, the introduction of $\mathcal{B}(t)$ as side formula for the designated premise of the $\vee \rightarrow$ preserves property P. If the succedent does not contain $\mathcal{A}$ as whole or part, the introduction of $\mathcal{A}$ as side formula for the designated premise preserves property P. CASE 3: $\mathcal{A} \vee \forall x\mathcal{B}(x)$ as the succedent. Since the conclusion has property P, the formula $\mathcal{A}$ does not occur among the antecedent formulas, by (1). Then the introduction of either $\mathcal{A}$ or $\forall x\mathcal{B}(x)$ into the succedent as the side formula of the $\rightarrow\vee$ preserves property P. CASE 4: $\forall x\mathcal{B}(x)$ as the succedent. By the restriction on variables for the $\rightarrow\forall$, the variable b of the side formula $\mathcal{B}$(b) must be a variable not occurring in the antecedent, which assures that (2) for property P remains satisfied.

(ii) Now consider instead $\neg\neg\{\forall x(\mathcal{A}\vee\mathcal{B}(x))\supset\mathcal{A}\vee\forall x\mathcal{B}(x)\}$; call it "$\neg\neg$C". We may now have in antecedents of sequents above the bottom line also the formula $\neg$C, as succedent also C. The induction for property P fails in the case for $\neg$C in the antecedent, as the $\neg\rightarrow$ can introduce C as the succedent after $\mathcal{A}$ has previously been introduced into the antecedent, leading to a violation of (1). By following out this loophole in the previous demonstration of unprovability, we are led to the following proof of $\rightarrow\neg\neg\{\forall x(\mathcal{A}\vee\mathcal{B}(x))\supset\mathcal{A}\vee\forall x\mathcal{B}(x)\}$, which we state in $G3$a. The designated branch, which except by using $\neg$C as the principal formula for an $\neg\rightarrow$ we would be unable to terminate in an axiom, is the left one.

11. $\mathcal{A}\rightarrow\mathcal{A}$
   ($\rightarrow\vee$)
10. $\mathcal{A}\rightarrow\mathcal{A}\vee\forall x\mathcal{B}(x)$
   ($\rightarrow\supset$)
9. $\mathcal{A}\rightarrow\forall x(\mathcal{A}\vee\mathcal{B}(x))\supset\mathcal{A}\vee\forall x\mathcal{B}(x)$
   ($\neg\rightarrow$)
8. $\neg C,\ \mathcal{A}\rightarrow$ $\qquad\qquad$ $\mathcal{B}(b)\rightarrow\mathcal{B}(b)$
   ($\vee\rightarrow$)
7. $\neg C,\ \mathcal{A}\vee\mathcal{B}(b)\rightarrow\mathcal{B}(b)$
   ($\forall\rightarrow$)
6. $\neg C,\ \forall x(\mathcal{A}\vee\mathcal{B}(x))\rightarrow\mathcal{B}(b)$
   ($\rightarrow\forall$)
5. $\neg C,\ \forall x(\mathcal{A}\vee\mathcal{B}(x))\rightarrow\forall x\mathcal{B}(x)$
   ($\rightarrow\vee$)
4. $\neg C,\ \forall x(\mathcal{A}\vee\mathcal{B}(x))\rightarrow\mathcal{A}\vee\forall x\mathcal{B}(x)$
   ($\rightarrow\supset$)
3. $\neg C\rightarrow C$
   ($\neg\rightarrow$)
2. $\neg C\rightarrow$
   ($\rightarrow\neg$)
1. $\rightarrow\neg\neg C.$

(iii) If we now change the formula to $\neg\neg\forall y\{\forall x(\mathcal{A}(y)\vee\mathcal{B}(x))\supset\mathcal{A}(y)\vee\forall x\mathcal{B}(x)\}$, the loophole is closed. For the $\mathcal{A}$ obtained in the antecedent before the $\neg\rightarrow$ becomes $\mathcal{A}$(c) for some variable c. Then the $\mathcal{A}$ obtained in the succedent after $\neg\rightarrow$ followed now by $\rightarrow\forall$ with respect to y will become $\mathcal{A}$(d) where d is a variable distinct from c by the restriction on variables for the $\rightarrow\forall$. The reader may work out the modifications in the demonstration given in (i) to establish the unprovability rigorously.

(c) For a given table, consider formulas A, B, C, D, where B is A or below A, C is immediately below B and separated from it by a line, and D is C or below C. Using *2, if $\vdash$ A $\supset$ B and $\vdash$ C $\supset$ D, but not $\vdash$ C $\supset$ B, then not $\vdash$ D $\supset$ A. Similarly, using *24 and *49a, if $\vdash$ A $\supset$ B and $\vdash$ C $\supset$ D, but not $\vdash \neg\neg$(C $\supset$ B), then not $\vdash \neg\neg$(D $\supset$ A) and not $\vdash$ D $\supset$ A. Hence it suffices to treat the upward implications between the six pairs of formulas immediately separated by a line, under double negation when the line is double.

Ib $\supset$ Ia, IIb $\supset$ IIa. If either were provable, by substituting $\mathcal{A}$ for $\mathcal{A}(x)$ (Theorem 15 § 34) and using *75 or *76, or by using Theorem 22 § 37 for $k = 1$, $\neg\neg\mathcal{A} \supset \mathcal{A}$ would be provable. Hence not $\vdash$ Ib $\supset$ Ia and not $\vdash$ IIb $\supset$ IIa.

$\neg\neg(\text{Ic}_1 \supset \text{Ib})$. Let "B($x$)" abbreviate $\mathcal{A}(x) \vee \neg\mathcal{A}(x)$. By *51a and $\forall$-introd., $\vdash \forall x\neg\neg B(x)$. Hence $\forall x\neg\neg B(x) \supset \neg\neg\forall x B(x) \vdash \neg\neg\forall x B(x)$. Thence by $\supset$-introd. and contraposition twice (*13, *12), $\vdash \neg\neg\{\forall x\neg\neg B(x) \supset \neg\neg\forall x B(x)\} \supset \neg\neg\forall x B(x)$. Thus if $\neg\neg\{\forall x\neg\neg B(x) \supset \neg\neg\forall x B(x)\}$ were provable, $\neg\neg\forall x B(x)$ would be. But by (a), not $\vdash \neg\neg\forall x B(x)$; hence not $\vdash \neg\neg\{\forall x\neg\neg B(x) \supset \neg\neg\forall x B(x)\}$; and hence by the substitution rule (Theorem 15) not $\vdash \neg\neg\{\forall x\neg\neg\mathcal{A}(x) \supset \neg\neg\forall x\mathcal{A}(x)\}$, i.e. not $\vdash \neg\neg(\text{Ic}_1 \supset \text{Ib})$.

$\neg\neg(\text{IIIc} \supset \text{IIIb}_2)$. Easily reduces to $\neg\neg(\text{Ic}_1 \supset \text{Ib})$.

$\text{IIc}_1 \supset \text{IIb}$. By Example 3 § 37 and Example 4 this section.

$\text{IIIb}_1 \supset \text{IIIa}$. Easily reduces to $\text{IIc}_1 \supset \text{IIb}$.

(d) *83—*85, *92. Included under (b) and (c) (with *25, *92a.)

*97. We show $(\mathcal{A} \supset \exists x\mathcal{B}(x)) \supset \exists x(\mathcal{A} \supset \mathcal{B}(x))$ unprovable, similarly to $\text{IIc}_1 \supset \text{IIb}$. (After applying Theorem 22 with $k = 2$, we obtain at Line 3: $\{\mathcal{A} \supset \mathcal{B}_1 \vee \mathcal{B}_2 \rightarrow \mathcal{A}$ and $\mathcal{B}_1 \vee \mathcal{B}_2$, $\mathcal{A} \supset \mathcal{B}_1 \vee \mathcal{B}_2 \rightarrow (\mathcal{A} \supset \mathcal{B}_1) \vee (\mathcal{A} \supset \mathcal{B}_2)\}$ or $\mathcal{A} \supset \mathcal{B}_1 \vee \mathcal{B}_2 \rightarrow \mathcal{A} \supset \mathcal{B}_1$ or $\mathcal{A} \supset \mathcal{B}_1 \vee \mathcal{B}_2 \rightarrow \mathcal{A} \supset \mathcal{B}_2$. In treating the first alternative, it suffices of course to show that the first premise $\mathcal{A} \supset \mathcal{B}_1 \vee \mathcal{B}_2 \rightarrow \mathcal{A}$ of the two is unprovable.) We prove $\neg\neg\{(\mathcal{A} \supset \exists x\mathcal{B}(x)) \supset \exists x(\mathcal{A} \supset \mathcal{B}(x))\}$, similarly to (b) (ii). (In Lines 4 — 9, use successively $\rightarrow\exists$, $\rightarrow\supset$, $\supset\rightarrow$, $\neg\rightarrow$, $\exists\rightarrow$.) Cf. *97a.

*98. Substituting $\mathcal{A}\ \&\ \neg\mathcal{A}$ for $\mathcal{B}$ in $\neg\neg\{(\forall x\mathcal{A}(x) \supset \mathcal{B}) \supset \exists x(\mathcal{A}(x) \supset \mathcal{B})\}$ and using *50 and *44, we get $\neg\neg(\text{IIIc} \supset \text{IIIa})$.

*99. Reduces to *98 (cf. the first method for Ib $\supset$ Ia).

Heyting (1930a p. 65) infers the unprovability of the formula of Theorem 58 (a) and of $\text{Ic}_1 \supset \text{Ib}$ from the interpretation of the intuitionistic predicate calculus in terms of Brouwer's theory of sets (end § 13).

The proof of Theorem 58 (a) by Kleene 1945 and Nelson 1947 is from results to be taken up in § 82.

The present treatment of (a) and (b) was reported in Kleene 1948; and some like applications of Gentzen's theorem are in Curry 1950 (already in press in 1948). de Iongh 1948 uses the method in establishing an intuitionistic classification of those formulas formed from $\mathcal{A}(x, y, z)$ by quantifying x, y, and z and possibly applying negation which are classically equivalent to $\forall x \exists y \forall z \mathcal{A}(x, y, z)$, analogous to each of the four tables of Heyting 1946 for one quantifier (Corollary Theorem 17 § 35 and Theorem 58 (c)). He takes this sequence of quantifiers for illustration, because of its role in formulating the notion of convergence of a sequence to a limit (cf. § 35 (i) or (ii), omitting the x's).

Mostowski 1948 demonstrates the unprovability of $\neg\neg(\mathrm{Ic}_1 \supset \mathrm{Ib})$, and (b) (i), by an interpretation of the intuitionistic predicate calculus in terms of "complete Brouwerian" lattices. Henkin 1950a extends Mostowski's results to obtain an algebraic characterization of quantifiers both for intuitionistic and for classical logic.

§ 81. Reductions of classical to intuitionistic systems.

For the rest of this chapter, we use the Hilbert-type systems H. When Γ is a sequence of zero or more formulas, $\neg\Gamma$, $\neg\neg\Gamma$, Γ°, etc. shall be the result of applying $\neg$, $\neg\neg$, $^\circ$ (as defined below), etc., respectively, to each of the formulas of Γ.

The main result of the first part of this section is given in several versions, though its significance can be seen from one. The reader desiring a simplified treatment may accordingly select: Theorem 59 and Proofs, Definition and Discussion of $^\circ$, Theorem 60 (a) for $^\circ$ only and (c), Lemma 43a and Proof, Proof of Theorem 60 (c), Corollary 2 (omitting the other material up to that point).

THEOREM 59. (a1) *If* $\Gamma \vdash \mathrm{E}$ *in the classical propositional calculus, then* $\neg\neg\Gamma \vdash \neg\neg\mathrm{E}$ *in the intuitionistic propositional calculus.* (a2) *If* $\neg\Gamma, \Delta \vdash \neg\mathrm{E}$ *in the classical propositional calculus, then* $\neg\Gamma, \neg\neg\Delta \vdash \neg\mathrm{E}$ *in the intuitionistic propositional calculus.* (Glivenko 1929.)

(b) *Likewise for the predicate calculus with Rule 9 omitted, and for the formal number-theoretic system with Rule 9 omitted.*

PROOFS. (a1) By induction on the length of the given classical deduction $\Gamma \vdash \mathrm{E}$ (i.e. the deduction of E from Γ which "$\Gamma \vdash \mathrm{E}$" asserts to exist, cf. § 22), using the following observations. If E is an axiom of the classical propositional calculus by any axiom schema except 8, then E is also an axiom intuitionistically, and by *49a § 27, $\vdash \neg\neg E$ in the intuitionistic system. If E is an axiom by the classical Axiom Schema 8, then by *51b, again $\vdash \neg\neg E$ intuitionistically. Moreover, corresponding to Rule 2, $\neg\neg A, \neg\neg(A \supset B) \vdash \neg\neg B$ intuitionistically, using *23 § 26. (a2) From (a1) using *49b.

(b) Because the additional axiom schemata and particular axioms belong to the intuitionistic as well as to the classical system, we need only add a treatment of the additional rule of inference 12. Using *23, Rule 12 and *49a: (i) $\neg\neg(A(x) \supset C) \vdash \neg\neg A(x) \supset \neg\neg C \vdash^x \exists x \neg\neg A(x) \supset \neg\neg C \vdash \neg\neg(\exists x \neg\neg A(x) \supset \neg\neg C)$. Using *49a, *70 § 32 and *49a: (ii) $\vdash \neg\neg(\exists x A(x) \supset \exists x \neg\neg A(x))$. By *51b: (iii) $\vdash \neg\neg(\neg\neg C \supset C)$. Combining (ii), (i) and (iii) by *24, $\neg\neg(A(x) \supset C) \vdash^x \neg\neg(\exists x A(x) \supset C)$.

Example 1. By (a1), each of the numbered results which were established in Chapter VI only for the classical propositional calculus (see Theorem 57 (b)) holds intuitionistically under double negation (applied in *14 and *15 to both formulas).

Example 2. That *97 holds intuitionistically under double negation (which we proved by another method for Theorem 58 (d)) now follows from (b) and Theorem 49 § 78.

Corollary (to (a2)). *If* E *is a proposition letter formula containing no logical symbols except* & *and* $\neg$, *and* $\vdash$ E *in the classical propositional calculus, then* $\vdash$ E *in the intuitionistic propositional calculus.* (Gödel 1932-3.)

Proof. Consider E as a conjunction of n formulas ($n \geq 1$) each of which is not a conjunction, and is therefore either a proposition letter or begins with the symbol $\neg$. By &-elim., each of these n components is provable classically. But no proposition letter is provable (by Theorem 9 § 28). So each component is a negation, and by Glivenko's theorem ((a2)) is also provable intuitionistically. Hence by &-introd., so is E.

Definition of °. For the rest of this section, the formulas Γ, the formula E, etc., shall be proposition letter formulas, predicate letter formulas, or number-theoretic formulas, according as we are considering propositional calculus, predicate calculus, or formal number theory. By a *prime part* of a formula, we mean a (consecutive) part which is a prime formula, i.e. one containing no logical symbol.

For any formula E, we define E° by the following recursion. 1. If P is a prime formula, P° is P. 2 — 5. If A and B are formulas, $(A \supset B)°$ is $A° \supset B°$, $(A \& B)°$ is $A° \& B°$, $(A \vee B)°$ is $\neg(\neg A° \& \neg B°)$, and $(\neg A)°$

is $\neg A^\circ$. 6—7. If x is a variable, and A(x) is a formula, $(\forall x A(x))^\circ$ is $\forall x A^\circ(x)$ (where $A^\circ(x)$ is $(A(x))^\circ$), and $(\exists x A(x))^\circ$ is $\neg\forall x\neg A^\circ(x)$.

Briefly, E° comes from E by replacing (or "translating") each part of E of the form shown below in the first line by the respective expression shown in the second.

$A \supset B$	$A \& B$	$A \vee B$	$\neg A$	$\forall x A(x)$	$\exists x A(x)$
"	"	$\neg(\neg A \& \neg B)$	"	"	$\neg\forall x\neg A(x)$

Example 3. Let A(x) and B be prime (and B not contain x free). If E is $[\forall x A(x) \supset B] \supset \exists x[A(x) \supset B]$ (cf. *98), then
E° is $[\forall x A(x) \supset B] \supset \neg\forall x\neg[A(x) \supset B]$.

Discussion of °. In the next theorem it is shown that the classical systems can be defined within the intuitionistic. In particular, for the number-theoretic system, if $\vdash$ E classically, then $\vdash$ E° intuitionistically. The converse holds obviously (since $\vdash E \sim E^\circ$ classically), as do the converses for Theorem 59 and the other parts of Theorem 60. So a formula E is provable in the classical system, if and only if the correlated formula E° is provable in the intuitionistic system. We can think of E° as resulting from E by changing the logical symbols $\supset, \&, \vee, \neg, \forall, \exists$ to $\supset^\circ, \&^\circ, \vee^\circ, \neg^\circ, \forall^\circ, \exists^\circ$, respectively, where "$A \supset^\circ B$" is an abbreviation for $A \supset B$, "$A \vee^\circ B$" for $\neg(\neg A \& \neg B)$, etc. The sense in which the classical formulas are thus "translated" into intuitionistic ones can be emphasized by using different logical symbols (say $\supset^C, \&^C, \vee^C, \neg^C, \forall^C, \exists^C$) for the classical system (upper row in the above translation table).

Definition of ′, etc. For the propositional and predicate calculi, we use other correlations. Let E′ be obtained from E like E° except that $A \supset B$ is translated as $\neg(A \& \neg B)$. Let $E^\dagger$ be obtained from E by replacing each prime part P by $\neg\neg P$; and $E^\ddagger$ likewise except that P is replaced by $\neg\neg P$ only where it is alone (i.e. when E itself is P), or immediately within the scope of an & or an $\forall$, or is the second part of the scope of an $\supset$; and E* like $E^\ddagger$ except without the replacements in the second part of the scope of $\supset$.

Example 3 (concluded).

E′ is $\neg\{\neg[\forall x A(x) \& \neg B] \& \neg\neg\forall x \neg\neg[A(x) \& \neg B]\}$,
$E^{\circ\dagger}$ is $[\forall x \neg\neg A(x) \supset \neg\neg B] \supset \neg\forall x \neg[\neg\neg A(x) \supset \neg\neg B]$,
$E^{\circ\ddagger}$ is $[\forall x \neg\neg A(x) \supset \neg\neg B] \supset \neg\forall x \neg[A(x) \supset \neg\neg B]$, and
$E^{*\prime}$ is $\neg\{\neg[\forall x \neg\neg A(x) \& \neg B] \& \neg\neg\forall x \neg\neg[A(x) \& \neg B]\}$.

For the propositional calculus, there can be no inverse theorem, giving a similar reduction of the intuitionistic to the classical system, in which the intuitionistic propositional connectives are defined explicitly from the classical. For that would give a truth table decision procedure for the intuitionistic propositional calculus, contradicting Gödel 1932.

THEOREM 60. (a) *For any formula* E, *in the propositional calculus, predicate calculus, or number-theoretic formal system,* $\vdash$ E $\sim$ E° $\sim$ E′ $\sim$ E°† $\sim$ E°‡ $\sim$ E*′ *classically* (by *56, *83, *58, *49).

(b1) *For the propositional calculus, if* $\vdash$ E *classically, then* $\vdash$ E′ *intuitionistically.* (b2) *For the number-theoretic formal system, if* Γ $\vdash$ E *classically, then* Γ′ $\vdash$ E′ *intuitionistically.* (Gödel 1932-3.)

(c) *For the number-theoretic formal system, if* Γ $\vdash$ E *classically, then* Γ° $\vdash$ E° *intuitionistically.* (Gentzen 1936 p. 532 and Bernays.)

(d) *For the propositional calculus, predicate calculus, or number-theoretic formal system, if* Γ $\vdash$ E *classically, then* Γ°† $\vdash$ E°† (*also* Γ°‡ $\vdash$ E°‡ *and* Γ*′ $\vdash$ E*′) *intuitionistically.*

PROOFS. (b1) Using (a), if $\vdash$ E classically, then $\vdash$ E′ classically. But E′ contains as operators only & and ¬. Thus (b1) follows from Corollary Theorem 59. (Conversely, Corollary Theorem 59 is implied by (b1).)

We shall prove (c) after the first lemma, and then infer (b2).

LEMMA 43a. *For the number-theoretic formal system, if* F *contains no logical symbols except* ⊃, &, ¬, ∀ (*in particular, if* F *is* E° *for some formula* E), *then* $\vdash$ ¬¬F ⊃ F (*and hence* $\vdash$ ¬¬F $\sim$ F) *intuitionistically.* (After Gödel 1932-3.)

PROOF OF LEMMA 43a, by induction on the number of (occurrences of) logical symbols in F.

BASIS: F is of the form s=t where s and t are terms. By *158 § 40, $\vdash$ s=t ∨ ¬s=t, whence by *49c, $\vdash$ ¬¬s=t ⊃ s=t.

IND. STEP. CASE 1: F is A ⊃ B. By hyp. ind.: (i) $\vdash$ ¬¬B ⊃ B. By *60g, h: (ii) ¬¬(A ⊃ B) $\vdash$ A ⊃ ¬¬B. From (ii) and (i) by chain inference (*2), ¬¬(A ⊃ B) $\vdash$ A ⊃ B, and by ⊃-introd., $\vdash$ ¬¬(A ⊃ B) ⊃ (A ⊃ B). CASE 2: F is A & B. By hyp. ind., $\vdash$ ¬¬A ⊃ A and $\vdash$ ¬¬B ⊃ B. Use *25. CASE 3: F is ¬A. By *49b. CASE 4: F is ∀xA(x). Use hyp. ind., *69 and $\vdash$ Ib ⊃ Ic_1 from Corollary Theorem 17.

PROOF OF THEOREM 60 (c). By induction on the length of the given classical deduction $\Gamma \vdash$ E, with cases as follows.

CASE 1: E is one of the particular axioms 14—21, or an axiom by any schema except 11. Then E° is E, or is an axiom by the same schema, or is deducible in the classical propositional calculus (using *56 with Theorem 6 § 26) from an axiom by the same schema; so E° is provable in the system of the classical propositional calculus with the other axioms and axiom schemata added. (For example, if E is an axiom A ⊃ (B ⊃ A) by Schema 1a, then E° is A° ⊃ (B° ⊃ A°), which is an axiom by the same schema. If E is an axiom A ⊃ A ∨ B by Schema 5a, then E° is A° ⊃ ¬(¬A° & ¬B°), which is deducible from A° ⊃ A° ∨ B° by *56 and Theorem 6, since the part to be replaced does not stand within the scope of a quantifier.) Hence by Theorem 59 (b), ⊢ ¬¬E° in the intuitionistic number-theoretic system; and hence by Lemma 43a, ⊢ E° in the same. CASE 2: Axiom Schema 11. Then E is A(t) ⊃ ∃xA(x), and E° is A°(t) ⊃ ¬∀x¬A°(x), which is provable intuitionistically by contraposition (*13) from the axiom ∀x¬A°(x) ⊃ ¬A°(t).

CASE 3: Rule 2. We must show that A°, (A ⊃ B)° ⊢ B° intuitionistically. But (A ⊃ B)° is A° ⊃ B°. CASE 4: Rule 9. Similarly. CASE 5: Rule 12. With the help of *12 and Lemma 43a.

PROOF OF THEOREM 60 (b2). By Lemma 43a with *58f § 27, any part of Γ°, E° of the form A ⊃ B is equivalent to ¬(A & ¬B).

LEMMA 43b. *For the propositional or predicate calculus, if* F *contains no logical symbols except* ⊃, &, ¬, ∀ *(in particular, if* F *is* E° *for some formula* E), *then* ⊢ ¬¬F† ⊃ F† *(and hence* ⊢ ¬¬F† ∼ F†) *intuitionistically.*

PROOF OF LEMMA 43b. Similarly to Lemma 43a, using in the basis *49b instead of *158 and *49c.

PROOF OF THEOREM 60 (d). For the number-theoretic system and °†, from (c) by Lemma 43a. For the propositional or predicate calculus and °†, from Lemma 43b in the same manner as (c) from Lemma 43a. (Using Lemma 43a or 43b, *58e and *49b, the result can be modified to $\Gamma^{\circ\ddagger} \vdash$ E°‡; using also *58f, to $\Gamma^{*\prime} \vdash$ E*′.)

REMARK 1. To show that Theorem 59 does not hold for the predicate calculus without the exclusion of Rule 9, and that Theorem 60 (b) does not hold for the predicate calculus, consider as an example $\forall x \neg\neg \mathcal{A}(x) \supset \neg\neg \forall x \mathcal{A}(x)$. Call this formula "E". Then ⊢ E classically, but intuitionistically neither $\vdash$ E nor $\vdash \neg\neg$E (Corollary Theorem 17 § 35 and Theorem 58 (c)), and moreover not $\vdash$ E′, as from E′ by *49b and *58b we can deduce E intuitionistically. The example $\neg\neg\mathcal{A} \supset \mathcal{A}$ shows that Theorem 60 (c) does not hold for the propositional or predicate calculus; and the example $\neg\neg\mathcal{A} \vdash \mathcal{A}$ that Corollary Theorem 59 and Theorem 60 (b1) do not hold with assumption formulas Γ. An example to show that Theorem 59 does not hold for the number-theoretic system without the exclusion of Rule 9 will have to wait until the next section (Theorem 63 (iii)), as we have yet no method of demonstrating an example of a classically provable but intuitionistically unprovable number-theoretic formula.

COROLLARY 1 (to (c)). *For the number-theoretic formal system, if* Γ, E *contain no logical symbols except* ⊃, &, ¬, ∀, *and* Γ $\vdash$ E *classically, then* Γ $\vdash$ E *intuitionistically.* (to (d) for °‡). *Likewise for the propositional or predicate calculus, provided also that* Γ, E *contain no letter unnegated other than as antecedent of an implication.*

COROLLARY 2 (to (b2), (c) or (d)). *The classical number-theoretic formal system is simply consistent, if the intuitionistic is.*

PROOF OF COROLLARY 2. If $1=0$ were provable in the classical system, it would also be in the intuitionistic.

DISCUSSION. Gödel remarks, "The theorem [60 (b2), or now (c)] ... shows that the intuitionistic arithmetic and number theory is only apparently narrower than the classical; in fact [it] includes the entire classical [number theory], merely with a somewhat differing interpretation." Heyting adds, "However for the intuitionists this interpretation is the essential thing." (1934* p. 18.)

de Iongh says, "In our significist opinion the most important advantage of intuitionistic mathematics is, that it distinguishes in every instance between directly and indirectly proved propositions and analyses the mathematical concepts into sequences of concepts with different degree of indirectness." (1948, p. 746.)

van Dantzig 1947 proposes to investigate how much further the development of classical mathematics can be carried within the intuitionistic, in the manner just shown to be possible for all of the usual elementary number theory. For this purpose, the classical formulas E are translated into classical equivalents F which are *stable* intuitionistically, i.e. such that $\vdash \neg\neg$F $\sim$ F (cf. Lemma 43a). van Dantzig suggests that it may be possible to interpret practically the whole of classical mathematics within this stable part of the intuitionistic system.

For the consistency problem, the present results can be regarded as showing that the intuitionistic number theory is equally in need of a metamathematical consistency proof with the classical, or, if one accepts the consistency of the intuitionistic system on the basis of its interpretation, as securing the consistency of the classical system.

Some formalists point out that the methods of intuitionistic elementary number theory go beyond what they consider as finitary (cf. Hilbert-Bernays 1934 p. 43 and Bernays 1935). It is said that the intuitionistic use of negations of complicated formulas, and of implications having in the antecedent a complicated formula (e.g. a generality formula, or another implication) involves the general logical notion of what is an intuitionistic proof. It is by such use of negation and implication that Brouwer and his followers are enabled to go much further in the development of a constructivistic mathematics than Brouwer's forerunner Kronecker.

The intuitionists do not attempt to give an exact description of their notion of a proof in general, and they say that in principle no such description is possible.

The intuitionists' use of negation and implication must then be understood as only requiring us to recognize, e.g., that a particular given proof is intuitionistically acceptable, or (when they prove a statement of the form $(A \rightarrow B) \rightarrow C$) that if one should produce an intuitionistically acceptable deduction of one statement B from another A, then on the basis of it one could by a given method surely construct an intuitionistically acceptable proof of a third C.

An attempt is made by Bernays 1938 to defend the Gentzen transfinite induction up to ε_0 (end § 79), as constituting less of an extension of the narrower finitary standpoint than the whole body of intuitionistic methods in number theory.

de Iongh 1948 touches briefly upon current discussions regarding intuitionism and related trends (particularly *significs*, represented by Mannoury 1909, 1925, 1934).

Now let us examine the way in which Corollary 2 Theorem 60 gives a consistency proof for classical elementary number theory from the intuitionistic standpoint. The second part of this proof is a tacit or explicit verification that the intuitionistic formal system for number theory is correct intuitionistically.

Since the proof of Corollary 2 Theorem 60 is entirely elementary, by Gödel's theorem on consistency proofs (Theorem 30 § 42) the second part cannot be.

It is interesting to note that, just as in the case of Gentzen's consistency proof using transfinite induction up to ε_0, the present consistency proof can be analyzed as depending for its sole non-elementary step on the use of a predicate defined by an induction with quantifiers of both sorts entering in the induction step, namely (here) the truth predicate for number-theoretic formulas. We shall define this predicate next.

Under the usual interpretation of the symbols 0, ′, +, ·, of the variables as natural number variables, and of the operations of building terms from them as corresponding to informal operations of explicit definition, any term $\mathrm{t}(\mathrm{x}_1, \ldots, \mathrm{x}_n)$ containing only the distinct variables $\mathrm{x}_1, \ldots, \mathrm{x}_n$ expresses a primitive recursive function $t(x_1, \ldots, x_n)$, or for $n = 0$ a number t. Under the usual interpretation of =, then every prime formula $\mathrm{P}(\mathrm{x}_1, \ldots, \mathrm{x}_n)$ containing only $\mathrm{x}_1, \ldots, \mathrm{x}_n$ expresses a primitive recursive predicate $P(x_1, \ldots, x_n)$, or for $n = 0$ a proposition P. For any closed prime formula P, the truth or falsity of P is determined (and effectively decidable) in our theory of primitive recursive functions, so we shall not elaborate upon this part of the truth definition. (Indeed, that theory would carry us somewhat further; cf. Example 4 below.)

(A) From this as basis, we define '*true*' as applied to any closed number-theoretic formula E, by induction on the number of (occurrences of) logical symbols in E. In this definition, of course "if" means "if and only if", as is common in definitions.

1. A closed prime formula P is *true*, if P, i.e. if P is a true proposition in the theory of recursive functions.

For Clauses 2 — 5, A and B are any closed formulas.

2. A & B is *true*, if A is *true* and B is *true*.

3. A ∨ B is *true*, if A is *true* or B is *true*.

4. A ⊃ B is *true*, if A is *true* implies B is *true* (i.e. when A is *true* only if B is *true*).

5. ¬A is *true*, if A is not *true*.

For Clauses 6 and 7, x is a variable, and A(x) is a formula containing only x free. (Then when x is a natural number, $\boldsymbol{x}$ is the corresponding numeral, § 41.)

6. ∃xA(x) is *true*, if, for some natural number x, A($\boldsymbol{x}$) is *true*.

7. ∀xA(x) is *true*, if, for every natural number x, A($\boldsymbol{x}$) is *true*.

(B) A number-theoretic formula $A(y_1, \ldots, y_m)$ containing free only the distinct variables $y_1, \ldots, y_m$ is *true*, if, for each m-tuple $y_1, \ldots, y_m$ of natural numbers, $A(\boldsymbol{y}_1, \ldots, \boldsymbol{y}_m)$ is *true*. (We need not stipulate here that $y_1, \ldots, y_m$ all occur free in $A(y_1, \ldots, y_m)$ or the order of occurrence, since if a formula is true for any one choice of the list $y_1, \ldots, y_m$, it is true for every other.)

EXAMPLE 4. Whether a formula E without variables is true or false (i.e. not true) can be decided using the 2-valued truth tables; and any formula $A(x_1, \ldots, x_n)$ without quantifiers and just $x_1, \ldots, x_n$ as variables expresses a primitive recursive predicate $A(x_1, \ldots, x_n)$ such that $A(x_1, \ldots, x_n) \equiv \{A(\boldsymbol{x}_1, \ldots, \boldsymbol{x}_n)$ is true$\}$. (Cf. before Theorem 51 § 79.) By (A), (C) and (D) § 41: *In the number-theoretic formal system every true formula without variables is provable, and every formula* $A(x_1, \ldots, x_n)$ *without quantifiers numeralwise expresses the predicate* $A(x_1, \ldots, x_n)$ *which it expresses under the interpretation.*

Using this definition, we can establish the following theorem, in much the same manner as Theorem 21 § 37, which corresponds to it for the predicate calculus.

THEOREM 61. (a)^{N} *If* $\Gamma \vdash E$ *in the intuitionistic formal system of number theory, and the formulas* Γ *are true, then* E *is true.* (b)^{C} *Similarly in the classical formal system of number theory.*

The only difference in the proofs of Parts (a) and (b) is that for (b) we need to use classical methods in the treatment of an axiom by the classical Axiom Schema 8. We label Part (a) with "N" to indicate that, although the reasoning is intuitionistic, non-elementary methods are used; and Part (b) with "C" to indicate that non-intuitionistic classical methods are employed (cf. § 37).

Since A and $\neg$A cannot both be true, Theorem 61 (a) (for Γ empty) implies the simple consistency of the intuitionistic number theory, and thence by Corollary 2 Theorem 60 of the classical number theory, as an "N" result. The gain by Theorem 60 is that we do not have to call the latter a "C" result, as we would in inferring it directly from Theorem 61 (b).

EXAMPLE 5. (a) *An* $\forall\exists$*-prenex formula, if true, is general recursively true* (§ 79). For example, if $\forall v \exists w_0 \exists w_1 C(v, w_0, w_1)$, where $C(v, w_0, w_1)$ contains no quantifiers and only the distinct variables shown, is true then $(v)\{C(\boldsymbol{v}, \boldsymbol{w}_0(v), \boldsymbol{w}_1(v))$ is t$\}$ when $w_i(v) = (\mu w C(v, (w)_0, (w)_1))_i$, which is general recursive using #19 § 45 and Theorem III § 57. (b)$^{N \text{ or } C}$ Hence by Theorem 61 (a) or (b): *In the number-theoretic formal system, every provable* ∀∃*-prenex formula is general recursively true.* (Cf. Remark 2 § 79.)

Under our Gödel numbering of the formulas, the predicate 'A is true' becomes a number-theoretic predicate $T(a)$, the values of which can be given as propositions constructed from primitive recursive predicates by the operations of the propositional calculus and quantifiers, the number of the latter used being unbounded. We see from Theorem 30 that this predicate $T(a)$ cannot be expressed, and its essential properties proved, in the system, as then we could formalize the above consistency proof in the system. (Cf. Hilbert-Bernays 1939 pp. 329—340.)

In fact, each of the predicates $(Ex)T_1(a, a, x)$, $(x)(Ey)T_2(a, a, x, y)$, $(Ex)(y)(Ez)T_3(a, a, x, y, z), \ldots$ (cf. Theorem V Part II (b) § 57) is expressible in the form $T(\psi(a))$ with a primitive recursive ψ, as can be seen by Corollary Theorem I § 49 (by which the formulas given by Corollary Theorem 27 to numeralwise express the predicates $T_1, T_2, T_3, \ldots$ express them also under the interpretation) with Example 2 § 52. Therefore by Theorems VII (d) and V, $T(a)$ is not arithmetical.

Truth definitions for formal systems were originally investigated by Tarski (1932, 1933). He established that, if an (effective) formal system including the usual number theory is consistent, it must be impossible to express the predicate $T(a)$ for the system by a formula T(a) so that $\mathrm{T}(\boldsymbol{a}) \sim \mathrm{A}_a$ is provable in the system whenever a is the Gödel number of a closed formula A_a. For then the reasoning of the Epimenides paradox (§ 11) could be carried out in the system. (For more detail, see Hilbert and Bernays 1939 pp. 254—269.)

The notions of truth for formulas intuitionistically and classically should differ. The above definition of truth however is phrased alike for the two, and any difference in the notions has to be made in our reading of the words used in the definition. In § 82, we shall give another truth definition, with a theorem for it corresponding to Theorem 61, which will apply selectively to the intuitionistic system. The first results, like Theorem 61 (a), will be intuitionistic though non-elementary ("ℵ"), but they lead to results which are metamathematical in the narrower sense.

§ 82. Recursive realizability. Our problem is to express the interpretation of the intuitionistic number theory in a way which makes explicit some feature in which it differs from the classical.

The meaning of an existential statement "$(Ex)A(x)$" for the intuitionists has been explained by saying that it constitutes an incomplete communication of a statement giving an x such that $A(x)$ (Hilbert-Bernays 1934 p. 32). But "$A(x)$" itself may in turn be an incomplete communication. Accordingly let us say that "$(Ex)A(x)$" is an incomplete communication, which is completed by giving an x such that $A(x)$ together with the further information required to complete the communication "$A(x)$" for that x.

The idea can be extended to the other logical operations. For example, we can regard a generality statement "$(x)A(x)$" intuitionistically as an incomplete communication, which is completed by giving an effective general method for finding, to any x, the information which completes the communication "$A(x)$" for that x.

Similarly, an implication "$A \rightarrow B$" can be regarded as an incomplete communication, which is completed by giving an effective general method for obtaining the information which completes "B", whenever that which completes "A" is given.

Negation can be reduced to implication (cf. Example 3 § 74).

Now effective general methods are recursive ones, when it is a natural number that is being given (§§ 60, 62, 63). Moreover, by the device of Gödel numbering, information can be given by a number.

Combining these ideas, we shall define a property of a number-theoretic formula which will amount to the formula's being true under the interpretation suggested. However, instead of saying 'true', we shall say '(recursively) realizable', to distinguish the property defined below from 'truth' as defined by using direct translations of the formal logical symbols by corresponding informal words (end § 81).

The interpretation of a term $\mathrm{t}(\mathrm{x}_1, \ldots, \mathrm{x}_n)$ containing only $\mathrm{x}_1, \ldots, \mathrm{x}_n$ free by a primitive recursive function $t(x_1, \ldots, x_n)$, or for $n = 0$ by a number t, and the interpretation of a prime formula $\mathrm{P}(\mathrm{x}_1, \ldots, \mathrm{x}_n)$ by a primitive recursive predicate $P(x_1, \ldots, x_n)$, or for $n = 0$ by a proposition P (end § 81), do not differ intuitionistically from classically. We build upon this in setting up the definition of 'realizability' which interprets the logical operators intuitionistically as applied to number-theoretic formulas.

First we define the circumstances under which a natural number e '(recursively) realizes' (or is a 'realization number' of) a closed number-theoretic formula E, by induction on the number of (occurrences of) logical symbols in E.

(A) 1. *e realizes* a closed prime formula P, if $e = 0$ and P is true (in other words, if $e = 0$ and P).

For Clauses 2 -- 5, A and B are any closed formulas.

2. *e realizes* A & B, if $e = 2^a \cdot 3^b$ where *a realizes* A and *b realizes* B.

3. *e realizes* A ∨ B, if $e = 2^0 \cdot 3^a$ where *a realizes* A, or $e = 2^1 \cdot 3^b$ where *b realizes* B.

4. *e realizes* A ⊃ B, if *e* is the Gödel number of a partial recursive function φ of one variable such that, whenever *a realizes* A, then $\varphi(a)$ *realizes* B.

5. *e realizes* ¬A, if *e realizes* A ⊃ 1=0.

For Clauses 6 and 7, x is a variable, and A(x) a formula containing free only x.

6. *e realizes* ∃xA(x), if $e = 2^x \cdot 3^a$ where *a realizes* A(**x**).

7. *e realizes* ∀xA(x), if *e* is the Gödel number of a general recursive function φ of one variable such that, for every *x*, $\varphi(x)$ *realizes* A(**x**).

Now we define '(recursive) realizability' for any number-theoretic formula, thus.

(B) A formula A containing no free variables is *realizable*, if there exists a number *p* which realizes A. A formula A($y_1, \ldots, y_m$) containing free only the distinct variables $y_1, \ldots, y_m$ ($m \geq 0$) is *realizable*, if there exists a general recursive function φ of *m* variables (called a *realization function* for A($y_1, \ldots, y_m$)) such that, for every $y_1, \ldots, y_m$, $\varphi(y_1, \ldots, y_m)$ realizes A($\boldsymbol{y}_1, \ldots, \boldsymbol{y}_m$). (Using § 44, if a given formula is realizable for one choice of the $y_1, \ldots, y_m$, it is for every other.)

The handling of the free variables in the present definition of realizability differs from that in Kleene 1945. It simplifies the proof of the first theorem (Theorem 62), after which the equivalence of the two definitions will follow (by Corollary 1).

The above definition of realizability refers only to our notion of number-theoretic formula, i.e. to the formation rules of our formal system.

A modified notion of realizability, referring to the postulate list of the system, and to assumption formulas Γ if desired, is obtained by altering three clauses, as follows. Clause 3: replace "*a realizes* A" by "*a realizes* A and Γ ⊢ A", and "*b realizes* B" by "*b realizes* B and Γ ⊢ B". Clause 4: replace "*a realizes* A" by "*a realizes* A and Γ ⊢ A". Clause 6: replace "*a realizes* A(**x**)" by "*a realizes* A(**x**) and Γ ⊢ A(**x**)". For 'realizes' ['realizable'] in this modified sense we say *realizes*-(Γ ⊢) [*realizable*-(Γ ⊢)].

THEOREM 62^N. (a) *If* $\Gamma \vdash E$ *in the intuitionistic number-theoretic formal system, and the formulas* Γ *are realizable, then* E *is realizable.* (David Nelson 1947 Part I.)

(b) *Similarly reading "realizable-*($\Gamma \vdash$)*" in place of "realizable".*

LEMMA 44^N. *If* x *is a variable,* A(x) *is a formula without free variables other than* x, *and* t *is a term without variables which hence expresses a number* t, *then* e *realizes* A(t) *if and only if* e *realizes* $A(\boldsymbol{t})$.

PROOF OF LEMMA 44. If A(x) is prime, then whether A(t) is true is equivalent to whether $A(\boldsymbol{t})$ is true. Hence by Clause 1, the lemma holds for a prime A(x). The lemma for any other A(x) follows from this basis by induction on the number of logical symbols in A(x), with cases corresponding to the other clauses in the definition of 'realizes'.

LEMMA 45^N. *If* E *is a closed formula, then* e *realizes* E *if and only if* e *realizes the result of replacing each part of* E *of the form* $\neg A$ *where* A *is a formula by* $A \supset 1=0$.

Lemmas 44 and 45 also hold reading "$\Gamma \vdash$" or "*e realizes*-($\Gamma \vdash$)" in place of "*e realizes*", when $\vdash$ refers to the intuitionistic number-theoretic system, and Γ are any formulas. (For Lemma 44 we then use (A) § 41 with Theorem 24 (b) § 38.)

PROOF OF THEOREM 62. We state the proof for (a), and (optionally) the reader, by taking slight extra care, can verify that the additional conditions are met for (b). The proof is by induction on the length of the given deduction $\Gamma \vdash E$, with cases corresponding to the postulates of our formal system.

First we consider AXIOMS. If $A(y_1, \ldots, y_m)$ is an axiom containing as its only free variables $y_1, \ldots, y_m$, then by (B) to establish its realizability we must give a general recursive function $\varphi(y_1, \ldots, y_m)$ such that, for every m-tuple of natural numbers $y_1, \ldots, y_m$, the number $\varphi(y_1, \ldots, y_m)$ realizes $A(\boldsymbol{y}_1, \ldots, \boldsymbol{y}_m)$. However, for each of the axiom schemata of the propositional calculus, we shall be able to find a number which realizes $A(\boldsymbol{y}_1, \ldots, \boldsymbol{y}_m)$ for any axiom $A(y_1, \ldots, y_m)$ by the schema. It will suffice to give this number (which realizes the closed axioms by the schema), because when free variables $y_1, \ldots, y_m$ are present, we can take as $\varphi(y_1, \ldots, y_m)$ the constant function of m variables with this number as value (§ 44). Similarly for the particular number-theoretic axioms, we shall merely give a number which realizes the result of any substitution of numerals for the free variables of the axiom. Similarly for Axiom Schema 13, we can give a realization number, as a general recursive function of x, which depends only on the numeral $\boldsymbol{x}$ substituted for x; and for each of Axiom Schemata 10 and 11 one can be given, as a general recursive function of $x_1, \ldots, x_n$, which depends only on the t and on the numerals $\boldsymbol{x}_1, \ldots, \boldsymbol{x}_n$ substituted for its variables $\mathrm{x}_1, \ldots, \mathrm{x}_n$. Then when the $\mathrm{y}_1, \ldots, \mathrm{y}_m$ include other variables, the $\varphi(y_1, \ldots, y_m)$ can be obtained by expanding that function into a function of the required additional variables by use of identity functions (§ 44).

For each of the axiom schemata and particular axioms (§§ 19, 23), we shall express our realization number or function using the notations of § 65. The proof that it is a realization number or function, and the necessary verifications of recursiveness, are left to the reader in cases not discussed in detail.

1a. In accordance with the preliminary remarks, consider an axiom $\mathrm{A} \supset (\mathrm{B} \supset \mathrm{A})$ by this schema containing no free variables. We show that $\Lambda a \Lambda b\, a$, i.e. $\Lambda a \Lambda b\, U_1^2(a, b)$ (§ 44), realizes $\mathrm{A} \supset (\mathrm{B} \supset \mathrm{A})$. For let a realize A; by Clause 4, we must show that $\{\Lambda a \Lambda b\, a\}(a)$, i.e. $\Lambda b\, a$ (by (71) § 65), realizes $\mathrm{B} \supset \mathrm{A}$. To show this, let b realize B; we must show that $\{\Lambda b\, a\}(b)$, i.e. a, realizes A. But a does realize A, by hypothesis.

1b. $(\mathrm{A} \supset \mathrm{B}) \supset ((\mathrm{A} \supset (\mathrm{B} \supset \mathrm{C})) \supset (\mathrm{A} \supset \mathrm{C}))$ is realized by $\Lambda p \Lambda q \Lambda a\, \{q(a)\}(p(a))$. For let p realize $\mathrm{A} \supset \mathrm{B}$; we must show that $\{\Lambda p \Lambda q \Lambda a\, \{q(a)\}(p(a))\}(p)$, i.e. $\Lambda q \Lambda a\, \{q(a)\}(p(a))$, realizes $(\mathrm{A} \supset (\mathrm{B} \supset \mathrm{C})) \supset (\mathrm{A} \supset \mathrm{C})$. To show this, let q realize $\mathrm{A} \supset (\mathrm{B} \supset \mathrm{C})$; we must show that $\Lambda a\, \{q(a)\}(p(a))$ realizes $\mathrm{A} \supset \mathrm{C}$. To show this, let a realize A; we must show that $\{q(a)\}(p(a))$ realizes C. Now by hypothesis, p realizes $\mathrm{A} \supset \mathrm{B}$ and a realizes A; hence $p(a)$ realizes B. Moreover q realizes $\mathrm{A} \supset (\mathrm{B} \supset \mathrm{C})$, and a realizes A; so $q(a)$ realizes $\mathrm{B} \supset \mathrm{C}$. But now $q(a)$ realizes $\mathrm{B} \supset \mathrm{C}$, and $p(a)$ realizes B; hence $\{q(a)\}(p(a))$ realizes C, as was to be shown.

3. $\mathrm{A} \supset (\mathrm{B} \supset \mathrm{A} \,\&\, \mathrm{B})$. $\Lambda a \Lambda b\, 2^a \cdot 3^b$.

4a. $\mathrm{A} \,\&\, \mathrm{B} \supset \mathrm{A}$. $\Lambda c\, (c)_0$ (cf. #19 § 45). 4b. $\mathrm{A} \,\&\, \mathrm{B} \supset \mathrm{B}$. $\Lambda c\, (c)_1$.

5a. $\mathrm{A} \supset \mathrm{A} \vee \mathrm{B}$. $\Lambda a\, 2^0 \cdot 3^a$. 5b. $\mathrm{B} \supset \mathrm{A} \vee \mathrm{B}$. $\Lambda b\, 2^1 \cdot 3^b$.

6. $(\mathrm{A} \supset \mathrm{C}) \supset ((\mathrm{B} \supset \mathrm{C}) \supset (\mathrm{A} \vee \mathrm{B} \supset \mathrm{C}))$.
$\Lambda p \Lambda q \Lambda r\, \chi(p, q, r)$ where
$\chi(p, q, r) \simeq [p((r)_1)$ if $(r)_0 = 0$, $q((r)_1)$ if $(r)_0 = 1]$, using Theorem XX (c). Suppose p realizes $\mathrm{A} \supset \mathrm{C}$, q realizes $\mathrm{B} \supset \mathrm{C}$, and r realizes $\mathrm{A} \vee \mathrm{B}$; we must show that $\chi(p, q, r)$ realizes C. Case 1: $r = 2^0 \cdot 3^a$ where a realizes A. Then $(r)_0 = 0$ and $(r)_1 = a$. Since p realizes $\mathrm{A} \supset \mathrm{C}$ and $(r)_1$ realizes A, $p((r)_1)$ realizes C. But $(r)_0 = 0$; so (and because $p((r)_1)$ is defined) $\chi(p, q, r) = p((r)_1)$, and so it realizes C, as was to be shown. Case 2: $r = 2^1 \cdot 3^b$ where b realizes B. Similarly.

7. $(A \supset B) \supset ((A \supset \neg B) \supset \neg A)$. Using Lemma 45, the number which realizes the closed axioms by Axiom Schema 1b (in particular those with $1=0$ as the C) realizes those by this schema.

8^I. $\neg A \supset (A \supset B)$. 0. For if p realizes $\neg A$, then by Clause 5, p realizes $A \supset 1=0$. But then no number a can realize A, since $p(a)$ would realize the false closed prime formula $1=0$, contradicting Clause 1. Thus vacuously, if p realizes $\neg A$ and a realizes A, then $\{0(p)\}(a)$ realizes B.

(The reader may find it instructive to verify that there is no apparent way to treat the classical Axiom Schema 8.)

10. Let the t for the axiom contain exactly the distinct variables $x_1, \ldots, x_n$ $(n \geq 0)$; denote it as "$t(x_1, \ldots, x_n)$", and let $t(x_1, \ldots, x_n)$ be the primitive recursive function (or for $n = 0$, the number) which it expresses. By the preliminary remarks, we suppose the axiom contains free only $x_1, \ldots, x_n$; if none of $x_1, \ldots, x_n$ is x, let it be $\forall x A(x, x_1, \ldots, x_n) \supset A(t(x_1, \ldots, x_n), x_1, \ldots, x_n)$. Since $t(x_1, \ldots, x_n)$ is free for x in $A(x, x_1, \ldots, x_n)$, the result of substituting numerals $\mathbf{x}_1, \ldots, \mathbf{x}_n$ for (the free occurrences of) $x_1, \ldots, x_n$ in the axiom is $\forall x A(x, \mathbf{x}_1, \ldots, \mathbf{x}_n) \supset A(t(\mathbf{x}_1, \ldots, \mathbf{x}_n), \mathbf{x}_1, \ldots, \mathbf{x}_n)$. We shall show that the number $\Lambda p\, p(t(x_1, \ldots, x_n))$, which as $x_1, \ldots, x_n$ vary is a general (in fact, primitive) recursive function of $x_1, \ldots, x_n$, realizes this formula. By Clause 4, for this purpose we must show that, if p realizes $\forall x A(x, \mathbf{x}_1, \ldots, \mathbf{x}_n)$, then $p(t(x_1, \ldots, x_n))$ realizes $A(t(\mathbf{x}_1, \ldots, \mathbf{x}_n), \mathbf{x}_1, \ldots, \mathbf{x}_n)$. But, if p realizes $\forall x A(x, \mathbf{x}_1, \ldots, \mathbf{x}_n)$, then by Clause 7, $p(t(x_1, \ldots, x_n))$ realizes $A(\mathbf{t}, \mathbf{x}_1, \ldots, \mathbf{x}_n)$ where $t = t(x_1, \ldots, x_n)$; and hence by Lemma 44, $p(t(x_1, \ldots, x_n))$ also realizes $A(t(\mathbf{x}_1, \ldots, \mathbf{x}_n), \mathbf{x}_1, \ldots, \mathbf{x}_n)$. — If say x_1 is x, the axiom is $\forall x_1 A(x_1, \ldots, x_n) \supset A(t(x_1, \ldots, x_n), x_2, \ldots, x_n)$, etc.

11. $A(t(x_1, \ldots, x_n), x_1, \ldots, x_n) \supset \exists x A(x, x_1, \ldots, x_n)$.
$\Lambda a\, 2^{t(x_1, \ldots, x_n)} \cdot 3^a$.

13. $A(0) \;\&\; \forall x(A(x) \supset A(x')) \supset A(x)$. We treat the case that the A(x) contains free only x, as the preliminary remarks will then take care of the general case. Let a partial recursive function $\rho(x, a)$ be defined by a primitive recursion thus,

$$\begin{cases} \rho(0, a) = (a)_0, \\ \rho(x', a) \simeq \{\{(a)_1\}(x)\}(\rho(x, a)). \end{cases}$$

Now we show that for every x the number $\Lambda a\, \rho(x, a)$, which is a primitive recursive function of x, realizes $A(0) \;\&\; \forall x(A(x) \supset A(x')) \supset A(\mathbf{x})$. To do so (Clause 4), we prove by induction on x that, if a realizes $A(0) \;\&\; \forall x(A(x) \supset A(x'))$, then $\rho(x, a)$ realizes $A(\mathbf{x})$. BASIS. If a realizes

A(0) & ∀x(A(x) ⊃ A(x′)), then by Clause 2, $\rho(0, a)$ [$= (a)_0$] realizes A(0). IND. STEP. Similarly $(a)_1$ realizes ∀x(A(x) ⊃ A(x′)), and hence (Clause 7) $\{(a)_1\}(x)$ realizes A(**x**) ⊃ A(**x**′). But by hyp. ind., $\rho(x, a)$ realizes A(**x**). Hence (Clause 4), $\rho(x', a)$ [$= \{\{(a)_1\}(x)\}(\rho(x, a))$] realizes A(**x**′).

14. After substitution of numerals, we have from this axiom $\boldsymbol{a}'=\boldsymbol{b}' \supset \boldsymbol{a}=\boldsymbol{b}$. This formula is realized by $\Lambda p\, 0$. For suppose p realizes $\boldsymbol{a}'=\boldsymbol{b}'$. We must show that then 0 realizes $\boldsymbol{a}=\boldsymbol{b}$. Since $\boldsymbol{a}'=\boldsymbol{b}'$ is prime, it is only realizable if it is true, i.e. if $a' = b'$. Then $a = b$, so $\boldsymbol{a}=\boldsymbol{b}$ is also true, and 0 realizes it.

Similarly, for the other particular axioms, after substituting numerals, we have realization numbers as follows.

15, 18 — 21: 0. 16: $\Lambda p \Lambda q\, 0$. 17: $\Lambda p\, 0$.

RULES OF INFERENCE. 2. We take advantage of the remark accompanying the definition of realizability to regard the formulas as each dependent on all of the variables occurring free in any of them. Thus we write the rule

$$\frac{\mathrm{A}(\mathrm{y}_1, \ldots, \mathrm{y}_m) \qquad \mathrm{A}(\mathrm{y}_1, \ldots, \mathrm{y}_m) \supset \mathrm{B}(\mathrm{y}_1, \ldots, \mathrm{y}_m)}{\mathrm{B}(\mathrm{y}_1, \ldots, \mathrm{y}_m).}$$

By hypothesis of the induction, the premises $\mathrm{A}(\mathrm{y}_1, \ldots, \mathrm{y}_m)$ and $\mathrm{A}(\mathrm{y}_1, \ldots, \mathrm{y}_m) \supset \mathrm{B}(\mathrm{y}_1, \ldots, \mathrm{y}_m)$ are realizable, i.e. there are general recursive functions α and ψ, such that, for every m-tuple of natural numbers $y_1, \ldots, y_m$, $\mathrm{A}(\boldsymbol{y}_1, \ldots, \boldsymbol{y}_m)$ is realized by the number $\alpha(y_1, \ldots, y_m)$ and $\mathrm{A}(\boldsymbol{y}_1, \ldots, \boldsymbol{y}_m) \supset \mathrm{B}(\boldsymbol{y}_1, \ldots, \boldsymbol{y}_m)$ by the number $\psi(y_1, \ldots, y_m)$. Then the number $\{\psi(y_1, \ldots, y_m)\}(\alpha(y_1, \ldots, y_m))$ realizes $\mathrm{B}(\boldsymbol{y}_1, \ldots, \boldsymbol{y}_m)$. Moreover, $\{\psi(y_1, \ldots, y_m)\}(\alpha(y_1, \ldots, y_m))$ is obviously a partial recursive function of $y_1, \ldots, y_m$. But its value is a realization number for every $y_1, \ldots, y_m$, so it must be defined for every $y_1, \ldots, y_m$; thus it is general recursive. Thus the conclusion $\mathrm{B}(\mathrm{y}_1, \ldots, \mathrm{y}_m)$ is realizable.

9. $$\frac{\mathrm{C}(\mathrm{y}_1, \ldots, \mathrm{y}_m) \supset \mathrm{A}(\mathrm{x}, \mathrm{y}_1, \ldots, \mathrm{y}_m)}{\mathrm{C}(\mathrm{y}_1, \ldots, \mathrm{y}_m) \supset \forall \mathrm{x}\mathrm{A}(\mathrm{x}, \mathrm{y}_1, \ldots, \mathrm{y}_m).}$$

By the hypothesis of the induction and the definition of realizability, there is a general recursive function ψ such that, for every $x, y_1, \ldots, y_m$, $\psi(x, y_1, \ldots, y_m)$ realizes $\mathrm{C}(\boldsymbol{y}_1, \ldots, \boldsymbol{y}_m) \supset \mathrm{A}(\boldsymbol{x}, \boldsymbol{y}_1, \ldots, \boldsymbol{y}_m)$. We shall prove that, for every $y_1, \ldots, y_m$, $\Lambda c \Lambda x \{\psi(x, y_1, \ldots, y_m)\}(c)$ realizes $\mathrm{C}(\boldsymbol{y}_1, \ldots, \boldsymbol{y}_m) \supset \forall \mathrm{x}\mathrm{A}(\mathrm{x}, \boldsymbol{y}_1, \ldots, \boldsymbol{y}_m)$. This will give the realizability of the conclusion, since $\Lambda c \Lambda x \{\psi(x, y_1, \ldots, y_m)\}(c)$ is a primitive recursive, a fortiori general recursive, function of $y_1, \ldots, y_m$. Accordingly suppose that

c realizes $C(\boldsymbol{y}_1, \ldots, \boldsymbol{y}_m)$; we must show that $\Lambda x\, \{\psi(x, y_1, \ldots, y_m)\}(c)$ realizes $\forall x A(x, \boldsymbol{y}_1, \ldots, \boldsymbol{y}_m)$. To do this, we must show that, for every x, $\{\psi(x, y_1, \ldots, y_m)\}(c)$ realizes $A(\boldsymbol{x}, \boldsymbol{y}_1, \ldots, \boldsymbol{y}_m)$. But since c realizes $C(\boldsymbol{y}_1, \ldots, \boldsymbol{y}_m)$, and by hyp. ind. $\psi(x, y_1, \ldots, y_m)$ realizes $C(\boldsymbol{y}_1, \ldots, \boldsymbol{y}_m) \supset A(\boldsymbol{x}, \boldsymbol{y}_1, \ldots, \boldsymbol{y}_m)$, $\{\psi(x, y_1, \ldots, y_m)\}(c)$ does realize $A(\boldsymbol{x}, \boldsymbol{y}_1, \ldots, \boldsymbol{y}_m)$. (Note how this treatment would break down, if the C contained x free, call it "$C(x, y_1, \ldots, y_m)$". Then, we would have to assume that c realizes $C(\boldsymbol{x}, \boldsymbol{y}_1, \ldots, \boldsymbol{y}_m)$ for some x, and we could conclude only that $\{\psi(x, y_1, \ldots, y_m)\}(c)$ realizes $A(\boldsymbol{x}, \boldsymbol{y}_1, \ldots, \boldsymbol{y}_m)$ for that x, whereas we would need to conclude it for every x.)

12. $$\frac{A(x, y_1, \ldots, y_m) \supset C(y_1, \ldots, y_m)}{\exists x A(x, y_1, \ldots, y_m) \supset C(y_1, \ldots, y_m).}$$

Similarly, using $\Lambda p\, \{\psi((p)_0, y_1, \ldots, y_m)\}((p)_1)$ as realization function for the conclusion, given that ψ is for the premise.

The theorem includes the simple consistency of the intuitionistic formal system of number theory (by using (a) with Γ empty and $1=0$ as the E), as does Theorem 61 (a). The additional interest in Theorem 62 in this connection stems from the different condition on new axioms Γ under which it is shown that the simple consistency is preserved (as we shall discuss further following Theorem 63).

Corollary 1^N. *If* $y_1, \ldots, y_m$ *are distinct variables, and* $A(y_1, \ldots, y_m)$ *is a formula, then* $A(y_1, \ldots, y_m)$ *is realizable, if and only if* $\forall y_1 \ldots \forall y_m A(y_1, \ldots, y_m)$ *is realizable.*

For $A(y_1, \ldots, y_m)$ and $\forall y_1 \ldots \forall y_m A(y_1, \ldots, y_m)$ are interdeducible in the intuitionistic formal system.

This corollary (applied to the case $y_1, \ldots, y_m$ are the free variables of the given formula in order of first free occurrence) gives the equivalence of the present version of the definition of realizability (Kleene 1948) to that of Kleene 1945.

Corollary 2^N. (a) *If* Γ *are realizable formulas,* $A(x_1, \ldots, x_n, y)$ *is a formula containing free only the distinct variables* $x_1, \ldots, x_n, y$, *and* $\Gamma \vdash \exists y A(x_1, \ldots, x_n, y)$ *in the intuitionistic number-theoretic formal system, then there is a general recursive function* $y = \varphi(x_1, \ldots, x_n)$ *such that, for every* $x_1, \ldots, x_n$, $A(\boldsymbol{x}_1, \ldots, \boldsymbol{x}_n, \boldsymbol{y})$ (*where* $y = \varphi(x_1, \ldots, x_n)$) *is realizable.*

(b) *Similarly reading in place of "realizable" any one of the following combinations of properties:* (i) *"realizable-*($\Gamma \vdash$) *and deducible from* Γ",

(ii) "*realizable-*(Γ ⊢), *deducible from* Γ, *and true*", (iii) "*realizable-*(Γ ⊢), *deducible from* Γ, *and realizable*", (iv) "*realizable-*(Γ ⊢), *deducible from* Γ, *true and realizable*".

PROOFS. (a) By (a) of the theorem with (B) and (A) 6 of the definitions. (b) (i) Using instead (b) of the theorem. (ii) Using further Theorem 61 (a) to infer that $\mathrm{A}(\boldsymbol{x}_1, \ldots, \boldsymbol{x}_n, \boldsymbol{y})$ is true. (iii) Using further (a) of the theorem to infer that $\mathrm{A}(\boldsymbol{x}_1, \ldots, \boldsymbol{x}_n, \boldsymbol{y})$ is realizable.

Realizability is intended as an intuitionistic interpretation of a formula; and to say intuitionistically that $\mathrm{A}(\boldsymbol{x}_1, \ldots, \boldsymbol{x}_n, \boldsymbol{y})$ is realizable should imply its being intuitionistically true, i.e. that the proposition $A(x_1, \ldots, x_n, y)$ constituting its intuitionistic meaning holds. The formula $\exists \mathrm{yA}(\mathrm{x}_1, \ldots, \mathrm{x}_n, \mathrm{y})$ asserts the existence, for every $x_1, \ldots, x_n$, of a y depending on $x_1, \ldots, x_n$, such that $A(x_1, \ldots, x_n, y)$; or in other words, the existence of a function $y = \varphi(x_1, \ldots, x_n)$ such that, for every $x_1, \ldots, x_n$, $A(x_1, \ldots, x_n, \varphi(x_1, \ldots, x_n))$. By (a) of the corollary for Γ empty, that formula can be proved in the intuitionistic formal system, only when there exists such a φ which is general recursive. In brief, only number-theoretic functions which are general recursive can be proved to exist intuitionistically. (We are here considering the assertion of the existence of a function value $\varphi(x_1, \ldots, x_n)$ for all n-tuples $x_1, \ldots, x_n$ of arguments, so this is not in conflict with our use intuitionistically of partial recursive functions.)

This result as inferred from (a) depends on accepting the thesis that the realizability of $\mathrm{A}(\boldsymbol{x}_1, \ldots, \boldsymbol{x}_n, \boldsymbol{y})$ implies its truth. However by using (b) for Γ empty (in which case, since we have no hypothesis on Γ to satisfy, we may take the strongest form (iv) in the conclusion, i.e. that $\mathrm{A}(\boldsymbol{x}_1, \ldots, \boldsymbol{x}_n, \boldsymbol{y})$ is realizable-(⊢), provable, true and realizable), we obtain the same result independently of that thesis.

The presence of the Γ in the corollary shows that the result will hold good upon enlarging the formal system by any suitable axioms Γ. If the thesis that realizability implies truth, intuitionistically, is accepted, these need only be realizable. Otherwise they should be realizable-(Γ ⊢) and true (deducibility from Γ holds automatically in the hypothesis on Γ).

The result provides a connection between Brouwer's logic as formalized by Heyting and Church's thesis (§ 62) that only general recursive functions are effectively calculable. Both developments arose from a constructivistic standpoint, but were previously unrelated in their details.

The formula $\exists \mathrm{yA}(\mathrm{x}_1, \ldots, \mathrm{x}_n, \mathrm{y})$ does not assert the uniqueness of the function $y = \varphi(x_1, \ldots, x_n)$ such that $A(x_1, \ldots, x_n, \varphi(x_1, \ldots, x_n))$; for this we need $\exists! yA(x_1, \ldots, x_n, y)$ (§ 41).

Classically, given the existence of some function φ such that, for all $x_1, \ldots, x_n$, $A(x_1, \ldots, x_n, \varphi(x_1, \ldots, x_n))$, the least number principle provides formally a method of describing a particular one (*149 § 40, *174b § 41). While we do not have the least number principle intuitionistically, we do know by Corollary 2 that, whenever a particular intuitionistic proof of a formula of the form $\exists yA(x_1, \ldots, x_n, y)$ is given, we can on the basis of that proof describe informally a particular general recursive function $\varphi(x_1, \ldots, x_n)$ such that, for all $x_1, \ldots, x_n$, $A(x_1, \ldots, x_n, \varphi(x_1, \ldots, x_n))$.

Example 1. (Cf. Example 8 (c) § 74.) Let S_1 be the intuitionistic number-theoretic system. Let A(x, y) be a formula containing free only x and y. Suppose that for each x, the formula $A(\boldsymbol{x}, \boldsymbol{y})$ is true for exactly one y. Then when (to obtain S_2) we introduce f with the axiom A(x, f(x)), the axiom characterizes f as expressing a certain function φ under the interpretation. By $\exists$-introd. from the new axiom, $\vdash_2 \exists yA(x, y)$. Now suppose f with the axiom A(x, f(x)) is eliminable. Then $\vdash_1 \exists yA(x, y)$. Then by Theorem 62 Corollary 2 (b) (ii) with Γ empty, there is a general recursive function $y = \varphi_1(x)$ such that, for each x, $A(\boldsymbol{x}, \boldsymbol{y})$ is true. But then $\varphi_1 = \varphi$. Thus *in the intuitionistic number-theoretic system, a new function symbol* f *(expressing a function* φ*) introduced with an axiom of the form* A(x, f(x)), *where* A(x, y) *contains free only* x *and* y, *and* $A(\boldsymbol{x}, \boldsymbol{y})$ *is true exactly when* $y = \varphi(x)$, *is eliminable only when* φ *is general recursive.*

Example 2. Let A(x, y) be any formula, containing free only x and y, such that $\vdash_1 \exists yA(x, y)$. Then as in Example 1, there is a general recursive function $y = \varphi_1(x)$ such that, for each x, $A(\boldsymbol{x}, \boldsymbol{y})$ is true. The demonstration of this (consisting mainly in the proof of Theorem 62 (b)) is constructive; given a proof of $\exists yA(x, y)$ (or the Gödel number of such a proof), we can find a system E of equations defining a φ_1 recursively (or a Gödel number of φ_1). Also it is effectively decidable whether a number a is the Gödel number of a proof of a formula of the form $\exists yA(x, y)$ where A contains free only x and y (Case 1), or not (Case 2). Let

$$\theta(a) = \begin{cases} \text{a Gödel number of } \varphi_1, \text{ in Case 1,} \\ \Lambda x\, x \text{ (i.e. a Gödel number of } U_1^1\text{), in Case 2,} \end{cases}$$

where ambiguity as to which Gödel number of which φ_1 (or which Gödel number of U_1^1) is chosen is removed by suitable conventions. Then $\theta(a)$ is effectively calculable. So by Church's thesis we may expect that $\theta(a)$

is general recursive. (In fact, it is easy to prove that $\theta(a)$ is primitive recursive, after establishing: (1) *There is a primitive recursive function* $\xi(a)$ *such that, if a is the Gödel number of a proof in the intuitionistic number-theoretic system, then* $\xi(a)$ *is a Gödel number of a realization-*($\vdash$) *function* $\varphi(y_1, \ldots, y_m)$ *for the endformula* $\mathrm{A}(\mathrm{y}_1, \ldots, \mathrm{y}_m)$, *where* $\mathrm{y}_1, \ldots, \mathrm{y}_m$ *are the free variables of the endformula in order of occurrence in our list of the variables.*) Let $\varphi(x) = \{\theta(x)\}(x)+1$. Then $\varphi(x)$ is general recursive. Now let A(x, y) be a formula such that $\mathrm{A}(\boldsymbol{x}, \boldsymbol{y})$ is true exactly when $y = \varphi(x)$ (e.g. one which numeralwise represents φ, cf. Theorem 32 (a) § 59). If we now take this formula as the A(x, y) of Example 1, we are led to a contradiction by supposing that f with the axiom A(x, f(x)) is eliminable. Thus: (2) *There is a general recursive function* φ *such that, in the intuitionistic number-theoretic system, a new function symbol* f *expressing* φ *with an axiom of the form* A(x, f(x)), *where* A(x, y) *contains free only* x *and* y, *and* $\mathrm{A}(\boldsymbol{x}, \boldsymbol{y})$ *is true exactly when* $y = \varphi(x)$, *is not eliminable* (*and* ∃yA(x, y) *is not provable for any such* A(x, y)).

THEOREM 63^{N}. *For suitably chosen formulas* A(x), B(x) *and* C(x, y), *the following classically provable formulas are unrealizable and hence* (by Theorem 62 (a)) *unprovable in the intuitionistic formal system of number theory.* (*Specifically, let* A(x, z) *numeralwise express the predicate* $T_1(x, x, z)$ *of* § 57, using Corollary Theorem 27 § 49. *Let* A(x) *be* ∃zA(x, z), B(x) *be* A(x) ∨ ¬A(x) *and* C(x, y) *be* y=1 ∨ (A(x) & y=0).)

(i) A(x) ∨ ¬A(x).

(ii) ∀x(A(x) ∨ ¬A(x)) (the closure of (i)).

(iii) ¬¬∀x(A(x) ∨ ¬A(x)) (the double negation of (ii)).

(iv) ∀x¬¬B(x) ⊃ ¬¬∀xB(x).

(v) ¬¬{∀x¬¬B(x) ⊃ ¬¬∀xB(x)} (the double negation of (iv)).

(vi) ∃yC(x, y) ⊃ ∃y[C(x, y) & ∀z(z<y ⊃ ¬C(x, z))] (cf. *149 § 40).

(vii) ∃y[y<w & C(x, y) & ∀z(z<y ⊃ ¬C(x, z))] ∨ ∀y[y<w ⊃ ¬C(x, y)] (cf. *148).

Also the closure, and the double negation of the closure, of (vi) *and of* (vii). ((i) — (v): Kleene 1945 with Nelson 1947.)

LEMMA 46^{N}. (a) *If* A *is realizable, and* B *is unrealizable, then* A ⊃ B *is unrealizable.* Hence: *If* A *is realizable, then* ¬A *is unrealizable.* (b) *If* A *is closed and unrealizable, then* A ⊃ B *and* (hence) ¬A *are realizable, and* (by (a)) ¬¬A *is unrealizable.*

PROOF OF LEMMA 46. (a) By Theorem 62 (a) or the case for Rule 2 in its proof, if A and A ⊃ B are realizable, so is B. (b) For a closed B, any number, e.g. 0, realizes A ⊃ B, since vacuously, whenever a realizes A (i.e. never), $0(a)$ realizes B.

LEMMA 47[N]. *If* $\mathrm{P}(\mathrm{x}_1, \ldots, \mathrm{x}_n)$ *numeralwise expresses a general recursive predicate* $P(x_1, \ldots, x_n)$ *in the intuitionistic formal system of number theory, then, for every* $x_1, \ldots, x_n$, $\mathrm{P}(\mathbf{x}_1, \ldots, \mathbf{x}_n)$ *is realizable if and only if* $P(x_1, \ldots, x_n)$.

PROOF OF LEMMA 47. If $P(x_1, \ldots, x_n)$, then by § 41 (i), $\vdash \mathrm{P}(\mathbf{x}_1, \ldots, \mathbf{x}_n)$, and hence by Theorem 62 (a), $\mathrm{P}(\mathbf{x}_1, \ldots, \mathbf{x}_n)$ is realizable. Conversely, suppose $\mathrm{P}(\mathbf{x}_1, \ldots, \mathbf{x}_n)$ is realizable. Because $P(x_1, \ldots, x_n)$ is a general recursive predicate, we have (constructively) that, for the given $x_1, \ldots, x_n$, either $P(x_1, \ldots, x_n)$ or $\overline{P}(x_1, \ldots, x_n)$. In the latter case, however, by § 41 (ii), $\vdash \neg\mathrm{P}(\mathbf{x}_1, \ldots, \mathbf{x}_n)$, and hence by Theorem 62 (a), $\neg\mathrm{P}(\mathbf{x}_1, \ldots, \mathbf{x}_n)$ is realizable, which by Lemma 46 (a) contradicts our supposition that $\mathrm{P}(\mathbf{x}_1, \ldots, \mathbf{x}_n)$ is realizable.

PROOF OF THEOREM 63. (i) Suppose (i), i.e. $\exists z\mathrm{A}(\mathrm{x}, \mathrm{z}) \vee \neg\exists z\mathrm{A}(\mathrm{x}, \mathrm{z})$, were realizable. Let $\varphi(x)$ be a realization function for it; and set $\rho(x) = (\varphi(x))_0$. Then $\rho(x)$ is general recursive, and takes only the values 0 and 1 (by (B) and (A) 3 of the definitions). Consider any fixed x. CASE 1: $\rho(x) = 0$. Then $(\varphi(x))_1$ realizes $\exists z\mathrm{A}(\mathbf{x}, \mathrm{z})$; and hence $(\varphi(x))_{1,1}$ realizes $\mathrm{A}(\mathbf{x}, \mathbf{z})$ where $z = (\varphi(x))_{1,0}$, in which case by Lemma 47, $T_1(x, x, z)$. Thus $(Ez)T_1(x, x, z)$. CASE 2: $\rho(x) = 1$. Then $(\varphi(x))_1$ realizes $\neg\exists z\mathrm{A}(\mathbf{x}, \mathrm{z})$, i.e. $(\varphi(x))_1$ realizes $\exists z\mathrm{A}(\mathbf{x}, \mathrm{z}) \supset 1=0$. We shall show that then $\overline{(Ez)}T_1(x, x, z)$. For if there were a z such that $T_1(x, x, z)$, by Lemma 47 $\mathrm{A}(\mathbf{x}, \mathbf{z})$ would be realizable; say k realizes it. Then $2^z \cdot 3^k$ would realize $\exists z\mathrm{A}(\mathbf{x}, \mathrm{z})$; and $\{(\varphi(x))_1\}(2^z \cdot 3^k)$ would realize $1=0$, which is impossible. The two cases show that the general recursive function $\rho(x)$ is the representing function of $(Ez)T_1(x, x, z)$. But $(Ez)T_1(x, x, z)$ is non-recursive ((15) Theorem V § 57); hence no such general recursive $\rho(x)$ can exist. By reductio ad absurdum, therefore (i) is unrealizable.

(ii), (iii). By ∀-elim. (i) is deducible intuitionistically from (ii), so by Theorem 62 (a) also (ii) is unrealizable; and by Lemma 46 (b) so is (iii), since (ii) is closed.

(iv) Since (iii) can be deduced from (iv), using *51a § 27 and ∀-introd.

(vi) We show as follows that (i) is deducible from (vi). From $1=1$ (which is provable) by ∨- and ∃-introd., $\exists y\mathrm{C}(\mathrm{x}, \mathrm{y})$. Using this, from (vi) by ⊃-elim., $\exists y[\mathrm{C}(\mathrm{x}, \mathrm{y}) \,\&\, \forall z(z<y \supset \neg\mathrm{C}(\mathrm{x}, \mathrm{z}))]$. Preparatory to &- and

$\exists$-elim., assume C(x, y), i.e.

(1) $$y=1 \vee (A(x) \& y=0)$$

and $$\forall z(z<y \supset \neg C(x, z)), \text{ i.e.}$$

(2) $$\forall z(z<y \supset \neg\{z=1 \vee (A(x) \& z=0)\}).$$

We use proof by cases from (1) to deduce (i) with the help of (2). CASE 1: assume y=1. For reductio ad absurdum, assume further A(x). From this and 0=0, by &- and $\vee$-introd., $0=1 \vee (A(x) \& 0=0)$. But also from y=1 by *135b, 0<y; and thence from (2) by $\forall$-elim. (with 0 as the t) and $\supset$-elim., $\neg\{0=1 \vee (A(x) \& 0=0)\}$. Hence by reductio ad absurdum, $\neg A(x)$. By $\vee$-introd., $A(x) \vee \neg A(x)$, which is (i) and does not contain free the variable y of our proposed $\exists$-elim. CASE 2: assume A(x) & y=0. By &-elim. and $\vee$-introd., $A(x) \vee \neg A(x)$. (This deduction is related to the intuitive reasoning of Example 6 § 64.)

(vii) From (vii) we can deduce (vi), as in the proof of *149 from *148.

Theorem 63 (i) — (v) imply that $\mathcal{A} \vee \neg \mathcal{A}$ is unprovable in the intuitionistic propositional calculus, and $\forall x(\mathcal{A}(x) \vee \neg \mathcal{A}(x))$, $\neg\neg\forall x(\mathcal{A}(x) \vee \neg \mathcal{A}(x))$, $\forall x \neg\neg \mathcal{A}(x) \supset \neg\neg\forall x \mathcal{A}(x)$ and $\neg\neg\{\forall x \neg\neg \mathcal{A}(x) \supset \neg\neg\forall x \mathcal{A}(x)\}$ in the intuitionistic predicate calculus, as we already knew from Theorem 57 (b) and Theorem 58 (a) and (c). The present proofs are less elementary than those based on Gentzen's normal form theorem, but contribute insight into the working of the intuitionistic logic as an instrument for number-theoretic reasoning. We succeed in showing $A \vee \neg A$ unprovable in intuitionistic number theory only in the presence of a free variable x.

COROLLARY (to (ii))[N]. *The formula* $\neg\forall x(A(x) \vee \neg A(x))$ *(although the negation of a classically provable formula) is realizable.*

By (ii) and Lemma 46 (b).

The formula $\forall x(A(x) \vee \neg A(x))$ is classically provable, and hence under classical interpretations true. But it is unrealizable. So if realizability is accepted as a necessary condition for intuitionistic truth, it is untrue intuitionistically, and therefore unprovable not only in the present intuitionistic formal system, but by any intuitionistic methods whatsoever.

This incidentally implies that our classical formal system reinforced by an intuitionistic proof of simple consistency cannot serve as an instrument of intuitionistic proof, as suggested in § 14, except of formulas belonging to a very restricted class (including those of the forms $B(\boldsymbol{x})$ and $\forall x B(x)$ end § 42, but not the present formula $\forall x(A(x) \vee \neg A(x))$).

The negation $\neg\forall x(A(x) \vee \neg A(x))$ of that formula is classically untrue, but (by the corollary) realizable, and hence intuitionistically true, if we accept realizability (intuitionistically established) as sufficient for intuitionistic truth.

So the possibility appears of asserting the formula $\neg\forall x(A(x) \vee \neg A(x))$ intuitionistically. Thus we should obtain an extension of the intuitionistic number theory, which has previously been treated as a subsystem of the classical, so that the intuitionistic and classical number theories diverge, with $\neg\forall x(A(x) \vee \neg A(x))$ holding in the intuitionistic and $\forall x(A(x) \vee \neg A(x))$ in the classical.

Such divergences are familiar to mathematicians from the example of Euclidean and non-Euclidean geometries, and other examples, but are a new phenomenon in arithmetic. The first example comes by adjoining $A_p(\boldsymbol{p})$ or $\neg A_p(\boldsymbol{p})$ to the number-theoretic formalism, cf. end §§ 42 and 75.

Not only is the formula $\neg\forall x(A(x) \vee \neg A(x))$ itself realizable, but by Theorem 62 (a) (taking it as the Γ), when we add it to the present intuitionistic formal system, only realizable formulas become provable in the enlarged system. So then every provable formula will be true under the realizability interpretation. In particular, the strengthened intuitionistic system is thus shown by interpretation to be simply consistent.

A fuller discussion is given in Kleene 1945, where the proposed adjunctions to the unstrengthened intuitionistic formal system of number theory S, to obtain a strengthened intuitionistic system S' diverging from the classical S_c, are in the form of an identification of truth with realizability.

Refinements of the results which we are basing here on interpretation are obtained by Nelson 1947 Parts II—IV (with Kleene 1945). Because they all involve the consistency of the number-theoretic formalism, no completely elementary treatment can be expected. But the non-elementariness is minimized in the results based on this further work of Nelson to the full extent that the results are proved in elementary metamathematics under the hypothesis of the simple consistency of S. In particular, by these results with those of Gödel 1932-3 (cf. Corollary 2 Theorem 60), it is demonstrated metamathematically that both S' and S_c are simply consistent if S is. (Nelson takes as his S not our intuitionistic formal system but one obtained, apart from an inessential difference in the equality postulates, by adjoining to ours some additional function symbols with their defining equations. These equations fit our schemata (I) — (V) § 43 or closely similar schemata, except that also a certain schema of course-of-values recursion is allowed. Using Nelson's (i) — (iv)

p. 332, to each application of that schema a pair of equations having the same form with f, g, h, t_i replaced by f′, g′, h′, t_i' is provable without the application; so the course-of-values recursion schema is eliminable. Then by Example 9 § 74 with the remarks preceding it, the additional function symbols are eliminable.)

Nelson 1949 introduces a notion of 'P-realizability', using which one can set up a number-theoretic system diverging from both the strengthened intuitionistic and the classical.

Gene Rose 1952 investigates realizability in relation to the intuitionistic propositional calculus.

Kleene 1950a plans the use of recursive functions in interpreting intuitionistic set theory.

Example 3. (a) *The operators* ⊃, ¬, &, ∨ *applied to closed formulas* A *and* B *obey the strong* 3-*valued truth tables* (§ 64, restated with the present symbols), *when* 𝔱, 𝔣, 𝔲 *are read as 'realizable', 'unrealizable', 'unknown (or value immaterial)', respectively*; i.e. the tables then give only correct information about the realizability or unrealizability of A ⊃ B, ¬A, A & B, A ∨ B, when entered from such information about A and B. Proof. Consider ⊃. If B is realizable, then by *11 § 26 with Theorem 62 (a), so is A ⊃ B, corresponding to the three 𝔱's in Column 1 of the table for ⊃. If A is unrealizable, then by Lemma 46 (b), A ⊃ B is realizable, corresponding to the three 𝔱's in Row 2. If A is realizable and B is unrealizable, then by Lemma 46 (a), A ⊃ B is unrealizable, corresponding to the 𝔣 in Row 1 Column 2. The table for ¬ is simply the 𝔣 column of that for ⊃; and & and ∨ are easily treated. (b) *A formula without variables is realizable, if and only if it is true.* Its realizability (and truth) or unrealizability (and falsity) is thus effectively decidable by the valuation procedure furnished by the usual interpretation of 0, ′, +, ·, = and the classical 2-valued truth tables for ⊃, ¬, &, ∨ (cf. § 79 before Theorem 51). Proof by using Example 4 § 81, or thus: For closed prime formulas, truth and realizability agree, and can be decided. In building thence composite formulas by the operations of the propositional calculus, we always remain within the first two rows and columns of the 3-valued tables. (c) We call a number e an R-*valuation number* of a closed formula E, if either $e = 2^0 \cdot 3^{e_1}$ (then $e_1 = (e)_1$) and e_1 realizes E, or $e = 2^1 \cdot 3^0$ and E is unrealizable. For open formulas, R-*valuation function* is defined in analogy to 'realization function'. *A formula* $C(z_1, \ldots, z_m)$ *containing no quantifiers and only the distinct variables* $z_1, \ldots, z_m$ $(m > 0)$ *has a primitive recursive* R-*valuation function* $\gamma(z_1, \ldots, z_m)$. Proof (omitting "$z_1, \ldots, z_m$"

to save space). CASE 1: C is a prime formula P. Then P expresses a primitive recursive predicate P, with representing function φ. Let $\gamma = 2^{\varphi}\cdot 3^{0}$. CASE 2: C is A ⊃ B, where by hyp. ind. there are primitive recursive R-valuation functions α and β for A and B, respectively. Let

$$\gamma = \begin{cases} 2^0\cdot[3 \text{ exp } \Lambda a\, (\beta)_1] \text{ if } (\beta)_0 = 0, \\ 2^0\cdot 3^0 \text{ if } (\alpha)_0 = (\beta)_0 = 1, \\ 2^1\cdot 3^0 \text{ otherwise.} \end{cases}$$

CASE 3: ¬A. Take $\beta = 2^1\cdot 3^0$ in Case 2. CASE 4: A & B. Let

$$\gamma = \begin{cases} 2^0\cdot[3 \text{ exp } 2^{(\alpha)_1}\cdot 3^{(\beta)_1}] \text{ if } (\alpha)_0 = (\beta)_0 = 0, \\ 2^1\cdot 3^0 \text{ otherwise.} \end{cases}$$

CASE 5: A ∨ B. Similarly. (d) *A prenex formula is realizable, if and only if it is general recursively true.* (Cf. Remark 2 § 79 and Example 5 § 81.) PROOF. Consider again the formula G used as illustration in § 79. Let $\alpha(y_1, x_1, y_2, x_2, y_3)$ be a primitive recursive R-valuation function for $A(y_1, x_1, y_2, x_2, y_3)$. Then if G is recursively true, it is realized by

$$2^{y_1}\cdot[3 \text{ exp } \Lambda x_1\, 2^{y_2(x_1)}\cdot[3 \text{ exp } \Lambda x_2\, 2^{y_3(x_1,x_2)}\cdot 3 \text{ exp } (\alpha(y_1, x_1, y_2(x_1), x_2, y_3(x_1, x_2)))_1]].$$

Conversely, if g realizes G, then G is recursively true with $y_1 = (g)_0$, $y_2(x_1) = (\{(g)_1\}(x_1))_0$ and $y_3(x_1, x_2) = (\{(\{(g)_1\}(x_1))_1\}(x_2))_0$ as the required number and general recursive functions.

EXAMPLE 4. Under the thesis that $(x)(Ei)B(x, i)$ holds intuitionistically only if there is a general recursive α such that $(x)B(x, \alpha(x))$ (cf. above, or Kleene 1943 p. 69 Thesis III), we show that

(a) $$(y)(Ei)_{i<a}A(i, (y)_i) \rightarrow (Ei)_{i<a}(y)A(i, y)$$

does not hold intuitionistically for all A (cf. (20) § 57). Using (51) § 61,

$$(x)(y)(Ei)_{i<2}\overline{W}_i(x, (y)_i).$$

Thence if we had (a) intuitionistically, we would get $(x)(Ei)_{i<2}(y)\overline{W}_i(x, y)$ intuitionistically; whence by the thesis, for some recursive α taking values < 2, $(x)(y)\overline{W}_{\alpha(x)}(x, y)$; whence $(x)\overline{(Ey)}W_{\alpha(x)}(x, y)$; whence for each x,

(b) $$(Ey)W_0(x, y) \rightarrow \alpha(x)=1, \qquad (Ey)W_1(x, y) \rightarrow \alpha(x)=0.$$

But we can take $\alpha(x)=1$ as the $R_0(x, y)$ and $\alpha(x)=0$ as the $R_1(x, y)$ of (57) and (58) § 61. Then either $\alpha(f) = 1$ or $\alpha(f) = 0$. If $\alpha(f) = 1$, then $(Ey)R_0(f, y)$, whence it follows as in § 61 that $(Ey)W_1(f, y)$, contradicting (b). Similarly, if $\alpha(f) = 0$.

BIBLIOGRAPHY

A date in medieval tailciphers (e.g. 1908, not 1908) appearing in conjunction with a name constitutes a reference to this bibliography (e.g. Brouwer 1908). The date is ordinarily the date of publication of the complete volume of the journal in which the article appears. There are exceptions; mainly, in the case of papers at international congresses, for which the date is usually that of the congress (e.g. Hilbert 1904). Letters a, b, etc. may be suffixed to the date to distinguish additional titles with the same date; or a star *, to indicate the presence of a note accompanying the title in this bibliography.

Only those works are listed which are cited from the text of the book (or in a few cases, from elsewhere in the bibliography). In quoting above from foreign-language works, we have translated into English.

Alonzo Church's *A bibliography of symbolic logic,* constituting vol. 1 (1936) no. 4 (pp. 121-218) of **The journal of symbolic logic,** with the *Additions and corrections* (and an index by subjects) in vol. 3 (1938) no. 4, pp. 178-212, are intended to give complete coverage of the literature on symbolic logic (including such related fields as recursive functions) up through 1935. These are available bound together. (A few additional items have come to light since, and are listed in subsequent volumes.)

The literature since 1935 is covered by critical reviews in **The journal of symbolic logic.** These are indexed by authors biennially (in odd-numbered years) and by subjects quinquennially (in 1940, 1945, etc.).

The present bibliography contains some items which are not widely available. For publications after 1935, information about their content can almost invariably be obtained by consulting the review sections of **The journal of symbolic logic,** or also for publications after 1938, from **Mathematical reviews** under the subject "Foundations" or (vols. 20-) "Logic and foundations".

The author has made use of Church's *Bibliography* and the review sections of **The journal of symbolic logic** in preparing the present bibliography, and also of the bibliographies in Fraenkel 1928 and Heyting 1934 (especially for items not within the field of the *Bibliography* and **Journal**).

Beginning with 1951 an international series of monographs is appearing under the title Studies in logic and the foundations of mathematics (North-Holland Pub. Co., Amsterdam), which includes research reports and expositions on many topics.

In the original printing of this book (1952), eleven works were cited which had not yet appeared. Now these eleven bibliographical items have been completed or corrected, but no new items have been added.

ACKERMANN, WILHELM

1924-5. *Begründung des "tertium non datur" mittels der Hilbertschen Theorie der Widerspruchsfreiheit.* **Mathematische Annalen,** vol. 93, pp. 1-36.

1928. *Zum Hilbertschen Aufbau der reellen Zahlen.* Ibid., vol. 99, pp. 118-133.

1940. *Zur Widerspruchsfreiheit der Zahlentheorie.* Ibid., vol. 117, pp. 162-194.

See Hilbert and Ackermann.

BEHMANN, HEINRICH

1922. *Beiträge zur Algebra der Logik, insbesondere zum Entscheidungsproblem.* Ibid., vol. 86, pp. 163-229.

BERECZKI, ILONA

1949 unpublished. Results reported to the author in a letter from Kalmár dated November 17, 1949. The author obtained (A) — (C) of Example 1 § 57 after receiving this letter; (D) was (in substance) mentioned (orally) to the author by Kalmár on August 18, 1948.

1952. *Nem elemi rekurzív függvény létezése* (*Existenz einer nichtelementaren rekursiven Funktion*). Comptes rendus du Premier Congrès des Math. Hongrois 27 août-2 sept. 1950, Budapest 1952, pp. 409-417. Cf. Péter 1951 pp. 61-67.

BERNAYS, PAUL

1935. *Sur le platonisme dans les mathématiques.* **L'Enseignement mathématique,** vol. 34, pp. 52-69.

1935a. *Hilberts Untersuchungen über die Grundlagen der Arithmetik.* **David Hilbert Gesammelte Abhandlungen,** vol. 3, Berlin (Springer), pp. 196-216.

1936. **Logical calculus.** Notes on lectures at the Institute for Advanced Study 1935-6, prepared with the assistance of F. A. Ficken. Mimeographed. Inst. for Adv. Study, Princeton, N.J., 1936, 125 pp.

1937-48. *A system of axiomatic set theory.* **The journal of symbolic logic,** vol. 2 (1937), pp. 65-77, vol. 6 (1941), pp. 1-17, vol. 7 (1942), pp. 65-89 and 133-145, vol. 8 (1943), pp. 89-106, vol. 13 (1948), pp. 65-79.

1938. *Sur les questions méthodologiques actuelles de la théorie hilbertienne de la démonstration.* **Les entretiens de Zurich sur les fondements et la méthode des sciences mathématiques, 6-9 Décembre 1938,** Exposés et discussions, published by F. Gonseth, Zurich (Leemann) 1941, pp. 144-152. Discussion on pp. 153-161.

See Hilbert and Bernays.

BERNSTEIN, FELIX

1898. See p. 104 of Borel 1898.

BERRY, G. G.

1906. See p. 645 of Russell 1906.

BLACK, MAX

1933. **The nature of mathematics. A critical survey.** London (Kegan Paul, Trench, Trubner) and New York (Harcourt, Brace), xiv+219 pp. Reprinted London (Routledge and Kegan Paul) and New York (The Humanities Press) 1950.

Boole, George

1847. **The mathematical analysis of logic, being an essay toward a calculus of deductive reasoning.** Cambridge (Macmillan, Barclay & Macmillan) and London (George Bell), 82 pp. Reprinted Oxford (Basil Blackwell) and New York (Philosophical Library, Inc.) 1948.

1854. **An investigation of the laws of thought, on which are founded the mathematical theories of logic and probabilities.** London (Walton and Maberly), v + iv + 424 pp. Reprinted as vol. 2 of George Boole's collected works, edited by Ph. E. B. Jourdain, Chicago & London 1916. Reprinted New York (Dover Publications) 1951.

Boone, William W.

1951. abstract. *An extension of a result of Post.* **The journal of symbolic logic,** vol. 16, pp. 237-238.

1952. Review of Turing 1950. Ibid., vol. 17, pp. 74-76.

Borel, Émile

1898. **Leçons sur la théorie des fonctions.** Paris (Gauthier-Villars).

Brouwer, L. E. J.

1908. *De onbetrouwbaarheid der logische principes* (The untrustworthiness of the principles of logic). **Tijdschrift voor wijsbegeerte,** vol. 2, pp. 152-158. Reprinted in **Wiskunde, waarheid, werkelijkheid,** by L. E. J. Brouwer, Groningen (P. Noordhoff) 1919, 12 pp.

1923. *Über die Bedeutung des Satzes vom ausgeschlossenen Dritten in der Mathematik, insbesondere in der Funktionentheorie.* **Journal für die reine und angewandte Mathematik,** vol. 154 (1925), pp. 1-7. Original in Dutch 1923.

1928. *Intuitionistische Betrachtungen über den Formalismus.* **Sitzungsberichte der Preussischen Akademie der Wissenschaften, Physikalisch-mathematische Klasse,** 1928, pp. 48-52. Also **Koninklijke Nederlandsche Akademie van Wetenschappen, Proceedings of the section of sciences,** vol. 31, pp. 374-379.

Burali-Forti, Cesare

1897. *Una questione sui numeri transfiniti.* **Rendiconti del Circolo Matematico di Palermo,** vol. 11, pp. 154-164. See also ibid., p. 260. Concerning Cantor's discoveries of the Burali-Forti and Cantor paradoxes, see Fraenkel 1932, p. 470.

Cantor, Georg

1874. *Über eine Eigenschaft des Inbegriffes aller reellen algebraischen Zahlen.* **Journal für die reine und angewandte Mathematik,** vol. 77, p. 258-262. Reprinted in **Georg Cantor Gesammelte Abhandlungen,** Berlin (Springer) 1932, pp. 115-118.

1895-7. *Beiträge zur Begründung der transfiniten Mengenlehre.* **Mathematische Annalen,** vol. 46 (1895), pp. 481-512, and vol. 49 (1897), pp. 207-246. Reprinted in **Georg Cantor Gesammelte Abhandlungen,** pp. 282-351. English translation by Ph. E. B. Jourdain entitled **Contributions to the founding of the theory of transfinite numbers,** Chicago and London (Open Court) 1915, ix + 211 pp.

CARNAP, RUDOLF

1931-2. *Die logizistische Grundlegung der Mathematik.* **Erkenntnis,** vol. 2, pp. 91-105.

1934. **The logical syntax of language.** New York (Harcourt, Brace) and London (Kegan Paul, Trench, Trubner) 1937, xvi+352 pp. Tr. by Amethe Smeaton from the German original 1934, with additions.

CHURCH, ALONZO

1932. *A set of postulates for the foundation of logic.* **Annals of mathematics,** second series, vol. 33, pp. 346-366.

1933. *A set of postulates for the foundation of logic (second paper).* Ibid., vol. 34, pp. 839-864.

1935. *A proof of freedom from contradiction.* **Proceedings of the National Academy of Sciences,** vol. 21, pp. 275-281.

1936. *An unsolvable problem of elementary number theory.* **American journal of mathematics,** vol. 58, pp. 345-363.

1936a. *A note on the Entscheidungsproblem.* **The journal of symbolic logic,** vol. 1, pp. 40-41. *Correction,* ibid., pp. 101-102.

1938. *The constructive second number class.* **Bulletin of the American Mathematical Society,** vol. 44, pp. 224-232.

1941. **The calculi of lambda-conversion.** Annals of Mathematics studies, no. 6. Lithoprinted. Princeton University Press, Princeton, N.J., ii+77 pp. Second printing 1951, ii+82 pp.

1951. *Special cases of the decision problem.* **Revue philosophique de Louvain,** vol. 49, pp. 203-221. *A correction,* ibid., vol. 50 (1952), pp. 270-272.

1956. **Introduction to mathematical logic.** Princeton University Press, Princeton, N.J., vol. I (1956) x + 376 pp., vol. II.

See Church and Kleene, Church and Quine.

CHURCH, ALONZO and KLEENE, S. C.

1936. *Formal definitions in the theory of ordinal numbers.* **Fundamenta mathematicae,** vol. 28, pp. 11-21.

CHURCH, ALONZO and QUINE, W. V.

1952. *Some theorems on definability and decidability.* **The journal of symbolic logic,** vol. 17, pp. 179-187.

CURRY, HASKELL B.

1929. *An analysis of logical substitution.* **American journal of mathematics,** vol. 51, pp. 363-384.

1930. *Grundlagen der kombinatorischen Logik.* Ibid., vol. 52, pp. 509-536, 789-834.

1932. *Some additions to the theory of combinators.* Ibid., vol. 54, pp. 551-558.

1939. *A note on the reduction of Gentzen's calculus LJ.* **Bulletin of the American Mathematical Society,** vol. 45, pp. 288-293.

1948-9. *A simplification of the theory of combinators.* **Synthese,** vol. 7, pp. 391-399.

1950. **A theory of formal deducibility.** Notre Dame mathematical lectures, no. 6, University of Notre Dame, Notre Dame, Ind., ix+126 pp.

1952. *The permutability of rules in the classical inferential calculus.* **The journal of symbolic logic**, vol. 17, pp. 245-248.

DANTZIG, D. VAN

1947. *On the principles of intuitionistic and affirmative mathematics.* **Koninklijke Nederlandsche Akademie van Wetenschappen, Proceedings of the section of sciences,** vol. 50, pp. 918-929, 1092-1103; also **Indagationes mathematicae,** vol. 9, pp. 429-440, 506-517.

1948. *Significs, and its relation to semiotics.* **Library of the Tenth International Congress of Philosophy (Amsterdam, Aug. 11-18, 1948),** vol. 2 **Philosophical essays,** Amsterdam (Veen) 1948, pp. 176-189.

DAVIS, MARTIN

1950 abstract. *Relatively recursive functions and the extended Kleene hierarchy.* **Proceedings of the International Congress of Mathematicians (Cambridge, Mass., U.S.A., Aug. 30-Sept. 6, 1950),** 1952, vol. 1, p. 723.

DEDEKIND, RICHARD

1872. **Stetigkeit und irrationale Zahlen.** Braunschweig (5th ed. 1927). Also in **Dedekind Gesammelte mathematische Werke,** vol. III, Braunschweig (Vieweg & Sohn) 1932, pp. 315-334. Eng. tr. by Wooster Woodruff Beman entitled *Continuity and irrational numbers*, pp. 1-24 of **Essays on the theory of numbers,** Chicago (Open Court) 1901, 115 pp.

1888. **Was sind und was sollen die Zahlen?** Braunschweig (6th ed. 1930). Also in **Werke,** vol. III, pp. 335-391. Eng. tr. by Beman, *The nature and meaning of numbers*, loc. cit., pp. 29-115.

DE MORGAN, AUGUSTUS

1847. **Formal logic: or, the calculus of inference, necessary and probable.** London, xvi+336 pp. Reprinted Chicago and London 1926 (ed. by A. E. Taylor).

1864. *On the syllogism, no. IV, and on the logic of relations* (read 23 April 1860). **Transactions of the Cambridge Philosophical Society,** vol. 10, pp. 331-358.

DIXON, A. C.

1906. *On "well-ordered" aggregates.* **Proceedings of the London Mathematical Society,** ser. 2, vol. 4, pp. 18-20. Cf. ibid., pp. 317-319.

EINSTEIN, ALBERT

1944. *Remarks on Bertrand Russell's theory of knowledge.* **The philosophy of Bertrand Russell,** ed. by Paul Arthur Schilpp, Northwestern University, Evanston and Chicago, pp. 277-291. (German with Eng. tr. by Schilpp.)

FEYS, ROBERT

1937-8. *Les logiques nouvelles des modalités.* **Revue néoscolastique de philosophie,** vol. 40 (1937), pp. 517-553, vol. 41 (1938), pp. 217-252.

1965. **Modal logics.** Ed. with some complements by Joseph Dopp, Louvain (E. Nauwelaerts) and Paris (Gauthier-Villars), xiv + 219 pp. This is the outcome of a plan for a joint work by Feys and J. C. C. McKinsey.

FINSLER, PAUL

1926. *Formale Beweise und die Entscheidbarkeit.* **Mathematische Zeitschrift**, vol. 25, pp. 676-682.

FRAENKEL, ADOLF

1922. *Der Begriff "definit" und die Unabhängigkeit des Auswahlaxioms.* **Sitzungsberichte der Preussische Akademie der Wissenschaften, Physikalisch-mathematische Klasse,** 1922, pp. 253-257.

1925. *Untersuchungen über die Grundlagen der Mengenlehre.* **Mathematische Zeitschrift,** vol. 22, pp. 250-273.

1928. **Einleitung in die Mengenlehre,** 3rd ed., Berlin (Springer) 1928, xiii+424 pp. Reprinted New York (Dover Publications) 1946.

1932. *Das Leben Georg Cantors.* **Georg Cantor Gesammelte Abhandlungen mathematischen und philosophischen Inhalts,** ed. by Ernst Zermelo, Berlin (Springer), pp. 452-483.

1953. **Abstract set theory.** Studies in logic and the foundations of mathematics, Amsterdam (North-Holland Pub. Co.), xii + 479 pp.

FREGE, GOTTLOB

1879. **Begriffsschrift, eine der arithmetischen nachgebildete Formelsprache des reinen Denkens.** Halle (Nebert), viii+88 pp.

1884. **Die Grundlagen der Arithmetik, eine logisch-mathematische Untersuchung über den Begriff der Zahl.** Breslau, xix+119 pp. Reprinted Breslau (M. & H. Marcus) 1934. Eng. tr. by J. L. Austin (with German original): **The foundations of arithmetic. A logico-mathematical enquiry into the concept of number.** Oxford (Basil Blackwell) and New York (Philosophical Library) 1950, (xii+XI+119) × 2 pages.

1893. **Grundgesetze der Arithmetik, begriffsschriftlich abgeleitet.** Jena (H. Pohle), vol. 1, xxxii+254 pp.

1903. Ibid., vol. 2, xv+265 pp. Eng. tr. of Sections 86-137 by Max Black entitled *Frege against the formalists* in **The philosophical review,** vol. 59 (1950), pp. 77-93, 202-219, 332-345.

GENTZEN, GERHARD

1934-5. *Untersuchungen über das logische Schliessen.* **Mathematische Zeitschrift,** vol. 39, pp. 176-210, 405-431. Apart from minor differences in the notion of formula, and for the Hilbert-type systems in the precise selection of the postulates, our classical "formal system *H*" for predicate calculus (cf. § 77) is Gentzen's "Kalkül *LHK*", our intuitionistic "*H*" is his "*LHJ*", our classical "*G*1" his "*LK*", and our intuitionistic "*G*1" his "*LJ*".

1936. *Die Widerspruchsfreiheit der reinen Zahlentheorie.* **Mathematische Annalen,** vol. 112, pp. 493-565. He uses 1, 2, 3, ... where we use 0, 1, 2, ...

1938. *Die gegenwärtige Lage in der mathematischen Grundlagenforschung.* **Forschungen zur Logik und zur Grundlegung der exakten Wissenschaften,** new series, no 4, Leipzig (Hirzel), pp. 5-18.

1938a. *Neue Fassung des Widerspruchsfreiheitsbeweises für die reine Zahlentheorie.* Ibid., pp. 19-44.

1943. *Beweisbarkeit und Unbeweisbarkeit von Anfangsfällen der transfiniten Induktion in der reinen Zahlentheorie.* **Math. Ann.,** vol. 119 no. 1, pp. 140-161.

GLIVENKO, V.

1929. *Sur quelques points de la logique de M. Brouwer.* **Académie Royale de Belgique, Bulletins de la classe des sciences,** ser. 5, vol. 15, pp. 183-188.

GÖDEL, KURT

1930. *Die Vollständigkeit der Axiome des logischen Funktionenkalküls.* **Monatshefte für Mathematik und Physik,** vol. 37, pp. 349-360.

1931. *Über formal unentscheidbare Sätze der Principia Mathematica und verwandter Systeme I.* Ibid., vol. 38, pp. 173-198.

1931-2. *Über Vollständigkeit und Widerspruchsfreiheit.* **Ergebnisse eines mathematischen Kolloquiums,** Heft 3 (for 1930-1, pub. 1932), pp. 12-13. This paper lists results without proofs.

1931-2a. Remarks contributed to a *Diskussion zur Grundlegung der Mathematik.* **Erkenntnis,** vol. 2, pp. 147-148.

1932. *Zum intuitionistischen Aussagenkalkül.* **Akademie der Wissenschaften in Wien, Mathematisch-naturwissenschaftliche Klasse, Anzeiger,** vol. 69 (1932), pp. 65-66. Reprinted in **Ergebnisse eines mathematischen Kolloquiums,** Heft 4 (for 1931-2, pub. 1933), p. 40.

1932-3. *Zur intuitionistischen Arithmetik und Zahlentheorie.* **Ergebnisse eines math. Koll.,** Heft 4 (for 1931-2, pub. 1933), pp. 34-38.

1934. **On undecidable propositions of formal mathematical systems.** Notes by S. C. Kleene and Barkley Rosser on lectures at the Institute for Advanced Study, 1934. Mimeographed, Princeton, N.J., 30 pp.

1936. *Über die Länge von Beweisen.* **Ergebnisse eines math. Koll.,** Heft 7 (for 1934-5, pub. 1936, with note added in press), pp. 23-24.

1938. *The consistency of the axiom of choice and of the generalized continuum-hypothesis.* **Proceedings of the National Academy of Sciences,** vol. 24, pp. 556-557. A full-length treatment is given in 1940.

1939. *Consistency-proof for the generalized continuum-hypothesis.* Ibid., vol. 25, pp. 220-224.

1940. **The consistency of the axiom of choice and of the generalized continuum-hypothesis with the axioms of set theory.** Lectures delivered at the Institute for Advanced Study 1938-9; notes by George W. Brown. Annals of Mathematics studies, no. 3. Lithoprinted. Princeton University Press, Princeton 1940, 66 pp. (In Axiom 4 insert "(u)" after "(∃z)". Also cf. Example 13 § 74 above.) Second printing 1951, v + 69 pp.

1944. *Russell's mathematical logic.* **The philosophy of Bertrand Russell,** ed. by Paul Arthur Schilpp, Northwestern University, Evanston and Chicago, pp. 123-153.

1947. *What is Cantor's continuum problem?* **American mathematical monthly,** vol. 54, pp. 515-525.

GONSETH, FERDINAND

1933. *La vérité mathématique et la réalité.* **L' Enseignement mathématique,** vol. 31 (for 1932, pub. 1933), pp. 96-114.
Also: *A propos d'un catalogue paradoxical. Réponse de M. Gonseth à M. Winants.* Ibid., pp. 269-271.

HALL, MARSHALL, JR.

1949. *The word problem for semigroups with two generators.* **The journal of symbolic logic,** vol. 14, pp. 115-118.

HASENJAEGER, GISBERT

1950. *Über eine Art von Unvollständigkeit des Prädikatenkalküls der ersten Stufe.* Ibid., vol. 15, pp. 273-276.

HAUSDORFF, FELIX

1914. **Grundzüge der Mengenlehre.** Leipzig (Viet), viii+476 pp. Reprinted New York (Chelsea) 1949.

1927. **Mengenlehre.** Göschens Lehrbucherei, 1 Gruppe Band 7, Berlin and Leipzig (Gruyter), a 2nd revised ed. of 1914 (but less complete in some respects), 285 pp. 3rd ed., 1935, 307 pp. Reprinted New York (Dover Publications) 1944.

HENKIN, LEON

1949. *The completeness of the first-order functional calculus.* **The journal of symbolic logic,** vol. 14, pp. 159-166.

1950. *Completeness in the theory of types.* Ibid., vol. 15, pp. 81-91.

1950a. *An algebraic characterization of quantifiers.* **Fundamenta mathematicae,** vol. 37, pp. 63-74.

HERBRAND, JACQUES

1928. *Sur la théorie de la démonstration.* **Comptes rendus hebdomadaires des séances de l'Académie des Sciences** (Paris), vol. 186, pp. 1274-1276.

1930. **Recherches sur la théorie de la démonstration.** Travaux de la Société des Sciences et des Lettres de Varsovie, Classe III sciences mathématiques et physiques, no. 33, 128 pp.

1931-2. *Sur la non-contradiction de l'arithmétique.* **Journal für die reine und angewandte Mathematik,** vol. 166, pp. 1-8.

HERMES, HANS

1938. *Semiotik. Eine Theorie der Zeichengestalten als Grundlage für Untersuchungen von formalisierten Sprachen.* **Forschungen zur Logik und zur Grundlegung der exakten Wissenschaften,** n.s., no. 5, Leipzig (Hirzel), 22 pp.

HEYTING, AREND

1930. *Die formalen Regeln der intuitionistischen Logik.* **Sitzungsberichte der Preussischen Akademie der Wissenschaften, Physikalisch-mathematische Klasse,** 1930, pp. 42-56.

1930a. *Die formalen Regeln der intuitionistischen Mathematik.* Ibid., pp. 57-71, 158-169.

1931-2. *Die intuitionistische Grundlegung der Mathematik.* **Erkenntnis,** vol. 2, pp. 106-115.

1934. **Mathematische Grundlagenforschung. Intuitionismus. Beweistheorie. Ergebnisse der Mathematik und ihrer Grenzgebiete,** vol. 3, no. 4, Berlin (Springer), pp. iv+73. Erratum: The theorem of Gödel 1932-3 does not hold for the predicate calculus quite as stated by Heyting on p. 18. Cf. Remark 1 § 81 above.

1946. *On weakened quantification.* **Jour. symbolic logic,** vol. 11, pp. 119-121.

HILBERT, DAVID

1899. **Grundlagen der Geometrie.** 7th ed. (1930), Leipzig and Berlin (Teubner), vii+326 pp. Eng. tr. by E. J. Townsend, **The foundations of geometry,** Chicago (Open Court) 1902, iv+143 pp.

1900. *Über den Zahlbegriff.* **Jahresbericht der Deutschen Mathematiker-Vereinigung** vol. 8, pp. 180-184. Reprinted with an omission in **Grundlagen der Geometrie,** 7th ed., Leipzig and Berlin (Teubner) 1930, pp. 241-246.

1904. *Über die Grundlagen der Logik und der Arithmetik.* **Verhandlungen des Dritten Internationalen Mathematiker-Kongresses in Heidelberg vom 8. bis 13. August 1904,** Leipzig 1905, pp. 174-185. Reprinted, loc. cit., pp. 247-261.

1918. *Axiomatisches Denken.* **Mathematische Annalen,** vol. 78, pp. 405-415. Reprinted in **David Hilbert Gesammelte Abhandlungen,** vol. 3, Berlin (Springer) 1935, pp. 146-156.

1926. *Über das Unendliche.* **Math. Ann.,** vol. 95, pp. 161-190. Reprinted in abbreviated form in **Jahresb. Deutschen Math.-Verein.,** vol. 36 (1927), pp. 201-215. Also with some revisions in **Grundlagen der Geometrie,** 7th ed., 1930, pp. 262-288.

1928. *Die Grundlagen der Mathematik.* **Abhandlungen aus dem Mathematischen Seminar der Hamburgischen Universität,** vol. 6, pp. 65-85. Reprinted with abridgements in **Grundlagen der Geometrie,** 7th ed., pp. 289-312.

See Hilbert and Ackermann, Hilbert and Bernays.

HILBERT, DAVID and ACKERMANN, WILHELM

1928. **Grundzüge der theoretischen Logik.** Berlin (Springer), viii+120 pp. 2nd ed. 1938, viii+133 pp. Reprinted New York (Dover Publications) 1946. 3rd ed. Berlin, Göttingen, Heidelberg (Springer) 1949, viii+155 pp. Eng. tr. of the 2nd ed. by L. M. Hammond, G. G. Leckie and F. Steinhardt, ed. with notes by R. E. Luce, **Principles of mathematical logic,** New York (Chelsea Pub. Co.) 1950, xii+172 pp.

HILBERT, DAVID and BERNAYS, PAUL

1934. **Grundlagen der Mathematik,** vol. 1, Berlin (Springer), xii+471 pp. Reprinted Ann Arbor, Mich. (J. W. Edwards) 1944.

1939. Ibid., vol. 2, Berlin (Springer), xii+498 pp. Reprinted Ann Arbor, Mich. (Edwards) 1944.

IONGH, JOHAN J. DE

1948. *Restricted forms of intuitionistic mathematics.* **Proceedings of the Tenth International Congress of Philosophy (Amsterdam, Aug. 11-18, 1948)**, Amsterdam (North-Holland Pub. Co.) 1949, pp. 744-748 (fasc. 2).

JAŚKOWSKI, STANISŁAW

1934. **On the rules of suppositions in formal logic.** Studia logica, no. 1, Warsaw, 32 pp.

1936. *Recherches sur le système de la logique intuitioniste.* **Actes du Congrès International de Philosophie Scientifique, VI Philosophie des mathématiques,** Actualités scientifiques et industrielles 393, Paris (Hermann & Cie.), pp. 58-61. Jaśkowski does not give his proofs in detail; a reconstruction of the proofs is in Gene Rose 1952 Part I.

KALMÁR, LÁSZLÓ

1934-5. *Über die Axiomatisierbarkeit des Aussagenkalküls.* **Acta scientiarum mathematicarum** (Szeged), vol. 7, pp. 222-243.

1943. *Egyszerü példa eldönthetetlen aritmetikai problémára (Ein einfaches Beispiel für ein unentscheidbares arithmetisches Problem).* **Matematikai és fizikai lapok,** vol. 50, pp. 1-23. Hungarian with German abstract. Kalmár takes, as his basis for elementary functions, the variables, 1, +, ·, $|a-b|$, $[a/b]$, $\sum_{y=w}^{z}$, $\prod_{y=w}^{z}$, but remarks that then · and $[a/b]$ are redundant. (Cf. Example 1 § 57 above.)

1948. *On unsolvable mathematical problems.* **Proceedings of the Tenth International Congress of Philosophy (Amsterdam, Aug. 11-18, 1948)**, Amsterdam (North-Holland Pub. Co.) 1949, pp. 756-758 (fasc. 2). Preprints 1948, pp. 534-536.

1950. *Eine einfache Konstruktion unentscheidbarer Sätze in formalen Systemen.* **Methodos,** vol. 2, pp. 220-226; Eng. tr. by Ernst v. Glasersfeld, pp. 227-231.

1950a. *Another proof of the Gödel-Rosser incompletability theorem.* **Acta scientiarum mathematicarum** (Szeged), vol. 12, pp. 38-43.

KEMENY, JOHN G.

1948. *Review of Mostowski 1947a.* **Jour. symbolic logic,** vol. 13, pp. 46-48.

KETONEN, OIVA

1944. *Untersuchungen zum Prädikatenkalkül.* **Annales Academiae Scientiarum Fennicae,** ser. A, I. **Mathematica-physica** 23, Helsinki, 71 pp.

KLEENE, STEPHEN C.

1934. *Proof by cases in formal logic.* **Ann. of math.,** 2 s., vol. 35, pp. 529-544. Relative to § 20 above, cf. p. 534. The use of "⊢" to express derivability by the rules of inference originated with Rosser; the modification to make ⊢ relative also to the axioms, with the author.

1935. *A theory of positive integers in formal logic.* **Amer. jour. math.**, vol. 57, pp. 153-173, 219-244.

1936. *General recursive functions of natural numbers.* **Math. Ann.**, vol. 112, pp. 727-742. For an erratum and a simplification, cf. **Jour. symbolic logic**, vol. 3 p. 152, vol. 2 p. 38 and vol. 4 top p. IV at end.

1936a. *λ-definability and recursiveness.* **Duke mathematical journal**, vol. 2, pp. 340-353.

1936b. *A note on recursive functions.* **Bull. Amer. Math. Soc.**, vol. 42, pp. 544-546.

1938. *On notation for ordinal numbers.* **Jour. symbolic logic**, vol. 3, pp. 150-155.

1943. *Recursive predicates and quantifiers.* **Transactions of the American Mathematical Society**, vol. 53, pp. 41-73. Omit § 15, because the proof of Theorem 1 of 1944 contains an error. — Footnote ([21]) cites only a function which is partial but not potentially recursive, though the text mentions predicates also. (This oversight was brought to the author's attention by J. C. E. Dekker, March 18, 1952.) For such a predicate, cf. Example 6 § 63 above.

1944. *On the forms of the predicates in the theory of constructive ordinals.* **Amer. jour. math.**, vol. 66, pp. 41-58. The stars should be omitted from (4) and (11) p. 43 (cf. *86 and *95 above). — The treatment of the example $P(a)$ in **8** is not complete. For (18) is not simply another way of writing the inductive definition of 'a is provable', but can have other solutions for $P(a)$ besides $P(a) \equiv \{a \text{ is provable}\}$ (e.g. $P(a) \equiv \{a \text{ is a formula}\}$). However for any solution of (18), $\{a \text{ is provable}\} \rightarrow P(a)$; and it is easily shown from (22) that for the particular solution $P(a) \equiv (Ex)R(a, x)$, $P(a) \rightarrow \{a \text{ is provable}\}$. — Similarly for all applications of the technique in which the particular solution contains only an existential quantifier (cf. end § 53). But in the application to $a \mathbin{8} Q$ in **14**, where there is also a generality quantifier, the treatment cannot be completed in this manner; and so Theorem 1 and the first half of Theorem 2 are not established. The author plans to discuss the situation in a second paper under the same title.

1945. *On the interpretation of intuitionistic number theory.* **Jour. symbolic logic**, vol. 10, pp. 109-124.

1948. *On the intuitionistic logic.* **Proceedings of the Tenth International Congress of Philosophy (Amsterdam, Aug. 11-18, 1948)**, Amsterdam (North-Holland Pub. Co.) 1949, pp. 741-743 (fasc. 2). Preprints 1948, pp. 185-187.

1950. *A symmetric form of Gödel's theorem.* **Koninklijke Nederlandsche Akademie van Wetenschappen, Proceedings of the section of sciences**, vol. 53, pp. 800-802; also **Indagationes mathematicae**, vol. 12, pp. 244-246.

1950a. *Recursive functions and intuitionistic mathematics.* **Proceedings of the International Congress of Mathematicians (Cambridge, Mass., U.S.A., Aug. 30-Sept. 6, 1950)**, 1952, vol. 1, pp. 679-685.

1952. *Permutability of inferences in Gentzen's calculi LK and LJ.* **Memoirs of the American Mathematical Society**, no. 10, pp. 1-26.

See Church and Kleene.

KREISEL, G.

1950. *Note on arithmetic models for consistent formulae of the predicate calculus.* **Fundamenta mathematicae**, vol. 37, pp. 265-285.

Kuznécov, A. V.

1950. *O primitivno rékursivnyh funkciáh bol'šogo razmaha* (On primitive recursive functions of large oscillation). **Doklady Akadémii Nauk SSSR**, n.s., vol. 71, pp. 233-236.

Langford, Cooper Harold

1927. *On inductive relations.* **Bull. Amer. Math. Soc.**, vol. 33, pp. 599-607.

See Lewis and Langford.

Lewis, Clarence Irving

1912. *Implication and the algebra of logic.* **Mind**, n.s., vol. 21, pp. 522-531.

1917. *The issues concerning material implication.* **The journal of philosophy, psychology and scientific method**, vol. 14, pp. 350-356.

See Lewis and Langford.

Lewis, Clarence Irving and Langford, Cooper Harold

1932. **Symbolic logic.** New York and London (The Century Co.), xi+506 pp. Reprinted New York (Dover Publications) 1951.

Löwenheim, Leopold

1915. *Über Möglichkeiten im Relativkalkül.* **Math. Ann.**, vol. 76, pp. 447-470.

Łukasiewicz, Jan

1920. *O logice trójwartościowej* (On three-valued logic). **Ruch filozoficzny** (Lwów), vol. 5, pp. 169-171.

1925. *Démonstration de la compatibilité des axioms de la théorie de la déduction.* **Annales de la Société Polonaise de Mathématique**, vol. 3 (for 1924, pub. 1925), p. 149.

See Łukasiewicz and Tarski.

Łukasiewicz, Jan and Tarski, Alfred

1930. *Untersuchungen über den Aussagenkalkül.* **Comptes rendus des seánces de la Société des Sciences et des Lettres de Varsovie**, Classe III, vol. 23, pp. 30-50.

MacLane, Saunders

1934. **Abgekürzte Beweise im Logikkalkul.** Dissertation Göttingen. 61 pp.

Mannoury, Gerrit

1909. **Methodologisches und Philosophisches zur Elementar-Mathematik.** Haarlem (P. Visser), viii+276 pp.

1925. **Mathesis en mystiek.** Amsterdam. French translation: **Les deux pôles de l'esprit.** Paris, 1933.

1934. *Die signifischen Grundlagen der Mathematik.* **Erkenntnis**, vol. 4, pp. 288-309, 317-345.

MARKOV, A. A.

1947. *Névozmožnost' nékotoryh algorifmov v téorii associativnyh sistém.* **Doklady Akadémii Nauk SSSR,** n.s., vol. 55, pp. 587-590. Eng. tr. *On the impossibility of certain algorithms in the theory of associative systems.* **Comptes rendus (Doklady) de l'Académie des Sciences de l'URSS,** n.s., vol. 55, pp. 583-586.

1947a. *O nékotoryh nérazréšimyh problémah kasaúščihsá matric* (On some unsolvable problems concerning matrices). Doklady Akadémii Nauk SSSR, n.s., vol. 57, pp. 539-542.

1947b. *Névozmožnost' nékotoryh algorifmov v téorii associativnyh sistém II* (Impossibility of certain algorithms in the theory of associative systems II). Ibid., vol. 58, pp. 353-356.

1947c. *O prédstavlénii rékursivnyh funkcij* (On the representation of recursive functions). Ibid., pp. 1891-1892.

1949. *O prédstavlénii rékursivnyh funkcij* (On the representation of recursive functions). **Izvéstiyá Akadémii Nauk SSSR, ser. mat.,** vol. 13, pp. 417-424. Eng. tr., **On the representation of recursive functions,** Amer. Math. Soc., translation no. 54, lithoprinted, New York 1951, 13 pp.

1951. *Névozmožnost' nékotoryh algoritmov v téorii associativnyh sistém* (Impossibility of certain algorithms in the theory of associative systems). **Doklady Akadémii Nauk SSSR,** n.s., vol. 77, pp. 19-20.

1951a. *Névozmožnost' algorifmov raspoznavaniá nékotoryh svojstv associativnyh sistém* (Impossibility of algorithms for distinguishing certain properties of associative systems). Ibid., pp. 953-956.

1951b. *Ob odnoj nérazréšimoj problémé, kasaúščéjsá matric* (An unsolvable problem concerning matrices). Ibid., vol. 78, pp. 1089-1092.

MCKINSEY, J. C. C.

1939. *Proof of the independence of the primitive symbols of Heyting's calculus of propositions.* **Jour. symbolic logic,** vol. 4, pp. 155-158.

See McKinsey and Tarski.

MCKINSEY, J. C. C. and TARSKI, ALFRED

1948. *Some theorems about the sentential calculi of Lewis and Heyting.* Ibid., vol. 13, pp. 1-15.

MOSTOWSKI, ANDRZEJ

1947. *On definable sets of positive integers.* **Fundamenta mathematicae,** vol. 34, pp. 81-112.

1947a. *On absolute properties of relations.* **Jour. symbolic logic,** vol. 12, pp. 33-42.

1948. *Proofs of non-deducibility in intuitionistic functional calculus.* Ibid., vol. 13, pp. 204-207.

1948a. *On a set of integers not definable by means of one-quantifier predicates.* **Annales de la Société Polonaise de Mathématique,** vol. 21, pp. 114-119.

1949. *An undecidable arithmetical statement.* **Fund. math.,** vol. 36, pp. 143-164.

1951. *A classification of logical systems.* **Studia philosophica,** vol. 4, pp. 237-274.

1952. **Sentences undecidable in formalized arithmetic. An exposition of the theory of Kurt Gödel.** Studies in logic and the foundations of mathematics, Amsterdam (North-Holland Pub. Co., viii+117 pp.

1952a. *Models of axiomatic systems.* **Fund. Math.**, vol. 39, pp. 133-158. Cf. Ryll-Nardzewski 1952.

See Mostowski and Tarski.

MOSTOWSKI, ANDRZEJ and TARSKI, ALFRED

1949 abstract. *Undecidability in the arithmetic of integers and in the theory of rings.* **Jour. symbolic logic,** vol. 14, p. 76.

NELSON, DAVID

1947. *Recursive functions and intuitionistic number theory.* **Trans. Amer. Math. Soc.,** vol. 61, pp. 307-368.

1949. *Constructible falsity.* **Jour. symbolic logic,** vol. 14, pp. 16-26.

NEUMANN, JOHN VON

1925. *Eine Axiomatisierung der Mengenlehre.* **Journal für die reine und angewandte Mathematik,** vol. 154, pp. 219-240. *Berichtigung,* ibid., vol. 155 (1926), p. 128.

1927. *Zur Hilbertschen Beweistheorie.* **Math. Zeit.,** vol. 26, pp. 1-46.

1928. *Die Axiomatisierung der Mengenlehre.* Ibid., vol. 27, pp. 669-752.

1931-2. *Die formalistische Grundlegung der Mathematik.* **Erkenntnis,** vol. 2, pp. 116-121.

1947. *The mathematician.* **The works of the mind,** ed. by Robert B. Heywood, Chicago (U. of Chicago Press), pp. 180-196.

PASCH, MORITZ

1882. **Vorlesungen über neuere Geometrie.** Leipzig (Teubner), iv+201 pp. Reprinted in **Vorlesungen über neuere Geometrie** by M. Pasch and Max Dehn, Berlin (Springer) 1926, viii+275 pp.

PEANO, GIUSEPPE

1889. **Arithmetices principia, nova methodo exposita.** Turin (Bocca), xvi+20 pp.

1891. *Sul concetto di numero.* **Rivista di matematica,** vol. 1, pp. 87-102, 256-267. Peano formulates his axioms for the positive integers. (In fact, some writers call these the "natural numbers".)

1894-1908. **Formulaire de mathématiques.** Introduction and five volumes. Turin. Edited by Peano and written by him in collaboration with Rodolfo Bettazzi, Cesare Burali-Forti, F. Castellano, Gino Fano, Francesco Giudice, Giovanni Vailati, Giulio Vivanti.

PEIRCE, CHARLES SANDERS

1867. *On an improvement in Boole's calculus of logic* (presented 12 March 1867). **Proceedings of the American Academy of Arts and Sciences,** vol. 7 (1865-8), pp. 250-261. Reprinted in **Collected papers of Charles Sanders Peirce,** ed. by

Charles Hartshorne & Paul Weiss, Cambridge, Mass. (Harvard University Press), vol. 3 (1933), pp. 3-15.

1880. *On the algebra of logic. Chapter I. — Syllogistic. Chapter II. — The logic of non-relative terms. Chapter III. — The logic of relatives.* **Amer. jour. math.**, vol. 3, pp. 15-57. Reprinted with corrections in **Collected papers**, vol. 3, pp. 104-157.

PÉTER, RÓZSA

1934. *Über den Zusammenhang der verschiedenen Begriffe der rekursiven Funktion.* **Math. Ann.**, vol. 110, pp. 612-632.

1935. *Konstruktion nichtrekursiver Funktionen.* Ibid., vol. 111, pp. 42-60.

1935a. *A rekurzív függvények elméletéhez* (*Zur Theorie der rekursiven Funktionen*). Hungarian with full German abstract. **Matematikai és fizikai lapok**, vol. 42, pp. 25-49.

1936. *Über die mehrfache Rekursion.* **Math. Ann.**, vol. 113, pp. 489-527.

1940. Review of Skolem 1939. **Jour. symbolic Logic**, vol. 5, pp. 34-35.

1950. *Zusammenhang der mehrfachen und transfiniten Rekursionen.* Ibid., vol. 15, pp. 248-272.

1951. **Rekursive Funktionen.** Akadémiai Kiadó (Akademischer Verlag) Budapest, 206 pp.

POINCARÉ, HENRI

1900. *Du role de l'intuition et de la logique en mathématiques.* **Compte rendu du Deuxième Congrès International des Mathématiciens, tenu a Paris du 6 au 12 aout 1900**, Paris (Gauthier-Villars) 1902, pp. 115-130.

1902. **La science et l'hypothèse.** Paris, 284 pp. Translated by G. Bruce Halstead as pp. 27-197 of **The foundations of science** by H. Poincaré, New York (The Science Press) 1913; reprinted 1929.

1905-6. *Les mathématiques et la logique.* **Revue de métaphysique et de morale**, vol. 13 (1905), pp. 815-835, vol. 14 (1906), pp. 17-34, 294-317. Reprinted in 1908 with substantial alterations and additions.

1908. **Science et méthode**, Paris, 311 pp. Translated by Halstead as pp. 359-546 of **The foundations of science**, New York 1913, reprinted 1929.

POST, EMIL L.

1921. *Introduction to a general theory of elementary propositions.* **Amer. jour. math.**, vol. 43, pp. 163-185.

1936. *Finite combinatory processes—formulation 1.* **Jour. symbolic logic**, vol. 1, pp. 103-105.

1943. *Formal reductions of the general combinatorial decision problem.* **Amer. jour. math.**, vol. 65, pp. 197-215.

1944. *Recursively enumerable sets of positive integers and their decision problems.* **Bull. Amer. Math. Soc.**, vol. 50, pp. 284-316.

1946. *A variant of a recursively unsolvable problem.* Ibid., vol. 52, pp. 264-268.

1946a. *Note on a conjecture of Skolem.* **Jour. symbolic logic**, vol. 11, pp. 73-74.

1947. *Recursive unsolvability of a problem of Thue.* Ibid., vol. 12, pp. 1-11.

1948 abstract. *Degrees of recursive unsolvability.* Preliminary report. **Bull. Amer. Math. Soc.** vol. 54, pp. 641-642.

PRANTL, CARL

1855. **Geschichte der Logik im Abendlande,** vol. 1, Leipzig (S. Hirzel), xii+734 pp. (Other volumes 1861, 1867, 1870.) Reprinted 1927.

PRESBURGER, M.

1930. *Über die Vollständigkeit eines gewissen Systems der Arithmetik ganzer Zahlen, in welchem die Addition als einzige Operation hervortritt.* **Sprawozdanie z I Kongresu Matematyków Krajów Słowiańskich** (Comptes-rendus du I Congrès des Mathématiciens des Pays Slaves), **Warszawa 1929,** Warsaw 1930, pp. 92-101, 395.

QUINE, WILLARD VAN ORMAN

1940. **Mathematical logic.** New York (Norton), xiii+348 pp. See Rosser 1942 and Quine 1941, concerning the fact that the Burali-Forti paradox arises in the system of this book (although Cantor's paradox apparently is avoided), as was discovered by Rosser and by Roger C. Lyndon. Revised ed., Harvard University Press, 1951, xii+346 pp.

1941. *Element and number.* **Jour. symbolic logic,** vol. 6, pp. 135-149.

See Church and Quine.

RAMSEY, F. P.

1926. *The foundations of mathematics.* **Proc. London Math. Soc.,** ser. 2, vol. 25, pp. 338-384. Reprinted as pp. 1-61 in **The foundations of mathematics and other logical essays** by F. P. Ramsey, ed. by R. B. Braithwaite, London (Kegan Paul, Trench, Trubner) and New York (Harcourt, Brace) 1931. The latter reprinted London (Routledge and Kegan Paul) and New York (Humanities Press) 1950.

RASIOWA, H. and SIKORSKI, R.

1950. *A proof of the completeness theorem of Gödel.* **Fund. math.,** vol. 37, pp. 193-200. For a simplification by Tarski, cf. **Jour. symbolic logic.,** vol. 17, p. 72.

RICHARD, JULES

1905. *Les principes des mathématiques et le problème des ensembles.* **Revue générale des sciences pures et appliquées,** vol. 16, pp. 541-543. Also in **Acta mathematica,** vol. 30 (1906), pp. 295-296.

ROBINSON, JULIA

1949 abstract. *Undecidability in the arithmetic of integers and rationals and in the theory of fields.* **Jour. symbolic logic,** vol. 14, p. 77.

1949. *Definability and decision problems in arithmetic.* Ibid., pp. 98-114. For § 48 above, her treatment for the positive integers can be adapted to the natural numbers.

1950. *General recursive functions.* **Proceedings of the American Mathematical Society,** vol. 1, pp. 703-718.

ROBINSON, RAPHAEL M.

1947. *Primitive recursive functions.* **Bull. Amer. Math. Soc.**, vol. 53, pp. 925-942.

1948. *Recursion and double recursion.* Ibid., vol. 54, pp. 987-993.

1949 abstract. *Undecidable rings.* Ibid., vol. 55, p. 1050.

1950 abstract. *An essentially undecidable axiom system.* **Proceedings of the International Congress of Mathematicians (Cambridge, Mass., U.S.A., Aug. 30-Sept. 6, 1950)**, 1952, vol. 1, pp. 729-730. Robinson's system is simpler than one we were using previously (since Mostowski and Tarski 1949 abstract) in §§ 41, 49 and 76 for the same purpose.

ROSE, GENE F.

1952. **Jaśkowski's truth-tables and realizability.** Doctoral dissertation, The University of Wisconsin.

ROSSER, BARKLEY (Rosser, J. B.; Rosser, J. Barkley)

1935. *A mathematical logic without variables.* **Ann. math.**, 2 s., vol. 36, pp. 127-150 and **Duke math. jour.**, vol. 1, pp. 328-355. Relative to § 20 above, cf. p. 130, p. 329, and the note accompanying Kleene 1934.

1936. *Extensions of some theorems of Gödel and Church.* **Jour. symbolic logic**, vol. 1, pp. 87-91.

1936a. Review of Gödel 1936. Ibid., vol. 1, p. 116.

1939. *On the consistency of Quine's "New foundations for mathematical logic".* Ibid., vol. 4, pp. 15-24.

1942. *The Burali-Forti paradox.* Ibid., vol. 7, pp. 1-17.

1942a. *New sets of postulates for combinatory logics.* Ibid., pp. 18-27. For a correction, cf. Curry 1948-9.

See Rosser and Turquette, Rosser and Wang.

ROSSER, J. B. and TURQUETTE, A. R.

1945. *Axiom schemes for m-valued propositional calculi.* **Jour. symbolic logic**, vol. 10, pp. 61-82. Cf. 1950.

1948-51. *Axiom schemes for m-valued functional calculi of first order. Part I. Definition of axiom schemes and proof of plausibility.* Ibid., vol. 13 (1948), pp. 177-192. *Part II. Deductive completeness.* Ibid., vol. 16 (1951), pp. 22-34.

1949. *A note on the deductive completeness of m-valued propositional calculi.* Ibid., vol. 14, pp. 219-225.

1952. **Many-valued logics.** Studies in logic and the foundations of mathematics, Amsterdam (North-Holland Pub. Co.), vii+124 pp.

ROSSER, J. BARKLEY and WANG, HAO

1950. *Non-standard models for formal logics.* **Jour. symbolic logic**, vol. 15, pp. 113-129.

RUSSELL, BERTRAND (Russell, B. A. W.)

1902. *On finite and infinite cardinal numbers* (Section III of A. N. Whitehead's *On cardinal numbers*). **Amer. jour. math.**, vol. 24, pp. 378-383.

1902-3. The Russell paradox appears in Frege 1903, in a postscript (dated by Frege October 1902), pp. 253-265. Concerning Zermelo's independent discovery of this paradox, see Zermelo 1908a p. 119 and Hilbert 1926 p. 169.

1906. *Les paradoxes de la logique.* **Revue de métaphysique et de morale**, vol. 14, pp. 627-650.

1908. *Mathematical logic as based on the theory of types.* **Amer. jour. math.**, vol. 30, pp. 222-262.

1910. *La théorie des types logiques.* **Rev. métaph. mor.**, vol. 18, pp. 263-301.

1919. **Introduction to mathematical philosophy.** London (G. Allen and Unwin) and New York (Macmillan), viii+208 pp.. 2nd ed. 1920.

See Whitehead and Russell.

RÜSTOW, ALEXANDER

1910. **Der Lügner, Theorie, Geschichte und Auflösung.** Leipzig (Teubner), v+147 pp.

RYLL-NARDZEWSKI, CZESŁAW

1952. *The role of the axiom of induction in elementary arithmetic.* **Fund. Math.**, vol. 39, pp. 239-263. Subsequently Mostowski obtained further results, 1952a.

SCHMIDT, ARNOLD

1938. *Über deduktive Theorien mit mehreren Sorten von Grunddingen.* **Math. Ann.**, vol. 115, pp. 485-506.

SCHÖNFINKEL, MOSES

1924. *Über die Bausteine der mathematischen Logik.* **Math. Ann.**, vol. 92, pp. 305-316.

SCHRÖDER, ERNST

1877. **Der Operationskreis des Logikkalkuls.** Leipzig, v+37 pp.

1890-1905. **Vorlesungen über die Algebra der Logik (exakte Logik).** Vol. 1, Leipzig (Teubner) 1890, xii+717 pp. Vol. 2 part 1, Leipzig 1891, xiii+400 pp. Vol. 3 **Algebra und Logik der Relative** part 1, Leipzig 1895, viii+649 pp. Vol. 2 part 2 appeared posthumously, ed. by Eugen Müller, Leipzig 1905, xxix+205 pp. **Abriss der Algebra der Logik,** ed. by Müller, part 1 **Elementarlehre** Leipzig and Berlin 1909, v+50 pp., part 2 **Aussagentheorie, Funktionen, Gleichungen und Ungleichungen,** Leipzig and Berlin 1910, vi+51+159 pp.

SCHÜTTE, KURT

1951. *Beweistheoretische Erfassung der unendlichen Induktion in der Zahlentheorie.* **Math. Ann.**, vol. 122, pp. 369-389.

SHEFFER, H. M.

1913. *A set of five independent postulates for Boolean algebras, with application to logical constants.* **Trans. Amer. Math. Soc.**, vol. 14, pp. 481-488. According to Quine 1940 p. 49, the definability of &, V and ¬ in terms of one operator was known to C. S. Peirce in 1880. (Cf. § 30 above.)

SKOLEM, THORALF

1919. *Untersuchungen über die Axiome des Klassenkalkuls und über Produktations- und Summationsprobleme, welche gewisse Klassen von Aussagen betreffen.* **Skrifter utgit av Videnskapsselskapet i Kristiania, I. Matematisk-naturvidenskabelig klasse 1919,** no. 3, 37 pp.

1920. *Logisch-kombinatorische Untersuchungen über die Erfüllbarkeit oder Beweisbarkeit mathematischer Sätze nebst einem Theoreme über dichte Mengen.* Ibid., **1920,** no. 4, 36 pp.

1922-3. *Einige Bemerkungen zur axiomatischen Begründung der Mengenlehre.* **Wissenschaftliche Vorträge gehalten auf dem Fünften Kongress der Skandinavischen Mathematiker in Helsingfors vom 4. bis 7. Juli 1922,** Helsingfors 1923, pp. 217-232.

1923. *Begründung der elementaren Arithmetik durch die rekurrierende Denkweise ohne Anwendung scheinbarer Veränderlichen mit unendlichem Ausdehnungsbereich.* **Skrifter utgit av Videnskapsselskapet i Kristiania, I. Matematisk-naturvidenskabelig klasse 1923,** no. 6, 38 pp.

1929. *Über einige Grundlagenfragen der Mathematik.* **Skrifter utgitt av Det Norske Videnskaps-Akademi i Oslo, I. Matematisk-naturvidenskapelig klasse 1929,** no. 4, 49 pp.

1929-30. *Über die Grundlagendiskussionen in der Mathematik.* **Den Syvende Skandinaviske Matematikerkongress i Oslo 19-22 August 1929,** Oslo (Brøggers) 1930, pp. 3-21.

1930-1. *Über einige Satzfunktionen in der Arithmetik.* **Skrifter utgitt av Det Norske Videnskaps-Akademi i Oslo, I. Matematisk-naturvidenskapelig klasse 1930,** no. 7, 28 pp. (1931).

1933. *Über die Unmöglichkeit einer vollständigen Charakterisierung der Zahlenreihe mittels eines endlichen Axiomensystems.* **Norsk matematisk forenings skrifter,** ser. 2, no. 10, pp. 73-82.

1934. *Über die Nicht-charakterisierbarkeit der Zahlenreihe mittels endlich oder abzählbar unendlich vieler Aussagen mit ausschliesslich Zahlenvariablen.* **Fund. math.,** vol. 23, pp. 150-161.

1936-7. *Über die Zurückführbarkeit einiger durch Rekursionen definierten Relationen auf "arithmetische".* **Acta litterarum ac scientiarum Regiae Universitatis Hungaricae Franscisco-Iosephinae, Sectio scientiarum mathematicarum** (Szeged), vol. 8, pp. 73-88.

1938. *Sur la portée du théorème de Löwenheim-Skolem.* **Les entretiens de Zurich sur les fondements et la méthode des sciences mathématiques, 6-9 Décembre 1938,** Exposés et discussions, pub. by F. Gonseth, Zurich (Leemann) 1941, pp. 25-47. Discussion on pp. 47-52.

1939. *Eine Bemerkung über die Induktionsschemata in der rekursiven Zahlentheorie.* **Monatshefte Math. Phys.,** vol. 48, pp. 268-276.

1944. *Some remarks on recursive arithmetic.* **Det Kongelige Norske Videnskabers Selskab, Forhandlinger,** vol. 17, pp. 103-106. This is the second of a series of four notes, the others of which appear in the same volume, pp. 89-92, pp. 107-109, pp. 126-129.

1951. Review of Rosser and Wang 1950. **Jour. Symbolic logic,** vol. 16, pp. 145-146.

TARSKI, ALFRED

1930. *Über einige fundamentalen Begriffe der Metamathematik.* **Comptes rendus des séances de la Société des Sciences et des Lettres de Varsovie,** Classe III, vol. 23, pp. 22-29.

1932. *Der Wahrheitsbegriff in den Sprachen der deduktiven Disziplinen.* **Akademie der Wissenschaften in Wien, Mathematisch-naturwissenschaftliche Klasse, Anzeiger,** vol. 69, pp. 23-25. A prospectus for 1933.

1933. *Der Wahrheitsbegriff in den formalisierten Sprachen.* **Studia philosophica,** vol. 1 (1936), pp. 261-405 (offprints dated 1935). Tr. by L. Blaustein from the Polish original 1933, with a postscript added.

1933a. *Einige Betrachtungen über die Begriffe der ω-Widerspruchsfreiheit und der ω-Vollständigkeit.* **Monatshefte Math. Phys.,** vol. 40, pp. 97-112.

1949 abstract. *On essential undecidability.* **Jour. symbolic logic,** vol. 14, pp. 75-76.

1949a abstract. *Undecidability of group theory.* Ibid., pp. 76-77.

1949b abstract. *Undecidability of the theories of lattices and projective geometries.* Ibid., pp. 77-78.

See Łukasiewicz and Tarski, McKinsey and Tarski, Mostowski and Tarski.

THUE, AXEL

1914. *Probleme über Veränderungen von Zeichenreihen nach gegebenen Regeln.* **Skrifter utgit av Videnskapsselskapet i Kristiania, I. Matematisk-naturvidenskabelig klasse 1914,** no. 10, 34 pp.

TRAHTÉNBROT, B. A.

1950. *Névozmožnost' algorifma dlá problémy razréšimosti na konéčnyh klassah* (Impossibility of an algorithm for the decision problem in finite classes). **Doklady Akadémii Nauk SSSR,** n.s., vol. 70, pp. 569-572.

TURING, ALAN MATHISON

1936-7. *On computable numbers, with an application to the Entscheidungsproblem.* **Proc. London Math. Soc.,** ser. 2, vol. 42 (1936-7), pp. 230-265. *A correction,* ibid., vol. 43 (1937), pp. 544-546.

1937. *Computability and λ-definability.* **Jour. symbolic logic,** vol. 2, pp. 153-163.

1939. *Systems of logic based on ordinals.* **Proc. London Math. Soc.,** ser. 2, vol. 45, pp. 161-228.

1950. *The word problem in semi-groups with cancellation.* **Ann. of math.,** 2 s., vol. 52, pp. 491-505. Some points in the proof require clarification, which can be given, as pointed out by Boone 1952.

VANDIVER, H. S.

1946. *Fermat's last theorem. Its history and the nature of the known results concerning it.* **Amer. math. monthly,** vol. 53, pp. 555-578.

VEBLEN, OSWALD

1904. *A system of axioms for geometry.* **Trans. Amer. Math. Soc.,** vol. 5, pp. 343-384.

See Veblen and Bussey.

VEBLEN, OSWALD and BUSSEY, W. H.

1906. *Finite projective geometries*. Ibid., vol. 7, pp. 241-259.

WAJSBERG, MORDECHAJ

1938. *Untersuchungen über den Aussagenkalkül von A. Heyting*. **Wiadomości matematyczne,** vol. 46, pp. 45-101.

WANG, HAO

1952. *Logic of many-sorted theories*. **Jour. symbolic logic,** vol. 17, pp. 105-116.

1953. *Certain predicates defined by induction schemata*. Ibid., vol. 18, pp. 49-59.

See Rosser and Wang.

WEYL, HERMANN

1918. **Das Kontinuum. Kritische Untersuchungen über die Grundlagen der Analysis.** Leipzig (Gruyter), iv+84 pp. Reprinted 1932.

1919. *Der circulus vitiosus in der heutigen Begründung der Analysis*. **Jahresbericht der Deutschen Mathematiker-Vereinigung,** vol. 28, pp. 85-92.

1926. **Die heutige Erkenntnislage in der Mathematik.** Sonderdrucke des Symposion, Erlangen (im Weldkreis-Verlag), Heft 3 (1926), 32 pp. Also in **Symposion** (Berlin), vol. 1 (1925-7), pp. 1-32.

1928. *Diskussionsbemerkungen zu dem zweiten Hilbertschen Vortrag über die Grundlagen der Mathematik*. **Abhandlungen aus dem Mathematischen Seminar der Hamburgischen Universität,** vol. 6, pp. 86-88.

1931. **Die Stufen des Unendlichen.** Jena (Fischer), 19 pp.

1944. *David Hilbert and his mathematical work*. **Bull. Amer. Math. Soc.,** vol. 50, pp. 612-654.

1946. *Mathematics and logic. A brief survey serving as a preface to a review of "The Philosophy of Bertrand Russell"*. **Amer. math. monthly,** vol. 53, pp. 2-13.

1949. **Philosophy of mathematics and natural science.** Princeton, N.J. (Princeton University Press), x+311 pp. Revised and augmented Eng. ed., based on a tr. by Olaf Helmer from the German original 1926.

WHITEHEAD, ALFRED NORTH and RUSSELL, BERTRAND

1910-13. **Principia mathematica.** Vol. 1 1910, xv+666 pp. (2nd ed. 1925). Vol. 2 1912, xxiv+772 pp. (2nd ed. 1927). Vol. 3 1913, x+491 pp. (2nd ed. 1927). Cambridge, England (University Press).

YOUNG, JOHN WESLEY

1911. **Lectures on fundamental concepts of algebra and geometry.** New York (Macmillan), vii+247 pp.

ZERMELO, ERNST

1904. *Beweis, dass jede Menge wohlgeordnet werden kann*. **Math. Ann.,** vol. 59, pp. 514-516. Also cf. 1908a.

1908a. *Neuer Beweis für die Möglichkeit einer Wohlordnung*. Ibid., vol. 65, pp. 107-128.

1908. *Untersuchungen über die Grundlagen der Mengenlehre I*. Ibid., pp. 261-281.

SYMBOLS AND NOTATIONS

Theory of sets

Mathematical logic and formal number theory

Recursive functions and informal number theory

INDEX